Pathways for Peace

Pathways for Peace
Inclusive Approaches to Preventing Violent Conflict

WORLD BANK GROUP

UNITED NATIONS

ISBN (paper): 978-1-4648-1162-3
ISBN (electronic): 978-1-4648-1186-9
DOI: 10.1596/978-1-4648-1162-3

Cover design: Takayo Muroga Fredericks.

Library of Congress Cataloging-in-Publication Data has been requested.

Contents

Boxes

Figures

Maps

Tables

In 2015, the United Nations Member States set ambitious goals for the world with the adoption of the 2030 Agenda for Sustainable Development, which offers a unique framework to come together around a renewed effort at preventing human suffering. The Agenda, which is universal, integrated and indivisible in nature, not only aims to end poverty and hunger, to ensure healthy lives and quality education and to protect the environment—but also to reduce inequalities and promote peaceful, just and inclusive societies.

Violent conflict is increasingly recognized as one of the big obstacles to reaching the Sustainable Development Goals (SDGs) by 2030. Its dramatic resurgence over the last few years has caused immense human suffering and has enormous global impact. Violent conflicts have also become more complex and protracted, involving more nonstate groups and regional and international actors. And they are increasingly linked to global challenges such as climate change, natural disasters, cyber security and transnational organized crime. It is projected that more than half of the people living in poverty will be found in countries affected by high levels of violence by 2030. This is utterly contrary to the promise contained in the 2030 Agenda to leave no one behind.

As the human, social and financial costs and complexity of violent conflict and its global impact grow, we must ask ourselves: how can the global community more effectively prevent violent conflict?

At the United Nations, we believe that prevention means doing everything we can to help countries avert the outbreak of crises that take a high toll on humanity, undermining institutions and capacities to achieve peace and development. We mean rededicating ourselves to the United Nations Charter, the mandate of Agenda 2030, protecting and respecting human rights, and ensuring that our assistance goes to those who need it the most. Prevention should permeate everything we do. It should cut across all pillars of the United Nations' work and unite us for more effective delivery. This study is a contribution to our internal reflection on the broader challenges of prevention.

At the World Bank Group, we believe that preventing fragility, conflict and violence is central to reducing poverty and achieving shared prosperity. Social and economic development have important roles to play in this effort, so we are doubling the amount of resources to address issues of fragility, conflict and violence as part of the 18th replenishment of the International Development Association (IDA), our fund for the poorest countries. We are ensuring that all of our operations can contribute to this effort in several ways: by introducing more flexibility and adaptability in our programs; by increasing our focus on the risks of fragility, conflict and violence, and on various crises faced by our clients; by improving our regional efforts; and by addressing some of the worst consequences of conflict such as forced displacement.

Each of our institutions brings a unique and complementary set of expertise and tools to the table in accordance with its mandate. We can already see the results of our intensified collaboration around conflict, violence and fragility in several countries. But we can achieve more together. We need to better harness our institutions' instruments and resources to support this shared agenda.

This joint study on the prevention of violent conflict—a first in the history of our institutions—was initiated in 2016 and conducted by a team of staff members from the United Nations and the World Bank Group, in a spirit of fostering closer collaboration to deliver at the country level. It reflects a process of research and intense global consultation aimed at providing ideas on how development approaches can better interact with other tools to prevent violent conflict.

This study, principally based on academic research, benefited immensely from consultations with a variety of actors including governments. It is therefore our hope that some of the findings will usefully inform global policy making.

This study is one element of a much broader partnership and a first step in working jointly to address the immense challenges of our time. We look forward to continuing the pursuit of knowledge together and to applying that knowledge together in support of the people we serve.

António Guterres
Secretary-General
United Nations

Jim Yong Kim
President
World Bank Group

Acknowledgments

Pathways for Peace: Inclusive Approaches to Preventing Violent Conflict was produced by an integrated team from the World Bank and the United Nations, including the Department of Peacekeeping Operations (DPKO), the Department of Political Affairs (DPA), the Peacebuilding Support Office (PBSO), and the United Nations Development Programme (UNDP). At the World Bank, the study was managed by the Fragility, Conflict, and Violence (FCV) Group in Global Themes. The study combined the efforts of several staff from both organizations, with inputs and reviews from dozens of experts and practitioners.

The integrated core team was led by Alexandre Marc (chief technical specialist, FCV Group, World Bank) and co-led by Jago Salmon (adviser, United Nations/World Bank Partnership on Conflict and Fragility, United Nations). The production of the study was overseen by Benjamin Petrini. Members of the joint core team included Lydiah Kemunto Bosire, Megan E. Carroll, Bledi Celiku, Catalina Crespo-Sancho, Djordje Djordjevic, Samhita Kumar, Michael Lund, Corey Pattison, Neelam Verjee, and Alys Willman. Extended team members and other chapter authors included Hannah Bleby Orford, Margherita Capellino, Nergis Gulasan, Eiko Ikegaya, Roudabeh Kishi, and Marco Zambotti. Charles "Chuck" Call, Gary Milante, Seth Kaplan, and David Steven acted as senior external advisers and provided critical contributions to the report. Other contributors included Ayham Al-Maleh, Holly Benner, Kevin Carey, Spyros Demetriou, Qurat Ul Ain Fatima, Sarah Hearn, Emilie Jourdan, Zainiddin Karaev, Joanna Kata-Blackman, Anne-Lise Klausen, Chris Mahony, Siobhan McInerney-Lankford, Vikram Raghavan, Alexandros Ragoussis, Irena Sargsyan, Tracy K. Washington, and Michael Woolcock. The communications and outreach strategy was overseen by Chisako Fukuda, Anna Liudmilova Stoyanova, Cynthia R. Delgadillo, and Justin Ticzon. The report was edited by Susan Sachs, Alys Willman, Michael Harrup, Elizabeth Forsyth, and Sherrie Brown, and references were edited by Lauri Scherer. The design of the cover and infographics was completed by Takayo Muroga Fredericks. Nancy Kebe and Janice Rowe-Barnwell provided administrative support. Special thanks are extended to Patricia Katayama and Aziz Gökdemir and the World Bank's Publishing Program.

The report was produced under overall guidance of a Steering Committee, the members of which also acted as peer reviewers. The Steering Committee was chaired by Oscar Fernandez-Taranco (assistant secretary-general for peacebuilding support, United Nations), and Franck Bousquet and Saroj Kumar Jha (respectively, current and former senior director, FCV Group, World Bank). Members included Pedro Conceicao (director, Strategic Policy, UNDP), Shantayanan Devarajan (senior director, Development Economics, World Bank), Renata Dwan (chief, Policy and Best Practices, Department of Policy, Evaluation, and Training, DPKO), Stephen Jackson (chief, Policy and Planning, DPA), Carlos Felipe Jaramillo (senior director, Macroeconomic and Fiscal Management, World Bank), Martin Rama (chief economist, South Asia region, World Bank), Lynne Sherburne-Benz (director, Social Protection and Jobs, World Bank), and Teresa Whitfield (director, Policy and Mediation Division, DPA).

The team appreciates the support and detailed guidance of additional peer reviewers, Edouard Al-Dahdah (senior public sector specialist, Governance, World Bank), Henk-Jan Brinkman (chief, Policy, Planning, and Application Branch, PBSO), Helene Grandvoinnet (lead governance specialist, Governance Global Practice, World Bank), and Markus Kostner (lead social development specialist, Social, Urban, Rural, and Resilience Global Practice, World Bank). The office of World Bank Group Senior Vice President Mahmoud Mohieldin provided valuable input and assistance, including through the World Bank Group offices in Geneva and New York. The International Finance Corporation (IFC) provided substantive inputs to the report.

The study benefited from the expertise of its Advisory Committee, bringing together internationally renowned experts from academia and leading organizations in the field of conflict and development. Members include Haroon Bhorat (director, Development Policy Research Unit, School of Economics, University of Cape Town); Sarah Cliffe (director, Center on International Cooperation [CIC], New York University); Meenakshi Gopinath (founder and director, Women in Security, Conflict Management, and Peace); Kristian Berg Harpviken (director, Peace Research Institute Oslo [PRIO]); Mushtaq Khan (professor of economics, SOAS, University of London); Andrew Mack (director, Human Security Report Project, Simon Fraser University); Olivier Ray (head, Crisis Prevention and Post Conflict Recovery, Agence Française de Développement [AFD]); Ambassador Gert Rosenthal (chair, Advisory Group of Experts on the Review of the United Nations Peacebuilding Architecture); Jacob N. Shapiro (co-director, Empirical Studies of Conflict Project [ESOC], Princeton University); and Frances Stewart (director, Centre for Research on Inequality, Human Security, and Ethnicity [CRISE], University of Oxford).

The team warmly thanks donors for their critical support toward the realization of this report and their generous contribution, including financial contribution, technical assistance through background research, and the hosting of seminars and consultations. Donors included Norway (Ministry of Foreign Affairs); United Kingdom (Department for International Development [DFID]); Sweden (Ministry of Foreign Affairs); France (AFD; Ministry of Foreign Affairs); Switzerland (Swiss Agency for Development and Cooperation [SDC]); the Netherlands (Ministry of Foreign Affairs); the Government of the Republic of Korea; and Germany (German Federal Foreign Office [AA]).

Consultations with partners, academia, regional organizations, and civil society organizations were instrumental in formulating the report and provided critical feedback at different stages of the study. Consultation events were held throughout the production of the report in the following countries: Belgium, the Arab Republic of Egypt, Ethiopia, France, Germany, Jordan, Kenya, Myanmar, the Netherlands, Norway, Senegal, Spain, Sweden, Switzerland, Thailand, the United Kingdom, and the United States. The team thanks the following organizations that were involved in consultations or that supported the study in different capacities: African Union, Berghof Foundation, Brookings Institution, CIC at New York University, Clingendael Netherlands Institute of International Relations, Club de Madrid, Dag Hammarskjöld Foundation (DHF), Economic Community of West African States (ECOWAS), ESOC at Princeton University, European Institute of Peace, European Union (EU), Freie Universitat Berlin, Geneva Centre for the Democratic Control of Armed Forces (DCAF), Geneva Peacebuilding Platform (GPP), German Development Institute/ Deutsches Institut für Entwicklungspolitik (DIE), Inclusive Peace & Transition Initiative (IPTI) at the Geneva Graduate Institute of

International and Development Studies, Institute of Development Studies at University of Sussex, Institute for Economic Analysis at Universitat Autònoma de Barcelona, Institute for Economics and Peace (IEP), Institute for Security Studies, Inter-Governmental Authority on Development (IGAD), League of Arab States (LAS), North Atlantic Treaty Organization (NATO), Norwegian Institute of International Affairs (NUPI), Oslo Governance Center (OGC-UNDP), Overseas Development Institute (ODI), Organisation for Economic Co-operation and Development (OECD), Peace Research Institute Oslo (PRIO), Quaker United Nations Office (QUNO), Stockholm International Peace Research Institute (SIPRI), United Nations University, United States Institute of Peace (USIP), and Wilton Park.

The team acknowledges those individuals within the two institutions and outside who supported the study in different capacities, including through enriching it with inputs, comments, or review of specific sections. The team would like to thank the following individuals from the World Bank and the United Nations as well as external colleagues, including Husam Abudagga, Andrea Aeby, Ozong Agborsangaya-Fiteu, Sakuntala Akmeemana, Fawah Akwo, Betsy Alley, Amatalalim Alsoswa, David Andersson, Diego Antoni, Jorge Araujo, Sakura Atsumi, Alexander Avanessov, Laura E. Bailey, Siaka Bakayoko, Salman Bal, Daniel Kiernan Balke, Luca Bandiera, Mary A. Barton-Dock, Sara Batmanglich, Viktoria Bechstein, Husam Mohamed Beides, Rachid Benmessaoud, Sandra Bloemenkamp, Michel Botzung, Robert Bou Jaoude, Monique Bouman, Parminder Brar, Armand-Michel Broux, Margot M. Brown, Colin Bruce, Dominique Bush, Susanna Campbell, Rubén Campos, Lars-Erik Cederman, Rodrigo Chaves, Nestor Coffi, Louise Cord, Sarah Cussen, Maitreyi Das, Pablo de Greiff, Jessica de Plessis, Bénédicte de la Brière, Jos De La Haye, Sascha Djumena, Sarah Douglas, Dirk Druet, Sebastian von Einsiedel, Marcelo Fabre, Faizaa Fatima, Abderrahim Fraiji, Diarietou Gaye, Kristalina Georgieva, Yashodhan Ghorpade, Maninder S. Gill, Bjorn Erik Gillsater, Ana Patricia Graca, Michele Griffin, Caren Grown, Sigrid Gruener, Thomas Guerber, Stephane Guimbert, Lobna Hadji, Maarten Halff, Daniel Ham, Lucia Hammer, Annika S. Hansen, Bernard Harborne, Malin Hedwig, Fabrizio Hochschild, Elena Ianchovichina, Ede Jorge Ijjasz-Vasquez, Deborah Isser, Alyssa Jackson, Regev Ben Jacob, Jenny Joelle, Bruce Jones, Steen Jorgensen, Patricia Justino, Mabruk Kabir, Takuya Kamata, Ellen Kang, Ethan Kapstein, Omer Karasapan, Michelle Keane, Mike Kelleher, Patrick Keuleers, Henrike Klau Panhans, Kate Almquist Knopf, Amara Konneh, Sahr Kpundeh, Aart Kraay, Marianne Krey-Jacobsen, Nandini Krishnan, Kathleen Kuehnast, Daniel Kull, Chetan Kumar, Heidi Kuttab, Romano Lasker, Marcus Lenzen, Larisa Leshchenko, Nancy Lindborg, Sarah Lister, Clare Lockhart, Ana Paula Lopez, Gladys C. Lopez-Acevedo, Rachel F. Madenyika, Marie-Francoise Marie-Nelly, David Marshall, Phil Matseza, Cecile Mazzacurati, Patrick McCarthy, Clem McCartney, Odhran McMahon, Oliver Meinecke, Erik Melander, Piers Merrick, Ivonne Astrid Moreno Horta, Hannes Mueller, Mamta Murthy, Ahmadou Moustapha Ndiaye, Florian Neutze, Akihiko Nishio, Håvard Mokleiv Nygård, Martin Ochoa, Helen Olafsdottir, Ozonnia Ojielo, Lisa Orrennius, Thania Paffenholz, Utz Pape, Gina Pattugalan, Laura Pereira, Nadia Piffaretti, Martin Ras, Sarah Rattray, Joel Reyes, Noella Richards, Hugh Riddell, Simon Ridley, Alberto Rodriguez, Paul Romer, Benjamin Rubin, Janice Ryu, Nika Saeedi, Carolina Sanchez-Paramo, Shinta Sander, Emanuele Sapienza, Livio Sarandrea, Hartwig Schafer, Julia Rosa Schoepp, Lotta Segerstrom, Ole Jacob Sending, Sajjad Ali Shah, Maryanne Sharp, Alex Shoebridge, Urban Sjöström, Alexander Slater, Ayat Soliman, Richard Spencer Hogg, Radhika Srinivasan, Victoria Stanley, Paul B. Stares, Endre Stiansen, Marcel Stoessel, R. Sudharshan Canagarajah, Isabelle Taylor, Tobias Techtenfeld, Jacobo Tenacio, Hans Timmer, Nana Oumou Toure-Sy, Maurizia Tovo, Carolyn Turk, James Turpin, Veronika Tywuschik, Oliver Ulich, Henrik Urdal, Jos Verbeek, Irene Vergara, Eckhard Volkmann, Mariska van

Beijnum, Henriette von Kaltenborn-Stachau, Joao Pedro Wagner De Acevedo, Victoria Walker, Asbjorn Haland Wee, Achim Wennmann, Deborah L. Wetzel, Alexandra Wilde, Ali Zafar, Giuseppe Zampaglione, William Zartman, Alexander Zuev, and Aly Zulficar Rahim.

Finally, we give special thanks to the authors of background papers and case studies commissioned for this study, including Daniel Arnon, Ghazia Aslam, Jonathan L. Austin, Mielna Bacalja Perianes, Karim Baghat, Guy Banim, Gray Barrett, Laura Bernal-Bermudez, Michelle Betz, Carl Black, Morten Bøås, George Bob-Milliar, Marco Boggero, Hans Born, Louise Bosetti, Rebecca Brubaker, John Bruce, Alexander Burian, Charles Call, Kevin Carey, David Cingranelli, James Cockayne, Nat J. Colletta, Virginia Comolli, Catalina Crespo-Sancho, Benjamin Crisman, Marianne Dahl, Adam Day, Catherine Defontaine, Spyros Demetriou, Constance Dijkstra, Thomas Dorfler, Elizabeth Drew, Kendra Dupuy, Stein Sundstøl Eriksen, Aissatou Fall, Quratul Ain Fatima, Charlotte Fiedler, Felix Fritsch, Tine Gade, Janel Galvanek, Scott Gates, Mark Gibney, Hans-Joachim Giessmann, Jorn Gravinghold, Patrick Hagan, David Hammond, Wissam Harake, Peter Haschke, Sarah Hearn, Solveig Hillesund, Andreas Hirblinger, Nazia Hussain, Daniel Hyslop, Sana Jaffrey, Patricia Justino, Suh Yoon Kang, Jocelyn Kelly, Farhad Khosrokhavar, Dana Landau, Igor Logvinenko, Louisa Lombard, Ingrid Magnusson, Chris Mahony, Aditi Malik, Brendan (Skip) Mark, Eric Min, Stephen Mogaka, Karina Mross, Hannes Mueller, Robert Muggah, Luise Müller, Taies Nezam, Havard Mokeiv Nygård, Ben Oppenheim, Gudrun Østby, Thania Paffenholz, Leigh Payne, Marc-Antoine Pérouse de Montclos, Alexandra Pichler Fong, Kristiana Powell, Olivia Rakotomalala, Andy Reiter, Simona Ross, Siri Aas Rustad, Cale Salih, Jon Harald Sande Lie, Irena L. Sargsyan, Christine Seifert, Ole Jacob Sending, Jacob N. Shapiro, Manu Singh, Timothy D. Sisk, Lucy Stackpool-Moore, David Steven, Håvard Strand, Gizem Sucuoglu, Silvana Toska, Henrik Urdal, Aly Verjee, Neelam Verjee, Sebastian von Einsiedel, Maurice Walsh, Barbara Walter, Asbjorn Haland Wee, Achim Wennmann, Stephan Wolff, Reed Wood, and Jisun Yi.

Executive Summary

A surge in violent conflicts in recent years has left a trail of human suffering, displacement, and protracted humanitarian need. In 2016, more countries experienced violent conflict than at any time in nearly 30 years.[1] Reported battle-related deaths in 2016 increased tenfold from the post–Cold War low of 2005, and terrorist attacks and fatalities also rose sharply over the past 10 years (GTD 2017).

This surge in violence afflicts both low- and middle-income countries with relatively strong institutions and calls into question the long-standing assumption that peace will accompany income growth and the expectations of steady social, economic, and political advancement that defined the end of the twentieth century (Fearon 2010; Humphreys and Varshney 2004; World Economic Forum 2016). If current trends persist, by 2030—the horizon set by the international community for the Sustainable Development Goals (SDGs)—more than half of the world's poor will be living in countries affected by high levels of violence (OECD 2015).

The benefit of preventive action, then, seems self-evident. Indeed, the global architecture for peace and security, forged in the aftermath of World War II, is grounded in the universal commitment to "save succeeding generations from the scourge of war" (United Nations Charter, preamble). Yet the changing scope and nature of today's conflicts pose a significant challenge to that system. With conflict today often simultaneously subnational and transnational, sustained, inclusive, and targeted engagement is needed at all levels.

This reality has accelerated momentum for countries at risk and for the international community to focus on improving efforts at preventing "the outbreak, escalation, recurrence, or continuation of conflict" (UN General Assembly 2016; UN Security Council 2016). Yet, at present, spending and efforts on prevention represent only a fraction of the amount spent on crisis response and reconstruction.[2] A shift away from managing and responding to crises and toward preventing conflict sustainably, inclusively, and collectively can save lives and greatly reduce these costs.

Pathways for Peace: Laying the Groundwork for a New Focus on Prevention

Pathways for Peace: Inclusive Approaches to Preventing Violent Conflict is a joint study of the United Nations and the World Bank. The study originates from the conviction on the part of both institutions that the attention of the international community needs to be urgently refocused on prevention. While the two institutions are governed by different, complementary mandates, they share a commitment, founded in the 2030 Agenda for Sustainable Development, to the prevention of conflict as a contribution to development progress, as expressed in the United Nations General Assembly and Security Council resolutions on sustaining peace[3] and the eighteenth replenishment of the World Bank Group's International Development Association.[4]

This study recognizes that the World Bank Group and the United Nations bring separate comparative advantages to approach the prevention of violent conflict and that they have different roles and responsibilities in the international architecture. Therefore, while a holistic framework is essential to implementing prevention, the findings and recommendations of this study do not apply to all organizations in the same way.

This study seeks to improve the way in which domestic development processes interact with security, diplomatic, justice, and human rights efforts to prevent conflicts from becoming violent. Its key audiences are national policy makers and staff of multilateral and regional institutions. The background research and literature reviews, including 19 case studies, were prepared in partnership with leading think tanks and academic institutions. Regional consultations were conducted throughout 2016–17 with policy makers, members of civil society, representatives of regional organizations, development aid organizations, and donor partners in Africa, Asia, Europe, the Middle East and North Africa, and North America.

Eight Key Messages for Prevention

The study's findings revolve around eight key messages:

- Violent conflict has increased after decades of relative decline. Direct deaths in war, numbers of displaced populations, military spending, and terrorist incidents, among others, have all surged since the beginning of the century. A rapidly evolving global context presents risks that transcend national borders and add to the complexity of conflict. This places the onus on policy makers at all levels, from local to global, to make a more concerted effort to bring

their tools and instruments to bear in an effective and complementary way.

- The human and economic cost of conflicts around the world requires all of those concerned to work more collaboratively. The SDGs should be at the core of this approach. Development actors need to provide more support to national and regional prevention agendas through targeted, flexible, and sustained engagement. Prevention agendas, in turn, should be integrated into development policies and efforts, because prevention is cost-effective, saves lives, and safeguards development gains.

- The best way to prevent societies from descending into crisis, including but not limited to conflict, is to ensure that they are resilient through investment in inclusive and sustainable development. For all countries, addressing inequalities and exclusion, making institutions more inclusive, and ensuring that development strategies are risk-informed are central to preventing the fraying of the social fabric that could erupt into crisis.

- The primary responsibility for preventive action rests with states, both through their national policy and their governance of the multilateral system. However, in today's shifting global landscape, states are often one actor among many. States are increasingly called to work with each other and with other actors to keep their countries on a pathway to peace.

- Exclusion from access to power, opportunity, services, and security creates fertile ground for mobilizing group grievances to violence, especially in areas with weak state capacity or legitimacy or in the context of human rights abuses. This study points to specific ways in which states and other actors can seek to avert violence, including through more inclusive policies.

- Growth and poverty alleviation are crucial but alone will not suffice to sustain peace. Preventing violence requires departing from traditional economic and social policies when risks are building up or are high. It also means seeking inclusive solutions through dialogue, adapted macroeconomic policies, institutional reform in core state functions, and redistributive policies.

- Inclusive decision making is fundamental to sustaining peace at all levels, as are long-term policies to address economic, social, and political aspirations. Fostering the participation of young people as well as of the organizations, movements, and networks that represent them is crucial. Women's meaningful participation in all aspects of peace and security is critical to effectiveness, including in peace processes, where it has been shown to have a direct impact on the sustainability of agreements reached.
- Alongside efforts to build institutional capacity to contain violence when it does occur, acting preventively entails fostering systems that create incentives for peaceful and cooperative behavior. In order to achieve more effective prevention, new mechanisms need to be established that will allow greater synergy to be achieved much earlier among the various tools and instruments of prevention, in particular, diplomacy and mediation, security, and development.

This study demonstrates that prevention works. Many countries have successfully managed high-risk conflicts and avoided descents into violence. These experiences offer lessons in prevention that can be applied to other contexts. There is no one formula, as each situation is specific to the actors, institutions, and structures of each society, but common threads can be teased out of these experiences.

This study also shows that prevention is cost-effective. Analysis undertaken for this study finds that a system for preventing the outbreak of violence would be economically beneficial. Even in the most pessimistic scenario, where preventive action is rarely successful, the average net savings are close to US$5 billion per year. In the most optimistic scenario, the net savings are almost US$70 billion per year (Mueller 2017).

The State of Violent Conflict

While interstate conflict remains rare, the number of violent conflicts within states has increased since 2010. Furthermore, high-intensity warfare in certain countries has increased the number of fatalities caused by these conflicts, with the number of reported battle-related deaths rising sharply and in 2014 reaching the highest numbers recorded in 20 years (Allansson, Melander, and Themnér 2017; Sundberg, Eck, and Kreutz 2012).

This increase in the number of conflicts is a surge, but not yet a trend. Most battle deaths occur in a small number of conflicts; the three deadliest countries in 2016 (Afghanistan, Iraq, and the Syrian Arab Republic) incurred more than 76 percent of all fatalities. However, even if battle deaths drop significantly as fighting declines in these countries, these conflicts are expected to be protracted and risks of new outbreaks remain high (Dupuy et al. 2017).

Much of this violence remains entrenched in low-income countries; however, some of today's deadliest and most complex conflicts are occurring in middle-income countries, underscoring the fact that income and wealth are not a guarantee of peace (Geneva Declaration Secretariat 2015; OECD 2016).

Armed groups have grown in number, diversity, and scope. Many of these groups are not linked to states. They include rebels, militias, armed trafficking groups, and violent extremist groups that may coalesce around a grievance, an identity, an ideology, or a claim to economic or political resources. Membership and alliances tend to evolve over time, depending on resources or leadership.

Violence is increasingly spreading beyond national borders: 18 out of 47 state-based violent conflicts were internationalized in 2016,[5] more than reported in any year since the end of World War II, except for 2015, when 20 were internationalized (UCDP 2017).

The costs of these conflicts are enormous. Battle deaths tell only part of the story of the damage inflicted. Civilians are increasingly vulnerable, and much recent violence has occurred in urban areas and targeted public spaces (ICRC 2017). Between 2010 and 2016 alone, the number of civilian deaths in violent conflicts doubled (UCDP 2017). Many more civilian deaths result from indirect effects of conflict, such as unmet medical needs, food insecurity, inadequate shelter, or contamination of water (Small Arms Survey 2011; UNESCWA 2017).

Violent conflict is forcibly displacing people in record numbers. An estimated 65.6 million people are now forcibly displaced from their homes, driven primarily by violence (UNHCR 2017). Between 2005 and 2016, the number of internally displaced persons increased more than fivefold (UNDP 2016; UNHCR 2017). The number of refugees nearly doubled over the same period, with the majority (55 percent) of refugees coming from Afghanistan, the Republic of South Sudan, and Syria (UNHCR 2017). More than half of the world's refugees are children, and many of them have been separated from their families (UNHCR 2017).

Violent conflict affects men and women differently. While men make up the majority of combatants during conflict and are more likely to die from the direct effects of violence, women also face a continuum of insecurity before, during, and after conflict (Crespo-Sancho 2017). Sexual and gender-based violence tends to be higher in conflict and postconflict settings, as does recruitment of girls into trafficking, sexual slavery, and forced marriage (Crespo-Sancho 2017; Kelly 2017; UNESCWA 2017; UN Secretary-General 2015; UN Women 2015). In insecure contexts, girls' mobility is often highly restricted, limiting their access to school, employment, and other opportunities (UN Women 2015). For children and youth, the long-term effects of exposure to violence and the adversities of daily life in a high-violence context are associated with a range of challenges (Miller and Rasmussen 2010). These include increased risk of perpetrating violence or being a victim of violence later in life, psychological trauma, and negative effects on cognitive and social development (Betancourt et al. 2012; Blattman 2006; Huesmann and Kirwil 2007; Leckman, Panter-Brick, and Salah 2014; Shonkoff and Garner 2012).

The costs associated with the economic losses caused by conflict put a severe strain on state capacity. Afghanistan's per capita income has remained at its 1970s level due to the continued war, and Somalia's per capita income has dropped by more than 40 percent over the same period (Mueller and Tobias 2016). Such effects can spread to surrounding countries in the region. On average, countries bordering a high-intensity conflict experience an annual decline of 1.4 percentage points in gross domestic product (GDP) and an increase of 1.7 points in inflation (Rother et al. 2016).

The Need for Prevention in an Interdependent World

The nature of violent conflict is not changing in isolation. The increase in violent conflicts has emerged in a global context where the balance of geopolitical power is in flux and a push for more inclusive governance is bringing new voices and new demands. Proxy wars are no longer the exclusive purview of traditional great powers. At the same time, the number of societies that have adopted more inclusive forms of political, economic, and cultural governance has grown rapidly over the last 30 years. While this transition has occurred peacefully in many countries, it can—when not managed carefully— also create a space for contestation and conflict to emerge.

At the same time, fast-emerging global trends are affecting the way people and societies operate and interact. Advances in information and communication technology (ICT) represent great opportunities for innovation, growth, and the unfettered exchange of ideas. However, alongside opportunities are risks. ICT benefits and access are not available to all, and the so-called "digital divide" threatens to widen the gaps between high- and low-income countries. New technologies and automation are rapidly transforming industries, with the effect of reducing the need for unskilled or semiskilled labor in industries. Interconnectivity also enables transnational organized crime to flourish, allows the rapid transmission of violent ideologies, and leaves economies vulnerable to cybercrime.

Climate change, too, presents new challenges, especially to poor and vulnerable countries and communities (Nordas and Gleditsch 2007). By itself, climate change does not cause violent conflict. However, it does create major stress, especially in fragile situations where governments have limited means to help their populations adapt. Risks associated with climate change can combine with and exacerbate risks of violence through factors such as food insecurity, economic shocks, and migration (Marc, Verjee, and Mogaka 2015; Schleussner et al. 2016).

This new global landscape features significant demographic shifts that may create new stresses, as well as opportunities, for global and national systems. Already there are more young people in the world than at any other time in history—1.8 billion people between the ages of 10 and 24—and the vast majority of young people live in low-income countries, many of them already affected by conflict (UN DESA 2015). In Africa, 60 percent of the population is under the age of 25 (UN DESA 2015). Harnessing the potential of a growing young population is an important challenge. In addition, population growth, while a positive force for economies, also puts pressure on labor markets, which will have to absorb the estimated 600 million new workers entering the workforce in the next 10 years (ILO 2016).

These demographic shifts are occurring against the backdrop of slow and uneven global economic growth. World trade value, merchandise exports, and commercial trade services all grew substantially over the past 70 years, contributing to consolidating peace in the aftermath of World War II. However, trade growth has been marked in recent years by downturns and a prolonged period of only modest improvement since the global financial crisis of 2007. In 2016, trade growth fell, for the fifth consecutive year, below 3 percent. Meanwhile, foreign direct investment has also been decreasing, adversely affecting growth and productivity (Hale and Xu 2016). These trends do not directly affect violent conflict; however, they do put additional stresses on systems and people and can increase the tendency for groups to mobilize for perceived grievances.

The Pathways for Peace Framework

Prevention is about creating incentives for actors to choose actions that resolve conflict without violence. An important corollary is that inclusive approaches to prevention should recognize and address group grievances early. Violence is highly path-dependent: once it takes hold, incentives and systems begin to reorient themselves in ways that sustain violence. Effective prevention requires acting before grievances harden and the threat of violence narrows the choices available for leaders and elites, understood as groups who hold power or influence in a society.

A society's ability to manage conflict constructively is tested continuously by risks that push it toward violence and by opportunities to advance sustainable development and peace. To help to visualize how these risks and opportunities act on and within a society, this book introduces the term "pathway" for the trajectory that every society shapes through the constant, dynamic interaction of its actors, institutions, and structural factors over time. As figure ES.1 illustrates, a society encounters many dimensions and levels of risks and opportunities that affect its pathway.

The pathway construct helps to conceptualize the temporal aspect of prevention. The behavior of domestic actors will adjust to changing events and the decisions of other actors. Reforming institutions to sustain peace and addressing structural factors that underpin grievances can take longer. This temporal aspect is important for international action. Development actors, for example, tend to decrease their engagement or withdraw altogether when risks escalate. Political actors tend to engage only when the risk of violence is high or violence is already present. Instead, viable, sustained action in support of preventing violence is needed throughout policies and programs.

FIGURE ES.1 Pathway between Sustainable Peace and Violent Conflict

Societies forge unique pathways as they negotiate competing pressures pushing toward violent conflict and sustainable peace. The figure illustrates how different forces can influence the direction of the pathway.

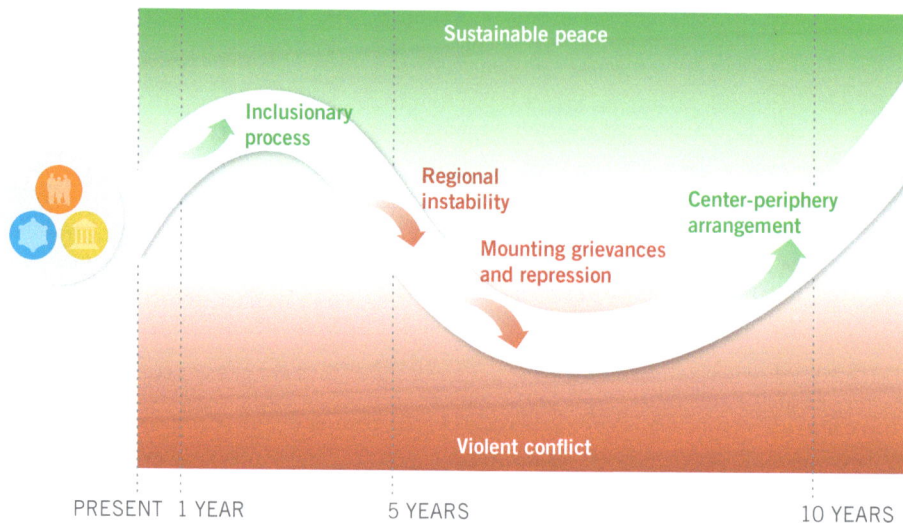

Sustainable peace

Inclusionary process

Regional instability

Center-periphery arrangement

Mounting grievances and repression

Violent conflict

PRESENT 1 YEAR   5 YEARS   10 YEARS

Why People Fight: Inequality, Exclusion, and Injustice

Some of the greatest risks of violence today stem from the mobilization of perceptions of exclusion and injustice, rooted in inequalities across groups (Collier and Hoeffler 2004; Cramer 2003; Fearon and Laitin 2003; Lichbach 1989; Østby 2013). When an aggrieved group assigns blame to others or to the state for its perceived economic, political, or social exclusion, then emotions, collective memories, frustration over unmet expectations, and a narrative that rouses a group to violence can all play a role in mobilization to violence (Cederman Wimmer, and Min 2010; Justino 2017; Nygård et al. 2017; Sargsyan 2017).

People come together in social groups for a variety of subjective and objective reasons. They may share feelings, history, narratives of humiliation, frustrations, or identities that motivate them to collective action in different ways, at different times, and in different situations. Perceptions of inequality between groups often matter more in terms of mobilization than measured inequality and exclusion (Rustad 2016; Stewart 2000, 2002, 2009). This pattern of exclusion includes inequality in the distribution of and access to political

opportunity and power among groups, including access to the executive branch and the police and military. Political exclusion provides group leaders with the incentive to mobilize collective action to force (or negotiate) change.

Exclusion that is enforced by state repression poses a grave risk of violent conflict (Bakker, Hill, and Moore 2016; Piazza 2017; Stewart 2002). Countries where governments violate human rights, especially the right to physical integrity, through practices such as torture, forced disappearances, political imprisonment, and extrajudicial killings, are at a higher risk for violent conflict (Cingranelli et al. 2017). In these contexts, repression creates incentives for violence by reinforcing the perception that there is no viable alternative for expressing grievances and frustration.

Societies that offer more opportunities for youth participation in the political and economic realms and provide routes for social mobility for youth tend to experience less violence (Idris 2016; Paasonen and Urdal 2016). With the global youth population increasing, the ability to harness the energy and potential of youth presents a strong opportunity for this "unique demographic dividend," as the 2015 United Nations Security Council Resolution 2250 notes (UN Security Council 2015).

Similarly, cross-country studies find evidence that high levels of gender inequality and gender-based violence in a society are associated with increased vulnerability to civil war and interstate war and the use of more severe forms of violence in conflict (Caprioli et al. 2007; GIWPS and PRIO 2017; Hudson et al. 2009; Kelly 2017). Changes in women's status or vulnerability, such as an increase in domestic violence or a reduction in girls' school attendance, often are viewed as early warnings of social and political insecurity (Hudson et al. 2012). Prevention of violent conflict requires a strong focus on women's experiences and on measures to ensure their participation in political, social, and economic life. Some evidence suggests that when women take leadership roles and are able to participate meaningfully in peace negotiations, the resulting agreements tend to last longer and there is greater satisfaction with the outcomes (O'Reilly, Ó Súilleabháin, and Paffenholz 2015; Paffenholz et al. 2017; Stone 2015; UN Women 2015).

What People Fight Over: Arenas of Contestation

Inequality and exclusion manifest most starkly in policy arenas related to access to political power and governance; land, water, and extractive resources; delivery of basic services; and justice and security. As the spaces where livelihoods and well-being are defined and defended, access to these arenas can become, quite literally, a matter of life or death. The arenas reflect the broader balance of power in society, and as such, they are highly contestable and often resistant to reform.

Competition for power is an age-old source of conflict. Power balances and imbalances can put a society at risk of violence. Experience shows that more inclusive and representative power-sharing arrangements lower the risk of violent conflict. Decentralizing, devolving, or allowing autonomy of subnational regions or groups can help to accommodate diversity and lower the risk of violence at the national level.

Resources such as land, water, and extractives are traditional sources of friction.

The effects of climate change, population growth, and urbanization are intensifying these risks. Disputes over resources have spilled over into violent conflict and instability across the world. Improving the sharing of resources and benefits derived from them as well as strengthening local conflict resolution mechanisms are important areas of focus.

Service delivery does not have a direct relationship with violence, but it affects state legitimacy and the ability of the state to mediate conflicts (Brinkerhoff, Wetterberg, and Dunn 2012; Sacks and Larizza 2012; Stel and Ndayiragiie 2014). The way in which services are delivered and the inclusiveness and perceptions of fairness in service delivery matter as much as—perhaps more than—the quality of services delivered (Sturge et al. 2017).

Security and justice institutions that operate fairly and in alignment with the rule of law are essential to preventing violence and sustaining peace. Accountability of security forces to the citizen, stronger community policing approaches, and improved efficiency of redress mechanisms are among the responses often needed.

What Works: How Countries Have Managed Contestation and Prevented Violent Conflict

Drawing on the pathways framework, the study describes the experience of national actors in three key areas: shaping the incentives of actors for peace, reforming institutions to foster inclusion, and addressing structural factors that feed into grievances. From the case studies analyzed for this report, common patterns emerge even if specific prescriptions do not. Overall, the studies suggest that effective prevention is a collective endeavor—led domestically, built on existing strengths, and with international and regional support.[6]

A central dilemma for all countries examined is that the incentives for violence are often certain and specific to an individual or group, while the incentives for peace are often uncertain, and diffuse (World Bank 2017). To shape incentives, governments took advantage of transition moments to introduce both long-term reforms or investments targeting structural factors, while implementing immediate initiatives that buttressed confidence in commitments to more inclusive processes.

The more successful cases mobilized a coalition of domestic actors to influence incentives toward peace, bringing in the comparative advantages of civil society, including women's groups, the faith community, and the private sector to manage tensions. Decisive leadership provided incentives for peaceful contestation, not least by mobilizing narratives and appealing to norms and values that support peaceful resolution (World Bank 2011).[7]

Nevertheless, before or after violence, countries that have found pathways to sustainable peace have eventually tackled the messy and contested process of institutional reform. Expanding access to the arenas of contestation has been key to increasing representation and alleviating grievances related to exclusion. Often, the transition moment that led to sustainable peace was based on a shift away from security-led responses and toward broader approaches that mobilized a range of sectors in support of institutional reforms.

Alongside institutional reform, however, in many cases, governments invested in addressing structural factors, launching programs targeting socioeconomic grievances, redistributing resources, and addressing past abuses even while violence was ongoing.

In these experiences, the greatest challenge lay not so much in accessing knowledge, but in the contentious process of identifying and prioritizing risks. Part of the reason for this difficulty is that violence narrowed the options for forward-looking decision making needed to invest in institutional or structural conditions for sustainable peace. Conflict did not bring a windfall of resources; instead it brought a move to equip and support police, military, or security operations that strained national budgets. Furthermore, preventive action was at times unpopular, with popular demands for visible and tangible security measures trumping longer-term, more complex responses addressing the causes of violence.

In these processes, formal political settlements, or at least durable settlements, have been important, but also rare events. In some cases, political settlements have been applied only to address specific aspects of conflict, while underlying causes were targeted more comprehensively through government action. In others, political settlements were not used as part of the prevention process at all.

A Global System for Prevention under Stress

Since the end of the Cold War, the multilateral architecture for conflict prevention and postconflict peacebuilding has struggled to adapt to a fast-changing situation in the field and globally. Despite many challenges, there have been clear achievements.

At a systemic level, comprehensive international normative and legal frameworks are in place to regulate the tools and conduct of war; protect human rights; address global threats including climate change, terrorism, and transnational criminal networks; and promote inclusive approaches to development (the SDGs).

Operationally, the United Nations and regional organizations such as the African Union and the European Union have provided global and regional forums to coordinate international responses to threats to peace and stability. The result has been important tools—including preventive diplomacy, sanctions, and peacekeeping—that have proven instrumental in preventing conflicts, mediating cease-fires and peace agreements, and supporting postconflict recovery and transition processes.

As conflicts have increasingly originated from and disrupted the core institutions of states, international and regional initiatives have accompanied these changes with greater coordination and resource pooling among development, diplomatic, and security efforts. While this evolution is welcome, with conflicts becoming more fragmented, more complex, and more transnational, these tools are being profoundly challenged by the emergence of nonstate actors, ideologies at odds with international humanitarian law, and the increased sponsorship of proxy warfare. These conclusions increase the need to focus on the endogenous risk factors that engender violence and on support for countries to address their own crises.

Building Inclusive Approaches for Prevention

Prevention is a long-term process of reinforcing and steering a society's pathway toward peace. This study amassed overwhelming evidence that prevention requires sustained, inclusive, and targeted attention and action. Deep changes are needed in the way national, regional, and international actors operate and cooperate so that risks of violent conflict are identified and addressed before they translate into crisis. However, few incentives now exist for this coordination, collaboration, and cooperation. Instead, preventive action often focuses on managing the accompanying crisis rather than addressing underlying risks, even when solutions to the underlying risk are available.

Pathways for Peace highlights three core principles of prevention.

- Prevention must be sustained over the time needed to address structural issues comprehensively, strengthen institutions, and adapt incentives for actors to manage conflict without violence. It is easy, but wrong, to see prevention as a trade-off between the short and long term. Sustainable results require sustained investment in all risk environments, while development investments should be integrated into overarching strategies with politically viable short-term and medium-term actions. The need for sustainability requires balancing effort and resources so that action does not reward only crisis management.
- Prevention must be inclusive and build broad partnerships across groups to identify and address grievances that fuel violence. Too often, preventive action is focused on the demands of actors that control the means of violence and positions of power. In complex, fragmented, and protracted conflicts,

an inclusive approach to prevention puts an understanding of grievances and agency at the center of national and international engagement. It recognizes the importance of understanding people and their communities: their trust in institutions, confidence in the future, perceptions of risk, and experience of exclusion and injustice.

- Prevention must proactively and directly target patterns of exclusion and institutional weaknesses that increase risk. Successful prevention depends on pro-active and targeted action before, during, and after violence. Modern conflicts arise when groups contest access to power, resources, services, and security; alongside efforts to mitigate the impacts of violence and de-escalate conflict, preventive action must actively and directly target grievances and exclusion across key arenas of risk.

Devising National Strategies for Prevention

The state bears the primary responsibility for preventing conflict and shaping a country's pathway toward sustainable development and peace. The following are some recommendations for effective national action in partnering for prevention.

Monitor the Risks of Conflict

Engaging early in preventive action requires a shift from early warning of violence and toward awareness of risk:

- Identify real and perceived exclusion and inequality, which requires strengthening the capacity for identifying, measuring, and monitoring SDG indicators[8]
- Strengthen national early warning systems and design systems that can effectively influence early response by national actors at various levels
- Harness technology to improve monitoring, especially in remote and conflict-affected areas, including through application of ICT and real-time data collection methods
- Ensure that surveys and data collection measure inequality, exclusion, and

perceptions and are conflict-sensitive and capacity-sensitive.[9]

Address Different Dimensions of Risk

National actors often deal with multiple risks simultaneously with limited budgets, political capital, and time:

- Bring institutions and actors together under a peace and development framework that prioritizes the risk of conflict
- Target risk spatially with investments and other actions in border and peripheral areas where grievances and violence may be more likely to exist
- Manage the impact of shocks when tensions are high
- Target action and resources to identified risks in arenas where exclusion and grievances arise over access to power, resources, services, and security and justice, and manage contestation and conflict by redistributive policies, among other possible actions.

Aligning Peace, Security, and Development for Prevention

One of the objectives of *Pathways for Peace* is to stimulate new thinking about the relationship of development, peace, and security—a relationship that takes concrete form in inclusive approaches to preventing conflict. A coherent strategy that can be sustained over time demands levels of integrated planning and implementation that are often challenging to development, security, humanitarian, and political actors. Each has comparative advantages at different stages of risk but sustained, inclusive, and targeted prevention requires that they coordinate more effectively. The following are some recommendations for better alignment.

Ensure that Security and Development Approaches Are Compatible and Mutually Supportive

Mutual support requires rebalancing growth and stability targets, as aggrieved groups whose exclusion poses a conflict risk may not be the poorest and may not be in areas of high potential for economic growth. Where security interventions are warranted, social services and economic support should also be provided so that security forces are not the only interface between the state and the population.

Build Capacity and Allocate Resources to Ensure that Grievances Are Mediated Quickly and Transparently

Capacity building can be addressed through training, development of guidance, and strengthening of institutions. Support for national and local-level mediation can be integrated into planning and programming at the local level (Rakotomalala 2017).

Engage Actors beyond the State in Platforms for Dialogue and Peacebuilding

Many actors involved in conflict today are not directly accessible to state institutions or agents. Inclusive prevention entails a focus on strengthening the capacity of the society, not just the state, for prevention. Inclusive prevention is a bottom-up process that should involve as broad a spectrum of people and groups as possible. Coalitions should reflect the importance of young people, women, the private sector, and civil society organizations.

Adopt a People-Centered Approach

A people-centered approach should include mainstreaming citizen engagement in development programs and local conflict resolution to empower underrepresented groups such as women and youth. Service delivery systems should seek to make people partners in the design and delivery of public services through mainstreaming participatory and consultative elements for all planning and programming in areas at risk of violent conflict.

Overcoming Barriers to Cooperation in Prevention

Development organizations need to adjust incentives toward prevention. International development actors and multilateral development banks are constrained by mandates, intergovernmental agreements, and institutional culture from engaging on sensitive risks with governments. Development organizations should ensure that prevention has a higher priority in their programming.

Share Risk Assessments

In the absence of a coherent process to share data, many organizations carry out assessments of different risks using different indicators. These data mostly remain internal to these organizations and are not shared with the national government or other relevant national actors, mostly because this information is often seen as politically sensitive. Risk monitoring and assessment methodologies also must become more widely shared, with specific focus on developing shared metrics across the various risks to development, peace, and security.

Commit to Collective Mechanisms to Identify and Understand Risks at Regional, Country, and Subnational Levels

The absence of effective mechanisms translates into ad hoc and fragmented actions among international partners.

Ensure That Joint Risk Assessments Articulate Jointly Agreed Priorities

Joint risk assessments should be based on agreed indicators that allow trends to be monitored over time. For example, the joint United Nations–European Union–World Bank Recovery and Peacebuilding Assessment offers one such approach for aligning priorities. Currently used mostly during and immediately following conflict, this approach could be used further upstream and developed into joint platforms for prioritizing risk.

Build Stronger Regional and Global Partnerships

Efforts should include the strengthening of regional analyses and strategies for prevention and the sharing of risk analyses to the extent possible at a regional level.

Explore New Investment Approaches for Prevention

Financing for prevention remains risk averse and focused on crises. As a result, current models are too slow to seize windows of opportunity and too volatile to sustain prevention. Complex and multilevel efforts are often constrained by the lack of needed and readily available resources, resulting in ad hoc resource mobilization attempts to generate financing from donors, often resulting in delayed and suboptimal responses. Options include strengthening support for financing national capacity for prevention, combining different forms of financing, and strengthening financing for regional prevention efforts.

Conclusion

A comprehensive shift toward preventing violence and sustaining peace offers life-saving rewards. *Pathways for Peace* presents national and international actors an agenda for action to ensure that attention, efforts, and resources are focused on prevention. Today, the consequences of failing to act together are alarmingly evident, and the call for urgent action has perhaps never been clearer. The time to act is now.

Notes

1. UCDP (2017). The UCDP/PRIO (Uppsala Conflict Data Program/Peace Research Institute Oslo) Armed Conflict Dataset 2017 records all state-based conflict in which at least one side is the government of a state and which results in at least 25 battle-related deaths in a calendar year. It covers the years 1946 to 2016. UCDP data that record nonstate and one-sided violence that results in at least 25 conflict-related deaths in a calendar year cover the years 1989 to 2016.

2. For example, official development assistance to countries with high risk of conflict averages US$250 million per year, only slightly higher than that to countries at peace, but increases to US$700 million during open conflict and US$400 million during recovery years. Similarly, peacekeeping support averages US$30 million a year for countries at high risk, compared with US$100 million

for countries in open conflict and US$300 million during recovery. See Mueller (2017).

3. UN General Assembly (2016); UN Security Council (2016). This study has been greatly informed by and builds on recent reviews by the United Nations and the World Bank. These include World Bank (2011, 2017); UN (2015a, 2015b, 2016); UN Women (2015).

4. National governments and other local actors are the foundation and point of reference for preventive action (see UN General Assembly 2016; UN Security Council 2016; Articles 2 and 3 of the United Nations Charter). The sustaining peace resolutions reaffirmed this principle. UN Security Council Resolution 2282 recognizes "the primary responsibility of national Governments and authorities in identifying, driving and directing priorities, strategies and activities for sustaining peace … emphasizing that sustaining peace is a shared task and responsibility that needs to be fulfilled by the Government and all other national stakeholders."

5. UCDP (2017) defines internationalized conflict as those where one side is a state and one side is nonstate, and where an outside state intervenes on behalf of one of these.

6. The insights are drawn from the background country case studies and research commissioned for this study and a review of broader relevant literature. The case studies cover Burkina Faso, Burundi, the Central African Republic, Côte d'Ivoire, the Arab Republic of Egypt, Ghana, Guatemala, Indonesia, Jordan, Kenya, the Kyrgyz Republic, Malawi, Morocco, Nepal, Niger, Northern Ireland, Sierra Leone, Republic of South Sudan, and Tunisia.

7. In addition to transition moments like a natural disaster or global economic shock, opportunities can arise when a society's tolerance for violence changes.

8. Several SDG targets and indicators could have relevance for assessing risks of horizontal inequality. Specifically, key core targets include SDG5 (5.1: End all forms of discrimination against all women and girls everywhere); SDG10 (10.2: By 2030, empower and promote the social, economic, and political inclusion of all, irrespective of age, sex, disability, race, ethnicity, origin, religion, or economic or other status; 10.3: Ensure equal opportunity and reduce inequalities of outcome, including by eliminating discriminatory laws, policies, and practices and promoting appropriate legislation, policies, and action in this regard); and SDG16 (16.3: Promote the rule of law at the national and international levels and ensure equal access to justice for all; 16.7: Ensure responsive, inclusive, participatory, and representative decision making at all levels).

9. Implementing the monitoring of perceptions and issues such as horizontal inequality requires several important safeguards to be in place. Governments and other actors can use questions on perceptions, identity, and aspirations to identify certain groups, target them for security purposes, deny people's rights, or support implementation of exclusionary policies. It is essential that very strong attention be given to protecting individual and collective rights of the population interviewed and the people collecting the information.

References

Allansson, M., E. Melander, and L. Themnér. 2017. "Organized Violence, 1989–2016." *Journal of Peace Research* 54 (4): 574–87.

Bakker, R., D. W. Hill, and W. H. Moore. 2016. "How Much Terror? Dissidents, Governments, Institutions, and the Cross-National Study of Terror Attacks." *Journal of Peace Research* 53 (5): 711–26.

Betancourt, T. S., R. McBain, E. A. Newnham, and R. T. Brennan. 2012. "Trajectories of Internalizing Problems in War-Affected Sierra Leonean Youth: Examining Conflict and Postconflict Factors." *Child Development* 84 (2): 455–70.

Blattman, C. 2006. *The Consequences of Child Soldiering*. Berkeley, CA: University of California.

Brinkerhoff, D., A. Wetterberg, and S. Dunn. 2012. "Service Delivery and Legitimacy in Fragile and Conflict-Affected States." *Public Management Review* 14 (2): 273–93.

Caprioli, M., V. Hudson, R. McDermott, C. Emmett, and B. Ballif-Spanvill. 2007. "Putting Women in Their Place." *Baker Journal of Applied Public Policy* 1 (1): 12–22.

Cederman, L.-E., A. Wimmer, and B. Min. 2010. "Why Do Ethnic Groups Rebel? New Data and Analysis." *World Politics* 62 (1): 87–119.

Cingranelli, D., M. Gibney, P. Haschke, R. Wood, D. Arnon, and B. Mark. 2017. "Human Rights Violations and Violent Conflict." Background paper for the United Nations–World Bank Flagship Study, *Pathways for Peace: Inclusive Approaches to Preventing Violent Conflict*, World Bank, Washington, DC.

Collier, P., and A. Hoeffler. 2004. "Greed and Grievance in Civil War." *Oxford Economic Papers* 56 (4): 563–95.

Cramer, C. 2003. "Does Inequality Cause Conflict?" *Journal of International Development* 15 (4): 397–412.

Crespo-Sancho, C. 2017. "Conflict Prevention and Gender." Background paper for the United Nations–World Bank Flagship Study, *Pathways for Peace: Inclusive Approaches to Preventing Violent Conflict*, World Bank, Washington, DC.

Dupuy, K., S. Gates, H. M. Nygård, I. Rudolfsen, S. A. Rustad, H. Strand, and H. Urdal. 2017. "Trends in Armed Conflict 1946–2016." PRIO Conflict Trends 02/2017, Peace Research Institute Oslo. https://www.prio .org/utility/DownloadFile.ashx?id=1373& type=publicationfile.

Fearon, J. D. 2010. "Governance and Civil War Onset." Background paper for *World Development Report 2011: Conflict, Security, and Development*, World Bank, Washington, DC.

Fearon, J., and D. Laitin. 2003. "Ethnicity, Insurgency, and Civil War." *American Political Science Review* 97 (1): 75–90.

Geneva Declaration Secretariat. 2015. *Global Burden of Armed Violence 2015: Every Body Counts.* Geneva: Geneva Declaration Secretariat.

GIWPS (Georgetown Institute for Women, Peace and Security) and PRIO (Peace Research Institute Oslo). 2017. *Women, Peace, and Security Index 2017/18: Tracking Sustainable Peace through Inclusion, Justice, and Security for Women.* Washington, DC: GIWPS and PRIO.

GTD (Global Terrorism Database). 2017. Global Terrorism Database. College Park: National Consortium for the Study of Terrorism and Responses to Terrorism, University of Maryland. https://www.start.umd.edu/gtd/.

Hale, G. and M. Xu. 2016. "FDI Effects on the Labor Market of Host Countries." Working Paper 2016-25, Federal Reserve Bank of San Francisco.

Hudson, V., B. Ballif-Spanvill, M. Caprioli, and C. Emmett. 2012. *Sex and World Peace.* New York: Columbia University Press.

Hudson, V., M. Caprioli, B. Ballif-Spanvill, R. McDermott, and C. Emmett. 2009. "The Heart of the Matter: The Security of Women and the Security of States." *International Security* 33 (3): 7–45.

Huesmann, L. R., and L. Kirwil. 2007. *Why Observing Violence Increases the Risk of Violent Behavior in the Observer.* New York: Cambridge University Press.

Humphreys, M., and A. Varshney. 2004. "Violent Conflict and the Millennium Development Goals: Diagnosis and Recommendations." Paper prepared for the Millennium Development Goals Poverty Task Force Workshop, Bangkok, June.

ICRC (International Committee of the Red Cross). 2017. *City at War.* Special Report. Geneva: ICRC.

Idris, I. 2016. Youth Unemployment and Violence: Rapid Literature Review. Birmingham, UK: Governance and Social Development Resource Centre, University of Birmingham.

ILO (International Labour Organization). 2016. *World Employment and Social Outlook 2016: Trends for Youth.* Geneva: ILO. http://www .ilo.org/wcmsp5/groups/public/---dgreports /---dcomm/---publ/documents/publication /wcms_513739.pdf.

Justino, P. 2017. "Linking Inequality and Political Conflict: The Role of Social Mobilization and Collective Action." Background paper for the United Nations–World Bank Flagship Study, *Pathways for Peace: Inclusive Approaches to Preventing Violent Conflict*, World Bank, Washington, DC.

Kelly, J. 2017. "Intimate Partner Violence and Conflict: Understanding the Links between Political Violence and Personal Violence." Background paper for the United Nations–World Bank Flagship Study, *Pathways for Peace: Inclusive Approaches to Preventing Violent Conflict*, World Bank, Washington, DC.

Leckman, J. F., C. Panter-Brick, and R. Salah, eds. 2014. *Pathways to Peace: The Transformative Power of Children and Families.* Cambridge, MA: MIT Press.

Lichbach, M. I. 1989. "An Evaluation of 'Does Economic Inequality Breed Political Conflict?' Studies." *World Politics* 41 (4): 431–70.

Marc, A., N. Verjee, and S. Mogaka. 2015. *The Challenge of Stability and Security in West Africa.* Africa Development Forum series. Washington, DC: World Bank; Paris: Agence Française de Développement.

Miller, K. E., and A. Rasmussen. 2010. "War Exposure, Daily Stressors, and Mental Health in Conflict and Post-Conflict Settings: Bridging the Divide between Trauma-Focused and Psychosocial Frameworks." *Journal of Social Science Medicine* 70 (1): 7–16.

Mueller, H. 2017. "How Much Is Prevention Worth?" Background paper for the United Nations–World Bank Flagship Study, *Pathways for Peace: Inclusive Approaches to Preventing Violent Conflict,* World Bank, Washington, DC.

Mueller, H., and J. Tobias. 2016. "The Cost of Violence: Estimating the Economic Impact of Conflict." Growth Brief, International Growth Centre, London. https://www.theigc.org/wp -content/uploads/2016/12/IGCJ5023 Economic Cost_of_Conflict_Brief_2211 v7 _WEB.pdf.

Nordas, R., and N. P. Gleditsch. 2007. "Climate Change and Conflict." *Political Geography* 26 (6): 627–38.

Nygård, H., K. Baghat, G. Barrett, K. Dupuy, S. Gates, S. Hillesund, S. A. Rustad, H. Strand, H. Urdal, and G. Østby. 2017. "Inequality and Armed Conflict: Evidence and Data." Background paper for the United Nations–World Bank Flagship Study, *Pathways for Peace: Inclusive Approaches to Preventing Violent Conflict*, World Bank, Washington, DC.

OECD (Organisation for Economic Co-operation and Development). 2015. *States of Fragility 2015: Meeting Post-2015 Ambitions.* Paris: OECD.

———. 2016. *States of Fragility Report 2016.* Paris: OECD.

O'Reilly, M., A. Ó Súilleabháin, and T. Paffenholz. 2015. *Reimagining Peacemaking: Women's Roles in Peace Processes.* New York: International Peace Institute.

Østby, G. 2013. "Inequality and Political Violence: A Review of the Literature." *International Area Studies Review* 16 (2): 206–31.

Paasonen, K., and H. Urdal. 2016. "Youth Bulges, Exclusion, and Instability: The Role of Youth in the Arab Spring." PRIO Conflict Trends, Peace Research Institute Oslo, March. http:// files.prio.org/Publication_files/prio/Paasonen, %20Urdal%20-%20Youth%20Bulges,%20Exc lusion%20and%20Instability,%20Conflict %20Trends%203-2016.pdf.

Paffenholz, T., A. Hirblinger, D. Landau, F. Fritsch, and C. Dijkstra. 2017. "Preventing Violence through Inclusion: From Building Political Momentum to Sustaining Peace." Background paper for the United Nations–World Bank Flagship Study, *Pathways for Peace: Inclusive Approaches to Preventing Violent Conflict,* World Bank, Washington, DC.

Piazza, J. A. 2017. "Repression and Terrorism: A Cross-National Empirical Analysis of Types of Repression and Domestic Terrorism." *Terrorism and Political Violence* 29 (1): 102–18.

Rakotomalala, O. 2017. "Local-Level Mechanisms for Violent Conflict Prevention." Background paper for the United Nations–World Bank Flagship Study, *Pathways for Peace: Inclusive Approaches to Preventing Violent Conflict,* World Bank, Washington, DC.

Rother, B., G. Pierre, D. Lombardo, R. Herrala, P. Toffano, E. Roos, G. Auclair, and K. Manasseh. 2016. "The Economic Impact of Conflicts and the Refugee Crisis in the Middle East and North Africa." Staff Discussion Note SDN/16/08, International Monetary Fund, Washington, DC.

Rustad, S. A. 2016. "Socioeconomic Inequalities and Attitudes toward Violence: A Test with New Survey Data in the Niger Delta." *International Interactions* 42 (1): 106–39.

Sacks, A., and M. Larizza. 2012. "Why Quality Matters: Rebuilding Trustworthy Local Government in Post-Conflict Sierra Leone." Policy Research Working Paper 6021, World Bank, Washington, DC.

Sargsyan, I. L. 2017. "Narrative, Perception, and Emotion: A Review of Recent Political Science Studies." Background paper for the United Nations–World Bank Flagship Study, *Pathways for Peace: Inclusive Approaches to Preventing Violent Conflict,* World Bank, Washington, DC.

Schleussner, C., J. F. Donges, R. V. Donner, and H. J. Schellnhuber. 2016. "Armed-Conflict Risks Enhanced by Climate-Related Disasters in Ethnically Fractionalized Countries." *Proceedings of the National Academy of Sciences* 113 (33): 9216–21.

Shonkoff, J. P., and A. P. Garner. 2012. *The Lifelong Effects of Early Childhood Adversity and Toxic Stress.* Technical Report. Elk Grove Village, IL: American Academy of Pediatrics. http://pediatrics.aappublications.org/content /pediatrics/early/2011/12/21/peds.2011-2663 .full.pdf.

Small Arms Survey. 2011. *Global Burden of Armed Violence.* Geneva: Small Arms Survey.

Stel, N., and R. Ndayiragiie. 2014. "The Eye of the Beholder: Service Provision and State Legitimacy in Burundi." *Africa Spectrum* 49 (3): 3–28.

Stewart, F. 2000. "Crisis Prevention: Tackling Horizontal Inequalities." *Oxford Development Studies* 28 (3): 245–62.

———. 2002. "Horizontal Inequalities: A Neglected Dimension of Development." QEH Working Paper 81, Centre for Research on Inequality, Human Security, and Ethnicity, Queen Elizabeth House, University of Oxford.

———. 2009. "Horizontal Inequalities as a Cause of Conflict." Bradford Development Lecture, University of Bradford. https://www .bradford.ac.uk/social-sciences/media/social-sciences/BDLStewart.pdf.

Stone, L. 2015. "Study of 156 Peace Agreements, Controlling for Other Variables, *Quantitative Analysis of Women's Participation in Peace Processes.*" In *Reimagining Peacemaking: Women's Roles in Peace Processes*, by M. O'Reilly, A. Ó Súilleabháin, and T. Paffenholz, annex I. New York: International Peace Institute.

Sturge, G., R. Mallett, J. Hagen-Zanker, and R. Slater. 2017. *Tracking Livelihoods, Services and Governance: Panel Survey Findings from the Secure Livelihoods Research Consortium*. London: Secure Livelihoods Research Consortium.

Sundberg, R., K. Eck, and J. Kreutz. 2012. "Introducing the UCDP Non-State Conflict Dataset." *Journal of Peace Research* 49 (2): 351–62.

UCDP (Uppsala Conflict Data Program). 2017. *UCDP Conflict Encyclopedia*. Uppsala University. www.ucdp.uu.se.

UN (United Nations). 2015a. *The Challenge of Sustaining Peace*. Report of the Advisory Group of Experts for the 2015 Review of the United Nations Peacebuilding Architecture. New York: UN.

———. 2015b. *Uniting Our Strengths for Peace: Politics, Partnership, and People*. Report of the High-Level Panel on Peace Operations. New York: United Nations, June 16.

———. 2016. *Too Important to Fail—Addressing the Humanitarian Financing Gap*. Report of the High-Level Panel on Humanitarian Financing to the Secretary-General. New York: UN.

UN DESA (United Nations Department of Economic and Social Affairs). 2015. "Population by Age and Sex (Thousands)." UN DESA, New York. https://esa.un.org /unpd/wpp/DataQuery/.

UNDP (United Nations Development Programme). 2016. *Arab Human Development Report: Youth and the Prospects for Human Development in a Changing Reality*. New York: UNDP. http://www.arab-hdr.org/ PreviousReports/2016/2016.aspx.

UNESCWA (UN Economic and Social Commission for Western Asia). 2017. "The Impact of Conflict over the Life Cycle: Evidence for the Arab Region." Forthcoming in *Trends and Impacts* 5.

UN General Assembly. 2016. "Review of United Nations Peacebuilding Architecture." Resolution A/RES/70/262, adopted April 27, New York.

UNHCR (United Nations High Commissioner for Refugees). 2017. *Global Trends: Forced Displacement in 2016*. Geneva: UNHCR. http://www.unhcr.org/en-us/statistics/unhcr stats/5943e8a34/global-trends-forced-dis-placement-2016.html.

UN Secretary-General. 2015. *Report of the Secretary-General: Conflict-Related Sexual Violence*, UN Doc. S/2015/203. New York: United Nations.

UN Security Council. 2015. "Youth, Peace, and Security." Resolution 2250, adopted December 9, New York.

———. 2016. "Postconflict Peacebuilding." Resolution S/RES/2282, adopted April 27, New York.

UN Women. 2015. *Preventing Conflict, Transforming Justice, Securing the Peace: Global Study on the Implementation of United Nations Security Council Resolution 1325*. New York: UN Women.

World Bank. 2011. *World Development Report 2011: Conflict, Security, and Development*. Washington, DC: World Bank.

———. 2017. *World Development Report 2017: Governance and the Law*. Washington, DC: World Bank.

World Economic Forum. 2016. *The Future of Jobs: Employment, Skills, and Workforce Strategy for the Fourth Industrial Revolution*. Global Challenge Insight Report. Geneva: World Economic Forum.

Additional Reading

Aall, P., and C. A. Crocker, eds. 2017. *The Fabric of Peace in Africa: Looking Beyond the State*. Wateloo: Centre for International Governance Innovation.

Bøås, M., S. Sundstøl Eriksen, T. Gade, J. H. Sande Lie, and O. J. Sending. 2017. "Conflict Prevention and Ownership: Limits and Opportunities for External Actors." Background paper for the United Nations–World Bank Flagship Study, *Pathways for Peace: Inclusive Approaches to Preventing Violent Conflict*, World Bank, Washington, DC.

Bob-Milliar, G. 2017. "Sustaining Peace: Making Development Work for the Prevention of Violent Conflicts: Ghana and Côte d'Ivoire Compared." Case study for the United Nations–World Bank Flagship Study, *Pathways for Peace: Inclusive Approaches to Preventing Violent Conflict*, World Bank, Washington, DC.

Brack, D., and G. Hayman. 2006. "Managing Trade in Conflict Resources." In *Trade, Aid, and Security*, edited by O. Brown, M. Halle, S. Pena-Moreno, and S. Winkler. London: Earthscan.

Call, C. 2012. *Why Peace Fails: The Causes and Prevention of Civil War Recurrence*. Washington, DC: Georgetown University Press.

Colletta, N., and B. Oppenheim. 2017. "Subnational Conflict: Dimensions, Trends, and Options for Prevention." Background paper for the United Nations–World Bank Flagship Study, *Pathways for Peace: Inclusive Approaches to Preventing Violent Conflict*, World Bank, Washington, DC.

DCAF (Geneva Center for the Democratic Control of Armed Forces). 2017. "The Contribution and Role of SSR in the Prevention of Violent Conflict." Background paper for the United Nations–World Bank Flagship Study, *Pathways for Peace: Inclusive Approaches to Preventing Violent Conflict*, World Bank, Washington, DC.

Drew, E. 2017. "Assessing the Links between Extractive Industries and the Prevention of Violent Conflict: A Literature Review." Background paper for the United Nations–World Bank Flagship Study, *Pathways for Peace: Inclusive Approaches to Preventing Violent Conflict*, World Bank, Washington, DC.

Griffin, M. Forthcoming. "The UN's Role in a Changing Global Landscape." In *The Oxford Handbook on the United Nations*. 2d ed., edited by T. G. Weiss and S. Daws. Oxford: Oxford University Press.

Gurr, T. R. 1970. *Why Men Rebel*. Princeton, NJ: Princeton University Press.

Jaffrey, S. 2017. "Sustaining Peace: Making Development Work for the Prevention of Violent Conflicts; Case Study: Indonesia." Case study for the United Nations–World Bank Flagship Study, *Pathways for Peace: Inclusive Approaches to Preventing Violent Conflict*, World Bank, Washington, DC.

Mogaka, S. 2017. "Competition for Power in Africa: Inclusive Politics and Its Relation to Violent Conflict." Background paper for the United Nations–World Bank Flagship Study, *Pathways for Peace: Inclusive Approaches to Preventing Violent Conflict*, World Bank, Washington, DC.

Langer, A., and K. Smedts. 2013. "Seeing Is Not Believing: Perceptions of Horizontal Inequalities in Africa." Working Paper 16, Centre for Research on Peace and Development, Leuven, Belgium.

Paffenholz, T. 2015. "Beyond the Normative: Can Women's Inclusion Really Make for Better Peace Processes?" Policy Brief, Graduate Institute of Geneva and Centre for Conflict Development and Peacebuilding, Geneva.

Parks, T., N. Colletta, and B. Oppenheim. 2013. *The Contested Corners of Asia: Subnational Conflict and International Development Assistance*. San Francisco: Asia Foundation.

UN (United Nations). 2013. *A New Global Partnership: Eradicate Poverty and Transform Economies through Sustainable Development*. Report of the High-Level Panel of Eminent Persons on the Post-2015 Development Agenda. New York: UN.

UN Secretary-General. 2013. *Securing States and Societies: Strengthening the United Nations Comprehensive Support to Security Sector Reform*. Report A/67/970. New York: United Nations.

———. 2017. *Restructuring of the United Nations Peace and Security Pillar*. Report A/72/525. New York: United Nations.

UNDP (United Nations Development Programme) and Department of Political Affairs. 2016. *Joint UNDP-DPA Programme on Building National Capacities for Conflict Prevention: Annual Report*. New York: UNDP. http://www.undp.org/content/undp/en/home/librarypage/democratic-governance/conflict-prevention/joint-undp-dpa-programme-on-building-national-capacities-for-con.html.

Abbreviations

3N Initiative	The Nigeriens Nourish the Nigeriens
ACLED	Armed Conflict Location and Event Data
CDD	community-driven development
CEWARN	Conflict Early Warning and Response Mechanism
CSO	civil society organization
DDR	disarmament, demobilization, and reintegration
ECOWARN	Early Warning and Response Network
ECOWAS	Economic Community of West African States
EITI	Extractive Industries Transparency Initiative
EU	European Union
EWS	early warning system
FARC	Revolutionary Armed Forces of Colombia
FDI	foreign direct investment
GCFF	Global Concessional Financing Facility
GDP	gross domestic product
GNI	gross national income
HACP	Haute Autorité à la Consolidation de la Paix
HIV/AIDS	human immunodeficiency virus/acquired immunodeficiency syndrome
I4P	infrastructures for peace
ICT	information and communication technology
IDA	International Development Association
IDP	internally displaced person
IGAD	Inter-Governmental Authority on Development
IRA	Irish Republican Army
KPCS	Kimberley Process Certification Scheme
MINUSCA	Multidimensional Integrated Stabilization Mission in the Central African Republic
NATO	North Atlantic Treaty Organization
NSP	National Solidarity Program
ODA	overseas development assistance
OSCE	Organization for Security and Co-operation in Europe
PDA	peace and development adviser
PER	public expenditure review
PRIO	Peace Research Institute Oslo
RPBA	Recovery and Peacebuilding Assessment
SDG	Sustainable Development Goal
SME	small or medium enterprise

SSR	security sector reform
TOC	transnational organized crime
UCDP	Uppsala Conflict Data Program
UN	United Nations
UNDP	United Nations Development Programme
UNHCR	United Nations High Commissioner for Refugees
UNOCA	United Nations Office for Central Africa
UNODC	United Nations Office on Drugs and Crime
UNOWA	United Nations Office for West Africa
UNOWAS	United Nations Office for West Africa and the Sahel
UNRCCA	United Nations Regional Center for Preventive Diplomacy in Central Asia
WTO	World Trade Organization

Introduction

Violent conflict has surged in recent years.[1] While this violence is concentrated in relatively few countries, its global impact is enormous. The spread of violence across previously stable regions, the increased use of terrorism as a tactic of war, and the deployment of remote tactics of warfare have exacted a terrible human toll. The global sense of security has been shaken far beyond any specific battlefield. For the countries directly affected by civil war, the impact of violence is measured not only in direct casualties but also in economic collapse, breaking apart of institutions, and tearing of the social fabric. The impacts of violence also reverberate globally. The flow of refugees from violent conflict has reached historic proportions. Attacks on civilian targets have increased significantly. Peace and security policies are changing dramatically in reaction to new threats.[2]

The majority of violent conflicts play out within the border of the countries where they originate. Yet violence has become increasingly complex, crossing borders and becoming protracted and intractable. In today's highly interconnected world, violent conflict can evolve rapidly, making traditional preventive tools obsolete and ineffective. Many armed conflicts today take place on the peripheries of states and do not directly involve government soldiers. Violence remains entrenched in low-income countries, yet some of today's deadliest conflicts are occurring in countries with higher income levels and stronger institutions.

This suggests that economic development alone is not a guarantee of peace. Armed groups increasingly act across borders and benefit from cross-border illicit economies, triggering foreign intervention and undermining regional stability.

An impediment to development and prosperity today and in the future, violent conflict also curtails the ability of governments to reduce poverty. By 2030—the horizon set by the international community for achieving the Sustainable Development Goals (SDGs)—more than 60 percent of the world's poor will live in countries affected by fragility and high levels of violence (OECD 2015; World Bank 2011). By the same year, the costs of humanitarian assistance will be a staggering US$50 billion per year (UN 2016).

The growing costs associated with violent conflict, the increasingly global impact of many contemporary conflicts, and their resistance to established settlement mechanisms make focusing on prevention a priority for the international community.

This study originates from the conviction on the part of the World Bank Group and the United Nations (UN) that the attention of the international community needs to be urgently refocused on prevention. It builds on the recognition that the end of violence should be both an objective and an enabler of development, as expressed in the 2030 Agenda for Sustainable Development, the recent commitments expressed in the UN resolutions on sustaining peace

(UN General Assembly 2016; UN Security Council 2016) and the eighteenth replenishment of the World Bank Group's International Development Association. This study also builds on the findings of the *World Development Report 2011: Conflict, Security, and Development* (World Bank 2011).

This study seeks to improve the way in which domestic development processes interact with security, diplomatic, justice, and human rights efforts to prevent conflicts from becoming violent. It recognizes that the World Bank Group and the United Nations bring separate comparative advantages to the prevention of violent conflict and have different roles and responsibilities in the international architecture. Therefore, while a holistic framework is essential to prevention, the findings and recommendations of this study do not apply to all organizations in the same way.

Prevention of Violent Conflict Works and Is Cost-Effective

Prevention is a rational and cost-effective strategy for countries at risk of violence and for the international community. Beyond the moral value associated with saving human lives and preventing atrocity, prevention minimizes the costs of destruction generated by cycles of violence (Chang and Luo 2013). By preserving a landscape free of large-scale armed violence, prevention also minimizes the indirect costs of violence, such as the diversion of resources toward military expenditures, international spillovers to neighboring countries and regions, and losses of human capital (De Groot, Brück, and Bozzoli 2009). Given the characteristic persistence of violence once it starts and the likelihood of relapse, the benefits of prevention accumulate over time (Mueller 2017).

Several studies have developed methodologies to estimate the cost-effectiveness of conflict prevention (Brown and Rosecrance 1999; Carnegie Commission on Preventing Deadly Conflict 1997; Chalmers 2007; IEP 2017; Mueller 2017). While the availability and quality of data remain a major issue, this recent body of literature provides evidence that the prevention of violent conflict is associated with enormous returns in terms of cost avoidance. These returns are particularly high for conflict-affected countries, but are equally meaningful for the international community as well. Existing patterns of spending on official development assistance and humanitarian aid—strongly focused on countries in or after conflict—suggest that the international community could save substantial resources by refocusing its efforts on preventing violence. The scholarly literature concurs that taking preventive action before the outbreak of violence is considerably cheaper for the international community than intervening during or after violence occurs (Foreign and Commonwealth Office 2003; Mueller 2017).

In their early attempt to estimate the cost-effectiveness of prevention, Brown and Rosecrance (1999) demonstrate that in Haiti, Rwanda, and Somalia, among other situations, preventive action by the international community would have saved considerable resources later on. Looking at a series of case studies, Chalmers (2007) similarly estimates the cost-effectiveness ratio of prevention to lie somewhere between 1:2 and 1:7. These figures suggest that, over the medium to long term, donors would save between US$2 and US$7 for each US$1 invested in prevention-related activities. The cost-effectiveness of prevention, however, becomes even clearer if the actual costs to conflict-affected countries and their neighbors are considered. Looking at data from Rwanda between 1995 and 2014, the Institute for Economics and Peace finds the cost-effectiveness ratio of peacebuilding to be 1:16. This means that US$1 invested in efforts to build peace and prevent the recurrence of violence in Rwanda has saved US$16 in costs over the past two decades (IEP 2017).

An analysis carried out for this study by Mueller (2017) presents a series of scenarios in which the costs and benefits of prevention are calculated considering different success rates of prevention efforts (see box I.1). In a conservative, neutral scenario where only 50 percent of efforts at prevention prove successful, the net returns from

BOX I.1 The Business Case for Prevention

Using a model and a series of scenarios, Mueller (2017) conducted a cost-benefit analysis of an effective system for preventing violent conflict. The expected returns on prevention will be positive as long as the costs of prevention are less than the damages or losses attributable to violence. Considering the highly destructive potential of war, this is almost always the case provided that prevention is minimally effective. The returns on prevention vary in optimistic, pessimistic, and neutral scenarios (table BI.1.1). The negative effects of war on economic growth and expenditures on postconflict aid and peacekeeping need to be weighed against the expected costs and efficacy of the three scenarios for prevention. The effects of prevention for each scenario are described in terms of economic damages, loss of life avoided (prevented damage), and cost savings in postconflict reconstruction and peacekeeping (saved costs).

Prevention benefits all actors involved:

- *Prevention is economically beneficial.* Even in the most pessimistic scenario, the average net savings is close to US$5 billion per year. In the most optimistic scenario, the net savings is almost US$70 billion per year.
- *The bulk of the savings accrue at the national level, where direct costs of conflict in terms of casualties and forgone economic growth are greatest.*

The lost growth from a year of conflict means that every subsequent year's economic growth starts from a lower base, so prevention leads to compounded savings over time.

- *Prevention is also good for the international community.* It saves on postconflict humanitarian assistance and peacekeeping interventions, which are much more expensive than preventive action itself. In the most optimistic scenario, yearly savings for the international community could amount to US$1.5 billion per year. In the most pessimistic scenario, yearly savings for the international community could amount to US$698 million.
- *The benefits of prevention increase over time, while the costs fall.* This means that the net savings (displayed in table BI.1.1) are much lower than the total benefits reached after 15 years.

The three scenarios are based on assumptions regarding lost gross domestic product (GDP) growth attributable to conflict (Lomborg 2013; Mueller 2017), the costs of prevention, and the effectiveness of prevention (Dunne 2012). The *optimistic scenario* assumes that the costs of prevention are low (US$100 million per intervention per year);

TABLE BI.1.1 Modeling the Returns to Prevention under Three Scenarios

Assumption	Optimistic	Neutral	Pessimistic
Lost GDP growth per conflict year (% points)	5.2	3.9	2.5
Cost of prevention[a]	100	500	1,000
Effectiveness of prevention (%)	75	50	25
Prevented damage[a]	68,736	34,251	9,377
Saved costs[b]	1,523	1,176	698
Additional cost[c]	−352	−2,118	−5,247
Net savings per year	**69,907**	**33,309**	**4,828**

Note: All figures for spending, damages, and costs are in US$, millions per year. GDP = gross domestic product.
a. The economic damage and deaths prevented.
b. Costs saved from peacekeeping and humanitarian assistance that become unnecessary with prevention.
c. Additional costs needed for prevention efforts.

(Box continued next page)

prevention is highly effective (succeeds in avoiding a conflict 75 percent of the time); and prevention avoids very high losses attributable to conflict (GDP growth is 5.2 percent lower during conflict). The *pessimistic scenario*, which uses the most conservative assumptions, assumes that prevention is rarely effective (25 percent of the time); the costs of prevention are very high (US$1 billion per intervention per year); and war affects GDP with lower growth of 2.5 percent per year. The *neutral scenario* uses assumptions between these two extremes: prevention is effective 50 percent of the time; it is moderately expensive (US$500 million per intervention per year); and GDP growth is 3.9 percent lower per year of active conflict.

Returns on prevention may be even greater than the conservative estimates that this simple model suggests. This model does not factor in many additional costs of war that may make prevention even more cost-effective. Costs associated with forced displacement, for instance, are not included. Military expenditure to fight civil wars, which is known to divert critical resources from productive activities in low-income countries (Collier and Hoeffler 2006), is not included either. The impact of "ungoverned spaces," which contribute to opportunities for violent extremism, organized crime, and trafficking, all have significant cost implications that are not accounted for in the model. Some of the persistent legacy effects of conflict due to refugees, interrupted trade, and illicit trade, among others, need to be factored in to gauge the real impact of prevention in terms of cost avoidance.

Sources: Collier and Hoeffler 2006; Dunne 2012; Lomborg 2013; Mueller 2017.

prevention are US$33 billion against an average cost of US$2.1 billion per year over 15 years. Put another way, for each US$1 invested in prevention, about US$16 is saved down the road.

Why, Then, Is There So Little Belief in the Prevention of Violent Conflict?

The vast majority of countries manage conflict peacefully most of the time and can prevent its violent manifestations. Both individuals and societies tend to cooperate to avoid the risk of violence. Many countries have established institutions for redistributive purposes, for security and justice, and for the management of political competition. These institutions support societies in resolving conflict peacefully and routinely provide effective governance (World Bank 2017), preventing conflict and tensions in society from turning violent. This study analyzes cases of countries at high risk of violent conflict that have successfully prevented violence through a combination of effective policies, programs, and political action.

While countries can be successful at reducing violence, the prevailing perception is that the international community's ability to tackle the risk of violent conflict effectively has been declining. Pessimism permeates the tone of public discourse when it comes to preventing conflict. Stories of successful prevention rarely receive the same public attention as conflicts that descend into violence. Prevention lacks positive publicity, as the existence of a direct link between specific policy actions and the resulting absence of violence is often hard to prove. Economists refer to this problem as "lack of counterfactuals." How can the positive impact of preventing a violent conflict be credited, if that conflict did not occur? It is difficult to prove that specific actions have addressed the high risk of violent conflicts. Many factors may be at play, and singling out specific causes and effects is often impossible.

Doubts about the effectiveness of prevention reflect the lack of clear *information* on what does, and does not, seem to work. The drivers of violent conflict are complex and so is the identification of the courses of action needed to prevent violence and sustain peace. There is no single, simple formula for prevention. Preventing violent conflict and building peace call for different approaches in different circumstances and in different contexts. Redirecting investments to a marginalized region, engaging youth in meaningful activities, investing in the education of women, and setting up grievance-redress mechanisms are all examples of actions that can foster inclusiveness and reduce the risk of violent conflict. At times, such courses of action may appear banal. Often, they do not even register as prevention in the minds of common citizens and policy makers.

Furthermore, effective preventive action requires justifying preemptive *investments* and allocating scarce resources to address risks before their potential impacts have become evident. It is part of human nature to hope, even in the face of clear risks, that the worst will be avoided. One may wonder, as a consequence, whether the political, economic, and social costs of early preventive actions are worth incurring. Conflict prevention, seen in this perspective, is not dissimilar from preventive health care (Stares 2017). It may take considerable effort to convince people that a healthy lifestyle is the most effective prescription for a long life and that tertiary care, with its sophisticated hospitals and technologies, can treat but not prevent illness.

Finally, *incentives* for acting collectively to prevent a crisis are often weaker than those for mobilizing a response to crisis. Crises mobilize societies and government much more effectively than early action. Crisis exerts a powerful and self-reinforcing attraction. Societies can become gripped by a cycle where conflict—and the response to that conflict—dominates the attention of leaders and citizens. Policy becomes increasingly reactive, reducing space for prevention. Cycles of crisis-to-crisis, short-term emergency responses create their own self-reinforcing appeal.

These three dilemmas of prevention hold at a global level. The international community has secured some degree of success in containing and ending conflicts, but its focus has been more on short-term crisis management than on the upstream prevention of violence. International efforts at preventive diplomacy and peacekeeping are aimed primarily at preserving international peace and security as well as preventing atrocities—the extremes of violence—while scarce resources are targeted at delivering tangible responses to the humanitarian crises that conflict causes. International action, deployed when a crisis is looming or when violence has escalated, is, arguably, overwhelming the capacity of the international system to respond.

Development policies that could effectively address early risks of violence by promoting structural and institutional change are often designed with limited consideration given to prevention. Risks of violent conflicts are rarely integrated in their design. Holistic and sustained approaches to maintaining peace and building local resilience are rare. When they succeed, they rarely attract attention.

What Is the Prevention of Violent Conflict?

The UN twin resolutions on sustaining peace define prevention as the avoidance of "the outbreak, escalation, recurrence, or continuation of violent conflicts" (UN General Assembly 2016; UN Security Council 2016). This study uses this definition and understands prevention to be a central component of what the United Nations Security Council and General Assembly describe "as a goal and a process to build a common vision of a society, ensuring that the needs of all segments of the population are taken into account … as a shared task and responsibility that needs to be fulfilled by the Government and all other national stakeholders … at all stages of conflict" (UN General Assembly 2016; UN Security Council 2016).

As violent conflict can potentially affect every society, risk needs to be a lens for the framing of development policies and be done routinely in each society and country. Prevention is about fostering societies in which it is easier to choose peace and where people can confidently expect to live without being exposed to violence over long periods of time. It is about building societies that offer opportunities and are inclusive. In this sense, prevention is a long-term approach in its time horizon, as it requires sustained efforts over time.

This study presents a framework (presented in chapter 3) for conceptualizing how societies forge unique pathways as they navigate risks of violence and harness opportunities for peace. The longer, and more intentionally, a society has worked to foster incentives for peace, the harder it will be to derail progress. Violence, too, is path-dependent. Once it takes hold, incentives reconfigure around the expectation that it will continue.

Prevention, then, is not only about avoiding or stopping repeated violent crises. While it is necessary to avoid crisis by mitigating the impact of shocks, prevention also requires proactively addressing deeper, underlying risks that prevent sustainable development and peace. In most conflicts, these deeper risks create fertile ground for mobilization to violence.

With the 2030 Agenda for Sustainable Development, the United Nations member states committed to build peaceful, just, and inclusive societies that are free from fear and violence; to eradicate poverty and hunger; to combat inequalities; and to protect and respect human rights (box I.2).[3] The 17 SDGs and 169 targets are seen as "integrated and indivisible, and balance the three dimensions of sustainable development: the economic, social, and environmental" (UN General Assembly 2015, preamble). This agenda provides an overarching framework for action for states and other actors to work together toward conflict prevention and peace. The SDGs contained in the 2030 Agenda offer entry points for implementing the recommendations of this study.[4]

Prevention is primarily an endogenous process, a responsibility of government and societies. In this sense, prevention enhances sovereignty, empowering each country to be

---

BOX I.2 The 2030 Agenda for Sustainable Development

In September 2015, UN member states adopted the 2030 Agenda for Sustainable Development and a new set of development goals as successors to the Millennium Development Goals. The 2030 Agenda is a universal agenda that commits all countries to work toward a peaceful and resilient world through inclusive and shared prosperity and the upholding of human rights. It puts people at the center and pledges to leave no one behind, to empower women, and to give special attention to countries in protracted crisis.

The 2030 Agenda emphasizes that peace, development, human rights, and humanitarian responses are inextricably linked and mutually reinforcing. It includes a focus on building peaceful, just, and inclusive societies, not only as an enabler but also as a fundamental component of development outcomes.

The 17 Sustainable Development Goals (SDGs) are integrated and indivisible in nature. Efforts to achieve one goal are seen as instrumental to achieving other goals. For example, actions to address goals such as eradicating poverty (SDG 1), reducing inequalities (SDG 10), promoting quality education (SDG 4), achieving gender equality (SDG 5), addressing climate change (SDG 13), supporting peace and strengthening institutions (SDG 16), and promoting partnerships (SDG 17) can have mutually reinforcing effects.

The SDGs provide a blueprint for scaling up investments to transform economies, build resilience, strengthen institutions, and bolster capacities. By integrating sustainability in all activities and promoting inclusivity, partnerships, and accountability, the 2030 Agenda can contribute to peace.

Source: UN General Assembly 2015.

---

in control of its own destiny and the state to build positive relationships with its citizens. International actors play a critical role in supporting endogenous preventive efforts. Their support is also instrumental in sustaining regional efforts by neighbors that have an interest in avoiding violence, the negative effects of which could spill over into their own countries.

Can Prevention of Violent Conflict Be Done Differently?

This study is about the prevention of violent conflict. Conflict is an essential component of societal dynamics and an expression of human interaction. Negotiation among groups over important issues, such as access to power, natural resources, and security, is a form of management of conflict. The process of contestation can be healthy. Conflict often produces positive outcomes, as it brings about change. When conflict becomes violent, however, it imposes human and economic costs that can become enormous and can strip away incentives for peaceful conflict resolution.

Violence and violent conflict have accompanied political, social, and economic change throughout history (Tilly 1990, 2003). Monuments to nation builders and war heroes often are the most visible and highly revered symbols in cities and communities across the world. Sacrifice and heroism in war are often celebrated as highly positive attributes of societies. Yet humans have constantly strived to avoid violence, developing sophisticated institutions to respond to its risk (Pinker 2012). This deep contradiction is not likely to disappear any time soon. Under certain circumstances, societies will always be tempted to resort to violence to achieve their goals. There is increasing recognition, however, that the human suffering and exorbitant costs associated with violent conflict can often be avoided, with positive change resulting from peaceful contestation.

This study is clear-eyed in its recognition that absolute prevention of all conflicts is beyond reach, if not impossible. To be sure, it looks beyond reach in the present, complex global context. It, nonetheless, argues that states and the international community can do a much better job of addressing the risks of violent conflicts and reducing their occurrence.

Prevention of conflict is a process whose benefits to both society and the actors within society unfold over time. Early efforts at prevention are often hardly visible. Successful implementation of inclusive economic and social policies rarely attracts much attention. Funds for humanitarian assistance and postconflict reconstruction will always be easier to mobilize than those for long-term preventive efforts. They are tangible. They can be broadcasted on television and make the donor feel successful. They sell politically in the country providing the funds. Effective, sustained prevention is not very interesting to watch on television.

The Importance of Agency to Prevention

Violence is the product of many factors. It is often difficult to attribute violence to a single root cause. Violence is like a fever in a human body: it can be caused by many different illnesses. The question is not why societies have conflict, but why some groups choose violence to resolve their differences with other groups or with the state. This study argues that a significant proportion of contemporary violent conflicts are rooted in group-based grievances around exclusion that forge deep-seated feelings of injustice and unfairness. Recent research supports this argument. Whether based on facts or perceptions, groups who feel excluded, relatively disadvantaged, or left out are much more likely to consider violence to be an acceptable response than those who do not.

Identity plays an important role in this context, as cohesive groups with a shared sense of historical grievance are more likely to unite in response. This does not mean that every group with grievances will turn violent. In fact, the opposite is true. Nor does it mean that other factors such as external support, proliferation of weapons, and absence of deterrents are irrelevant.

On the contrary, they can and do play a critical role. Group-based grievances, nonetheless, are an important precursor to collective mobilization to violence. They need to be tackled head on and made a central component of prevention. This is why this study stresses the centrality of inclusion in prevention approaches.

The accumulation of grievances around exclusion and how leaders and groups choose to deal with them largely determine whether a society steers a pathway toward violence or peace. Actors are constantly faced with choices, weighing responses to a variety of pressures and changes along their society's pathway. Prevention, then, involves identifying and creating incentives for actors to make choices that lead to peaceful outcomes. Structural change and institutional reform within a society take time and require sustained investment. Actors in a society tend to behave and operate based on shorter timelines. They may need to show fast results, which prevention may not always provide. The need to balance actors' short- and medium-term incentives with a long-term time horizon is thus one of the crucial challenges of prevention.

Once collective violence starts, incentives are reconfigured in ways that sustain and possibly escalate violence, making efforts to restore peace especially challenging. Actors' changing interests, societal dynamics, and social norms also may prolong violence and increase the likelihood of recurrence. They play a strong role in the escalation and geographic expansion of violence. As violence spreads, it also creates incentives for more actors to engage in or profit from it. The result is a very complex situation that calls for a multifaceted approach to restoring peace.

This study is divided into eight chapters. Chapter 1 describes the new profile of violent conflict, which affects more countries, occurs more often within states and among a proliferation of armed groups, and increasingly involves foreign intervention. Chapter 2 looks at rapidly evolving global trends and changing geopolitical balance that affect the risk of violent conflict, including climate change, movements of people, and a push for more inclusive governance.

Chapter 3 introduces the concept of "pathways" to illustrate how societies shape pathways toward violence, or sustainable peace, by the way they mitigate risk and navigate conflict. Chapter 4 examines the association between violent conflict and exclusion, inequality, and unfairness and discusses how resulting grievances may be mobilized to collective violence. Chapter 5 looks at the policy arenas where most contemporary violent conflicts have arisen and discusses approaches to lower the risk. Chapter 6 summarizes lessons from successful prevention at the country level and, in particular, how successful prevention builds on coalitions, supports inclusive political arrangements, and addresses economic and social grievances. Chapter 7 reviews the instruments that the international community has in place to prevent conflict and its recent efforts to adapt these tools and instruments to new conditions. Chapter 8 discusses recommendations for improving prevention at all levels.

Notes

1. Conflicts are inherent in all societies and are managed, mitigated, and resolved in nonviolent manners through, for example, political processes (see, for example, UN General Assembly 2015), formal and informal judicial systems, local dispute mechanisms, or dialogue. But sometimes conflict may turn violent, causing enormous human and economic loss. Violent conflict can take various forms, including interstate war, armed conflict, civil war, political and electoral violence, and communal violence, and can include many actors, including states and nonstate actors, such as militias, insurgents, terrorist groups, and violent extremists. This study—while looking at conflict in general— focuses on conflicts that are becoming violent and explores pathways that prevent conflicts from escalating.

2. While battle-related deaths will likely decline after the spike of 2014–15, largely related to fewer casualties from the Syrian Arab Republic conflict, the risks of violent conflict remain high at the global level. Many of the underlying issues that are triggering conflict in different regions, such as Africa and

the Middle East, for example, are not changing drastically. This study demonstrates that the complexity of today's violent conflict and the risks associated with it go beyond yearly trends and warrant long-term attention.

3. UN General Assembly (2015), including the preamble, para. 3, and SDGs 10 and 16.
4. UN General Assembly (2015), including SDGs 4, 5, 10, 11, 12, 13, 14, 15, and 16.

References

Brown, M. E., and R. N. Rosecrance. 1999. *The Costs of Conflict: Prevention and Cure in the Global Arena.* New York: Carnegie Commission on Preventing Deadly Conflict.

Carnegie Commission on Preventing Deadly Conflict. 1997. *Preventing Deadly Conflict: Report.* New York: Carnegie Commission on Preventing Deadly Conflict.

Chalmers, M. 2007. "Spending to Save? The Cost-Effectiveness of Conflict Prevention." *Defence and Peace Economics* 18 (1): 1–23.

Chang, Y., and Z. Luo. 2013. "War or Settlement: An Economic Analysis of Conflict with Endogenous and Increasing Destruction." *Defence and Peace Economics* 24 (1): 23–46.

Collier, P., and A. Hoeffler. 2006. "Military Expenditure in Post-Conflict Societies." *Economics of Governance* 7 (1): 89–107.

De Groot, O. J., T. Brück, and C. Bozzoli. 2009. "How Many Bucks in a Bang: On the Estimation of the Economic Costs of Conflict." Economics of Security Working Paper 21, Economics of Security, Berlin.

Dunne, J. Paul. 2012. "Third Copenhagen Consensus: Armed Conflict Assessment." Assessment Paper, Copenhagen Consensus Center, Tewksbury, MA.

Foreign and Commonwealth Office. 2003. *The Global Conflict Prevention Pool: A Joint U.K. Government Approach to Reducing Conflict.* London: Foreign and Commonwealth Office.

IEP (Institute for Economics and Peace). 2017. *Measuring Peacebuilding Cost-Effectiveness.* Sydney: IEP.

Lomborg, B., ed. 2013. *Global Problems, Smart Solutions: Costs and Benefits.* Cambridge, U.K.: Cambridge University Press.

Mueller, H. 2017. "How Much Is Prevention Worth?" Background paper for the United Nations–World Bank Flagship Study, *Pathways for Peace: Inclusive Approaches to Preventing Violent Conflict,* World Bank, Washington, DC.

OECD (Organisation for Economic Co-operation and Development). 2015. *States of Fragility 2015: Meeting Post-2015 Ambitions.* Paris: OECD.

Pinker, S. 2012. *The Better Angels of Our Nature: Why Violence Has Declined.* New York: Viking.

Stares, P. 2017. *Preventive Engagement: How America Can Avoid War, Stay Strong, and Keep the Peace.* New York: Columbia University Press.

Tilly, C. 1990. *Coercion, Capital, and European States, AD 990–1992.* Cambridge, U.K.: Blackwell.

———. 2003. *The Politics of Collective Violence.* Cambridge, U.K.: Cambridge University Press.

UN (United Nations). 2016. *Too Important to Fail—Addressing the Humanitarian Financing Gap.* Report by the High-Level Panel on Humanitarian Financing to the Secretary-General. Geneva: United Nations Office for the Coordination of Humanitarian Affairs. http://www.unocha.org/sites/dms/Documents/[HLP%20Report]%20Too%20important%20to%20fail—addressing%20the%20humanitarian%20financing%20gap.pdf.

UN General Assembly. 2015. "Transforming Our World: The 2030 Agenda for Sustainable Development." Resolution A/RES/70/1, adopted September 25, New York.

———. 2016. "Review of United Nations Peacebuilding Architecture." Resolution A/RES/70/262, adopted April 27, New York.

UN Security Council. 2016. "Post-Conflict Peacebuilding." Resolution S/RES/2282, adopted April 27, New York.

World Bank. 2011. *World Development Report 2011: Conflict, Security, and Development.* Washington, DC: World Bank.

———. 2017. *World Development Report 2017: Governance and the Law.* Washington, DC: World Bank.

Additional Reading

Coleman, P. T., and R. Ferguson. 2014. *Making Conflict Work: Harnessing the Power of Disagreement.* New York: Houghton-Mifflin-Harcourt.

Cramer, C., J. Goodhand, and R. Morris. 2016. *Evidence Synthesis: What Interventions Have Been Effective in Preventing or Mitigating*

Armed Violence in Developing and Middle-Income Countries? London: Department for International Development.

Giessmann, H. J., J. B. Galvanek, and C. Seifert. 2017. "Curbing Violence: Development, Application, and Sustaining National Capacities for Prevention." Background paper for the United Nations–World Bank Flagship Study, *Pathways for Peace: Inclusive Approaches to Preventing Violent Conflict*, World Bank, Washington, DC.

Geneva Convention (IV). 1949. *Geneva Convention (IV) Relative to the Protection of Civilian Persons in Time of War*. Geneva, August 12. http://www.un.org/en/genocide prevention/documents/atrocity-crimes/Doc .33_GC-IV-EN.pdf.

Goodhand, J. 2004. "From War Economy to Peace Economy? Reconstruction and Statebuilding in Afghanistan." *Journal of International Affairs, Special Edition on International Institutions and Justice* 58 (1): 155–74.

ICRC (International Committee of the Red Cross). 2008. "How Is the Term 'Armed Conflict' Defined in International Humanitarian Law?" Opinion Paper, ICRC, Geneva, March.

IEP (Institute for Economics and Peace). 2013. *The Economic Cost of Violence Containment: A Comprehensive Assessment of the Global Cost of Violence*. Sydney: IEP.

———. 2016. *The Economic Value of Peace: 2016*. Sydney: IEP.

Mueller, H. 2013. "The Economic Cost of Conflict." ICG Working Paper, International Growth Centre, London.

UN (United Nations). 2004. "Promotion of Religious and Cultural Understanding, Harmony, and Cooperation." A/RES/59/201, note by the Secretary-General, United Nations, New York.

———. 2017. "Secretary-General, in First Address to Security Council since Taking Office, Sets Restoring Trust, Preventing Crises as United Nations Priorities." Security Council 7857th Meeting SC/12673, January 10.

CHAPTER 1

A Surge and Expansion of Violent Conflict

The threats facing the world today are different from those of decades ago. Violent conflict is now occurring in middle-income countries as well as in both low-income countries and fragile contexts, opening space for violent extremist groups and spilling over borders.

This chapter surveys the state of violent conflict across several indicators, showing that, in recent years, more countries are affected by violent conflict, more armed groups are fighting, and more outside actors are intervening. The chapter also examines trends beyond the numbers both to understand factors contributing to the new conflict dynamics and to adapt prevention policy on national, regional, and international levels.

The cost of *not* preventing violent conflict is extremely high. Beyond its incalculable human cost, violent conflict reverses hard-won development gains, stunts the opportunities of children and young people, and robs economies of opportunities for growth. Preventable diseases become more difficult to treat in and around violent conflict, and there is a higher risk of famine. Forced displacement has reached a level not seen since the immediate aftermath of World War II. Violent conflict and the humanitarian crises it spawns cost the world billions of dollars a year, outpacing the capacity of states to respond.

From roughly 1950 to 1990, parts of Africa and Asia experienced anti- and postcolonial violent conflicts and superpower proxy wars over influence and control of the state. The end of the Cold War brought a pause in the interstate tensions that characterized the bipolar international order. A window of opportunity opened to focus on intrastate conflicts. Despite the escalation of some ethnic conflicts and prompted by the atrocities that took place in Rwanda and the former Yugoslavia, a surge in peacekeeping and prevention, among other factors, reduced violent conflict to unprecedented levels by the mid-2000s (Human Security Report Project 2005; Pinker 2011). That more peaceful lull was broken in 2007, when violent conflict began to increase in scope and number of fatalities, particularly beginning in 2010.

What makes people fight and what they fight over are not new, but the fighting is happening in a new context. Violent conflict has spread to middle-income countries that have, or had, functioning institutions (such as Iraq, Syria, and Ukraine), upending assumptions that violent conflict is an exclusive problem of low-income countries. In a world where communications, finance, crime, and ideas flow across borders, many conflicts have evolved into complex systems with international, regional, national, and communal links. Such conflicts are resistant to resolution through negotiated settlement, tending to play out in regions where other countries are already at risk of violent conflict (Walter 2017b). The proliferation of nonstate armed groups has also resulted in conflicts with less state involvement, making them impervious to the settlement mechanisms deployed in the past. More external countries are intervening in violent conflicts, which could present opportunities for mediation, yet also complicates conflict dynamics.

Violent Conflict in the Twenty-First Century

Until recently, the world was becoming more peaceful (Pinker 2011). Following the end of the Cold War, the number and intensity[1] of most types of violent conflict steadily declined. That trend stalled in 2007 and has reversed since 2010. The incidence of violent conflict between states is still low (see box 1.1), but conflict within states—among a ballooning number of armed groups, between nonstate armed groups and the state, and increasingly involving some form of external intervention—is spreading. More countries were experiencing some form of violent conflict in 2016 than at any time in the previous 30 years (Allansson, Melander, and Themnér 2017; Gleditsch et al. 2002; Sundberg, Eck, and Kreutz 2012).

While much of today's violence is entrenched in low-income countries, neither wealth nor income renders countries immune. Some of the deadliest and seemingly most intractable conflicts are occurring in middle-income countries, reversing hard-won human development gains. In addition, violence in various forms has reached epidemic proportions in countries not considered fragile (Geneva Declaration Secretariat 2015; OECD 2016). The highest rates of homicide and violent crime in the world are found in Latin America and the Caribbean, where urban gang violence and drug-related crime are features of everyday life.

A few of these violent conflicts—whether in low- or middle-income countries—produce the preponderance of fatalities, and most conflicts are broadly concentrated in a few regions (Africa, the Middle East, and South Asia).

BOX 1.1 The Decline of Violent Conflict between States

Interstate violent conflict has been at historically low levels since the end of the Cold War. The Uppsala Conflict Data Program (UCDP) reported just two active interstate violent conflicts in 2016, one between India and Pakistan and the other between Ethiopia and Eritrea. In 1987, five interstate wars were recorded, but since 1992, no more than two interstate wars were recorded in any given year, and several years experienced no such wars.

The reasons for these low levels are varied. The end of the Cold War marked a shifting disposition of the great powers from conducting proxy warfare to preventing conflicts around the world. Enhanced cooperation translated into a greater role for the United Nations (UN) Security Council as a mechanism for resolving disputes. In parallel, "International norms, legal regulations, and treaties [have created] a situation today where invasion and conquest are not only outlawed, but also actively proscribed through deterrence" (Thompson 2014). Casualty avoidance has become a factor, with national leaders acutely sensitive to the perceptions of their domestic constituents and less willing to risk their soldiers' lives or engage in warfare when it can be avoided. Today, outright military victory has become less feasible. Increasing economic interdependence may also contribute to the declining trend in interstate conflict because it creates mutual vulnerabilities that act as disincentives to going to war. In this calculus, "The opportunity costs of conflict greatly outweigh any potential economic gains" (Thompson 2014), which is one of the reasons why trade linkages between countries help to promote peace (Hegre, Oneal, and Russett 2010).

The decline in interstate conflict does not mean that disagreements between states have disappeared. Real interstate tensions also persist, leaving open the possibility for a potentially devastating violent conflict to come. The number of unresolved boundary issues across the world is a further cause of persistent interstate tensions. The South China Sea is but one of these. The African Union alone is involved in mediating 19 separate contested border claims.

Sources: Haass 2017; Hegre, Oneal, and Russett 2010; Human Security Report Project 2005; Pinker and Mack 2014; Thompson 2014; Allansson, Melander, and Themnér 2017; Gleditsch et al. 2002.

Violent extremist groups also contribute to the increase in conflicts, feeding off local grievances and exploiting transnational financial and crime networks.

Today's violent conflicts are not confined to national borders. Energized by regional and international links among groups, violent conflicts often spill across borders or reflect the transnational aims and organization of such groups (OECD 2016, ch. 1). At the same time, countries are increasingly intervening in another country's conflict in support of a party or parties, giving these conflicts an additional regional or international dimension. These new dynamics have significant implications for preventing violent conflict and building sustainable peace.

Number of Violent Conflicts within States

The number of internal state-based conflicts—involving state and nonstate forces within the boundaries of a state—has risen sharply.[2] After peaking at 50 in 1991, the number of these conflicts declined for some years but then shot up again. In 2016, 47 internal state-based violent conflicts were recorded—the second-highest number in the post–Cold War era after 2015, when UCDP recorded 51 violent state-based conflicts (Allansson, Melander, and Themnér 2017; Gleditsch et al. 2002; see figure 1.1).[3] The number of conflicts that reach the threshold of war, resulting in at least 1,000 battle deaths a year, has more than tripled since just 2007 (Allansson, Melander, and Themnér 2017; Gleditsch et al. 2002; Sundberg, Eck, and Kreutz 2012).[4] The number of lower-intensity conflicts (both state-based and nonstate), meaning those resulting in between 25 and 999 battle deaths a year, has risen by more than 60 percent since 2007 (Allansson, Melander, and Themnér 2017; Gleditsch et al. 2002; Sundberg, Eck, and Kreutz 2012).[5]

FIGURE 1.1 **Violent Conflict Worldwide, by Type of Conflict, 1975–2016**

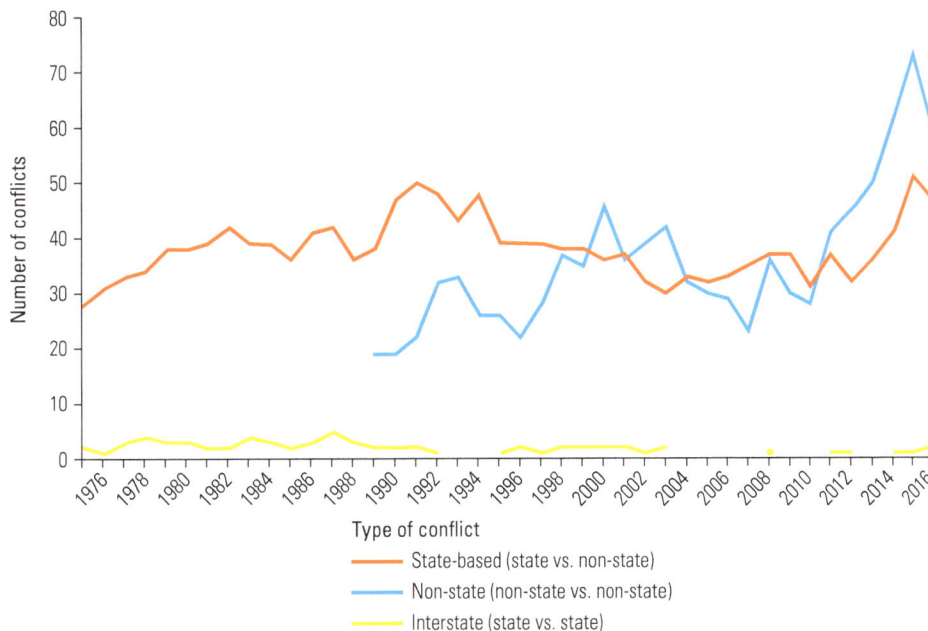

Sources: For interstate and state-based conflicts, data from Uppsala Conflict Data Program (UCDP) and Peace Research Institute Oslo (Allansson, Melander, and Themnér 2017; Gleditsch et al. 2002); for nonstate conflicts, data from UCDP (Sundberg, Eck, and Kreutz 2012; Allansson, Melander, and Themnér 2017).

Number of Fatalities Associated with Violent Conflict

Violent conflict is resulting in more fatalities. The number of reported battle-related deaths has risen sharply since 2010 to the highest numbers recorded in 20 years (see figure 1.2).[6] From the post–Cold War low in 2005, reported battle-related deaths have increased tenfold (Allansson, Melander, and Themnér 2017; Sundberg, Eck, and Kreutz 2012). A few conflicts are largely responsible for the overall increase and result in the greatest proportion of battle-related deaths; the three deadliest countries in 2016 (Afghanistan, Iraq, and Syria) incurred more than 76 percent of all fatalities recorded that year (Sundberg and Melander 2013; Croicu and Sundberg 2017; also see figure 1.3). However, the true cost of a violent conflict should be measured not by its intensity (number of conflict-related fatalities) or duration alone, but also by its human, social, and economic impact.

Minor conflicts within countries may be less visible to outside observers and may result in relatively fewer battle-related deaths; their costs also may be harder to measure. But they are just as destructive and can have devastating consequences for people and economies, not least contributing to instability and fragility within countries and fueling other intrastate or regional conflicts.

Number of Armed Groups and Violent Conflict

Violent conflict between nonstate armed groups has been rising, as has the number of armed groups. The number of violent conflicts between nonstate armed groups[7]

FIGURE 1.2 Number of Battle-Related Deaths Worldwide, by Type of Conflict, 1989–2016

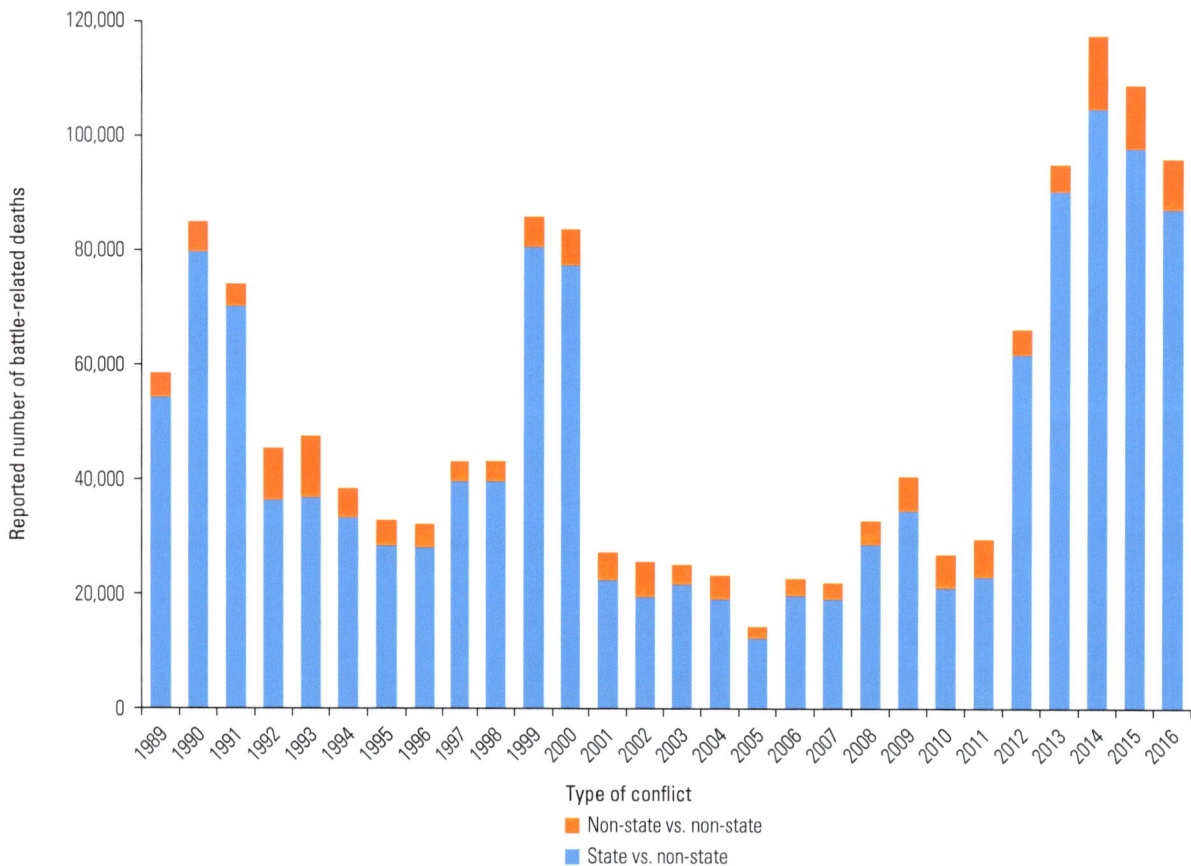

Source: Uppsala Conflict Data Program (Allansson, Melander, and Themnér 2017; Sundberg, Eck, and Kreutz 2012).

FIGURE 1.3 Number of Conflict-Related Deaths Worldwide, by Country, 2016

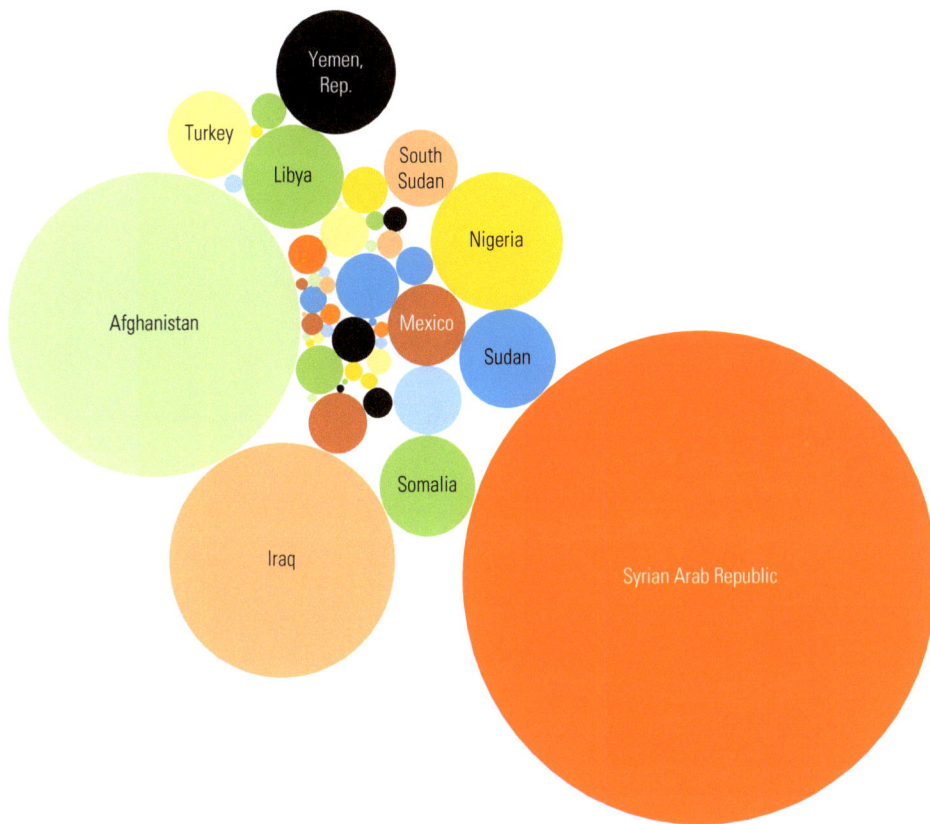

Source: Uppsala Conflict Data Program (UCDP) (Sundberg and Melander 2013; Croicu and Sundberg 2017).
Note: This figure is based on the UCDP definition of conflict (Sundberg and Melander 2013; Croicu and Sundberg 2017).

has more than doubled since 2010, as shown in figure 1.1 (Sundberg, Eck, and Kreutz 2012; Allansson, Melander, and Themnér 2017). In 2016, 60 violent conflicts were reported between nonstate armed groups, and 73 were reported in 2015, compared with only 28 in 2010 (Sundberg, Eck, and Kreutz 2012; Allansson, Melander, and Themnér 2017). In 1950, there were an average of eight armed groups in a civil war; by 2010 the average had jumped to 14 (Walter 2017b).

The proliferation of nonstate actors—armed groups that are not formally state actors—has been rising steadily especially since 2010 (see figure 1.4). These groups include rebels, militias, armed trafficking groups, and violent extremist groups, among others, that may coalesce around a grievance, an identity, an ideology, or a claim to economic or political resources.

Box 1.2 outlines the limitations of current data sets, including the fact that categorizations of "nonstate" and other actors have not yet become as nuanced as current realities. The composition and alliances of these armed groups are fluid and may evolve over time, depending on resources or leadership. Some nonstate armed groups have been able to seize and hold terrain from state militaries, despite a lack of sophisticated weaponry.

The proliferation of such groups, which may fight each other and the state in different configurations at different times, complicates violent conflicts and efforts to end them. One example is the conflict in Syria, which was responsible for the greatest number of fatalities of any single war or country in 2016 (UCDP 2017). It has involved the government of Syria, Syrian opposition groups, violent extremist groups including

FIGURE 1.4 **Number of Nonstate Groups Active in Violent Conflict Worldwide, 1989–2016**

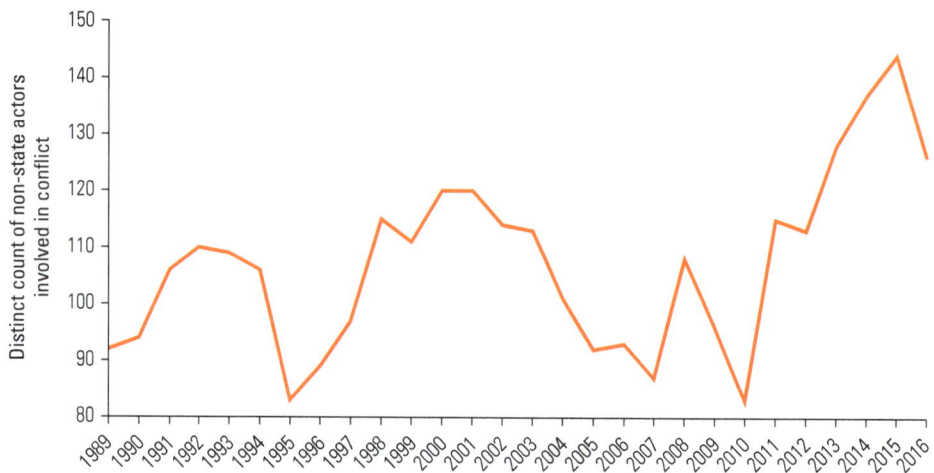

Source: Uppsala Conflict Data Program (Sundberg, Eck, and Kreutz 2012; Allansson, Melander, and Themnér 2017).

BOX 1.2 Adapting Conflict Data to Today's Violent Conflicts

The shift in trends of violent conflict is difficult to quantify with the measures used or available now. The structure of many of the quantitative data sets relied on to understand conflict dynamics are better suited for understanding the conflicts of decades ago, when conflicts predominantly involved fighting between the state militaries of two countries or when conflicts occurring within a state (as opposed to between states) consisted largely of rebel groups seeking to overthrow a government. Today's conflicts are increasingly complex and multidimensional, and available measurements may not be capturing their true extent and costs.

Both the number of nonstate conflicts that do not involve a country's formal forces and the number of nonstate armed groups have been rising. Yet data sets—for example, the Uppsala Conflict Data Program (UCDP)—often lump all nonstate groups into a single category. Such armed groups are increasingly diverse and have varied goals. Putting all of them into one overarching category— one that includes rebel groups seeking to overthrow a state, armed trafficking groups, violent extremist groups with goals beyond the overthrow of a single

state, and militias doing the bidding of elites yet not seeking formal state power, among others—conflates these groups. These groups exhibit different patterns of conflict as a result of their diverse goals, capacities, incentives, and other factors. The Armed Conflict Location and Event Data (ACLED) project makes some distinctions among nonstate armed groups.

Data sets are organized according to the perpetrator of violence, and the perpetrator is not always evident. When a perpetrator is not or cannot be identified, the violence often goes unrecorded, and the data may depict a region as nonviolent when in fact it is very violent. UCDP data dramatically undercount fatalities related to nonstate conflict, as it is often difficult, if not impossible, to identify the victims and the perpetrators. Armed groups may exploit anonymity to carry out violence on behalf of others.

Conflicts are coded as dyadic events, pitting two sides against each other, despite the fact that conflicts are becoming increasingly complex and multidimensional. The goals, capacities, and incentives of actors may shift as conflicts become reframed or internationalized. Alliances can form and

(Box continued next page)

BOX 1.2   **Adapting Conflict Data to Today's Violent Conflicts** *(continued)*

disband or shift among various actors within a single conflict. Especially in cases where conflicts are coded as full campaigns of violence that can last years, it can be difficult to capture these shifts and nuances accurately—resulting in a much simpler view of a very complex context.

As conflicts adapt, data sets should adapt and anticipate their complexity. The structure of data sets today corresponds to the dynamics of conflicts in previous eras. While many

of these data sets have been refined over the years to respond to new needs and contexts, they should continue to adapt.

Not all data sets code conflicts as full campaigns of violence. ACLED, for example, relies on an atomic format, coding only a single day of conflict at a time, which can later be aggregated into a larger context. However, ACLED also relies on a dyadic format where two sides are coded as being in combat with one another.

foreign fighters, and the so-called Islamic State,[8] with the state fighting these groups and these groups fighting each other. Their interplay contributes to the intractability of the Syrian conflict and overall instability in the region.

Violent conflict between nonstate armed groups does not indicate the strength or weakness of such groups, nor does it preclude indirect state involvement. Progovernment militias, for example, fall under the umbrella of nonstate actors, as governments recruit militias to carry out violence on their behalf.[9] Communities or powerful actors (for example, gangs and drug cartels) may also create militias or armed groups when state security forces are absent or to protect their trade routes or control territory. These groups can be used to carry out violence on behalf of a regime seeking to distance itself from particularly shameful acts; militia violence may even be used to exercise influence in competitive democratic contexts, aggravating grievances and exacerbating local and subnational conflicts (Alvarez 2006; Raleigh 2016; Ron 2002).

This proliferation of nonstate armed groups challenges state-based models of conflict prevention, mediation, and peacekeeping. Many of today's armed actors operate in areas where state presence is too limited and fragmented or diffuse for traditional, leader-based approaches to negotiated political solutions to be effective

(Raleigh and Dowd 2013). Some groups may explicitly reject international humanitarian law as well as the international institutions established to uphold it, placing themselves outside the ambit of traditional peacemaking processes (Walter 2017b). Many groups thrive in environments of weak rule of law or profit from illicit economies; they have little incentive to end violence.

More external actors are intervening more often. Proxy wars with internationalized involvement from the Soviet Union or the United States were commonplace during the Cold War. Today, emerging powers are also intervening in violent conflicts in pursuit of regional or strategic interests. In 2016, 18 violent conflicts were internationalized,[10] more than reported in any year since the end of World War II and second only to 2015, when 20 conflicts were internationalized (Allansson, Melander, and Themnér 2017; Gleditsch et al. 2002; see figure 1.5).

The involvement of outside countries can also provide additional avenues to influence combatants, whether a state or an armed group, in favor of a settlement. Current studies, which have largely focused on the impact of direct intervention, find that it extended the duration of violent conflicts and can complicate peace negotiations (Regan 2002; Walter 2017a). Less focus has been placed on indirect intervention, such as nonmilitary involvement by outside actors.

FIGURE 1.5 Number of Internationalized Violent Conflicts, Global, 1946–2016

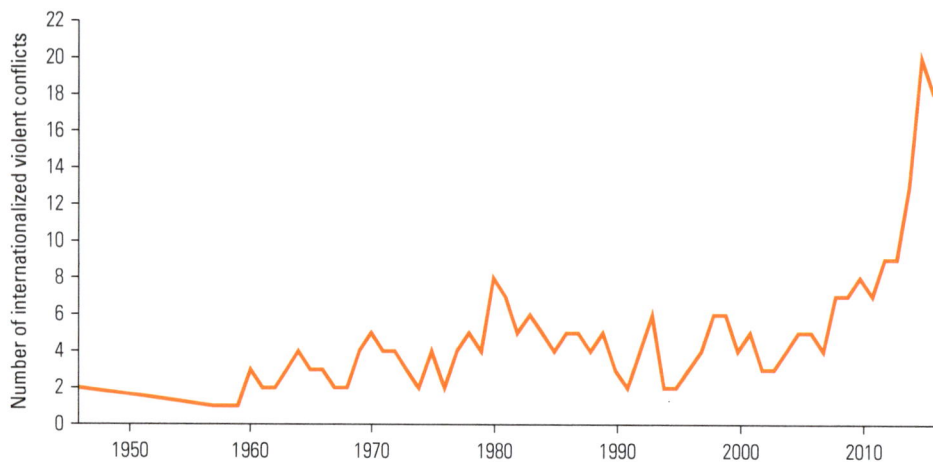

Source: Uppsala Conflict Data Program and Peace Research Institution Oslo (Allansson, Melander, and Themnér 2017; Gleditsch et al. 2002).

The rise of private external funding may play a role in conflict dynamics. In the context of Syria, for example, private funding complicates the dynamics of the conflict and any potential settlement.

Engagement by outsiders, however, does not necessarily have a negative impact. According to Walter (2017a, 3), "Outside intervention that occurs after a peace treaty has been signed has a strong positive effect on the successful resolution of these [violent conflicts]. . . . External intervention also tends to have a positive effect on reducing the risks of an additional [violent conflict] once the first [violent conflict] has ended" (see also Doyle and Sambanis 2000; Fortna 2002). In cases where an outside state or international organization has been willing to enforce or verify the terms of a peace treaty, "negotiations almost always lead to peace"; when external actors do not do so, "negotiations almost always result in renewed [conflict]" (Walter 2017a, 1).[11]

Violent conflicts have become more protracted and more difficult to resolve, with many violent conflicts relapsing. Even violent conflicts that may seem to stop (that is, where few or no battle-related fatalities are reported in the following year) often involve neither peace agreements nor ceasefires nor victories, meaning that fighting could begin again. The Peace Research Institute Oslo reports that, since the mid-1990s,

most conflicts have been recurrences of old conflicts rather than new conflicts (Gates, Nygård, and Trappeniers 2016). On average, peace lasts only seven years after a conflict ends. In the post–World War II era, 135 countries experienced the recurrence of conflict, with 60 percent of all conflicts recurring (Gates, Nygård, and Trappeniers 2016). In many violent conflicts, gray zones appear, where a conflict becomes less intense, yet is not fully resolved (National Intelligence Council 2017).

The average duration of violent conflicts involving state forces has been trending upward since 1971. Violent conflicts involving state forces that ended in 2014 lasted, on average, 26.7 years, and those that ended in 2015 lasted, on average, 14.5 years.[12] By comparison, conflicts that ended in 1970 lasted, on average, 9.6 years (Allansson, Melander, and Themnér 2017; Gleditsch et al. 2002; see figure 1.6).

The longer a conflict lasts, the more difficult it becomes to resolve (Fearon 2004), given that the involved parties tend to fragment and mutate with time (ICRC 2016). Prolonged violent conflict may become more complex and multidimensional. Also, as a conflict continues, the original drivers are more likely to transform and require different solutions (Wolff, Ross, and Wee 2017).[13] Protracted conflicts also tend to vary over the course of their life cycle,

FIGURE 1.6 Average Duration of Conflict Worldwide, 1970–2015

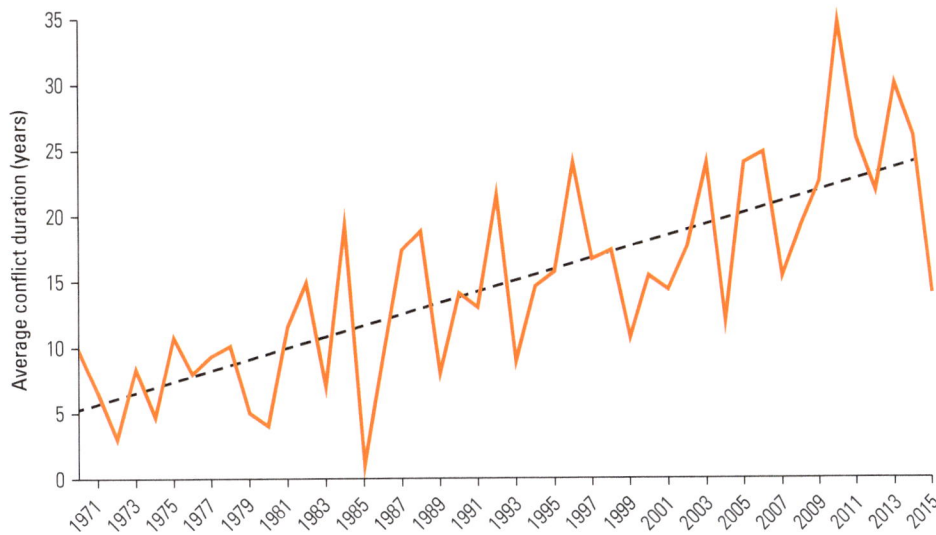

Source: Uppsala Conflict Data Program and Peace Research Institute Oslo (Allansson, Melander, and Themnér 2017; Gleditsch et al. 2002).

both spatially (that is, where conflict occurs within countries) and in intensity (for example, number of battle-related fatalities). The implications for prevention are significant. Once a country or society is on a violent path, changing the trajectory becomes more difficult and gets more difficult with time.

Understanding Trends in Violent Conflict

The regional concentration of violent conflict is shifting. Most violent conflicts today are occurring in Africa, the Middle East, and South Asia (see figure 1.7); the number of violent conflicts in other parts of Asia and Europe, previously epicenters of conflict, has been decreasing (Allansson, Melander, and Themnér 2017; Gleditsch et al. 2002; Sundberg, Eck, and Kreutz 2012). In 2016, more than 24 percent of all violent conflicts occurred in the Middle East, an increase from 2010, when the region experienced less than 11 percent of the total. These trends are predicted to continue (National Intelligence Council 2017).

There are variations, however, in the kind of violent conflict that is most prevalent in a region. Conflicts between nonstate actors represented more than 63 percent of the violent conflicts in Africa in 2016 (33 violent conflicts). The largest proportion, or more than 24 percent of these, occurred in Somalia, followed by the Democratic Republic of Congo (more than 12 percent) and Nigeria (more than 11 percent) (ACLED 2016; Raleigh et al. 2010). Conflict between nonstate actors is also the primary form of violent conflict occurring in the Middle East and in the Americas,[14] where it makes up more than 63 percent (17 violent conflicts) and 80 percent (8 violent conflicts) of all violent conflicts in the region, respectively (Sundberg, Eck, and Kreutz 2012; Allansson, Melander, and Themnér 2017).

Subnational conflict, or "violent contestation aimed at securing greater political autonomy [often] for an ethnic minority group" (Colletta and Oppenheim 2017, 1), affects nearly every part of the world, but some regions more than others. It is the most common form of violent conflict in Asia, yet it has also been on the rise in Europe, the Middle East, and in recent years in Sub-Saharan Africa. Between 2000 and 2015, subnational conflict affected 24 countries, resulting in more than 100,000 battle-related deaths in the period. Several countries faced multiple clusters of separatist conflicts (Colletta and Oppenheim 2017).

FIGURE 1.7 Conflict Events Worldwide, by Type of Conflict and Region, 1989–2016

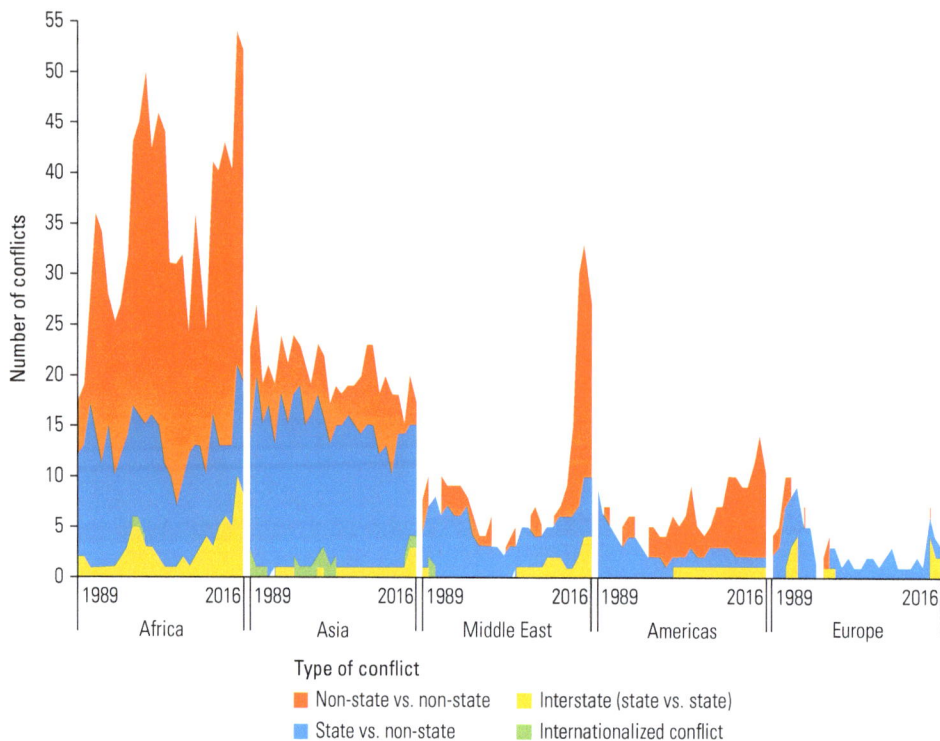

Sources: For interstate and state-based conflicts (including internationalized conflicts), data from Uppsala Conflict Data Program (UCDP) and Peace Research Institute Oslo (Allansson, Melander, and Themnér 2017; Gleditsch et al. 2002); for nonstate conflicts, data from UCDP (Sundberg, Eck, and Kreutz 2012; Allansson, Melander, and Themnér 2017).

Each of the many varieties of conflict in the world today has different implications for prevention approaches. Some of the deadliest conflicts are over control of the central state or over internal power arrangements, as in Iraq, South Sudan, and Syria.[15] Protracted subregional conflicts might not disrupt the functionality of the central state in most of its territory—as in Myanmar, the Philippines, and Thailand, among others— yet these conflicts still have an impact on the operation of the state (Parks, Colletta, and Oppenheim 2013). Moreover, a large number of intercommunal conflicts over extractive or natural resources or land can flare up before declining in intensity. Other events of political violence may occur around electoral periods, such as in Jamaica and Kenya (Malik 2017). Chapter 5 discusses in greater detail these arenas of contestation, where societies negotiate access to resources and political power and where the risk of violence is intensified.

Factors Contributing to the Increase in Violent Conflict

Three broad, interrelated factors have contributed to the increased number, resulting fatalities, and reach of violent conflict:

- The eruption of violent conflict in the Middle East and North Africa in the wake of the Arab Spring
- The spread of violent extremism
- The increase in power contestation in Sub-Saharan Africa.

Each, separately and in combination with the other underlying factors, can have different implications for prevention. This is especially evident in the case of violent extremism, which has expanded rapidly by exploiting preexisting violent conflicts related to sectarian grievances and power struggles that may have nothing to do with extremism, yet provide a space for these movements to grow.

Violent Conflict in the Wake of the Arab Spring

Increased levels of violent conflict have most affected the Middle East and North Africa (Gleditsch and Rudolfsen 2016). Arab countries are home to only 5 percent of the world's population, but in 2014 they accounted for 45 percent of the world's terrorist incidents, 68 percent of its battle-related deaths,[16] 47 percent of its internally displaced population, and 58 percent of its refugees (UNDP 2016a). The United Nations Development Programme's *Arab Human Development Report 2016* predicts that by 2020, "Almost three out of four Arabs could be living in countries vulnerable to violent conflict" (UNDP 2016a).

The violent conflicts emerging after the Arab Spring—in Libya, Syria, and the Republic of Yemen, in particular—originated in domestic unrest influenced by the regional upheavals of 2011. These conflicts quickly drew in regional and global powers, which may "influence or support—but rarely fully control—those fighting on the ground" (Guéhenno 2016). Coupled with their internal nature, some of these conflicts have become proxy wars in which both regional and international players pursue their geopolitical rivalries, and in some cases nonstate armed groups linked with transnational criminal networks embrace ideologies of violent extremism that cannot be accommodated in peace agreements (International Peace Institute 2016).

One of the factors contributing to the Arab Spring of 2011 and to the destabilization of long-standing Arab autocracies was the broken social contract between governments and citizens (Toska 2017). Challenges to state legitimacy across the region also played an important role and emanated from shortcomings in economic opportunity, social mobility, democracy, rule of law, human rights, and gender equality. The social contract between several Arab governments and citizens that had persisted since independence consisted of the state providing public sector jobs, free education and health care, and subsidized food and fuel. In return, citizens were expected to keep their voices low and to tolerate some level of elite capture in the private sector

(Devarajan and Ianchovichina 2017). This mechanism became less and less sustainable starting in the 2000s, as persistent fiscal imbalances undermined the ability of governments to keep their part of the social bargain. Once mass protests sparked the political transition in Tunisia, contagion to the rest of the region was quick, enabled by technology and a common language and rooted in economic problems and popular grievances that were common throughout the Middle East and North Africa (Ianchovichina 2017).[17]

Worsening polarization between groups recurred across different contexts, whether between Islamists and their opponents in the Arab Republic of Egypt and Tunisia; politicization of cross-sectarian divides involving Sunnis and Shi'ites in Iraq[18] and some of the Gulf states; or tribal and local forces in Libya and the Republic of Yemen (Lynch 2016, 37). The lack of institutional confidence and the failure to secure a predictable transition toward new stable institutions further exacerbated social and political polarization. External interventions stoking sectarian or ethnic hatred inflamed intergroup polarization.

Countries that managed to stay peaceful distinguished themselves from those that were affected by violence in terms of the quality of governance institutions, the ability to use redistribution to address grievances, and the presence or absence of external military interference (Devarajan and Ianchovichina 2017). The difference in how governments responded to demonstrations and memories of past violence (in the case of Algeria) were also contributing factors (Brownlee, Masoud, and Reynolds 2015).

The Spread of Violent Extremism

One of the most significant recent developments is the proliferation and transnational reach of violent extremist groups. While the twentieth century is full of examples of violent extremist groups, violent extremism presently displays some new features.

Contemporary violent extremist groups, often making use of twenty-first-century technology, embed themselves into communities while simultaneously forming strategic alliances with transnational networks (World Bank 2015). This allows them to spread across borders, hooking into local grievances and connecting them to a global identity. Many also have proven adept at exploiting local violent conflict to expand and recruiting well beyond conflict-affected countries.[19] They tend to thrive in areas with political disorder and at heightened risk of violence. Indeed, the growing reach of violent extremist groups in recent years "is more a product of instability than its primary driver" (ICG 2016a). They differ from their predecessors in at least three ways (World Bank 2015).

First, some of today's violent extremist groups have greater global appeal than violent extremist groups of earlier times. Some are adept at connecting very local grievances—frustration with a discriminatory or predatory state, for example—with a global identity that posits youth as heroes in ostensibly a movement for global justice. Such groups harness technology to promote their narrative and recruit globally in ways that are often far ahead of state efforts to rein them in (World Bank 2015).

Second, many of today's violent extremist groups form strategic alliances with different groups in the areas in which they operate. This engagement can take different forms. There have always been some true believers, some who join for material or political gain, and others who condone such groups but do not actively participate. However, today's violent extremist groups are taking advantage of local divisions among groups and building opportunistic alliances to an unprecedented degree (ICG 2016a).

Third, some violent extremist groups today have been able to use transnational networks to facilitate financing. This includes mobilizing financing from states and private donors to an unprecedented level. For example, oil revenue has contributed a great deal of financing for the Islamic State (Heibner et al. 2017). Drug trafficking has been an important resource for both insurgent and extremist groups in Afghanistan and northern Mali (Comolli 2017). Extracting rents in exchange for providing protection to many other types of

trafficking networks—in particular, human trafficking networks—has also been a source of income. Finally, ransom and hostage taking have been a source of revenue for some groups.

A few violent extremist groups, especially over the last decade, have tried to establish a de facto state presence in large areas of territory. For example, groups like Al Shabaab, Boko Haram, and the Islamic State claim to be recreating a caliphate with some of the elements of state structure. Looking for territorial control, these groups make much stronger efforts to connect with local communities, who at times support them out of fear or economic opportunity (ICG 2016a).[20] This suggests that focusing solely on the recruitment of violent extremist groups is shortsighted.[21] Overall, "preventing crises will do more to contain violent extremists than countering violent extremism will do to prevent crises" (ICG 2016a, v).

Violent Conflict in the Midst of Rapid Transformation in Sub-Saharan Africa

Violent conflict in Sub-Saharan Africa has increased against the backdrop of the continent's fast-paced economic and political changes (Williams 2017). Poverty, and to some extent inequality, is decreasing, and economic growth has enabled several countries to graduate to middle-income status (Beegle et al. 2016). Democratization has expanded at the same time, although with some reversals in 2015 (Mogaka 2017). Against this positive background, rapid changes are also creating tensions. Three dynamics play out in this context: violent competition for political power and associated electoral-related violence; the spread of violent extremism that in most cases derives from conflicting identity; and the persistence of violent intercommunal conflict in many parts of East and Central Africa that often does not involve states.

Conflict around weak political settlements in the region and power contestation is clearly exemplified by the dramatic developments in South Sudan. Since 2013, the violent conflict that resulted from a leadership division within the Sudan People's

Liberation Movement, antagonized by deep ethnic structural divisions, has taken a disastrous turn. By March 2016, at least 50,000 people had reportedly been killed (Reuters 2016), and millions of people had been forcibly displaced both as refugees and as internally displaced persons (IDPs).[22] Since South Sudan's independence in 2011, enormous challenges have constrained the effort of building institutions. The absence of legitimate political institutions beyond liberation politics, which was masked during the years of the common struggle against the Sudanese central government—combined with the lack of a security apparatus apart from the rebel movements that had led the fight for independence—was at the origin of the outbreak of the conflict (ICG 2016b).

Mali and Nigeria are two examples of identity-based conflicts that have turned into violent extremist insurrections, as seen in other parts of the world. These conflicts grew out of tensions that had little to do with ideology and were built up over time. For example, the Boko Haram insurrection in northern Nigeria, which started in the 1990s, developed slowly, building on a sentiment of marginalization fueled by large inequalities between regions that left the population of the poorest state (Borno) feeling excluded from the country's overall relative prosperity (Comolli 2015). Similarly, the spread of violent extremism in northern Mali in 2012 started as a nationalist Tuareg rebellion, a recurrent phenomenon since colonial times, that turned into a violent extremist insurrection involving Al-Qaeda in the Islamic Maghreb, the Movement for Unity and Jihad in West Africa, Harakat Ansar Al-Dine, and others (ICG 2015).

The high level of violence in the eastern Democratic Republic of Congo is a clear illustration of intercommunal conflict connected to the absence of a positive state presence. In this region, many forms of conflict overlap. External influence has played a role in sustaining violent conflict in the region. Yet eastern Democratic Republic of Congo has experienced a relentlessly high number of both battle and other deaths and a particularly high number of civilian casualties, coupled with the use of

conflict-related sexual violence as a weapon of war since the 1990s (Stearn 2011; UN 2017). To a lesser degree, the Central African Republic presents a similar situation involving the multiplication of intercommunal conflict and the incapacity of the state to project a positive presence (Lombard 2016). This is the case as well in many subregions of African states, such as in Sudan's Darfur region and parts of South Sudan, among others (De Waal 2007).

In addition to these three factors, other rising trends include the following.

The tactics of violence are evolving. The number of weapons in circulation around the world has dramatically increased since the beginning of the twenty-first century (Pavesi 2016). The Small Arms Survey reports that an estimated 875 million small arms are in circulation worldwide. This is certainly a conservative estimate, given that accurate assessments are difficult. From 2001 to 2011, the value of the trade in small arms and light weapons nearly doubled globally, from $2.38 billion to $4.634 billion (Small Arms Survey 2014). From 2012 to 2013 the global small arms trade rose to US$6 billion—an increase of US$1 billion, or 17 percent, in a single year (Dutt 2016).

Remote violence tactics are also becoming increasingly common and deadlier in conflict zones around the world. This type of violence refers to instances in which a spatially removed group determines the time, place, and victims of an attack using an explosive device such as a bomb, an improvised explosive device (IED), or missiles, among others (ACLED 2016; Raleigh et al. 2010). For non-state-armed actors that may control a limited amount of territory compared to government forces, "remote violence is an ideal tactic to either damage state forces with minimal risk or to coerce the state without controlling it. This tactic also fits into a strategy of groups resorting to so-called 'weapons of the weak' after losing territory and influence," or being in an objective disadvantageous position compared to state forces (Kishi, Raleigh, and Linke 2016, 30; see also McCormick and Giordano 2007; Merari 1993; and Denselow 2010).

Drone strikes also have become increasingly prevalent and deadly and are likely to become even more so (Action on Armed Violence 2017). Cyberattacks may begin to have kinetic effects in the contexts of violent conflicts, and weaponizable biotechnologies too may become a reality. At the same time, many conflicts are waged with few sophisticated weapons, and many events featuring terrorist tactics rely on artisanal bombs, trucks, or knives. The genocide in Rwanda was carried out using machetes.

The tactic of terror. Terrorist incidents have risen sharply over the last 10 years, as have the number of resulting fatalities (see figure 1.8).[23]

Interpersonal and gang violence and violent conflict. Interpersonal, gang, and drug-related violence may reflect or exacerbate grievances that ultimately lead to violent conflict. Conflicts may degenerate into violence more rapidly in societies with high levels of interpersonal violence or with a culture of resolving interpersonal issues violently, especially along the lines of gender (see boxes 1.3 and 1.8). Political figures or groups can finance or co-opt gangs to foment targeted violence against opponents, particularly in periods of intense political competition (for example, election periods) or when there are external shocks.

In some conflicts, the sale of drugs can provide a ready stream of revenue for non-state actors in their battles against more powerful and resource-rich state forces.[24] Examples include the links between Colombia's illegal armed groups and different stages of the illegal drug industry (including taxation, production, and trafficking), and the sale of illegal amphetamines in the Middle East by groups involved in conflict (Otis 2014; NPR 2013). Violence that may stem from these exchanges is therefore at least indirectly linked to larger ongoing conflicts, can result in the destabilization of the state, and can contribute to cycles of persistent violence.

The Unacceptable Costs of Violent Conflict

"A full accounting of any war's burdens cannot be placed in columns on a ledger" (Crawford 2016, 1). It is clear, however, that violent conflict exacts an incalculably high cost in direct and indirect damage to

FIGURE 1.8 Terrorism Prevalence and Reported Fatalities, Global, 1995–2015

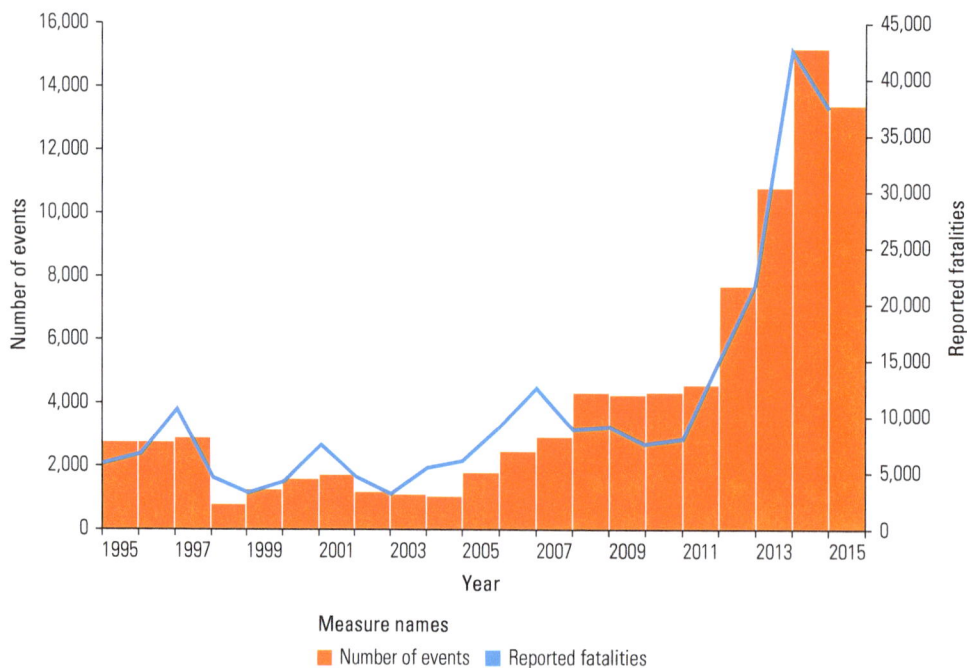

Source: Global Terrorism Database (National Consortium for the Study of Terrorism and Responses to Terrorism 2016).

societies, economies, and people (see box 1.4 on the impacts of the Syrian conflict). It kills and injures combatants and civilians alike and inflicts insidious damage to bodies, minds, and communities that can halt human and economic development for many years. Violent conflict has a major impact on the ability of the world to improve the well-being of populations and to reduce poverty, disease, and other catastrophic risks. Its long-term effects on the countries involved, and on their neighbors, include monetary costs such as reduced economic growth, minimized trade and investment opportunities, and the added cost of reconstruction.[25]

The Direct Human Cost of Violent Conflict

Today's violent conflicts do not necessarily play out within the confines of a distinct battleground. Nor are their impacts confined to the combatants. Civilians overwhelmingly bear the brunt of today's violent conflicts (see box 1.5). The number of

atrocities committed worldwide—defined as "the deliberate killing of noncombatant civilians in the context of a wider political conflict" (Schrodt and Ulfelder 2016)[26]—has increased rapidly since 2010, as has the number of civilians reportedly killed in such contexts (Eck and Hultman 2007; Allansson, Melander, and Themnér 2017; see also Action on Armed Violence 2017).

About twice as many civilians were reportedly killed by one-sided violence during conflict in 2016 than in 2010. These numbers were even higher in 2014, driven largely by attacks carried out by Boko Haram and the Islamic State (Eck and Hultman 2007; Allansson, Melander, and Themnér 2017). In some instances, nonstate actors may have an incentive to target civilians—for example, "as a cheaper strategy of imposing costs on the adversary"—especially at times when a settlement may be imminent (Hultman 2010).[27] States are also responsible for high rates of civilian deaths, although they may often "contract" this violence out to militias (Raleigh 2012).

The Syrian conflict is one of the defining crises of the contemporary era. At least 400,000 persons have been killed, about 5 million have fled the country, and, according to the United Nations Office for the Coordination of Humanitarian Affairs, 6.3 million have been internally displaced. Many of the individuals remaining in the country cannot access the help they need, as more than 50 percent of hospitals have been partially or completely destroyed, and the supply of doctors, nurses, and medical supplies is woefully inadequate (UNICEF 2015; UNOCHA 2017; World Bank 2017a).

Children have been intensely affected: the United Nations Children's Fund reports more than 1,500 grave human rights violations against children in 2015 alone, of which more than one-third occurred while children were in or on their way to school (UNICEF 2015). The proportion of children under 15 being recruited by armed groups increased from 20 percent in 2014 to more than 50 percent in 2015, and there has been an alarming increase in child marriage: a 2017 United Nations Population Fund survey estimates that the number of child brides (under 18 years of age) in Syria has quadrupled since the war began (UNFPA 2017). Women have taken on a large burden not only of dealing with the impacts

of conflict—caring for injured or orphaned family members—but also of providing humanitarian assistance and participating in processes to resist and transform the conflict.

The economic impacts of the conflict are enormous. In real terms, Syria's gross domestic product (GDP) contracted an estimated 63 percent between 2011 and 2016. In cumulative terms, the loss in GDP amounted to an estimated US$226 billion between 2011 and 2016—approximately four times the country's 2010 GDP. According to the World Bank, even if the conflict ends this year, the cumulative losses in GDP will reach 7.6 times the preconflict GDP by the twentieth year after the beginning of the conflict. If the conflict continues, this loss will stand at 13.2 times the country's preconflict GDP (World Bank 2017a).

The impacts of the conflict have spread to neighboring countries, which feel the brunt of the crisis acutely. Jordan, for example, has registered 654,903 Syrian refugees, while Lebanon has registered 997,905 (as of December 2017; UNHCR 2017). Neighboring Turkey has registered 3,400,195 Syrian refugees (as of December 2017; UNHCR 2017). The quality of care for basic public services in health care and education has also declined, for both refugee and host communities.

Much of the violence occurs in urban areas and often targets civilian spaces, including those considered sanctuaries under international humanitarian law, such as schools, hospitals, and places of worship (ICRC 2017).[28] This impact is facilitated by the increasing use of "remote violence"[29] both in civil wars and in acts of terrorism in countries far from conflict. In addition to the doubling of the number of civilian deaths in violent conflicts between 2010 and 2016, many more civilian deaths result from the indirect effects of conflict,

such as unmet medical needs, food insecurity, inadequate shelter, or contamination of water (Geneva Declaration on Armed Violence and Development 2011; UNESCWA 2017).

Vulnerable populations, such as children, are at particularly high risk (Economist 2015; Guha-Sapir and van Panhuis 2004). Nearly one-third of the 11,418 noncombatants killed or wounded in Afghanistan in 2016 were children (UNAMA 2017).[30] This is due to the nature of the indiscriminate tactics used, such as suicide bombings, IEDs, and urban terrorist attacks by the Taliban and other groups, as well as the increased use of air support by Afghan and international military forces. It is important to note that "when children are targeted or killed, it is often in an attempt to instill terror in populations or to reaffirm brutality and gain (global) notoriety, given that the targeting of children is meant to send a message to (adult) adversaries and/or the international community at-large. In addition to attacks, there are also numerous instances in which children are abducted and forced to fight in violent conflict" (Kishi 2015; see also Economist 2015; SOS Children's Village 2015).

The deliberate targeting of civilians overall may be creating a perverse corollary. It is becoming more accepted that civilians in conflict zones are an inevitable part of violent conflict casualties. Although a majority of people still say that it is wrong to violate the international norms regarding the rules of war, support for these norms has dropped from 68 to 59 percent since 1999 (ICRC 2016).

Regional Trends in Civilian Fatalities and Atrocities

Between 1980 and 2016, Africa had by far the highest proportion of civilian fatalities, with nearly 87 percent (676,625 fatalities in the region) of all reported civilian fatalities (Eck and Hultman 2007; Allansson, Melander, and Themnér 2017). Some 500,000 of these fatalities were a direct result of the Rwandan genocide of 1994, although the estimates vary among sources (Eck and Hultman 2007; Allansson, Melander, and Themnér 2017).[31]

Map 1.1 shows reported civilian fatalities in Africa between 2002 and 2016 (ACLED 2016; Raleigh et al. 2010). Countries experiencing the most civilian fatalities during this time period include the Democratic Republic of Congo (especially the eastern region), Nigeria (where Boko Haram was responsible for almost half of all reported civilian fatalities in the country), Sudan (especially in the Darfur region), and South Sudan (especially in recent years during its civil war). While nonstate armed groups were responsible for the majority (more than 86 percent) of civilian fatalities in Africa during this time period (ACLED 2016; Raleigh et al. 2010; Kishi, Raleigh, and Linke 2016), state forces were involved as well, even if indirectly in some cases. Raleigh and Kishi (2017) estimate that, in Africa, progovernment militias commit more violence against civilians, with at least 10 percent more of their activities targeting civilians than other militias.

In recent years, civilians also have been at heightened risk in the Middle East, accounting for around two-thirds of all civilian fatalities reported in 2016 (Eck and Hultman 2007; Allansson, Melander, and Themnér 2017). This increase has been driven by an increase in the rate of conflict involving nonstate armed groups, which spiked in 2012 in conflicts following the Arab Spring.

Conflict, Famine, and Displacement

Violent conflict scatters populations and disrupts livelihoods. Conflict, famine, and displacement are deeply interrelated (see box 1.6). Famine and food crises further contribute to the involuntary mass movement of people, especially in cases where violent conflict, mismanagement, and insufficient responses to previous disasters have exacerbated the negative impact of a food crisis (Raleigh 2017). Violent conflict disrupts trade routes and markets for food and other necessities, causing further direct and indirect costs. IDPs are particularly vulnerable to the effects of famine and disproportionately affected by food insecurity, often due to barriers to accessing labor markets and reliance on humanitarian assistance for survival.

An estimated 65.6 million people are currently forcibly displaced from their homes, driven primarily by violence (UNHCR 2017). Between 2005 and 2016, the number of IDPs increased more than fivefold (UNDP 2016b; UNHCR 2017; World Bank

MAP 1.1 Reported Civilian Fatalities in Africa, 2002–16

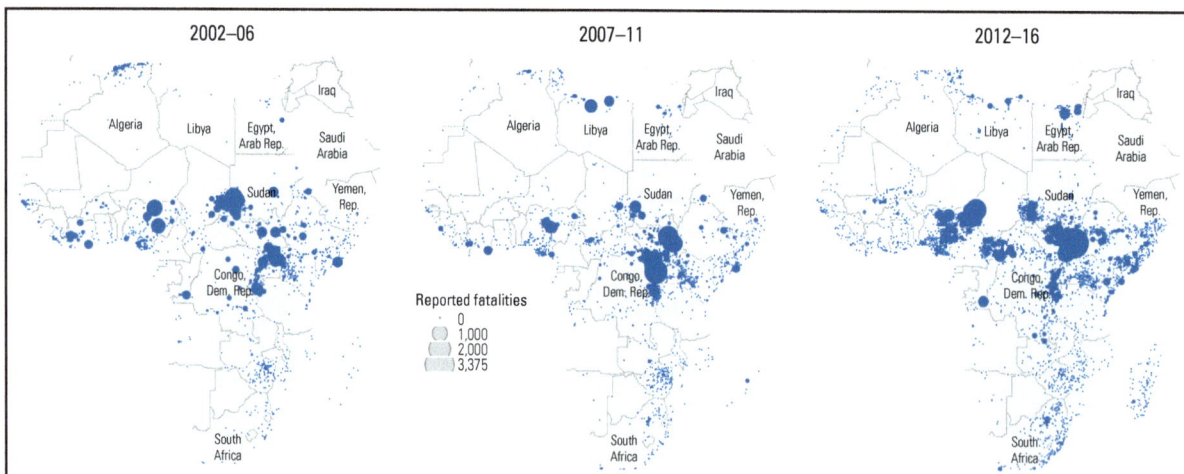

Source: Raleigh et al. 2010.

BOX 1.6 Famine and Fragility, Conflict, and Violence

The four-decade declining trend of famine and famine-related deaths has reversed since 2011. Throughout history, famines have been associated with violent conflicts, particularly in recent decades as our knowledge of how to prevent famine and instruments for doing so in peaceful contexts have improved dramatically. Yet famines and severe food insecurity have resulted in hundreds of thousands of deaths in Nigeria, Somalia, South Sudan, and Yemen, with millions more people left food insecure, partly because of violent conflicts.

In fragile situations, shocks such as drought, conflict, and economic insecurity can lead to increased food insecurity and famine. Drought destroys agricultural output, and violent conflict disrupts agriculture and trade of food crops between areas of surplus and deficit. The *Global Report on Food Crises 2017* reports that in 2016, violent conflict and civil insecurity left more than 63 million people acutely food insecure and in need of urgent humanitarian assistance in 13 countries (Food Security Information Network 2017).

Food insecurity can increase the risk of conflict, particularly when caused by rising food prices, by displacing populations, by exacerbating grievances, and by increasing competition for scarce food and water resources. Internally displaced persons and refugees often rely on host communities, placing a strain on already-scarce resources and heightening the risk for tension. The 2008 and 2011 global food crises triggered more than 40 food riots across the world: it arguably contributed to the breakdown of the social contract that led to the Arab Spring, to the fall of the government of Haiti in 2008, and to the fueling of grievances underpinning the 2009 coup in Madagascar. For each added percentage point in undernourishment, the likelihood for violent conflict increases by 0.24 percent per 1,000 population.

Famine and food insecurity particularly affect rural and agriculture-based workers, women, and children, partly because social safety nets might be more prevalent. In addition to short-term suffering, famine victims are more likely to experience serious health problems and have significantly worse financial prospects over the long term.

Modern famines are largely man-made and avoidable. In fragile contexts, alleviating poverty, strengthening social safety nets, and preventing violent conflict lower the risk of famine and food insecurity. Long-term stability also increases these states' chances of weathering shocks that potentially cause famines.

Sources: World Bank 2017a, 2017b; World Food Programme 2017a, 2017b; von Uexkull et al. 2016; Brinkman and Hendrix, 2011.

2016a; see figure 1.9). Approximately 40.3 million IDPs were recorded in 2016 (UNHCR 2017).[32] These are likely conservative estimates given the difficulty of collecting accurate data (see box 1.7). The number of refugees nearly doubled over the same period, with the majority (55 percent) of refugees coming from just three countries: Afghanistan, South Sudan, and Syria (UNHCR 2017). More than half of the world's refugees are children, many of whom have been separated from family (UNHCR 2017).

Extreme poverty is now increasingly concentrated in vulnerable groups displaced by violent conflict, and the presence of these populations can affect development prospects in the communities hosting them (World Bank 2016a). Often host countries and countries with internally displaced persons may be fragile themselves, and housing additional vulnerable populations can impose an added strain. Indeed, 95 percent of refugees and IDPs live in low- and middle-income countries (World Bank 2016a).

FIGURE 1.9 Number of Refugees and IDPs Worldwide, 1951–2016

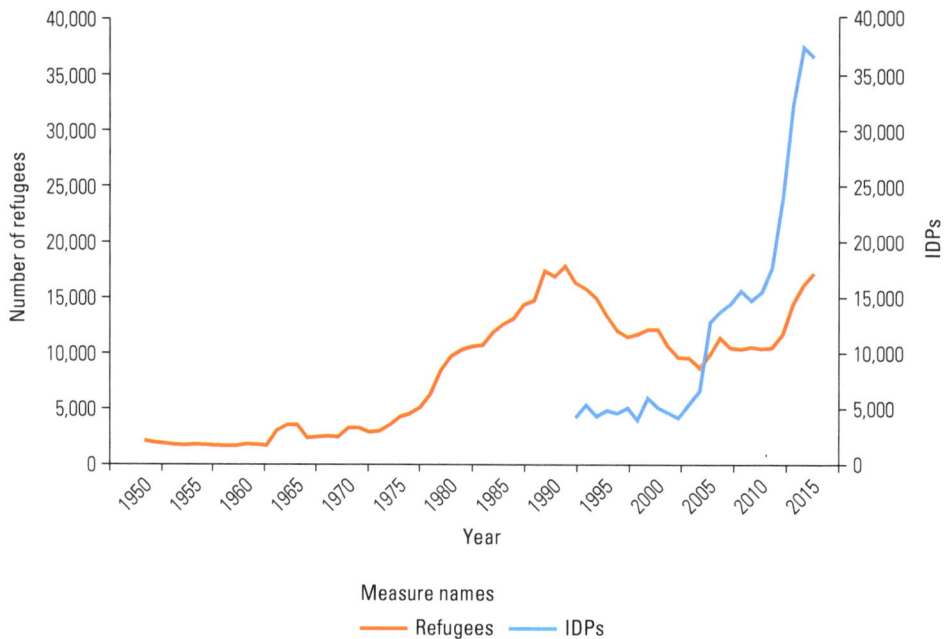

Source: UNHCR 2017.
Note: IDP = internally displaced person.

BOX 1.7 Limitations of the Data on Forced Displacement

Insecurity can constrain direct access to displaced populations, making it difficult, if not impossible, to verify reported numbers. It can be especially difficult to compile accurate data, as crisis situations resulting in large displaced populations are often dynamic and changing rapidly, making static snapshots quickly out of date.

Various sources are used to collect data on displaced populations. Within protracted crises, large numbers of assessments and surveys often are undertaken for both protection and assistance purposes. Government agencies, United Nations High Commissioner for Refugees

field offices, and nongovernmental organizations compile and collect data using mainly registers, surveys, registration processes, or censuses. Each method of data collection has both strengths and weaknesses.

The use of different methodologies and inconsistent sharing of information, however, can weaken systematic data collection. Logistically, it is also difficult to know when displacement ends. For example, should internally displaced persons (IDPs) who have lived in an area for several years and who have achieved a durable solution still be considered IDPs?

Sources: IDMC 2016; UNHCR 2013.

The Gender Impacts of Violent Conflict

The impacts of violent conflict on civilians are gendered. Women and men experience conflict and violence differently, and there are both direct and indirect effects on each group. Mortality rates on the battlefield are higher in men, especially in young adult males, but women tend to experience violence and its effects in significantly greater proportions. Women often face a continuum of violence before, during, and after conflict. Sexual and gender-based violence tends to be higher in conflict and

BOX 1.8 Intimate Partner Violence and Violent Conflict

Violent conflict may exacerbate all forms of violence against women and girls and rebound particularly on them. In a comparative study looking at cross-sectional variation in self-reported intimate partner violence before and after conflict in three Sub-Saharan African countries (Côte d'Ivoire, Kenya, and Liberia), Kelly (2017) finds that, despite differences in the nature of violent conflict in each country, there is a significant relationship between intimate partner violence and previous violent conflict in all three countries. In Kenya and Liberia, women living in a district with reported deaths from violent conflict were 50 percent more likely to experience intimate partner violence than women in districts without reported fatalities. When levels of conflict are split into low, medium, and high levels, Côte d'Ivoire and Kenya had significantly higher levels of intimate partner violence in high- compared to low-conflict districts. Using Demographic and Health Survey data for periods before and after conflict in Kenya, Kelly (2017) also finds that districts with higher levels of intimate partner violence before the conflict were 30 percent more likely to be associated with fatal violence after the conflict broke out.

postconflict settings, as does recruitment of girls into trafficking, sexual slavery, or forced marriage (Kelly 2017; UN Secretary-General 2015; UN Women 2015; UNFPA 2017; UNESCWA 2015). Girls' mobility is often highly restricted, limiting their access to school, employment, and other opportunities, and this can be exacerbated during and after violent conflict (UN Women 2015). Intimate partner violence—whose victims are more often women—can also be linked to violent conflict more largely (see box 1.8).

The Lifetime Impacts of Violent Conflict

Exposure to conflict can generate impacts all along the life cycle. As illustrated in box 1.9, living in a setting where violence is present can have myriad impacts, some of which continue to manifest throughout the life cycle. These impacts can be generated both by the direct exposure to violence or by the witnessing of violence. For children and youth, the long-term effects of exposure to violence, combined with the adversities of daily life in a high-violence context, are associated with a range of challenges (Miller and Rasmussen 2010). These include increased risk of perpetrating or being a victim of violence later in life (Child Trends 2017; Finkelhor et al. 2009; Margolin and Elana 2004) as well as negative effects on cognitive and social development (Betancourt et al. 2012; Blattman 2006; Calvete and Orue 2011; Huesmann and Kirwil 2007; Leckman, Panter-Brick, and Salah 2014; Shonkoff and Garner 2012; Weaver, Borkowski, and Whitman 2008).

The experience of traumatic events can lead to serious mental health and behavioral problems that hinder people's ability to function in life. The World Bank has found that 30–70 percent of people who have lived in conflict zones suffer from symptoms of post-traumatic stress disorder and depression (CDC 2014; Murthy and Lakshminarayana 2006; World Bank 2016b). Children who are orphaned or separated from family often experience pressure to provide for themselves or become heads of households, which can make them vulnerable to exploitation by trafficking networks or armed groups (World Vision International 2017). The impacts on human capital can extend over generations (Mueller and Tobias 2016).

The harmful effects of violent conflict are especially insidious for children's potential development. According to Save the Children (2013), "Almost 50 million children and young people living in conflict areas are out of school, more than half of them primary age, and reports of attacks on education are rising" (reported in Tran 2013).

BOX 1.9 The Impact of Conflict over the Life Cycle

Conflict causes disruption and destruction far beyond the loss of life. Famine and disease, the closure of public services, and the collapse of labor market opportunities create lasting impacts that affect the overall pathway of a society and the development opportunities of its citizens. Figure B1.9.1 shows how conflict can affect the skill formation process.

The rise in violent conflict in the Middle East, for example, has interrupted critical investments in the development of human capital. Children exposed to conflict will carry the effects of conflict throughout their lives, as the destruction of family assets has devastating long-term consequences on future possibilities and the destruction of education halts critical interventions designed to enhance the opportunities of individuals and improve society.

Even if conflict across the region came to an end today, the effects of conflict on human development would likely be felt for generations to come.

The impact of conflict on the nutritional status of children is of particular concern. Stunting, through which nutritional disadvantages translate into weaker physical and cognitive health in childhood and adulthood, is associated with cognitive development, long-term productivity, and overall adult health. These risks produce a lifetime of lower productivity and opportunity. The persistence of economic and educational inequalities, which often manifest in low educational attainment and low employment opportunities for a large fraction of the population, may contribute to grievances that pose a risk of future violence.

FIGURE B1.9.1 Skill Formation Process over the Life Cycle

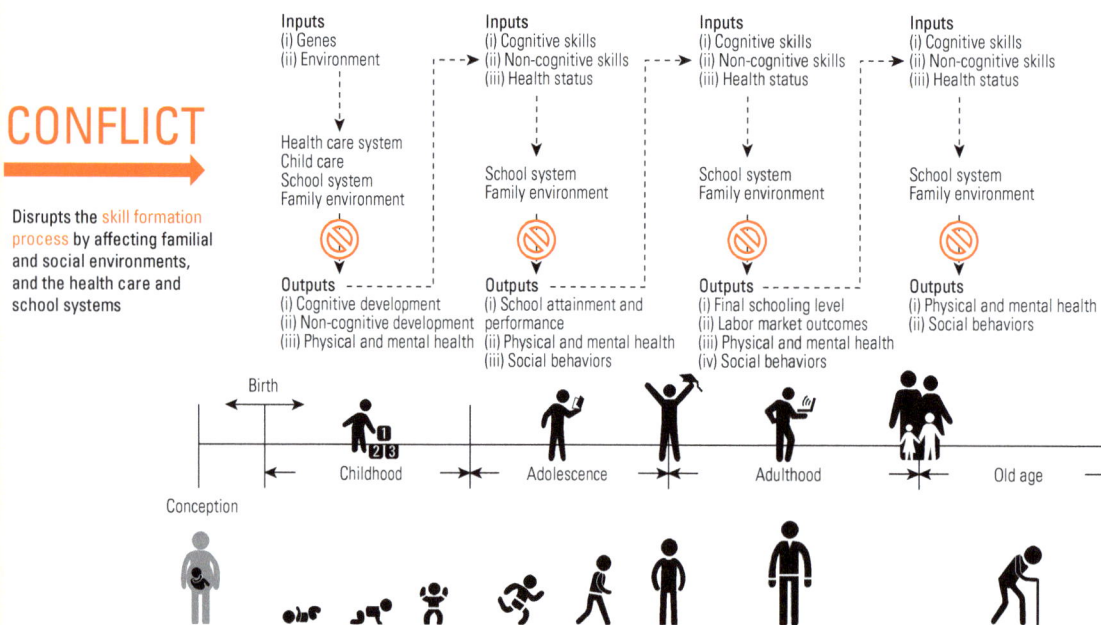

Source: Based on Urzúa 2016.

Source: UNESCWA 2017.

Years of violent conflict in Syria "have reversed more than a decade of progress in children's education. Today over 2 million of Syria's 4.8 million school-aged children are not in school" (SOS Children's Village 2014). Children who have to leave school as a result of the hardships of violent conflict may never resume their education or acquire needed workforce training after the conflict (World Vision International 2017). These impacts underscore the need for investment in human capital development, which can help build a country's future workforce and thereby enhance its competitiveness in the global economy.

The Health Impacts of Violent Conflict

Violent conflicts affect health in direct and indirect ways. In Liberia, 354 of 550 medical facilities were destroyed during the Liberian Civil War, affecting how it coped with the Ebola epidemic (Murphy and Ricks 2014). In the Democratic Republic of Congo, violent conflict worsened pregnancy outcomes (Ahuka, Chabikuli, and Ogunbanjo 2004). Conflict can also exacerbate the spread of infectious diseases. For example, the onset of recent conflict has resulted in a resurgence of polio in Syria, a disease that had been nearly eradicated worldwide (Tajaldin et al. 2015). The World Health Organization has called the recent cholera outbreak in the Republic of Yemen "unprecedented" due to its quick appearance in the conflict zone (Al Jazeera 2017). Tuberculosis is also a major health problem, and conflict-affected countries have lower capacity to run tuberculosis control programs (Waldman 2001).

The Economic Costs of Violent Conflict

The economic costs of violent conflict are staggering. However, the overall costs of conflict are unevenly distributed, contributing to global inequality between countries. In the absence of violent conflict, global income inequality would be significantly lower. In fact, violent conflict is an integral part of the world economic structure (De Groot, Bozzoli, and Brück 2012), resulting in certain high-income countries' benefiting from the prevalence of violent conflict, while certain low- and middle-income countries bear a disproportionate amount of the costs.

The Institute for Economics and Peace states in a 2016 report that the cost of containing violence is US$13.6 trillion a year globally, a figure "equivalent to 13.3 [percent] of world GDP or US$1,876 PPP [purchasing power parity] per annum, per person.[33] To further break it down, that figure is US$5 per person, per day, every day

of the year. When you consider that according to the most recent World Bank estimates 10.7 [percent] of the world's population are living on less than US$2 per day, it shows an alarming market failure" (IEP 2016; Schippa 2017).

Prolonged violent conflict increases economic costs. Violent conflict can also result in opportunity costs that have long-term ramifications for countries. The resources and money spent fighting wars can result in lost employment opportunities, creating pressures and grievances that pose risks for future violent conflict (Garrett-Peltier 2014). The adverse economic cost of violent conflict increases with the length of exposure to violence; with the duration of conflicts increasing over time, these economic costs will have an increasingly adverse effect on affected countries and their futures (Röther et al. 2016). Beyond the impacts on countries at the macro-level, violent conflict also has economic impacts at the micro-level; loss of livelihoods and assets of households are essential in understanding the dynamics of conflict traps.

Violent conflict is a major cause of the reversals in economic growth that many low- and middle-income countries have experienced in recent decades. Indeed, recessions experienced during periods of violent conflict in fragile countries are a key reason for much lower average growth rates over time (Mueller and Tobias 2016). The consequences are hugely negative for fragile contexts. Afghanistan's per capita income, for example, has barely changed since 1970 as the result of multiple violent conflicts, while Somalia's per capita income dropped by more than 40 percent in the same period (IEP 2015). Recurrent and protracted violent conflict, therefore, decimates the ability of states to rebuild their economies and thus potentially prevent future violent conflict.

The macroeconomic costs of violent conflict are also high. Violent conflict can undermine confidence in an economy by altering investors' expectations about political risks, particularly the risk of violence recurrence (Mueller and Tobias 2016). Investors seek political stability for their investments because it entails lower risk.

Following violent conflict, states can have a difficult time attracting new investors who are willing to incur the higher risks of doing business in a postconflict environment.

The impacts on the overall economy can be substantial. Mavriqi (2016) finds that countries experiencing violent conflict suffer a reduction in annual GDP growth of 2–4 percent and up to 8.4 percent if the conflict is severe. Violent conflict is also associated with an acceleration of inflation; on average, the consumer price index increases by 1.6 percentage points during years of violent conflict (Röther et al. 2016). Economic growth can be severely affected in countries relying on trade or natural resources, if these resources are destroyed during conflict; a country relying on tourism may lose or have limited growth in that potential source of income as a result of violent conflict.

Political, social, and economic risks are rife in postconflict periods. Postconflict economies often exist in power vacuums that allow organized crime to flourish and create black market economies, which can include both drug and human trafficking. Human trafficking explodes during violent conflict, spilling into neighboring states, but the situation persists once the conflict ends. Grievances can fester and grow in this environment.

Many countries affected by violent conflict also have had enormous difficulties rebuilding institutions. A principal reason is that trust and capacity must first be built up before new institutions can succeed in fragile situations (Chen, Ravallion, and Sangraula 2008; World Bank 2011). Mueller and Tobias (2016) find that countries with a history of intrastate conflict collect a smaller share of taxes relative to GDP than countries that have not experienced violent conflict, which can make rebuilding after a conflict that much more difficult.

Societies also pay the costs of conflict in their security structures. Military costs, especially for large armies, can be very high (Nordhaus 2002), hurting opportunity costs in particular. When resources are diverted toward security costs, states may forgo opportunities to invest in other sectors, such as manufacturing, clean energy, or increasing access to social services like education (Garrett-Peltier 2014).

Violent conflict usually exacts a very high toll on infrastructure and production systems (Mueller and Tobias 2016). For example, electoral violence surrounding the 2007 Kenyan presidential election drove up labor costs by 70 percent (Ksoll, Rocco, and Morjaria 2009); insecurity stemming from the Somali pirates in the Gulf of Aden and the Indian Ocean increased shipping costs by about 10 percent (Besley, Fetzer, and Mueller 2012; Mueller and Tobias 2016).

Neighboring countries often shoulder the burden of spillover effects from violent conflict. On average, countries that border a high-intensity conflict zone experience an annual decline of 1.4 percentage points in their GDP and an acceleration in inflation of 1.7 percentage points (Röther et al. 2016). In the Middle East, the conflicts in Iraq and Syria are associated with a drop in economic growth of 1 percentage point in Jordan in 2013. Similar dynamics were at work in Lebanon, where GDP growth slowed from 2.8 percent in 2012 and 2.6 percent in 2013 from an average of 9.2 percent in 2007–10. Prices for basic needs such as food or housing also increased at the beginning of the conflicts (Röther et al. 2016).

The Costs of Responding to Conflict

In 2017, an estimated 141.1 million people living in 37 countries were in need of international humanitarian assistance (UNOCHA 2017). The costs of this assistance are high and rising. They include the cost of increasing humanitarian assistance during conflict and postconflict aid to assist reconstruction and recovery and to support resilience as well as prevention and intervention strategies (Dancs 2011; Demekas, McHugh, and Kosma 2002; Ndikumana 2015).[34] The estimated economic cost of efforts to contain violence in 2012 was US\$9.46 trillion or 11 percent of world gross product (IEP 2015). To put this into perspective, spending on conflict containment is 2.4 times the total GDP of Africa; the majority of this spending goes to militaries, with just 0.1 percent spent on UN peacekeeping (IEP 2015).

The costs of responding to conflict have climbed significantly in parallel with the rapid growth and changing nature of conflict.

- Total funding requirements for humanitarian action in 2016 reached US$22.1 billion, an increase of US$2.2 billion over the previous year and a staggering US$13.3 billion (nearly 70 percent) over 2012.[35] This upward trend seems bound to continue in the future, with estimated requirements for 2017 reaching new highs at US$23.5 billion. Funding secured for humanitarian action has gradually adjusted in response to growing demand. The gap between requested and secured funding, however, has widened steadily over time. In 2016, total funding secured fell short of requests by US$9 billion or more than 40 percent of the total.[36]
- A large majority of resources requested for humanitarian action are directed to areas of violent conflict. A report by the UN Secretary-General states that, between 2002 and 2013, US$83 billion out of US$96 billion (or 86 percent) of total requests for humanitarian assistance through UN appeals was to assist people affected by conflicts (United Nations 2014). Since then, mega-crises such as in Iraq and Syria have further reinforced the link between conflict and humanitarian action. In 2015, approximately 97 percent of total humanitarian action targeted complex emergencies—situations in which a total or considerable breakdown of authority results from internal or external conflict (UNOCHA 2016).
- In the last two decades, peacekeeping operations expanded in mandate, size, and length. So-called "traditional" peacekeeping missions involving observational tasks performed by military personnel have evolved into what the United Nations Capstone Doctrine referred to as complex "multidimensional" enterprises (United Nations 2008). As of mid-2017, 16 peacekeeping operations were deployed and operational, while the number of police and military personnel in missions had nearly tripled from 34,000 in 2000 to 94,000 in August 2017.[37] By 2016, the total cost of maintaining peacekeeping missions in the field had climbed to almost US$8 billion a year, also reflecting the fact that missions today "last on average three times longer than their predecessors"[38] (United Nations 2015, 11). At the same time, the number, size, and responsibilities of smaller civilian political missions have grown; 21 political missions are now in place, with more than 3,000 personnel.[39]
- Costs for humanitarian action not directly linked to conflict have risen as well. In 2015, for instance, roughly 1.5 million refugees sought asylum in Organisation for Economic Co-operation and Development countries, nearly twice as many as in the previous year. Funding for the immediate response to this crisis came in large part from official development assistance. Development aid spent on refugees in host countries doubled between 2014 and 2015 and increased sixfold since 2010, reaching a total of US$12 billion (9.1 percent of total overseas development assistance).[40]

The evolving geography of conflict is driving these cost increases as much as the escalation of violence. Conflict is becoming more concentrated in middle-income countries, presenting a unique set of difficulties from those of lower-income countries.

How Violent Conflicts End

Violent conflicts tend either to end in victory for one side or another or to fade into a state of chronic but low-intensity armed hostilities. Permanent settlements through mediation, particularly for intrastate conflicts, have been rarer. In the decades after World War II, the bipolar international order focused on interstate wars. The end of the Cold War ushered in a new era of cooperation among global powers and a renewed effort to peacefully resolve violent conflicts that were previously seen only through the prism of the competition between the

Soviet Union and the United States. Between 1946 and 1991, more than 23 percent of conflicts were brought to an end by means of permanent peace settlements or ceasefire agreements; the proportion increased to almost 29 percent between 1991 and 2014 (Kreutz 2010; see figure 1.10).

The use of mediation declined in the early 2000s, yet remains well above Cold War levels (Wallensteen and Svensson 2014). While the long-term effectiveness of the mediation of violent intrastate conflict has been challenged (Beardsley 2008, 2011; Fortna 2003), recent research suggests that negotiated settlements are effective at reducing violence in at least the first few years after an agreement is signed (De Rouen and Chowdhury 2016; see figure 1.11).

Indeed, negotiated settlements can have a transformative effect on conflict dynamics even when they fail. For example, violent conflicts that restart after collapse of a negotiated settlement result in significantly fewer fatalities relative to the presettlement death toll. This was the case in 10 out of 11 cases in which peace agreements collapsed between 1989 and 2004 (Mack 2012). The average annual death toll of intrastate conflicts drops by more than 80 percent if they recur after a peace agreement (Human Security Report Project 2012). Notwithstanding its positive impacts, the use of mediation to negotiate the peaceful resolution of conflicts has not become a stable feature of the international system. A recent analysis suggests that the proliferation of negotiated settlements has ended, with the violent conflicts in today's world challenging existing international mechanisms and hence being increasingly difficult to resolve with agreements (Walter 2017a).

Indeed, many of the intrastate conflicts and civil wars that have erupted since 2007 share characteristics that make them

FIGURE 1.10 **Termination of Violent Conflicts Worldwide before and after the Cold War, 1946–2014**

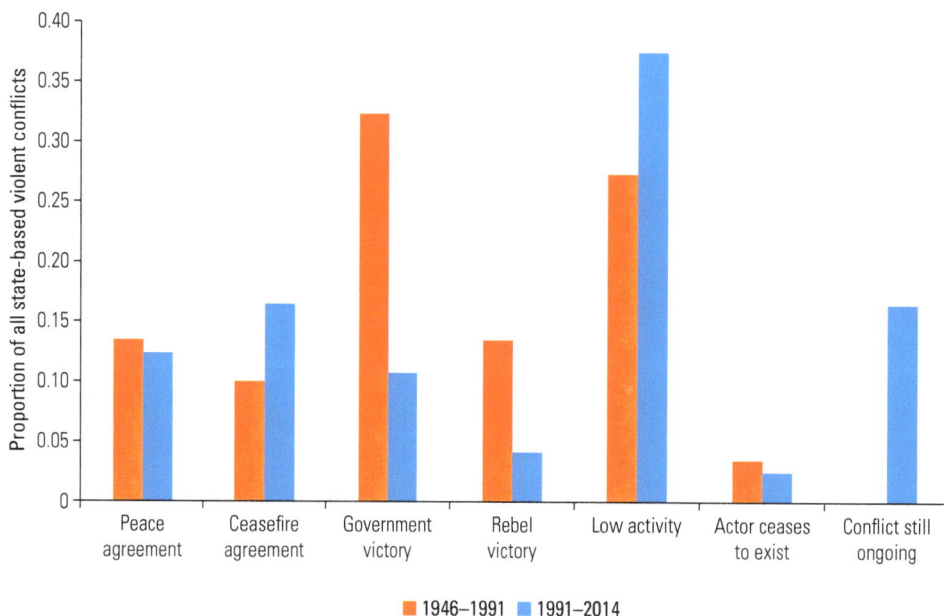

Source: Uppsala Conflict Data Program (Kreutz 2010).

Note: The Cold War period extends from 1945 to 1991; the post–Cold War period extends from 1991 to 2014. Peace agreement = an agreement concerned with resolving or regulating the incompatibility (completely or a central part of it) that is signed or accepted by all or the main parties active in the last year of conflict. Ceasefire agreement = an agreement typically concerned with ending the use of force by the warring sides. It can also offer amnesty for participation in the conflict. It does not include any resolution of the incompatibility. Government victory = the state manages to defeat comprehensively or eliminate the opposition. Rebel victory = the rebel group manages to oust the government. Low activity = conflict activity continues but does not reach the Uppsala Conflict Data Program threshold with regard to fatalities. Actor ceases to exist = conflict activity continues, but at least one of the parties ceases to exist or becomes another conflict actor.

FIGURE 1.11 The Onset and End of Armed Conflict Worldwide, 1950–2013

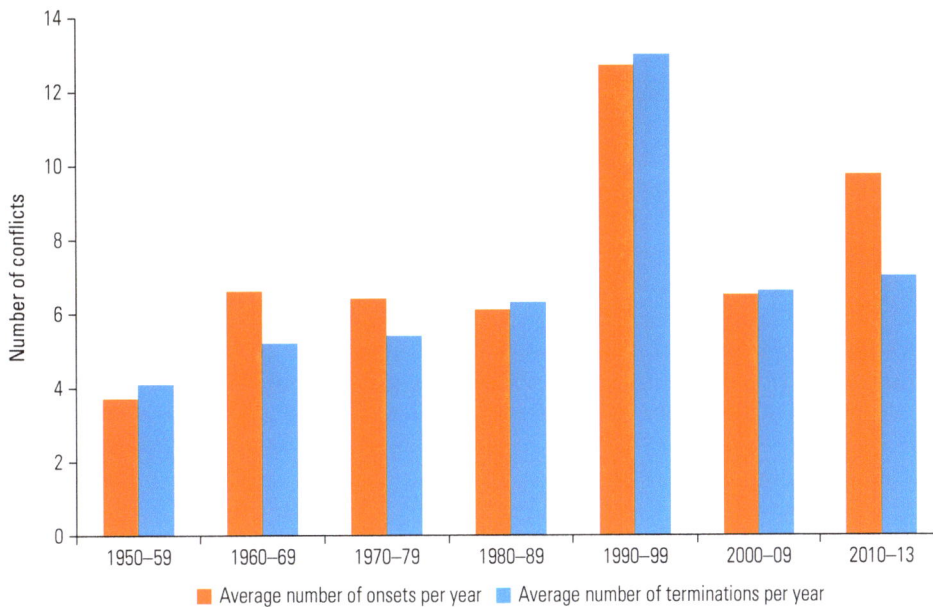

Source: Uppsala Conflict Data Program (Kreutz 2010).

particularly resistant to negotiated settlements.[41] For example, international consensus on how they should end is lacking, as demonstrated in the absence of UN Security Council action (UN Security Council 2017). Moreover, the nature of these wars—with multiple fighting factions, significant involvement of outside states, and the deep societal divisions that the conflicts feed and reflect—challenges the existing international and state-based conflict-resolution mechanisms (Walter 2017a).

Conclusion

Violent conflict remains the exception, not the rule, in today's world. But it remains a significant threat to the stability of countries and regions. Violent conflict has become more complex, more internationalized, and more multidimensional. It affects more middle-income countries, but is also stubbornly entrenched in low-income countries. In both cases, violent conflicts are contagious.

The international system created after World War II is rooted in the collective desire to prevent violent conflict through norms, values, and peace mechanisms. But

it is challenged on many fronts in a world where communication, finance, crime, and ideas flow seamlessly across borders. Responding to violence after it has broken out is more expensive than ever, underscoring the need to move beyond crisis response and recovery to a focus on prevention.

This chapter has reviewed current trends in violent conflict, the nature of the risks, and the opportunities for prevention. The study turns next to an exploration of the context in which violent conflicts are happening, focusing on some of the key systemic risks posed by global trends, and the implications for prevention.

Notes

1. Intensity is defined as the number of conflict-related deaths and injuries.
2. Most of the numbers referred to in this chapter are based on the UCDP and Peace Research Institute Oslo (PRIO) definitions of state-based armed conflict as "a contested incompatibility which concerns government and/or territory where the use of armed force between two parties, of which at least one is the government of a state, results in at least 25 battle-related deaths" and nonstate

violent conflict as a conflict between non-state (that is, not state-based) armed groups, which may have ties to one or more states. The data on state-based conflicts cover the years 1946–2016 (Allansson, Melander, and Themnér 2017; Gleditsch et al. 2002), while the data on nonstate violent conflicts cover the years 1989–2016 (Sundberg, Eck, and Kreutz 2012; Allansson, Melander, and Themnér 2017). UCDP is the source for the majority of trends on the character and intensity of violent conflicts in this chapter. Figure 1.1 includes conflicts that have resulted in at least 25 battle-related deaths in a given year.

3. Pinker and Mack (2014) note, "The end of the Cold War … saw a steep reduction in the number of armed conflicts of all kinds, including civil wars." While it is true that the rate of violent conflicts between state forces and a nonstate actor had been decreasing since the end of the Cold War, it has been increasing in recent years, as has the rate of conflicts between nonstate actors—although the latter is not explored in Pinker and Mack (2014), given the low number of battle deaths reported by these conflicts.

4. UCDP reports four conflicts with more than 1,000 fatalities each for 2007 and 13 for 2016 (Allansson, Melander, and Themnér 2017; Gleditsch et al. 2002; Sundberg, Eck, and Kreutz 2012).

5. UCDP reports 63 state-based and nonstate conflicts with between 25 and 999 battle-related deaths for 2007 and 101 for 2016 (Allansson, Melander, and Themnér 2017; Gleditsch et al. 2002; Sundberg, Eck, and Kreutz 2012).

6. Figures 1.2 and 1.3 use the best estimate for battle-related deaths in violent conflicts, including those that involve state forces and those that do not; figure 1.3 also includes fatalities stemming from one-sided violence.

7. Nonstate armed groups include rebel organizations and violent extremist groups; political militias or "armed gangs" operating on behalf of political actors; and communal and ethnic militias, which can act as local security providers or can engage in intercommunal conflict, often not engaging with the state (for example, the Fulani ethnic militia in Nigeria).

8. The Islamic State is known by several other names, including the Islamic State of Iraq and the Levant, the Islamic State of Iraq and Syria, and its Arabic language acronym with a negative connotation, Daesh.

9. The use of progovernment militias does not necessarily signify that a state lacks the capacity to carry out violence using its own forces. In fact, the use of such militias is often a sign of strong state capacity (see Kishi, Aucoin, and Raleigh 2016; Raleigh and Kishi 2017).

10. UCDP/PRIO defines internationalized conflict as those where one side is a state and one side is a nonstate and where an outside state intervenes on behalf of one of these (Allansson, Melander, and Themnér 2017; Gleditsch et al. 2002).

11. "This appears to be because credible guarantees on the terms of an agreement are almost impossible to design by the combatants themselves" (Walter 2017a, 1).

12. UCDP does not report any violent conflicts involving state forces ending in 2016 (Allansson, Melander, and Themnér 2017; Gleditsch et al. 2002). As this study was being prepared, it was too early to say which conflicts that were active in 2016 might or might not be active in 2017. Hence, figure 1.6 extends only to 2015. Several factors account for the stark difference in the duration (number of years, on average) of violent conflicts involving state forces that ended in 2014 versus those that ended in 2015. In 2014, 56 percent of violent conflicts had lasted more than 20 years and 44 percent had lasted less than 10 years. In 2015, in contrast, 31 percent had lasted more than 20 years and 69 percent had lasted less than 10 years.

13. "Conflict duration is [also] likely to change power balances that need to be reflected in the institutional designs of political settlements; [as such] stability can only be achieved if underlying causes are sufficiently addressed as well. Otherwise, conflict is likely to recur" (Wolff, Ross, and Wee 2017).

14. Gang violence, which is prevalent in the Americas, is not systematically included here, as it was mentioned previously in the analysis of armed groups.

15. Political-religious divides and territorial claims are also major drivers, both of which may conflate with issues related to political power.

16. In 2015, approximately 19 percent of battle-field deaths occurred in the Arab world.

17. These states also had highly repressive human rights policies and practiced capital punishment, among other commonalities (see Gleditsch and Rudolfsen 2016).

18. In Iraq, long-standing grievances are increasingly manifesting themselves in the creation of cross-sectarian alliances as an expression of widespread and diverse popular dissatisfaction with the ruling elites. Iraq also has a history of long-standing tensions between Arabs and Kurds.

19. For example, the global recruitment of Western foreign fighters through technology and other means (ICG 2016a).

20. While the international recruitment of young people by groups such as the Islamic State has received much attention, the strength of such groups in Iraq, for example, has come from the local co-optation of the old Ba'athist apparatus as well as from collaboration with tribes that have been frightened by a formal state structure they perceive to be serving as an instrument of retribution for the years of Sunni domination in Iraq. Al Shabaab has also co-opted many people who had been excluded by the domination of clans in Somali politics, especially many youths.

21. Chapter 4 presents the findings of studies of the motivations of individuals who join violent extremist groups (see box 4.4).

22. See the United Nations High Commissioner for Refugees (UNHCR) data portal, "South Sudan Situation," http://data.unhcr.org/SouthSudan/regional.php; Internal Displacement Monitoring Centre database, "South Sudan," http://www.internal-displacement.org/countries/south-sudan.

23. Terrorism is understood here as "the threatened or actual use of illegal force and violence by a non-state actor to attain a political, economic, religious or social goal through fear, coercion or intimidation" (National Consortium for the Study of Terrorism and Responses to Terrorism 2016). This definition renders it difficult to distinguish events from warfare during violent conflict (Hoffman 2006).

24. Illicit financing of nonstate actors is not limited to the sale of drugs.

25. "An exact estimate for the economic cost of violent conflict is hard to derive. The very existence of a conflict makes measurement of economic activity problematic ... [and so numbers] ought to be interpreted with this in mind. . . . [Regardless of the estimate used,] the impact of civil war on output is disastrous" (Mueller 2013).

26. Definitions and data set are available at http://eventdata.parusanalytics.com/data.dir/atrocities.html.

27. Hultman (2010) suggests three mechanisms that may result in this behavior: "First, if an intervention makes the warring parties expect a settlement of the conflict, they might target civilians as a last-minute strategy to establish territorial control. Second, if the intervention alters the balance of power between the warring parties or hinders military clashes, the warring parties might turn to violence against civilians as a cheaper strategy of imposing costs on the adversary. Third, if an intervention challenges the warring parties' ability to extract natural resources or to engage in criminal economic activity, it might trigger them to increase violent looting behavior in order to maintain control over resources."

28. Attacks on schools and hospitals are considered one of the six grave violations under the August 1999 UN Security Council Resolution (S/RES/1261) on Children and Armed Conflict (see also ICRC 2017; Sassoli 2004).

29. See ACLED for definitions and discussion, http://www.crisis.acleddata.com/category/remote-violence/.

30. This was also the highest number of civilian casualties that the UN has ever recorded over the protracted conflict in the country.

31. Other estimates put the figure in excess of 800,000, suggesting that UCDP underestimates the scale of the genocide. No genocide has been comparable in scale to that of Rwanda for more than 20 years. However, several massive genocides occurred between 1955 and 1994.

32. The numbers reported here reflect the numbers released in UNHCR's report, *Global Trends: Forced Displacement in 2016* (UNHCR 2017). The trends depicted in figure 1.9 are based on data downloaded from UNHCR. The numbers reported in the UNHCR report differ because IDP numbers come from the Internal Displacement Monitoring Centre and refugee numbers

come from the United Nations Relief and Works Agency for Palestine Refugees in the Near East in addition to UNHCR.

33. This figure is based on the Global Peace Index, which includes 16 separate categories with estimated costs, including the losses from crime and interpersonal violence ($2.5 trillion) and losses from conflict ($742 billion), as well as the costs of containing violence through internal security spending ($4.2 trillion) and military spending ($6.2 trillion) (IEP 2015).

34. Does the outcome of prevention and intervention justify its cost? In cases where it is not deemed "successful," arguing its justification can be more difficult. Valentino (2011), for example, argues, "Intervening militarily to save lives abroad often sounds good on paper, but the record has not been promising. The ethical calculus involved is almost always complicated by messy realities on the ground, and the opportunity costs of such missions are massive. Well-meaning countries could save far more lives by helping refugees and victims of natural disasters and funding public health."

35. See http://interactive.unocha.org/publication/globalhumanitarianoverview/, section on funding requirements.

36. See http://interactive.unocha.org/publication/globalhumanitarianoverview/, section on funding requirements.

37. See https://www.unmissions.org/#block-views-missions-peacekeeping-missions.

38. Based on the planned closure of peacekeeping missions in Haiti and Liberia, peacekeeping missions' budgets have been reduced to approximately US$6.8 billion in 2017.

39. See https://www.unmissions.org/#block-views-missions-political-missions.

40. See http://www.oecd.org/dac/development-aid-rises-again-in-2015-spending-on-refugees-doubles.htm.

41. With the notable exception of some new wars in the Middle East, for instance, most conflicts initiated in the twenty-first century represent a relapse of conflict (Walter 2010).

References

ACLED (Armed Conflict Location and Event Data Project). 2016. ACLED-Africa, v.7. http://www.acleddata.com.

Action on Armed Violence. 2017. "Explosive Truths: Monitoring Explosive Violence in 2016." https://aoav.org.uk/2017/explosive-truths-monitoring-explosive-violence-2016/.

Ahuka, O. L., N. Chabikuli, and G. A. Ogunbanjo. 2004. "The Effects of Armed Conflict on Pregnancy Outcomes in the Congo." *International Journal of Gynecology and Obstetrics* 84 (1): 91–92.

Al Jazeera. 2017. "WHO: Speed of Yemen Cholera Outbreak 'Unprecedented.'" May 19. http://www.aljazeera.com/news/2017/05/speed-yemen-cholera-outbreak-unprecedented-170519110837434.html.

Allansson, M., E. Melander, and L. Themnér. 2017. "Organized Violence, 1989–2016." *Journal of Peace Research* 54 (4): 574–87.

Alvarez, A. 2006. "Militias and Genocide." *War Crimes, Genocide and Crimes Against Humanity* 2 (1): 1–33.

Bastick, M., K. Grimm, and R. Kunz. 2007. *Sexual Violence in Armed Conflict: Global Overview and Implications for the Security Sector.* Geneva: Centre for the Democratic Control of Armed Forces.

Beardsley, K. 2008. "Agreement without Peace? International Mediation and Time Inconsistency Problems." *American Journal of Political Science* 52 (4): 723–40.

———. 2011. "Peacekeeping and the Contagion of Armed Conflict." *Journal of Politics* 73 (4): 1051–64.

Beegle, K., L. Christiaensen, A. Dabalen, and I. Gaddis. 2016. *Poverty in a Rising Africa.* Washington, DC: World Bank.

Besley, T., T. Fetzer, and H. Mueller. 2012. "One Kind of Lawlessness: Estimating the Welfare Cost of Somali Piracy." Working Paper 626, Barcelona Graduate School of Economics.

Betancourt, T. S., R. McBain, E. A. Newnham, and R. T. Brennan. 2012. "Trajectories of Internalizing Problems in War-Affected Sierra Leonean Youth: Examining Conflict and Postconflict Factors." *Child Development* 84 (2): 455–70.

Bevins, V. 2015. "In Brazil, Homicide Rate Still High Despite Increased Prosperity." *Los Angeles Times*, May 22. http://www.latimes.com/world/brazil/la-fg-ff-brazil-crime-20150522-story.html.

Blattman, C. 2006. *The Consequences of Child Soldiering.* Berkeley: University of California Press.

Brinkman, H.-J., and C. S. Hendrix. 2011. "Food Insecurity and Violent Conflict: Causes, Consequences, and Addressing the Challenges." Occasional Paper 24, World Food Programme, Rome.

Brownlee, J., T. Masoud, and A. Reynolds. 2015. The Arab Spring: Pathways of Repression and Reform. Oxford: Oxford University Press.

Calvete, E., and I. Orue. 2011. "The Impact of Violence Exposure on Aggressive Behavior through Social Information Processing in Adolescents. *American Journal of Orthopsychiatry* 81 (1): 38.

CDC (Centers for Disease Control and Prevention). 2014. "Mental Health in Conflict-Affected Populations: Fact Sheet." ERRB Scientific Publications, CDC, Atlanta.

Chen, S., M. Ravallion, and P. Sangraula. 2008. "Dollar a Day Revisited." *World Bank Economic Review* 23 (2): 163–84.

Child Trends. 2017. "Children's Exposure to Violence." https://www.childtrends.org/indi cators/childrens-exposure-to-violence/.

Chioda, L. 2017. *Stop the Violence in Latin America: A Look at Prevention from Cradle to Adulthood*. Washington, DC: World Bank.

Citizens Council for Public Security and Criminal Justice. 2016. "Caracas, Venezuela, the Most Violent City in the World." Seguridad, Justicia, y Paz. http://www.seguri dadjusticiaypaz.org.mx/biblioteca/prensa /download/6-prensa/231-caracas-venezuela -the-most-violent-city-in-the-world.

Colletta, N., and B. Oppenheim. 2017. "Subnational Conflict: Dimensions, Trends, and Options for Prevention." Background paper for the United Nations–World Bank Flagship Study *Pathways for Peace: Inclusive Approaches to Preventing Violent Conflict*, World Bank, Washington, DC.

Comolli, V. 2015. *Boko Haram, Nigeria Islamist Insurgency*. London: Hurst.

———. 2017. "Transnational Organized Crime and Conflict." Background Paper for the United Nations–World Bank Flagship Study, *Pathways for Peace: Inclusive Approaches to Preventing Violent Conflict*, World Bank, Washington, DC.

Crawford, N. C. 2016. "US Budgetary Costs of War through 2016: $4.79 Trillion and Counting: Summary of Costs of the US Wars in Iraq, Syria, Afghanistan, and Pakistan and Homeland Security." Costs of War Working Paper, Watson Institute for International Studies, Brown University, Providence, RI.

Croicu, M., and R. Sundberg. 2017. *UCDP GED Codebook,* version 17.1. Department of Peace and Conflict Research, Uppsala University, Uppsala, Sweden.

Dancs, A. 2011. "International Assistance Spending due to War on Terror." Costs of War Working Paper, Watson Institute for International Studies, Brown University, Providence, RI.

De Groot, O. J., C. Bozzoli, and T. Brück. 2012. "The Global Economic Burden of Violent Conflict." HiCN Working Paper 199, Institute of Development Studies, University of Sussex, Falmer, UK.

De Rouen, K., and I. Chowdhury. 2016. "Peacekeeping and Civil War Peace Agreements." *Defence and Peace Economics* (May 9): 1–17.

De Waal, A. 2007. *War in Darfur and the Search for Peace*. Cambridge, MA: Harvard University Press.

Demekas, D. G., J. McHugh, and T. Kosma. 2002. "The Economics of Post Conflict Aid (Vol. 2)." IMF Working Paper 02/198, International Monetary Fund, Washington, DC.

Denselow, J. 2010. "Roadside Bombs: Weapons of the Weak. *The Guardian*, June 18. http:// www.theguardian.com/commentisfree/2010 /jun/18/roadside-bombs-afghanistan.

Devarajan, S., and E. Ianchovichina. 2017. "A Broken Social Contract, Not High Inequality, Led to the Arab Spring." *Review of Income and Wealth* [online version of record]. http://onlinelibrary.wiley.com/doi/10.1111 /roiw.12288/abstract.

Doyle, M. W., and N. Sambanis. 2000. "International Peacebuilding: A Theoretical and Quantitative Analysis." *American Political Science Review* 94 (4): 779–801.

Dutt, A. 2016. "UN-Backed Findings Reveal Startling Small Arms Trade Increase." Inter Press Service News Agency, June 8. http://www .ipsnews.net/2016/06/un-backed-findings -reveal-startling-small-arms-trade-increase/.

Eck, K., and L. Hultman. 2007. "One-Sided Violence against Civilians in War: Insights from New Fatality Data." *Journal of Peace Research* 44 (2): 233–46.

Economist. 2015. "War Child." June 3.

Fearon, J. 2004. "Why Do Some Civil Wars Last So Much Longer than Others?" *Journal of Peace Research* 41 (3): 275–301.

Finkelhor, D., H. A. Turner, R. Ormrod, S. Hamby, and K. Kracke. 2009. *Children's Exposure to Violence: A Comprehensive National Survey.* Washington: U.S. Department of Justice.

Food Security Information Network. 2017. *Global Report on Food Crisis 2017.* Brussels: European Union, World Food Programme, and Food and Agricultural Organization, March.

Fortna, V. P. 2002. "Does Peacekeeping Keep Peace after Civil War? And If So How?" Unpublished paper, Columbia University, New York.

———. 2003. "Scraps of Paper? Agreements and the Durability of Peace." *International Organization* 57 (2): 337–72.

Garrett-Peltier, H. 2014. "The Job Opportunity Cost of War." Costs of War Working Paper, Watson Institute for International Studies, Brown University, Providence, RI.

Gates, S., H. M. Nygård, and E. Trappeniers. 2016. "Conflict Recurrence." PRIO Conflict Trends 2/2016, Peace Research Institute Oslo. www.prio.org/ConflictTrends.

Geneva Declaration on Armed Violence and Development. 2011. *Global Burden of Armed Violence 2011.* http://www.genevadeclaration .org/measurability/global-burden-of-armed -violence/global-burden-of-armed-violence -2011.html. Small Arms Survey, Geneva.

Geneva Declaration Secretariat. 2015. *Global Burden of Armed Violence 2015: Every Body Counts.* Geneva: Geneva Declaration Secretariat.

Gleditsch, N. P., and I. Rudolfsen. 2016. "Are Muslim Countries More Prone to Violence?" *Research and Politics* 3 (2): 1–9.

Gleditsch, N. P., P. Wallensteen, M. Eriksson, M. Sollenberg, and H. Strand. 2002. "Armed Conflict 1946–2001: A New Dataset." *Journal of Peace Research* 39 (5): 615–37.

Guéhenno, J.-M. 2016. "The Transformation of War and Peace." Carnegie Corporation of New York. www.carnegie.org/news/articles /international-day-peace/.

Guha-Sapir, D., and W. G. van Panhuis. 2004. "Conflict-Related Mortality: An Analysis of 37 Datasets." *Disasters* 28 (4): 418–28.

Haass, R. 2017. *A World in Disarray: American Foreign Policy and the Crisis of the Old Order.* New York: Penguin.

Hegre, H., J. R. Oneal, and B. Russett. 2010. "Trade Does Promote Peace: New Simultaneous Estimates of the Reciprocal Effects of Trade and Conflict." *Journal of Peace Research* 47 (6): 763–74.

Heibner, S., P. Neumann, J. Holland-McCowan, and R. Basra. 2017. "Caliphate in Decline: An Estimate of Islamic State's Financial Fortunes." Ernst & Young.

Hoffman, B. 2006. *Inside Terrorism.* New York: Columbia University Press.

Huesmann, L. R., and L. Kirwil. 2007. *Why Observing Violence Increases the Risk of Violent Behavior in the Observer.* Cambridge, U.K.: Cambridge University Press.

Hultman, L. 2010. "Keeping Peace or Spurring Violence? Unintended Effects of Peace Operations on Violence against Civilians." *Civil Wars* 12 (1–2): 29–46.

Human Security Report Project. 2005. *Human Security Report 2005: War and Peace in the 21st Century.* Burnaby, BC: Simon Fraser University Press.

———. 2011. *Human Security Report 2009/2010: The Causes of Peace and the Shrinking Costs of War.* Burnaby, BC: Simon Fraser University Press.

———. 2012. *Human Security Report 2012: Sexual Violence, Education, and War; Beyond the Mainstream Narrative.* Burnaby, BC: Simon Fraser University Press.

———. 2013. *Human Security Report 2013: The Decline in Global Violence; Evidence, Explanation, and Contestation.* Burnaby, BC: Simon Fraser University Press.

Ianchovichina, E. 2017. *Eruptions of Popular Arab Anger: The Economics of the Arab Spring, Its Aftermath, and the Way Forward.* Washington, DC: World Bank.

ICG (International Crisis Group). 2015. "The Central Sahel: A Perfect Sandstorm." Africa Report 227, ICG, Brussels.

———. 2016a. "Exploiting Disorder: Al-Qaeda and the Islamic State." Special Report 1, ICG, Brussels.

———. 2016b. "South Sudan: Rearranging the Chess Board." Africa Report 243, ICG, Brussels.

ICRC (International Committee of the Red Cross). 2016. *People on War: Perspectives from 16 Countries.* Geneva: ICRC.

———. 2017. *I Saw My City Die: Voices from the Front Lines of Urban Conflict in Iraq, Syria and Yemen.* Geneva: ICRC.

IDMC (Internal Displacement Monitoring Centre). 2016. "Somalia IDP Figures Analysis."

IDMC, Geneva. http://www.internal-displacement.org/sub-saharan-africa/somalia/figures-analysis.

IEP (Institute for Economics and Peace). 2015. *Global Peace Index 2015: Measuring Peace, Its Causes, and Its Economic Value.* Sydney: IEP.

———. 2016. *The Economic Value of Peace: Measuring the Global Economic Impact of Violence and Conflict.* Sydney: IEP. http://economicsandpeace.org/wp-content/uploads/2016/12/The-Economic-Value-of-Peace-2016-WEB.pdf.

International Peace Institute. 2016. *Lost in Transition: UN Mediation in Libya, Syria, and Yemen.* New York: International Peace Institute. http://reliefweb.int/sites/reliefweb.int/files/resources/1611_Lost-in-Transition.pdf.

Kelly, J. 2017. "Violence: From the Public to the Domestic; Examining the Relationship between Political Instability and Intimate Partner Violence." Background paper for the United Nations–World Bank Flagship Study, *Pathways for Peace: Inclusive Approaches to Preventing Violent Conflict*, World Bank, Washington, DC.

Kishi, R. 2015. "The Targeting of Children in Conflict Zones, Part 1: General Trends." ACLED Crisis Blog, March 13. http://www.crisis.acleddata.com/the-targeting-of-children-in-conflict-zones-part-1-general-trends/.

Kishi, R., C. Aucoin, and C. Raleigh. 2016. "Are Pro-Government Political Militias Evidence of a Strong State?" *Angle Journal*, March 13. https://anglejournal.com/article/2015-12-conflict-data-and-policymaking-in-the-era-of-the-sustainable-development-goals/.

Kishi, R., C. Raleigh, and A. M. Linke. 2016. "Patterns and Trends of the Geography of Conflict." In *Peace and Conflict*, edited by D. Backer, R. Bhavnani, and P. Huth, 25–41. New York: Routledge.

Kreutz, J. 2010. "How and When Armed Conflicts End: Introducing the UCDP Conflict Termination Dataset." *Journal of Peace Research* 47 (2): 243–50.

Ksoll, C., M. Rocco, and A. Morjaria. 2009. "Guns and Roses: The Impact of the Kenyan Post-Election Violence on Flower Exporting Firms." CSAE Working Paper 2009/06, Centre for the Study of African Economies, Oxford University, Oxford, UK.

Leckman, J. F., C. Panter-Brick, and R. Salah, eds. 2014. *Pathways to Peace: The Transformative Power of Children and Families.* Cambridge, MA: MIT Press.

Lombard, L. 2016. *State of Rebellion, Violence, and Intervention in the Central African Republic.* Chicago: University of Chicago Press.

Lynch, M. 2016. *The New Arab Wars: Uprisings and Anarchy in the Middle East.* New York: PublicAffairs.

Mack, A. 2012. "Even Failed Peace Agreements Save Lives." Political Violence at a Glance, August 10. https://politicalviolenceataglance.org/2012/08/10/even-failed-peace-agreements-save-lives/.

Malik, A. 2017. "Electoral Violence and the Prevention of Violent Conflict." Background paper for the United Nations–World Bank Flagship Study, *Pathways for Peace: Inclusive Approaches to Preventing Violent Conflict*, World Bank, Washington, DC.

Margolin, G., and B. G. Elana. 2004. "Children's Exposure to Violence in the Family and Community." *Current Directions in Psychological Science* 13 (4): 152–55. http://www.jstor.org/stable/pdfplus/20182938.pdf.

Mavriqi, R. R. 2016. "Global Economic Burden of Conflict." Unpublished manuscript.

McCormick, G. H., and F. Giordano. 2007. "Things Come Together: Symbolic Violence and Guerrilla Mobilization." *Third World Quarterly* 28 (2): 295–320.

Merari, A. 1993. "Terrorism as a Strategy of Insurgency." *Terrorism and Political Violence* 5 (4): 213–51.

Miller, K. E., and A. Rasmussen. 2010. "War Exposure, Daily Stressors, and Mental Health in Conflict and Post-conflict Settings: Bridging the Divide between Trauma-Focused and Psychosocial Frameworks." *Journal of Social Science Medicine* 70 (1): 7–16.

Mogaka, S. 2017. "Competition for Power in Africa: Inclusive Politics and Its Relation to Violent Conflict." Background paper for the United Nations–World Bank Flagship Study, *Pathways for Peace: Inclusive Approaches to Preventing Violent Conflict*, World Bank, Washington, DC.

Mueller, H. 2013. "The Economic Cost of Conflict." IGC Working Paper, International Growth Centre, London.

Mueller, H., and J. Tobias. 2016. "The Cost of Violence: Estimating the Economic Impact of

Conflict." Growth Brief, International Growth Centre, London.

Murphy, M., and A. Ricks. 2014. "After Ebola: Rebuilding Liberia's Health Care Infrastructure." *Boston Globe*, September 17. https://www.bostonglobe.com/opinion/2014/09/17/ebola-outbreak-liberia-health-care-infrastructure-underdeveloped/lTN5s8n77upOQkMclDIseK/story.html.

Murthy, R. S., and R. Lakshminarayana. 2006. "Mental Health Consequences of War: A Brief Review of Research Findings." *World Psychiatry* 5 (1): 25–30.

National Consortium for the Study of Terrorism and Responses to Terrorism. 2016. Global Terrorism Database. National Consortium for the Study of Terrorism and Responses to Terrorism, Department of Homeland Security, University of Maryland, College Park. https://www.start.umd.edu/gtd.

National Intelligence Council. 2017. *Global Trends: Paradox of Progress.* Washington, DC: National Intelligence Council.

Ndikumana, L. 2015. "The Role of Foreign Aid in Post-Conflict Countries." CRPD Working Paper 30, Center for Research on Peace and Development, Katholieke Universiteit Leuven, Leuven, Belgium.

Nordhaus, W. D. 2002. "The Economic Consequences of a War in Iraq." NBER Working Paper w9361, National Bureau of Economic Research, Cambridge, MA.

NPR (National Public Radio). 2013. "Syrian Drug Sales Fuel Country's Civil War." *All Things Considered*, October 29. http://www.npr.org/templates/story/story.php?storyId=241667347.

OECD (Organisation for Economic Co-operation and Development). 2016. *States of Fragility Report 2016.* Paris: OECD.

Ormhaug, C. M. 2009. "Maternal Health in the Aftermath of Civil Conflict." Book chapter, Peace Research Institute Oslo (PRIO), Oslo.

Otis, J. 2014. *The FARC and Colombia's Illegal Drug Trade.* Washington, DC: Wilson Center Latin American Program. https://www.wilsoncenter.org/sites/default/files/Otis_FARCDrugTrade2014.pdf.

Parks, T., N. Colletta, and B. Oppenheim. 2013. *The Contested Corners of Asia: Subnational Conflict and International Development Assistance.* San Francisco: Asia Foundation.

Pavesi, I. 2016. *Trade Update 2016: Transfers and Transparency.* Geneva: Small Arms Survey, Graduate Institute of International and Development Studies. http://www.smallarmssurvey.org/fileadmin/docs/S-Trade-Update/SAS-Trade-Update.pdf.

Pinker, S., 2011. "Violence Vanquished." *Wall Street Journal*, 24. https://www.wsj.com/articles/SB1000142405311190410670457658320 3589408180.

Pinker, S., and A. Mack. 2014. "The World Is Not Falling Apart." *Slate*, December 22. http://www.slate.com/articles/news_and_politics/foreigners/2014/12/the_world_is_not_falling_apart_the_trend_lines_reveal_an_increasingly_peaceful.html.

Raleigh, C. 2012. "Violence against Civilians: A Disaggregated Analysis." *International Interactions* 38 (4): 462–81.

————. 2016. "Pragmatic and Promiscuous: Explaining the Rise of Competitive Political Militias across Africa." *Journal of Conflict Resolution* 60 (2): 283–310.

————. 2017. "The Links between Food Crises and Violence in East, South, and West Africa: An ACLED Briefing Note." ACLED Crisis Blog, March 23. http://www.crisis.acleddata.com/the-links-between-food-crises-and-violence-in-east-south-and-west-africa-an-acled-briefing-note/.

Raleigh, C., and C. Dowd. 2013. "Governance and Conflict in the Sahel's 'Ungoverned Space.'" *Stability: International Journal of Security and Development* 2 (2).

Raleigh, C., and R. Kishi. 2017. "Hired Guns: Using Pro-government Militias for Political Competition." Working Paper, Armed Conflict Location and Event Data Project (ACLED), University of Sussex.

Raleigh, C., A. Linke, H. Hegre, and J. Karlsen. 2010. "Introducing ACLED—Armed Conflict Location and Event Data." *Journal of Peace Research* 47 (5): 651–60.

Regan, P. M. 2002. "Third-Party Interventions and the Duration of Intrastate Conflicts." *Journal of Conflict Resolution* 46 (1): 55–73.

Reuters. 2015. "Violent Deaths in Brazil Surge to Peak of 58,000 amid Olympic Safety Fears." *Guardian* (Manchester), October 9. https://www.theguardian.com/world/2015/oct/09/violent-deaths-in-brazil-surge-to-peak-of-58000-amid-olympic-safety-fears.

————. 2016. "U.N. Official Says at Least 50,000 Dead in South Sudan War." Reuters, March 2.

https://www.reuters.com/article/us-southsudan
-unrest-un/u-n-official-says-at-least-50000
-dead-in-south-sudan-war-idUSKCN0W503Q.

Ron, J. 2002. Territoriality and Plausible Deniability: Serbian Paramilitaries in the Bosnian War. In *Death Squads in Global Perspective*, edited by B. B. Campbell and A. D. Brenner, 287–312. New York: Palgrave Macmillan.

Röther, B., G. Pierre, D. Lombardo, R. Herrala, P. Toffano, E. Roos, G. Auclair, and K. Manasseh. 2016. "The Economic Impact of Conflicts and the Refugee Crisis in the Middle East and North Africa." IMF Staff Discussion Note SDN/16/08, International Monetary Fund, Washington, DC.

Sassoli, M. 2004. "Legitimate Targets of Attack under International Humanitarian Law, Harvard Humanitarian Initiative." Background paper prepared for the Informal High-Level Expert Meeting on the Reaffirmation and Development of International Humanitarian Law, Cambridge, MA, January 27–29, 2003.

Save the Children. 2013. *Attacks on Education: The Impact of Conflict and Grave Violations on Children's Future.* London: Save the Children.

Schippa, C. 2017. "Conflict Costs Us $13.6 Trillion a Year. And We Spend Next to Nothing on Peace." World Economic Forum, Geneva, January 5. https://www.weforum.org/agenda/2017/01/how-much-does-violence-really-cost-our-global-economy/.

Schrodt, P. A., and J. Ulfelder. 2016. *Political Instability Task Force Atrocities Event Data Collection Codebook,* Version 1.1b1. Washington, DC: Political Instability Task Force.

Seddon, D., and J. Adhikari. 2003. "Conflict and Food Security in Nepal: A Preliminary Analysis." RN Report Series, Rural Reconstruction Nepal, Kathmandu.

Shonkoff, J. P., and A. P. Garner. 2012. "The Lifelong Effects of Early Childhood Adversity and Toxic Stress." Technical Report, American Academy of Pediatrics, Elk Grove Village, IL. http://pediatrics.aappublications.org/content/pediatrics/early/2011/12/21/peds.2011-2663.full.pdf.

Small Arms Survey. 2014. "Small Arms Survey 2014." Small Arms Survey, Graduate Institute of International and Development Studies, Geneva. http://www.smallarmssurvey.org/de/publications/by-type/yearbook/small-arms-survey-2014.html.

SOS Children's Village. 2014. "Syria: War Has Denied Children Their Right to Education." SOS Children's Village, October 21. http://www.sos-childrensvillages.org/publications/news/syria-war-denying-children-right-to-education.

———. 2015. "Children in Conflict: Child Soldiers." SOS Children's Village. http://www.child-soldier.org'.

Stearn, J. 2011. *Dancing in the Glory of Monsters.* New York: PublicAffairs.

Sundberg, R., K. Eck, and J. Kreutz. 2012. "Introducing the UCDP Non-state Conflict Dataset." *Journal of Peace Research* 49 (2): 351–62.

Sundberg, R., and E. Melander. 2013. "Introducing the UCDP Georeferenced Event Dataset." *Journal of Peace Research* 50 (4): 523–32.

Tajaldin, B., K. Almilaji, P. Langton, and A. Sparrow. 2015. "Defining Polio: Closing the Gap in Global Surveillance." *Annals of Global Health* 81 (3): 386–95.

Tegel, S. 2016. "Venezuela's Capital Is World's Most Murderous City." *USA Today*, January 29. http://www.usatoday.com/story/news/world/2016/01/29/venezuelas-capital-worlds-most-murderous-city/79508586/.

Thompson, P. G. 2014. *Armed Groups: The 21st Century Threat.* Lanham, MD: Rowman and Littlefield.

Toska, S. 2017. "Sustaining Peace: Making Development Work for the Prevention of Violent Conflicts Cases; Egypt, Tunisia, Morocco, and Jordan." Case study for the United Nations–World Bank Flagship Study, *Pathways for Peace: Inclusive Approaches to Preventing Violent Conflict*, World Bank, Washington, DC.

Tran, M. 2013. "War Denying Millions of Children an Education." *Guardian* (Manchester), July 11. https://www.theguardian.com/global-development/2013/jul/12/war-denying-children-education.

UCDP (Uppsala Conflict Data Program). 2017. *UCDP Conflict Encyclopedia.* Uppsala University. http://www.ucdp.uu.se.

UN (United Nations). 2008. *United Nations Peacekeeping Operations Principles and Guidelines.* New York: UN. http://www.un.org/en/peacekeeping/documents/capstone_eng.pdf.

———. 2014. "Strengthening of the Coordination of Emergency Humanitarian Assistance of the United Nations." Report of the UN Secretary-General (A/69/80 – E/2014/68), New York.

———. 2015. *Report of the High-Level Independent Panel on United Nations Peace Operations: Uniting Our Strengths for Peace—Politics, Partnership, and People.* New York: United Nations.

———. 2017. "Report of the Secretary-General on Conflict-Related Sexual Violence." Report S/2017/249, United Nations, New York.

UN Secretary-General. 2015. "Report on Women and Peace and Security." Report of the Secretary-General S/2015/716, United Nations, New York, September 16.

UN Security Council. 2017. "Can the Security Council Prevent Conflict?" Research Report 1. UN Security Council, New York.

UN Women. 2015. *Preventing Conflict, Transforming Justice, Securing the Peace: Global Study on the Implementation of United Nations Security Council Resolution 1325.* New York: UN Women.

UNAMA (United Nations Assistance Mission in Afghanistan). 2017. *Afghanistan: Protection of Civilians in Armed Conflict; Annual Report 2016.* Kabul: UNAMA. https://unama.unmissions.org/sites/default/files/protection_of_civilians_in_armed_conflict_annual_report_2016_final280317.pdf.

UNDP (United Nations Development Programme). 2016a. *Arab Human Development Report: Youth and the Prospects for Human Development in a Changing Reality.* New York: UNDP. http://www.arab-hdr.org/PreviousReports/2016/2016.aspx.

———. 2016b. "Development Approaches to Migration and Displacement." Position Paper, UNDP, New York. http://www.undp.org/content/undp/en/home/librarypage/poverty-reduction/position-paper-for-the-2016-un-summit-for-refugees-and-migrants-.html.

UNESCWA (United Nations Economic and Social Commission for Western Asia). 2017. *The Impact of Conflict over the Life Cycle: Evidence for the Arab Region.* Trends and Impacts 5. New York: United Nations.

UNFPA (United Nations Population Fund). 2017. "New Study Finds Child Marriage Rising among Most Vulnerable Syrian Refugees." UNFPA, New York. http://www.unfpa.org/news/new-study-finds-child-marriage-rising-among-most-vulnerable-syrian-refugees.

UNHCR (United Nations High Commissioner for Refugees). 2013. "UNHCR Statistical Online Population Database: Sources, Methods, and Data Considerations." UNHCR, Geneva. http://www.unhcr.org/en-us/statistics/country/45c06c662/unhcr-statistical-online-population-database-sources-methods-data-considerations.html#OTHER_DATA_CONSIDERATIONS.

———. 2017. *Global Trends: Forced Displacement in 2016.* Geneva: UNHCR. http://www.unhcr.org/en-us/statistics/unhcrstats/5943e8a34/global-trends-forced-displacement-2016.html.

UNICEF (United Nations Children's Fund). 2015. *No Place for Children: The Impact of Five Years of War on Syria's Children and Their Childhoods.* New York: UNICEF.

UNOCHA (United Nations Office for the Coordination of Humanitarian Affairs). 2016. *World Humanitarian Data and Trends 2016.* New York: UNOCHA.

———. 2017. "Global Humanitarian Overview 2017." June Status Report, UNOCHA, New York.

UNODC (United Nations Office on Drugs and Crime). 2016. "Global Homicide Data." UNODC, Brussels.

Urzúa, S. 2016. "Do Skills/Abilities Matter? The Life Cycle Approach." Keynote address at "Conference on the Socio-economic Ramifications of Conflict: A Life Cycle Approach," UN ESCWA and the American University of Beirut, Beirut.

Valentino, B. A. 2011. "The True Costs of Humanitarian Intervention." *Foreign Affairs* 90 (6): 60–73.

von Uexkull, N., M. Croicu, H. Fjelde, and H. Buhaug. 2016. "Civil Conflict Sensitivity to Growing-Season Drought." *Proceedings of the National Academy of Sciences* 113(44): 12391–96.

Waldman, R. J. 2001. "Public Health in Times of War and Famine: What Can Be Done? What Should Be Done?" *Journal of the American Medical Association* 286 (5): 588–90. doi:10.1001/jama.286.5.588.

Wallensteen, P., and I. Svensson. 2014. "Talking Peace: International Mediation in Armed Conflicts." *Journal of Peace Research* 51 (2): 315–27.

Walter, B. 2010. "Conflict Relapse and the Sustainability of Post-Conflict Peace." Background paper for the *World Development Report 2011: Conflict, Security, and Development.* Washington, DC: World Bank.

———. 2017a. "External Intervention and Civil Wars." Unpublished paper, University of California, Berkeley.

———. 2017b. "The New Civil Wars." *Annual Review of Political Science* 20 (May): 469–86.

Weaver, C. M., J. G. Borkowski, and T. L. Whitman. 2008. "Violence Breeds Violence: Childhood Exposure and Adolescent Conduct Problems." *Journal of Community Psychology* 36(1): 96–112.

Williams, P. 2017. "Continuity and Change in War and Conflict in Africa." *PRISM* 6 (4): 33–45.

Wolff, S., S. Ross., and A. Wee. 2017. "Subnational Governance and Conflict." Background paper for United Nations–World Bank Flagship Study, *Pathways for Peace: Inclusive Approaches to Preventing Violent Conflict,* World Bank, Washington, DC.

World Bank. 2011. *World Development Report 2011: Conflict, Security, and Development.* Washington, DC: World Bank.

———. 2015. "Preventing Violent Extremism with Development Interventions: A Strategic Review." Unpublished, World Bank, Washington, DC.

———. 2016a. *Forcibly Displaced: Toward a Development Approach Supporting Refugees, the Internally Displaced, and Their Hosts.* Washington, DC: World Bank.

———. 2016b. "Psychosocial Support in Fragile and Conflict-Affected Settings." World Bank, Washington, DC, May 9. http://www.world bank.org/en/topic/fragilityconflictviolence /brief/psychosocial-support-in-fragile-and -conflict-affected-settings.

———. 2017a. *The Toll of War: The Economic and Social Consequences of the Conflict in Syria.* Washington, DC: World Bank.

———. 2017b. "Toward Zero Tolerance for Famine: Fragility and Famine Response and Prevention." World Bank and United Nations Discussion Draft, World Bank, Washington, DC.

World Food Programme. 2017a. "Global Report on Food Crises 2017." https://www.wfp.org /content/global-report-food-crisis-2017.

———. 2017b. "At the Root of Exodus: Food Security, Conflict and International Migration." http://documents.wfp.org/stel-l e n t / g r o u p s / p u b l i c / d o c u m e n t s /communications/wfp291884.pdf.

World Vision International. 2017. "Children in Conflict." World Vision International, New York. http://www.wvi.org/disaster -management/children-conflict.

Additional Reading

Alesina, A., and R. Perotti. 1995. "Income Distribution, Political Instability, and Investment." Department of Economics Discussion Paper 751, Columbia University, New York.

Ghobarah, H. A., P. Huth, and B. Russett. 2003. "Civil Wars Kill and Maim People—Long after the Shooting Stops." *American Political Science Review* 97 (2): 189–202.

Jensen, N. 2008. "Political Risk, Democratic Institutions, and Foreign Direct Investment." *Journal of Politics* 70 (4): 1040–52.

Kishi, R. 2015. "Rape as a Weapon of Political Violence, Part 2: Where, When, and by Whom Is This Tactic Used?" ACLED Crisis Blog, February 25. http://www.crisis.acleddata.com /rape-as-a-weapon-of-political-violence-part -2-where-when-and-by-whom-is-this-tactic -used/.

Security Council Report. 2017. *Can the Security Council Prevent Conflict*? Research report 2017 1. http://www.securitycouncilreport.org /atf/cf/%7B65BFCF9B-6D27-4E9C-8CD3 -CF6E4FF96FF9%7D/research_report_con flict_prevention_2017.pdf.

UN (United Nations). 2016. "Violence, Conflict Cost World $13.6 Billion Annually, Secretary-General Says, Urging Member States to Shore Up Financially Strapped Peacebuilding Fund." Press Release, September 21. https:// www.un.org/press/en/2016/sgsm18113.doc .htm.

CHAPTER 2

The Need for Prevention in an Interdependent World

The changing profile of violent conflict in the world today is not taking place in isolation. This chapter explores how the trend of violence without borders has emerged in a global context where the balance of geopolitical power is in flux and transnational factors like advances in information and communication technology (ICT), population movements, and climate change create risks and opportunities to be managed at multiple levels.[1] It highlights the centrality of the 2030 Agenda for Sustainable Development as an organizing template for prevention and examines patterns of governance, pressures at all levels for more inclusive forms of political organization, and changing economic structures. It also reviews the complexity of these global trends that form the landscape against which states and other actors navigate change in pursuit of sustainable peace.

The international system designed to save the world from "the scourge of war" at the conclusion of World War II was formed in the context of still-pressing threats and dark memories of war between nations (UN 1945, 1). The adoption of global norms and values, including those pertaining to human rights, further embodied the collective commitment to managing problems through international governance institutions. As noted in chapter 1, those systems and norms are being called on to respond to a resurgence of violent conflict that is testing the postwar order.

The geopolitical balance in the world is shifting. The rise of new global powers affects not only political and economic equilibriums but also peace efforts (Call and de Coning 2017). Rising tensions among great powers affect the multilateral system at its core, most notably in the United Nations (UN) Security Council, and increasingly tend to spill over into proxy wars. Proxy wars, moreover, are not the exclusive purview of traditional or emerging great powers. A multipolar international system is consolidating, where regional powers easily find room to pursue their own strategic interests independently.

A push for political inclusion is clearly visible within nations as well as in the international system. The number of societies that have adopted more inclusive forms of political and economic governance over the last 30 years has grown rapidly. Inclusive societies, this study argues, are better equipped to develop the incentives that give momentum to prevention and to peace. However, the transition toward inclusion can itself increase the risks of violence, at least in the short term, if not handled carefully. As chapters 4 and 5 discuss in more detail, this transition can open space for new contestation among groups demanding or resenting a change in their relative status.

The shifts in the international balance of power are taking place against a backdrop of changes in the way people and societies operate and interact. Rapid advances in ICT present opportunities for innovation, growth, and the unfettered exchange of ideas and inclusive narratives. But these advances have negative aspects too. Interconnectivity enables transnational organized crime to flourish, allows the rapid transmission of violent ideologies, and leaves economies vulnerable to cybercrime. Climate change, mass movements of people, and the unmet expectations of a growing population of young people in low- and middle-income countries also present risks that challenge governments on all levels. The ability of global systems to distribute the opportunities equitably and to manage the risks that accompany these rapid changes is increasingly in question.

Changes in the global landscape as well as within societies have major implications for the prevention of violent conflict. Prevention, as elaborated throughout this study and in line with the joint UN Sustaining Peace Resolutions (UNSC 2016; UN General Assembly 2016), is a process aimed at minimizing incentives for violence, while boosting incentives for peace. In such a process, actors continually adjust to changes in the local landscape and beyond in ways that solidify social cohesion and ultimately peace. Countries and the international community urgently need to leverage global trends and better manage the associated risks, building on new and existing approaches that enhance collaboration, inclusiveness, and conflict prevention.

An International System in Search of a New Equilibrium

A Transition in the World Order

The framework of multilateralism, international law, and treaties dedicated to managing peace and security has weathered many storms over the past 70 years, and global institutions continue to adapt to new challenges. The global balance of power and the environment in which global institutions operate are also shifting.

It is widely argued that a transition to a multipolar world is underway (Guterres 2017), with new centers of political, economic, and military power emerging. Today, growing economic power for emerging economies and the achievement by many countries of middle-income status bring demands for the redistribution of global political influence. Pressure to redraw normative boundaries in key areas of international law (such as human rights or the status of women) is mounting. Many countries seek to renegotiate power sharing in multilateral forums, such as the UN and international financial institutions (Griffin, forthcoming; Haass 2017). The pressure for greater inclusion and wider representation in global governance is marked by the emergence of informal and more flexible forums such as the G-20, which facilitates economic and financial cooperation among countries representing more than 80 percent of the world's gross domestic product (GDP) and almost two-thirds of the world's population.[2]

The growing need for flexible instruments is also apparent when it comes to preventing violent conflict and sustaining peace. On the one hand, the United Nations remains the pivotal institution in this sector. The 2030 Agenda for Sustainable Development, including its 17 Sustainable Development Goals (SDGs), not only confirms that sustainable development is the overaching goal in its own right, but also provides a universal framework for addressing the root causes of conflict, recognizing the deep complexity and interconnectedness on the path to peace and progress.

On the other hand, regional organizations play an increasingly central role in preventing conflict (Verjee 2017).[3] As violent conflict has evolved, with a decline in wars between states and a sharp increase in intrastate conflicts, some regional organizations in Sub-Saharan Africa are taking a distinctive, more active role in ensuring peace and security in their neighborhoods. Even when their initial purpose was to foster economic integration and trade links, as in the case of the Economic Community of West African States (ECOWAS), some of these organizations have become the lynchpin of stability and security in their regions, working also in the field of conflict prevention, resolution, and peacekeeping. Regional responses to the risk of violent conflict, however, have been uneven in their ability to sustain peace. Furthermore, regional competition can fuel unilateral action, prolonging and aggravating conflicts and weakening the capacity of regional organizations to play a role in preventing violent conflicts.

The international law on conflict has evolved as well, becoming increasingly sophisticated (see box 7.2). Commitment to prevention has also been renewed, including at the 2005 World Summit. The United Nations and its partners have built consensus around challenging issues, producing major international agreements such as the 2015 Paris Accord on Climate Change. A series of high-level reports have consistently recognized the need for a stronger focus on prevention. This analytical effort has been consolidated into important resolutions, including the twin Security Council and General Assembly resolutions on sustaining peace (UNSC 2016; UN General Assembly 2016).

Global Drive for More Inclusive Societies

Some states are becoming progressively more open to sharing power and including citizens in political participation. This has been happening in extended waves since the eighteenth century and continues today. A new wave began in the 1970s and broadened after the end of the Cold War with a strong increase in the number of countries with more democratic forms of government (Strand et al. 2012). The number of states with democratic forms of government grew from 45 among 150 states in 1974 to 121 among 193 states in 2003 (Menocal, Fritz, and Rakner 2007).

The 2015 Global Attitudes Survey finds support for democratic values in countries across all regions, although the support varies. Large majorities tend to value religious freedom and an impartial judicial system, while smaller majorities tend to support multiparty elections, free speech, and censorship-free media (Pew Research

Center 2015). The World Values Survey, a global survey of basic values and beliefs, similarly concludes, "Democracy has an overwhelming positive image throughout the world" (Freedom House 2004, 5) and has become, over the last decade, "virtually the only political model with global appeal, no matter what the culture" (Freedom House 2004, 5). The sixth round of the World Values Survey, which collected data from 2010 to 2014, finds that on average people ranked living in a democratically governed country as "highly important," with the lowest average of the distribution being 6.4 out of 10 (World Values Survey Association 2014).

This recent push for more inclusive politics has been driven partly by the availability of social media and communication tools. The growth in interconnectivity and transparency in the world has opened windows, showing people how others live, raising awareness of global inequality, and providing a platform for expression. These tools have been important factors in many political transformations, coming more from the middle class and educated youth than from the poor or marginalized (Devarajan and Ianchovichina 2017).

While this push for more inclusive and transparent government is a positive sign for long-term, sustainable peace (Doyle 1986; Russett 1993; Tomz and Weeks 2013) and has occurred peacefully in many countries, it also carries increased risk. Chapters 4 and 5 explore in more detail some of these risks and opportunities and their implications for prevention.

Data from the Polity IV project (Marshall, Gurr, and Jaggers 2015) clearly illustrate changing trends in national governance (see figure 2.1) and the risk of instability associated with political systems with varying degrees of openness (see figure 2.2). As figure 2.1 shows,

- The number of autocracies across the world has been declining since 1984.
- The number of democracies has increased since 1980.
- Many countries can be defined as anocracies, meaning that they are either highly imperfect democracies or

FIGURE 2.1   Global Trends in Governance, 1946–2008

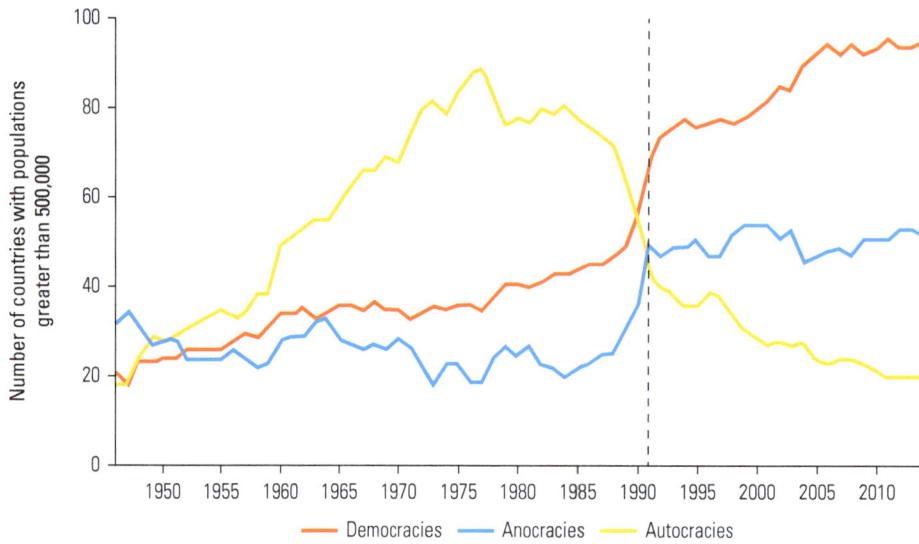

Source: Center for Systemic Peace 2014.

hybrid regimes. As countries that are transitioning or stationed between one mode of governance and another, anocracies present situations where "odd combinations of democratic and autocratic authority patterns could be observed" (Center for Systemic Peace 2014).

Figure 2.2 illustrates the annual likelihood of political instability (y-axis) plotted

FIGURE 2.2   Polity and the Onset of Political Instability, 1955–2006

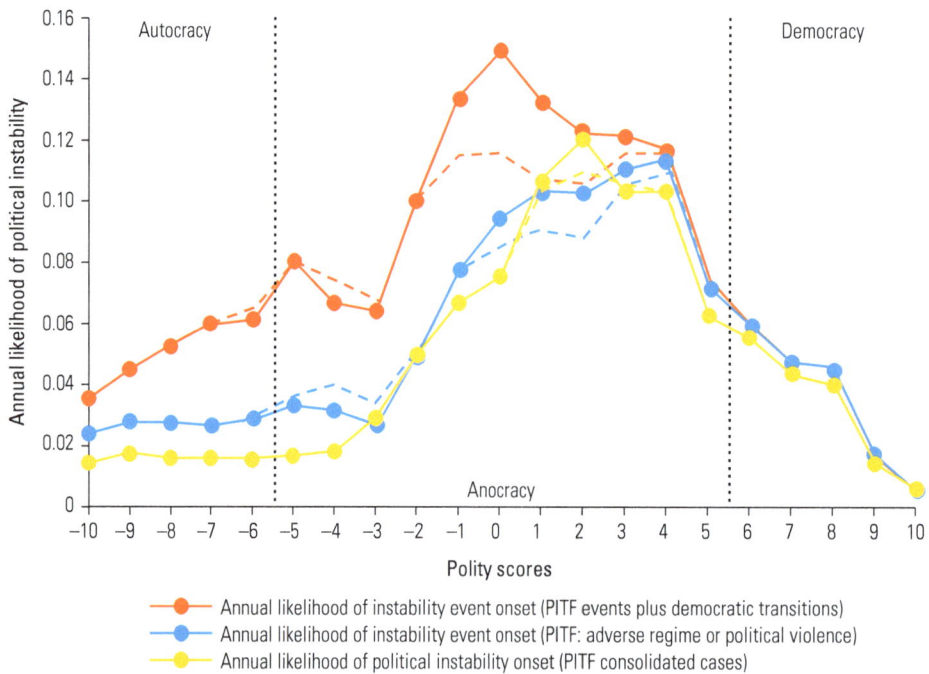

Source: Center for Systemic Peace 2014.
Note: PITF = Political Instability Task Force.

against the polity scores of 167 independent countries.[4] The five categories of instability events are adverse regime change, revolutionary war, ethnic war, genocide or politicide, and major democratic transition (Marshall, Gurr, and Jaggers 2015). The figure plots the annual likelihood for the following:

- Onset of any of these five categories
- Onset of all categories excluding major democratic transition
- A period of political instability or "consolidated cases."

Across all plots, "anocracies have the greatest risk of instability, while autocracies and unconsolidated democracies have a lesser, yet still substantial, risk" (Center for Systemic Peace 2014). The rising number of anocracies and the high degree of instability associated with periods of anocracy have important implications for prevention, in that they intensify the risk of conflict that might escalate to violence.

Political transitions can be bidirectional. Freedom House suggests that in 2016, scores for freedom declined in 67 countries but rose in 36 and that 2016 was the eleventh consecutive year in which declines in freedom outnumbered improvements (Puddington and Roylance 2017). Most striking is that, as opposed to earlier years, established democracies[5]—not autocracies or dictatorships—dominated the list of countries suffering setbacks as measured by the Freedom House rankings (Freedom House 2017). This alludes to the fact that democracies are not homogenous and that issues like inequality are on the rise even in democratic systems.

Changing Economic Structures

The global economy has grown substantially since the end of World War II. Global GDP growth has been associated with increasing trade openness and poverty reduction. Between 1990 and 2014, for instance, the share of world GDP encompassing international trade grew from US$3.5 trillion to US$18.9 trillion. The correlation between trade openness and per capita GDP growth at the global level is firmly established (see figure 2.3).

While trade and technology have provided "ladders" for rapid growth, individual countries' ability to benefit fully from advances in trade and technology critically depends on their own characteristics (Bartley Johns et al. 2015). Trade and technology have acted in a complementary way, in large part due to several technological and logistical advances that have improved mobility, communications, and financial systems, such as containerization and information technology.

There are also fewer barriers to global trade and finance. Trade agreements and trade and financial deepening have multiplied in tandem, with the World Trade Organization (WTO) playing an important role in advocating and managing an inclusive global trading system and setting the "rules of the game" for regional trade agreements. Overall, trade dynamics since 1990 have been one of the contributors to the historic improvement in living standards across the world and to a reduction in the share of the world population living in extreme poverty (below $1.90 a day, in 2011 dollars at purchasing power parity) from 35 percent in 1990 to around 11 percent in 2013 (Ferreira, Joliffe, and Prydz 2015).

The global economy, nonetheless, continues to face many challenges. While global trade has grown, growth has not been evenly spread. Rather, trade growth has been marked by downturns and a prolonged period of only modest improvement since the global financial crisis of 2007, falling, for the fifth consecutive year, below 3 percent in 2016. These values are well below the average of 7 percent between 1987 and 2007. Although the volume of global trade has increased, the value of global trade has fallen as a result of shifting exchange rates and lower commodity prices (WTO 2017). Meanwhile, foreign direct investment (FDI) to developing countries, which has been empirically found to contribute to higher wages, productivity, and employment, has also been decreasing since 2011 (United Nations 2017a), adversely affecting growth and productivity (Hale and

FIGURE 2.3 Global Gross Domestic Product per Capita and World Exports, 1960–2014

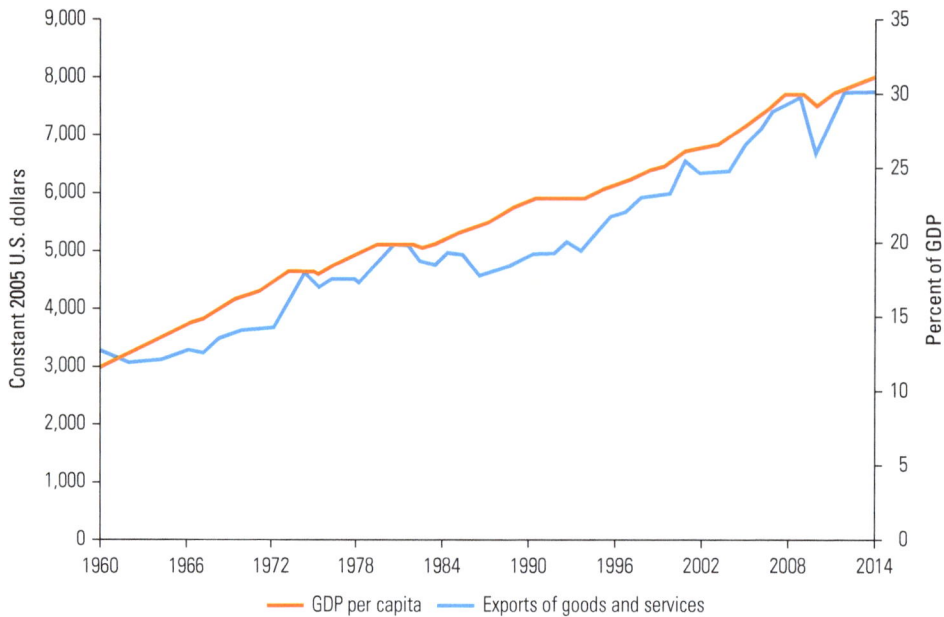

Sources: World Bank Group and World Trade Organization 2015; data from World Bank, *World Development Indicators.*
Note: GDP = gross domestic product.

Xu 2016). From 2015 to 2016, global FDI flows decreased by 7 percent to US$1.625 billion and stayed below their precrisis peak, representing approximately 2.2 percent of global GDP compared with 3.6 percent in 2007 (OECD 2017; see figure 2.4).

These trends and others create additional challenges for development. For example, the reduction in the incidence of extreme poverty since 1981 has relied heavily on the strong and rapid growth of the global economy. But given the current slow pace of global economic growth and the potential for this trend to persist, many countries face issues in sustaining poverty reduction at the same rhythm as in previous decades. This trend may jeopardize progress toward attainment of the SDGs (SDG 1), calling on the international community to intensify its efforts to combat extreme poverty.

Despite the fact that inequality between countries has decreased globally, inequality within countries remains high (World Bank 2016b) because economic interdependence and globalization have increased without equal distribution of the gains. The 2030 Agenda for Sustainable Development (SDG 10) identifies the reduction of inequality, both within countries as well as globally, as a priority of the international community (UN 2015). Recent analysis by the International Monetary Fund shows that the labor share of income has been on a downward trend in high-income economies since the 1980s and in low- and middle-income countries since the early 1990s (IMF 2017).[6] This decline in the labor share of income has been associated with an increase in income inequality in many parts of the world. In addition, unemployment rates remain high in many regions, especially in those with high populations of youth.

Challenges to reducing in-country inequality include technological change, such as the increase in automation and routinization of tasks. Although technological progress and the globalization of trade and capital have contributed strongly to overall global growth and prosperity as well as to income convergence in low- and middle-income countries, they have had disproportionate and asymmetric impacts across countries, industries, and workers of different skill groups.

FIGURE 2.4 Global Flows of Foreign Direct Investment, 1999–2016

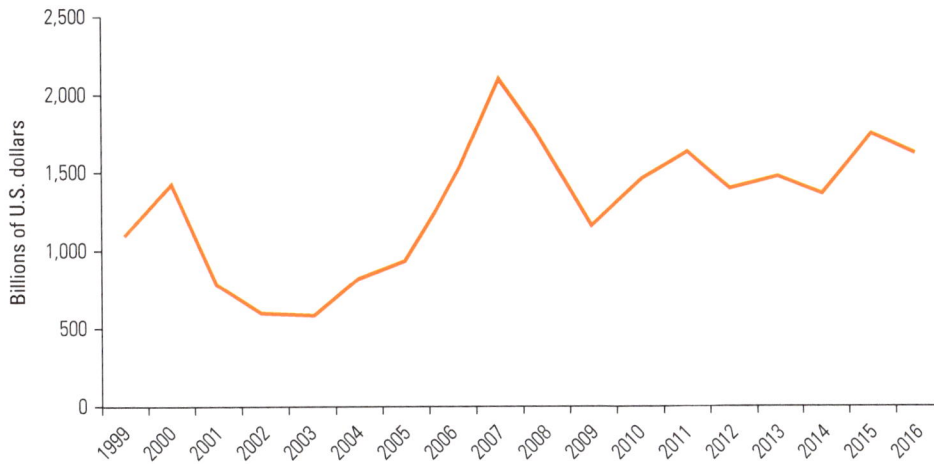

Source: Data from OECD, International Direct Investment Statistics database.

Moreover, technological change happens quickly, requiring fast adaptation on the part of industries and people to new markets and jobs. The speed of change leads many to believe that technological change, including automation shifts, is, in the long term, "the most important force shaping the labor market and income inequality" (Hallward-Driemeier and Nayyar 2017).

While all of these recent trends pose challenges, they do not directly affect violent conflict. Instead, they put additional stresses on systems and people and can increase the tendency for groups to mobilize to address perceived grievances, which can culminate in violence. In a world where interconnectivity is stronger than ever and transparency is possible through an ever-increasing number of ICT platforms, in most societies the growth of the global economy has generated greater expectations and aspirations for the future. When these expectations and aspirations are unmet, because of the weak capacity of governments to provide for their constituents, the inability of labor markets to provide jobs, or the uneven distribution of global wealth, frustration and tensions associated with job creation, employment, and wages can rise (Piketty 2013).

It is at this moment that the threat of protectionism weighs heavily. Rising uncertainty about receiving one's fair share of national or global wealth and being able to achieve individual aspirations has led to mixed feelings regarding the benefits of globalization. A poll of 19 countries shows that globalization is met with increasing skepticism, with mixed views on immigration and trade (see figure 2.5). While enthusiasm for economic globalization is high among people from lower- and middle-income countries that are experiencing higher growth rates, people from high-income countries with modest growth are more apprehensive (Pew Research Center 2007).

Thus, while changing economic structures and the reduction of the role of labor as an economic factor of production in the postindustrial age are not a direct cause of violent conflict, they generate stress while systems and people adapt. The problem is particularly complex in low- and lower-middle-income countries that have only partially gone through an industrial transition and that have a labor force with low skills. These countries now face the question of whether a path of convergence to higher income levels through manufacturing is viable. In turn, these countries place immense pressure on job creation and employment, and many people are not able to acquire skills for the higher-quality jobs that are being generated (such as in modern services).

FIGURE 2.5 Attitudes toward Globalization and Change in Gross Domestic Product per Person, Selected Countries, 2011–15

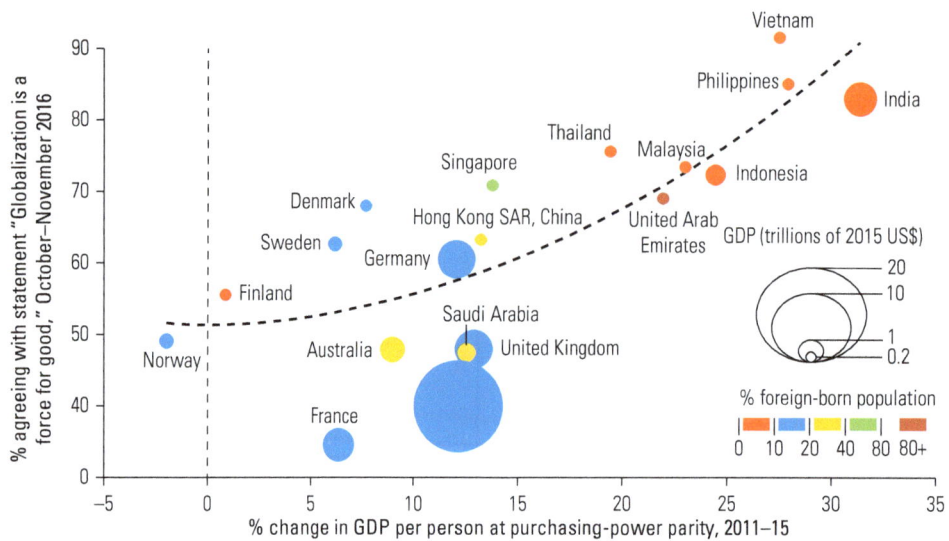

Source: Economist 2016b.
Note: GDP = gross domestic product.

Such adjustments would likely require countries to work together at global and local levels to ensure that their capacities are leveraged to realign jobs and reskill workers and to provide training for different tasks and skills that complement jobs for which machines are substitutes (Hallward-Driemeier and Nayyar 2017; Economist 2016a). As with previous waves of technological change, automation and related technologies enhance overall productivity growth and therefore increase the resources available to redistribute to adversely affected groups. Key elements of the social safety net and distributive policies such as unemployment insurance and progressive taxation remain integral to mitigating the social conflict arising from these potential changes. Addressing changing economic structures and associated inequality through global collaboration also supports attitude changes toward an integrated global economy.

Risk and Opportunity in an Increasingly Connected World

Against this backdrop of geopolitical flux and the charged movement regarding inclusive governance, some new and fast-evolving trends are altering the environment that international and domestic actors must negotiate. Many of these transnational processes will pose risks to individual societies and the institutions in place. But, if well managed, they will also create opportunities for greater inclusion and peace. Collective and collaborative action is needed by all countries to address these trends in the interest of preventing violent conflict.

Challenges of the Revolution in Information and Communication Technology

Societies have transformed over centuries with the help of technology, but the unprecedented pace and reach of technological innovation in recent decades make this phenomenon a defining global trend. Technological advancements in food and water security, health, education, climate action, disaster response, and economies have saved lives and helped to lift many people out of poverty. Not only has their role as an important means for implementing the Sustainable Development Goals been underscored in the 2030 Agenda, but their potential for advancing peace has also been widely recognized by the global community.

Fast-moving advancements in ICT, however, also have problematic consequences. While more people are connected to ICT than ever before—with an estimated 3.2 billion now using the Internet (ITU 2015)—access remains uneven, exacerbating tensions related to exclusion (World Economic Forum 2015). ICT tools for monitoring and managing conflict such as early-warning systems and crowdsourcing technologies can improve the flow of information and, in some ways, facilitate direct communication between state and society. Similarly, new ICT tools, like social media, offer new platforms for expressing grievances and finding common ground or potentially channeling those grievances toward violence (Mor, Ron, and Maoz 2016). By lowering the cost of collective action, advances in ICT enable armed groups, and violent extremist groups in particular, to recruit globally on an unprecedented scale (Smith et al. 2015).

The Digital Divide

Technology has increased global interconnectivity and access to opportunities that improve well-being. There has been a massive increase in the number of mobile devices with cameras, mobile network coverage, and quantity of data available from so-called "smart" technologies (Pew Research Center 2017). Mobile cellular subscriptions worldwide jumped from less than 1 billion in 2000 to more than 7 billion in 2016 (ITU 2015). By 2020, it is projected that 70 percent of the world's population, or 5.5 billion people, will be using mobile technology (CISCO 2017). With the advent of Web 2.0, social media platforms, and other ICT tools, the number of people using the Internet globally has risen steeply (figure 2.6).

Nevertheless, 3.9 billion people in low- and middle-income countries, equivalent to 53 percent of the world's population, are not connected (see map 2.1). The penetration rate in the poorest countries is only 9.5 percent, or 89 million out of 940 million people (ITU 2015). ICT use continues to

vary among men and women: Internet penetration rates are higher among men than women in all regions of the world, with the gender gap in global Internet use rising from 11 to 12 percent from 2013 to 2016 (ITU 2016). In many contexts, the unconnected are often the poor and excluded. Data that show income levels as a critical barrier to Internet access also point to the fact that countries with low GDP per capita often have low Internet penetration. For example, Internet penetration is five times lower in India than in Europe (Deloitte 2014). Additionally, many people are unable to access or use available ICTs because electricity is minimal or absent or because they lack technological literacy. This digital divide cuts people off from the potential cross-cultural exchange and discourse that come with increasing interconnectivity.

Internet penetration has direct implications for economic progress. Every 10 percent increase in broadband penetration in low- and middle-income countries is estimated to have a 1.38 percent increase in GDP (Independent Commission on Multilateralism 2016). The digital divide can aggravate exclusion and inequality, since "some segments of the population may be exposed differently than others to labor market shifts induced by technological innovation, which can aggravate inequalities across groups with different skill levels. In the absence of close monitoring, ICTs could contribute to inequality, thus exacerbating tensions rather than mitigating them" (World Economic Forum 2015).

The Potential Role of ICT in Peacebuilding

The international community and the multilateral system increasingly recognize the role of ICT in preventing violent conflict. The 2005 Tunis Commitment, a statement from the World Summit on the Information Society (2005), highlights ICTs as "effective tools to promote peace, security, and stability and to enhance democracy, social cohesion, good governance, and the rule of law, at national, regional, and international levels." In addition, it argues that ICTs can and should be used for multiple purposes along the conflict prevention

FIGURE 2.6 Global Mobile Network Coverage, 2007–16

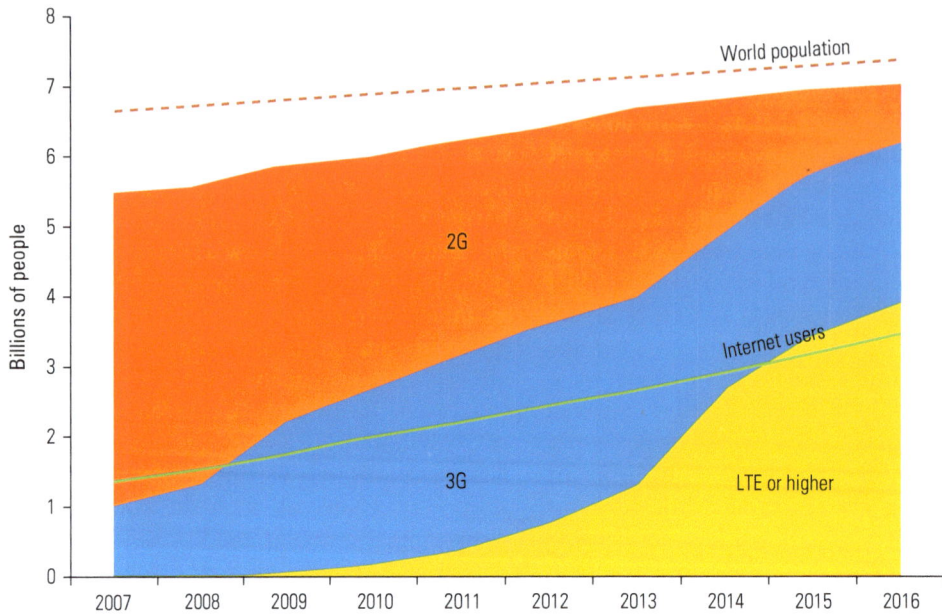

Source: UNITU 2016.
Note: 2016 data are estimates. "Mobile network coverage" refers to population covered by a mobile network.
LTE = long-term evolution.

MAP 2.1 Percentage of Individuals Not Using the Internet, by World Region

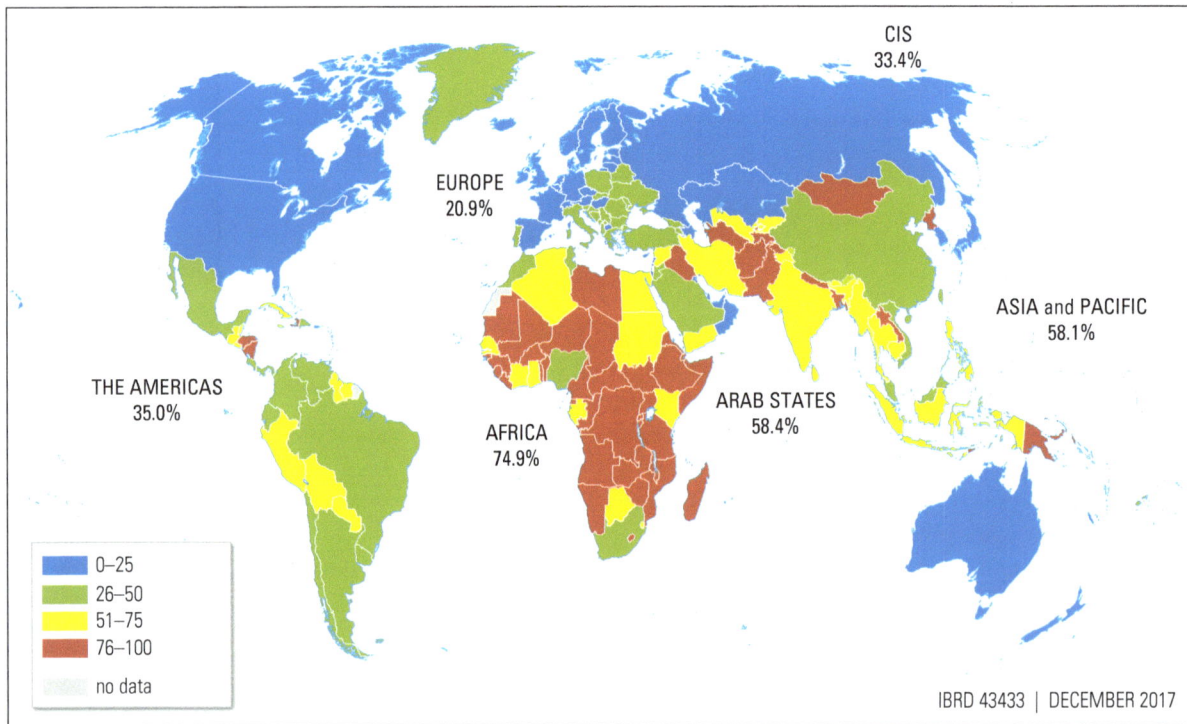

Source: UNITU 2016.
Note: CIS = Commonwealth of Independent States.

arc, including identifying conflict situations through early-warning systems, preventing conflicts, promoting peaceful resolution, and assisting postconflict peacebuilding and reconstruction (see box 2.1).

Indeed, early-warning systems are useful for collecting data, analyzing risk, and providing information with recommendations to targeted stakeholders on the escalation and potential occurrence of violent conflict. Greater capacity to mine and manage big data provides opportunities to improve conflict analysis as well as to test the effectiveness of early-warning systems and refine program selection, design, and implementation accordingly. Geographic information systems, crisis mapping, and crowdsourcing are just some of the tools that can generate data to identify risk and patterns of conflict and violence. Techniques like crowdsourcing can promote inclusion and transparency regarding decision-making processes and enable citizens to "better assess their outcomes, indirectly increasing their

legitimacy" (Independent Commission on Multilateralism 2016). Many nongovernmental and civil society organizations, such as those that tracked postelection violence in Kenya in 2008, use these technologies (World Economic Forum 2016).

Recent analyses of the application of ICT to peacebuilding and peacekeeping highlight the examples of Kenya's violence prevention network, Uganda's election monitoring, Sudan's low-tech adaptations for community communications, and Cyprus's civil society empowerment to illustrate that "ICTs can facilitate peace, not because they directly empower the local over the national and international, or the marginalized over the elites, but because they can be used for the mobilization of grassroots actors, which may affect peacebuilding's balances of power" (Tellidis and Kappler 2016, 80). Participatory peacekeeping is another example that enables local residents to share their observations, alerts, and insights. This process helps to foster

---

BOX 2.1 **Examples of New Technologies Assessing Violent Conflict Risks**

Information and communication technologies (ICT) and the data they generate can support efforts to prevent crisis and tackle the causes of violence using cell phones and tablets, social media, crowdsourcing and crowd seeding, crisis mapping, blogging, and big data analytics. ICT help collect quantitative and qualitative data more frequently in remote areas, through digital surveys, SMS-administered polling, geo-spatial mapping, photographs, videos, and satellite imagery.

For instance, in Sudan and South Sudan, the Crisis and Recovery Mapping and Analysis project (CRMA) undertook participatory mapping of threats and risks. For that purpose, UNDP developed a GIS-enabled desktop database tool, and used geo-referenced analysis to work with state governments, as well as national security, development, and informal actors to identify preemptive interventions based on perceptions of

risk and tension after the Comprehensive Peace Agreement. During the 2015 elections in Nigeria, a team used Artificial Intelligence for Monitoring Elections (AIME), a free and open source solution that combines crowdsourcing with Artificial Intelligence to automatically identify tweets of interest during major elections. Crowdsourcing systems such as Ushahidi have the potential to be used in early warning if the system is designed to produce consistent and complete data frequently.

Technologies have also changed the way people respond to crisis. Following the 2010 Haiti earthquake, for the first time, thousands of people volunteered online to support rescue operations. This has given rise to "Digital Humanitarians," who, through crowdsourcing, created a digital crisis map that showed the real-time evolution of the situation on the ground.

Sources: Blattman 2014; Letouzé 2012a, 2012b; Letouzé, Meier, and Vinck 2013; Mancini 2013; Meier 2013, 2015; Morel 2016; Scharbatke-Church and Patel 2016; and Puig Larrauri 2013.

confidence and trust between peacekeepers and local populations (Independent Commission on Multilateralism 2016).

ICT as a Means to Achieve the Unfiltered Exchanges of Views

Tools like social media can mitigate the risk of violent conflict through online platforms for dialogue and conciliation (Mor, Ron, and Maoz 2016). A study of Israelis and Palestinians using the Facebook platform showed that Facebook posts emphasizing moderate Palestinian voices promoting peace elicited higher sympathy and acceptance (Mor, Ron, and Maoz 2016). Social media can encourage and enable back and forth communications among people, differentiating them from traditional media communications and mass media outreach that are typically one way and susceptible to power control. Social media are a means, therefore, to mobilize people collectively to nonviolent or violent action. Social media messaging services like Twitter also can serve as outlets for people to express their views and discontent peacefully, by providing access to larger networks and freedom to speak or associate (Davison 2015). They can present an opportunity for whistleblowing on corrupt, unethical, or other practices contrary to the public interest. However, they potentially also can constitute a harmful instrument for spoilers seeking to procure and disclose communications selectively for divisive purposes. Chapters 3 and 4 discuss in greater detail collective mobilization in terms of the risk and prevention of violent conflict.

ICT and the Risk of Violence

ICTs can put inequalities into sharp relief and create a space for inciting violence. Recent research on the effect of ICTs on violence indicates that the most important impact is through collective action (Weidmann 2015). But traditional media can play significant roles as well. In the Rwandan genocide, approximately 10 percent of the participation in the violence was attributed to the effects of radio broadcasts (Boggero 2017; Yanagizawa-Drott 2014). Mobile long-distance communication also changes the way information

flows, with varying effects on violent activity (Pierskalla and Hollenbach 2013). For example, one analysis finds that the diffusion of cell phones affected the propensity for political violence in Iraq, where the location of cell phone towers was negatively associated with violence (Shapiro and Weidmann 2015); another shows that the availability of cell phones substantially increased the probability of violent conflict and can amplify the effect of economic downturns on political mobilization (Manacorda and Tesai 2016).

ICT and the Reach of Violent Extremist Groups

It is broadly recognized that violent extremist ideologies have harnessed the "technological revolution," adversely affecting international, regional, and state stability (Boggero 2017). Social media have played multiple roles in violent extremism (Smith et al. 2015), including allowing violent extremist groups to use the online space to coordinate group behavior on a large scale and catalyze grassroots action from anywhere in the world (Veilleux-Lepage 2016). Groups, including but not limited to violent extremist groups, can use social media platforms to mobilize support among persons whose grievances and anxieties about the future have already reached or are close to reaching a critical level. Excluded identity groups and youth are prime targets (Allan et al. 2015; Crenshaw 1981; Fjelde and Østby 2014; Miodownik and Nir 2016; Ross 1993). Logistically, technology platforms are used for data mining, networking, recruiting, mobilization, instruction, planning, and fundraising, among others.

The Cyber Security Threat

Overall, the systemic challenges posed by ICT suggest that action is needed at national, regional, and global levels. International collaboration is needed on issues such as governing cyberspace and addressing cybercrime (see box 2.2), as well as providing international support to countries that are not able to afford equitable access to these technologies.

The answer is not to restrict the use of ICT. Instead, countries could ensure that mechanisms for equitable access are in

BOX 2.2 Cyberspace, the Fifth Domain of Warfare

Cyber insecurity is a new threat to stability. The increased use of cyberspace as a domain for hostilities has been increasingly apparent (Singer and Friedman 2014), and the North Atlantic Treaty Organization (NATO) has declared it the fifth domain of warfare. Research suggests, "As the barriers to entry in the cyber domain are low, cyberspace includes many and varied actors—from criminal hackers to terrorist networks to governments engaged in cyber espionage" (Independent Commission on Multilateralism 2016). Moreover, cybercrime and cyberattacks can "undermine the safety of Internet users, disrupt economic and commercial activity, and threaten military effectiveness" (Independent Commission on Multilateralism 2016).

Many have argued for a treaty addressing cyber security that is more comprehensive than those that govern nuclear, chemical, and biological weapons. In 2001, the Budapest Convention—or Convention on Cybercrime—required "parties to harmonize domestic criminal legislation and promote international collaboration in addressing transnational cybercrime" (Council of Europe 2001). However, the UN Working Group on Countering the Use of the Internet for Terrorist Purposes has concluded thus far that cyber terrorism is "not yet a threat serious enough to warrant separate legislation" (Independent Commission on Multilateralism 2016).

Privacy rights play a prominent role in developing legal frameworks around cyber security. Big data can be a severe risk not just to privacy but also to individual security. This is a critical area for attention, as privacy in conflict-affected areas can be a question of life or death. What constitutes a cybercrime and how existing international law is to be applied are heated elements of this debate. Some initiatives have aimed to provide clarity in this matter, resulting in an emerging consensus that international law, and specifically the UN charter, is applicable to cyberspace. These include a report by the Group of Governmental Experts[a] as well as the Tallinn Manual created by the NATO Cooperative Cyber Defense Center of Excellence.

[a]The third Group of Governmental Experts on Developments in the Field of Information and Telecommunications in the Context of International Security.

place at the local level, in line with the SDGs, and that strong normative frameworks for the prevention of cyber security threats exist. This may entail enforcement of existing norms or creation of new norms where needed (G7 2017).

Additionally, they should ensure that technology is leveraged in the many ways that it can be for building peace, addressing risks of conflict, and communicating narratives that create incentives for peace rather than violence. This will allow societies to realize the potential of ICT as an instrument for sustaining peace and mitigate the risks of violent conflict that are too often easily exploited. Indeed, navigating change by fostering inclusiveness and, thus, social cohesion is the essence of prevention, as this study argues throughout.

Demographic Change and Populations on the Move

Population Growth, Youth, and Aging

Demographic shifts may create new stresses on global and national systems that carry implications for prevention. The good news is that more than 1 billion people exited extreme poverty between 1990 and 2015, even as the world's population increased by 2 billion (UNDP 2017). Looking ahead, half of the world's population growth during 2015–50 is expected to be concentrated in just nine countries, including several conflict-affected countries such as the Democratic Republic of Congo and Nigeria (UNDESA 2015b). The shift is already striking in some areas.

One of the fastest-growing areas in the world, for example, is the Sahel in Africa, which is also one of the most challenged because of the direct impact of climate change, violent extremism, and illegal trafficking (World Bank 2014).

Already there are more young people in the world than at any other time in history—1.8 billion people between the ages of 10 and 24—and the vast majority of young people live in low- and middle-income countries (UNDESA 2015b). In Africa, 60 percent of the population is under the age of 25 (UNDESA 2015a), compared with around 40 percent in Asia and in Latin America and the Caribbean (UNDESA 2015c).

Populations are also aging in parallel with this population growth: 12 percent of the global population is now 60 years or older. Rapidly aging populations create pressures on societies with low fertility rates. Europe has the largest percentage of older persons (24 percent), but by 2050, all regions except for Africa will have around one-quarter or more of their population 60 years of age or older (UNDESA 2015c). Having more old and young people rely on a disproportionately smaller working-age population places a heavy burden on the share of the population that is of working age (Griffin, forthcoming). The varying stages of demographic transition are also correlated with the income level of countries (see figure 2.7).

Greater Expectations and Pressures Due to Demographic Shifts

Major demographic shifts are creating potential vulnerabilities and risks. While demographic change in itself does not cause conflict, it can potentially put pressure on systems and societies, increasing the risk for conflict. A large youth population puts huge pressure on education systems to provide decent learning and skills that will allow young people to become more meaningfully engaged and included in their societies. Many countries with high demographic growth are seeing their education system struggle to provide even quality basic education (World Bank 2018). Population growth, while a positive force for

economies, also puts pressure on labor markets, which will have to absorb the estimated 600 million new workers entering the markets in the next 10 years (ILO 2016).

Similarly, increasing levels of educational attainment create greater aspirations; compounded with increasing transparency of the world via the ICT revolution, young people are more aware of how others live and succeed. The middle-class dream has become universal. These rising expectations are difficult for many societies to meet, creating the risk that people will grow dissatisfied with the social contract in their country because they have come to expect services and opportunities that are not provided to them. For instance, research on aspirations and well-being in the Middle East shows that many young people, better educated than their parents and previous generations, aspire to meet social and economic milestones like finding a good job after school, getting married, and being socially recognized as important (Devarajan and Ianchovichina 2017). However, they are often unable to do so because of a lagging economy, skills mismatch, and lack of mobility, and so they grow increasingly frustrated (Cammett and Diwan 2013).

Addressing these challenges requires not only creating a societal framework that integrates people successfully, but also investing directly in children and youth. Education is key for poverty reduction and sustainable development. It gives individuals access to information and the knowledge to use it. The 2030 Agenda for Sustainable Development, specifically SDG 4, makes access to inclusive and equitable quality education a global priority. Furthermore, it promotes lifelong learning opportunities for all, focusing on the need to provide citizens with skills that are valuable and valued on the labor market. Investing in the right skills is particularly critical, as the demands of the labor market are changing rapidly and proving to be a risk for tension. A survey of nine broad industry sectors in 15 economies at various stages of development shows that by 2020 more than a third of the core skills that will be considered essential in most

FIGURE 2.7 Correlation between Country Income Level and Stage of Demographic Transition, 2015

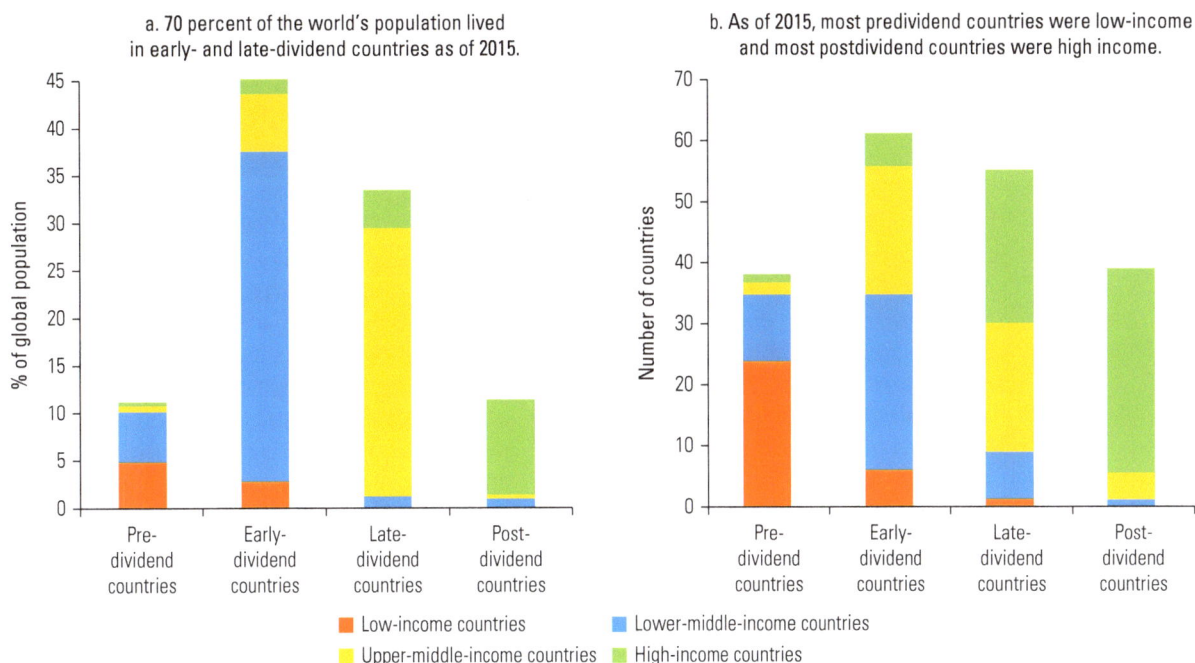

a. 70 percent of the world's population lived in early- and late-dividend countries as of 2015.

b. As of 2015, most predividend countries were low-income and most postdividend countries were high income.

■ Low-income countries   ■ Lower-middle-income countries
■ Upper-middle-income countries   ■ High-income countries

Source: World Bank and IMF 2016.
Note: See appendix C.5 of World Bank and IMF 2016 for classifications of country groupings.

occupations were not yet considered crucial to the job in 2015 (World Economic Forum 2016). With these challenges in mind, many individuals migrate to other places in search of better socioeconomic opportunities.

Record-Breaking Migration

Migration and the historic movement of people in recent years is a defining trend in today's world (UNDESA 2016). In 2015, there were approximately 250 million international migrants throughout the world (World Bank 2016a), up from 173 million in 2000 (UNDESA 2016), and women constituted 48 percent of the total (World Bank 2016a). Well-managed migration can offer many benefits and is an alternative to enduring the constraints felt by demographic transitions. Migrants contribute to their host countries by filling critical labor shortages, paying taxes and social security contributions, and creating jobs as entrepreneurs. Globally, a vast majority of migrants (72 percent) are of working age (UNDESA 2016). Migration also can

contribute to reducing the pace of population aging and, hence, old-age dependency ratios.

Migration can be important for home communities as well. For instance, since 2000 remittances sent to low- and middle-income countries have increased by more than 500 percent, reaching US$441 billion in 2015 (Dugarova and Gulasan 2017). These funds constitute important sources of foreign exchange earnings and help recipient households to increase consumption, invest in education and health, and support small businesses. In origin countries, emigration can often lead to the loss of valuable human resources such as doctors, nurses, and teachers, but it can also lower unemployment and facilitate trade, investment, and technology transfers. Moreover, some migrants who become successful abroad invest in their home countries, bringing home capital, trade, ideas, skills, and technology (UN 2017b).

In particular, the global community needs to address the challenge presented by rapidly growing younger populations and populations on the move. This requires providing urgent help to countries that have not yet undergone a demographic transition, especially those with scarce resources. Giving children security and the opportunity to receive a quality education is vital and a core element of early conflict prevention. Moreover, migration needs better management, within countries, intraregionally, and internationally. Better management cannot be achieved without the right legal frameworks and processes for migrants, such as the provision of identity cards and papers. Along with improving legislation on asset ownership, such as land and housing (see chapter 5 on land), conflict management systems at the local level need to be strengthened.

While much attention is focused on migration across continents, intraregional migration and rural-urban migration constitute the bulk of the population movements. In Sub-Saharan Africa, for example, intraregional migration is higher (67 percent) than migration to other regions (World Bank 2016a). Often this migration has beneficial aspects because it brings people closer to resources and livelihoods. In West Africa, for instance, where a large amount of intraregional migration takes place among ECOWAS states (see map 2.2), 70 percent of migration is linked to employment (Marc, Verjee, and Mogaka 2015).

Intraregional migration can be a source of major tension and can give rise to civil war or severe cases of violence. Growing numbers of people looking for resources and livelihoods can exacerbate tensions across fault lines, as in the conflict in Mindanao, one cause of which is thought to have been the mass migration of Christian populations to ancestral Muslim lands (Parks, Colletta, and Oppenheim 2013), or in Nigeria's Middle Belt, which was caused mostly by nomadic herders searching for water and fodder in areas largely populated by sedentary farmers (Marc, Verjee, and Mogaka 2015). In Côte d'Ivoire, conflicts over land management were ignited between migrants from the north of the country as well as from other

countries and local communities during and after the civil war (McGovern 2011).

In places like the semiarid regions of northern Kenya and the Sahel region of West Africa (Marc, Verjee, and Mogaka 2015), conflicts are endemic between nomadic herders moving southward and farmers in the southern areas. Pastoral and agricultural livelihoods depend on mutually beneficial and negotiated, nonexclusive access to water and reciprocal land use agreements. Conflicts arise when access to water points, grazing lands, and pastoral corridors are restricted and crops are damaged. Increased herd sizes and environmental degradation have increased the frequency and intensity of these conflicts.

Migration also has impacts on the areas left behind. If a large proportion of the working-age population migrates, they often leave behind family members of either younger or older generations. This may create a gap in the labor force and social fabric. Resulting low-density areas may experience challenges with service provision and local governance mechanisms, dynamics that some armed groups could see as an opportunity.

The Flow of Forcibly Displaced Persons

Another major challenge today is the large-scale forced displacement across countries and regions as well as the flow of internally displaced persons (IDPs). As noted in chapter 1, conflict, generalized violence, and persecution are forcibly uprooting people on a large scale. At the end of 2016, 65.6 million individuals were forcibly displaced (UNHCR 2017). These individuals include 40.8 million IDPs, 21.3 million refugees, and 3.2 million asylum seekers (UNHCR 2017).

Low- and middle-income countries host the great majority of forcibly displaced persons: by the end of 2015, these countries hosted 99 percent of IDPs and 89 percent of refugees, including Palestinian refugees (World Bank 2017). Africa and the Middle East accounted for almost 60 percent of all forcibly displaced persons by the end of 2015 (World Bank 2017). The 10 countries hosting the largest numbers of

MAP 2.2 Intraregional Migration within the Economic Community of West African States

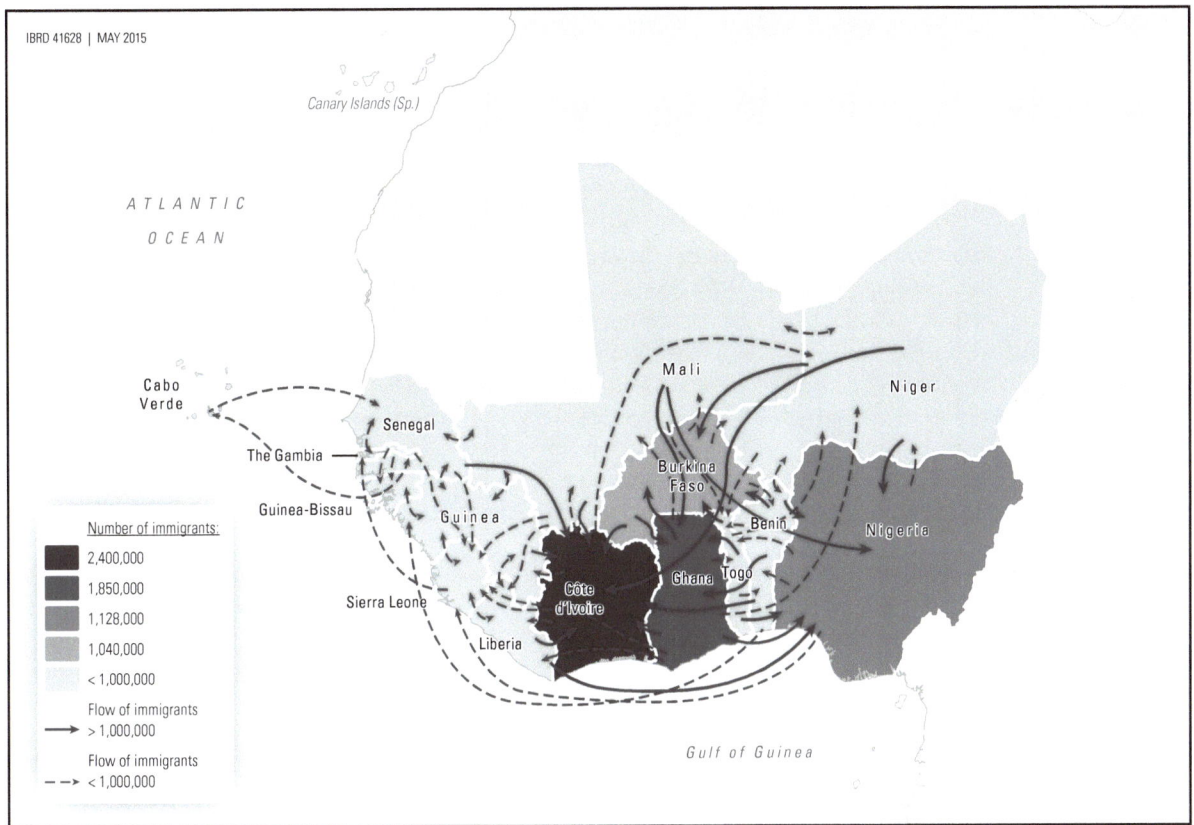

IBRD 41628 | MAY 2015

Canary Islands (Sp.)

ATLANTIC
OCEAN

Mali

Niger

Cabo
Verde

Senegal

The Gambia

Burkina
Faso

Benin

Nigeria

Guinea-Bissau

Guinea

Number of immigrants:
2,400,000
1,850,000
1,128,000
1,040,000
< 1,000,000
Flow of immigrants
→ > 1,000,000
Flow of immigrants
--→ < 1,000,000

Ghana Togo

Sierra Leone

Côte
d'Ivoire

Liberia

Gulf of Guinea

Source: Marc, Verjee, and Mogaka 2015.

refugees by the end of 2015[7] were all low- and middle-income countries, and five of these were in Sub-Saharan Africa (UNHCR 2016).

While these flows can strain the economic resources and capacities of many host countries, including conflict-affected countries, forcibly displaced persons rarely spread conflict to host communities and countries (World Bank 2017). A review of 82 countries that received more than 25,000 refugees for at least a year between 1991 and 2014 finds that about 68 percent of these countries did not experience any conflict (World Bank 2017). In the 32 percent of hosting countries that did experience conflict, refugees were determined to have a role in causing conflict in only 0.8 percent of cases (World Bank 2017). In addition, the wage and employment effects were small because refugees and natives did not compete for the same jobs. Instead, refugees

often have a net positive effect on government budgets (World Bank 2017).

The Trend of Increasing Urbanization

An estimated 66 percent of the world's population will live in urban areas by 2050, up from 54 percent in 2014 (UNDESA 2014). Population growth projections for this period estimate that 2.5 billion people will be added to urban centers, with almost 90 percent of the increase concentrated in Africa and Asia (UNDESA 2014). Between 2014 and 2050, just three countries (China, India, and Nigeria) are expected to account for 37 percent of the growth of the world's urban population (UNDESA 2014).

Rapid urbanization raises an array of risks and challenges. Many armed conflicts are now taking place in cities rather than rural areas, as in many past conflicts. The International Committee of the Red Cross (ICRC) estimates that 50 million people are affected by war in cities around the world (ICRC 2017). The increasing trend of conflict taking place in urban centers, including violent extremism, which can find fertile breeding ground in cities, will have important implications for the risk of violence and the number of civilian casualties that result from conflict.

Still, urbanization offers many opportunities for conflict prevention. Historically, the development of urban centers has helped to facilitate contact across different identity groups, creating a stronger sense of citizenship, building social networks, and stimulating trade and exchange. Social systems have also evolved the fastest in urban centers. Such potential needs to be leveraged for peacebuilding to a much greater extent than it is currently, including through urban planning that, in line with SDG 11, reflects risks in full and identifies factors of increased vulnerability to violence, making cities inclusive, safe, resilient, and sustainable.

The Stress of Climate Change

The ability of climate change to disrupt societies has become increasingly evident with more extreme weather events, water and soil stress, and food insecurity (National Intelligence Council 2017). Climate change poses immense threats to sustainable development, affecting people through changes in mean conditions such as temperature, precipitation, and sea level (Barnett and Adger 2007) over long periods of time and through greater frequency and severity of extreme weather events (Hallegatte et al. 2016). The 2030 Agenda for Sustainable Development (SDG 13) commits the international community to take urgent action to combat climate change and its impact. In the absence of preventive action, global warming may exceed 4°C by the end of the twenty-first century, facilitating "severe, widespread, and irreversible" impacts on poverty reduction and development (Hallegatte et al. 2016; IPCC 2014, 17).

The impacts of climate change cut across both the short and long term. Environmentally, climate change leads to rising sea levels, ocean acidification, melting glaciers and polar ice caps, and increased pollution that affects both animal and human health (National Intelligence Council 2017). Increasing pressure on environmental systems also affects the availability of water and biodiversity, threatening livelihoods and intensifying competition for natural resources such as farm and grazing land. Economically, climate change can affect household consumption by leading to spikes in food prices, decreasing productivity, and eroding financial, physical, human, social, and natural capital assets (Burke, Hsiang, and Edward 2015).

Climate change unevenly affects certain places and people, including fragile and conflict-affected settings. A largely uncontested evidence base indicates that, regardless of the exact nature and magnitude of change, climate change has a disproportionate impact on poor and vulnerable countries and communities (Nordas and Gleditsch 2007). This is especially true for people who are more dependent on natural resources for their livelihoods and jobs and who cannot easily adapt to fluctuations in their supply. For example, a decline in precipitation can be dangerous for people around the world already working at subsistence levels. In Timor Leste, 85 percent of the population relies on agriculture as the main source of income, with most of the population being subsistence farmers (Barnett and Adger 2007). A lack of rainfall in the dry season can reduce crop production by up to one-third, increasing the risk for pervasive hunger and famine as well as migration and competition for resources (Barnett and Adger 2007).

Climate change increases the frequency and intensity of extreme weather events, thus increasing the risk of complex crises and human insecurity (USAID 2014). It may reduce access to natural resources important for sustaining livelihoods, or it may degrade the quality of those resources. In such contexts, direct resource competition from relative scarcity or abundance of a specific natural resource can create tensions within and among groups. Schleussner et al. (2016) examine data on outbreaks of violent conflict and climate-related natural disasters for the 1980–2010 period, finding that climate-related disasters coincided with approximately 23 percent of the outbreaks of armed conflict in ethnically fractionalized countries.

There is also strong evidence that climate change acts as a threat multiplier, indirectly escalating the risk of conflict through mechanisms such as food insecurity, economic shocks, and migration. Evidence in a growing body of literature on the impact of climatic variability on violent conflict shows that low water availability and very high and low temperatures are associated with organized political conflicts. Studies using country-level data show a correlation between changes in temperature and precipitation associated with economic contraction and destabilization of the political balance (Hsiang, Burke, and Miguel 2013).

Overall, climate change does not automatically cause violent conflict. However, there is no doubt that climate change creates major stress, especially in fragile situations where governments have limited means to help their population to adapt (see box 2.3). Climate change requires global collaboration, from reducing the emission of carbon dioxide to preparing for climate shocks (which can trigger violent conflicts in tense environments, as discussed in chapter 5) to investing in and building up social and economic resilience. In some countries—in particular, those on the fringes of the Sahara Desert—addressing climate change remains at the core of early conflict prevention strategies (Marc, Verjee, and Mogaka 2015).

Transnational Organized Crime

Trafficking and transnational organized crime (TOC) contribute directly and indirectly to violent conflict. The detrimental impacts of TOC are increasingly recognized,[8] as are the negative ripple effects of various illicit flows such as drug, human, and natural resource trafficking, smuggling of migrants, illicit trade of firearms and wildlife, counterfeit medicines, and cybercrime. The United Nations High-Level Panel on Threats, Challenges, and Change has identified TOC as a top priority, on par with civil wars, nuclear weapons, and terrorism (Comolli 2017; UN 2004).

The financial consequences of TOC are serious. The United Nations Office on Drugs and Crime (UNODC) (n.d.) estimates that

---

BOX 2.3 The Impacts of Climate Change on the Lake Chad Region

Since 1970, temperatures across the Sahel have increased by almost 1°C, which is nearly double the global average. The Inter-Governmental Panel on Climate Change expects temperatures in the Sahel to increase by 1°C over the next 20 years, 2.1°C by 2065, and 4°C by the end of the twenty-first century. Despite limited data on changes in environmental conditions, the Sahel has experienced more severe and recurrent droughts and floods in past years. Combined with political, economic, and social instability; poverty; historical grievances; poor governance; and weak institutions, Sahelian states face many challenges in managing the detrimental impacts of climate change.

Lake Chad is one such example that highlights the links between environmental, social, and political vulnerability. Situated between Cameroon, Chad, Niger, and Nigeria, Lake Chad is a vital resource for more than 50 million people. The lake and its drainage basin provide not only jobs through food production and a rich trading economy, but also water and land for agriculture. The region itself is a focal point for agricultural production, encompassing both expanses of shallow water, vegetation, and rich soil used for a variety of purposes.

In recent years, the ability of the lake region to be a net exporter of food and a source of employment has

(Box continued next page)

come under threat. Climate change challenges the biodiversity growing in the lake, creating a fragile ecosystem and increasing the vulnerability of the Sahel, which relies heavily on the resources of Lake Chad. Rising population growth rates have also generated an increasing number of incoming migrants, such as refugees and displaced persons fleeing Boko Haram. Although these groups have historically been welcomed into the area, food, water, job insecurity, and land saturation have created tensions over access to available resources. With 2.8 million displaced people in the Sahel, these tensions may rise between host and displaced communities over competition for scarce resources. Traditional conflict resolution mechanisms may no longer be adequate to help residents to cope with the scale of the growing challenge.

The Sahel has experienced major tensions and violent conflicts directly related to these climatic changes. Pastoralists from the northern fringes of the Sahara, who have to use transhumance to sustain their herds, increasingly move southward in search of pasture. In these areas, agriculturists are already struggling with less predictable rainfall. Pastoralists also tend to stay in these areas over a longer period of time, including when crops are ready to be harvested. These situations have created serious conflict and destruction of both crops and cattle. Herders increasingly form militias to protect their cattle, look for protection from various armed groups, and get drawn into violent conflict. In the Central African Republic and Mali, for instance, militia groups were created for protection purposes and have played a strong role in local conflict dynamics. Nigeria has also seen this dimension of conflict increasingly in the north of the country.

Sources: Crawford 2015; Ferdi 2016; Guichaoua and Pellerin 2017; Marc, Verjee, and Mogaka 2015.

in 2009, TOC generated US$870 billion, equivalent to 1.5 percent of the global GDP. Trafficking of drugs, arms, and people—the most lucrative manifestations of transnational organized crime—generates large criminal proceeds. Illicit drugs alone account for 17–25 percent of the total generated by TOC. It is difficult to measure illicit financial flows, such as money that is illegally earned, transferred, or used and that crosses borders, including transfer pricing and tax avoidance by multinational corporations. Still, Global Financial Integrity estimates that 15 low- and middle-income countries lose almost US$1 trillion per year and lost US$7.8 trillion from 2004 to 2013 (Spanjers and Salomon 2017). The yearly amount of illicit financial flows from low- and middle-income countries exceeded the sum of FDI and official development assistance that those countries received in 2013 (Spanjers and Salomon 2017).

The magnitude of TOC also puts the stability of many countries at risk, given increased mobility and interconnectedness

today and the global impacts of illicit trafficking (see map 2.3). As UNODC (2010, v) notes, "Most TOC flows begin on one continent and end on another, often by means of a third." For instance, drug production and trade have an impact not only on countries of origin but also on consumer markets, as in the case of the Andean region, where drugs are transmitted through West and North Africa and into Europe (Marc, Verjee, and Mogaka 2015). West Africa also provides an example of how drug trafficking undermines stability, governance, development, and health in transit regions (UNODC 2008, 35–48).

The scale and reach of illicit trafficking contribute to many elements that can increase the risk of conflict or allow it to persist. Its transnational nature means that it can generate or perpetuate instability across borders (see map 2.4). Illicit trafficking activities can make it more likely for local conflict to spill into surrounding areas and countries, thus contributing to its regionalization. The Balkans provide a good illustration of the regional dimension of trafficking networks and their ramifications (Grillot et al. 2004). Criminal networks are actors, with agency, that should be taken into account in assessing the risk of violent conflict. They may act to undermine the legitimacy and capacity of their rivals, including the state. (Chapter 3 discusses actors and their interrelationship in greater detail.) Drug cartels in Latin America changed their behavior to avoid confrontation with the state and seek alternative markets, shifting cocaine trafficking to West Africa (Cockayne 2013, 14–16; 2016, 267–89). By establishing parallel structures that provide economic opportunities and services to the local population, criminal networks (like other actors) can also degrade the image of the state in the eyes of the population.

Criminal activities can underwrite parties in violent conflict, prolonging or changing the nature of the conflict. Revenues from these activities can enable parties to attract more fighters and purchase more sophisticated weapons (Felbab-Brown 2009) and thus to fight longer. Analyzing 128 civil wars between 1945 and 1999, Fearon (2004, 284) finds, "Contraband has clearly played a role in several of the longest-running civil wars since 1945, such as Colombia (cocaine; 37 years to 2000 as coded here), Angola (diamonds; 25 years to 2000), Myanmar (opium; off and on for many years, especially in Shan State), and Sierra Leone (diamonds; 9 years to 2000). In 17 cases where there was major evidence of rebel groups relying on production or trafficking on contraband, the estimated median and mean civil war durations were 28.1 and 48.2 years, respectively, as compared to 6.0 and 8.8 years for the remaining civil wars."

Violent conflict also opens up opportunities for criminality. Illicit activities tend to thrive in contexts of weak rule of law and where other forms of violence are present (World Bank 2011). In conflict settings, goods and supplies may not be easily accessible, and criminals adapt to fill the demand.

MAP 2.3 **Global Flows of Transnational Organized Crime**

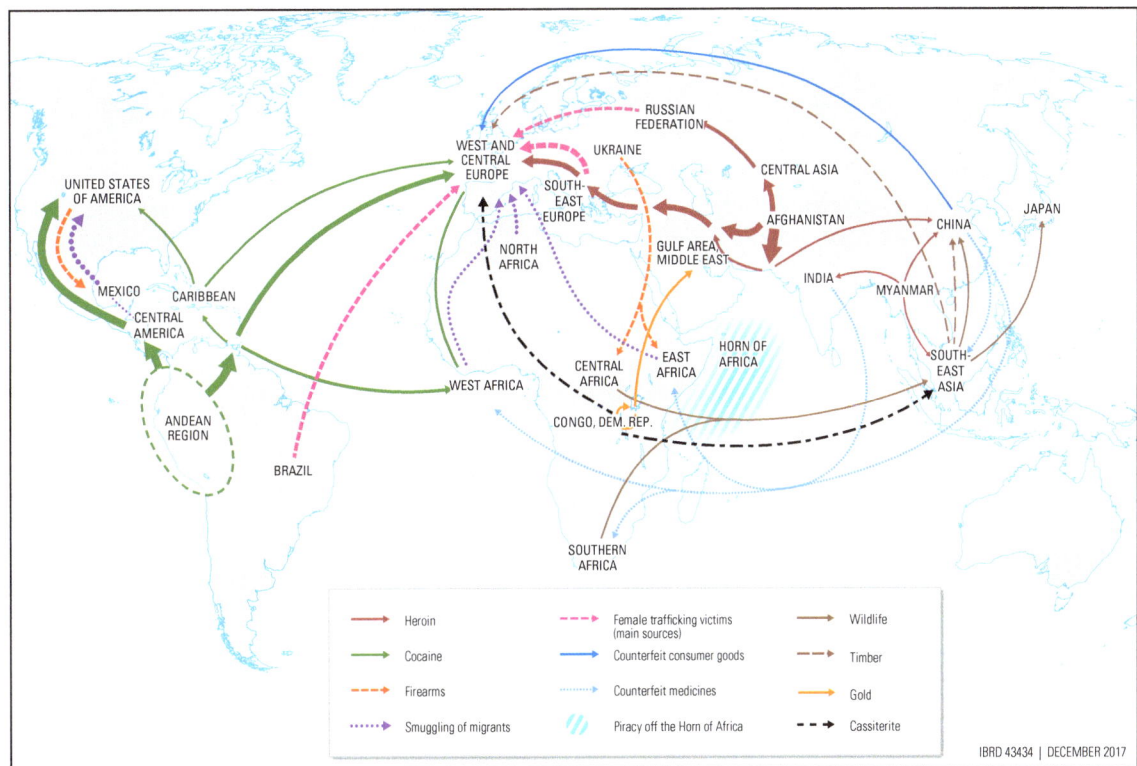

Source: UNODC 2010.

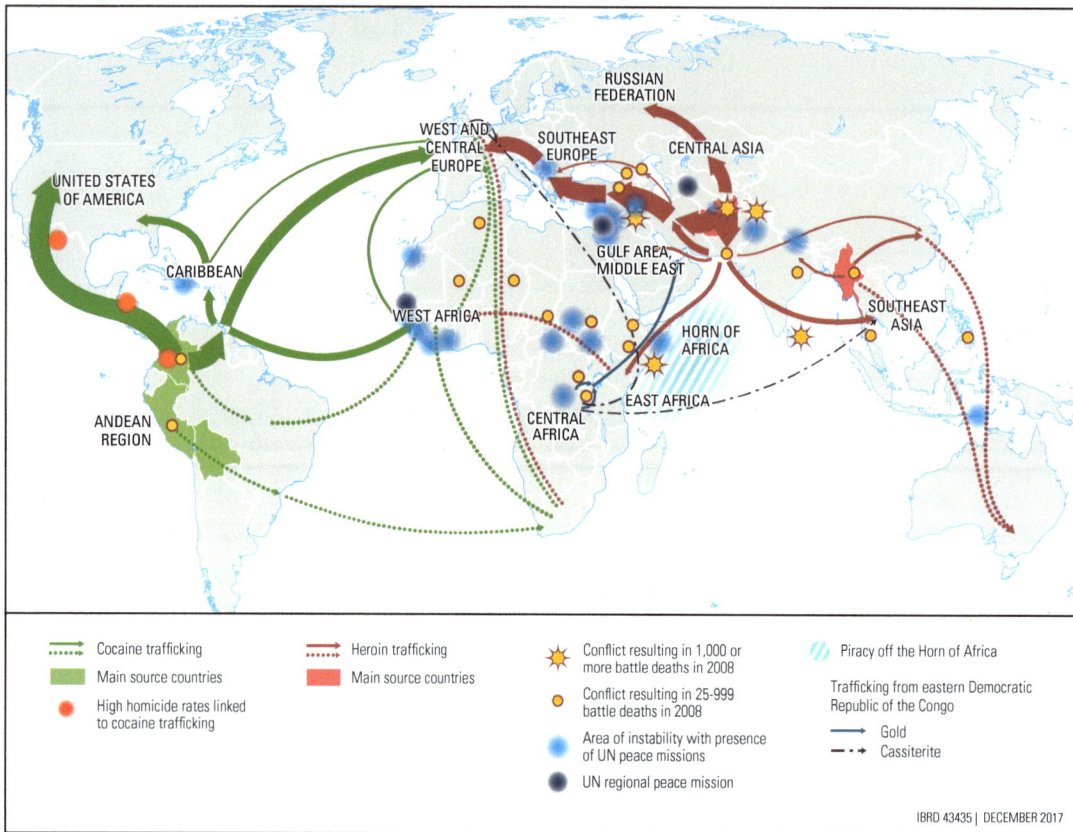

Source: UNODC 2010.

In this regard, more attention should be paid to the trafficking of illicit commodities versus "survival smuggling" of basic goods such as food that have long been the lifeline of nomadic communities in the Sahel-Sahara region (Reitano and Shaw 2015).

In spite of these dynamics, the existence of criminal economies and illicit trafficking networks in conflict situations does not automatically translate into higher levels of violence. Certain criminal groups may choose instead to operate by coercion and intimidation, especially where markets are stable and a clear hierarchy is identified. For instance, despite the large size of the narcotics economy in Afghanistan, drug-related violence remains relatively low and sizably lower than in Latin American drug markets such as in the Northern Triangle (Byrd and Mansfield 2014, 75). In addition, state responses to crime and preconditions, like the nature of local gang culture, are important factors in assessing the potential escalation of violence (IISS 2011).

Like other trends discussed in this chapter, TOC needs to be addressed at national, regional, and global levels. Globally, UNODC and other institutions have made important advancements, including the United Nations Convention against Transnational Organized Crime adopted by General Assembly Resolution 55/25, which has been ratified by 170 parties. This convention provides "a universal legal framework to help identify, deter, and dismantle organized criminal groups" (UNODC 2012, 3). In addition, the global community has adopted specific frameworks, such as the Protocol against the Illicit Manufacturing of and Trafficking in Firearms, Their Parts and Components, and Ammunition. These agreements represent the commitment of states to address a complex global challenge in partnership with the international community.

As discussed in chapter 3, prevention rests on the incentives of actors to choose behavior leading toward peace rather than violence and to limit the harm done by actors who choose violence. This understanding is particularly relevant in relation to the risks posed by TOC. At the country and regional levels, focus should be placed not only on changing the incentives of actors operating in areas where transnational organized crime is present, but also on fighting corruption within the state and reinforcing its accountability prerequisites for action to be effective. The security and justice sector is particularly crucial in this regard. It is also important to ensure that no geographic areas are left out of an accountable and positive governance system, because TOC preys on vulnerable areas, including those far from the center or difficult to reach regions with low density, urban slums where the state is absent, and any area with weak governance. Addressing TOC requires working with the community, as many organized crime networks are entrenched in the communities themselves.

Conclusion

The scale and pace of change in the world today are striking. The world is at once more interconnected and interdependent than ever, which means that many countries acutely feel the stresses of global changes like population movements, climate change, advancements in new technologies, and shifting patterns of governance.

Now there is pressure on global institutions and individual societies to improve their management of the risks and opportunities that arise as a result of so many concurrent, interlinked, and impactful global trends. The current international system, both states and multilateral institutions, has been dedicated to preventing interstate war and, increasingly, intrastate conflict. But the changing nature of warfare and violence (as shown in chapter 1) and the changes in transnational phenomena and the global landscape (described here) warrant a different approach. With several opportunities for peace, as well as risks for violence, global collaboration is critical.

Specifically, it requires working at national, regional, and international levels together, as no country alone can manage the risks that arise from these trends.

In this challenging global framework, the 2030 Agenda for Sustainable Development provides an organizing framework for achieving global development goals that are sustainable in part because they recognize the deep complexity and interconnectedness on the path to peace and progress.

Notes

1. The concept of risk is discussed in more detail in chapter 3. It is understood in this study as a combination of the probability of an event and the severity of the event if it does occur and is strongly mediated by the capacity of a society to manage its impacts.
2. See https://www.g20.org/en/g20/faqs.
3. Regional organizations include, among others, the European Union, League of Arab States (1945), Organization of American States (1948), Association of Southeast Asian Nations (1967), Organization of Islamic Cooperation (1969), Economic Community of West African States (1975), and Southern African Development Community (1992).
4. The Center for Systemic Peace (2014) notes that these countries had total populations greater than 500,000 in 2015 along a 21-point scale. Polity scores range from −10 (hereditary monarchy) to +10 (consolidated democracy). Countries can also be grouped into three categories of regime: autocracies (−10 to −6), anocracies (−5 to +5), and democracies (+6 to +10).
5. The United Nations does not have a specific definition of "democracy." The General Assembly asserts that "democracy is a universal value based on the freely expressed will of the people to determine their own political, economic, social and cultural systems and their full participation in all aspects of their lives. . . . [W]hile democracies share common features, there is no single model of democracy and . . . democracy does not belong to any country or region, and reaffirming further the necessity of due respect

for sovereignty and the right to self-determination" (UN General Assembly 2015).

6. Labor share of income is defined as the share of national income paid in wages, including benefits, to workers.

7. Chad, the Democratic Republic of Congo, Ethiopia, the Islamic Republic of Iran, Jordan, Kenya, Lebanon, Pakistan, Turkey, and Uganda.

8. UNODC broadly defines TOC as encompassing all criminal activities motivated by profit and with international scope.

References

Allan, H., A. Glazzard, S. Jesperson, S. Reddy-Tumu, and E. Winterbotham. 2015. *Drivers of Violent Extremism: Hypotheses and Literature Review.* London: Royal United Services Institute (RUSI).

Barnett, J., and W. N. Adger. 2007. "Climate Change, Human Security, and Violent Conflict." *Political Geography* 26 (2): 639–55.

Bartley Johns, M., P. Brenton, M. Cali, M. Hoppe, and R. Piermartini. 2015. *The Role of Trade in Ending Poverty.* Geneva: World Trade Organization.

Blattman, C. 2014. "Can We Use Data and Machine Learning to Predict Local Violence in Fragile States? As It Turns Out, Yes." https://chrisblattman.com/2014/10/02/can-use-data-machine-learning-predict-local-violence-fragile-states-turns-yes/.

Boggero, M. 2017. "Technologies for Conflict." Background paper for the United Nations–World Bank Flagship Study, *Pathways for Peace: Inclusive Approaches to Preventing Violent Conflict,* World Bank, Washington, DC.

Burke, M., S. M. Hsiang, and M. Edward. 2015. "Climate and Conflict." *Annual Review of Economics* 7 (1): 577–617.

Byrd, W. A., and D. Mansfield. 2014. "Afghanistan's Opium Economy: An Agricultural, Livelihoods, and Governance Perspective." Report prepared for the Afghanistan Agriculture Sector Review, World Bank, Washington, DC.

Call, C. T., and C. de Coning. 2017. *Rising Powers and Peacebuilding.* London: Palgrave.

Cammett, M., and I. Diwan. 2013. *A Political Economy of the Arab Uprisings. Polity IV User Manual.* Vienna, VA: Center for Systemic Peace.

Center for Systemic Peace. 2014. "Polity and the Onset of Political Instability by Polity Score, 1955–2006." Center for Systemic Peace, Vienna, VA.

CISCO. 2017. "Visual Networking Index Global Mobile Data Traffic Forecast Report, 2016–2021." White Paper, CISCO, San Jose, CA, February 7.

Cockayne, J. 2013. "Chasing Shadows." *RUSI Journal* 158 (2): 10–24.

———. 2016. *The Hidden Power: The Strategic Logic of Organized Crime.* London: C. Hurst.

Comolli, V. 2017. "Transnational Organized Crime and Conflict." Background paper for the United Nations–World Bank Flagship Study, *Pathways for Peace: Inclusive Approaches to Preventing Violent Conflict,* World Bank, Washington DC.

Council of Europe. 2001. "Convention on Cybercrime, Budapest, 23.XI.2001." ETS185, Council of Europe, Budapest.

Crawford, A. 2015. "Climate Change and State Fragility in the Sahel." Policy brief no. 205, FRIDE, Madrid.

Crenshaw, M. 1981. "The Causes of Terrorism." *Comparative Politics* 13 (4): 379–99.

Davison, S. 2015. "An Exploratory Study of Risk and Social Media: What Role Did Social Media Play in the Arab Spring Revolutions?" *Journal of Middle East Media* 11 (Fall): 1–33.

Deloitte. 2014. "Value of Connectivity: Economic and Social Benefits of Expanding Internet Access." Deloitte, London, February.

Devarajan, S., and E. Ianchovichina. 2017. "A Broken Social Contract, Not High Inequality, Led to the Arab Spring." *Review of Income and Wealth,* online version of record, February 20. doi:10.1111/roiw.12288.

Doyle, M. 1986. "Liberalism and World Politics." *American Political Science Review* 80 (4): 1151–69.

Dugarova, E., and N. Gulasan. 2017. "Global Trends: Challenges and Opportunities in the Implementation of the Sustainable Development Goals." United Nations Development Programme and United Nations Research Institute for Social Development, Geneva.

Economist. 2016a. "Automation and Anxiety: Will Smarter Machines Cause Mass Unemployment." Special report, June 25.

———. 2016b. "Global Politics: League of Nationalists—All around the World, Nationalists Are Gaining Ground. Why?" November 19. https://www.economist.com

/news/international/21710276-all-around
-world-nationalists-are-gaining-ground-why
-league-nationalists.

Fearon, J. D. 2004. "Why Do Some Civil Wars Last So Much Longer Than Others?" *Journal of Peace Research* 41 (3): 275–301.

Felbab-Brown, V. 2009. *Shooting Up: Counterinsurgency and the War on Drugs.* Washington, DC: Brookings Institution.

Ferdi (Fondation pour les études et recherches sur le développement international). 2016. "Linking Security and Development—A Plea for the Sahel." Ferdi, Clermont-Ferrand, France. http://www.ferdi.fr/sites/www.ferdi.fr/files/publication/sahel_anglais-_vol1-final.pdf.

Ferreira, F., D. M. Joliffe, and E. B. Prydz. 2015. "The International Poverty Line Has Just Been Raised to $1.90 a Day, but Global Poverty is Basically Unchanged. How Is That Even Possible? World Bank, Washington DC.

Fjelde, H., and G. Østby. 2014. "Socioeconomic Inequality and Communal Conflict: A Disaggregated Analysis of Sub-Saharan Africa, 1990–2008." *International Interactions* 40 (5): 737–62.

Freedom House. 2004. *Freedom in the World 2004: The Annual Survey of Political Rights and Civil Liberties.* Lanham, MD: Rowman and Littlefield.

———. 2017. *Freedom in the World 2017: Populists and Autocrats: The Dual Threat to Global Democracy.* Washington, DC: Freedom House. https://freedomhouse.org/report/freedom-world/freedom-world-2017.

G7 (Group of Seven). 2017. "On Responsible States Behavior in Cyberspace." Lucca, April 11.

Griffin, M. Forthcoming. "The UN's Role in a Changing Global Landscape." In *The Oxford Handbook on the United Nations,* 2d ed., edited by T. G. Weiss and S. Daws, ch. 45. Oxford: Oxford University Press.

Grillot, S. R., W. Paes, H. Risser, and S. O. Stoneman. 2004. *A Fragile Peace: Guns and Security in Post-conflict Macedonia.* Geneva: United Nations Development Programme and the Small Arms Survey.

Guichaoua, Y., and M. Pellerin. 2017. "Faire la paix et construire l'etat: Les relations entre pouvoir central et périphéries sahéliennes au Niger et au Mali." Study 51, Institute de Recherche Stratégique de l'Ecole Militaire (IRSEM), Paris. http://www.defense.gouv.fr/content/download/509288/8603319/file/Etude_IRSEM_n51_2017.pdf.

Guterres, A. 2017. "Remarks to Munich Security Conference." United Nations Secretary-General, February 18.

Haass, R. 2017. *A World in Disarray: American Foreign Policy and the Crisis of the Old Order.* New York: Penguin Press.

Hale, G. and M. Xu. 2016. "FDI Effects on the Labor Market of Host Countries." Working Paper 2016-25, Federal Reserve Bank of San Francisco.

Hallegatte, S., M. Bangalore, L. Bonzanigo, M. Fay, T. Kane, U. Narloch, J. Rozenberg, D. Treguer, and A. Vogt-Schilb. 2016. *Shock Waves: Managing the Impacts of Climate Change on Poverty.* Climate Change and Development. Washington, DC: World Bank.

Hallward-Driemeier, M., and G. Nayyar. 2017. *Trouble in the Making? The Future of Manufacturing-Led Development.* Washington, DC: World Bank.

Hsiang, S. M., M. Burke, and E. Miguel. 2013. "Quantifying the Influence of Climate on Human Conflict." *Science* 341 (6151): 1212.

ICRC (International Committee of the Red Cross). 2017. *I Saw My City Die.* Special report. Geneva: International Committee of the Red Cross.

IISS (International Institute for Strategic Studies). 2011. "West Africa's 'Cocaine Coast.'" *Strategic Comments* 21 (May 11).

ILO (International Labour Organization). 2016. "World Employment and Social Outlook 2016: Trends for Youth." ILO, Geneva.

IMF (International Monetary Fund). 2017. *World Economic Outlook, April 2017: Gaining Momentum?* Washington, DC: IMF.

Independent Commission on Multilateralism. 2016. "The Impact of New Technologies on Peace, Security, and Development." Independent Commission on Multilateralism, New York.

IPCC (Intergovernmental Panel on Climate Change). 2014. *Synthesis Report,* edited by R. K. Pachauri and L. A. Meyer. Contribution of Working Groups I, II, and III to the Fifth Assessment Report of the Intergovernmental Panel on Climate Change. Geneva: IPCC.

ITU (International Telecommunications Union). 2015. "ICT Facts and Figures." ITU, Geneva.

———. 2016. "ICT Facts and Figures." ITU, Geneva.

Letouzé, E. 2012a. "Big Data for Development: Challenges and Opportunities." UN Global Pulse, New York.

———. 2012b. "Can Big Data from Cellphones Help Prevent Conflict?" IPI Global Observatory, International Peace Institute, New York. https://theglobalobservatory.org/2012/11/can-big-data-from-cellphones-help-prevent-conflict/.

Letouzé, E., P. Meier, and P. Vinck. 2013. "Big Data for Conflict Prevention: New Oil and Old Fires," in *New Technology and the Prevention of Violence and Conflict*, edited by F. Mancini. New York: International Peace Institute.

Manacorda, M., and A. Tesai. 2016. *Liberation Technology: Mobile Phones and Political Mobilization in Africa*. Princeton, NJ: Princeton University Press.

Mancini, F., ed. 2013. *New Technology and the Prevention of Violence and Conflict*. New York: International Peace Institute.

Marc, A., N. Verjee, and S. Mogaka. 2015. *The Challenge of Stability and Security in West Africa*. Africa Development Forum series. Washington, DC: World Bank; Paris: Agence Française de Développement.

Marshall, M. G., T. Gurr, and K. Jaggers. 2015. *Polity IV Project: Political Regime Characteristics and Transitions, 1800–2015; Dataset Users' Manual*. Vienna, VA: Center for Systemic Peace.

McGovern, M. 2011. "Popular Development Economics: An Anthropologist among the Mandarins." *Perspectives on Politics* 9 (2): 345–55.

Meier, P. 2013. "Artificial Intelligence for Monitoring Elections (AIME)." iRevolutions. https://irevolutions.org/2013/04/17/ai-for-election-monitoring/.

———. 2015. *Digital Humanitarians: How Big Data Is Changing the Face of Humanitarian Response*. New York: Routledge.

Menocal, A., V. Fritz, and L. Rakner. 2007. "Hybrid Regimes and the Challenges of Deepening and Sustaining Democracy in Developing Countries." Background Note 2 prepared for the Wilton Park Conference on Democracy and Development, October 10–12.

Miodownik, D., and L. Nir. 2016. "Receptivity to Violence in Ethnically Divided Societies: A Micro-Level Mechanism of Perceived Horizontal Inequalities." *Studies in Conflict and Terrorism* 39 (1): 22–45.

Mor, Y., Y. Ron, and I. Maoz. 2016. "Likes for Peace: Can Facebook Promote Dialogue in the Israeli-Palestinian Conflict?" *Media and Communication* 4 (1): 15–26.

Morel, A. 2016. *Violent Incidents Monitoring Systems: A Methods Toolkit*. San Francisco: Asia Foundation.

National Intelligence Council. 2017. "Global Trends: Paradox of Progress." National Intelligence Council, Washington, DC.

Nordas, R., and N. P. Gleditsch. 2007. "Climate Change and Conflict." *Political Geography* 26 (6): 627–38.

OECD (Organisation for Economic Co-operation and Development). 2017. "FDI in Figures." OECD, Paris.

———. Various years. International Direct Investment Statistics. Paris: OECD.

Parks, T., N. Colletta, and B. Oppenheim. 2013. *The Contested Corners of Asia: Subnational Conflict and International Development Assistance*. San Francisco: Asia Foundation.

Pew Research Center. 2007. "Global Views on Life Satisfaction, National Conditions, and the Global Economy: Highlights from the 2007 Pew Global Attitudes 47-Nation Survey." Pew Research Center, Washington, DC.

———. 2015. "Global Support for Principle of Free Expression, but Opposition to Some Forms of Speech." Pew Research Center, Washington, DC.

———. 2017. "The Internet of Things Connectivity Binge: What Are the Implications?" Pew Research Center, Washington, DC. http://www.pewinternet.org/2017/06/06/the-internet-of-things-connectivity-binge-what-are-the-implications/.

Pierskalla, J. H., and F. M. Hollenbach. 2013. "Technology and Collective Action: The Effect of Cell Phone Coverage on Political Violence in Africa." *American Political Science Review* 107 (2): 207–24.

Piketty, T. 2013. *Capital in the 21st Century*. Paris: Éditions du Seuil.

Puddington, A., and T. Roylance. 2017. *Freedom in the World 2017: Populists and Autocrats: The Dual Threat to Global Democracy*. Washington, DC: Freedom House.

Puig Larrauri, H. 2013. "New Technologies and Conflict Prevention in Sudan and South Sudan." In *New Technology and the Prevention of Violence and Conflict*, edited by F. Mancini. New York: Insternational Peace Institute.

Reitano, T., and M. Shaw. 2015. *Fixing a Fractured State: Breaking the Cycles of Crime, Corruption and Conflict in Mali and the Sahel*. Geneva:

Global Initiative against Transnational Organized Crime.

Ross, J. I. 1993. "Structural Causes of Oppositional Political Terrorism." *Journal of Peace Research* 30 (3): 317–29.

Russett, B. 1993. *Grasping the Democratic Peace: Principles for a Post–Cold War World*. Princeton, NJ: Princeton University Press.

Scharbatke-Church, C., and A. Patel. 2016. "Technology for Evaluation in Fragile and Conflict Affected States: An Introduction for the Digital Immigrant Evaluator." Working Paper, Fletcher School, Tufts University, Medford, MA.

Schleussner, C., J. F. Donges, R. V. Donner, and J. H. Schellnhuber. 2016. "Armed-Conflict Risks Enhanced by Climate-Related Disasters in Ethnically Fractionalized Countries." *Proceedings of the National Academy of Sciences* 113 (33): 9216–21.

Shapiro, J. N., and N. B. Weidmann. 2015. "Is the Phone Mightier Than the Sword? Cellphones and Insurgent Violence in Iraq." *International Organization* 69 (2): 247–74.

Singer, P. W., and A. Friedman. 2014. *Cybersecurity: What Everyone Needs to Know*. Oxford: Oxford University Press.

Smith, C., H. Burke, C. de Leiuen, and G. Jackson. 2015. "The Islamic State's Symbolic War: Da'esh's Socially Mediated Terrorism as a Threat to Cultural Heritage." *Journal of Social Archaeology* 16 (2): 164–88.

Spanjers, J., and M. Salomon. 2017. "Illicit Financial Flows to and from Developing Countries: 2005–2014." *Global Financial Integrity*, May 1.

Strand, H., H. Hegre, S. Gates, and M. Dahl. 2012. "Why Waves? Global Patterns of Democratization, 1816–2008." Paper presented at third International Conference on Democracy as Idea and Practice, Oslo, January 12–13.

Tellidis, I., and S. Kappler. 2016. "Information and Communication Technologies in Peacebuilding: Implications, Opportunities and Challenges." *Cooperation and Conflict* 51 (1): 75–93.

Tomz, M., and J. Weeks. 2013. "Public Opinion and Democratic Peace." *American Political Science Review* 107 (4): 849–65.

UN (United Nations). 1945. "Charter, June 26, 1945." UN, New York.

———. 2004. "*A More Secure World: Our Shared Responsibility.*" Report of the High-Level Panel on Threats, Challenges and Change. New York: United Nations.

———. 2015. "Transforming Our World: The 2030 Agenda for Sustainable Development." (A/RES/70/1). Resolution adopted by the General Assembly on September 25.

———. 2017a. *World Economic Situation and Prospects 2017*. New York.

———. 2017b. *Report of the Special Representative of the Secretary-General on Migration*. Report A/71/728. New York: UN.

UN General Assembly. 2015. "Strengthening the Role of the United Nations in Enhancing Periodic and Genuine Elections and the Promotion of Democratization." Resolution A/RES/70/168, adopted February 17, New York.

———. 2016. "Review of United Nations Peacebuilding Architecture." Resolution A/RES/70/262, adopted April 27, New York.

UNDESA (United Nations Department of Economic and Social Affairs). 2014. *World Urbanization Prospects: The 2014 Revision*. New York: UNDESA.

———. 2015a. "Percentage of Total Population by Broad Age Group, Both Sexes (per 100 Total Population)." UNDESA, New York.

———. 2015b. "Population by Age and Sex (Thousands)." UNDESA, New York.

———. 2015c. *World Population Prospects: The 2015 Revision*. New York: UNDESA.

———. 2016. *International Migration Report 2015*. New York: United Nations.

UNDP (United Nations Development Programme). 2017. *Human Development Report 2016*. New York: UNDP.

UNHCR (United Nations High Commissioner for Refugees). 2016. *Global Trends: Forced Displacement in 2015*. Geneva: UNHCR.

———. 2017. *Global Trends: Forced Displacement in 2016*. Geneva: UNHCR. http://www.unhcr.org/en-us/statistics/unhcrstats/5943e8a34/global-trends-forced-displacement-2016.html.

UNITU (United Nations International Telecommunication Union). 2016. *UN ITU Facts and Figures 2016*. Geneva: UNITU.

UNODC (United Nations Office on Drugs and Crime). 2008. "Drug Trafficking as a Security Threat in West Africa." UNODC, Vienna.

———. 2010. "The Globalization of Crime: A Transnational Organized Crime Threat Assessment." UNODC, Vienna.

———. 2012. "Transnational Organized Crime: The Globalized Illegal Economy." Fact Sheet, UNODC, Vienna.

———. n.d. "Transnational Organized Crime: The Globalized Illegal Economy." https://www.unodc.org/toc/en/crimes/organized-crime.html.

UNSC (United Nations Security Council). "Review of United Nations Peacebuilding Architecture." 2016. Resolution S/RES/2282, adopted April 27, New York.

USAID (U.S. Agency for International Development). 2014. "Climate Change and Conflict in the Sahel." Policy Brief, USAID, Washington, DC.

Veilleux-Lepage, Y. 2016. "Retweeting the Caliphate: The Role of Soft Sympathizers in the Islamic State's Social Media Strategy." *Turkish Journal of Security Studies* 18 (1): 53–69.

Verjee, N. 2017. "Regional Economic Communities in Conflict Prevention and Management." Background paper for the United Nations–World Bank Flagship Study, *Pathways for Peace: Inclusive Approaches to Preventing Violent Conflict*, World Bank, Washington, DC.

Weidmann, N. B. 2015. "Communication, Technology, and Political Conflict: Introduction to the Special Issue." *Journal of Peace Research* 52 (3): 263–68.

World Bank. 2011. *World Development Report 2011: Conflict, Security, and Development.* Washington, DC: World Bank.

———. 2014. "Africa: Sahel Demography and Development." Report ACS 11786, World Bank, Washington, DC, November 10.

———. 2016a. "Migration and Development: A Role for the World Bank Group." Washington, DC: World Bank.

———. 2016b. *Poverty and Shared Prosperity 2016: Taking on Inequality.* Washington, DC: World Bank.

———. 2017. *Forcibly Displaced: Toward a Development Approach Supporting Refugees, the Internally Displaced, and Their Hosts.* Washington, DC: World Bank.

———. Various years. *World Development Indicators.* Washington, DC: World Bank.

———. 2018. *World Development Report 2018: Learning to Realize Education's Promise.* Washington, DC: World Bank.

World Bank and IMF (International Monetary Fund). 2016. *Global Monitoring Report 2015/2016: Development Goals in an Era of Demographic Change.* Washington, DC: World Bank.

World Bank Group and World Trade Organization. 2015. *The Role of Trade in Ending Poverty.* Geneva: World Trade Organization.

World Economic Forum. 2015. *Global IT Report.* Geneva: World Economic Forum.

———. 2016. *The Future of Jobs: Employment, Skills, and Workforce Strategy for the Fourth Industrial Revolution.* Global Challenge Insight Report. Geneva: World Economic Forum.

World Summit on the Information Society. 2005. "Tunis Commitment." ITU, Geneva.

World Values Survey Association. 2014. "World Values Survey Round 6." World Values Survey Association, Vienna.

WTO (World Trade Organization). 2017. "World Trade and GDP Growth in 2016 and Early 2017." Chapter 3 in *World Trade Statistical Review 2017.* Geneva: World Trade Organization. https://www.wto.org/english/res_e/statis_e/wts2017_e/WTO_Chapter_03_e.pdf.

Yanagizawa-Drott, D. 2014. "Propaganda and Conflict: Evidence from the Rwandan Genocide." *Quarterly Journal of Economics* 129 (4): 1947–94.

Additional Reading

Collier, P., and A. Hoeffler 2006. "Military Expenditure in Post-conflict Societies." *Economics of Governance* 7 (1): 89–107.

Dunne, J. P. 2012. "Third Copenhagen Consensus: Armed Conflict Assessment." Assessment Paper, Copenhagen Consensus Center, Tewksbury, MA.

Lomborg, B., ed. 2013. *Global Problems, Smart Solutions: Costs and Benefits.* Cambridge: Cambridge University Press.

World Bank. Various years. Povcalnet. Washington, DC: World Bank.

CHAPTER 3

Pathways for Peace

A society's ability to manage conflict constructively is tested continuously by risks that push it toward violence and opportunities to move toward sustainable peace. These challenges emerge from the fast-shifting global and regional landscape, as highlighted in chapter 2, and they reflect each society's unique composition.

This study views prevention, in line with the United Nations (UN) sustaining peace resolutions (UN General Assembly 2016a; UN Security Council 2016a), as "activities aimed at preventing the outbreak, escalation, continuation, and recurrence of conflict, addressing root causes, assisting parties to conflict to end hostilities, ensuring national reconciliation, and moving towards recovery, reconstruction, and development."

This chapter presents a framework for understanding prevention as part of a comprehensive strategy for sustaining peace. Societies are complex systems in which change follows nonlinear trajectories created by the interaction, decisions, and actions of multiple actors. The framework is based on the concept of pathways for peace and focuses on three core elements of society: actors, the individuals and groups whose decisions ultimately define the pathway a society takes; institutions, which shape the incentives for peace or violence and therefore influence the society's overall capacity to mitigate conflict; and structural factors, which are the foundational elements of a society that define its organization and

constitute the overall environment in which actors make decisions.

Violent conflict cannot be adequately understood using state-centric perspectives because, as discussed in chapters 1 and 2, many of the world's violent conflicts take place on the peripheries of, or outside, the community of states and do not involve government soldiers. Instead, conflicts involving a variety of actors, structures, and processes are playing out at multiple levels, with governments and partners increasingly challenged with identifying and addressing risks, simultaneously, but to varying degrees, at local, national, regional, and global levels.

The concept of pathways for peace helps to illustrate how the risk of violence and the opportunities for peace emerge and change over time. It is possible for a single event to cause an abrupt shift in a society's pathway; however, in most cases pathways change relatively slowly, as risks intensify, accumulate, or are mitigated. Underlying risks related to the exclusion of particular groups—for example, based on identity or geography—tend to play a role in most violent conflicts.

While the calculus of actors is driven strongly by incentives in the short term, the incentives to use violence may accumulate or dissipate over months, years, or even decades. Often violence exists in different forms before being recognized and labeled as a violent conflict. In some cases, actions result in violence even when this is not the preferred outcome of any single actor.

The pathways for peace framework allows for the identification of entry points over time for efforts to address risks and take advantage of opportunities for peace. In line with the 2030 Agenda on Sustainable Development and the UN sustaining peace resolutions, prevention in this model requires a constant process of mitigating shocks, while making sustained investments to reduce underlying structural and institutional risks.

A Framework for Peaceful Pathways

A society's pathway moves through a variety of situations that present risks and opportunities for maintaining a peaceful path (figure 3.1). These pathways are never linear. In the words of North, Wallis, and Weingast (2009, 12), "The dynamism of social order is a dynamic of change, not a dynamic of progress. Most societies move backward and forward with respect to political and economic development." Because they are shaped by the complex relationships among the core elements of society, the pathways are extremely difficult to predict.

Pathways move through a myriad of situations. The ideal state of affairs, shown as the darker shade of green in figure 3.1, can be understood as sustainable peace, a situation without violence and built on sustainable development, justice, equity, and protection of human rights as defined in the 2030 Agenda for Sustainable Development.[1] The opposing situation, shown as the darker shade of red, is one of overt, collective violence.

Between sustainable peace and overt violence is a range of situations where risks to peace and violence manifest together. Some of these situations can be quite stable and predictable, in the sense that a certain power equilibrium is maintained (Galtung 1969) and there is an apparent absence of tension (King 1963, 1). Yet, such situations do not constitute sustainable peace as long as underlying tensions remain unaddressed or actively suppressed (World Bank 2011).

At times, temporary bargains have helped to stave off overt violence in the short term, potentially buying time for broader reforms that can direct a pathway toward more sustained peace. For example, the increase in public sector employment in the Arab Republic of Egypt and Tunisia in

FIGURE 3.1 Pathway between Sustainable Peace and Violent Conflict

Societies forge unique pathways as they negotiate competing pressures pushing toward violent conflict and sustainable peace. The figure illustrates how different forces can influence the direction of the pathway.

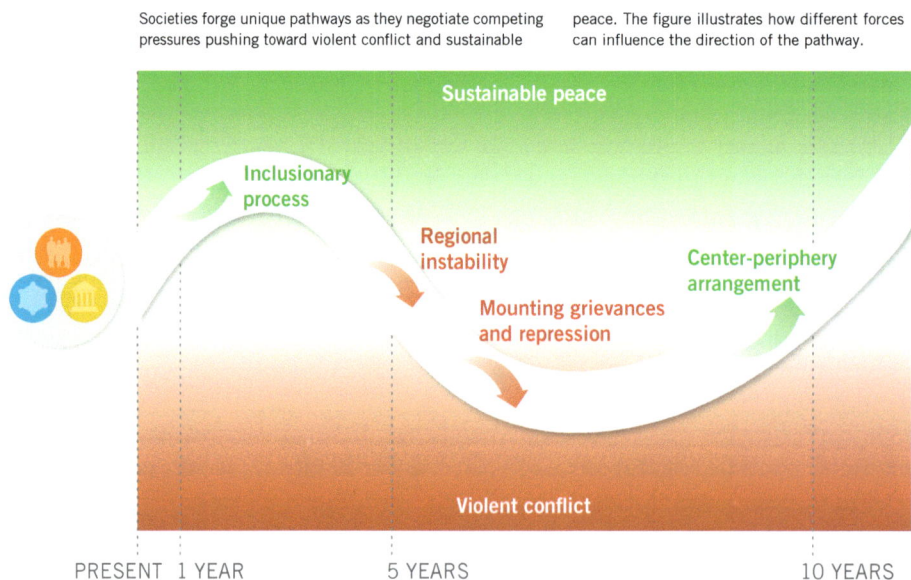

the period after the Arab Spring has achieved some stability in the immediate term, although its long-term sustainability is unclear (World Bank 2017, 16). Some societies have exited violent conflict and transitioned into long periods during which conflicts are suppressed by force more than resolved. Yet, this relative stability does not equate with sustainable peace. Thus, the lack of open violence should not be confused with peace but rather understood as conditions of varying risk.

Sudden changes in a pathway are relatively rare. Instead, cross-country studies of violent conflict have consistently demonstrated that some societies appear particularly vulnerable to violence, with histories characterized by either prolonged violence or repeated episodes of violence, while others tend to be resilient and experience protracted periods of peace (Jones, Elgin-Cossart, and Esberg 2012). Min et al. (2017), relying on the Armed Conflict Dataset of Peace Research Institute Oslo (PRIO), reviewed data for 161 countries during the 1995–2015 period and found that violent conflict is often cyclical or episodic and that vulnerability to violence relates less to specific shocks than to slow-changing institutional and structural factors. Similarly, Fearon and Laitin (2013) examined data for all countries over the 1816–2007 period, finding that violent conflict tends to concentrate and persist in certain countries[2] and, conversely, that a large set of countries, roughly 60, did not experience violent conflict at all.

Given the global trends discussed in chapter 1, this pattern can be expected to continue. A relatively small number of countries experience violent conflict at any given time. That said, risks of conflict will remain high in many countries as long as underlying drivers are not addressed and systemic risks continue to intensify, with the potential for new conflicts to break out and existing conflicts to become protracted or internationalized (Dupuy et al. 2017). Efforts to encourage peaceful pathways continue to be critical both in ending violence as well as in reducing the risk to these countries of violence breaking out.

The pathways concept is applicable at multiple levels—that is, to specific areas within a country or areas that extend beyond the borders of a single country. It aids in understanding the risks and opportunities around subregional conflict and in regions like the Sahel, where risks and opportunities are linked across countries. These different levels, although often treated as separate, are in reality fluid and interlinked. In an increasingly interdependent world, risks intersect across levels. In the same way, pathways, in principle, also exist at different levels. A key analytical challenge is to define the boundaries between the levels and the relative weight that should be assigned to them, which Williams terms the "level of analysis problem" (Williams 2016, 43).

Recognizing this challenge, the framework presented in this study takes the national-level pathway as the dominant path, highlighting the centrality of the state in determining national outcomes. The framework underscores that the different levels formally intersect through the rights and responsibilities of the state. The state has local, national, and international responsibilities, and the failure of the state in those responsibilities can fuel the spread of conflict across borders. The focus on national pathways does not mean a focus solely on state institutions, but rather a focus on the national level of analysis, in which the state is a key actor, as discussed later in this chapter. A key variable in this analysis is, therefore, the capacity of a state to govern risks across levels within its territory.

The framework for this study understands societies as comprising three core elements—actors, institutions, and structural factors—whose interactions influence the pathway a society takes (figure 3.2).

The pathway that a society takes is a product of the decisions of critical *actors*, who are enabled or constrained by *structural factors* and influenced by the *institutions* that help to define the incentives for their behavior. To understand how pathways are forged, it is critical to examine the interactions among these three elements.

FIGURE 3.2 Actors, Structural Factors, Institutions

ACTORS are individuals, social groups, or small organizations who make decisions, in cooperation or competition with one another, that determine the pathway.

ACTORS

STRUCTURAL FACTORS

INSTITUTIONS

STRUCTURAL FACTORS are the foundational elements of society that determine its essential organization.

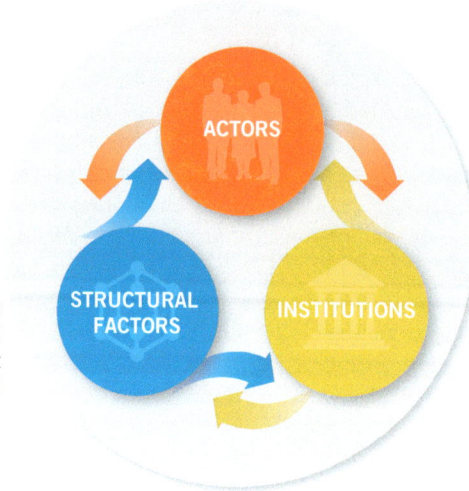

INSTITUTIONS provide the "rules of the game," both formal, legal frameworks and informal social norms and values that can determine actors' behavior, incentives, and capacity to work together.

Because they operate in relationship to one another, a shift in one will have impacts on the others.

Structural factors are the foundational elements of society that determine its essential organization. They include, for example, geography, economic systems, political structures, demographic composition, or distribution of resources. In general, structural factors do not change easily, and when they do, they do so only over relatively long periods of time. Structural factors shape the overall environment in which actors make decisions. As highlighted in chapter 2, they may include systemic stresses, such as the influence of transnational illicit markets or the impacts of climate change.

Some structural factors are more malleable than others. For example, geography can rarely be altered, although societies can find ways to mitigate its impacts (Fearon and Laitin 2013; Raleigh and Urdal 2007), as reflected in Sustainable Development Goal (SDG) 13 of the 2030 Agenda. High levels of aid dependence and excessive reliance on natural resources for economic growth tend to be associated with greater risk of violence

and can usually be changed only over longer periods of time (Blattman and Miguel 2010; Collier and Hoeffler 2004; OECD 2016). In the social realm, structural factors such as legacies of violence, trauma, and the societal divisions left by violence, can persist over generations and often take significant effort and time to change (Hegre and Sambanis 2006; Volkan 2004; World Bank 2011). Conversely, societies that possess more cohesion, higher income levels, more inclusive economic and political regimes, a more diversified economy, and a history of peaceful cooperation across groups and that are located in more stable regions experience less violence (Collier et al. 2003; Easterly, Ritzen, and Woolcock 2006; Østby 2008; Parks, Colletta, and Oppenheim 2013; Stewart 2004, 2008, 2010).

While structural factors are clear influences on the overall health of a society, *institutions* have been described as the "immune system," charged with defending a society from pressures toward violence and promoting overall resilience (World Bank 2011, 72). Just as a healthy immune system mounts a quick, targeted response to a pathogen, effective institutions can respond and contain the actions of individuals or groups that threaten overall societal well-being.

Institutions provide the "rules of the game"—both formal legal frameworks and informal social norms and values—that govern actors' behavior and limit the damage that individual actors can do (North 1990, 3). Formal law enforcement institutions do this directly, by capturing and containing individuals who behave violently. Informal social norms also perform this role, by influencing people's expectations about how other people will behave. If individuals believe that others are obeying the laws and rules of society, they are more likely to do so as well. However, if an individual does not have solid reason to expect that rules will be enforced, the payoffs to violence are higher. In these cases, ineffective institutions can enable—rather than contain—behavior that threatens societal well-being. The larger a society, the greater the number of institutions (as "enforcers" of rules) needed (North, Wallis, and Weingast 2009).

In defining the "rules" for actors' behavior, institutions shape the overall incentive structure for peace. In high-risk situations or in the presence of violent conflict, capable institutions provide commitment mechanisms for armed groups to hold to a cease-fire by raising the costs of reneging on the agreement. In "Somaliland," trusted governing bodies that encompass actors from various sectors, including clan leaders and elders, have contributed to more than two decades of relative stability and peace, despite ongoing violent conflict in southern Somalia (World Bank 2017). The longer peace endures, the greater the disincentives for any of the groups to resort to violence.

Institutions also structure incentives by managing the expectations of actors. One of the key tasks of institutions is to temper the sense of relative deprivation and frustrated expectations of groups who do not see themselves as benefiting fairly from overall economic advancement and ensuring that these frustrations are addressed peacefully (Gurr 1970; Huntington 1968). As more countries shift toward open political systems, they raise expectations about access to certain freedoms and services. As discussed in more detail in chapter 4, grievances across groups can arise if expectations remain unmet due to constrained resources or lack of political will (Brinkerhoff 2011).

Effective institutions are impersonal. Rather than being confined to the influence of individual leaders or special interest groups, they possess sufficient depth to include diverse groups in a society and have the staying power to outlast political terms or temporary agreements between elites (World Bank 2011). This generates trust in the institutions themselves, even when people do not feel trust or legitimacy toward a particular leader representing that institution. In this way, the impersonal nature of effective institutions can produce a legitimizing effect, which is itself an incentive for maintaining peace and stability. Effective, accountable, and inclusive institutions at all levels are an explicit goal within the 2030 Agenda.

To some degree, inclusive institutions can also protect against the impact of unfavorable structural factors, for example, by embodying greater voice and accountability in decision making or redistribution of resources (Fearon and Laitin 2013; Raleigh and Urdal 2007). Social norms that promote gender inclusion, for instance, can help to equalize power relations in decision-making processes and lead to more optimal outcomes; as detailed in chapter 6, women's participation in peace negotiations has improved the quality and staying power of peace agreements across a range of countries (Anderlini 2007; O'Reilly, Ó Súilleabháin, and Paffenholz 2015; Paffenholz et al. 2017; Stone 2015).

Actors are the central component of this framework. Actors can include individuals (especially influential leaders), social groups, or small organizations who make decisions in competition or cooperation with one another. Capable institutions and favorable structural factors can make peaceful pathways more likely and easier to maintain; but, at the end of the day, it is actors—working together or individually— who determine the direction society will take (Chesterman, Ignatieff, and Thakur 2004; Faustino and Booth 2014; MacGinty 2010). Actors' behaviors, in turn, shape the incentives for other actors to choose violence or peace. For example, as chapter 4 highlights, leaders may develop narratives that increase the incentives for violence or promote peace.

The boundaries between organizations of actors and institutions are difficult to define. At what point does a group of people, acting together, become an institution? For the purposes of this framework, institutions are understood as possessing a level of structure that transcends personal relationships, with rules and norms that apply broadly to all constituents. An organization of actors becomes an institution when it establishes norms and rules that go beyond the immediate influence of one or a few members. Some organizations and even some states are in reality not institutions if they are effectively controlled by a small group of individuals or the rules or norms are not endorsed or followed by the majority of citizens. They do not provide what an institution is supposed to provide, and the small group of individuals may not represent the interests of all social groups, deepening the perception that an organization is exclusionary by design. Box 3.1 illustrates how this framework can be applied to a particular society—in this case, Mali—to aid in understanding how pathways are formed.

BOX 3.1 Applying the Framework to the Northern Mali Conflict, 2012–13

Structural factors

- Some of the populations of the extreme north of Mali have historically been connected more with the Sahara and Northern Africa than with the population of the south, through commercial routes and cultural ties.
- Some of the populations of the extreme north have a long history of conflict with the south, including raiding for slaves, and during colonization and after independence have been in regular rebellion against the central government.
- The extreme north has been deeply affected by climate change, drought, and the collapse of Saharan trade.
- The civil war in Algeria (1991–2002) and collapse of the central Libyan state have brought about the installation of small violent extremist groups in the region and increased illicit trafficking of arms, people, and weapons.
- There are few economic opportunities aside from illicit trade and some limited herding and agriculture activities.
- The low population density of the north makes the provision of services and infrastructure development very costly and difficult.

Institutions

- Although it is a democratic state with an active political life, Mali has struggled with accountability, corruption, clientelism, and personalization of institutions.
- The military was terribly weakened during prior regimes by fear of military coup and reliance on ethnic militias. The army has been poorly trained and equipped and lacks cohesiveness and leadership. This has created a security vacuum in various parts of the country, especially the border region.
- Decentralization, a central factor in giving the regions more autonomy, has been marred by corruption and lack of accountability of local politicians. It has also upset the ethnic balance. Additionally, political decentralization has never been well accepted by the central government bureaucracy.
- Competition among clans and families has weakened traditional institutions regulating the Tuareg and Fulani groups. Youth, in particular, do not have effective means of participating in these institutions, contributing to a loss in moral authority.

(Box continued next page)

Path Dependency of Violence

All societies experience some violence. Yet, high-intensity violent conflict is a relatively rare phenomenon; most societies are at peace most of the time. Being at peace brings a certain inertia; societies at peace tend to remain at peace. The longer and more intentionally a society has worked to address structural factors and create the incentives for peace, the harder it is to derail that society from a peaceful path.

Episodes of violence, nevertheless, can happen at any point along the pathway, even when the path is headed in the direction of peace. Violence tends to emerge more gradually than is often assumed, with risks building up over periods of months and years (box 3.2).

Like peace, violence is highly path-dependent. As violent conflict continues, societies can get caught in a "conflict trap," where incentives are reconfigured in ways that sustain conflict, and many actors—the state, private sector, communities—start to organize themselves with the view that violent conflict will continue (Collier et al. 2003, 1). As discussed in chapter 1,

many of today's conflicts are more protracted and involve an increasing number of armed groups, including self-defense militias, rebel groups, illicit trafficking networks, and urban gangs. The "original causes" often evolve and transform as new generations of actors get involved and as war economies become more entrenched (Bøås 2015; Wolff, Ross, and Wee 2017).

Over time, violent conflict can deepen grievances and divisions between groups. These emotional legacies can be transferred from generation to generation to justify continued violence. In addition, social norms meant to limit violence often relax, as violence becomes normalized as a means of resolving conflict or enforcing power relationships. Women and children are particularly affected by these dynamics, as violence against them tends to become more common and more brutal as conflict continues (Boudet et al. 2012; Crespo-Sancho 2017; Kelly 2017; Slegh, Barker, and Levtov 2014). Because of the way these psychosocial impacts accumulate, even building the "right" institutions cannot ensure a linear path out of conflict (World Bank 2017).

The path dependency of violence is reinforced by the damage it often inflicts on

Overall, outbreaks and cycles of violence are rare. This is demonstrated using a model developed for this study and drawing on Uppsala Conflict Data Program (UCDP) data for the 1975–2014 period (Mueller 2017). The model predicts that the average likelihood of a country at peace transitioning to an outbreak is 2.3 percent for a lower-intensity conflict (defined as 25–999 battle deaths a year) and just 0.09 percent for a civil war.

As risks build and accumulate, the probability of violence increases, but not as quickly as often assumed. Only 4 percent of countries at peace are likely to escalate to either a high-risk conflict (in which an early warning system warns of an outbreak of violence) or a low-intensity conflict in a given year. Of countries already at high risk, 11 percent are likely to transition to a high-intensity conflict (1,000 or more battle deaths a year).

Once violence takes root, however, the likelihood it will continue is relatively high. In 78 percent of cases, the first year of civil war is followed by a second year of war. Risk continues to be high even after violence has stopped; in the first year of recovery after civil war, the likelihood of relapse is 18 percent.

institutions (Jones, Elgin-Cossart, and Esberg 2012). During protracted conflict, political systems reorient around wartime dynamics. The need to prioritize security often results in large security forces that are difficult to demobilize and reintegrate later. Trust and legitimacy in state institutions can be eroded, as people lose faith in institutions that cannot protect them or provide the basic services they need. Protracted conflict also fuels the brain drain of national talent and skills, as those with the means to do so look for opportunities elsewhere.

Even after violence has taken root, it is still possible for societies to change course. Intermittently along the pathways, opportunities appear when actors' decisions have more impact to define a pathway. These "transition moments" are events that open up the possibility for a marked change in direction (figure 3.3)—for example, a national political transition, a new leader in

FIGURE 3.3 Transition Moments

The graphic illustrates the way transition moments can shift the direction of the pathway, Here, a change in leadership provides an example of an event that can shift the pathway toward sustainable peace, via a power-sharing agreement, or toward greater risk of conflict, via increased competition for power and grievances.

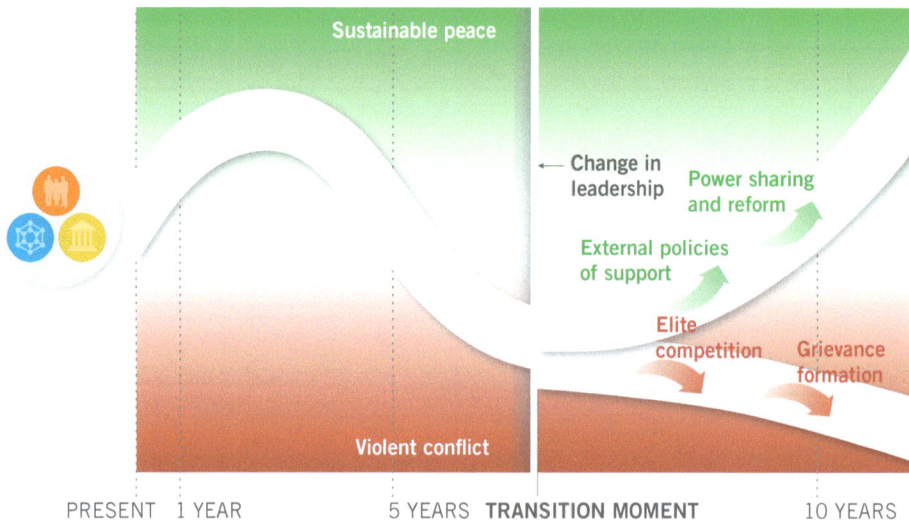

Sustainable peace

← Change in leadership   Power sharing and reform

External policies of support

Elite competition   Grievance formation

Violent conflict

PRESENT   1 YEAR   5 YEARS   **TRANSITION MOMENT**   10 YEARS

power, a new international alliance—or smaller-scale shifts such as policy reform in one sector (World Bank 2011, 12). During transition moments, coalitions can be formed, leadership demonstrated, and reforms launched. In most cases, a peaceful pathway results from actions taken in many transition moments, rather than a single event. However, as risks escalate—and especially after violence has begun—opportunities for transition moments are less frequent. As explored further below, early monitoring of risks helps in identifying potential transition moments.

The Centrality of Actors

As noted throughout this study, the decisions, calculations, and leadership shown (or not) by actors ultimately determine the pathways societies take. Actors can shape structural factors and influence the way institutions are built and reformed. Understanding the central role that different actors play in driving conflict is especially crucial now, given the multiplicity and complexity of the actors involved in violent conflict today.

Actors can change their behavior relatively abruptly. In contrast, although institutions can sometimes change course quickly, in most cases they take several years, even decades, to reform—thus changing the rules of the game and the incentives for action. It may take a generation or more to achieve the deeper institutional transformations needed to reach recognized standards of governance like civilian oversight of the military, anticorruption measures, or a functioning state bureaucracy (Pritchett and de Weijer 2010).

In most settings, actors tend to make decisions that privilege visible beneficial impact in the short to medium term over actions that may only bear fruit in the longer term. This is often as true in contexts with democratic systems that require a periodic transfer of power between parties as in less democratic settings where leaders often feel a strong need to maintain popular support.

The actions of one individual, or a small group, can bring enormous, often swift, consequences for society. In some cases, just one or a few actors can derail progress toward peace. To draw on the public health analogy (Stares 2017) used in the study introduction, individuals can make unhealthy choices—to smoke or engage in unprotected sex, for instance—that threaten not only their health but also the health of others. This can occur even in people with strong immune systems and favorable environmental conditions that facilitate healthy choices. One terrorist attack by a small group of individuals can abruptly shift the overall political, security, and economic trajectory of a country or a region.

Likewise, the decisive actions of particular leaders and small groups can create incentives for peace, helping to push a society out of a cycle of violence. Leaders can spearhead initiatives that can change a pathway quickly, such as activating coalitions and invoking or shaping norms and values for prevention. They may provide a long-term vision of a society's peaceful future that engages a large audience. Taking such actions often involves risk, especially for political leaders, because political capital or even survival may be at stake in the short term. As chapter 6 illustrates, in high-risk or violent situations, it most often falls to individual leaders to weigh and act on the inevitable political, social, economic, and security trade-offs that prevention entails and to balance the effects of other actors, institutions, and structural factors.

It is now broadly acknowledged that actors do not always behave "rationally"—considering all possible contingencies and making a calculated decision based on self-interest—as economic models would predict (World Bank 2015). People and groups are rarely able to process all of the available information or to consider every possible contingency when making a decision. Actors "think automatically" rather than deliberately (World Bank 2015). Stress and tension limit agency further by constraining the capacity for deliberative thinking (Mani et al. 2013; Mullainathan and Shafir 2013; Narayan et al. 2000). For example, the experience of poverty can stress mental resources, simply through the many decisions that need to be made to meet basic needs—keeping children safe or obtaining food, for example. The stress of poverty focuses attention on the present, making it hard to plan for the future, like investing in education, or opening a small business. This "cognitive tax"[3] is exacerbated in conflict-affected environments, where the threat or experience of violence combines with the daily challenges of meeting basic needs (World Bank 2015, 81).

Actors also "think socially," that is, they are heavily influenced by social norms that determine their expectations about how others will respond to a decision they make. Instead, the behavior of actors is shaped by their social and emotional environment (Halliday and Shaffer 2015; Simon 1997 [1947]). In this way, social norms help to shape the incentives of actors because they help actors to anticipate how others will behave. Expectations of shame or loss of reputation, for example, can be more powerful enforcers of contracts than legal regulations.

Domestic Actors

The pathway a society takes depends greatly on the way actors in that society—what this report calls "domestic actors"—cooperate or compete with one another. Domestic actors may be part of the state or outside it, including groups or individuals, members of civil society, and the private sector, and they may be formal, informal, or traditional leaders. Most often, the state is central among them, but a constellation of actors plays roles in various combinations at different times.

Domestic actors can promote a virtuous cycle of long-term peace and development. For example, community or religious groups and nongovernmental organizations have played pivotal roles in promoting and sustaining peace. They can also push a society toward violence. As mentioned in chapter 1, violent conflict in recent years is characterized by a proliferation of nonstate actors such as militias, rebel groups, criminal groups, violent extremist groups, and many others. Oftentimes the stated grievances used to justify their movements evolve over time.

In addition, these groups do not always represent the interests of the people whom they claim to represent. This is particularly evident in the emergence of criminal networks operating in contexts of violence.

Domestic actors hold the highest stake in mitigating and preventing violent conflict, even when a conflict has global significance; possess the deepest understanding of their history and causes (although that understanding may be deeply biased); and have the most legitimacy, whether formal or informal, to act (Mcloughlin 2015). External actors can play critical and sometimes decisive roles (see chapter 7) in high-risk and violent situations, but ultimately internal actors can go beyond preventing imminent or existing violence itself to address underlying grievances or causes, including by engaging international support and mobilizing domestic coalitions, including around the 2030 Agenda.

The range of domestic actors is too vast to treat exhaustively. Here, the chapter focuses on some of the key domestic actors that matter for understanding violence and violence prevention: the state, civil society and community organizations, and the private sector.

The State

In most societies, the state is the central domestic actor influencing a society's pathway. While the extent of its agency and power vary vis-à-vis other actors in society, the state ultimately holds responsibility for many of the decisions that shape the pathway and has the authority to negotiate and navigate agreements or political settlements, reform institutions, and direct policy. On top of this, the state also has the legal responsibility to implement international treaties that it has ratified, including in relation to human rights, and international agreements such as the 2030 Agenda and the sustaining peace resolutions. The state's role is not always positive; history is full of examples of states perpetrating violence directly through state forces or failing to quell violence within their borders (Elias 1982; Tilly 1985, 2003).

As an abstract concept, the "state" comprises not only the institutions that represent its more formal and "visible" structure, but also the social interactions that create and sustain that structure. The state is not a unitary actor, but an organization of heterogeneous individuals, all of whom bring varying motivations, interests, and degrees of commitment to shaping the character and functioning of the state. For example, the bureaucrats that make up state institutions are driven by a variety of motivations, from a vocation for public service, desire to advance their careers, need to provide for their families or accumulate wealth, as well as political interests. All of these motivations and interests are constantly negotiated; they shape, and are shaped by, the institutions that result from them (Marc et al. 2012).

The state is a product of its interaction with society and continually evolves in the context of that relationship. Predatory states prey on social groups, extracting resources with little or no compensation. States can be captured or work in collusion with powerful interests that undermine peaceful pathways. For example, some drug cartels now command financial flows that rival those of national governments and heavily influence key state institutions.[4] More authoritarian states may strike a bargain with society in which the state distributes resources in exchange for limits on civil freedoms. Others essentially contract out the delivery of basic services to nonstate actors, such as nonprofit organizations and external partners.

Many states—including many in fragile and conflict-affected contexts—garner support and ensure their existence through informal patronage networks that distribute resources and privileges to key constituencies (Evans 2004).[5] In these cases, political authority is diffuse and informal, rather than formalized through state institutions (Bøås et al. 2017). The relationship between these networks and the state may be quite stable, as long as the power balance is maintained (Brinkerhoff and Goldsmith 2005). Attempts to reform institutions will inevitably bump up against this reality and can lead to instability when the balance of power across groups is disrupted (Hameiri 2007).

Where the state has not established its presence in a convincing way, nonstate actors often step into the breach and provide alternative forms of governance (box 3.3). Most policy makers and academics now

---

BOX 3.3 Alternatively Governed Spaces

The concept of ungoverned spaces, defined as "areas of limited or anomalous government control inside otherwise functional states," emerged out of the policy debates following the September 11, 2001 terrorist attacks in the United States (Keister 2014, 1; Nezam 2017). These spaces are not necessarily limited to a defined geographic area. The Internet, for instance, has been described as an ungoverned space because it offers an unregulated, virtual haven and a platform for recruiting to violent extremist groups (Patrick 2010).

In reality, ungoverned spaces are not so much ungoverned as alternatively governed. In many cases, they represent populations on the political or geographic peripheries of a country that have never been meaningfully integrated into state-building projects. Where the state is absent or unwilling to assert its presence, other actors step into the void. These can include a range of actors, from tribal leaders and elders to criminal networks, insurgent groups, and extremist groups. In a study of the Sahel region, Raleigh and Dowd (2013) argue that the challenges faced by political and geographic peripheries are a result not of too little governance but of many overlapping forms of governance.

Rabasa et al. (2007) define three main forms of alternate governance:

- With *contested governance*, a territory does not recognize the legitimacy of the government and is loyal to another

(Box continued next page)

BOX 3.3 **Alternatively Governed Spaces** *(continued)*

type of social organization such as an identity group or insurgent movement. These groups or movements usually want to establish their own state.

- With *incomplete governance*, a state wants to project its authority over its territory and provide public goods and services for its population but lacks the competence and resources to do so. Where officials are present, they are often intimidated, inept, or corrupt.

- With *abdicated governance*, the government refuses to extend its authority or provide security, infrastructure, and services because doing so is not cost-effective. Instead, authority for delivering basic services is ceded to subnational groups such as local tribes.

The chief concern has been that alternatively governed spaces may facilitate the entry and operations of nonstate actors such as illicit trafficking networks, gangs, or violent extremist

groups (Clunan and Trinkunas 2010; Keister 2014; Nezam 2017). While weak state presence is often an attractive condition for these actors, it is insufficient on its own. Criminal and extremist groups require a certain level of infrastructure (transport and communications, in particular) as well as some support from local populations, in order to operate effectively. For this reason, weak states may be more vulnerable than failed states to these types of networks (Menkhaus and Shapiro 2010).

All three forms of alternative governance ultimately undermine state capacity and legitimacy, even though they may bring some stability over the short term. The presence of these spaces also offers varying degrees of opportunity to integrate them into broader society by increasing the representation of local populations in the arenas where access to power, resources, and security are negotiated. Chapter 5 discusses these issues in greater detail.

agree that what have often been called "ungoverned spaces" are not actually ungoverned; rather, they are "differently governed" by alternative authorities or nonstate actors—traditional or customary, tribal or clan, religious, criminal, and insurgent, among others (Keister 2014; Nezam 2017). These actors may provide state-like services such as security, employment, and education, as armed groups have done in contexts ranging from the Philippines to Afghanistan, Jamaica, and cities in Brazil (Arias 2013; Clunan and Trinkunas 2010; Keister 2014; Sacks 2009).

Alternatively governed spaces can present a challenge to sustainable peace when the presence and activities of nonstate actors undermine state capacity and legitimacy (Nezam 2017). Illicit trafficking networks are a good example. These networks can have a variety of relationships with the state and with society (Cockayne 2016).

When these groups are able to establish control and set up parallel state structures, especially when they deliver security that the state cannot, or will not, deliver, the state loses credibility and its capacity is undermined. When elites accept bribes or participate directly in trafficking networks, legitimacy suffers, and resources that could go to deliver basic services are diverted (Kemp, Shaw, and Boutellis 2013; Stearns Lawson and Dininio 2013).

In general, states based on open access and contestation tend to forge more peaceful pathways (North, Wallis, and Weingast 2009). Conversely, states that employ coercive tactics that limit people's agency in expressing identity and accessing opportunities for social and economic mobility tend to see a hardening of identities and increased risk of violence (Benford and Snow 2000; Fearon 2010).

Countries experiencing fragility are often hard-pressed to act preventively. In some cases, elites may discount actions whose consequences, while grave, are not immediate and clear, in order to ensure regime survival. In other cases, the state may lack the requisite legitimacy in the eyes of particular groups to address underlying risks. Capacity is another factor; states that are unable to formulate and implement policies, collect taxes, provide basic services, or ensure a minimum of security are often limited in the extent to which they can monitor and address risks. A particular effort is needed to support the capacity of countries experiencing situations of fragility so that they can more effectively undertake prevention policies and programs and implement the 2030 Agenda, which provides a pathway to sustainable development and peace.

Civil Society and Community-Based Organizations

Civil society actors comprise a wide range of associations and nonstate entities, including charities, nongovernmental organizations, community groups, faith-based organizations, trade guilds and unions, professional associations, and advocacy groups, among others (Aslam 2017; Marc et al. 2012). The category also includes informal decision-making bodies, such as tribal councils or elders, that provide many of the basic services to people in transition or postconflict settings (UNDP 2012). While civil society is often seen as consisting of organizations that may be competing for the same pool of resources, their underlying norms and values have been assumed to be largely shared, facilitating potential broad-based solidarity. With an increasing multiplicity and diversity of actors engaging in the civic space, this space is also becoming a more contested domain of public life (Poppe and Wolff 2017). In addition, civic space has received a digital dimension, which provides space for different modes of both solidarity and contestation (Dahlgren 2015).

Civil society actors can promote confidence and build trust, which encourages cooperation among members of society and creates incentives for collective action. Where trust is forged across groups, it can apply to society more broadly (Boix and Posner 1996; Yamagishi and Yamagishi 1994). This ability to build bottom-up trust gives civil society an instrumental role in forming coalitions for peace.

Civil society and community-based actors, in particular, are central to both the resolution and prevention of conflict (Giessmann, Galvanek, and Seifert 2017). At the most basic level, civil society actors may help to provide basic services to local communities, an important function in maintaining stability during a crisis. Civic associations, such as neighborhood or community organizations, often contribute to cohesion that helps to buffer against risk of violence, especially when they build relationships across different social groups (Aslam 2017; Varshney 2002). Civil society groups also play an important role in promoting social norms that discourage violence, for example, by increasing awareness of the costs of violent conflict and showcasing opportunities that can come from engagement across rival groups (Barnes 2009).

Beyond these roles, civil society organizations (CSOs) play a crucial part in mediating the state-society relationship by maintaining space for dialogue and expression of dissent (Marc et al. 2012). CSOs, in many cases, play a role in holding the state accountable, which becomes increasingly important in high-risk situations, when the space for dialogue often narrows (Chenoweth and Stephan 2011), including to ensure that the state implements international agreements such as the 2030 Agenda. They may help to mediate conflict directly, through local peace committees, or by participating in national peace processes (Nilsson 2012; Wanis-St. John and Kew 2008). They can also work indirectly, by helping to shift norms and behaviors to increase commitment to peace (Barnes 2009). Once violence takes hold, civil society actors can help to prevent further escalation (Dahl, Gates, and Nygård 2017). Over the longer term, they can help to build more responsive state institutions, contributing to sustaining peaceful pathways (Dahl, Gates, and Nygård 2017). Chapter 6 covers the experiences of civil society actors in shaping societies' pathways in more detail.

As with all actors, the role of CSOs has its limitations and is not uniformly positive or effective. Many actors make a transition from civil society to operate in state institutions or move to civil society after their role in the government. These career paths often facilitate better relations between state institutions and communities, but can also damage the perception of independence. Where CSOs are insufficiently independent or represent narrow interest groups, they can cause more harm than good in the absence of appropriate countervailing forces.

CSOs can also contribute to division when they exclude other groups, either unintentionally or by design. CSOs can use their grassroots appeal and convening power as a way to mobilize for violence against other groups. For instance, before the 1994 genocide in Rwanda, CSOs including the Hutu Power groups excluded parts of the population and tended not to cross group divides, and some community organizations were active in the genocide (Aslam 2017; Human Rights Watch 1999; UN General Assembly and UN Security Council 1999). By building intergroup cohesion and "perverse social capital" that isolates them from other social groups, CSOs can also work to counter positive social goals (Posner 2004). This methodology is present in groups as diverse as urban gangs, paramilitary organizations, and student associations that became the first vigilante groups active during the 2002 conflict in Côte d'Ivoire (Sany 2010).

Private Sector Actors

Private enterprises have been an integral part of society for millennia and play an important role in shaping peaceful pathways. The private sector is a primary source of livelihoods for the majority of the population today as well as an important avenue by which to foster inclusion and social cohesion. Private enterprises, both formal and informal, have the flexibility to provide jobs, services, and tax revenue, as well as public goods such as infrastructure and enhanced environmental and governance standards, all of which shape incentives for maintaining peace. In addition, by supporting markets, the private sector enables interaction across social groups and communities that helps to build trust—a critical ingredient for prevention. A thriving private sector mitigates tensions and remedies their consequences by increasing economic opportunity and helping to address exclusion (IFC 2018).

Both large corporations and small and medium enterprises may play crucial roles in prevention. Small firms provide services and jobs to the local population, including the most marginalized. Small and medium enterprises can be collectively powerful in shaping peace incentives by contributing to social and economic interactions and attracting and making investments that are conducive to peace. They play an important role as flexible, adaptable entities. Large domestic and multinational firms can act as a major force for peace too. Leadership from businesses—setting examples of conduct, developing standards, negotiating concessions, and consolidating international partnerships—can go a long way toward mitigating tensions. Global companies, for example, have made positive contributions to stability and peace around problems such as conflict minerals or oil spills, by developing new rules and investing in social programs.

The leadership potential of private firms is exemplified by private companies' direct participation in peacebuilding processes, reflecting their understanding that a stable operating environment is essential for a prosperous business community. This has been seen in many contexts, such as in Kenya, where the Kenya Private Sector Alliance, together with other civil society groups, swiftly mobilized to help end election-related violence in 2007–08 and worked to prevent a recurrence of violence during the 2013 general elections (Goldstein and Rotich 2008). Some of these experiences are described in more detail in chapter 6.

However, the role of the private sector, like that of all other actors, is nuanced and not uniformly positive. Just as private sector actors can help shape peaceful pathways, they can also contribute to and benefit from violent conflict (Peschka 2011). When conflict starts, individual companies or groups of companies may seek to profit from the opportunities that conflict provides, for instance, by trafficking or trading in weapons and other goods with various armed factions (Comolli 2017). In some cases, private companies have become embroiled directly in conflict by supporting trade in minerals that may be trafficked by armed groups (Campbell 2002; Rettberg 2015). Corporations can also contribute to grievances and tensions through land grabs for agriculture, extractives, or commercial projects, while large-scale mining companies have fed into conflicts in Bougainville and Samoa. The proliferation of private security companies and private military firms in recent decades has also raised questions of conflicts of interest, as in some cases these firms have contributed to undermining state capacity to control violence and citizen trust in state law enforcement (Singer 2010). In Papua New Guinea, for example, the private security sector has grown to be larger than the state law enforcement forces, supplanting the state's monopoly on violence (Lakhani and Willman 2014).

The interaction of businesses with other actors in a given institutional context determines to a large extent their impact on conflict dynamics. For this reason, transparency, on the one hand, and accountability, on the other hand, are critical for fostering a positive contribution of the private actors to peace; these issues are elaborated in chapter 6.

Voluntary standards play a similarly critical role in that respect. Conflict-sensitive business practices have gathered momentum as a way for private companies to carry out their activities with a commitment to do-no-harm principles (UN Global Compact 2017). Operating in a conflict-sensitive manner is a preventive strategy deeply rooted in understanding the local context. Lack of such understanding

stands to aggravate local tensions unintentionally by disproportionally employing staff from one community or another, providing revenue or capacity that can later be deployed in conflicts. Businesses can also actively engage to stabilize the environment in high-risk contexts. To that end, the former UN Secretary-General Ban Ki Moon launched the United Nations Global Compact "Business for Peace" platform, which boosts the participation of the private sector in support of peace and supports local actors to adopt responsible business practices (UN Global Compact 2017). The UN Global Compact's "Guidance on Responsible Business and in Conflict-Affected and High-Risk Areas" (UN Global Compact 2010) helps companies to operate in challenging contexts and seeks to aid their operations to contribute positively to peace and development.

International Actors

While domestic actors drive change on the ground, international actors have a strong role to play, primarily in helping to shape the incentives and actions of national actors. International actors include national governments external to the conflict, regional organizations, the private sector,[6] and the multilateral system of political, security, and development institutions. Their actions can be decisive, especially where domestic actors are too fractured, inclined by their own interests or history, or incapable of acting. The most constructive external role has usually been to create space and, in some cases, safety nets—fiscal and economic, security, human and social capacity, or political—into which domestic actors can step forward and direct their society on a peaceful pathway. International actors can also play a role in setting and enforcing norms and supporting the implementation of international treaties and agreements, including the 2030 Agenda.

The very presence of international actors has an influence on the pathway a society takes. In the more extreme cases, international actors manipulate violence to further their own interests. Chapter 1 describes the growing trend of internationalization of conflicts, as outside states finance or send military support for proxy wars in other countries.

In other cases, international actors contribute indirectly to the forces pushing toward violence, by failing to understand their own role in conflict dynamics. International actors bring their own expectations and ideas of what domestic action should look like, which are in turn shaped by their individual experiences and backgrounds. It can be difficult for international actors to "see" domestic institutions and relationships, especially if they are culturally and socially different from their own. This tension between formal structures, which are often more visible and understood by international actors, and the (usually) informal institutions and norms that govern daily life for much of society influences every aspect of the involvement of international actors: from who gets invited to the table for decision making to the information international actors receive and how international support is prioritized and directed. International actors can help to neutralize the impact of their presence by being aware of the biases they bring and the makeup of the society they are entering (Barron, Woolcock, and Diprose 2011).

In recent years, regional organizations have emerged as important international actors for peacebuilding. Regional actors have provided channels for navigating the effects of systemic risks such as broader political and economic trends and global issues such as trade, climate change, transnational crime or terrorism, or natural disasters. They also are taking more active roles in conflict mitigation and prevention. Regional actors are likely to have deeper interests in the outcomes, to have greater understanding of and interest in regional stability, and therefore to be seen as more legitimate mediators or conveners than multilateral actors. Countries at risk of violent conflict also are often more receptive to talking to neighbors and governments from the same region. However, regional actors are not without challenges. Regional organizations' mandates, capacity, and resources do not always match the demand for their support, or they may be perceived as partial

toward certain actors. Chapter 7 discusses these experiences in more detail.

International organizations face particular constraints in supporting national actors for violent conflict prevention, but nonetheless have found effective means to do so in some cases, working in concert with regional partners. Following on the principle of state sovereignty, as enshrined in the mandates and procedural rules of international organizations, international actors require an interlocutor at the national level in order to operate in any environment. This is almost always the national government. In turn, national governments may depend on international actors to supply the resources and in some cases technical capacity to ensure regime survival. This support can take many forms, including strengthening the security apparatus or targeted delivery of public services to certain constituencies on which the regime depends.

The terms of this mutually dependent relationship represent constraints on the agency of both parties, to differing degrees (Barnett and Zurcher 2010; Bøås et al. 2017). National governments encounter limits on the degree to which they can maintain stability through coercion and repression, lest they risk losing the external financial or military support that allows them to sustain power. Additionally, they must balance the demands of the constituencies that keep them in power with the requirements for international support. This dual accountability represents a critical dilemma for many states, especially when the nature of the demands makes it impossible to satisfy expectations from both international and domestic consistencies simultaneously (Englebert and Tüll 2008; Ghani and Lockhart 2008).

In turn, international actors' reliance on states as interlocutors for conflict prevention limits their room for maneuver, since their presence depends on the discretion of national governments. Any support they provide happens relative to the state's relationship with the constituencies that maintain it. Thus, international actors are often constrained in the degree to which they can engage nonstate actors who may be strong influences on the pathway. In cases where states derive support and legitimacy from

BOX 3.4 The Interface of Violent Conflict with Exogenous Dimensions of Risk

The experience of the Syrian Arab Republic helps to illustrate how a shock can contribute to more intense disruption when other risks are present. Recent studies have looked at the intersection of risks related to climate change and violent conflict (Schleussner et al. 2016; von Uexkulla et al. 2016). Some authors have drawn a relation between the drought in Syria and the beginning of the uprising.

Beginning in 2005 and intensifying through the winter of 2006–07, the Fertile Crescent region witnessed the worst drought in its recorded history (Kelleya et al. 2015). There is very strong evidence that the drought resulted from anthropogenic climate change. The drought, which lasted more than five years with peak intensity during the first three, was an extreme event; however, longer-term trends toward warming, reduction of soil moisture, and decreases in precipitation in the Fertile Crescent are also consistent with climate change dynamics in the region.

The drought affected Syria with particular intensity. Agriculture in the northeastern region of Syria—the breadbasket of the country, producing two-thirds of its total cereal output—

collapsed. In 2008, during the driest winter in the country's recorded history, wheat production failed and almost all the livestock was lost. Food prices more than doubled between 2007 and 2008. Unable to afford food, the population in the northeast provinces of Syria experienced a dramatic increase in nutrition-related diseases, and school enrollment dropped by 80 percent in some areas. It is claimed that as many as 1.5 million people were internally displaced in Syria as a result of the drought.

Along with many Iraqi refugees fleeing from the war across the border, the population gravitated to peripheral urban areas. By 2010, 20 percent of Syria's urban population was composed of internally displaced persons and Iraqi refugees. Bereft of options other than illegal settlement and confronted by a combination of overcrowding, an absence of access to basic services, and rampant crime, these peripheral urban areas became the locus of grievances against the state. Dissatisfaction focused on the lack of decisive action on the part of the Syrian government to address the food crisis (Lynch 2016). It was also in these poor, urban areas that Syria witnessed its first demonstrations of the Arab Spring.

Sources: Kelleya et al. 2015; Lynch 2016; Pearlman 2013; Schleussner et al. 2016; von Uexkulla et al. 2016.

patronage systems that distribute favors and privileges to informal networks of elites rather than from formal institutions, international support may simply maintain these systems at the expense of broader institutional reform. In the process, international actors frequently opt for reinforcing these networks—especially when the state maintains them with minimal repression—over pressuring for the long-term reforms needed to ensure greater inclusion. Chapter 6 explores this dilemma further.

Understanding Risk and Opportunity

Different points along the pathways exhibit varying degrees of risk and present

opportunities. The concept of risk has been well developed in the fields of disaster risk management and finance. It is generally understood as the probability of an event combined with the severity of its impact if it does occur (Hammond and Hyslop 2017, 17–18; UN General Assembly 2016b). Risk is mediated by the capacity to manage it. A central premise of the *World Development Report 2011* is that the capacity of institutions provides the necessary buffer for societies to manage risk and navigate conflict without violence (World Bank 2011).

Sometimes, risks can be relatively isolated. More often than not, however, risks are multidimensional and interconnected (box 3.4)— that is, they interact with other risks, which can increase not only the probability of their occurrence, but also their impact if they do occur (Hammond and Hyslop 2017; OECD 2016). A drought can exacerbate food insecurity, which by itself may be manageable. However, if the risk posed by the drought combines with other risks—loss of livelihoods, perceived discrimination in the state response, or the presence of armed groups who can mobilize grievances—the overall risk of violence increases. The more risks are present or the more intense the risks are, the more they can strain the capacity of a society to respond effectively.

All along the pathways, societies experience shocks of different types. A shock is a neutral event. It can be understood simply as a change in the world that brings consequences of some kind (Hammond and Hyslop 2017). A shock may occur suddenly, in the form of a price spike, for example, or could unfold over time, such as a drought.

Most of the time, capable institutions weather shocks and a society stays on a peaceful path. However, in situations where risk is already high or multiple risks are present, shocks can act as triggers by causing a particular effect, such as violence. In these cases, the presence of multiple risks—or very intense risks—and a sudden shock overwhelms the capacity to manage them and triggers violence (box 3.5). For example, rainfall variability in certain climates may pose little risk by itself, but when it coincides with other risks,

---

BOX 3.5 Economic Shocks and Violent Conflict

If not mitigated effectively, economic shocks can act as triggers for violence, especially in settings that are already at high risk. Studies examining the relationship between economic shocks and violent conflict yield mixed findings. Min et al. (2017) reviewed data for 161 countries during the 1995–2015 period and found a significant relationship between economic downturns and the onset of conflict. Similarly, in a study of 44 countries in Africa, Aguirre (2016) found that commodity price shocks had a significant effect on the onset of conflict. Similarly, Calì and Mulabdic (2017), in a study of developing countries between 1960 and 2010, found that an increase in a country's export prices increased the risk of intrastate conflict. However, Bazzi and Blattman (2014), in a global, longitudinal study of all low- and middle-income countries from 1957 to 2007, found that price shocks—even intense shocks in high-risk countries—had no significant effect on outbreak of conflict, but did have a mild, negative impact in countries where violent conflict was ongoing.

Three main theories guide the literature in this area. The "rapacity effect" theory posits that a sharp increase in the price of exports, especially capital-intensive products such as extractives, sparks violence because the benefits of the increase can be more easily appropriated (Bazzi and Blattman 2014). Calì and Mulabdic (2017) find support for this theory, as violence in their sample is more likely to be associated with increases in the price of natural resource exports. Others have argued that whether increased rents provide incentive for violence depends on the extent to which the state can control access to them (the "state-deterrence theory"). If the state exerts control over resources, a price rise generates increased tax revenue, whereas if state control is weak, nonstate armed groups have greater incentive to appropriate resources (Dube and Vargas 2013; Fearon and Laitin 2003). According to the "opportunity cost" theory, economic shocks lower the risk of conflict by increasing the opportunity cost of participating in violence (Collier and Hoeffler 2004; Dal Bo and Dal Bo 2011). This is especially the case with changes in the price of agricultural products, which are more labor-intensive. For example, in Colombia, falling coffee prices were associated with increased violence in regions producing more coffee, while increasing oil prices coincided with higher

(Box continued next page)

levels of violence in municipalities where landowners sought to appropriate oil rents (Dube and Vargas 2013).

Economic shocks are more likely to trigger violence when they are not accompanied by mitigation measures. For example, Calì and Mulabdic (2017) find that countries with strong trading relationships with neighbor countries are less likely to experience violence associated with price shocks. These benefits can be enhanced when accompanied by measures to facilitate trade across borders, such as easing logistics or reducing transaction costs.

In some cases, economic shocks put increased pressure on governments to make up for lost resources. The state may struggle to pay civil servants or security forces or may need to make fiscal adjustments by slashing subsidies, which can cause a rapid increase in the price of basic goods. Accordingly, cuts in subsidies can be accompanied by a properly considered and communicated safety net program to buffer the impacts. Additionally, special provisions or protections may be needed for vulnerable groups, such as internally displaced people or minority groups.

it can undermine the ability of institutions to cope. A study of the relationship between rainfall and civil conflict in 41 African countries between 1981 and 1999 concludes that civil conflict is more likely to occur following years of poor rainfall (Miguel, Satyanath, and Sergenti 2004). If shocks occur when conflict is already under way, they can exacerbate or prolong it (Bazzi and Blattman 2014).

The risks that societies face along their pathways can be exogenous or endogenous. Some *exogenous risks* arise from the systemic trends detailed in chapter 2, including climate change, advancements in information and communication technology (ICT), demographic shifts, or the increase in illicit trafficking. While these risks may originate outside national borders, they exert powerful impacts on national dynamics.

As noted in chapter 1, a key exogenous risk is that an increasing number of conflicts are internationalized, involving the direct assistance of an external state actor. In these situations, the knowledge that outside actors can, or might, intervene at any time influences the incentives of domestic actors to commit to peace or to disrupt stability (World Bank 2011).

Spillover effects of conflict from neighboring countries pose additional risks, including direct incursions from armed groups, increased availability of arms, disruption of trade, and sudden and heavy flows of refugees across borders, among others (Min et al. 2017; World Bank 2011). These risks are more likely to overwhelm the capacity to mitigate them when other endogenous risks are present. In Central Africa, armed groups have exploited areas of weak governance to set up bases, recruit new members, and take advantage of looting opportunities (Raleigh et al. 2010). Likewise, extremist groups have often exploited the existence of internal divisions between identity groups and the lack of consistent or credible state presence to gain territory and support from local populations (ICG 2016). As another example, international illicit trafficking networks often capitalize on internal instability, buying off elites or offering financing to armed groups in exchange for the freedom to operate with impunity (Comolli 2017).

Institutional capacity can mitigate the impact of exogenous risks. For example, in Nicaragua, security reforms and relatively inclusive institutions built during the war and postwar period have been credited with stemming the influence of international drug trafficking networks in that country compared with its neighbors (Cruz 2011).[7] As another example, Calì and Mulabdic (2017) show that price shocks are less likely to coincide with violence when the country enjoys strong trade relationships with neighboring countries. This effect is enhanced when governments take measures to facilitate trade—for example, by easing tariffs or logistics costs—and when trade policy is informed by analysis of the distribution of gains and losses across society, with specific focus on whether trade exacerbates existing societal cleavages.

Endogenous risks to peaceful pathways tend to emanate from relationships among actors and often involve the state in some way. Perhaps not surprising, grievances tend to arise in arenas where access to power, resources, and security is negotiated. Chapter 5 includes a rich discussion of these arenas and the risks and opportunities present in them.

Some of the most powerful *endogenous risks* relate to social, economic, and political exclusion of different social groups (box 3.6). Exclusionary systems that are perceived to privilege some groups at the expense of others[8] create fertile ground for violence. This is underscored by a growing body of literature arguing that policies promoting inclusion are a source of stability and legitimacy (Barnett 2006; Brinkerhoff 2007; Call 2008; Chesterman, Ignatieff, and Thakur 2004; Fukuyama 2004; Ghani and Lockhart 2008; Keating and Knight 2004; Stewart et al. 2006).

Cross-country studies consistently identify policies to promote inclusion as a key factor reducing the risk of violence. Collier and Hoeffler (2004) find that stronger economic performance has a pacifying effect on countries by creating greater economic interdependence across groups. Call (2012, 99) applied mixed methods to study the causes

of conflict recurrence in 15 countries, identifying exclusionary policies and behavior as the most important causal factor in 11 cases and chronic exclusion as important in 2 of the 15, concluding that exclusion is the "consistently most important" factor in violence relapse. Hegre et al. (2016) examined data from all countries between 1960 and 2013, drawing on the UCDP data set and on a set of five scenarios for policy choices drawn from the Shared Socio-Economic Pathways initiative (O'Neill et al. 2014), predicting that countries with higher levels of inequality face greater challenges in mitigating the risk of conflict as well as those associated with climate change. Similarly, Min et al. (2017) find that countries with policies to increase the participation of previously excluded groups, to influence government policy, and to increase political engagement during economic downturns experience less conflict. These findings build on prior work by Fearon (2010) and Fearon and Laitin (2013) emphasizing the importance of inclusive governance to mitigating the risk of conflict.

Gender inclusion, in particular, shows a robust, empirical relationship with peace, from the local to the international level (Caprioli and Tumbore 2003; Caprioli et al. 2007; Herbert 2017; Hudson et al. 2009). Governments of countries with more equitable gender relations, as measured by levels of violence against women, labor market participation, and income disparities, for example, are significantly less likely to initiate interstate conflict or escalate civil conflict (Hudson et al. 2012). In contrast, countries with higher levels of gender

BOX 3.6 Inclusion and Risk

Inclusion defies easy measurement. This study follows the World Bank's definition of inclusion as "the process of improving the ability, opportunity, and dignity of people, disadvantaged on the basis of their identity, to take part in society" (World Bank 2013, 7). This definition privileges identity as the source of discrimination,

drawing on the work of Stewart (2000, 2002, 2009), which notes that the more rigid identities are in a society, the harder it is for an individual to move across identity groups and the greater the chance for group-based discrimination and thus for grievances to accumulate. This subject is explored further in chapter 4.

inequality are associated not only with increased risk of international or civil war, but also with higher levels of violence in conflict (Caprioli and Boyer 2001).

Inclusion of youth also strongly affects a society's pathway. Societies that offer youth opportunities to participate in the political and economic realms and routes for social mobility tend to experience less violence (Idris 2016; Paasonen and Urdal 2016). With the youth population increasing globally, the ability to harness the energy and potential of youth presents a strong opportunity to realize a "demographic dividend" (UN Security Council 2016b). This topic is explored in depth in chapter 4.

Other forms of exclusion that heighten the risk of conflict relate to relationships between central states and populations located on geographic or political peripheries within a state. Subnational conflicts of this nature are on the rise in various regions, especially Asia, Europe, and the Middle East as well as Sub-Saharan Africa (Colletta and Oppenheim 2017; Parks, Colletta, and Oppenheim 2013). These conflicts tend to revolve around center-periphery tensions, with a subregion opposing a state-building project or responding to exclusion from political and economic systems. They are increasingly common in middle-income countries (World Bank 2016).

Center-periphery tensions tend to be rooted in historical patterns of exclusion and are therefore heavily entrenched in state institutions. For a variety of reasons, states often deem the costs of integrating peripheral regions via improved infrastructure or services to be too high for the potential benefits it could bring (Keister 2014). Some peripheral regions continue to receive minimal investment as part of colonial legacies of neglect of certain areas that were previously buffer zones between rival powers. In many cases, populations in peripheral areas are minorities with strong, separate cultural identities, who were forcibly incorporated into national structures during moments of state consolidation. In these cases, populations may resist efforts by the state to forge a national identity or to consolidate power as existential threats to

ethnic identity (Parks, Colletta, and Oppenheim 2013).

Exclusion along center-periphery lines not only fuels conflict with the state, but also creates fertile ground for other forms of violence to emerge and escalate, including localized intercommunal and intra-elite violence. In some cases, center-periphery conflicts have become interlinked with cross-border violence and large-scale internationalized conflicts as well (Colletta and Oppenheim 2017; Parks, Colletta, and Oppenheim 2013).

Many peripheral regions fall into the category of "alternatively governed spaces" as discussed in box 3.3. In these cases, integration efforts can exacerbate instability if they disturb the existing power balances between the vested interests in peripheral regions (Keister 2014).

Prevention and Sustaining Peace: Building Peaceful Pathways

Understanding the pathways and the ways in which risk and opportunity manifest along them helps to better define prevention. At its core, prevention is the process of influencing systems so that it is *easier* for actors to forge a pathway toward peace, by reinforcing the elements of the system pulling toward peace and mitigating the elements that push it toward violent conflict. This proactive approach is in line with the 2030 Agenda for Sustainable Development and the UN sustaining peace resolutions. Consistent with the framework of the *World Development Report 2017*, prevention requires a rethinking of the process in which state and nonstate actors make decisions and negotiate different outcomes to create the mechanisms needed for them to commit, cooperate, and coordinate along peaceful pathways (World Bank 2017).

Effective prevention requires a delicate balancing of efforts to address risks that may provoke crises in the short term, while maintaining the necessary attention to deeper structural and institutional risks. Many times, immediate measures are needed to manage shocks or alter the calculus of actors—a cease-fire, an elite bargain, or sanctions to prevent violence from escalating. The challenge for all societies is to monitor and mitigate these risks, while not losing sight of the sustained investments in institutional reform and addressing the underlying risks, especially those associated with inequalities and exclusion. These underlying risks are taken up in more detail in chapter 4.

Addressing underlying risks and enhancing the capacity to mitigate shocks entail tackling institutional reform. Risk and opportunity tend to accumulate in critical spaces, which this study calls arenas of contestation, where access to power, resources, services, and security are determined. Institutional reform is the entry point for addressing risk in the arenas; this issue is discussed in detail in chapter 5. As chapter 6 explains, all countries that significantly reduced violent conflict eventually undertook institutional reform to manage risk.

Drawing on the framework presented here, five key implications are evident:

First, prevention entails promoting favorable structural conditions, where possible, by fostering a social and political environment where the deeper drivers of conflict can be addressed (Giessmann, Galvanek, and Seifert 2017). As chapter 4 argues, many of today's conflicts are rooted in perceptions of exclusion related to inequalities across groups. Addressing these and the narratives that often form around them is critical. The 2030 Agenda provides a framework for addressing some of these issues.

Second, prevention means shaping incentives for peace. This can happen both through institutions, as they change their rules and policies, and through key decisions by influential actors. As noted earlier, broad institutional changes often take years, if not decades. That said, sometimes measures that signal bigger changes can send powerful messages to the population and influence the behavior of actors quickly, even if the reforms take much longer to take full effect. Domestic institutions play a central role here, both in mitigating conflict and in sanctioning violent behavior. For example, governments

have sent strong messages of change by announcing power-sharing arrangements or nominating a member of an opposition party to the governing administration, adopting reforms that equalize spending across geographic regions, or launching new grievance-redress mechanisms (World Bank 2011). Chapter 5 develops this argument in more detail.

Third, actions that influence short-term decisions by actors are a very important part of a prevention strategy. Decisions by actors alter incentive structures. Mediation efforts can immediately influence the calculus of armed actors, encouraging them to commit to a cease-fire or peace settlement, for example. These are especially important in conveying a change in direction in situations where violence has already escalated and addressing the short-term incentives for violence during a crisis. Promoting peaceful narratives can also play a big role in creating incentives for peace, as chapter 4 explains. Chapter 6 explores how domestic actors have mobilized incentives for peacebuilding.

Fourth, shaping incentives for peace also requires a strong focus on arenas where access to power, resources, and security are contested. These arenas define who has access to political power and representation, natural resources (in particular, land and extractives), security and justice, and basic services. Because existing power dynamics determine access to these arenas, prevention means making the arenas more inclusive, particularly to groups that have traditionally been left out of decision-making processes, especially women and youth. However, as chapter 5 notes, reform in the arenas is often fraught with setbacks and backlashes, as groups who hold power do not often relinquish it easily.

Fifth, systemic prevention is very important. In today's globalized world, systemic trends like climate change, demographic shifts, advancements in ICT, and the rise of transnational criminal networks present risks and opportunities that must be managed carefully. It is necessary to energize global coalitions to tackle systemic risks and take advantage of the opportunities posed by today's global trends. This subject is discussed further in chapter 8.

Scenarios for Pathways to Peace or Violence

Effective prevention has a strong temporal dimension. Not everything can—or should—be done at once. Rather, the scale and nature of prevention changes along a society's pathway. Prevention requires flexibility, adaptability, and a good sense of the right timing and sequencing. Prevention also relies on systematic monitoring of risks and their potential interactions, in order to address underlying and emerging risks and preempt and manage shocks.

Every decision point along the pathway presents trade-offs that must be managed carefully. For example, stability and a ceasefire today can open the space for movement toward a sustainable peace in the future. Likewise, short-term crisis prevention to avert violence may postpone, or even undermine, efforts to make the structural changes for sustained peace. Long-term efforts to develop institutions and mechanisms that will systematically address previously identified social, economic, and political factors contributing to conflict and create resilience toward outbreaks of collective violence should be done in parallel with identifying and providing timely response to emerging risks. Ideally, prevention efforts represent a continuum of mutually reinforcing actions, from early monitoring and action on risks, to consistent strengthening of social resilience to invest in peace for future generations.

In *environments of emerging risks*, the greatest number of options are still on the table, and medium- to long-term policies can have an important impact. For domestic actors, dealing with underlying and emerging risks entails development planning that will address structural imbalances contributing to social polarization and establishing inclusive systems of risk assessment and response. The 2030 Agenda provides multiple entry points to address several risks. To ensure sustainability of these efforts, the reform of existing legislation and institutions and,

potentially, the creation of new ones are needed to bolster resilience against risk of violence. Institutional safeguards can enable the monitoring of grievances and their potential for mobilization as well as efforts to address violence and norms that tolerate it, especially against at-risk groups, such as women, children, and minorities. However, prevention may be more difficult to sell politically because actors see the payoffs as relatively low.

Among the international actors, development actors have the widest space to maneuver in environments with emerging risks because the security situation has not deteriorated to the extent that it limits their activities. To address underlying and emerging risk, indicators of conflict risk can be embedded within broader monitoring of macroeconomic trends, paying special attention to countries with structural factors associated with risk of violence, such as high dependence on aid or natural resources. In these moments, conflict-sensitive development policies will have the most impact in mitigating the risk of violence. International political and security actors have a smaller presence in these environments.

In *high-risk contexts*, risks have intensified or compounded to the point that they are picked up by early warning systems. For domestic actors, the incentives for violence are tangible, and the opportunity costs for engaging in violence are decreasing. Meanwhile, the incentives to reverse course are less evident, contributing to an overall environment of uncertainty. In these situations, a failure to prevent violence can lead to permanent losses in social and economic development. This is where diplomatic efforts and local-level mediation are central, but development action can also play a strong role by signaling willingness by the state to change its stance and restore confidence among the population. Do-no-harm, conflict-sensitive approaches take on greater salience in these situations.

In *contexts of open violence*, preventing escalation of violence takes priority. In many cases, efforts are focused on mitigating the impact of violence on civilians, the economy, and state institutions—once a state has collapsed or atrocities have been committed, violence is often irreversible in the short term. In these situations, development actors often halt or cease operations in high-risk areas; yet, maintaining development projects is critical for buffering populations against the risk of violence. In these moments, it is critical for development actors to identify ways to work through local partners and to employ more flexible delivery systems, in order to ensure a minimum of basic service delivery.

Finally, in *contexts where violence is halted*, preventing recurrence is paramount. This is the time where the window of opportunity reopens, providing some space for structural factors to be addressed and institutions to be rebuilt. However, the forces of path dependence remain strong. During this time, it is essential to restore trust and confidence by rebuilding the core functions of the state. Often, reforms are needed in arenas of contestation where conflict has played out (for example, land or security sector reform). Attention needs to be given to addressing the grievances of particular groups, especially those mobilized during the conflict, including former combatants, as well as to the processes of accountability and reconciliation, including the prosecution of war crimes. Taking on illicit economies that can fuel the resurgence of conflict is also essential, though more likely to be effective through global coalitions.

Preventing recurrence in conflict-affected environments requires sustained attention and resources from international actors, because conflict has, in most cases, overwhelmed the capacity and legitimacy of many domestic actors to take the actions needed to address conflict drivers. Preventing recurrence is where special financing facilities can have an important impact.

Conclusion

Investing in prevention of violent conflict requires a long-term view of how violent conflict emerges and evolves in societies in order to identify and act on appropriate entry points. The organizing framework presented here helps to define how societies shape unique pathways toward different outcomes as they manage the forces pushing for peace or violence. The pathway is formed by the decisions of actors, who respond to the structural factors and incentives present in society.

Within this framework, prevention is a process of building systems where actors are more likely to choose peaceful pathways, by taking advantage of favorable structural factors or mitigating the impacts of unfavorable ones, building incentive structures that encourage peace, and containing violence when it does occur. The longer and more intentionally a society has built a path toward peace, the higher the probability that it will stay on that path. The scope and nature of possible actions changes along the pathway, in response to the risks and opportunities that are present at different moments.

Drawing on this understanding of violence, prevention of violence, and risk, the study turns next to a deeper discussion of some of the factors and processes that often push actors toward violence. In particular, understanding the relationships among groups in a society and their perceptions of whether they are treated fairly is key to understanding the risk of violence. Chapter 4 looks deeply at what makes people fight and the importance of exclusion, inequality, and perceptions of unfairness.

Notes

1. See UN General Assembly (2015, 2016a) and UN Security Council (2016a).
2. Comparing the historical periods of pre- and post-1945, Fearon and Laitin (2013) find that the experience of an "extra-state" (imperial or colonial) war pre-1945 is associated with an increase in the occurrence of intrastate war in later years. Intrastate war pre-1945 was not associated with violent conflict after 1945.
3. A cognitive tax is a metaphor for stresses that compromise mental resources.
4. On Latin America, see Briscoe, Perdomo, and Burcher (2014); on Afghanistan, see Felbab-Brown (2017).

5. In Peter Evans' formulation, "informal structures of power and practice render the formal structures ineffectual" (Evans 2004).

6. For sake of convenience, international private sector actors are discussed together with domestic private sector actors in the "private sector" section of this chapter.

7. Drug flows have increased through Nicaragua in recent years, calling the long-term sustainability of this situation into question.

8. Galtung (1969) defines these conditions as "structural violence."

References

Aguirre, A. 2016. "Fiscal Policy and Civil Conflict in Africa." Paper prepared as part of the World Bank Regional Study, *Africa's Macroeconomic Vulnerabilities,* World Bank, Washington, DC. http://alvaroaguirre .weebly.com/uploads/1/3/2/9/13298570/pf _conflict.pdf.

Anderlini, S. N. 2007. *Women Building Peace: What They Do; Why It Matters.* Boulder, CO: Lynne Rienner.

Antil, A. 2011. "*Mali et Mauritanie, pays sahéliens fragiles et Etats résilients.*" *Revue Politique Etrangère* 2011/1 (Spring): 59. https://www .cairn.info/revue-politique-etrangere-2011- 1-page-59.htm.

Arias, E. D. 2013. "The Impacts of Differential Armed Dominance of Politics in Rio de Janeiro, Brazil." *Studies in Comparative International Development* 48 (3): 263–84.

Aslam, G. 2017. "Civic Associations and Conflict Prevention: Potential, Challenges, and Opportunities—A Review of the Literature." Background paper for the United Nations–World Bank Flagship Study, *Pathways for Peace: Inclusive Approaches to Preventing Violent Conflict,* World Bank, Washington, DC.

Barnes, C. 2009. "Civil Society and Peacebuilding: Mapping Functions in Working for Peace." *International Spectator* 44 (1): 131–47.

Barnett, M. 2006. "Building a Republican Peace: Stabilizing States after War." *International Security* 30 (4): 87–112.

Barnett, M., and C. Zurcher. 2010. "The Peacebuilder's Contract." In *The Dilemmas of Statebuilding,* edited by R. Paris and T. Sisk, 23–52. London: Routledge.

Barron, P., M. Woolcock, and R. Diprose. 2011. *Contesting Development: Participatory Projects and Local Conflict Dynamics in Indonesia.* New Haven, CT: Yale University Press.

Bazzi, S., and C. Blattman. 2014. "Economic Shocks and Conflict: Evidence from Commodity Prices." *American Economic Journal: Macroeconomics* 6 (4): 1–38.

Benford, R. D., and D. A. Snow. 2000. "Framing Processes and Social Movements: An Overview and Assessment." *Annual Review of Sociology* 26 (August): 611–39.

Blattman, C., and E. Miguel. 2010. "Civil War." *Journal of Economic Literature* 48 (1): 3–57.

Bøås, M. 2015. *The Politics of Conflict Economies: Miners, Merchants and Warriors in the African Borderland.* New York: Routledge.

Bøås, M., S. S. Eriksen, T. Gade, J. H. S. Lie, and O. J. Sending. 2017. "Conflict Prevention and Ownership: Limits and Opportunities for External Actors." Background paper for the United Nations–World Bank Flagship Study, *Pathways for Peace: Inclusive Approaches to Preventing Violent Conflict,* World Bank, Washington, DC.

Boix, C., and D. Posner. 1996. "Making Social Capital Work: A Review of Robert Putnam's 'Making Democracy Work: Civic Traditions in Modern Italy.'" Weatherhead Center for International Affairs, Harvard University, Cambridge, MA. https://wcfia.harvard.edu /publications/making-social-capital-work -review-robert-putnams-making-democracy -work-civic.

Boudet, A. M. M., P. Petesch, C. Turk, and A. Thumala. 2012. *On Norms and Agency Conversations about Gender Equality with Women and Men in 20 Countries.* Washington, DC: World Bank.

Brinkerhoff, D. W. 2007. *Capacity Development in Fragile States.* European Centre for Development Policy Management, Maastricht.

———. 2011. "State Fragility and Governance: Conflict Mitigation and Subnational Perspectives." *Development Policy Review* 29 (2): 131–53.

Brinkerhoff, D., and A. Goldsmith. 2005. "Institutional Dualism and International Development. A Revisionist Interpretation of Good Governance." *Administration and Society* 37 (2): 199–224.

Briscoe, I., C. Perdomo, and C. U. Burcher, eds. 2014. *Illicit Networks and Politics in Latin America.* Stockholm: International IDEA; The Hague: Clingendael Institute; and The Hague: Netherlands Institute for Multiparty

Democracy. https://www.idea.int/sites/default /files/publications/illicit-networks-and -politics-in-latin-america.pdf.

Calì, M., and A. Mulabdic. 2017. "Trade and Civil Conflict: Revisiting the Cross-Country Evidence." Policy Research Working Paper 7125. World Bank, Washington, DC.

Call, C. 2008. "Knowing Peace When You See it: Setting Standards for Peacebuilding Success." *Civil Wars* 10 (2): 173–94.

———. 2012. *Why Peace Fails: The Causes and Prevention of Civil War Recurrence.* Washington, DC: Georgetown University Press.

Campbell, B. 2002. *Blood Diamonds: Tracing the Deadly Path of the World's Most Precious Stones.* Boulder, CO: Westview Press.

Caprioli, M., and M. Boyer. 2001. "Gender, Violence, and International Crisis." *Journal of Conflict Resolution* 45 (4): 503–18.

Caprioli, M., V. Hudson, R. McDermott, C. Emmett, and B. Ballif-Spanvill. 2007. "Putting Women in Their Place." *Baker Journal of Applied Public Policy* 1 (1): 12–22.

Caprioli, M., and P. F. Tumbore. 2003. "Ethnic Discrimination and Interstate Violence: Testing the International Impact of Domestic Behavior." *Journal of Peace Research* 40 (1): 5–23.

Chenoweth, E., and M. Stephan. 2011. *Why Civil Resistance Works: The Strategic Logic of Nonviolent Conflict.* New York: Columbia University Press.

Chesterman, S., M. Ignatieff, and R. Thakur. 2004. *Making States Work: State Failure and the Crisis of Governance.* Tokyo: United Nations University Press.

Clunan, A., and H. A. Trinkunas. 2010. *Ungoverned Spaces: Alternatives to State Authority in an Era of Softened Sovereignty.* Stanford, CA: Stanford University Press.

Cockayne, J. 2016. *The Hidden Power. The Strategic Logic of Organized Crime.* London: C. Hurst.

Colletta, N., and B. Oppenheim. 2017. "Subnational Conflict: Dimensions, Trends, and Options for Prevention." Background paper for the United Nations–World Bank Flagship Study, *Pathways for Peace: Inclusive Approaches to Preventing Violent Conflict.* World Bank, Washington, DC.

Collier, P., V. L. Elliott, H. Hegre, A. Hoeffler, M. Reynal-Querol, and N. Sambanis. 2003. *Breaking the Conflict Trap: Civil War and Development Policy.* Washington, DC: World Bank and Oxford University Press.

Collier, P., and A. Hoeffler. 2004. "Greed and Grievance in Civil War." *Oxford Economic Papers* 56 (4): 563–95.

Comolli, V. 2017. "Transnational Organized Crime and Conflict." Background paper for the United Nations–World Bank Flagship Study, *Pathways for Peace: Inclusive Approaches to Preventing Violent Conflict,* World Bank, Washington, DC.

Crespo-Sancho, C. 2017. "Conflict Prevention and Gender." Background paper for the United Nations–World Bank Flagship Study, *Pathways for Peace: Inclusive Approaches to Preventing Violent Conflict,* World Bank, Washington, DC.

Cruz, J. M. 2011. "Criminal Violence and Democratization in Central America: The Survival of the Violent State." *Latin American Politics and Society* 53 (4): 1–33.

Dahl, M., S. Gates, and H. M. Nygård. 2017. "Securing the Peace." Background paper for the United Nations–World Bank Flagship Study, *Pathways for Peace: Inclusive Approaches to Preventing Violent Conflict,* World Bank, Washington, DC.

Dahlgren, P. 2015. "Internet as Civic Space." In *Handbook of Digital Politics,* edited by S. Coleman and D. Freelon. Cheltenham: Elgin.

Dal Bo, E., and P. Dal Bo. 2011. "Workers, Warriors, and Criminals: Social Conflict in General Equilibrium." *Journal of the European Economic Association* 9 (4): 646–77.

Dube, O., and J. Vargas. 2013. "Commodity Price Shocks and Civil Conflict: Evidence from Colombia." *Review of Economic Studies* 80 (4, October 1): 1384–421.

Dupuy, K., S. Gates, H. M. Nygård, I. Rudolfsen, S. A. Rustad, H. Strand, and H. Urdal. 2017. "Trends in Armed Conflict 1946–2016." PRIO Conflict Trends 02/2017. Peace Reaearch Institue Oslo. https://www.prio .org/utility/DownloadFile.ashx?id=1373 &type=publicationfile.

Easterly, W., J. Ritzen, and M. Woolcock. 2006. "Social Cohesion, Institutions, and Growth." Working Paper 94, Center for Global Development, Washington, DC.

Elias, N. 1982. *The Civilizing Process.* Vol. 2: *State Formation and Civilisation.* Oxford: Blackwell.

Englebert, P., and D. Tüll. 2008. "Postconflict Reconstruction in Africa: Flawed Ideas about

Failed States." *International Security* 32 (4): 106–39.

Evans, P. 2004. "Development as Institutional Change: The Pitfalls of Monocropping and the Potentials of Deliberation." *Studies in Comparative International Development* 38(4): 30–52.

Faustino, J., and D. Booth. 2014. *Development Entrepreneurship: How Donors and Leaders Can Foster Institutional Change.* London: Overseas Development Institute. http://www .odi.org/publications/9118-development -entrepreneurship.

Fearon, J. 2010. "Governance and Civil War Onset." Background paper for *World Development Report 2011: Conflict, Security, and Development,* World Bank, Washington, DC.

Fearon, J., and D. Laitin. 2003. "Ethnicity, Insurgency, and Civil War." *American Political Science Review* 97 (1): 75–90.

———. 2013. "How Persistent Is Armed Conflict?" Working Paper, Empirical Studies of Conflict. Stanford University, Stanford, CA.

Felbab-Brown, V. 2017. "How to Break Political-Criminal Alliances in Contexts of Transition." Crime-Conflict Nexus 7, United Nations University, Centre for Policy Research Crime, Tokyo.

Fukuyama, F. 2004. *State-Building: Governance and World Order in the 21st Century.* Ithaca: Cornell University Press.

Galtung, J. 1969. "Violence, Peace and Peace Research." *Journal of Peace Research* 6 (3): 167–91.

Ghani, A., and C. Lockhart. 2008. *Fixing Failed States.* Oxford, U.K.: Oxford University Press.

Giessmann, H. J., J. Galvanek, and C. Seifert. 2017. "Curbing Violence Development, Application, and the Sustaining of National Capacities for Conflict Prevention." Background paper for the United Nations–World Bank Flagship Study, *Pathways for Peace: Inclusive Approaches to Preventing Violent Conflict,* World Bank, Washington, DC.

Goldstein, J., and J. Rotich. 2008. *Digitally Networked Technology in Kenya's 2007–2008 Post-Election Crisis.* Cambridge, MA: Berkman Klein Center for Internet and Society. http:// cyber.harvard.edu/sites/cyber.harvard.edu /files/Goldstein&Rotich_Digitally_Net worked_Technology_Kenyas_Crisis.pdf.pdf.

Grémont, C. 2012. "Villages and Crossroads. Changing Territorialities among the Tuareg of Northern Mali." In *Saharan Frontiers,* edited by J. McDougall and J. Scheele. Bloomington: Indiana University Press.

Guichaoua, Y., and M. Pellerin. 2017. "Faire la paix et construire l'etat: Les relations entre pouvoir central et périphéries sahéliennes au Niger et au Mali." Study 51, Institute de Recherche Stratégique de l'Ecole Militaire (IRSEM), Paris. http://www.defense.gouv.fr /content/download/509288/8603319/file /Etude_IRSEM_n51_2017.pdf.

Gurr, T. R. 1970. *Why Men Rebel.* Princeton, NJ: Princeton University Press.

Halliday, T. C., and G. Shaffer. 2015. *Transnational Legal Orders.* Cambridge Studies in Law and Society. Cambridge, U.K.: Cambridge University.

Hameiri, S. 2007. "Failed State or a Failed Paradigm? State Capacity and the Limits of Institutionalism." *Journal of International Relations and Development* 10 (2): 122–49.

Hammond, D., and D. Hyslop. 2017. "Understanding Multi-Dimensional Risks and Violent Conflict Lessons for Prevention." Background paper for the United Nations–World Bank Flagship Study, *Pathways for Peace: Inclusive Approaches to Preventing Violent Conflict,* World Bank, Washington, DC.

Hegre, H., H. Buhaug, K. V. Calvin, J. Nordkvelle, S. T. Waldhoff, and E. Gilmore. 2016. "Forecasting Civil Conflict along the Shared Socioeconomic Pathways." *Environmental Research Letters* 11 (5): 054002.

Hegre, H., and N. Sambanis. 2006. "Sensitivity Analysis of Empirical Results on Civil War Onset." *Journal of Conflict Resolution* 50 (4): 508–35

Herbert, S. 2017. *Links between Women's Empowerment (or Lack of) and Outbreaks of Violent Conflict.* Birmingham, U.K.: University of Birmingham.

Hudson, V., B. Ballif-Spanvill, M. Caprioli, and C. Emmett. 2012. *Sex and World Peace.* New York: Columbia University Press.

Hudson, V., M. Caprioli, B. Ballif-Spanvill, R. McDermott, and C. Emmett. 2009. "The Heart of the Matter: The Security of Women and the Security of States." *International Security* 33 (3): 7–45. doi:10.1162/isec.2009 .33.3.7.

Human Rights Watch. 1999. *Leave None to Tell the Story: Genocide in Rwanda.* https://www. hrw.org/reports/1999/rwanda/Geno4-7-03. htm.

Huntington, S. 1968. *Political Order in Changing Societies*. New Haven, CT: Yale University Press.

ICG (International Crisis Group). 2014. *Reform or Relapse*. Africa Report 201. Brussels: ICG. https://d2071andvip0wj.cloudfront.net/mali -reform-or-relapse.pdf.

———. 2016. "Exploiting Disorder: Al-Qaeda and the Islamic State." Special Report 1, ICG, Brussels.

Idris, I. 2016. *Youth Unemployment and Violence: Rapid Literature Review*. Birmingham, U.K.: GSDRC, University of Birmingham.

IFC (International Finance Corporation). 2018. *Private Enterprises in Conflict-Related Situations*. Washington, DC: World Bank.

Jones, B., M. Elgin-Cossart, and J. Esberg. 2012. *Pathways Out of Fragility: The Case for a Research Agenda on Inclusive Political Settlements in Fragile States*. New York: Centre for International Cooperation.

Keating, T. F., and W. A. Knight. 2004. *Building Sustainable Peace*. Tokyo: United Nations University Press.

Keister, J. 2014. "The Illusion of Chaos: Why Ungoverned Spaces Aren't Ungoverned, and Why that Matters." Policy Analysis 766, Cato Institute, Washington, DC.

Kelleya, C. P., S. Mohtadib, M. A. Canec, R. Seagerc, and Y. Kushnirc. 2015. "Climate Change in the Fertile Crescent and Implications of the Recent Syrian Drought." *Proceedings of the National Academy of Sciences* 112 (11): 3241–46.

Kelly, J. 2017. "Intimate Partner Violence and Conflict: Understanding the Links between Political Violence and Personal Violence." Background paper for the United Nations–World Bank Flagship Study, *Pathways for Peace: Inclusive Approaches to Preventing Violent Conflict*, World Bank, Washington, DC.

Kemp, W., M. Shaw, and A. Boutellis. 2013. *The Elephant in the Room: How Can Peace Operations Deal with Organized Crime?* New York: International Peace Institute.

King, M. L., Jr. 1963. "Letter from a Birmingham Jail." Stanford University, Stanford, CA. https://kinginstitute.stanford.edu/king -papers/documents/letter-birmingham-jail.

Lakhani, S., and A. Willman. 2014. "Gates, Hired Guns and Mistrust—Business Unusual: The Cost of Crime and Violence to Businesses in Papua New Guinea." Working Paper 88544, World Bank, Washington, DC.

Lynch, M. 2016. *The New Arab Wars. Uprisings and Anarchy in the Middle East*. New York: Perseus Group.

MacGinty, R. 2010. "Hybrid Peace: The Interaction between Top-Down and Bottom-Up Peace." *Security Dialogue* 41 (4): 391–412.

Mani, A., S. Mullainathan, E. Shafir, and J. Zhao. 2013. "Poverty Impedes Cognitive Function." *Science* 341 (6149): 976–80.

Marc, A., A. Willman, G. Aslam, M. Rebosio, and K. Balasuriya. 2012. *Societal Dynamics and Fragility: Engaging Societies in Responding to Fragile Situations*. New Frontiers of Social Policy. Washington, DC: World Bank.

Mcloughlin, C. 2015. "When Does Service Delivery Improve the Legitimacy of a Fragile or Conflict-Affected State?" *Governance: An International Journal of Policy, Administration, and Institutions* 28 (3): 341–56.

Menkhaus, K., and J. N. Shapiro. 2010. "Non-State Actors and Failed States: Lessons from Al-Qa'ida's Experiences in the Horn of Africa." In *Ungoverned Spaces: Alternatives to State Authority in an Era of Softened Sovereignty*, edited by A. Clunan and H. A. Trinkunas. Stanford, CA: Stanford University Press.

Miguel, E., S. Satyanath, and E. Sergenti. 2004. "Economic Shocks and Civil Conflict: An Instrumental Variables Approach." *Journal of Political Economy* 112 (4): 725–53.

Min, E., M. Singh, J. N. Shapiro, and B. Crisman. 2017. "Understanding Risk and Resilience to Violent Conflicts." Background paper for the United Nations–World Bank Flagship Study, *Pathways for Peace: Inclusive Approaches to Preventing Violent Conflict*, World Bank, Washington, DC.

Mueller, H. 2017. "How Much Is Prevention Worth?" Background paper for the United Nations–World Bank Flagship Study, *Pathways for Peace: Inclusive Approaches to Preventing Violent Conflict*, World Bank, Washington, DC.

Mullainathan, S., and E. Shafir. 2013. *Scarcity: Why Having Too Little Means So Much*. New York: Times Books.

Narayan, D., R. Chambers, M. K. Shah, and P. Petesch. 2000. *Voices of the Poor: Crying Out for Change*. Washington, DC: World Bank.

Nezam, T. 2017. "Alternatively Governed Spaces." Background paper for the United Nations–World Bank Flagship Study, *Pathways for*

Peace: Inclusive Approaches to Preventing Violent Conflict, World Bank, Washington, DC.

Nilsson, D. 2012. "Anchoring the Peace: Civil Society Actors in Peace Accords and Durable Peace." *International Interactions* 38 (2): 258.

North, D. 1990. *Institutions, Institutional Change, and Economic Progress*. Cambridge, U.K.: Cambridge University Press.

North, D. C., J. J. Wallis, and B. R. Weingast. 2009. *Violence and Social Orders*. Cambridge, U.K.: Cambridge University Press.

OECD (Organisation for Economic Co-operation and Development). 2016. *States of Fragility*. Geneva: OECD.

O'Neill, B. C., E. Kriegler, K. Riahi, K. L. Ebi, S. Hallegatte, T. R. Carter, R. Mathur, and D. P. van Vuuren. 2014. "A New Scenario Framework for Climate Change Research: The Concept of Shared Socioeconomic Pathways." *Climate Change* 122 (3): 387–400.

O'Reilly, M., A. Ó Súilleabháin, and T. Paffenholz. 2015. *Reimagining Peacemaking: Women's Roles in Peace Processes*. New York: International Peace Institute.

Østby, G. 2008. "Inequalities, the Political Environment, and Civil Conflict: Evidence from 55 Developing Countries." In *Horizontal Inequalities and Conflict: Understanding Group Violence in Multiethnic Societies*, edited by F. Stewart, 252–81. London: Palgrave Macmillan UK

Paasonen, K., and H. Urdal. 2016. "Youth Bulges, Exclusion and Instability: The Role of Youth in the Arab Spring." PRIO Conflict Trends. Prevention Research Institute Oslo, March.

Paffenholz, T., A. Hirblinger, D. Landau, F. Fritsch, and C. Dijkstra. 2017. "Preventing Violence through Inclusion: From Building Political Momentum to Sustaining Peace." Background paper for the United Nations–World Bank Flagship Study, *Pathways for Peace: Inclusive Approaches to Preventing Violent Conflicts*, World Bank, Washington, DC.

Parks, T., N. Colletta, and B. Oppenheim. 2013. *The Contested Corners of Asia: Subnational Conflict and International Development Assistance*. San Francisco, CA: The Asia Foundation.

Patrick, S. M. 2010. "Are Ungoverned Spaces a Threat?" *Foreign Affairs*, January 11.

Pearlman, W. 2013. "Emotions and the Microfoundations of the Arab Uprisings." *Perspectives on Politics* 11 (2): 387–409.

Peschka, M. 2011. "The Role of the Private Sector in Fragile and Conflict-Affected States." Background paper for *World Development Report 2011: Conflict, Security, and Development*, World Bank, Washington, DC.

Poppe, A. E., and J. Wolff. 2017. "The Contested Spaces of Civil Society in a Plural World: Norm Contestation in the Debate about Restrictions on International Civil Society Support." *Contemporary Politics* 23 (4): 468–88.

Posner, D. 2004. "Civil Society and the Reconstruction of Failed States." In *When States Fail: Causes and Consequences*, edited by R. I. Rotberg. Princeton, NJ: Princeton University Press.

Pritchett, L., and F. de Weijer. 2010. "Fragile States: Stuck in a Capability Trap?" Background paper for the *World Development Report 2011: Conflict, Security, and Development*, World Bank, Washington, DC.

Rabasa, A., S. Boraz, P. Chalk, K. Cragin, T. W. Karasik, J. D. P. Moroney, K. A. O'Brien, and J. E. Peet. 2007. *Ungoverned Territories: Understanding and Reducing Terrorism Risks*. Santa Monica, CA: Rand Corporation.

Raleigh, C., and C. Dowd. 2013. "Governance and Conflict in the Sahel's 'Ungoverned Space.'" *Stability: International Journal of Security and Development* 2 (2): Art. 32.

Raleigh, C., A. Linke, H. Hegre, and J. Carlsen. 2010. "Introducing ACLED: An Armed Conflict Location and Event Dataset." *Journal of Peace Research* 47 (5): 651–60.

Raleigh, C., and H. Urdal. 2007. "Climate Change, Environmental Degradation, and Armed Conflict." *Political Geography* 26 (6): 674–94.

Rettberg, M. 2015. *Gold, Oil and the Lure of Violence: The Private Sector and Post-Conflict Risks in Colombia*. The Hague: Clingendael.

Sacks, A. 2009. "Non-State Actor Provision of Services, Government Legitimacy, and the Rule of Law." Paper presented at the annual meeting of the American Sociological Association, San Francisco, CA.

Sany, J. 2010. *Education and Conflict in Côte d'Ivoire. Special Report 235*. Washington, DC: United States Institute of Peace.

Schleussner, C.-F., J. F. Donges, R. V. Donnera, and H. J. Schellnhuber. 2016. "Armed-Conflict Risks Enhanced by Climate-Related Disasters in Ethnically Fractionalized Countries." *Proceedings of the National Academy of Sciences* 113 (33): 9216–21.

Simon, H. 1997 [1947]. *Administrative Behavior: A Study of Decision-Making Processes in Administrative Organization.* 4th ed. New York: The Free Press.

Singer, P. W. 2010. "Private Military Firms: The Profit Side of VNSAs." In *Violent Non-State Actors in World Politics,* edited by K. Mulaj. New York: Columbia University Press.

Slegh, H., G. Barker, and R. Levtov. 2014. *Gender Relations, Sexual and Gender-Based Violence and the Effects of Conflict on Women and Men in North Kivu, Eastern Democratic Republic of the Congo: Results from the International Men and Gender Equality Survey (IMAGES).* Washington, DC: Promundo-US and Sonke Gender Justice.

Stares, P. 2017. *Preventive Engagement: How America Can Avoid War, Stay Strong, and Keep the Peace.* New York: Columbia University Press.

Stearns Lawson, B., and P. Dininio. 2013. *The Development Response to Drug Trafficking in Africa: A Programming Guide.* Washington, DC: USAID.

Stewart, F. 2000. "Crisis Prevention: Tackling Horizontal Inequalities." *Oxford Development Studies* 28 (3): 245–62.

———. 2002. "Horizontal Inequalities: A Neglected Dimension of Development." QEH Working Paper 81, Centre for Research on Inequality, Human Security, and Ethnicity, Queen Elizabeth House, University of Oxford.

———. 2004. "Development and Security." *Conflict, Security and Development* 4 (3): 261–88.

———. 2008. *Horizontal Inequalities and Conflict: Understanding Group Violence in Multiethnic Societies.* London: Palgrave Macmillan UK.

———. 2009. "Horizontal Inequalities as a Cause of Conflict." Bradford Development Lecture, University of Bradford. https://www.bradford.ac.uk/social-sciences/media/social-sciences/BDLStewart.pdf.

———. 2010. *Horizontal Inequalities as a Cause of Conflict.* Washington, DC: World Bank. http://siteresources.worldbank.org/EXTWDR2011/Resources/6406082-1283882418764/WDR_Background_Paper_Stewart.pdf.

Stewart, F., M. Barron, G. Brown, and M. Hartwell. 2006. *Social Exclusion and Conflict: Analysis and Policy Implications.* Centre for Research on Inequality, Human Security, and Ethnicity, Oxford University.

Stone, L. 2015. "Study of 156 Peace Agreements, Controlling for Other Variables, Quantitative Analysis of Women's Participation." In *Peace Processes in Reimagining Peacemaking: Women's Roles in Peace Processes,* by M. O'Reilly, A. Ó Súilleabháin, and T. Paffenholz, annex II. New York: International Peace Institute.

Tilly, C. 1985. "War Making and State Making as Organized Crime." In *Bringing the State Back In,* edited by P. Evans, D. Rueschmeyer, and T. Skocpol, 169–91. Cambridge, U.K.: Cambridge University Press.

———. 2003. *The Politics of Collective Violence.* Cambridge, U.K.: Cambridge University Press.

UNDP (United Nations Development Programme). 2012. *Informal Justice Systems.* New York: UNDP. http://www.undp.org/content/undp/en/home/librarypage/democratic-governance/access_to_justiceandruleoflaw/informal-justice-systems.html.

UN General Assembly. 2015. "Transforming Our World: The 2030 Agenda for Sustainable Development." Resolution A/RES/70/1, adopted September 25, New York.

———. 2016a. "Review of United Nations Peacebuilding Architecture." Resolution A/RES/70/262, adopted April 27, New York.

———. 2016b. "Report of the Open-Ended Intergovernmental Expert Working Group on Indicators and Terminology Relating to Disaster Risk Reduction." Resolution A/RES/71/644, adopted December 1, New York.

UN General Assembly and UN Security Council. 1999. *Report of the International Criminal Tribunal for the Prosecution of Persons Responsible for Genocide and Other Serious Violations of International Humanitarian Law Committed in the Territory of Rwanda and Rwandan Citizens Responsible for Genocide and Other Such Violations Committed in the Territory of Neighbouring States between 1 January and 31 December 1994.* Report A/54/315 S/1999/94. New York: United Nations, September 7. http://www.un.org/ga/54/doc/tcir.pdf.

UN Global Compact. 2010. "Guidance on Responsible Business in Conflict-Affected and High-Risk Areas: A Resource for Companies."

UN Global Compact and Principles for Responsible Investing, New York.

———. 2017. "Take Action: Business Advancing Peace." UN Global Compact, New York. https://www.unglobalcompact.org/take-action/action/peace.

UN Security Council. 2016a. "Postconflict Peacebuilding." Resolution S/RES/2282, adopted April 27, New York.

———. 2016b. "Youth, Peace, and Security." Resolution S/RES/2250, adopted December 9, New York.

Varshney, A. 2002. *Ethnic Conflict and Civic Life: Hindus and Muslims in India*. New Haven, CT: Yale University Press.

Volkan, V. 2004. *Blind Trust: Large Groups and Their Leaders in Times of Crisis and Terror*. Durham, NC: Pitchstone Publishing.

von Uexkulla, N., M. Croicua, H. Fjelde, and H. Buhaug. 2016. "Civil Conflict Sensitivity to Growing-Season Drought." *Proceedings of the National Academy of Sciences* 113 (44): 12391–96.

Wanis-St. John, A., and D. Kew. 2008. "Civil Society and Peace Negotiations: Confronting Exclusion." *International Negotiation* 13 (2008): 11–36.

Williams, P. 2016. *War and Conflict in Africa*. Cambridge, U.K.: Polity Press.

Wolff, S., S. Ross, and A. Wee. 2017. *Subnational Governance and Conflict*. Washington, DC: World Bank.

World Bank. 2011. *World Development Report 2011: Conflict, Security, and Development*. Washington, DC: World Bank.

———. 2013. "Inclusion Matters: The Foundation for Shared Prosperity." Washington, DC: World Bank Group.

———. 2015. *World Development Report 2015: Mind, Society, and Behavior*. Washington, DC: World Bank. https://openknowledge.worldbank.org/handle/10986/20597 License: CC BY 3.0 IGO.

———. 2016. *Independent Evaluation Group (IEG), World Bank Group Engagement in Situations of Fragility, Conflict, and Violence: An Independent Evaluation*. Washington, DC: World Bank.

———. 2017. *World Development Report 2017: Governance and the Law*. Washington, DC: World Bank.

Yamagishi, T., and M. Yamagishi. 1994. "Trust and Commitment in the United States and Japan." *Motivation and Emotion* 18 (2): 129–66.

Additional Reading

Bloom, M. 2011. *Bombshell: Women and Terrorism*. Philadelphia, PA: University of Pennsylvania Press.

Bøås, M. 2014. "Guns, Money, and Prayers: AQIM's Blueprint for Securing Control of Northern Mali." *CTC Sentinel* 7 (4): 1–7.

Botha, A. 2013. "Assessing the Vulnerability of Kenyan Youths to Radicalism and Extremism." ISS Paper 245, Institute for Security Studies, Pretoria. http://www.issafrica.org/uploads/Paper245.pdf.

Brown, K. 2014. "Why Are Western Women Joining Islamic State?" *BBC News Online*, October 4. http://www.bbc.com/news/uk-29507410.

Byrd, W. A., and D. Mansfield. 2014. "Afghanistan's Opium Economy. An Agricultural, Livelihoods, and Governance Perspective." Report, Afghanistan Agriculture Sector Review, World Bank, Washington, DC.

Colletta, N. J., and M. L. Cullen. 2000. *Violent Conflict and the Transformation of Social Capital: Lessons from Cambodia, Rwanda, Guatemala, and Somalia*. Washington, DC: World Bank.

Colletta, N., T. G. Lim, and A. Kelles-Viitanen. 2001. *Social Cohesion and Conflict Prevention in Asia*. Washington, DC: World Bank.

Cramer, C., J. Goodhand, and R. Morris. 2016. *Evidence Synthesis: What Interventions Have Been Effective in Preventing or Mitigating Armed Violence in Developing and Middle-Income Countries?* London: Department for International Development.

Curle, A. 1971. *Making Peace*. Durham, NC: Tavistock.

Easterly, W. 2001. "Can Institutions Resolve Ethnic Conflict?" *Economic Development and Cultural Change* 49 (4): 687–706.

Fiedler, C., J. Gravinghold, and K. Mross. 2017. "Identifying Pathways to Peace: How Post-Conflict Support Can Help Prevent Relapse of War." Background paper for the United Nations–World Bank Flagship Study, *Pathways for Peace: Inclusive Approaches to Preventing Violent Conflict*, World Bank, Washington, DC.

Haggard, S. 2004. "Institutions and Growth in East Asia." *Studies in Comparative International Development* 38 (4): 53–81.

Hegre, H., J. Karlsen, H. M. Nygård, H. Strand, and H. Urdal. 2013. "Predicting Armed Conflict, 2010–2050." *International Studies Quarterly* 57 (2): 250–70.

Ladbury, S. 2015. "Women and Extremism: The Association of Women and Girls with Jihadi Groups and Implications for Programming." Independent paper prepared for the Department of International Development (DFID) and the Foreign and Commonwealth Office. January 23.

Lederach, J. P. 1997. *Building Peace*. Washington, DC: United States Institute of Peace.

Leftwich, L. 2005. "Politics in Command: Development Studies and the Rediscovery of Social Science." *New Political Economy* 10 (4): 573–607.

Moser, C., and C. McIlwaine. 2004. *Encounters with Violence in Latin America: Urban Poor Perceptions from Colombia and Guatemala*. London: Routledge.

UN General Assembly. 2000. "UN Convention against Transnational Organized Crime." Resolution S/RES/55/25, adopted November 10, New York.

Urdal, H. 2006. "A Clash of Generations? Youth Bulges and Political Violence." *International Studies Quarterly* 50 (3): 607–30.

Wallensteen, P., and I. Svensson. 2014. "Talking Peace: International Mediation in Armed Conflicts." *Journal of Peace Research* 51 (2): 319–20.

Warschauer, M. 2003. *Technology and Social Inclusion: Rethinking the Digital Divide*. Cambridge, MA: MIT Press.

WHO (World Health Organization) and World Bank. 2011. *World Report on Disability*. Geneva: World Health Organization. http://www.refworld.org/docid/50854a322.html.

CHAPTER 4

Why People Fight: Inequality, Exclusion, and a Sense of Injustice

Many of today's violent conflicts relate to group-based grievances arising from inequality, exclusion, and feelings of injustice. Every country has groups who believe they suffer one or all of these ills in some measure. Most of the time, the attendant tensions and conflicts may simmer for long periods without boiling over into violence. It is when an aggrieved group assigns blame to others or to the state for its perceived economic, political, or social exclusion that its grievances may become politicized and risk tipping into violence.

On their own, inequality among groups and group-based exclusion do not generate violence. But they can create fertile ground upon which grievances can build. In the absence of incentives to avoid violence or address grievances, group leaders may mobilize their cohort to violence. Emotions, collective memories, frustration over unmet expectations, and a narrative that rouses a group to violence can all play a role in this mobilization.

The chances of violence are higher if leaders in a group can both frame the intergroup inequality as unfair and assign blame to another actor, usually a different identity group or the state. Elites, as discussed later in this chapter, can play a significant role in collective mobilization by shaping narratives. In Indonesia, conflict escalated in one of three resource-rich provinces where elites engaged in "hard ideological work [...] to transform unfocused resentments about

natural resources into grievances that would mandate violence" (Aspinall 2007, 968). Prevention efforts need to pay special attention to perceptions of inequality and injustice (Nygård et al. 2017). The 2030 Agenda for Sustainable Development provides a framework through which various social and economic inequalities can be addressed, not only through Sustainable Development Goal (SDG) 10, which is focused on inequalities, but also through other SDGs.

This chapter is organized around a comprehensive review of the multiple strands of research into the relationship between inequality and exclusion and the risk of violent conflict. It looks at how social groups coalesce—around identity, status, feelings of humiliation, and the perception they are being politically shortchanged, among others—and the conditions under which their grievances can be mobilized. The chapter also highlights the important roles the state may play and reviews evidence that reducing inequality and exclusion, particularly of women and young people, is fundamental to forging pathways for sustainable peace.

Inequality and Violent Conflict

The link between inequality and violent conflict is one of the oldest issues in political economy. "At least since Aristotle, theorists have believed that political discontent and its consequences—protest, instability, violence, revolution—depend not only on the absolute level of economic well-being, but also on the distribution of wealth" (Østby 2013, 4). Two dimensions of inequality are relevant here: inequality among individuals or households (vertical inequality) and inequality among groups (horizontal inequality) (Stewart 2002a). The evidence that horizontal inequality is linked to a higher risk of violent conflict is stronger than that for vertical inequality (Østby 2013). Nevertheless, although the relationship between inequality and conflict is not clear or direct, there is reason to believe that reducing inequality may help ease conflict between groups and thereby lower the risk of violence.

Vertical Inequality

As noted above, scholars have long argued that economic inequality is fundamentally linked to violent conflict (Muller 1985). Lichbach (1989, 432) finds that "it often appears that the principal political contest and debate in a nation involves a polarization of social groups around distributional issues." This view is reflected in conflict theory, which argues that conflict arises between the "haves" who wish to maintain the status quo distribution of resources and the "have-nots" who seek to challenge the existing system and its resource distribution. For decades, the notion that prosperous societies will be peaceful societies has underpinned development programming and spending.

Indeed, the gap between "haves" and "have-nots" remains at the center of much heated contemporary political and academic discussion on the growing income and wealth inequality in some developing and developed countries (Lichbach 1989; Piketty 2013; Justino 2017). The gap has widened to the point where the top 9 percent of the world's population earns half of all global income, while the bottom half controls only about 7 percent of global income (Milanovic 2016).

Some income and wealth inequality is inevitable because people start out with different natural endowments of physical, social, and human capital and abilities. However, these differences do not explain the differences in individuals' access to power and opportunity or social exclusion (Stiglitz 2013; Krishnan et al. 2016). Rising income and wealth inequality seems to be due largely to these factors of unequal access and opportunity (Stewart 2002b). Persistent inequality driven by these factors could impede economic growth; it also may sometimes lead to social and political instability and violent conflict (Justino and Moore 2015).

Numerous studies have looked at the relationship between vertical inequality, such as individuals' relative wealth or poverty, and conflict, with mixed findings (Lichbach 1989; Cramer 2003; Østby 2013; Nygård et al. 2017). As Cramer (2003) notes, links between vertical inequality and violent conflict are elusive. Various studies find that higher inequality increases the likelihood of conflict, decreases it, or has no impact at all (Russett 1964; Sigelman and Simpson 1977; Lichbach 1989; Bartusevičius 2014). Some studies have found a positive relationship between inequality in income (or land tenure) and conflict (Nagel 1976). Others argue for a positive relationship between income inequality and the likelihood of popular rebellion (Bartusevičius 2014) or the risk of violence, particularly under semi-repressive regimes (Schock 1996). In some studies, particular forms of inequality are found to matter—for example, household asset inequality that increased the propensity of civil strife in Uganda (Deininger 2003)—and vertical inequality is found to have a different impact on different conflict and violence types (Besançon 2005; Nepal, Bohara, and Gawande 2011). Recent cross-country studies find no significant relationship between income inequality measured by the Gini coefficient and violent conflict (Fearon and Laitin 2003; Collier and Hoeffler 2004).

It should be noted, however, that cross-country studies that examine the effect of vertical inequality on the onset of violent conflict are constrained by major data limitations, both in the availability and reliability of vertical inequality data and in the way conflict onset is measured.[1] In addition, little empirical testing has been undertaken of the causal mechanisms that have been put forward by the theoretical and qualitative literature on the relationship between vertical inequality and conflict.

Horizontal Inequality

Horizontal inequalities are differences in access and opportunities across culturally defined (or constructed) groups based on identities such as ethnicity, region, and religion. They create fertile ground for grievances, especially when they accumulate across multiple realms, such as economic and political, and social (Østby 2008a; Justino 2017).[2]

The hypothesis that horizontal inequality makes countries more vulnerable to conflict derives from the idea that political, economic, and social inequalities are likely to create grievances among a relatively disadvantaged group whose members can mobilize along ethnic (or other identity-based) lines to cause violent conflict. Much research has been done on measurement and quantitative evidence related to this hypothesis.

Horizontal inequality as an explanatory factor for violent conflict rests on three points (Nygård et al. 2017). First, there is a positive relationship between horizontal inequality and the onset of violent conflict. Second, this positive relationship is due to the presence of group identity and of a subjective, collective sense of inequality that creates group grievances. Third, group grievances can lead to violent conflict when the group has the opportunity to collectively mobilize around its feeling of injustice (Gurr 1993; Østby 2013).

For horizontal inequality to spur collective action—which may or may not involve violence—objective inequality must be translated into an "inter-subjectively perceived grievance" (Nygård et al. 2017, 12); that is, the grievance is experienced collectively by the group. Gurr's (1970) pioneering theory of relative deprivation builds a conceptual model to provide an understanding of the conditions under which individuals resort to violence. He argues that relative deprivation will lead to frustration and aggression that will motivate individuals to rebel. As this chapter discusses, this reasoning could arguably apply as well to social groups, with relative deprivation defined as actors' perceptions of discrepancy between what they think they are rightfully entitled to achieve and what they are actually capable of achieving.[3] Additionally, while most of the focus in this line of research to date has been on the impact of objective inequality among groups, some recent studies have tried to address *perceived* grievances as well.[4]

Economic Inequality among Groups

Most of the cross-country literature that discusses horizontal inequality examines economic inequality that occurs along ethnic and religious lines. Ethnicity is broadly defined along ethnoreligious and ethnolinguistic groups (Østby, Nordås, and Rød 2009; Cederman, Gleditsch, and Buhaug 2013). Issues related to measuring and defining ethnicity, including questions related to endogeneity, are discussed throughout this chapter.

Scholars have tried to understand the relationship quantitatively by building summary indices of economic horizontal inequality and by measures of relative position. Cross-country studies that construct summary indices of economic horizontal inequality generally find a positive and statistically significant relationship between horizontal inequality and conflict (Østby 2008a, 2008b). These studies mostly use data from a range of countries, such as data from the Demographic and Health Survey, to measure the difference in asset ownership between each country's two largest ethnic groups and to study its relationship with violent conflict (Østby 2008a, 2008b). Nepal, Bohara, and Gawande (2011) use village-level data to evaluate the relationship between intergroup inequalities and violence during the Maoist armed conflict in Nepal, which began in 1996 and has killed 10,000 people and displaced more than 200,000 people. They find that intergroup horizontal inequalities—measured according to religion, caste, and language—are associated with Maoist killings.

In a study measuring horizontal inequality, Alesina, Michalopoulos, and Papaioannou (2016) take a new approach. They combine satellite images of nighttime luminosity with historical homelands of ethnolinguistic groups and find that ethnic inequality has a significant and negative association with socioeconomic development. Celiku and Kraay (2017) find that this measure of horizontal economic inequality is a good predictor of the outbreak of conflict.

Other cross-country studies focus on measures of the relative position an identity group holds within the wealth distribution in a geographic area (Cederman, Weidmann, and Gleditsch 2011; Cederman, Gleditsch, and Buhaug 2013). These studies allow the likelihood that each group will take part in conflict in a given area to be examined. One important advantage these studies have in comparison with the summary indices mentioned above is that they create the opportunity to disentangle the effect of relative deprivation from the effect of relative privilege. This is an important distinction that relies on different theoretical underpinnings for why certain groups would want to incite violent conflict. These studies find robust evidence of a positive relationship between relatively disadvantaged groups and violent conflict (Cederman, Weidmann, and Gleditsch 2011; Cederman, Gleditsch, and Buhaug 2013; Cederman, Weidmann, and Bormann 2015). Deprivation is measured as the distance between the deprived group's estimated gross domestic product (GDP) per capita and the average GDP per capita of all groups. However, there is evidence that sometimes relatively privileged groups are the ones that initiate violence, a finding discussed at greater length later in this chapter.

Political Inequality among Groups

Recent quantitative studies and qualitative analysis support a strong and positive link between political exclusion of certain groups and violent conflict, making political inclusion a particularly significant goal for prevention of violence (Jones, Elgin-Cossart, and Esberg 2012; Cederman, Gleditsch, and Buhaug 2013). This is a key message of this study and is discussed in greater detail in chapters 5 and 6. Political horizontal inequality can be broadly defined to include inequalities in the distribution and access to political opportunity and power among groups, including access to

the executive branch and the police and military. It also relates to the ability of individuals to participate in political processes. Theories of political horizontal inequality draw on literatures of ethnonationalism and self-determination, as well as on the idea that ethnic capture of the state provides politically excluded groups with motivation to challenge the state (Wimmer, Cederman, and Min 2009; Cederman, Wimmer, and Min 2010; Cederman, Gleditsch, and Buhaug 2013).

Early empirical investigations used data from the Minorities at Risk project, which considers indices of political discrimination among ethnic groups and political differentials measured by political status between groups. Results using the Minorities at Risk data set were mixed, in part because of the quality of the data (Gurr 1993).

More recent quantitative studies have used the Ethnic Power Relations data set, which includes measures of the exclusion of ethnic groups from executive power (Buhaug, Cederman, and Gleditsch 2014; Vogt et al. 2015).[5] Several of these studies find that group-level exclusion from the executive branch increases the risk that these groups will participate in conflict; an ethnic group's recent loss of power also increases that risk (Cederman, Wimmer, and Min 2010; Cederman, Weidmann, and Gleditsch 2011; Cederman, Gleditsch, and Buhaug 2013; Cederman, Weidmann, and Bormann 2015). When aggregated to the country level, political inequality has been found to increase the risk of violent conflict (Cederman, Gleditsch, and Buhaug 2013). By disaggregating conflict types into territorial and governmental conflict, Buhaug, Cederman, and Gleditsch (2014) find that the presence of large groups that are discriminated against boosts the probability of governmental civil wars. They attribute this to the discrepancy between a group's demographic power and its political privileges.

Social Inequality among Groups

While most of the quantitative literature on horizontal inequalities has focused on the economic and political dimensions, social inequality among groups is also important to any discussion of conflict risk.

Social inequality can be broadly defined to include inequalities in access to basic services, such as education, health care, and benefits related to educational and health outcomes, which could be monitored through the 2030 Agenda for Sustainable Development. Education is particularly relevant, given that it is strongly connected to future economic activity and well-being and plays an important role in national identity and social cohesion. Although quantitative evidence on the social dimension of horizontal inequality is rather limited,[6] studies have sought to examine the association between social inequality and conflict (Omoeva and Buckner 2015).

Omoeva and Buckner (2015), for example, build a cross-country panel data set of educational attainment and find a robust relationship between higher levels of horizontal inequality in education among ethnic and religious groups and the likelihood of violent conflict. They find that a one standard deviation increase in horizontal inequality in educational attainment more than doubles the odds that a country will experience a conflict in the next five years; this relationship was statistically significant in the 2000s and was robust to multiple specifications while not being present in earlier decades (Omoeva and Buckner 2015). The authors hypothesize that in the 1970s and 1980s, high levels of education inequality were not perceived as a sufficient reason for grievances to build. It could also be that large differences between ethnic or religious groups in educational attainment signal higher levels of exclusion of specific groups (Omoeva and Buckner 2015). Social differences between ethnic groups can sometimes represent group discrimination. Education policies have been used to discriminate against minorities or other ethnic groups, as has been shown in postapartheid South Africa and Sri Lanka, for example (Gurr 2000; Stewart 2002b).

Using Demographic and Health Survey data on a set of developing countries, Østby (2008b) finds that for a country with low levels of horizontal social inequality (5th percentile), the probability of onset of civil conflict in any given year is 1.75 percent. This probability increases to 3.7 percent when the level of horizontal social inequality rises to the 95th percentile. Horizontal social inequality is measured by the total years of education completed. Murshed and Gates (2005) find that horizontal inequalities were significant in explaining violent conflict in Nepal. Specifically, they find that higher life expectancy and educational attainment, the latter measured by average years of schooling, were associated with a lower risk of civil war. However, reverse causality can be a potential problem because conflict can sometimes increase horizontal social inequality. Box 4.1 elaborates on the issue of reverse causality.

A district-level study of Indonesia finds that horizontal inequality in child mortality rates was positively associated with ethnic-based communal violence (Mancini, Stewart, and Brown 2008). Other measures of horizontal inequality include civil service employment, unemployment, education, and poverty among farmers. The study finds these factors were also linked to the incidence of conflict, but that the effects were much less pronounced. In another analysis, Østby et al. (2011) find that in Indonesian districts with high population growth, horizontal inequality in infant mortality rates is related to violence.

Relatively Privileged Groups and Violent Conflict

While there is robust evidence that high levels of horizontal inequality among the relatively deprived increase the likelihood of conflict, evidence on relatively privileged groups is mixed. Relatively privileged groups may initiate violence to preserve their power and their access to important resources (Stewart 2002a). A privileged group that produces wealth may develop a sense of injustice if it sees a redistribution of that wealth as an unfair benefit to another region or group. Asal et al. (2016) find that ethnic groups that face political exclusion and live in an area that produces oil wealth are more likely to experience violent conflict than groups that experience only exclusion. Economically privileged groups have more resources with which to sustain violent conflict, but their higher opportunity cost means they also have more to lose by participating

Studies of the relationship between inequality and violent conflict are subject to the issue of endogeneity, and specifically reverse causality, with implications for prevention policy. Greater inequality may increase the likelihood of violent conflict, and violent conflict may worsen inequality. Collier et al. (2003) call this "development in reverse," where violent conflict may deepen the problems that led groups to take up arms in the first place. However, overall case study evidence is mixed on whether conflict indeed widens or reduces horizontal inequality. In fact, Bircan, Bruck, and Vothknecht (2017) find that conflict increases vertical inequality, but the impact is not permanent.

Fearon (2010) includes variables that measure the extent of the population that is excluded or discriminated against in regression analysis and argues that including such variables effectively results in the running of a "policy regression." This means that a variable that is a direct policy choice is used as an independent variable in regression analysis, thus allowing the researcher to explore the effect of specific policy choices. Policy makers who anticipate that a particular group is likely to mobilize for violence can enact policies that reduce certain inequalities.

Endogeneity can lead to over- or underestimating the causal impact in a specific country with more exclusionary policies. Wucherpfennig, Hunziker, and Cederman (2016) argue that empirical analysis that does not correct for endogeneity will overestimate the effect of political exclusion on the risk of violent conflict. They suggest that governments then may strategically exclude conflict-prone ethnic groups or regions. If conflict-prone groups are included in a government, empirical analysis that does not correct for endogeneity will artificially underestimate this effect. A few studies have used an instrumental variables approach to correct for endogeneity, but this remains an area for further exploration and research. Improving the link between different types of horizontal inequality and higher risk of violent conflict would contribute to better informing prevention policies. However, drawing policy recommendations and entry points from associations between two different phenomena is challenging because evidence of an association is not enough to draw specific causal inference and policy entry points. Hence, policies that address the potential risks of violent conflict have to be context specific and informed by evidence that tries to go beyond simple association.

in violence (Nygård et al. 2017). There is also evidence that in the case of separatist movements, relatively privileged groups sometimes initiate violence (Brown 2010).

Whether relatively wealthier groups are more likely to participate in conflicts is debatable. Several authors find that this is the case by conducting studies comparing a group's GDP per capita to the GDP per capita of all groups (Cederman, Weidmann, and Gleditsch 2011; Cederman, Weidmann, and Bormann 2015), but other studies fail to find a significant relationship (Buhaug, Cederman, and Gleditsch 2014; Fjelde and Østby 2014). In their theoretical model of

conflict and economic change, Mitra and Ray (2014) show that increasing a specific group's income lowers the chances of that group's participating in violence. Meanwhile, it is worth noting that they also find that raising one group's income may increase the chance that that same group will be the target of violence because other privileged groups would perceive that increase as losing their own comparative advantage.

As explored in more detail below, steep changes in the relative status of groups can foment new grievances that increase the risk of violence, even if the change reduces inequalities.

The Multiple and Intersecting Dimensions of Exclusion

Inequality among groups is not a sufficient condition for collective action toward violence. A deep-rooted sense of exclusion and a perception of injustice seem to be present in many violent conflicts. These factors are key in grievance formation. Changes in status and political exclusion are especially potent. The perception of exclusion is also persuasive, even when it is at odds with a group's objective situation in relation to other groups'. Although exclusion and inequality based on gender and age are not linked to conflict risk in a direct way, the participation and inclusion of women and young people strengthen a country's capacity to manage and avert conflict (Paffenholz et al. 2017).

The Importance of Political Exclusion in Conflict Risks

Some qualitative case studies and quantitative evidence suggest that political exclusion is very important in fostering between-group tensions that can lead to violence. Political exclusion provides leaders of deprived groups with an incentive to act to change the situation. Some have argued that political exclusion is more visible—and therefore groups can more easily assign blame, one of the steps considered essential in stirring grievances to violence—than economic disadvantage (Jones, Elgin-Cossart, and Esberg 2012; Vogt et al. 2015).

Data limitations regarding political exclusion, however, are even more severe than they are for economic exclusion. Some recent work tries to address the limitations. The latest Ethnic Power Relations data set compiles data for the period 1946–2013 that includes all "politically relevant ethnic groups"[7] in 141 countries and their access to power in the executive branch, including cabinet positions and control of the army (Cederman, Wimmer, and Min 2010).[8] The indicator for SDG target 16.7, which is being developed, will provide additional possibilities for measuring political inclusion.

Cederman, Gleditsch, and Buhaug (2013) show that politically excluded groups experience conflict at a much higher frequency in comparison with included groups. They also show that the less included a group is politically, the more likely it is to fight the incumbent government. This effect is even more pronounced when groups have experienced a change of power.

The size of the politically incumbent group makes little to no difference to the probability of conflict. But size has a strong positive effect toward violence for excluded groups. This finding is interpreted as evidence that conflict is to a large extent driven by grievances, since one would expect the perceived injustice to increase with the size of the excluded population, rather than group size being regarded as simply a proxy for resource endowment (Cederman, Gleditsch, and Buhaug 2013). Other evidence suggests that excluded groups will be more likely to engage in collective violent action when they perceive the political system to be completely closed to their group, as opposed to when they believe they have minimum representation (Jost and Banaji 2004).

A group may well suffer exclusion in several dimensions at once, and the overlap of different types of exclusion can heighten the risk of violent conflict. Cederman, Gleditsch, and Buhaug (2013) find that groups excluded both economically and politically will be more likely to participate in violent conflict than groups excluded in only one dimension. They conclude that the effect of economic horizontal inequality on violent conflict is conditional on political exclusion. In fact, economic horizontal inequalities can be compensated for by a politically inclusive society. Østby (2008a), in a study at the country level, finds a strong link between asset inequality and violent conflict, especially for countries with higher levels of political discrimination.

Different types of exclusion tend to reinforce each other. Political exclusion often leads to social and economic exclusion. Social exclusion is related to power relations and tends to involve discrimination against or exclusion of groups from the regular activities of society. There are causal connections between educational access and income: lack of access to education, lack of education, or both, lead to fewer economic opportunities, which is correlated with low income. At the same time, the low income of certain groups leads to lower educational attainment, which creates a vicious cycle for relatively deprived groups. Exclusion in recognition of culture, especially related to language use, can also affect educational and economic opportunities and outcomes as a result. It also reinforces group identities.

Stewart (2009) suggests that conflict is less likely when a particular group that is relatively deprived in one dimension is privileged in another. In cases in which a group is economically or socially excluded (or both), but the group's elite holds power or participates in the government, the elite are less likely to organize or lead a rebellion. She cites the examples of Malaysia and Nigeria, suggesting that after their civil wars the group that was economically disadvantaged held a numerical majority and was also politically advantaged. Having political power reduces the elites' motives to rebel and gives them an opportunity to correct the inequalities faced by their group.

Inclusion of Women and Gender Equality

The degree to which women are included in political, economic, and social life is a key factor influencing a society's propensity for conflict. Gender inequality is often a reflection of overall levels of exclusion in a society and its tendency to resort to violence as a means of resolving conflict (GIWPS and PRIO 2017; Tessler and Warriner 1997; Caprioli and Tumbore 2003; Caprioli 2005; Melander 2005; Caprioli et al. 2007; Hudson et al. 2009; O'Reilly 2015; UNSC 2015a; Crespo-Sancho 2017; Kelly 2017; Nygård et al. 2017).

Several large-sample, quantitative studies have explored the relationship between gender exclusion and violent conflict, finding that women's status relative to men's, especially their vulnerability to violence, is a significant predictor of the country's propensity for violent conflict overall (Caprioli 2000;

Caprioli and Boyer 2001; Caprioli and Tumbore 2003; Regan and Paskeviciute 2003; Hudson et al. 2012). In a global, longitudinal study relying on the WomanStats database,[9] which includes data from 175 countries (1960–2001), and using fertility rates and labor force participation as proxies for gender equality, Caprioli and Boyer (2001) find a significant and positive relationship between levels of gender inequality in a country and the likelihood of that country's being the first to use military force in disputes with other countries. Hudson et al. (2012), also relying on the WomanStats database, compares indicators of gender-based violence with macro-level indicators of peace and stability, as well as legislation protecting women's rights. They find that the higher the level of violence against women, the more likely a country may be not to comply with international norms and treaty agreements, and the less peacefully it will operate in the international system.

Changes in women's experiences can be viewed as early warning signs of social and political insecurity. These signs may include an increase in domestic violence, increased risk of gender-based violence outside the home, an increase in the number of female-headed households, a decrease in girls' attending school because of security concerns, and an increase in pregnancy terminations (Hudson et al. 2012). This finding underscores the importance of monitoring indicators of gender equality within broader systems to prevent violence.

Gender inclusion offers important potential for reducing the risk of violence. Caprioli (2005) finds that countries with 10 percent of women in the labor force compared with countries with 40 percent of women in the labor force are nearly 30 times more likely to experience internal conflict. She also finds that a 5 percent increase in females in the labor force is associated with a fivefold decrease in the probability that a state will use military force to resolve international conflict. Caprioli and Boyer (2001) find that states with higher levels of gender inequality (using labor force participation as a proxy) also tend to use more extreme forms of violence in conflict.

Mobilizing women's leadership and participation in peace processes and in conflict resolution has also been instrumental in shifting toward peaceful pathways in many countries (UN Women 2015) (see box 4.2). Some of these experiences are discussed further in chapter 6.

However, gender equality by itself is not a panacea or absolute bulwark against the risk of violent conflict. Even countries where women enjoy relatively solid access to the political, social, and economic spheres may be affected by violent conflict. Indeed, in one of the trends in contemporary violent conflict discussed in chapter 1, conflict has spread to middle-income countries with relatively developed institutions. Among these countries is the Syrian Arab Republic, where women, or at least urban women, had relatively wide educational and professional opportunities (UNICEF 2011).

Gender exclusion is maintained by social norms that prescribe certain roles for women and men. These norms affect not only the propensity for conflict, but the experience of conflict by women and men, as discussed in chapter 1.

In some cases, violent conflict can relax rigid gender norms, at least temporarily. Women may join armed groups, move into new livelihood opportunities, and take leadership roles as peacemakers. In many cases, however, the potential to take advantage of these roles is limited, especially in the postconflict period. In a study of six conflict and postconflict countries, Justino et al. (2012) find that although women increased their participation in new labor markets during conflict, and in some cases overall household welfare improved in economic terms, they earned less than male colleagues and often lost their jobs in the postconflict period. In addition, the increased participation in new jobs was not accompanied by any reduction in their household labor; on the contrary, these responsibilities tended to increase as women took over as heads of household while male partners and family members were recruited or abducted into armed groups. Once conflict ended, they faced pressure to return to more traditional roles, and were often tasked with caring for male relatives injured during conflict or orphaned children.

BOX 4.2 Mobilizing Women's Leadership for Peacebuilding

In October of 2000 the UN Security Council adopted Resolution 1325 on Women, Peace, and Security. Recognizing women's important role in peace and the disproportionate effects of violence on women during conflict, Resolution 1325 urges states to ensure increased representation of women at all decision-making levels in national, regional, and international institutions as well as in mechanisms for the prevention, management, and resolution of conflicts (UN Women 2015). Empirical studies have documented the positive role women can play:

- Paffenholz (2015) establishes that meaningful participation of women in peace negotiations results in participants being more satisfied with the outcomes, and thus, agreements that tend to be longer lasting.

- Women's inclusion in peace processes has a positive impact on the durability of peace agreements (O'Reilly, Ó Súilleabháin, and Paffenholz 2015).

- Stone (2015) shows that the inclusion of women as negotiators, mediators, signatories, and witnesses increases the probability of an agreement's lasting at least two years by 20 percent, and the probability of an agreement's lasting at least 15 years by 35 percent.

- Increasing the number of women at the negotiating table, although necessary and helpful, is not enough; rather, increasing the number of women with quality participation should be the target (Anderlini 2007; Paffenholz 2015).

Gender norms affect the experience of conflict for men as well. The perpetrators of violence are predominantly men, as are most members of violent extremist groups, gangs, militias, and armies. Even so, the vast majority of men do not perpetrate violence, young men are not inherently violent, men actively participate in peace building, and men are the primary direct victims of violent conflict (with more men dying on the battlefield) (Spiegel and Salama 2000; Reza, Mercy, and Krug 2001; Obermeyer, Murray, and Gakidou 2008). All this suggests that masculinity is in large part a social construct, and that men create violent identities because of social, cultural, and political expectations and pressures placed upon them (Bannon and Correia 2006; Vess et al. 2013). A corollary explored below is that masculinity does not drive violence so much as do environments where men are unable to assert and fulfill other nonviolent masculine identities.

In a study of nine violence-affected countries UNDP (forthcoming) identifies four common and interrelated roles associated with manhood. These "four Ps of manhood" follow:

- Provider for his family
- Procreator or father
- Prestige through being respected in the community, which also brings social status
- Protector of family and community.

Important differences in men's abilities to assert these roles appear in a noncrisis setting as compared with a crisis setting (see figure 4.1). In a crisis setting, men are unable to assert their roles of provider and procreator and to acquire social standing. A demand for traditional, patriarchal masculinities that advocates for the use of violence can surge within young men who seek to reassert their threatened masculinity. Although men's roles are challenged in conflict settings, not all men will develop violent behaviors.

Norms do not change quickly or easily. Indeed, although formal, institutional changes, such as legislation protecting women's rights, can occur relatively quickly, norms require much more time to change, and tend to be more resistant to change (Petesch 2012). When they are in flux, those who step outside the older, more rigid norms into new roles—from women who leave their households or communities to study or work in the city, to men who take on more domestic responsibilities—face a heightened risk of violence if their communities persist in enforcing more traditional norms (Boudet et al. 2012). As discussed further in chapter 6, this entrenchment of norms underscores the importance of focusing not only on the objective of equality but also on the processes that lead there.

FIGURE 4.1 Masculinities in Noncrisis and Crisis Settings

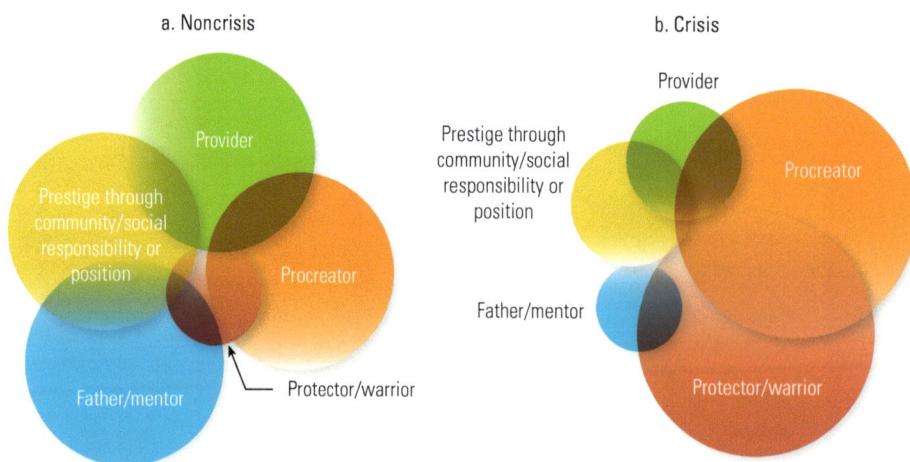

Source: UNDP, forthcoming.

Youth Inclusion

Young people are productive workers, engaged citizens, and peace builders. The 2015 United Nations Security Council resolution on Youth, Peace and Security (SCR 2250) was groundbreaking on this score, recognizing the role of youth in the prevention of violence and the resolution of conflicts for the first time, and calling for increased representation of youth in decision-making at all levels (see box 4.3).[10]

At the same time, a growing field of study for researchers and policy makers alike is the relationship between youth and violence, particularly the role that youth exclusion may play in increasing a country's risk of violent conflict, as well as the question of what drives a minority of young people to participate in violence. These questions are particularly salient in light of the global trends described in chapter 2, such as the historically high number of young people in the world today, the high levels of youth unemployment, and the growing transnational reach of violent extremist groups that actively recruit youth.

While many have hypothesized that a demographic "youth bulge" is a structural risk of conflict (Collier 2000; Urdal 2006), more recent, cross-country work finds that whether a large youth population constitutes a threat or, to the contrary, a "demographic

---

BOX 4.3 Youth Aspirations and Exclusion

Half of the global population is age 24 years or younger (World Bank 2017a). Young people face a wide array of development challenges. They are often victims of multiple and interlocking forms of discrimination that can lead to an imbalance of power that excludes young people from being recognized socially as adults, undermining their needs and aspirations. Intergenerational inequality, and youth perceptions of lower status and fewer opportunities than their parents had at the same age, can also contribute to frustration (Ginges et al. 2007; Atran and Ginges 2012; Höhne 2013; Honwana 2013; Idris 2016; UNDP 2017b).

Youth exclusion is often highlighted as a key factor in violent conflict. Programs around the world have focused on increasing employment opportunities for youth, but they have had mixed results. Evidence shows that employment can, in some cases, contribute to protecting youth against mobilization to violence, but that the motivations for joining armed groups are not limited to economics. They often stem from frustration with the rigidity of intergenerational social structures (Ginges et al. 2007; Atran and Ginges 2012; Höhne 2013; Idris 2016), frustrated aspirations for social and economic mobility, discrimination, and unmet needs for recognition and respect (Idris 2016; Devarajan and Ianchovichina 2017). Although it is true that the majority of fighters in all types of armed groups are young men, they only ever represent a minority of the youth population in any given country. At the same time, youth groups are important parts of civil society and are forces for effective prevention of violent conflict.

Empowering youth is essential for violence-prevention and peacebuilding efforts. In 2015, the UN Security Council unanimously adopted its Resolution 2250 on Youth, Peace, and Security, recognizing the important and positive contribution of young people in efforts for the maintenance and promotion of peace and security. The Security Council called for active engagement of youth because they represent "a unique demographic dividend that can contribute to lasting peace and prosperity" if inclusive policies are put in place. These policies include, for example, those related to youth employment, vocational training, educational opportunities, and promoting youth entrepreneurship and meaningful participation in decision making. The Security Council highlighted that the disruption of young people's access to educational and economic opportunities has a dramatic impact on durable peace and reconciliation.

dividend" (UNSC 2015b), depends largely on the degree to which youth are included in economic, social, and political life (Paasonen and Paasonen and Urdal 2016). More micro-level analysis finds that economic, social, and political exclusion prevents young peoples' transition into adulthood in countries at all income levels, and is often cited as a risk factor for joining armed groups (Ginges et al. 2007; Atran and Ginges 2012; Höhne 2013; Honwana 2013; Mercy Corps 2015; Idris 2016). Indeed, studies from various contexts show that youth's motivations to join armed groups extend beyond more practical needs for employment or income to a broader frustration with the rigidity of intergenerational social structures, frustrated aspirations for social and economic mobility, discrimination, and unmet needs for recognition and respect (Ginges et al. 2007; Atran and Ginges 2012; Botha 2013; Höhne 2013; Mercy Corps 2015; Idris 2016, 40; Devarajan and Ianchovichina 2017). These motivations vary somewhat by gender; generally speaking, male youth are more likely to be motivated to join armed groups out of a need for economic or social mobility, whereas young women may join for protection, the chance for greater autonomy than allowed by mainstream society, to avenge the loss of a loved one, or perceptions of injustice and frustration (Bloom 2005, 2011; Brown 2014; Ladbury 2015). As noted earlier in this chapter, unequal access to education and the quality of education can become sources of frustration, feelings of injustice, and grievances that can all increase a society's risk of violent conflict.

Barriers to meaningful and inclusive youth participation in governance are also important risk factors. The disenfranchisement of young people from formal political systems leaves them not only frustrated but also mistrustful of political systems and institutions (UNDP 2017a). In countries with more rigid, conservative power structures and social hierarchies, youth tend to express their dissatisfaction by blaming older generations, thus creating an intergenerational drift. In these settings, youth feel disempowered and frustrated and assert that they receive little attention from those in power, including teachers, elders, and politicians (Abbink 2005).

Recruitment of Youth by Violent Armed Groups

In recent years, much attention has turned to recruitment of youth by violent groups, especially violent extremist groups. The research suggests that the motivations and experiences of people in violent extremist groups is similar to that for other types of armed groups. Empirical work on youth motivations, and on extremist groups' recruiting strategies, is scarce—although increasing in some areas—because of several important limitations (World Bank 2015; UNDP 2017b). These constraints include, first, the difficulties of accessing members of clandestine groups, resulting in a bias toward people who have left such groups or who have been imprisoned for crimes committed while members (Barrett 2011; Atran and Stone 2015; Mercy Corps 2015; Stern and Berger 2015; ISS 2016). A strong bias toward male fighters contributes to a limited understanding of women's involvement (Ladbury 2015) as well as of the various roles that people can play in these groups. Most studies tend to focus on one group in one setting, which has given rise to some rich case studies, but often offers little in the way of generalizability for orienting policy in other contexts or toward other groups (ISS 2016; Mercy Corps 2016; CeSID 2017; EIP 2017). A small number of studies have been able to interview members of extremist groups—the Islamic State, or ISIS, in particular—to offer a glimpse into the group's internal organization (Atran and Stone 2015; Stern and Berger 2015; Weiss and Hassan 2015), and some journalist reports offer some detail on the profiles of recruits, particularly foreign fighters (Weaver 2015). However, many violent extremist groups, such as Boko Haram and al-Shabaab, do not keep formal records of their members. There is little information on members' sociodemographic profiles or on the roles they play once recruited.

No single characteristic, identity, or motivation appears to draw individuals to become part of violent groups. In a study of violent extremism in six countries across Africa, including interviews with 718 people, of which 495 were former or current self-identified members of extremist groups, UNDP (2017b) finds that certain vulnerabilities tended to be present in those who joined extremist groups, especially a lack of exposure to people of other religious and ethnic identities, low levels of literacy or quality of education, and a perceived lack of parental involvement during childhood. Grievances against the state were an important motivating factor; frustration with perceived corruption or lack of access to political representation was key. One of the most striking findings relates to grievances against security actors: 78 percent of the sample reported low levels of trust in the police or military, and 71 percent said that the killing or arrest of a family member or friend prompted them to join an extremist group (UNDP 2017b).

Far from all members join armed groups voluntarily; groups also use violence and threats to coerce people to join. For extremist groups, coercion as a means of recruitment and payment for services become much more common when such a group controls territory (see box 4.4).

BOX 4.4 A Multiplicity of Motivations Drives People to Join Violent Extremist Groups

Individuals who join violent extremist groups do not fit a single profile or follow a single trajectory. A growing body of empirical research on violent extremism across different regions and groups finds that motivations are complex and context specific, and that coercion by armed groups plays a strong role as well.

Motivations when individuals join voluntarily

- *Perception of injustice at the hands of the state is suggested to be a strong motivation,* along with a sense of frustration with the state. These grievances toward the state may revolve around elite corruption and perceptions that the state is illegitimate. Members of social groups who feel marginalized or excluded experience such grievances most acutely. The narrative offered by some violent extremist groups of an egalitarian and moral order, marked by justice and fairness, may appear to be an attractive alternative.

- *Experience of violence, persecution, and repression from the state,* notably by its police and military forces against family members and friends, is a documented tipping point for individuals to voluntarily join violent extremist groups. In UNDP's (2017b) study, 71 percent of respondents cited the killing or arrest of a family member or friend as the incident that motivated them to join an extremist group.

- *Desire for a sense of community, social belonging, and recognition* is a motivation, particularly when family members or friends already are members of a group. Alternatively, the group may fill a gap in social belonging, especially for individuals who report low parental involvement during their childhood, a lack of friends, and poor integration with peers and the community at large. Recruiters often appeal to this desire for social membership and social recognition by portraying the group as a fellowship.

- *Prospects for earning income and economic empowerment* are rarely the main reason for joining, but in some cases may motivate poor youth and educated middle-class youth with higher expectations of social mobility.

- The need for *physical protection* is cited as a motivating factor. In a conflict context that is dangerous and unstable, and notably when the presence of the state is weak, individuals may join an extremist group to protect themselves or their family, broader group, or property.

- Women or girls may seek other ways to *assert their identity and independence* as a result of gender-based inequality,

(Box continued next page)

Perceptions of Exclusion and Unfairness in Violent Conflict Risk

Perceptions play a powerful role in creating feelings of exclusion and injustice that may be mobilized toward violence. Indeed, evidence suggests that *perceptions* of exclusion and inequality often matter more for their potential for mobilization than do measured inequality and exclusion (Gurr 1970). Studies that find a relationship between objective horizontal inequality and violent conflict assume that the relationship is mediated through perceptions (Østby 2008a; Cederman, Wimmer, and Min 2010; Cederman, Gleditsch, and Buhaug 2013).[11] However, the correlation between objective and perceived horizontal inequality is not as high as might be expected (see box 4.5). Better data are needed to provide more conclusive evidence on perceptions and their importance in relation to objective inequality and exclusion measures.

Recent studies have shifted from measuring group-level grievances expressed by leaders to measuring individual-level perceptions assessed from survey questions. The shift reflects the view that objective inequality results in violent conflict only if a sufficient number of group members view the inequality as unjust and can cast blame on another group or on the state (Cederman, Gleditsch, and Buhaug 2013).

Most studies that use these various types of perception measures find a positive correlation between perceptions and behavior or attitudes that would favor violence. For example, respondents' perception that the government was treating their group unfairly was found to be associated with an increased rate of participation in demonstrations and also higher levels of support for violence. Hillesund (2015) finds that Palestinians were more likely to support violent over nonviolent actions when they assessed the political and human rights situation as poor (Kirwin and

Cho 2009; Miodownik and Nir 2016). Cross-country studies find support for the idea that perceptions affect people's willingness to engage in conflict. Using all the measures described in box 4.5 as well as data from Afrobarometer and the World Values Survey, Must (2016) finds that perceptions of political inequality and unfair treatment by the government also motivate people toward violence. Devarajan and Ianchovichina (2017) find that the Arab Spring uprisings can be explained in part by subjective feelings of a decline in life satisfaction, driven by perceived declining living standards related to a shortage of formal sector jobs, corruption, and dissatisfaction with the quality of public services.

Not all empirical results point to the same conclusion, however. Miodownik and Nir (2016) construct a measure of horizontal inequality from survey questions in the third and fourth Afrobarometer[12] rounds that asked respondents whether they considered their ethnic group's economic and political condition to be worse, the same, or better than that of other groups in their country. The authors find the following:

- Perceptions of group political deprivation were associated with a lower risk of participation in demonstrations among African individuals, along with lower support for violence.
- Perceptions of group economic deprivation had no discernable effect. A study across four states in Nigeria (Rustad 2016) finds evidence that individuals who rated their conditions as poor were more likely to express support for violence in their attitudes. However, the findings were different when aggregated to the group level: belonging to a district or ethnic group where the average score of self-reported conditions was much poorer than that in the richest or largest group was associated with lower support for violence. This finding could be evidence that members of relatively privileged groups are more likely to support violence.

There is more evidence of a robust relationship between perceptions and violent conflict when perceptions are couched as unfair government treatment rather than in direct or aggregate measures of perceived material inequality.

The Gap between Objective and Perceived Inequalities

As discussed earlier, perceptions are crucial in explaining the effect of inequality and exclusion on conflict. However, in the absence of data, it is commonly assumed that perceptions of inequality will likely correspond to objective measures of inequality (Stewart 2002a; Cederman, Gleditsch, and Buhaug 2013). Studies therefore have focused on the relationship of the objective inequality to violent conflict—with mixed conclusions. Some find support for the argument that there is a correspondence (Gurr 1993; Holmqvist 2012); yet other studies find instead that often perceptions do not correspond to the objective reality (Langer and Smedts 2013). In a survey that includes Nigeria and Ghana, Langer and Ukiwo (2008) find a discrepancy between objective actual conditions and group members' perceptions of access to political power and education. Rustad's (2016) study in the Niger Delta also finds little overlap between the objective and perceived income levels of different ethnic groups (see figure 4.2).[13]

FIGURE 4.2 **Perceived and Objective Horizontal Inequality of Ethnic Groups in Nigeria**

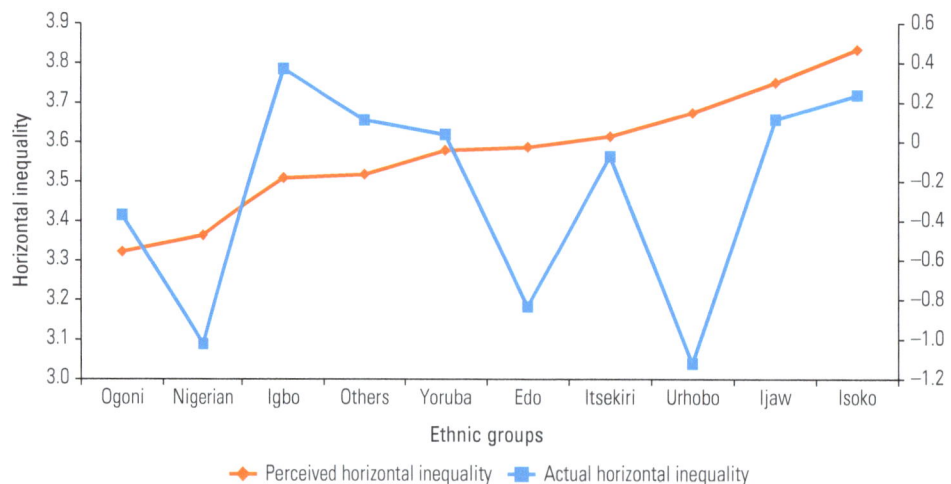

Source: Rustad 2016.

Exclusion, Identity, Grievances, and Mobilization to Violence

Violent conflict is not the inevitable outcome in a society or state in which there is horizontal inequality among groups, exclusion, and perceived exclusion. Many social groups may feel excluded or may objectively suffer from exclusion; inequality is present in most, if not all, countries. But only in very few countries will these circumstances lead first to group-based grievances and then to violent conflict. Despite the relatively little in-depth research around these transformations, this section explores evidence that has emerged on the progression from exclusion to grievance, and then from grievance to violent conflict.

Exclusion based on identity is at the heart of many conflicts. It is generally recognized that identity is fungible, neither static nor exclusive (Woolcock 2014). Different identities tend to become salient at different times and in different circumstances, and thus are context specific in their importance to mobilization to violent conflict (see box 4.6). For example, castes became politically salient in India only after the British began conducting national censuses, which required respondents to be placed into fixed demographic categories that were determined by the British themselves (Dirks 2001; Woolcock 2014). Similarly, Posner (2007) documents how leaders in Zambia and Kenya emphasized national-level ethnic cleavages to incite violence.

BOX 4.6 Identity and Mobilization to Violence: The Demographics and the Dynamics of Difference

Many studies on the association of horizontal inequality with violent conflict use social factors such as ethnicity, religion, and language as group identifiers. For example, contrary to prevailing belief, recent evidence suggests that conflict may be more likely within linguistic dyads than within religious ones. Moreover, Bormann, Cederman, and Vogt (2015) find no support for the thesis that Muslim groups are particularly conflict prone. Social identity, however, is not a static demographic characteristic. Individuals have multiple, overlapping forms and sources of identity that only become politically salient under particular conditions. For example, Kingston, Jamaica, is essentially monoethnic from a demographic perspective, is vibrantly democratic, and does not have unduly high economic inequality. Yet it is one of the most violent cities in the world. Why? Because political leaders are able to mobilize politically salient (but statistically unobservable) forms of social identity to protect their space and expand their markets (Duncan-Waite and Woolcock 2008).

Rather than looking at *demographics of difference*, some social scientists are increasingly studying what might be called the *dynamics of difference*—the conditions under which particular aspects of people's identities can be mobilized for large-scale collective action, whether for constructive or harmful purposes (Weber 1976; Mamdani 1996; Marx 1998; Baiocchi 2010). Needless to say, this juxtaposition—between the demographics and the dynamics of difference—is perhaps overly simplified (indeed, students of ethnicity seem to revel in creating ever-finer distinctions when locating themselves in the theoretical landscape), but for present purposes it is a fruitful one for elucidating the key differences between most economists and many other social scientists studying ethnicity and violence.

For example, careful micro-level studies of the conditions under which ethnicity can or cannot be mobilized for the purposes of violence (Varshney 2002; Posner 2004) suggest, as McGovern (2011, 350) notes, "that participants in violent politics are operating according to rational and irrational choice models at once. Such 'irrational choice' models must account for the presence and significance of actors' desires for respect, honor, adulation, and revenge."

The existence of diverse identity groups does not, by itself, move people to collective action. Nor does the prevalence of inequalities across those groups. There are plenty of examples of diverse societies with distributional differences on various dimensions that do not create frustration and that are accepted by people.

The process of grievance formation around inequalities appears to be the link between the existence of those inequalities and whether they generate some kind of collective action. Cederman, Gleditsch, and Buhaug (2013) explore this process, arguing that inequalities have to be politicized to become grievances. They identify three necessary steps for this politicization of grievances: First, there must be well-defined and separate identifiable groups in society.[14] Second, a group must be able to compare itself and its status to other groups, either by objective measures or perceptions. Finally, groups must frame the intergroup inequality as unfair and assign blame to another group

The wider literature on social movements includes some similar discussion of grievance formation. For example, a feeling of injustice and assignment of blame have been identified as necessary to the transformation of inequality and exclusion into grievance (Tarrow 2011). However, group perceptions may differ in different contexts, and what one group perceives as just at one time may be perceived as unjust by the same group at a different time.[15]

The severity of polarization among groups in a society also influences how or whether inequalities and perceived exclusion translate into grievances, and then into violent conflict. Scholars generally agree that ethnic polarization is a strong predictor of violent conflict (Montalvo and Reynal-Querol 2012; Bader and Ianchovichina 2017). Some studies suggest a strong relationship between polarization and the risk of genocide (Montalvo and Reynal-Querol 2008). Horowitz (2000) argues that more homogeneous societies tend to be less violent than highly heterogeneous societies, and that more conflicts occur in societies in which a large ethnic minority faces an ethnic majority. Similarly, Easterly, Ritzen, and Woolcock (2006) find that the polarization

of two large groups of similar size—for example, when a large minority is in conflict with a large minority—presents the highest likelihood of violent conflict.

Exclusion and grievances can result in collective mobilization; however, collective mobilization does not always result in violence. Some movements take a nonviolent approach, using tactics such as boycotts, marches, sit-ins, strikes, and silent vigils. Societies in which people feel the system is just and responsive to their grievances are societies most likely to be able to peacefully express grievances. In turn, social movements that do not use violence tend to be more successful. Chenoweth and Stephan (2011) find that nonviolent movements with political aims are twice as successful, on average, in achieving their objectives than those that use violence, and pave the way to more durable and internally peaceful societies.

What, then, are the factors that influence whether collective mobilization involves violence? Justino (2017, 3) argues that "whether social mobilization motivated by inequalities may turn violent is ultimately conditional on how people, individually or in groups, perceive themselves in relation to others in society" (see figure 4.3). She distinguishes four types of collective mobilization ranging from peaceful to violent:

- *Peaceful social mobilization* is a feature of democratic settings in which citizens and groups express their grievances and demands through peaceful means, including legal demonstrations, petition signing, and contacting government officials.[16]
- *Covert social resistance* tends to take place in settings of weak democratic institutions in which power rests mainly in the hands of strong elites and less privileged groups are excluded. Mobilization tends to be informal or less organized and reflects some sort of agreement among less privileged groups at the bottom of the distribution to resist the power of elites.
- *Fragmented social mobilization* occurs when social agreements are not possible.
- *Violent social mobilization* occurs when different groups engage in violent action to resolve disputes with other groups or with the state.

FIGURE 4.3 A Typology of Social Mobilization

		Within-group coordination	
		High	Low
Between-group relations	Cooperation	Peaceful social mobilization	Convert social resistance
	Antagonism	Violent social mobilization	Fragmented social mobilization

Source: Justino 2017.

Most often, collective mobilization driven by grievances is channeled toward conflict with the state rather than against another group or groups (Stewart 2002a). This occurs especially if the state is seen as "captured" for the economic benefit or interest of a specific socioeconomic group, or when the state is seen as acting solely to protect its own interests. Cederman, Wimmer, and Min (2010) suggest conflict with the government is more likely when the following three conditions prevail:

1. *A group or its representatives are excluded from executive power, especially after a loss of power.* The recent loss of power or prestige of excluded groups produces feelings of anger and resentment and increases the impulse to fight to change the situation. Call (2012) finds that perceived exclusionary behavior after internal armed conflicts correlates highly with conflict recurrence. Ghatak (2016) finds that exclusion of small numbers of people from state power likely results in domestic terrorism; civil war is highly likely when the number of politically excluded groups increases. Cederman, Wimmer, and Min (2010) find that the likelihood of violent conflict decreases when social or cultural group leaders gain access to state power.

2. *The group can mobilize large numbers of people.* Mobilization and violent contestation require both motivation and organizational capacity (Gurr 2000). Larger groups not only enjoy more legitimacy but also can draw on their networks for recruitment and resources to sustain their cause (McCarthy and Zald 1977; Cederman, Buhaug, and Rød 2009). For example, Posner (2004) finds that the main reason Chewas and Tumbukas are allies in Zambia and adversaries in Malawi stems from the different size of each group relative to each country's national political arena. In Malawi, he notes, Chewas and Tumbukas are large groups, and thus serve as viable bases for political coalition building. In Zambia, both groups are relatively small compared with the country as a whole, thus making it more difficult and less useful to mobilize for political support.

3. *The group has experienced violent conflict in the past.* Historical memories of past conflicts influence the likelihood of current conflict. They enable group members to see violence as a possibility, in that they have already experienced violence. Narratives of past conflicts also play an important role in the likelihood of present conflict. Having a group history that narrates a one-sided story and that perpetuates past violent experiences through oral histories, public rituals, or in official textbooks can create structures and identities that can be reactivated for violent purposes.

The way the state relates to different groups in society greatly determines how and whether grievances form against it (box 4.7). The literature has long examined the relationship between abuse by the state and popular dissent, and it is quite clear on how

State Violence and Conflict Risk

An analysis developed for this study (Cingranelli et al. 2017) considers how torture, disappearance, political imprisonment, and extrajudicial killing contributed to the risks of onset and escalation (or de-escalation) of three types of violent conflict within states: violent protests, domestic terrorism, and civil war. This analysis, based on samples of nearly 150 nation-states during the period 1990–2015, shows that countries with fewer violations of physical integrity rights witnessed, on average, 37 percent fewer violent protests, 79 percent fewer terrorist attacks, and 86 percent fewer civil war deaths (see figure B4.7.1).

FIGURE B4.7.1 Risks to Onset and Escalation of Violent Conflict

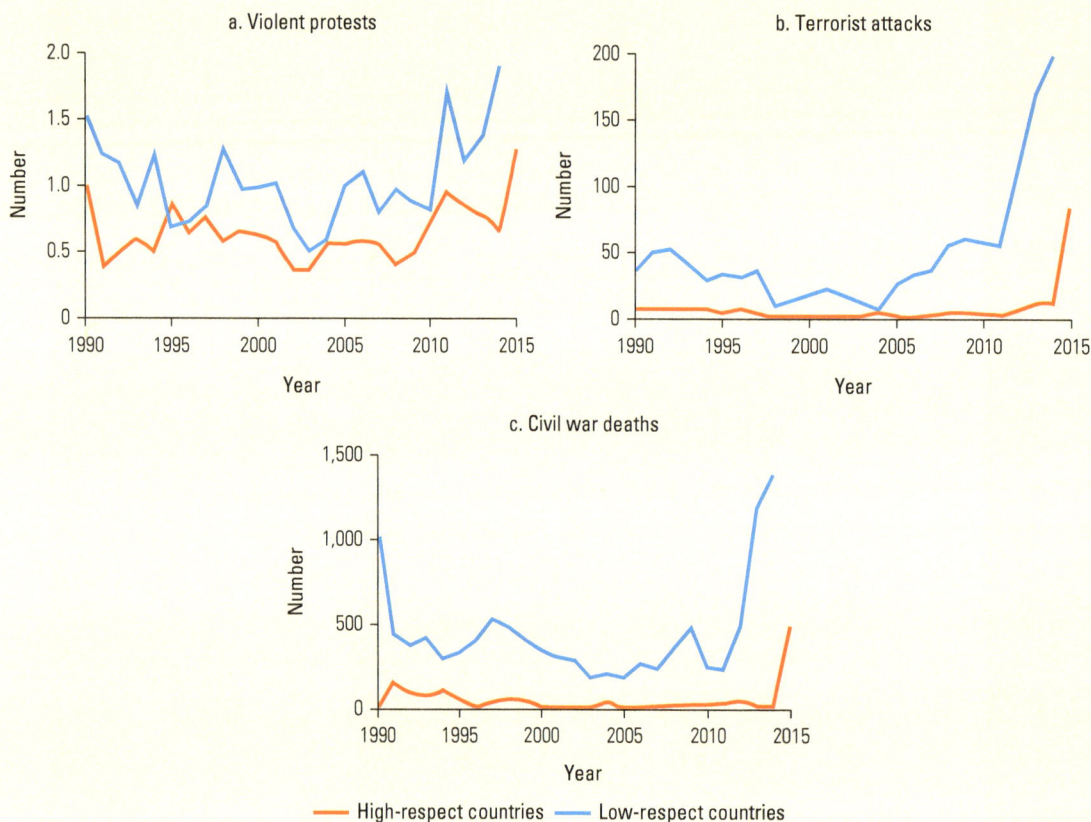

Source: Cingranelli et al. 2017.

government abuse increases both the scope and intensity of the population's grievances and the risk of onset and escalation of violent conflict. Goodwin (2001) concludes that government abuse creates the belief among the population that armed revolt against an unjust and abusive regime is the only alternative. Thoms and Ron (2007) show that violations of physical integrity by state actors are associated with the escalation of existing political conflicts. Work by Mason and Krane (1989) and by Kalyvas and Kocher (2007) shows how indiscriminate state violence against civilian populations generates grievances and pushes civilians into violence. Cederman et al. (2017) find evidence that the state-led civilian victimization of particular ethnic groups increases the likelihood that the group becomes involved in ethnic civil war.

Furthermore, studies by Piazza (2017) and Bakker, Hill, and Moore (2016) note that as state actors engage in higher levels of violent coercion and physical repression against the population, the risk of terrorist violence directed against the state and its population increases steeply.

The Role of Emotions in Mobilizing Groups

People come together in social groups for a kaleidoscope of subjective and objective reasons. They may share feelings, history, narratives of pain, frustrations, or identities that motivate them to collective action in different ways, at different times, and in the face of different situations. A body of scholarly literature argues that these reasons may contribute, alone or in combination with inequality and exclusion, to the mobilization of groups to violent action. Understanding how emotions, among other causes, play a role in the production of violent conflict can also provide policy makers with an understanding of how emotions can also play a role in the creation of more peaceful societies.

Emotions are intertwined with grievances, both triggering and sustaining collective violence (Horowitz 2001; Petersen 2002; Sargsyan 2017). Fear, for instance, can bond people into a group that mobilizes for violence, as when an attack or shock from outside results in a collective response to the perceived threat. Petersen (2002) suggests that fear, rage, hatred, and resentment all play a role in ethnic violence, but that different emotions result in different outcomes. He argues that resentment over loss of political power or a decline in status is especially potent, while violent experiences result in fear and anger, and prejudice and stigma bring about contempt and hatred. For example, Serbs' change in status in Kosovo resulted in feelings of resentment that fueled repression against Kosovo-Albanians.[17]

Collective memory, too, plays into the mobilization of group grievances (Durkheim, Pocock, and Peristiany 1953; Le Goff 1992). As Ross (2007) argues, interpretations of events are as important as the events themselves, and in conflict situations,

collective memories can trigger emotional and violent reactions. For example, during the conflict in Chechnya in the 1990s, Chechen leaders evoked collective memories of past wars and mass deportations, recalling feelings of humiliation to justify a violent struggle for self-determination (Campana 2009).

Collective feelings of humiliation and injustice, as indicated in the Chechen case, can be especially potent motivating factors. Khosrokhavar (2017) suggests that collective mobilization is more likely when feelings of injustice are coupled with resentment.

Unmet expectations and thwarted aspirations can be a source of frustration that drives mobilization to violence. As discussed in chapter 2 and earlier in this chapter, limited access to employment and livelihood opportunities can affect the rites of passage to adulthood, including marriage and starting families, and leaves many young people feeling frustrated, uncertain, and angry (Kraetsch 2008). Some authors suggest that radicalism can emerge among the highly educated young people that go through these experiences (Al-Azmeh 2006). However, these same frustrations can lead some, including young people, to become activists and peace builders.[18]

The Power of Elites and Narratives

Elites and leaders play a critical role in mobilizing grievances and shaping narratives that may steer groups toward, or away from, violent action. Elite theories of conflict suggest that collective violence is not a result of spontaneous eruptions of anger, but rather, in some cases, that elites plan and organize violence with the objective of increasing group cohesion and maintaining a loyal support base (Demmers 2016). Fearon and Laitin (2000, 853) argue that "elites foment ethnic violence to build support [and that] this process has the effect of constructing more antagonistic identities, which favors more violence." When elites feel threatened, often because of "past oppression," they tend to organize and defend themselves, giving rise to internal security stresses (World Bank 2011). Horowitz (2000) suggests that elites may initiate conflict along ethnic lines to deep ethnic divisions—thus increasing polarization—to strengthen their position in society and to exploit power. Failing to act can also be an elite tactic: in some cases, elites decide not to act or not to implement certain beneficial policies because doing so would challenge the status quo (World Bank 2017b).

Elites exert strong influence on collective mobilization through the narratives they create around their group's experiences. Narratives are stories that represent "the ways in which we construct disparate facts in our own worlds and weave them together cognitively in order to make sense of our reality" (Patterson and Monroe 1998, 315). They appeal to emotions, and an especially charismatic leader can invest the narrative with great power. Elites and other actors can use narratives to build social cohesion, as described in chapter 6. A narrative around inclusion, such as around the 2030 Agenda for Sustainable Development, could avert mobilization to violence when there is risk of conflict.

Elites also may use narratives to manipulate perceptions and memories to mobilize individuals toward collective violence. Shesterinina (2016), for example, finds that a narrative can lead civilians to fight and others to freeze or flee, and that the response depends upon how local elites translate national threats and on how populations perceive such narratives.

Collective experiences of injustice or violence and coercive measures by the state that are perceived as targeting certain groups only reinforce the power of narratives and harden group boundaries. Media, both private and government controlled, play a large role today in shaping narratives that can either reduce or inflame grievances (Sargsyan 2017), a role that is more salient than ever with the rapid growth of information and communication technology, as discussed in chapter 2.

Conclusion

Horizontal inequalities and exclusion are important factors in modern violent conflict, although in and of themselves they are not sufficient to mobilize groups to violence. The available research does not provide evidence of a straightforward path between the two. Nevertheless, this study argues that inequality and exclusion—even merely the *perception* of exclusion—can evolve into group-based grievances.

Whether collective mobilization becomes violent depends on a variety of factors, but is greatly influenced by whether aggrieved groups perceive themselves to have viable, peaceful alternatives for expressing grievances. Risks are heightened if leaders are able to hook into grievances and assign blame to another group. Oftentimes emotions are called upon in narratives that incite violence.

Very often the state is perceived to be the source of grievance, and becomes the target of collective mobilization. An aggrieved group may see the state as acting in its own interest or as controlled by a group that is using the state for its exclusive benefit. The state also may be incapable of dealing with intergroup grievances or, in the worst-case scenario, may aggravate these tensions through abuses or discriminatory behavior toward specific groups. Addressing exclusion and horizontal inequality is therefore important as a prevention strategy. Chapter 5 now turns to key spaces where exclusion is felt most acutely, and where grievances tend to concentrate.

Notes

1. Chapter 1 of this report assesses the limitations and challenges of measuring violent conflict.
2. On education, see UNICEF (2015). On infant mortality (for Indonesia only), see Østby et al. (2011); Cederman, Gleditsch, and Buhaug (2013).
3. See the subsection "Perceptions of Exclusion and Unfairness in Violent Conflict Risk" in this chapter for more discussion.
4. This is addressed in the "The Multiple and Intersecting Dimensions of Exclusion" section.
5. See "Ethnic Power Relations Dataset Family 2014" at https://icr.ethz.ch/data/epr/.
6. Most quantitative studies use education as a proxy for inequality generally and do not distinguish between the impacts of economic and social inequalities. It is difficult

in this case to assess the importance solely of social inequalities.

7. "Politically relevant groups" are defined as those that are active in national politics or discriminated against by the government. They comprise a subset of all groups observed, and are potentially subject to bias because, for example, excluded groups that are not active are not represented in the data.

8. The data set produces 32,567 "group-years."

9. WomanStats (n.d.).

10. The United Nations uses the range of 15–24 years of age for statistical reasons when discussing youth, and recognizes national and regional definitions of youth. However, SCR 2250 (UNSC 2015b) uses 18–29 years to avoid overlap with resolutions on children in armed conflict.

11. The assumption is that objective inequality leads to perceived deprivation, which increases the likelihood to take part in conflict.

12. Afrobarometer is a pan-African, nonpartisan research network that conducts public attitude surveys on democracy, governance, economic conditions, and related issues in more than 35 countries in Africa.

13. Objective horizontal inequality is measured as a wealth index of items that the survey respondent owns.

14. As Stewart (2000) notes, the presence of horizontal inequalities already, to a certain extent, assumes the existence of well-defined groups.

15. Marc et al. (2012) discuss different criteria for assessing fairness.

16. Nonviolent movements use tactics such as marches, consumer boycotts, sit-ins, labor strikes, and silent vigils. Examples of nonviolent movements in history include the U.S. civil rights movement and the Yellow Revolution in the Philippines.

17. All references to Kosovo shall be understood in the context of UN Security Council Resolution 1244 (1999).

18. For most, feelings of frustration do not lead to violence.

References

Abbink, Jon. 2005. "Being Young in Africa: The Politics of Despair and Renewal." In *Vanguard or Vandals: Youth, Politics and Conflict in Africa*, edited by J. Abbink and I. Kessel, 1–34. Boston, MA: Brill.

Al-Azmeh, A. 2006. *Making Governance Work against Radicalisation*. Copenhagen: Danish Institute for International Studies.

Alesina, A., S. Michalopoulos, and E. Papaioannou. 2016. "Ethnic Inequality." *Journal of Political Economy* 124 (2): 428–88.

Anderlini, Sanam Naraghi. 2007. *Women Building Peace: What They Do, Why It Matters*. Boulder, CO: Lynne Rienner.

Asal, V., M. Findley, J. A. Piazza, and J. I. Walsh. 2016. "Political Exclusion, Oil, and Ethnic Armed Conflict." *Journal of Conflict Resolution* 60 (8): 1343–67.

Aspinall, E. 2007. "The Construction of Grievance: Natural Resources and Identity in a Separatist Conflict." *Journal of Conflict Resolution* 51 (6): 950–72.

Atran, Scott. 2016. "The Devoted Actor: Unconditional Commitment and Intractable Conflict across Cultures." *Current Anthropology* 57 (S13): S192–S203.

Atran, Scott, and J. Ginges. 2012. "Religious and Sacred Imperatives in Human Conflict." *Science* 336 (6083): 855–57. http://www.princeton.edu/~acoman/Projects_files/Science-2012-Scott-Jeremy.pdf.

Atran, Scott, and Douglas M. Stone. 2015. "The Kurds' Heroic Stand against ISIS." *New York Times*, March 16. http://www.nytimes.com/2015/03/16/opinion/the-kurds-heroic-stand-against-isis.html.

Bader, S. A., and E. Ianchovichina. 2017. "Polarization, Foreign Military Interventions, and Civil Conflicts." Working Paper, World Bank, Washington, DC. http://siteresources.worldbank.org/INTMENA/Resources/PolarizationForeignMilitaryInterventionsandCivilConflictspaper.pdf.

Baiocchi, G. A. 2010. "The Politics of Habitus: Publics, Blackness and Community Activism in Salvador, Brazil." *Qualitative Sociology* 33 (3): 369–88.

Bakker, Ryan, Daniel W. Hill, and Will H. Moore. 2016. "How Much Terror? Dissidents, Governments, Institutions, and the Cross-National Study of Terror Attacks." *Journal of Peace Research* 53 (5): 711–26.

Bannon, Ian, and Maria Correia. 2006. *The Other Half of Gender: Men's Issues in Development*. Washington, DC: World Bank. https://openknowledge.worldbank.org/handle/10986/7029.

Barrett, Robert S. 2011. "Interviews with Killers: Six Types of Combatants and Their Motivations for Joining Deadly Groups." *Studies in Conflict and Terrorism* 34 (10): 749–64.

Bartusevičius, H. 2014. "The Inequality-Conflict Nexus Re-examined: Income, Education and Popular Rebellions." *Journal of Peace Research* 51 (1): 35–50.

Besançon, Marie L. 2005. "Relative Resources: Inequality in Ethnic Wars, Revolutions, and Genocides." *Journal of Peace Research* 42 (4): 393–415.

Bhatia, Kartika, and Hafez Ghanem. 2017. "How Do Education and Unemployment Affect Support for Violent Extremism? Evidence from Eight Arab Countries." Global Economy and Development Working Paper 102, Brookings Institution, Washington, DC.

Bircan, C., T. Bruck, and M. Vothknecht. 2017. "Violent Conflict and Inequality." *Oxford Development Studies* 45 (2): 125–44.

Bloom, M. 2005. *Dying to Kill: The Allure of Suicide Terror.* New York: Columbia University Press.

———. 2011. *Bombshell: Women and Terrorism.* Philadelphia, PA: University of Pennsylvania Press.

Bormann, Nils-Christian, Lars-Erik Cederman, and Manuel Vogt. 2015. "Language, Religion, and Ethnic Civil War." *Journal of Conflict Resolution* 61 (4): 1–28.

Botha, Anneli. 2013. "Assessing the Vulnerability of Kenyan Youths to Radicalism and Extremism." ISS Paper 245, Institute for Security Studies, Pretoria. http://www.issafrica.org/uploads/Paper245.pdf.

Boudet, A. M. M., P. Petesch, C. Turk, and A. Thumala. 2012. *On Norms and Agency: Conversations about Gender Equality with Women and Men in 20 Countries.* Washington, DC: World Bank.

Brown, G. 2010. "The Political Economy of Secessionism: Identity, Inequality and the State." Bath Paper in International Development 9, University of Bath, Bath, UK.

Brown, K. 2014. "Why Are Western Women Joining Islamic State?" *BBC News Online,* October 4. http://www.bbc.com/news/uk-29507410.

Buhaug, H., L.-E. Cederman, and K. S. Gleditsch. 2014. "Square Pegs in Round Holes: Inequalities, Grievances, and Civil War." *International Studies Quarterly* 58 (2): 418–31.

Call, Charles T. 2012. "UN Mediation and the Politics of Transition after Constitutional Crises." International Peace Institute Policy Papers, International Peace Institute, New York. https://www.ipinst.org/2012/02/un-mediation-and-the-politics-of-transition-after-constitutional-crises-2.

Campana, A. 2009. "Collective Memory and Violence: The Use of Myths in the Chechen Separatist Ideology, 1991–1994." *Journal of Muslim Minority Affairs* 29 (1): 43–56. doi: 10.1080/13602000902726756.

Caprioli, M. 2000. "Gendered Conflict." *Journal of Peace Research* 37 (1): 51–68.

———. 2005. "Primed for Violence: The Role of Gender Inequality in Predicting Internal Conflict." *International Studies Quarterly* 49 (2): 161–78. doi: 10.1111/j.0020-8833.2005.00340.x.

Caprioli, M., and M. Boyer. 2001. "Gender, Violence, and International Crisis." *Journal of Conflict Resolution* 45: 503–18.

Caprioli, M., V. Hudson, R. McDermott, C. Emmett, and B. Ballif-Spanvill. 2007. "Putting Women in Their Place." *Baker Journal of Applied Public Policy* 1 (1): 12–22.

Caprioli, M., and P. F. Tumbore. 2003. "Ethnic Discrimination and Interstate Violence: Testing the International Impact of Domestic Behavior." *Journal of Peace Research* 40 (1): 5–23.

Cederman, Lars-Erik, Halvard Buhaug, and Jan Ketil Rød. 2009. "Ethno-Nationalist Dyads and Civil War: A GIS-Based Analysis." *Journal of Conflict Resolution* 53 (4): 496–525. doi:10.1177/0022002709336455.

Cederman, Lars-Erik, K. Gleditsch, and H. Buhaug. 2013. *Inequality, Grievances, and Civil War.* New York: Cambridge University Press.

Cederman, Lars-Erik, Simon Hug, Livia I. Schubiger, and Francisco Villamil. 2017. "Civilian Victimization and Ethnic Civil War." Paper prepared for the Annual Meeting of the American Political Science Association, San Francisco, CA, August 31–September 3.

Cederman, Lars-Erik, N. B. Weidmann, and N.-C. Bormann. 2015. "Triangulating Horizontal Inequality: Toward Improved Conflict Analysis." *Journal of Peace Research* 52 (6): 806–21.

Cederman, Lars-Erik, N. B. Weidmann, and K. S. Gleditsch. 2011. "Horizontal Inequalities and Ethnonationalist Civil War: A Global

Comparison." *American Political Science Review* 105 (3): 478–95.

Cederman, Lars-Erik, Andreas Wimmer, and Brian Min. 2010. "Why Do Ethnic Groups Rebel? New Data and Analysis." *World Politics* 62 (1): 87–119.

Celiku, B., and A. C. Kraay. 2017. "Predicting Conflict." Policy Research Working Paper 8075, World Bank, Washington, DC.

CeSID (Center for Free Elections and Democracy). 2017. "Survey of the Drivers of Youth Radicalism and Violent Extremism in Serbia." Report prepared in cooperation with UNDP Serbia, Belgrade.

Chenoweth, E., and M. J. Stephan. 2011. *Why Civil Resistance Works*. New York: Columbia University Press.

Christmann, Kris. 2012. "Preventing Religious Radicalisation and Violent Extremism: A Systematic Review of the Research Evidence." Research Report. Youth Justice Board for England and Wales.

Cingranelli, D., M. Gibney, P. Haschke, R. Wood, D. Arnon, and B. Mark. 2017. "Human Rights Violations and Violent Conflict." Background paper for the United Nations–World Bank Flagship Study, *Pathways for Peace: Inclusive Approaches to Preventing Violent Conflict*, World Bank, Washington, DC.

Collier, P. 2000. "Doing Well Out of War: An Economic Perspective." In *Greed and Grievance: Economic Agendas in Civil Wars*, edited by M. Berdal and D. M. Malone, 91–111. Boulder, CO: Lynne Rienner.

Collier, P., V. L. Elliot, H. Hegre, A. Hoeffler, M. Reynal-Querol, and N. Sambanis. 2003. *Breaking the Conflict Trap: Civil War and Development Policy*. Washington, DC: World Bank.

Collier, P., and A. Hoeffler. 2004. "Greed and Grievance in Civil War." *Oxford Economic Papers* 56 (4): 563–95.

Cramer, Christopher. 2003. "Does Inequality Cause Conflict?" *Journal of International Development* 15 (4): 397–412.

Crespo-Sancho, Catalina. 2017. "Conflict Prevention and Gender." Background paper for the United Nations–World Bank Flagship Study, *Pathways for Peace: Inclusive Approaches to Preventing Violent Conflict*, World Bank, Washington, DC.

Deininger, Klaus. 2003. "Causes and Consequences of Civil Strife: Micro-Level Evidence from Uganda." *Oxford Economic Papers* 55 (4): 579–606.

Demmers, J. 2016. *Theories of Violent Conflict*. Milton, UK: Taylor and Francis.

Devarajan, S., and E. Ianchovichina. 2017. "A Broken Social Contract, Not High Inequality, Led to the Arab Spring." *Review of Income and Wealth* 18 (2): 1–4.

Devarajan, Shantayanan, Lili Mottaghi, Quy-Toan Do, Anne Brockmeyer, Clement Jean Edouard Joubert, Kartika Bhatia, Mohamed Abdel Jelil, Radwan Ali Shaban, Isabelle Chaal-Dabi, and Nathalie Lenoble. 2016. *MENA Economic Monitor: Economic and Social Inclusion to Prevent Violent Extremism*. Washington, DC: World Bank Group. http://documents.worldbank.org /curated/en/409591474983005625/Economic -and-social-inclusion-to-prevent-violent -extremism.

Dirks, N. 2001. *Castes of Mind: Colonialism and the Making of Modern India*. Princeton, NJ: Princeton University Press.

Duncan-Waite, I., and M. Woolcock. 2008. "Arrested Development: The Political Origins and Socioeconomic Foundations of Common Violence in Jamaica." Brooks World Poverty Institute Working Paper 2008/6/1, University of Manchester.

Durkheim, E., D. Pocock, and J. Peristiany. 1953. *Sociology and Philosophy*. London: Routledge.

Easterly, W., J. Ritzen, and M. Woolcock. 2006. "Social Cohesion, Institutions, and Growth." Working Paper 94, Center for Global Development, Washington, DC.

EIP (European Institute of Peace). 2017. "Molenbeek and Violent Radicalization: 'A Social Mapping.'" EIP, Brussels.

Fearon, James. 2010. "Governance and Civil War Onset." Background paper for *World Development Report 2011: Conflict, Security, and Development*, World Bank, Washington, DC.

Fearon, James, and David Laitin. 2000. "Violence and the Social Construction of Ethnic Identity." *International Organization* 54 (4): 845–77.

———. 2003. "Ethnicity, Insurgency, and Civil War." *American Political Science Review* 97: 75–90.

Fjelde, H., and G. Østby. 2014. "Socioeconomic Inequality and Communal Conflict: A Disaggregated Analysis of Sub-Saharan Africa, 1990–2008." *International Interactions* 40 (5): 737–62.

Ghatak, S. 2016. "The Role of Political Exclusion and State Capacity in Civil Conflict in

South Asia." *Terrorism and Political Violence* 1–23. doi: 10.1080/09546553.2016.1150840.

Ginges, Jeremy, Scott Atran, Douglas Medin, and Khalil Shikaki. 2007. "Sacred Bounds on Rational Resolution of Violent Political Conflict." *Proceedings of the National Academy of Sciences* 104 (18): 7357–60.

GIWPS (Georgetown Institute for Women, Peace and Security) and PRIO (Peace Research Institute Oslo). 2017. *Women, Peace and Security Index 2017/18: Tracking Sustainable Peace through Inclusion, Justice, and Security for Women.* Washington, DC: GIWPS and PRIO.

Goodwin, Jeff. 2001. *No Other Way Out: States and Social Movements, 1945–1991.* Cambridge, MA: Cambridge University Press.

Gurr, T. R. 1970. *Why Men Rebel.* Princeton, NJ: Princeton University Press.

———. 1993. "Why Minorities Rebel: A Global Analysis of Communal Mobilization and Conflict since 1945." *International Political Science Review* 14 (2): 161–201.

———. 2000. *Peoples versus States: Minorities at Risk in the New Century.* Washington, DC: United States Institute of Peace Press.

Hillesund, S. 2015. "A Dangerous Discrepancy: Testing the Micro-Dynamics of Horizontal Inequality on Palestinian Support for Armed Resistance." *Journal of Peace Research* 52 (1): 76–90.

Höhne, Markus. 2013. "Minorities in Somalia." In *Somalia: Security, Minorities and Migration*, edited by Alexander Schahbasi and Thomas Schrott, 63–86. Vienna: Austrian Federal Ministry of the Interior.

Holmqvist, G. 2012. "Inequality and Identity: Causes of War." Discussion Paper 72, Nordic Africa Institute, Uppsala, Sweden.

Honwana, Alcinda. 2013. *The Time of Youth: Work, Social Change and Politics in Africa.* Boulder, CO: Lynne Rienner.

Horowitz, D. L. 2000. *Ethnic Groups in Conflict.* Berkeley, CA: University of California Press.

———. 2001. *The Deadly Ethnic Riot.* Berkeley, CA: University of California Press.

Hudson, V., B. Ballif-Spanvill, M. Caprioli, and C. Emmett. 2012. *Sex and World Peace.* New York: Columbia University Press.

Hudson, V., M. Caprioli, B. Ballif-Spanvill, R. McDermott, and C. Emmett. 2009. "The Heart of the Matter: The Security of Women and the Security of States." *International Security* 33 (3): 7–45. doi: 10.1162/isec.2009.33.3.7.

Idris, I. 2016. *Youth Unemployment and Violence: Rapid Literature Review.* Birmingham, UK: GSDRC, University of Birmingham.

ISS (Institute for Security Studies). 2016. "Mali's Young 'Jihadists'—Fuelled by Faith or Circumstance?" Policy Brief 89, ISS, Pretoria.

Jones, B., M. Elgin-Cossart, and J. Esberg. 2012. *Pathways Out of Fragility: The Case for a Research Agenda on Inclusive Political Settlements in Fragile States.* New York: Center on International Cooperation.

Jost, J., and M. Banaji. 2004. "A Decade of System Justification Theory: Accumulated Evidence of Conscious and Unconscious Bolstering of the Status Quo." *Political Psychology* 25 (6): 881–919.

Justino, Patricia. 2017. "Linking Inequality and Political Conflict: The Role of Social Mobilization and Collective Action." Background paper for the United Nations–World Bank Flagship Study, *Pathways for Peace: Inclusive Approaches to Preventing Violent Conflict*, World Bank, Washington, DC.

Justino, Patricia, Ivan Cardona, Rebecca Mitchell, and Catherine Müller. 2012. "Quantifying the Impact of Women's Participation in Post-Conflict Economic Recovery." HiCN Working Paper 131, Households in Conflict Network, University of Sussex, Brighton, UK.

Justino, Patricia, and M. Moore. 2015. *Inequality: Trends, Harms and New Agendas.* IDS Evidence Report 144. Brighton, UK: Institute of Development Studies.

Kalyvas, Stathis N., and Matthew Adam Kocher. 2007. "How 'Free' Is Free Riding in Civil Wars? Violence, Insurgency, and the Collective Action Problem." *World Politics* 59 (2): 177–216.

Kelly, Jocelyn. 2017. "Intimate Partner Violence and Conflict: Understanding the Links between Political Violence and Personal Violence." Background paper for the United Nations–World Bank Flagship Study, *Pathways for Peace: Inclusive Approaches to Preventing Violent Conflict*, World Bank, Washington, DC.

Khosrokhavar, Farhad. 2017. "Humiliation and Its Multiple Dimensions." Background paper for the United Nations–World Bank Flagship Study, *Pathways for Peace: Inclusive Approaches to Preventing Violent Conflict*, World Bank, Washington, DC.

Kirwin, M., and W. Cho. 2009. "Weak States and Political Violence in Sub-Saharan Africa." Working Paper 111, Afrobarometer. http://afrobarometer.org/sites/default/files/publications/Working%20paper/AfropaperNo111.pdf.

Kraetsch, M. 2008. "Middle East Youth Initiative." Paper presented at the Peace Research Institute Oslo, "Youth Exclusion and Political Violence," Oslo, December 4–5.

Krishnan, N., C. Ibarra, A. Narayan, S. Tiwari, and T. Vishwanath. 2016. *Uneven Odds, Unequal Outcomes: Inequality of Opportunity in the Middle East and North Africa.* Washington, DC: World Bank.

Ladbury, Sarah. 2015. *Women and Extremism: The Association of Women and Girls with Jihadi Groups and Implications for Programming.* Independent paper prepared for the Department of International Development (DFID) and the Foreign and Commonwealth Office. https://www.gov.uk/dfid-research-outputs/women-and-extremism-the-association-of-women-and-girls-with-jihadi-groups-and-implications-for-programming.

Langer, A., and K. Smedts. 2013. "Seeing Is Not Believing: Perceptions of Horizontal Inequalities in Africa." Working Paper 16, Centre for Research on Peace and Development, Leuven, Belgium.

Langer, A., and U. Ukiwo. 2008. "Ethnicity, Religion and the State in Ghana and Nigeria: Perceptions from the Street." In *Horizontal Inequalities and Conflict: Understanding Group Violence in Multiethnic Societies*, edited by F. Stewart, 205–26. London: Palgrave Macmillan UK.

Le Goff, J. 1992. *History and Memory.* New York: Columbia University Press.

Lichbach, M. I. 1989. "An Evaluation of 'Does Economic Inequality Breed Political Conflict?' Studies." *World Politics* 41 (4): 431–70.

Mamdani, Mahmood. 1996. *Citizen and Subject: Contemporary Africa and the Legacy of Late Colonialism.* Princeton, NJ: Princeton University Press.

Mancini, L., F. Stewart, and G. K. Brown. 2008. "Approaches to the Measurement of Horizontal Inequalities." In *Horizontal Inequalities and Conflict: Understanding Group Violence in Multiethnic Societies*, edited by F. Stewart, 85–105. London: Palgrave Macmillan.

Marc, Alexandre, Alys Willman, Ghazia Aslam, Michelle Rebosio, and Kanishka Balasuriya. 2012. *Societal Dynamics and Fragility: Engaging Societies in Responding to Fragile Situations.* New Frontiers of Social Policy Series. Washington, DC: World Bank.

Marx, A. 1998. *Making Race and Nation: A Comparison of South Africa, the United States and Brazil.* Cambridge, UK: Cambridge University Press.

Mason, T. David, and Dale A. Krane. 1989. "The Political Economy of Death Squads: Toward a Theory of the Impact of State-Sanctioned Terror." *International Studies Quarterly* 33 (2): 175–98.

McCarthy, J., and M. Zald. 1977. "Resource Mobilization and Social Movements: A Partial Theory." *American Journal of Sociology* 82 (6): 1212–41. doi: 10.1086/226464.

McCauley, Clark, and Sophia Moskalenko. 2008. "Mechanisms of Political Radicalization: Pathways toward Terrorism." *Terrorism and Political Violence* 20 (3): 415–33.

McGovern, M. 2011. *Making War in Côte d'Ivoire.* Chicago, IL: University of Chicago Press.

Melander, E. 2005. "Gender Equality and Intrastate Armed Conflict." *International Studies Quarterly* 49 (4): 695–714. doi: 10.1111/j.1468-2478.2005.00384.x.

Mercy Corps. 2015. *Youth & Consequences: Unemployment, Injustice and Violence.* Portland, OR: Mercy Corps.

———. 2016. *"Motivations and Empty Promises:" Voices of Former Boko Haram Combatants and Nigerian Youth.* Portland, OR: Mercy Corps.

Milanovic, B. 2016. *Global Inequality: A New Approach for the Age of Globalization.* Cambridge, MA: Harvard University Press.

Miodownik, D., and L. Nir. 2016. "Receptivity to Violence in Ethnically Divided Societies: A Micro-Level Mechanism of Perceived Horizontal Inequalities." *Studies in Conflict and Terrorism* 39 (1): 22–45.

Mitra, A., and D. Ray. 2014. "Implications of an Economic Theory of Conflict: Hindu-Muslim Violence in India." *Journal of Political Economy* 122 (4): 719–65.

Montalvo, J., and M. Reynal-Querol. 2008. "Discrete Polarisation with an Application to the Determinants of Genocides." *Economic Journal* 118 (533): 1835–65. doi: 10.1111/j.1468-0297.2008.02193.x.

———. 2012. *Inequality, Polarization, and Conflict.* Oxford: Oxford University Press.

Muller, E. 1985. "Income Inequality, Regime Repressiveness, and Political Violence." *American Sociological Review* 50: 47–67.

Murshed, S. M., and S. Gates. 2005. "Spatial–Horizontal Inequality and the Maoist Insurgency in Nepal." *Review of Development Economics* 9 (1): 121–34.

Must, E. 2016. "When and How Does Inequality Cause Conflict? Group Dynamics, Perceptions and Natural Resources." PhD thesis, Department of Government, London School of Economics.

Nagel, J. H. 1976. "Erratum." *World Politics* 28 (2): 315.

Nepal, M., A. Bohara, and K. Gawande. 2011. "More Inequality, More Killings: The Maoist Insurgency in Nepal." *American Journal of Political Science* 55 (4): 886–906.

Nygård, Havard Mokeiv, Karim Baghat, Gray Barrett, Kenra Dupuy, Scott Gates, Solveig Hillesund, Siri Aas Rustad, Håvard Strand, Henrik Urdal, and Gudrun Østby. 2017. "Inequality and Armed Conflict: Evidence and Data." Background paper for the United Nations–World Bank Flagship Study, *Pathways for Peace: Inclusive Approaches to Preventing Violent Conflict*, World Bank, Washington, DC.

Obermeyer, Z., C. Murray, and E. Gakidou. 2008. "Fifty Years of Violent War Deaths from Vietnam to Bosnia: Analysis of Data from the World Health Survey Programme." *British Medical Journal* 336 (7659): 1482–86. http://dx.doi.org/10.1136/bmj.a137.

Omoeva, C., and E. Buckner. 2015. *Does Horizontal Education Inequality Lead to Violent Conflict? A Global Analysis.* New York: UNICEF.

O'Reilly, M. 2015. *Why Women? Inclusive Security and Peaceful Societies.* Washington, DC: Inclusive Security.

O'Reilly, M., A. Ó Súilleabháin, and T. Paffenholz. 2015. "Reimagining Peacemaking: Women's Roles in Peace Processes." International Peace Institute, New York.

Østby, Gudrun. 2008a. "Inequalities, the Political Environment and Civil Conflict: Evidence from 55 Developing Countries." In *Horizontal Inequalities and Conflict: Understanding Group Violence in Multiethnic Societies*, edited by F. Stewart, 252–81. London: Palgrave Macmillan UK.

———. 2008b. "Polarization, Horizontal Inequalities and Violent Civil Conflict." *Journal of Peace Research* 45 (2): 143–62.

———. 2013. "Inequality and Political Violence: A Review of the Literature." *International Area Studies Review* 16 (2): 206–31.

Østby, G., R. Nordås, and J. Rød. 2009. "Regional Inequalities and Civil Conflict in Sub-Saharan Africa." *International Studies Quarterly* 53 (2): 301–24.

Østby, G., H. Urdal, M. Z. Tadjoeddin, S. M. Murshed, and H. Strand. 2011. "Population Pressure, Horizontal Inequality and Political Violence: A Disaggregated Study of Indonesian Provinces, 1990–2003." *Journal of Development Studies* 47 (3): 377–98.

Paasonen, K., and H. Urdal. 2016. "Youth Bulges, Exclusion and Instability: The Role of Youth in the Arab Spring." PRIO Conflict Trends. http://files.prio.org/Publication_files/prio/Paasonen,%20Urdal%20-%20Youth%20Bulges,%20Exclusion%20and%20Instability,%20Conflict%20Trends%203-2016.pdf.

Paffenholz, Thania. 2015. "Beyond the Normative: Can Women's Inclusion Really Make for Better Peace Processes?" Policy Brief, Graduate Institute of International and Development Studies, Centre for Conflict Development and Peacebuilding, Geneva.

Paffenholz, Thania, Andreas Hirblinger, Dana Landau, Felix Fritsch, and Constance Dijkstra. 2017. "Preventing Violence through Inclusion: From Building Political Momentum to Sustaining Peace." Background paper for the United Nations–World Bank Flagship Study, *Pathways for Peace: Inclusive Approaches to Preventing Violent Conflict*, World Bank, Washington, DC.

Patterson, M., and K. Monroe. 1998. "Narrative in Political Science." *Annual Review of Political Science* 1 (1): 315–31. doi: 10.1146/annurev.polisci.1.1.315.

Petersen, R. D. 2002. *Understanding Ethnic Violence: Fear, Hatred, and Resentment in Twentieth-Century Eastern Europe.* Cambridge, UK: Cambridge University Press.

Petesch, P. 2012. "Unlocking Pathways to Women's Empowerment and Gender Equality: The Good, the Bad and the Sticky." Ethics and Social Welfare 6 (3): 233–46.

Piazza, James A. 2017. "Repression and Terrorism: A Cross National Empirical Analysis of Types of Repression and Domestic Terrorism." *Terrorism and Political Violence* 29 (1): 102–18.

Piketty, T. 2013. *Capital in the Twenty-First Century.* Translated by A. Goldhammer. Cambridge, MA: Belknap.

Posner, Daniel. 2004. "The Political Salience of Cultural Difference: Why Chewas and Tumbukas are Allies in Zambia and Adversaries in Malawi." *American Political Science Review* 98 (4): 529–45.

———. 2007. "Regime Change and Ethnic Cleavages in Africa." *Comparative Political Studies* 40 (11): 1302–27.

Regan, P., and A. Paskeviciute. 2003. "Women's Access to Politics and Peaceful States." *Journal of Peace Research* 40 (3): 287–302. doi: 10.1177/0022343303040003003.

Reza, A., J. Mercy, and E. Krug. 2001. "Epidemiology of Violent Deaths in the World." *Injury Prevention* 7 (2): 104–11. doi: 10.1136/ip.7.2.104.

Ross, M. 2007. *Cultural Contestation in Ethnic Conflict*. Cambridge, UK: Cambridge University Press.

Russett, B. M. 1964. "Inequality and Instability." *World Politics* 16 (3): 442–54.

Rustad, S. A. 2016. "Socioeconomic Inequalities and Attitudes toward Violence: A Test with New Survey Data in the Niger Delta." *International Interactions* 42 (1): 106–39.

Sargsyan, Irena L. 2017. "Narrative, Perception and Emotion: A Review of Recent Political Science Studies." Background paper for the United Nations–World Bank Flagship Study, *Pathways for Peace: Inclusive Approaches to Preventing Violent Conflict*, World Bank, Washington, DC.

Schock, Kurt. 1996. "A Conjunctural Model of Political Conflict: The Impact of Political Opportunities on the Relationship between Economic Inequality and Violent Political Conflict." *Journal of Conflict Resolution* 40 (1): 98–133.

Shesterinina, A. 2016. "Collective Threat Framing and Mobilization in Civil War." *American Political Science Review* 110 (3): 411–27.

Sigelman, L., and M. Simpson. 1977. "A Cross-National Test of the Linkage between Economic Inequality and Political Violence." *Journal of Conflict Resolution* 21 (1): 105–28.

Sjoberg, Laura, and C. E. Gentry. 2016. "It's Complicated: Looking Closely at Women in Violent Extremism." *Georgetown Journal of International Affairs* 17 (2): 23–30. doi: 10.1353/gia.2016.0021.

Sjoberg, Laura, and Reed Wood. 2015. "People, Not Pawns: Women's Participation in Violent Extremism across MENA." United States Agency for International Development, Washington, DC. http://www.tinyurl.com/lbhunw9.

Spiegel, P., and P. Salama. 2000. "War and Mortality in Kosovo, 1998–99: An Epidemiological Testimony." *Lancet* 355 (9222): 2204–09. doi: 10.1016/s0140-6736(00)02404-1.

Stern, J., and J. M. Berger. 2015. *ISIS: The State of Terror*. New York: HarperCollins.

Stewart, Frances. 2000. "Crisis Prevention: Tackling Horizontal Inequalities." *Oxford Development Studies* 28 (3): 245–62.

———. 2002a. "Horizontal Inequalities: A Neglected Dimension of Development." QEH Working Paper Series 81, Queen Elizabeth House, University of Oxford.

———. 2002b. "Roots of Violent Conflict in Developing Countries." *British Medical Journal* 324 (7333): 342–45.

———. 2009. "Horizontal Inequalities as a Cause of Conflict." Bradford Development Lecture, University of Bradford, West Yorkshire, UK.

Stiglitz, J. 2013. *The Price of Inequality: How Today's Divided Society Endangers Our Future*. New York: Norton.

Stone, Laurel. 2015. "Study of 156 Peace Agreements, Controlling for Other Variables, Quantitative Analysis of Women's Participation in Peace Processes." In "Reimagining Peacemaking: Women's Roles in Peace Processes," by M. O'Reilly, A. Ó Súilleabháin, and T. Paffenholz, International Peace Institute, New York.

Tarrow, Sidney. 2011. *Power in Movement: Social Movements and Contentious Politics*. Cambridge, UK: Cambridge University Press.

Tessler, M., and I. Warriner. 1997. "Gender, Feminism, and Attitudes toward International Conflict: Exploring Relationships with Survey Data from the Middle East." *World Politics* 49 (02): 250–81. doi: 10.1353/wp.1997.0005.

Thoms, O., and J. Ron. 2007. "Public Health, Conflict and Human Rights: Toward a Collaborative Research Agenda." *Conflict and Health* 1 (11). doi: 10.1186/1752-1505-1-11

UNDP (United Nations Development Programme). 2017a. *Fact Sheet: Youth Political Participation and Decision-Making*. New York: UNDP. http://www.un.org/esa/socdev/documents/youth/fact-sheets/youth-political-participation.pdf.

———. 2017b. *Journey to Extremism in Africa: Drivers, Incentives and the Tipping Point for Recruitment*. New York: UNDP.

———. Forthcoming. "Vulnerable and Violent, Agency and Aspirations: Men as Perpetrators and Victims of Violence; A UNDP Framework for Dialogue, Policy and Programming on Engaging Men in Fragile and Conflict-Affected Settings." UNDP, New York.

UNICEF (United Nations Children's Fund). 2011. *MENA Gender Equality Profile*. New York: UNICEF.

———. 2015. *Does Horizontal Education Inequality Lead to Violent Conflict?* New York: UNICEF. https://www.fhi360.org/sites/default/files/media/documents/resource-education-inequality_0.pdf.

UNSC (UN Security Council). 1999. "Resolution on the Situation in Kosovo." Resolution S/RES/1244, adopted June 19, New York.

———. 2015a. *Report of the Secretary-General on Women and Peace and Security*. New York: UN Security Council. http://www.un.org/ga/search/view_doc.asp?symbol=S/2015/716&Lang=E.

———. 2015b. *S/RES/2250 (2015) [on Youth, Peace and Security]*. New York: UN Security Council.

UN Women. 2015. *Preventing Conflict, Transforming Justice, Securing the Peace: Global Study on the Implementation of United Nations Security Council Resolution 1325*. New York: UN Women.

———. 2016. "Women and Violent Radicalization in Jordan." Technical Report, UN Women, New York.

Urdal, H. 2006. "A Clash of Generations? Youth Bulges and Political Violence." *International Studies Quarterly* 50 (3): 607–30.

Varshney, Ashutosh. 2002. *Ethnic Conflict and Civic Life: Hindus and Muslims in India*. New Haven, CT: Yale University Press.

Vess, J., G. Barker, S. Naraghi-Anderlini, and A. Hassink. 2013. *The Other Side of Gender*. Special Report. Washington, DC: United States Institute of Peace. https://www.usip.org/publications/2013/12/other-side-gender.

Vogt, M., N.-C. Bormann, S. Rüegger, L.-E. Cederman, P. Hunziker, and L. Girardin. 2015. "Integrating Data on Ethnicity, Geography, and Conflict: The Ethnic Power Relations Dataset Family." *Journal of Conflict Resolution* 59 (7): 1327–42.

Weaver, Mary Anne. 2015. "Her Majesty's Jihadists." *New York Times*, April 14. http://www.nytimes.com/2015/04/19/magazine/her-majestys-jihadists.html.

Weber, E. 1976. *Peasants into Frenchman: The Modernization of Rural France, 1870–1914*. Palo Alto, CA: Stanford University Press.

Weiss, Michael, and H. Hassan. 2015. *ISIS: Inside the Army of Terror*. New York: Regan Arts.

Wimmer, Andreas, Lars-Erik Cederman, and Brian Min. 2009. "Ethnic Politics and Armed Conflict: A Configurational Analysis of a New Global Data Set." *American Sociological Review* 74 (2): 316–37.

WomanStats. n.d. "The WomanStats Project." http://www.womanstats.org/aboutoverview.html.

Woolcock, Michael. 2014. "Culture, Politics and Development." Policy Research Working Paper 6939, World Bank, Washington, DC.

World Bank. 2011. *World Development Report 2011: Conflict, Security, and Development*. Washington, DC: World Bank.

———. 2015. "Preventing Violent Extremism with Development Interventions: A Strategic Review." Briefing Note, World Bank, Washington, DC.

———. 2017a. *Atlas of Sustainable Development Goals*. Washington, DC: World Bank. http://www.datatopics.worldbank.org/sdgatlas.

———. 2017b. *World Development Report 2017: Governance and the Law*. Washington, DC: World Bank.

World Bank Group IEG (Independent Evaluation Group). 2016. *World Bank Group Engagement in Situations of Fragility, Conflict, and Violence*. Washington, DC: World Bank.

Wucherpfennig, J., P. Hunziker, and L.-E. Cederman. 2016. "Who Inherits the State? Colonial Rule and Postcolonial Conflict." *American Journal of Political Science* 60 (4): 882–88.

Additional Reading

Cramer, Christopher. 2010. *Unemployment and Participation in Violence*. Washington, DC: World Bank.

Fair, C., R. Littman, N. Malhotra, and J. Shapiro. 2016. "Relative Poverty, Perceived Violence, and Support for Militant Politics: Evidence from Pakistan." *Political Science Research and Methods* 6 (1): 1–25. doi: 10.1017/psrm.2016.6.

Hegre, H., G. Østby, and C. Raleigh. 2009. "Poverty and Civil War Events: A Disaggregated Study of Liberia." *Journal of Conflict Resolution* 53 (4): 598–623.

Holmes, R., A. McCord, and J. Hagen-Zanker. 2013. *What Is the Evidence on the Impact of Employment Creation on Stability and Poverty Reduction in Fragile States.* London: Overseas Development Institute. https://www.odi.org /publications/7447-what-evidence-impact -employment-creation-stability-and-poverty -reduction-fragile-states.

ICG (International Crisis Group). 2013. *Women and Conflict in Afghanistan.* Asia Report 252. Brussels: ICG. https://d2071andvip0wj. cloudfront.net/women-and-conflict-in-af ghanistan.pdf.

Interpeace. 2016. *Beyond Ideology and Greed— Understanding New Forms of Violence in Côte d'Ivoire and Mali.* Executive Summary. Geneva: Interpeace. http://3n589z370e6o-2eata9wahfl4.wpengine.netdna-cdn.com /wp-content/uploads/2016/11/2016-Au-del %C3%A0-de-lid%C3%A9ologie-et-de-lap-p%C3%A2t-du-gain-ExecSum-ENG-002. pdf.

Krueger, A. 2008. *What Makes a Terrorist.* Princeton, NJ: Princeton University Press.

Nordhaus, W. 2006. "Geography and Macroeconomics: New Data and New Findings." *Proceedings of the National Academy of Sciences* 103 (10): 3510–17.

Pearlman, W. 2013. "Emotions and the Microfoundations of the Arab Uprisings." *Perspectives on Politics* 11 (02): 387–409. doi: 10.1017/s1537592713001072.

Piazza, James A. 2006. "Rooted in Poverty? Terrorism, Poor Economic Development, and Social Cleavages." *Terrorism and Political Violence* 18 (1): 159–77. doi: 10.1080/095465 590944578.

Sargsyan, Irena L., and Andrew Bennett. 2016. "Discursive Emotional Appeals in Sustaining Violent Social Movements in Iraq, 2003–11." *Security Studies* 25 (4): 608–45.

UNSC (United Nations Security Council). 2000. "On Women and Peace and Security." Resolution S/RES/1325, adopted October 31, New York.

World Bank. 2001. *Social Protection Strategy: From Safety Net to Springboard.* Washington, DC: World Bank.

———. 2011. *Violence in the City: Understanding and Supporting Community Responses to Urban Violence.* Washington, DC: World Bank.

CHAPTER 5

What People Fight Over: Arenas of Contestation

Maintaining a peaceful pathway entails the constant management of underlying grievances and the monitoring of shocks that could trigger violence. Where risks accumulate or intensify, they can overwhelm a society's coping resources, with violence as a frequent result. As chapter 4 argues, certain risks deserve special attention because they underlie most violent conflict. These risks relate to perceptions of injustice deriving from social, economic, and political exclusion.

This chapter explores the accumulation and intensification of risks and opportunities in critical spaces, called *arenas of contestation*. These arenas involve what groups care about in their relationships with each other and with the state and thus what they tend to fight over—access to power, land, and resources, equitable delivery of services, and responsive justice and security.

These four broad arenas are by no means an exhaustive list, but they have been selected because they have consistently recurred in violent conflict in various contexts.[1] Competition for power, for example, is an age-old source of conflict, while balances and imbalances of power can put a society in danger of violence. Experience shows that more inclusive and representative power-sharing arrangements increase the likelihood of peaceful pathways. Land and resources, too, are traditional sources of friction, and this arena is now under more stress with the effects of climate change,

population growth, urbanization, and the expansion of large-scale agriculture. The service delivery arena is critical because state legitimacy hinges, in part, on whether the population deems that the processes of service delivery are fair. In this arena, again, inclusiveness and *perceptions* of fairness matter as much—perhaps more—than the quality of services. Finally, security and justice institutions that operate fairly and in alignment with the rule of law are fundamental. Conflict in this arena that is not managed can have long-term impacts on a society's pathway.

The salience of these arenas is demonstrated by the changing profile of violent conflict, as described in chapter 1, and by influential global trends that may increase risk or open opportunities in these arenas, as discussed in chapter 2. Moreover, contestation in these arenas is shaped by the degree of inequality, exclusion, and unfairness in a society, as noted in chapter 4, and can increase the risk of violence.

The arenas of power, resources, services, and security are defined by the interaction of the unique structural factors, institutions, and actors in a society. The state is critical in each of the arenas. While the state may not exercise full authority in all the arenas, it does bear ultimate responsibility for coordinating the actions of other actors there. Through its actions or inaction, the state can reinforce a broad-based belief that social, economic, and political arrangements and outcomes are accessible to all. Alternatively, it can reinforce perceptions of exclusion that deepen tensions among groups.

The 2030 Agenda for Sustainable Development includes various goals and targets related to these four arenas. For example, Sustainable Development Goal (SDG) target 10.2 addresses political inclusion, while target 16.7 addresses responsive, inclusive, participatory, and representative decision making at all levels. With regard to access to services, targets 1.4, 5.4, and 11.1 address basic or public services, targets 3.7 and 3.8 address health, and targets 4.2, 4.3, and 4.5 address education. Targets 5.2, 16.1, and 16.2 address security and violence. In the area of resources, targets 1.4, 2.3, and 12.2 address land, target 6.5 addresses water, SDG 14 addresses oceans, seas, and marine resources, and SDG 15 addresses terrestrial ecosystems.

Targeted, flexible, and sustained attention to these arenas is an important component of governance in general (World Bank 2017c) and is particularly critical to prevention. The more strategically that risks are addressed and shocks are managed, the better the chances for peaceful pathways. Policy changes alone are insufficient; even the most technically sound actions often fall short because they cannot, by themselves, address the underlying incentive structures that drive behavior. Measures are needed to assess and address risk, especially by fostering incentives and norms for peaceful bargaining and negotiation within the arenas.

This chapter begins by introducing the concept of arenas of contestation as areas for risk and opportunity. Next, it discusses each of the arenas of contestation in more detail, exploring the risks of violence and opportunities for peace that can build up there, the trade-offs that are present when managing them, and the conditions that may amplify risk (for example, attempting major reform during the transition to a more inclusive political system). As substantially broad fields in themselves, it is impossible to treat the arenas in a comprehensive manner here. Instead, key messages and ideas are summarized, with examples drawn from the case studies where appropriate. Chapter 6 contains a more detailed description of the experiences of different societies in managing risks and opportunities in the arenas.

Risk and Opportunity in the Arenas of Contestation

Conflict that arises in the arenas of contestation is especially prone to escalate to violence. Risk is high chiefly because the stakes are high. As the sites where, ultimately, people and groups bargain for access to the basic means of livelihoods and well-being, exclusion from one or more arenas can, often literally, become a matter of life or death.

Moreover, the broader balance of power in society is defined and defended in these arenas (World Bank 2017c). This balance of power has an impact on the incentives that are so critical for prevention. Actors who are already at the table must agree to change the rules, institutions, or structural factors that define the balance of power in the arenas, and they may see little benefit in altering the status quo. Leaders who perceive reform as an unfair loss of power for themselves or their group, then, have few incentives to propose or support any change in the existing arrangements. Exclusion and inequality often persist, not because leaders lack the technical knowledge or capacity for reform, but because they have insufficient incentives to allow greater access to the arenas.

Contestation here is fraught, too, because exclusion and inequality among groups, the precursors of grievance, often manifest most visibly in the arenas. As the evidence presented in chapter 4 suggests, an identity-based group that perceives itself unfairly deprived relative to other groups—whether because of unequal access to political representation, unequal distribution of basic services, insecure tenancy of land, exclusion from justice and security, or some other exclusionary situation—may develop grievances. Both perceived exclusion and objective exclusion are important.

Finally, the arenas overlap substantially, such that any shift in one arena can trigger ripple effects in others. An election that upsets the political balance of power can trigger a land reform, or judicial reforms aiming to address legal discrimination against one group may increase their claim on political power. Measures to mitigate a crisis in the short term can affect the conditions needed for lasting reforms. For example, the relocation of a community after a natural disaster can complicate efforts for land reform over the long term. Côte d'Ivoire illustrates how conflict can spill over from one arena and activate conflict in another (box 5.1).

At the same time, the overlap of the arenas means that actions taken in one arena can mitigate risks in another. For example, more inclusive political arrangements have been shown to decrease the risk of violence associated with the "resource curse" around extractives, as discussed in detail in this chapter (Drew 2017). In West Africa, there is evidence that power sharing has had a "mediating effect" on the relationship between natural resources and stability (Vogt 2012).

The state plays a key role in governing the arenas by embodying constraints and opportunities to influence different actors. The state bears ultimate responsibility for setting the rules that govern relationships and access in these important policy arenas, which it does through laws and the system of formal institutions. Its overall legitimacy in the eyes of citizens is determined by how well it does this. In this way, governance of the arenas is central to the social contract.

This does not mean that, in practice, the state must be active and present in all the arenas. As chapters 2 and 3 note, nonstate actors generally fill the void where the state is unable or unwilling to provide needed services. In many cases, community organizations, traditional leadership, the private sector, and civil society are better placed than the state to mediate and address risks as they manifest. In others, armed groups and organized criminal networks may supplant the state and undermine its legitimacy. Ultimately, however, the state needs to exert a minimum presence as a credible facilitator in the arenas if it is to maintain a modicum of legitimacy.

BOX 5.1 **Conflict across Arenas of Contestation: The Political Crisis and Civil War in Côte d'Ivoire**

During the civil war in Côte d'Ivoire between 2002 and 2011, conflict in the political arena spilled over to the arena of land and natural resources. While some localized land conflicts were prevailing in the country, they have been exacerbated by the conflict in the political arena. Violence came about initially in response to attempts to exclude specific groups from central power by denying a northerner the opportunity to participate in presidential elections. These attempts aggravated long-standing resentments related to the political exclusion of northerners. The conflict quickly revived resentments related to an influx of migrants and the contestation of their rights to access, own, and benefit from land and its related resources. Rents from trade in natural resources, from coffee production to timber and diamonds, provided sources of financing to all sides of the conflict. A fall in the price of the country's main export crops, particularly cocoa, exacerbated competition for these resources and further fueled conflict. Regional disparities in poverty and access to services between the north and south also played an important role.

Sources: Marc, Verjee, and Mogaka 2015; McGovern 2011.

The Arena of Power and Governance

Since the beginning of recorded history, blood has been spilled over who holds the proverbial keys to the castle. Political power gives individuals and the groups they represent those keys or at least a seat at the table inside the castle. Political power largely determines how economic and other resources are distributed, and therefore, it is difficult for actors to increase access to the other policy arenas unless they have some presence (and relative power) in the political realm.

Greater inclusion and representation of different groups in the political arena tend to be associated with reduced violence over the longer term. However, as discussed in chapter 2, the transition to a more open and democratic political system is often fraught with risk of violence because it can disrupt power dynamics and bring forth new groups seeking influence.

Political Settlements and Mitigation of Risk

Political settlements help to manage conflicts over political power that risk becoming violent, particularly in transitional settings. A political settlement can be an explicit or an implicit bargain among elites over the distribution of rights and entitlements. It is often viewed as a prerequisite to avoiding violence in situations of high risk or to reducing the intensity of violent conflict (Lindemann 2008). A peace agreement is a political settlement whose objective is to manage the risks of violence and reach some form of stability.

The risk of relapse into conflict is elevated where elites have not sought to accommodate or include former opponents in a political settlement, but have instead moved to exclude rivals on the basis of ethnicity, religion, or other dimension of identity (Call 2012; Elgin-Cossart, Jones, and Esberg 2012). An agreement among elites is likely to be unsustainable if it is not underpinned by policy that addresses the grievances of the populations that these elites represent or if it includes only elites and excludes the rest of the population.

While political settlements are a very important component of any peace process, their ability to contribute to sustained peace is more elusive. Many recent peace processes appear to have produced an uncertain—sometimes transitory—peace that features recurrence of violence, absence of security, and political stalemate (Bell 2017). Many of today's peace agreements are characterized as a "formalized political unsettlement," where the root causes of the conflict are carried into the new institutional arrangements without being resolved (Bell and Pospisil 2017, 1). The preeminent focus on a narrow set of elites reinforces this tendency of many peace agreements to create highly unsustainable political settlements. The absence of a discussion of longer-term development issues as a key dimension of these settlements is also often part of the problem. Translating a political settlement into a more sustainable process of constitutional change, institutional reform, and modified legal frameworks is complicated and often requires multiple iterations (Bell and Zulueta-Fülscher 2016).

Ensuring that a political settlement is genuinely inclusive is essential to steering a society on a peaceful pathway, as it constitutes an important part of the process of renegotiating access to power among different groups. Democratic instruments and the electoral process are often insufficient to bring about the inclusion of excluded groups, especially excluded minority groups, in a sustainable manner. Often, new political settlements are needed as institutions and political frameworks change. A political settlement can rarely be a one-off effort. It requires sustained, long-term attention and periodic renegotiation, even as institutions are undergoing reform and development policies are being adapted, so that the reach of the settlement extends beyond a small elite. Otherwise, the sustainability of the settlement will be uncertain (Bell 2015).

Power-sharing arrangements[2] allocate a share of political power to different groups in society and can be an important aspect of political settlements. They can regulate offices, territorial governance, or decision making in the arenas of contestation to ensure that no single group or party has a monopoly over all government functions and branches (McEvoy and O'Leary 2013).[3]

Political power sharing can take several forms. At the national level, these forms include creating so-called "grand coalitions" of all major parties, as in Austria (Lijphart 2008); reserving political positions such as president and prime minister for certain religious communities, as in Lebanon (Bahout 2016); alternating the presidency between parties every four years, as in Colombia (Mazzuca and Robinson 2009); and setting quotas for marginalized groups in institutions, as in India (Gates et al. 2016). Inclusive elite bargains and the distribution of positions of state power among different groups in Zambia since independence has helped to avoid violent conflict over the last decades in spite of the existence of multiple fissures in society (Lindemann 2008). Other types of power sharing include security (military, police, or security forces), economic (access to resources or processes of decision making), and territorial (forms of territorial autonomy) arrangements (Hartzell and Hoddie 2006; Hoddie and Hartzell 2005). These arrangements are not static. Rather, they involve continual negotiating, bargaining, and contestation of relations between elites over time and mediation of relations between elites and the broader society (Putzel and Di John 2012; World Bank 2011).

While the long-term effects of power sharing on peace and stability are hard to discern, a substantial body of evidence suggests that power sharing helps to prevent recurrence of violent conflict (Putzel and Di John 2012; World Bank 2011) and is associated with greater stability overall (Gleditsch and Ruggeri 2010; Linder and Bächtiger 2005; Vreeland 2008). For example, in Africa, between 1970 and 1990, rulers faced a 72 percent chance of being forced out of office under violent circumstances, but after 1990 and owing in part to multiparty elections, the chance fell to 41 percent (Reno 2002).

However, power sharing is not a guaranteed means of addressing the underlying risks associated with exclusion. It has limitations and cannot easily adapt to changing realities, for instance, such as when a change in structural factors prompts one group to seek an increase in its share of power (Call 2012). Colombia's National Front Pact between 1958 and 1974 helped to alleviate tensions between the Liberal and Conservative parties, but its exclusion of other groups contributed to the armed conflict there (Felter and Renwick 2017). As demographics or allegiances shift, actors might be reluctant to adapt power-sharing arrangements accordingly, as in Lebanon, where power sharing has contributed to a deadlock in the implementation of policies, along with sectarian-based allocation of power and the resistance of political leaders to cede power (Bahout 2016; Rosiny 2016). If power is distributed according to group identity, the power-sharing arrangement can reinforce certain identities relative to others and thus can negate the potential of these arrangements to minimize violent conflict.

Translating a power-sharing arrangement into a new constitution after a conflict can lower the risk of violence recurrence. A cross-country study using the Comparative Constitutions Project database, which includes data on constitutions from all independent states over the years 1789–2015, finds that the process of creating a new constitution after the conclusion of violent conflict is associated with an approximately 60 percent reduction in potential recurrence of violence (Elkins, Ginsburg, and Melton 2014). The amendment of an existing constitution has no statistically significant impact, suggesting that the process of writing a constitution and the existing postconflict political, security, economic, or other conditions that enable this process are important for sustaining peace (Elkins, Ginsburg, and Melton 2014).

Other factors that could be influential include the makeup of coalitions that participate in the process, how representative they are of the groups they head up, and the duration of constitutional negotiations. Many studies show that the process of writing a constitution—particularly the extent to which different groups are consulted in a genuine fashion—is at least as important as the content of the document produced. This work also suggests that a constitutional process can serve as a means of addressing intergroup grievances and inequality, as in the peace process after the end of apartheid in South Africa (Samuels 2005). The chance of peace is enhanced when multiple forms of power sharing are adopted together (Jarstad and Nilsson 2008).

Federalism, Decentralization, and Devolution

Power-sharing arrangements often extend across multiple levels of governance through the transfer of power and resources to the subnational level. Some of the most common mechanisms for this are decentralization, devolution, and federalism, discussed here in general terms. Chapter 6 provides more specific examples of countries that have overcome violent conflict by means of devolution and government restructuring.

Decentralization refers to the process and result of structuring a system so that multiple layers share authority and deliver goods and services (Wolff, Ross, and Wee 2017). It denotes territorial-based autonomous political authority and decentralized political systems. Where ethnic, linguistic, religious, and cultural groups concentrate in distinct geographic regions, decentralization can reduce the potential for violence by addressing center-periphery tensions and accommodating diversity (USAID 2009). Subnational governance arrangements proposed as part of peace negotiations can signal moderation by the majority and temper fears of the minority (Lake and Rothchild 2005). When further institutionalized in national law, such arrangements can help to protect the rights and interests of both minority and majority groups, to manage regional horizontal inequalities, and to ensure a balance of power among groups, thereby reducing the risk of violent conflict.

Self-governance arrangements such as federalism have proven effective in many cases in reducing local violent conflict where there is horizontal inequality among groups, such as in Bangsamoro in Mindanao in the Philippines (Colletta and Oppenheim 2017). The effectiveness of self-rule is greatly enhanced when self-governance arrangements are paired with a proportional representation system that ensures that power is shared across groups (Neudorfer, Theuerkauf, and Wolff 2016) and when they are supported by sufficient guarantees against the recentralization of power (Lake and Rothchild 2005). Territorial self-governance in combination with a proportional representation system "can improve the quality of governance, make government more responsive to minorities and disgruntled groups, and guarantee minority groups' physical security and identity survival" (Nygård et al. 2017, 14).

Power-sharing arrangements between national and subnational levels carry their own risks. Just as concentrating power in a centralized system can raise tensions, decentralizing or devolving power to the local level raises the stakes among local groups and creates new avenues for violence. Devolution can exacerbate the risks of violence where local political parties reinforce ethnic identities, foster interethnic and intergroup tensions, and mobilize groups for violent conflict (Wolff, Ross, and Wee 2017). Chapter 6 focuses more specifically on the experience of decentralization as a peacebuilding strategy.

The Risk of Election-Related Violence

The peaceful transfer of power is regarded as a cornerstone of democratic and inclusive governance (Diamond 2006). Elections are a means to accomplish this transfer openly and transparently. In this way, they can strengthen the legitimacy of governments and, over time, consolidate democracy, especially in postconflict states (Diamond 2006). By nature a high-stakes contest, elections can bring forth demands, grievances, and expectations and are a frequent focus for mitigating the risks of violence (Malik 2017).

While publicly linked to elite contestation of outcomes or confidence in the result, elections can also trigger violence, especially in the presence of multiple preexisting risks. Electoral violence is associated with long-standing and unresolved grievances (real or perceived). As elections, by definition, produce winners and losers, they can fuel concerns that political or constitutional order will not respond to demands for reform.

As discussed in chapter 2, the risk of election-related violence is amplified in fledgling democracies (Bates 2008; Gagnon 1994; Snyder 2000), where winner-take-all outcomes, real or perceived, can leave groups outside the circle of power (Chabal and Daloz 1999; Mamdani 1996). In certain cases, even attempts to amend the rules can lead to violence, as in Niger in 2010, when a military coup followed an attempt by the president to remain in power beyond the terms set by the constitution.

The overriding responsibility for a successful election lies with political leaders, from both government and opposition parties. Incumbents and challengers can see elections as a chance to manipulate the system and structures to exclude rival groups and can use violence as a tactic to influence the outcome, with different actors and mechanisms appearing in pre- and postelection violence. Studies suggest that pre-election violence is more frequent than postelection conflict and is usually mobilized by actors in favor of an incumbent, often using the coercive apparatus of the state to retain power (Arriola and Johnson 2012, 10; Straus and Taylor 2012).

Ensuring peaceful elections depends on how risks are managed. First, it is critical to foster conditions that avoid zero-sum politics well before an election. This often requires managing exclusionary dynamics across arenas and beyond elections—for example, in the distribution of natural resources—as well as placing a premium on national leadership, to refrain from threats of violence or harassment of political opponents. Managing such dynamics may be particularly important when legal authority and political power are heavily concentrated and in presidential and semipresidential systems, which some studies show demonstrate greater risks of violence (Malik 2017).

In contrast, electoral systems based on proportional representation are sometimes associated with fewer incidents of violence (Fiedler 2017; Mukherjee 2006). In Sub-Saharan Africa, for example, countries with majoritarian (that is, so-called "first past the post") electoral rules have a higher incidence of election-related violence (number of incidents) than countries with proportional electoral rules (Fjelde and Höglund 2016). Power-sharing agreements have also been shown to help to ensure that groups that lose an election nevertheless have meaningful representation in government, access to state resources, and some degree of autonomy (Brancati and Synder 2012). However, such power-sharing agreements, often struck between elites to manage a specific crisis, can undermine popular will and trust in the political system.

Beyond individual leaders and forms of institutions, electoral processes matter. Often, election-related violence is influenced by perceptions of unfairness in how elections are managed and held. Elections are most likely to succeed when citizens have confidence that electoral results reflect their choices. When there are perceived inconsistencies in the process or when the results are contested, particularly when perceptions evoke memories of historical injustices and elites or group leaders mobilize around these memories, the risk of election-related violence may be heightened. The effectiveness and legitimacy of the institutions that manage the electoral process are very important—in particular, transparent and trusted electoral commissions.

Protecting people's right to vote is equally critical. In many cases, women or minority groups are vulnerable to intimidation or exclusion from elections and face adversity when running for political office (Berry, Bouka, and Kamuru 2017). Special measures to protect voting rights—including increasing access to voter registration, remote or early voting options, and physical security at polling stations—can help to ensure the full participation of marginalized groups in elections. SDG target 5.5 recognizes the importance of women's full and effective participation and equal opportunities for leadership at all levels of decision making in political, economic, and public life, while SDG target 16.7 recognizes the importance of responsive, inclusive, participatory, and representative decision making at all levels.

The potential for violence around elections can also be managed through mechanisms for dialogue and transparency as part of a broader approach to promoting peace and stability. Responses to electoral violence are not necessarily, or exclusively, contingent on the quality of the electoral process itself. Most elections produce results that lead to acceptance even in the face of varying degrees of imperfections.

Nonstate actors and new media can play a role in defusing tensions. Civil society and private sector actors in Kenya during and after the violence of 2007–08 lobbied the warring parties to come together and acted as a channel for the views of the public (Lindenmayer and Kaye 2009). These actors also provided a pressure valve to ease tensions in subsequent elections. Social media and communications strategies can help to educate and inform the population ahead of elections. Technology can support early warning systems as well as efforts to counter hate speech and to improve communication between the government and citizens (IDS 2017). Again, in Kenya, policy makers, citizens, and the government have used the Internet and communications tools, which played a destructive role in postelection violence in 2013 (IDS 2017), to raise awareness of, monitor, and respond to violence.

The findings of electoral fraud may also create opportunities for violence in protest of the results, and independent electoral observers may announce aspects of electoral conduct that were previously not public, as in the 2005 legislative elections in Ethiopia. Similarly, studies highlight that the timing of elections influences the risk of violence. Holding elections early in a political transition may increase the chance of violence because institutions are weak and trust is low (Brancati and Synder 2012).

This risk has to be weighed against the benefit of elections, which is that that they tend to confer legitimacy on a new government when they are based on a sufficiently robust and inclusive political settlement. These experiences point to the need to foster creative forms of electoral support and monitoring as part of comprehensive preventive strategies.

The Arena of Land and Natural Resources

Land-Related Disputes in Today's Conflicts

Land is deeply evocative. It is essential to personal and communal economic well-being, livelihoods, and identity. A major resource for most economies, land is part of the social fabric. Social control of land is central to most systems of governance. Even in cases where land has not played a direct role in violent conflict, the breakdown of institutions and societal structures during conflict can revive latent frustrations or a sense of unfairness around land and resources (Marc, Verjee, and Mogaka 2015). In the wake of conflict, land-related disputes can center on a clash of rights between returnees and current occupiers of the land (Maze 2014). Scholars have argued that conflicts fought over land tend to be more prolonged, more stubborn to negotiation, and thus more likely to recur than conflicts related to other arenas (Maze 2014).

Violent conflict around land is typically stoked by grievances related to land scarcity, insecurity of tenure, and historical injustices. These grievances can play out individually or in combination. They pose a higher risk where they overlap with exclusion along identity lines and when ethnic groups that compete over land call on exclusionary narratives to justify their claims. Scarcity is often the symptom of a larger problem of access and distribution of land, with smaller numbers of people owning larger pieces of property, leaving much of the population to live on degraded land (UNDP 2003, 2013).

Confrontations around land are set to increase in the coming years because of demographic pressures, growing demands for land from large-scale agricultural production and conservation, deterioration of land quality, displacement through war and subsequent attempts to regain lost land, and the adverse effects of climate change. This projected rise in violent conflict around land will be most evident across Africa, which already sees the bulk of land-related conflict (Bruce 2017).

Urbanization is another global trend that may fuel conflict over land. Many societies are already struggling to extend basic services and governance to rapidly growing populations in urban and peri-urban areas. This urbanization puts a strain on land and service delivery (ICRC 2016a, 2016b; World Bank 2010). The civil unrest in Ethiopia that began in late-2015 was underscored by tensions between the Oromian population and the seat of power in Addis Ababa. The expansion of the city into surrounding farmland reignited concerns among the Oromo population over their lack of control in managing the suburbs that lie in Oromia and regarding fair compensation for land (Global Voices 2015).

Tenure insecurity can take the form of a lack of transparency in transactions, the risk of land loss for groups with secondary rights, a lack of clarity in agreements, an increase in formalized land grabbing by the state of land held under customary and informal tenure for the large-scale commercial production of food crops and biofuels, and displacement (Marc, Verjee, and Mogaka 2015). In Liberia, numerous disputes over local landownership, compounded by the loss of land records during the civil war, remain unresolved (World Bank 2008). The recent surge in state sales of land is exacerbating tensions between local communities and the state and agribusiness companies (Brown and Keating 2015). Tenure insecurity also reflects the failure of the state to recognize customary or informal property rights.

Women can be especially vulnerable to insecurity of tenure. Although women have legal entitlement to own land in some regions, they often continue to be denied land rights for political and cultural reasons. Under customary systems, women often have access to land only through a male intermediary. Women also have difficulty retaining land in the event of divorce or after the death of their husbands (Deininger and Castagnini 2006). SDG 5 recognizes women's equal rights to own and control land and other forms of property and natural resources.

Nevertheless, there are examples of successful efforts to increase women's access to land. In Rwanda, land-related issues contributed to the 1994 genocide (Gillingham and Buckle 2014). Consequently, to prevent further cycles of violence and to address grievances such as those related to ethnic division and gender discrimination in land access, the government moved to clarify land rights and launched a program of land tenure regularization (Gillingham and Buckle 2014). An assessment found that participants in the program doubled their investment in soil conservation, with a larger increase for females (Ali, Deininger, and Goldstein 2014). In addition, the program increased the tenure security of legally married women. In Peru, land titling programs have enabled women to join the formal labor market, increasing income levels and reducing child labor (Field 2007).

As chapter 2 notes, the global trends of migration and climate change may exacerbate tensions related to land. While migration can be a source of resilience, migrants often find themselves at the center of competition over land and resources. Political manipulation, weak mechanisms for integration, and unclear property rights can deepen tensions over land and power between indigenous communities and migrants. Disputes over access to, ownership of, and use of land often emerge from a clash of identities. The scarcity of formal documentation (identity cards, national passports) among migrant populations, especially in rural areas, poses a further challenge to achieving security of tenure. It adds complexity to the already precarious situation facing migrants, which includes corruption, poverty, and illiteracy (Adepoju, Boulton, and Levin 2007). Competition between migrants and host communities can be especially pronounced when coupled with political and social marginalization and the spillover from regional ethnic, religious, and political tensions (Marc, Verjee, and Mogaka 2015).

Pastoralists face particular challenges related to the right of passage. They rely on mobility to cope with variations in rainfall. Pastoral and agricultural livelihoods depend on mutually beneficial and negotiated nonexclusive access to water and reciprocal land use agreements. Conflicts arise when access to waterpoints, grazing lands, and pastoral corridors are restricted and crops are damaged. Larger herd sizes and environmental degradation, as well as larger farms, especially large agribusinesses, have increased the frequency and intensity of these conflicts. In the Darfur region of Sudan, tensions between nomadic pastoralist herders and settled farmers over livestock migration routes and waterholes have become a flashpoint for wider differences and have contributed to

violent conflict there (Brown and Keating 2015; box 5.2).

Land reform has rarely taken place without incurring "a high degree of conflict" ranging from nonviolent conflict to systemic violence that seeks to overthrow the government (Bruce 2017, 43). Land reform is high risk and often has unintended consequences. It is rarely effective when undertaken in so-called "shock-therapy" style. To be implemented and accepted, such far-reaching reforms require time, patience, and the buy-in of the various interested groups and actors. Reforms can benefit from consultations with communities and other interested actors such as the private sector. Institutions and structural factors within a society are often resistant to change, as noted in chapter 3. Vested interests often hold sway; in some countries, corruption can help to entrench the status quo.

BOX 5.2 Darfur: A Case of Land Management Systems and Environmental Change

The Darfur conflict originated in the impact of drought on African settled farmers and Arab nomadic herders and in the breakdown of agreements over the right of passage for pastoralists. Previously amicable relationships among groups unraveled as drought and famine created new migration patterns, including the migration of camel-owning Zaghawa pastoralists of North Darfur southward beyond their traditional grazing ranges. As they moved south, they displaced others, including Masalit cattle herders and farmers.

Farmers from the Fur group, whose lands the pastoralists traversed, had traditionally accommodated these herds. A local governance system had evolved to mediate conflicts over resources, facilitate farming and grazing on the same plots of land, and to accommodate new arrivals. The Native Administration and officials appointed by the ruling tribes administered this system. Each man received a hut and a plot of land to farm, while grazing rights and access

to waterpoints remained communal. Nomads were given temporary access to land to enable them to reach grazing routes but were obligated to prevent crop damage. Migrants were also given land, and the terms of their stay were negotiated by the village sheik.

The decline of central government control over the region stripped customary rulers of their authority to manage grazing patterns. Historically, once annual rainfall patterns became clear, customary authorities would meet to negotiate adjustments in the grazing patterns of different tribal groups. Comity was a key principle. A tribe struggling with poor rainfall would be allowed to use land in the territory (dar) of another tribe, which in return had a reasonable expectation of receiving the same assistance in case of need. The vacuum in effective local authority caused the collapse of intertribal social control of land use and eliminated the best hope of peaceful mediation of the climate crisis.

Sources: Charney 1975; Edwards 2008; Giannini, Biasutti, and Verstraete 2008; Null and Risi 2016.

For prevention, reforms are most valuable before the onset of violence. However, the experience of reform and its success in preventing violent conflict vary by type of reform and context. Early experiences of land reform in East Asia were quite positive, while the experience in Latin America in the 1970s was more complex (Bruce 2017).

Efforts to manage conflict and to prevent violent conflict related to land tend to be most effective where they combine the reform of land with more immediate conflict and dispute resolution measures. Supports involving the empowerment of communities, the improvement of land governance and administration, and the more effective resolutions of land disputes fall short of addressing the structural causes of conflict, yet they can manage tensions and help to avoid violence (Bruce 2017). These initiatives have often been used in lieu of longer-lasting reforms or better-directed reform efforts. These initiatives are valuable in their own right and can improve security of tenure, but more than that they pave the way for deeper reforms. In Afghanistan, dispute resolution councils that bring tribal leaders and government officials together in the two eastern provinces of Kunar and Nangarhar demonstrate the potentially positive role of local leaders in solving local land-related disputes (Coburn 2011).

The efficacy of each reform needs to be examined individually. One type of reform is the resettlement of citizens onto public lands as a way of alleviating land pressure in densely populated areas (Bruce 2017). This often brings brief, if any, respite from competition over land and can be a significant cause of conflict in itself, with new tensions emerging on the periphery in an attempt to address grievances at the center. Another type of reform is the regulation and reform of tenancy, which uses legislation to improve the situation of tenants. Tenancy reform can be an important step toward more meaningful reform, but on its own, it has largely failed as a comprehensive reform strategy.

Programs of land titling and registration can be effective peacebuilding tools in post-conflict contexts. The increasing acceptance of a range of legitimate forms of land tenure as being on a continuum of land rights can help to overcome tensions between formal and informal tenure systems (UN Human Settlements Programme 2016). Titling and registration can increase security of tenure and provide protection by recognizing full rights for communities under customary law. "Formalizing" the rights of informal settlers and customary landholders is widely accepted as being important for preventing conflict, although there is little agreement on when and how it should be implemented (Bruce 2017). The significant potential of these programs to prevent conflict relies on careful planning, implementation, and targeting. Experiences from Cambodia show that, while titling can bring about security of tenure, corruption in implementation can exclude vulnerable groups from the benefits (Sekiguchi and Hatsukano 2013). In Cambodia, the program was ineffective where the risks of violence were greatest (Cambodian Center for Human Rights 2013). Titling and registration can also facilitate land grabs by making land more valuable. This has been a recurrent risk in urban land reform, especially in slum-upgrading efforts.

Land tenure reform prevents conflict by providing new land rights, but usually only as part of a broader package of reforms. It is particularly relevant in contexts where land is mostly held under customary law. Land that is not formally titled under statutory law is considered public land. Effective land tenure reform needs to be accompanied by a program of systematic titling and registration of rights to give these new rights some sense of reality and grounding.

So-called "land to the tiller" reforms make land available to the people working it. These reforms either take land from landlords and provide tenants with titles to the land they have been farming or break up large farms. Such reforms usually come in response to escalating tenant demands for land and can be applied where tenancy reforms have failed. They have been effective in some countries, including China; Japan (under U.S. military occupation after World War II); the Republic of Korea; and Taiwan, China. In all cases, they took place under great external pressure, with external support, and often where the state was seeking to defuse the risks of violent conflict (Dorner and Thiesenhusen 2005).

Market-mechanism redistribution and community-based land reform rely on the government to facilitate the purchase and sale of land. The government provides credit to buyers; when the credit has been repaid, the land is titled to beneficiary households. This model is being implemented in Brazil, Malawi, and South Africa (Bruce 2017). This model presents less risk of conflict because it does not compel landowners to sell land.

In addition, agricultural land reform holds a much higher chance of success when accompanied by increased access to credit and markets for new landholders. In areas where this has not been the case, land reforms have been effectively reversed, as new landowners face difficulties in maintaining livelihoods or keeping up with property taxes. In El Salvador, unequal access to land was an important structural driver of the 12-year civil war and a critical area for the eventual peace accords (Binford 1993; Seligson 1995; Thiesenhusen 1995). The failure to increase access to credit and markets was an important factor limiting the sustainability of the land reform process (Binford 1993; Seligson 1995; Thiesenhusen 1995).[4]

Managing land as an arena of contestation is not limited to agricultural reform. In urban areas, access to housing enables broader access to livelihoods. There are many and diverse examples of efforts to increase access to affordable housing. The state may provide low-cost housing directly, as in Brazil up until the 1980s, or it may offer subsidies to facilitate the purchase or rental of housing (Magalhaes 2016). Many countries throughout Latin America, including Bolivia, Chile, Colombia, El Salvador, Mexico, and Peru, adopted these market-based approaches during the 1970s and 1980s, all with the strong participation of the private sector (Magalhaes 2016). Results have been mixed, with some countries experiencing a virtual reversal of the intended reforms toward even stronger segregation in slums (Magalhaes 2016).

Tensions around Access to Water

Access to water, which Fergusson (2015) describes as the "petroleum of the next century," is a factor in both intra- and interstate conflict where threats have accumulated and where the failure to achieve water security multiplies the risk (World Bank 2017b). Water-related contestations can take place at multiple levels: between herders and farmers over a shared waterpoint, between communities over allocation of irrigation water, between citizens and the state over the displacement impact of a new dam, and between neighboring states over the sharing of transnational waters. These disputes may also interconnect at different levels. For instance, local disputes over water may mirror, contribute to, and complicate wider disputes over water allocation (Brown and Keating 2015). Managing local-level disputes is thus as critical as resolving interstate water-related confrontations.

Improving access to water can help to promote women's safety. In many societies, gender-based divisions of work leave women with the primary responsibility for organizing and undertaking domestic work, including cooking, cleaning, and taking care of children and elderly family members—all of which require access to water (Cleaver and Elson 1995). Women are at risk of harassment and violence when fetching water. Girls are more likely to miss school because of the responsibility of obtaining water for the family, and both women and girls are more likely to be punished if they are not able to bring back water (in a drought, for instance) or return home late after waiting in line at the well. The prevalence of these challenges has prompted international guidelines to include safety and protection measures for women and girls within humanitarian efforts and broader water and sanitation projects (IASC 2015; UN Women 2015).

Climate change, population growth, urbanization, and large-scale agriculture combine to strain limited water resources. It is predicted that, by the middle of the twenty-first century, global water demand will be up 55 percent over 2012 levels (Global Water Forum 2012). Water scarcity is expected to cost some regions up to 6 percent of their gross domestic product (GDP) by 2050 (World Bank 2016). The effects of scarcity are felt most keenly in the Middle East and North Africa, which has only 1 percent of the world's renewable water resources despite hosting about 5 percent of the world's population (Pedraza and Heinrich 2016). Often, it is not the scarcity of water that leads to tensions, but the way in which it is governed and administered. Inefficient use and management of water, outdated infrastructure, and inappropriate legal, political, and economic frameworks all exacerbate tensions arising from the scarcity of water (Pedraza and Heinrich 2016).

Climate change is a "threat multiplier which exacerbates existing tensions and instability" and magnifies the challenge of managing the resource (EU 2008). The impacts of climate change will be detected primarily through water use, creating uncertainty in food, energy, urban, and environmental systems (World Bank 2016). Shifts in the availability and variability of water can induce migration and ignite civil conflict. The conflict that has torn the Syrian Arab Republic apart is an example of how water insecurity can multiply risk (Gleick 2014; World Bank 2017b).

Risks of violence around water are more pronounced at the local or subnational levels than at the national level (Gleick 1993; Postel and Wolf 2001). However, relatively few mechanisms are available for managing subnational contestations around water. One local option is dialogue among stakeholders facilitated by civil society (OECD 2005). Where dialogue occurs, actions should situate the conflict in the broader context of prevailing power and political arrangements. Increasing women's participation in governance of water is particularly important, given the links between access to water and women's safety and the improved sustainability of projects that involve women as key stakeholders (UN Water 2006).

An understanding of shared needs and mutual concern over water supplies may encourage cooperation in water sharing between different communities or countries. An attempt to impose a technical solution on warring parties in the Ferghana Valley in Central Asia failed because it disregarded the wider socioeconomic context and viewed irrigation disputes simply as local issues between communities of different ethnic origins (Brown and Keating 2015). Strengthening institutions and local conflict resolution mechanisms may help to manage contestations (box 5.3).

At the international level, several mechanisms can help to ease water-related tensions between states. These mechanisms include transboundary cooperation principles, shared data, information systems,

BOX 5.3 Collaboration over Water: EcoPeace Middle East

EcoPeace Middle East adopts grassroots and community approaches, as well as advocacy, to create cooperative management of water resources in Israel, Jordan, and the West Bank and Gaza. It works with individuals and communities to build relationships between communities and to foster trust and cooperation at a local level. The environmental peacebuilding organization hosts camps, organizes activities such as role playing, and brings together people of all ages "to develop long-term common solutions [and] gain a broader understanding of their long-term impact on nature and on future generations." EcoPeace Middle East bases its approach on the belief that solutions in natural resource management and water security typically require long-term collaboration. It complements government-to-government water diplomacy efforts and cultivates local capacity to deal with the complexity of interdependent regional environmental resources at the community, national, and regional levels.

Source: EcoPeace Middle East (http://ecopeaceme.org).

water management institutions, and legal frameworks. Disputes between riparian states can be resolved through consultations, mediation, negotiation, and judicial means, such as recourse to the International Court of Justice (Strategic Foresight Group 2013). Technology can also help to manage the risks around the scarcity of water by finding innovative ways in which to reuse and recycle water. Desalination and reprocessing of sewage water are two examples of how technology can help to manage the supply of water.

However, conflict over water is infrequent at the international level, and in most cases, countries share transboundary water resources without violence (Wolf et al. 2006). Relations among riparian states tend to be more cooperative in the presence of international water institutions that can accommodate changing political, hydrological, or other basin conditions (Ho 2017). The Indus Waters Treaty, which codified the sharing of water from the Indus River between India and Pakistan in 1960, is often cited as a successful case of resource sharing between countries in a constant state of tension (Strategic Foresight Group 2013). It also underscores the effectiveness of having a third party in the dialogue, in this case the World Bank. The treaty has continued to be honored even through times of war, and disputes are resolved within the framework of the treaty.

The Challenge of Extractive Resources

Extractive resources have developed a reputation as being a poisoned chalice for economic and institutional stability and peace. While resources such as oil, natural gas, and minerals have the potential to confer significant benefits onto populations and to improve development outcomes, they can also fuel tremendous instability and violence. This combination of risks of violence together with the opportunity for increased revenue and development, known as the "resource curse," has a large influence on the pathway a society takes (Drew 2017). Simply put, the economic benefits of natural resource extraction create incentives for

competition that, if well managed, can be directed toward broader society. If not well managed, the benefits concentrate among specific groups, with the potential to fuel violent conflict. Research suggests that 40–60 percent of intrastate armed conflicts over the past 60 years have been triggered, funded, or sustained by natural resources (Brown and Keating 2015, 4; Drew 2017; Matthew, Brown, and Jensen 2009).[5]

Violence related to extractive resources can take place at the national and subnational levels. It can take many forms, ranging from community-based contestations over the access to profits from extraction or its environmental impacts to civil war that is funded by resources open to being looted. The degree of risk of conflict over natural resources depends, in part, on the type of resource, its location, and the mode of exploitation (Lujala 2010; Ross 2012). The connection between minerals, including alluvial diamonds (Lujala 2009; Ross 2003, 2006), other alluvial gemstones (Fearon 2004), and other nonfuel minerals (Besley and Persson 2011; Collier, Hoeffler, and Rohner 2009; Sorens 2011), and the risk of violent conflict has been especially pronounced.

The destructive potential of misappropriated, misused, and poorly managed extractive resources has been under scrutiny since the beginning of the so-called "greed versus grievance" debate of the last decade and even before (Drew 2017). Greed was argued to provide both the opportunity and the cause of conflict (Collier and Hoeffler 2004), while grievance as a motivation was said to derive from a sense of injustice and the complex interplay of factors that led to violent conflict (Homer-Dixon 1999). While this debate has since become more nuanced, extractive resources can contribute to the risk of violence, both directly and indirectly, in several ways.

Whether a society rich in natural resources follows a peaceful pathway or not depends on how the associated risks are managed. The role of the state and the interaction of institutions with the extractives industry and affected communities are important mediating factors. Extractives can create incentives for corruption and can enable elite co-option or suppression of political opposition, leading to the entrenchment of undemocratic, kleptocratic regimes (Drew 2017). Extractives may be both a structural facilitator of such regimes and a focal point for group-based grievances where the perception of an unfair distribution of benefits is felt to reflect an unjust social contract (Drew 2017). This is especially the case in the absence of fair, robust, and competent governing institutions that are able to deter corruption or respond to the seizure of resources by powerful actors.

The capture of resources by elites, which deprives the general population of revenues and the potential development opportunities they may have derived from these revenues, is a major source of grievance. Diverting revenues from resources can fuel tensions, especially when combined with corruption and mismanagement or where revenues benefit only certain groups and exclude others. In this case, the "unrealized potential" of extractives revenues to increase opportunities for all and contribute to development can feed into preexisting grievances (Le Billon 2014).

The resource curse can be particularly acute in oil-, gas-, and mineral-rich countries (Drew 2017). Oil-dependent states sometimes become rentier states characterized by authoritarianism, repression, poor governance, and high levels of corruption. Oil, in particular, makes corruption more entrenched and authoritarian regimes more durable (Ross 2015). In countries where political elites have captured resources, the exclusion of specific ethnic communities from patronage networks can deepen economic inequalities, create distortions in the political process, and weaken political systems (Sargsyan 2017). States can also use extractives as concessions to finance violent conflict, while royalties and bonus payments made to repressive or unaccountable governments by transnational companies can support counterinsurgency or suppress dissent (Ballentine and Nitzschke 2004).

The risk of violent conflict tends to rise in the presence of so-called "lootable" resources and those that can be extracted with relatively little access to technology or capital, such as alluvial diamonds, gemstones, or hydrocarbons (Drew 2017). Such resources may become the focus of armed movements searching for sources of revenue to finance their operations (Brack and Hayman 2006). Some armed movements are primarily rent seeking; others are primarily political, religious, or ideological; and many have mixed or shifting motives, for example, when economic incentives supplant a group's original aims. The existence of these sources of income for armed groups and organized crime networks can prolong and entrench violent conflict.

At the local level, land and natural resources often constitute the primary means of income and livelihood for communities. This creates high stakes for contestation over resources. Often, conflict stems from grievances where communities are excluded from decisions about extraction or where the distribution of project benefits is perceived to be unfair or unequal.

Grievances can coalesce around the environmental impacts of extraction, especially if these are perceived to fall disproportionately on certain groups. In Nigeria, environmental degradation associated with oil extraction has impinged on the livelihoods of local fishermen and farmers in the Niger delta and contributed to oil-related violent conflict over the last two decades (Marc, Verjee, and Mogaka 2015). In Bougainville, Papua New Guinea, environmental damage caused by mining activities at the Panguna copper mine in the 1980s helped to trigger a civil war, which evolved into a secessionist conflict (Brown and Keating 2015).

Grievances can also relate to the distribution of benefits, including compensation, investment, or preference toward contracting workers or businesses from the surrounding areas, known as "local content" (Vasquez 2016).[6] Often, the jobs created by extractives projects are insufficient in number and are very technical or require a different skill set than that held by local communities and thus are unable to appease the local population and offset the negative impacts of the industry (Marc, Verjee, and Mogaka 2015). These projects affect men and women in different ways, including in relation to access to employment, decision making, disruption of established social patterns, and changes in the environment (World Bank 2013). In some cases, however, communities have been able to win important concessions from extractives companies. In Papua New Guinea's North Fly District, women leaders organized to negotiate community mine continuation agreements with the Ok Tedi mine. Their seat at the negotiating table eventually won them an agreement guaranteeing their community 10 percent of all compensation, 50 percent of scholarships, cash payments to families (including women as co-signatories), and a quota of seats on the bodies charged with implementing the agreement (Menzies and Harley 2012).

Several instruments and mechanisms have been developed to respond to the challenge of extractives-related violent conflict. These include international frameworks of voluntary standards and principles, such as the Extractive Industries Transparency Initiative (EITI)[7] and the Kimberley Process Certification Scheme (KPCS).[8] The 2030 Agenda also calls for accountable and transparent institutions and includes specific targets to reduce illicit financial flows significantly by 2030 (target 16.4) and reduce corruption and bribery substantially (target 16.5). Other mechanisms include international and national legal instruments that mandate compliance from states and companies, including section 1504 of the U.S. Dodd-Frank Act and the European Union Transparency Directive (Drew 2017). Companion initiatives also call for greater transparency and accountability across the industry, including the Publish What You Pay initiative and the Revenue Watch Institute (Drew 2017). Other initiatives include due diligence schemes in supply chain management and government-led initiatives by producing nations toward the equitable and peaceful management of resources, such as the creation of the Office of the Ombudsman in Peru (Vasquez 2016; box 5.4). At the community level, corporate social responsibility initiatives introduced by extractives companies have had some success in offsetting the risk of local-level

contestations by managing company-community conflict. Here too, the government has a role to play in ensuring that communities are consulted.

Although international instruments and other voluntary frameworks generally have made a positive contribution to the governance of extractives, there are challenges in assessing their impact, including the absence of agreement on key dimensions. Their drawbacks also include the fact that, as voluntary arrangements, they are by nature nonbinding and their instruments are sometimes too abstract and theoretical to have a real impact or are only effective in concert with other initiatives. Moreover, frameworks that only deal with national governments, reinforce the status quo, or undermine an ongoing process of change risk creating new forms of violence (Drew 2017). Insufficiently inclusive EITI government representation can reinforce conflict dynamics, especially in highly divided societies with preexisting perceptions of exclusion.

At the subnational level, where the risk of conflict is often pronounced, subnational implementation of EITI is currently being piloted in six countries as a way to foster greater inclusivity for conflict prevention. The theory is that EITI facilitates the empowerment of regional institutions or local actors, while providing greater transparency through project-level reporting (Wilson and Van Alstine 2014). However, decentralized extractive management can also expose regions to boom-and-bust cycles and deepen regional inequalities. Brazil's revenue-sharing system "disproportionately benefits oil-rich Rio de Janeiro, the nation's third wealthiest state in terms of GDP per capita" (NRGI 2016). It can also create contestations over control of mines and extractives sites, as in Peru (NRGI 2016). Furthermore, windfalls for local governments do not inevitably lead to better development outcomes or lessen grievances, as in Brazil, Colombia, and Peru (Drew 2017).

For greater efficacy, decentralized revenue management or revenue transfers could be coupled with capacity support to local government and checks and balances in the form of active civil society and community participation. This, along with transparency systems promoted by the private sector and international organizations, could help to increase the success of decentralization approaches (Vasquez 2016). Well-structured community development planning processes can constructively channel devolved revenue for conflict prevention benefits and can help to address risks around horizontal inequalities. Gradualism in the decentralization of development planning to producing regions can also help to build institutional capability and local ownership, as in Peru (Vasquez 2016), while participatory development planning processes can help to calibrate corporate social responsibility initiatives to local priorities.

Ultimately, the idea of addressing the risks of extractives-related conflict through devolution and the transfer of wealth to subnational entities has been mooted as a potential prevention mechanism (Cordella and Onder 2016). A recent investigation of the devolution of oil windfalls finds that redistributing oil revenues does prevent conflict in some cases, but can stoke violence in other cases by decreasing the opportunity cost of mobilization (Cordella and Onder 2016). Even small transfers in countries with large oil wealth can have this effect. Furthermore, the same research shows that the transfer of oil wealth directly to people is more effective as a means of preventing violent conflict than fiscal transfers to subnational governments, even though the latter typically generates greater welfare through higher levels of consumption (Cordella and Onder 2016).

The Arena of Service Delivery

Service delivery can affect the risk of violence in that it affects state legitimacy (Omoeva and Buckner 2015; World Bank 2017a). While service delivery is not the only determinant of state legitimacy,[9] it is a primary way by which many citizens directly encounter the state and shapes their overall perception of it. In the hierarchy of political goods, the relevance of services has been referred to as giving "content to the social contract between the ruler and ruled" (Rotberg 2004). Specifically, the delivery of education, health care, water, sanitation, and even justice and security have been described as "the glue" that binds state and society together (Milliken and Krause 2002). These services are the most tangible expression of the basic minimum that citizens expect from the state in exchange for their deference to the state's rule over them (Gilley 2009).

However, the relationship between service delivery and legitimacy is neither simple nor direct (Brinkerhoff, Wetterberg, and Dunn 2012; Fisk and Cherney 2016; Mcloughlin 2015b; Sacks and Larizza 2012; Stel and Abate 2014; Stel and Ndayiragiie 2014; Sturge et al. 2017). The degree of legitimacy that the state enjoys depends on people's expectations, which are, in turn, shaped by their prior experiences (Nixon, Mallett, and McCullough 2017), geography, identity, and culture (Sturge et al. 2017). In South Africa, perceptions of state legitimacy vary according to age, race, and gender; along rural-urban divides; and by their experiences of apartheid (Carter 2011).

Uneven coverage of services can undermine state legitimacy, when it is viewed as a manifestation of group exclusion. Perceptions of unequal or exclusionary access to services influence the way citizens regard the "rightfulness" of the state (Dix, Hussmann, and Walton 2012). According to one study, patronage politics in Sri Lanka has meant that poorer and less well-connected individuals fail to access social protection transfers as a result of a bargain forged among wealthier and more powerful members of society (Nixon, Mallett, and McCullough 2017).

In Colombia, Liberia, and Nepal, unequal or exclusionary access to public goods has also been detrimental to perceptions of state legitimacy (Dix, Hussmann, and Walton 2012).

In these cases, uneven service delivery can stoke grievances against the state or against groups that are seen to be receiving unfairly disproportionate access. Perceived favoritism toward one group may boost the favored group's trust in the state, but also it may undermine other groups' trust in the state (Mcloughlin 2015a). Reforms of service delivery can generate grievances that lead to violent conflict "when the rules and patterns of distribution are perceived by some to be unjustifiable and unfair" (Sturge et al. 2017, ix).

The legitimizing effect of service delivery also depends heavily on *how* services are delivered. A five-country study of citizen perceptions and service delivery in conflict-affected contexts finds that, with regard to state legitimacy, fairness and inclusiveness in the service delivery process matters as much as, if not more than, the quality of services or who delivers them (Sturge et al. 2017). Similarly, other research across different contexts finds that "the perceived fairness of the process by which authorities and institutions make decisions and exercise authority is a key aspect of people's willingness to comply with it" (Mcloughlin 2015a; Tyler 2006).

When services are not delivered appropriately, state legitimacy suffers. Service delivery that falls short can undermine perceptions of government and can have a delegitimizing effect (Sturge et al. 2017). Legitimacy is grounded in justifiable rules and can unravel when power is used in ways that are not justified (Mcloughlin 2015a). Delegitimation can happen when institutions or individuals charged with exercising authority breach social norms or when these norms change in relation to governing rules and practices (Mcloughlin 2015a).

Corruption Related to Basic Services

Where inefficient or inappropriate service delivery overlaps with corruption, it can exclude certain populations within society, particularly those who are already marginalized. This can lead to civil unrest, protests, and even outright violence, as in South Africa's informal settlements in 2009 (Burger 2009; Corruption Watch 2014). In Nepal, corruption, lack of information about the availability of services, and the exclusion of some groups from their share undermined the credibility of the state institutions (Ndaruhutse et al. 2012). Where corruption is endemic, political legitimacy is weakened and the risk of conflict rises (Baker 2017).

At its simplest, corruption is defined as the misuse of public offices and resources for private gain (Sargsyan 2017). However, corruption can occur at different levels and in many different forms. Corruption has an indirect connection to violence in that it can fuel grievances between groups that are seen to be benefiting and those that are not. Additionally, corruption ultimately undermines national institutions and social norms because some are seen to be above the rules set by those institutions (World Bank 2011). In combination with weak rule of law and where the institutions charged with delivering services are politicized or captured, corruption can generate popular "distrust, dissatisfaction, and grievances with the existing political system" (Taydas, Peksen, and James 2010). These feelings can contribute to delegitimizing the state and invalidating disincentives for violent protest (Sargsyan 2017). In Afghanistan, endemic corruption and elite impunity undermined the image of the government and was one of the factors that enabled the resurgence of the Taliban in the countryside (World Bank 2017a).

Some research suggests that corruption can have a stabilizing role, depending on the context and the form it takes (Hussmann, Tisne, and Mathisen 2009). "Classic" patronage politics can be a source of social and political cohesion, in that it promotes a certain consistency (Brinkerhoff and Goldsmith 2005) and trying to eliminate it can destabilize power dynamics (Hameiri 2007). In certain cases, public investments can enhance inclusive service delivery, despite the presence of corruption. In the midst of armed conflict in Nepal, Maoists allowed health services to operate in exchange for rents, and district-level officials understood that they needed to maintain the flow of medicine to villages to enhance their local legitimacy (World Bank 2017a).

Service Delivery in Alternatively Governed Spaces

As discussed in chapter 3, nonstate actors often provide alternative forms of governance, especially in areas where the state has not established its presence in a convincing way. These actors may be traditional or communal leaders and institutions that step in to fill the vacuum, or they may include criminal networks, traffickers, militants, and extremists. While not all of the latter may directly oppose the state, they may undermine the state, either indirectly by supplanting the state's authority or more directly by using these spaces to launch attacks, build up operations, and traffic narcotics, arms, and contraband.

The dominant narrative across such contexts is to "securitize" these spaces, to link them to multiple emerging security threats, and to view them as safe havens for rogue elements (Abrahamsen 2005; Keenan 2008). While one of the state's primary responsibilities is to provide security, a purely security-focused approach in such contexts is often ineffective. It fails to address the core reason that such spaces emerge in the first place: namely, poor governance and weak state presence (Keister 2014). To assert its presence and gain the trust of citizens, which is a prerequisite for legitimacy, the state needs to maintain a positive, visible presence. Delivery of services provides the means to do so and can have particular resonance for women, who are primarily responsible for providing education, health, clothing, and food for the household (MacPherson 2008). The state does not need to be involved in every aspect of the provision of services. However, being recognized as ultimately responsible for providing services and for organizing the contributions of other actors bolsters its legitimacy and authority (Bellina et al. 2009).

Building state legitimacy requires, among other measures, the visible presence of state institutions, also referred to as "penetration" (Nixon, Mallett, and McCullough 2017, 4). Often, however, the state chooses to allocate limited resources in a rational manner, only extending authority when the benefits outweigh the costs. The state may decide not to integrate areas where its presence is already low or weak if integration promises few benefits and meager returns on the investment (Keister 2014). For example, limited infrastructure and fiscal constraints in the north of Mali, along with high per capita cost of services in proportion to low population density, make the delivery of services very expensive and challenging (Wee et al. 2014). However, a growing sense of marginalization among the local population (despite data showing that service provision in some sectors is compatible with or higher than in the south) necessitates finding innovative ways to deliver services (Wee et al. 2014).

Government strategies to compete with alternative governance and service providers by making the state a more attractive option have had some success. A policy of "peaceful penetration" in Pakistan between 1951 and 1955 and between 1972 and 1977 saw the government provide Pashtun areas with a variety of development projects to demonstrate the value of closer relations with the government; this helped to lessen the appeal of an independent Pashtunistan and to improve citizens' perceptions of the government (Keister 2014). Using existing structures that emerge locally and organically to form the "building blocks" of administration in areas such as the remote regions of Somalia can also be effective (Bryden 1999; Keister 2014).

The extension of authority and legitimacy through local intermediaries in this way forms "mediated states" or "hybrid regimes" (Boege et al. 2008; Keister 2014, 9; Menkhaus 2006, 7). Hybrid arrangements can involve public and private as well as formal and informal arrangements. These arrangements can be effective in remote communities with a high level of diversity,

helping service delivery to adapt to local preferences and building trust between the center and the periphery. Furthermore, in remote and sparsely populated areas where state presence is scarce, security, justice, basic, and livelihood services can be delivered with a smaller government presence "so long as mechanisms are nested within customary practices, ad hoc community structures, and communities themselves are invested in the success of delivery modalities" (Wee et al. 2014).

Inclusion and Consultation in Service Delivery

Providing a platform for inclusion, participation, and voice to citizens and involving them directly in the provision of services can significantly improve citizens' perceptions of the state. Citizens' perceptions of and regard for the state, particularly at the local level, are improved when they are consulted, when they feel heard, and, most important, when they are brought directly into the process itself (Sturge et al. 2017). The presence of grievance mechanisms and possibilities of civil participation strongly influence perceptions of government, which suggests that public services can act as a channel through which citizens and public authorities interact (Van de Walle and Scott 2011).

In Nepal, Pakistan, and Uganda, including citizens in the process of service delivery through grievance mechanisms improved the perceptions among citizens of national actors and reinforced feelings that both local and national government actors care about the opinion of citizens (Sturge et al. 2017). In Nepal, Sri Lanka, and Uganda, community meetings have had the same effect (Sturge et al. 2017). Although problematic service delivery can also negatively affect attitudes to and relationships with both local-level service providers and the government, embedding grievance mechanisms into the service can have the opposite effect (Nixon, Mallett, and McCullough 2017).

The strongest results show up where people are involved directly in running a service, particularly at the local level.

Indeed, direct involvement matters more than the mere presence of services, when it comes to the way in which people think about the government. Experiences of corruption in service delivery and poor treatment by staff, especially when repeated, undermine trust in the capacity of government to provide decent care. In Sierra Leone, decentralization of service delivery was intended to give local communities a greater say and stake in outcomes (Sacks and Larizza 2012). However, this was insufficient in and of itself for building trust in local authorities. What beneficiaries cared about in reality was how fair and free of corruption they perceived the process to be, combined with the quality of services (Sacks and Larizza 2012). The state can gain legitimacy by fencing in disagreements, opening up space for voice and arbitration, providing services in a fair and inclusive manner, and offering institutionalized arrangements for service provision.

The Arena of Security and Justice

The security and justice arena is central to understanding and preventing violent conflict. Security and justice institutions, whether formal or informal, impose sanctions on violence and limit the harm that violence can cause. Severe deficits in the governance of this arena, including lack of accountability, transparency, and responsiveness, can result in a breakdown in the rule of law and, consequently, impunity. If rules and norms regarding violence are discriminatory or poorly enforced, groups may cease to rely on institutionalized security and justice sectors and may seek security and justice elsewhere (World Bank 2011). These issues are specifically addressed in the 2030 Agenda. SDG 16 emphasizes effective, accountable, transparent, and inclusive institutions and specifically aims to reduce all forms of violence (target 16.1), particularly against children (target 16.2), and to promote the rule of law and ensure equal access to justice for all (target 16.3). This study argues throughout that designing incentives for peace and limiting the harm that violent actors can cause are key

elements in the prevention of violent conflict throughout the conflict cycle.

This chapter discusses security and justice individually, although they are deeply interconnected both conceptually and as practical policy domains. Measures to provide better security will not be sustainable if they are not combined with improvements in access to justice—and vice versa. Together, security and justice form the basis for the enjoyment of access to all the other arenas—security as the system responsible for protecting the basic right to life and personal integrity and justice as the system responsible for resolving conflict. Each is treated separately here to give greater attention to their respective contributions to the overall risk of conflict.

The Role of the Security Sector in Sustaining Peace

The monopoly of the use of force is a main characteristic of the state's authority, and the state almost always has a strong role in governance and the provision of security, even if this role is uneven across a country's territory. The state cannot delegate security functions to nonstate actors without eventually sacrificing sovereignty. Nevertheless, hybrid models, with mixed arrangements of informal, nonstate, and formal state security providers, are the norm in many low-capacity contexts, for example, rural Liberia, where community watch teams constitute a large component of security provision. While extending the reach of security provision, despite being "rooted in local custom and practice, [informal institutions] can sometimes be just as exclusive and oppressive as formal security provision" (Bagayoko, Hutchful, and Luckham 2016, 20).

The security arena offers opportunities for conflict prevention. Security is a necessary precondition for other public goods and freedoms, such as freedom of movement and expression. When security is provided inclusively, access to the other arenas is enhanced. Security enables economic development and overall development by providing the conditions necessary for people to invest in new businesses, obtain and maintain employment, and send children to school. Risks increase when security provision is weak, exclusionary, or predatory. Where security actors do not behave in a manner consistent with the rule of law, they can pose a threat to the very populations they are charged with protecting (World Bank 2011).

Noting the trends in violent conflict elaborated in chapter 1, this section focuses largely on internal security forces, for example, police, gendarmes, and wildlife forces. However, even if designed to manage external security, military forces can nonetheless have significant direct and indirect impacts on the prevention of conflict. While very few military regimes remain in place in the world, the military still plays a very strong role in politics and the economy in many countries. In some cases, this situation can be a source of stability, especially when the army manages to stay out of political infighting. However, military penetration of society and the economy can make reform of the security sector itself challenging. Where the military owns corporations or controls economic sectors or, more precisely, where military and security personnel derive benefits from their rank that are not directly related to their role as security providers, reform of the security sector often requires much broader reform of the state too.

As noted, where the state's presence is weak or the authority of the state is contested, nonstate security providers and informal mechanisms can proliferate and become the preferred alternative for local populations.[10] Such nonstate providers can take many shapes and often change form over time, including as rogue local-level units of formal security institutions, criminal gangs, violence entrepreneurs, rebel groups, self-defense militias, or vigilante groups. In some fragile contexts, there is no clear distinction between state and nonstate security providers, with the relationship of armed groups to state security forces changing and evolving over time. The shifting alliances in the Democratic Republic of Congo, where rebels were integrated into the armed forces, only to revert to their established practices and structures once

they returned home, are a case in point (Stearns 2012).

In other contexts, the proliferation of nonstate armed groups and formal providers of security can fragment the provision of security. For example, in South Sudan, the Sudan People's Liberation Army and the Sudan People's Liberation Movement-in-Opposition constitute "a conglomerate of various ethnic factions with different goals and trajectories; groups that at times have fought each other, and that have come together to fight a joint enemy only to split up again and again, forming various allegiances throughout South Sudan's long journey towards self-determination" (Breitung, Paes, and van de Vondervoort 2016). In many countries, political elites essentially arm private militias to garner power and influence around key moments, such as elections.

Even when managed by formal institutions, security actors—be they police units, individual patrols, or intelligence officers—are motivated by a range of political, social, cultural, and economic incentives. Exclusionary and biased security forces pose an especially high risk if access to and control of the tools to maintain security are instead used to maintain loyalty or dispense favors. Although the state should provide security, as a service, to its citizens, it may use security forces less to further the public good than to defend its own power and protect allied private interests. As such, decision making, the allocation of resources, and the use of force may reflect private, group, or partisan interests. Risks increase, for example, when police operations are conducted in accordance with private agendas and political and economic interests, rather than being operationally independent from political decision making and conducted in response to the population's concerns and demands for public safety.

In more extreme cases, security forces are predatory toward the populations they are meant to protect. Examples of police and military forces participating in or facilitating mass atrocities abound, as do abuses during so-called "crackdowns" and other muscular approaches to security threats or even common crime. As discussed in chapter 4, abuse of identity groups by security forces will deepen grievances and may be a strong factor motivating people to identify with and join violent groups.

The overall risk of weak, fragmented, exclusionary, or predatory security provision is popular disenchantment and loss of confidence in a society's willingness and ability to deliver security. Reform of the security sector, understood as the structures, institutions, and personnel responsible for managing, providing, and overseeing security, including informal or traditional security providers, can build the credibility, legitimacy, and effectiveness of a society.[11] When security services have no legitimacy, they will struggle to be effective, and that effort will further undermine their credibility and delegitimize them in the eyes of the population.

Reform of security institutions can signal a change in approach, even when results from such reforms require sustained investment. From its beginnings in the mid-1990s, lessons on security sector reform (SSR) highlight three key entry points for reform: (a) the development of an institutional framework of organizations and policies; (b) governance and civilian oversight; and (c) the establishment of capable, professional, and accountable security forces.

In addition to security sector reforms, demilitarization of society is also important. In recognition of the critical nexus between security and development, SSR processes have sometimes been undertaken in conjunction with disarmament, demobilization, and reintegration (DDR) programs, especially in postconflict countries. The DDR-SSR nexus is manifested in the integration of former combatants into national security and defense forces, at both the strategic and operational levels. Some countries tie development goals specifically to security goals or develop joint programs for security and development, for example, through integrated rule of law and DDR programs.[12] If done effectively, DDR and SSR provide vital support to peace agreements and other transitional agreements by building confidence in postconflict institutions and processes. DDR contributes to immediate security and stability, allowing recovery and development to begin. In turn, SSR processes can help to contain the risk of future violence by building institutions that support the welfare of former members of national armed services, creating new employment opportunities in reformed security institutions, reducing incentives for future violence, and reestablishing trust between the security and defense forces and the population (McFate 2010).

In an increasing number of contexts, international and regional actors are playing important roles in accompanying and monitoring security forces, supplying equipment, and providing technical training.[13] This support has been instrumental in monitoring and addressing short-term threats to stability, as evidenced by international counterterrorism support to the Sahel (DeYoung 2017). However, addressing the deeper constraints to inclusive and effective security requires sustained and flexible support for a fuller reform process, with strong national ownership. Chapter 7 discusses the role of international actors in helping to calibrate incentives for peace, to reform institutions, and to change structural factors in the field of security.

The UN Security Council recently recognized that a professional, accountable, and effective security sector is critical to consolidating peace and stability and to preventing countries from lapsing or relapsing into conflict (UN Security Council 2014, 2016). A representative security force, which is the face of the state, is a basic ingredient for effective security provision in a society. Groups need to see themselves represented in the makeup of the police force, for example. Incorporating greater numbers of marginalized ethnic or religious groups into the military and police forces and fostering a cultural shift toward nondiscriminatory policing can help to alleviate grievances around security. Increasing the number of female police officers and setting up women's police stations have, in some cases, contributed to higher reporting of crimes against women, especially assault and domestic violence (DCAF 2017). Community policing programs also have increased the representativeness of police forces, with important gains in citizen perceptions of security and state legitimacy. Chapter 6 discusses specific examples drawn from country experiences with preventing violent conflict.

SSR also needs to bring about a cultural shift in how authorities display and use their power. It is essential to establish mechanisms to signal and implement the shift in institutional culture to make it real and visible to citizens. To reduce risk in the security arena, SSR should establish civilian oversight of security forces as well as of the responsible ministries, parliament, and civil society.[14] This requires that the chain of command for policy decisions is ultimately in the hands of a civilian, that this official is responsible for decisions to systematic oversight process, and that a legal regime exists to empower civil society to highlight concerns and abuses. Public expenditure reviews (PERs) provide a useful tool for establishing civilian oversight and monitoring (Harborne, Dorotinsky, and Bisca 2017; box 5.5). To date, these oversight mechanisms have received much less external funding than the security forces themselves have (Bryden and Olonisakin 2010; Donnelly 1997).

SSRs are also more sustainable when they include all of the security agencies and forces. There is often a reluctance to include certain bodies in reform efforts—elite forces or intelligence units, for example. Where these agencies are perpetuating some of the worst human rights violations, holding them accountable is essential for the overall credibility of the security architecture. However, because they operate more clandestinely and with impunity, they have proven to be the most elusive. In addition, including all agencies poses practical challenges to sequencing, prioritizing, and financing. Even in South

---

BOX 5.5 Public Expenditure Analysis of the Security Forces

A framework for analyzing the expenditure for military, police, and criminal justice institutions should resemble that for other elements of the public sector. It involves testing the underlying rationale for state engagement, policy alignment of resource allocations, and effectiveness and efficiency in spending. Recent work has also emphasized the need to mobilize domestic resources and strengthen public expenditures in fragile states. However, most central finance agencies and development institutions are ill-equipped to undertake this analysis. Similarly, most decision makers in national security have little or no informed dialogue with their counterparts in finance. This is largely due to a poor understanding of the specific requirements of the security sector as well as a poor articulation between decision-making processes in public finance and in security and justice.

Security sector public expenditure reviews (PERs) fill this gap. The PER is a tried and tested tool that has been used over the last few decades in helping governments to examine key questions of economic policy and public financial management regarding their budgets. A PER examines government resource allocations within and among sectors, assessing the equity, efficiency, and effectiveness of those allocations in the context of a country's macroeconomic framework and sectoral priorities.

Building on their complementary mandates in economic management and security sector reform (SSR), recent work by the World Bank and United Nations provides national and international stakeholders with (a) the information needed to engage in dialogue on security expenditure policy; (b) a framework for analyzing financial management, financial transparency and oversight, and expenditure policy issues; and (c) advice on entry points for integrating expenditure analysis into SSR and broader governance reform processes.

Sources: Development Committee 2015; Harborne, Dorotinsky, and Bisca 2017; OECD 2015; World Bank 2011.

Africa, where public consultations substantially contributed to the 1996 Defense White Paper to great acclaim, there was no willingness to subject the Intelligence White Paper to the same scrutiny (Nathan 2007).[15] A notable exception was the State Information and Protection Agency in Bosnia and Herzegovina, which was created from scratch and therefore not saddled with the crimes of a predecessor organization (Vetschera and Damian 2006).

Finally, reform processes tend to be more sustainable when based on citizen involvement, through consultations, joint oversight with communities, or similar mechanisms. In Kosovo, local public safety committees and municipal community safety councils, consisting of a wide range of representatives ranging from local authorities to nongovernmental organizations and the community, were established to enhance cooperation between the police and communities (OSCE 2008). Public safety concerns of minority groups and women were emphasized in order to address specific violations against and needs of women and girls.[16] Strengthening these dialogues has been a key role for international action (Mahmoud 2017). In the same vein, SSR programs have at times promoted national dialogue, but national dialogues are labor- and time-intensive undertakings and depend on a tolerable security situation.[17]

Justice and Fairness in Prevention

This study incorporates the definition of two aspects of justice from the *World Development Report 2011* (World Bank 2011). First, the term justice refers to "the broadly held notion of fairness," which, despite differences in context, is a universally relevant, albeit subjective, concept relating to just processes and outcomes regarding the distribution of power, resources, opportunities, and sanctions. A perception of unfairness is a key aspect of the relationship between grievances and mobilization to violence, as discussed in chapter 4.

Second, the institutional side of justice refers to "the institutions that are central to resolving conflicts arising over alleged violations or different interpretations of the rules that societies create to govern members' behavior and that, as a consequence, are central to strengthening the normative framework (laws and rules) that shapes public and private actions" (World Bank 2011). Justice systems include the framework of institutions that determine how power is acquired and distributed, and they define the sanctions against abuses. They also adjudicate grievances in society and are the primary mechanism for redressing disputes and wrongs done. As such, justice systems go beyond the rule of law, which refers to the general compliance with laws in a society. The distinction is important, in that it is possible for a regime to act in accordance with the rule of law for its particular context and still violate, and be accountable to, the international system of justice.

Lack of legal identity is a major cause of exclusion from justice, and target 16.9 of the 2030 Agenda focuses specifically on providing legal identity for all, including birth registration, by 2030. Approximately 12 million people globally are stateless and without effective citizenship rights.[18] In addition, some 27 states around the world do not allow women to transfer nationality to their children, and statelessness can occur where fathers are stateless, missing, or deceased. For example, the Rohingya are Muslims living in Rakhine (historically known as Arakan) State, a geographically isolated area in western Myanmar, bordering Bangladesh. There are different, irreconcilable narratives of who the Rohingya are and the length of time they have resided in Rakhine State. Since independence in 1948, the community has been gradually marginalized. The 1982 Citizenship Law designated three categories of citizens: (1) full citizens, (2) associate citizens, and (3) naturalized citizens. None of the categories applies to the Rohingya, who are not recognized as one of the 135 "national races" by the Myanmar government (Human Rights Watch 2017). While many remain stateless in Rakhine State today, many more are stateless refugees residing in other countries. They have been forced to flee as a result of widespread discrimination and persecution rooted in the deprivation of citizenship.

The justice system, especially the *formal* justice system, is the space where rules and power are ultimately defined. These rules protect the basic rights that allow individuals to enjoy the benefits from the other arenas. The justice system is the ultimate guarantor of the right to physical integrity, which underlies all other rights through the sanctions it imposes on violators. Most governments have strong written policies that guarantee the right to physical integrity, which includes the right of protection from extrajudicial killing, torture, political or wrongful imprisonment, or enforced disappearance (box 5.6). If the state violates these rights or tolerates impunity for their violation, it can exacerbate grievances, particularly when these manifestations of injustice overlap with perceptions of exclusion, unfairness, or inequality (Cingranelli et al. 2017).

By extension, access to the justice arena partly determines fair access to the other arenas. Perceptions of injustice can be situated or can originate in the other arenas, but are ultimately resolved within the justice and conflict resolution systems. For example, unfair outcomes in access to natural resources and their benefits are addressed within the justice system. Put another way, the credibility and legitimacy of the justice system has an impact on the functioning of other arenas and on the population's perceptions of fairness and legitimacy overall. Durable institutions that are perceived as just are crucial to broad-based, inclusive development (World Bank 2011). The 2030 Agenda includes targets on equal access both to natural resources (targets 1.4, 2.3, 5a) and to justice (target 16.3).

A robust justice system creates incentives for peaceful behavior. It can settle disputes in a peaceful manner, ensure accountability of power, promote respect for human rights, combat corruption through the enforceability of contracts and property rights, and

---

BOX 5.6 Human Rights as a Basis for Normative Change

Many countries have used the universal, interrelated, and interdependent rights set out in the Universal Declaration of Human Rights and the universal treaties that derive from it as well as a range of regional human rights instruments as a shared foundation for normative and legal change.

All 193 UN member states have ratified at least two of the nine core human rights treaties, and more than 80 percent of states have ratified seven. The primary responsibility for respecting, protecting, and fulfilling human rights rests with states, who translate the international norms into laws, policies, and programs. In many states, human rights have also underpinned institutional reforms—for example, constitutional reforms, creation of national human rights institutions, or transitional justice mechanisms. National human rights institutions serve as mechanisms,

independent from government, for monitoring respect for human rights nationally. Civil society organizations have made vital contributions to human rights instruments and their implementation.

International tools like fact-finding missions, routine reporting, investigative commissions, and special rapporteurs have often focused on maintaining dialogue with governments on violations of rights, discrimination, and abuse as part of efforts to reduce the risks of conflict. The Universal Periodic Review undertaken by the Human Rights Council is the main institutional review mechanism for all 193 UN member states. Its potential to contribute to prevention and peacebuilding efforts was acknowledged in the recent sustaining peace resolutions (UN General Assembly 2015a, para. 11; UN Security Council 2016).

Sources: OHCHR 2010; Payne et al. 2017.

ensure checks and balances (World Bank 2017c). Conversely, a breakdown of justice systems and the rule of law generally can inflame the grievances that may be mobilized for conflict and create incentives for violent behavior.[19] The relationship between weak rule of law and violence is underscored by the poor perceptions of justice systems often found in regions suffering from or at risk of violent conflict, as people lose confidence in institutions that cannot, or will not, protect them from injustices (Logan 2017). Grievances can accumulate with prolonged conflict, as the capacity of justice systems is strained by the need to respond to ongoing violence; the often-elevated levels of criminality and abuses during violent conflict can further weaken the capacity of formal justice stystems.

Prevention of violent conflict requires identifying why justice system processes and outcomes may discriminate against certain groups. In many cases, the formal justice system may be inaccessible. In others, it may be irrelevant to the justice-related needs of the population. Many people rely, voluntarily or out of necessity, on informal or customary justice systems that are rooted in traditional authority. Indeed, this is the case for roughly 80 percent of the population in transition or postconflict settings (UN 2017). A cross-country study of Afghanistan, Guatemala, Iraq, Liberia, Mozambique, South Sudan, and Timor-Leste finds that customary systems are often more trusted and used by people because they are more sensitive to the political and social realities and therefore faster and more effective in solving the everyday problems that people face (Isser 2011). Also, where formal rules diverge greatly from local norms and customs, these customary systems of justice are much more likely to be respected (Isser 2011).

Any reform of the formal system can undermine public confidence in the justice system—and in the state more generally—if it does not engage meaningfully with informal and customary justice systems. Time and again, experience has shown the critical importance, especially in countries transitioning out of violent conflict, of understanding the role that customary systems play in responding to the problems people face.

Reforms that fail to recognize this context may waste time and resources in building a formal system that the population later rejects and may also deepen resentment of the overall project of state building (Isser 2011).

An important first step is to understand how people are solving the problems they face and the role that customary institutions play in those processes. This understanding helps to identify the gap between the way laws and policies are written, on the one hand, and the way conflicts are resolved and needs are met in reality, on the other hand. Starting with understanding as a point of departure challenges the notion that legal authority needs to originate in the state. It also opens up the possibility for more inclusive and credible processes and offers the potential to anticipate trade-offs and unintended consequences. In many contexts, including in contexts where violent conflict has already begun, local-level mechanisms for resolving conflicts have helped to ensure stability and to reduce violence. In the 1990s, the Islamic Courts in Somalia started to develop a level of popular legitimacy, and by 2006, various armed groups were using the principle of credible law and order to form an Islamic Courts Union, which increased the stability in the territories under their control (Barnes and Hassan 2007; box 5.7). Chapter 6 discusses practical experiences with local peace committees.

Reform of justice systems requires two parallel courses of action. On the one hand, it is important to ensure that current challenges receive equitable attention in order to build trust and reestablish a sense of normalcy. At the same time, particularly in postconflict environments, perpetrators must be equally held to account for past abuses in order to send a strong signal of change. Balancing these needs is one of the most formidable challenges of conflict-affected environments. Weighing the equality of accountability processes against the imperative to bring perpetrators to book is critical to the challenge of advancing stabilization and justice in conflict-affected environments under SDG 16 (UN General Assembly 2015b). Accountability processes may exacerbate grievances related to specific social groups if they are perceived to discriminate between groups (Mahony 2015a). How and why the real or perceived unequal treatment of social groups actually occurs varies from one process to another. Frameworks to identify how accountability processes treat groups differently can help to identify ways in which to preempt spoilers and mitigate risks of conflict (Mahony 2016).

Responding to current needs implies expanding access to justice, especially for those who have been excluded. Strengthening the capacity of local-level mechanisms to resolve disputes that originate in the other arenas, as discussed in previous sections of this chapter, can go a long way toward building confidence. For example, promoting more effective resolution of local-level conflicts over land or water access helps to address the everyday problems people face. It also builds useful bridges between customary or informal and formal processes. Strengthening the capacity of formal institutions to process judicial caseloads and increasing the efficiency of investigations and prosecutions also need to be prioritized (World Bank 2011).

Addressing everyday justice needs also entails dealing with manifestations of violence that tend to increase in situations of violent conflict, especially common crime

and domestic violence. In some contexts, efforts to address this violence draw on customary norms to challenge the rules and practices of formal institutions. For example, women's advocacy groups in India's Gujarat and Utter Pradesh states set up informal women's courts (*nari adalat*) as an alternative to formal systems for resolving domestic violence cases (Kethineni, Srinivasan, and Kakar 2016). By drawing on community norms, international human rights laws, and state laws, they were able to expand access to justice and help to prevent further violence by contesting unequal gender power structures (Merry 2012; World Bank 2017c).

Promoting accountability is pursued through transitional justice measures.[20] These include a wide range of mechanisms, such as vetting of government agencies and especially security forces, truth and reconciliation commissions, public apologies,[21] memorialization or local healing processes, prosecution of human rights abuses, and material or symbolic reparations.[22] In some cases, transitional justice measures enable high-level prosecutions to take place. These measures aim to establish a clear public record of the past and to reassert respect for the rule of law, and they usually rely on heavy support from civil society and international actors (Payne et al. 2017).

There is widespread debate over the value of transitional justice measures in reducing the risks of conflict recurrence, in part due to the range of actions included in this category (Mallinder and O'Rourke 2016; Thoms, Ron, and Paris 2010). Some have argued that prosecutions for past crimes are essential to preventing conflict recurrence because they create deterrents for spoilers (Sikkink 2011); others argue that mechanisms to appease spoilers, such as amnesty, are more effective (Snyder and Vinjamuri 2003).

The Transitional Justice Research Collaborative examines the relationships between five variables—trials, truth commissions, amnesties, reparations, and vetting—that have been implemented following 119 transitions from authoritarian rule or civil war in 86 countries since 1970 (Payne et al. 2017). It finds that implementing domestic criminal prosecutions[23] for past human rights violations has a significant relationship with nonrecurrence of intrastate conflict. It also finds that the rate of recurrence decreases by approximately 70 percent when trials are pursued of middle- and low-level actors (Payne et al. 2017), holding all other factors constant. Paradoxically, the prosecution of high-ranking individuals is associated with a 65 percent increase in the rate of conflict recurrence, suggesting that "coming together after a war to initiate a major legal process (much like writing a new constitution) has important effects" (Payne et al. 2017, 19).

The number of cases of international criminal justice engagement with country situations is insufficient to make statistically significant findings about their impact on conflict recurrence or nonrecurrence (Payne et al. 2017). The International Criminal Court defers jurisdiction to states that are able and willing to prosecute international crimes domestically. There is debate over whether this relationship to domestic processes prompts improved domestic trials or if it enables governments to engage in selective prosecution targeting specific social groups while avoiding others (Hyeran and Simmons 2014; Mahony 2015b). Although the relationship between

peace and justice has been debated, the focus of debate has generally been the willingness of spoilers to reengage in violence in response to the threat of prosecution (Vinjamuri 2010).

Effective reckoning with the past via transitional justice measures requires a gendered approach. This implies accounting for the multiple roles and experiences of women during conflict as combatants, victims of violence, widows, or mothers whose children die (Tabak 2011). It is also important to consider the challenges that women, after a conflict, face in accessing livelihoods, recovering from physical and emotional trauma, and obtaining justice. In many cases, focusing on sexual violence as the sole form of violence women face during conflict ignores nonconflict-related violence and its impacts.

Similar debates exist over the effectiveness of truth-telling processes as part of transitional justice (Mendeloff 2009). A recent quantitative study finds that certain truth-telling and reconciliation processes are associated with a decline in mental health, but higher levels of social integration (Cilliers, Dube, and Siddiqi 2016). Some qualitative studies, moreover, suggest that deeply contested narratives associated with truth telling may revive societal cleavages (Kelsall 2005). The intervention of traditional elders in Sierra Leone's Truth Commission has been credited with enabling reconciliation and defusing tensions relating to contested truths there (Kelsall 2005). However, such processes often require participants to subordinate to the very power structures (traditional elites) that may have been at the root of the conflict, so they may not sufficiently address underlying causes over the longer term (Mahony and Sooka 2015).

Transitional justice measures can have a broader impact on social relationships. Some measures have been used to engage with previously marginalized communities or secessionist movements in order to address political polarization and prevent an outbreak. For example, the Tunisian Truth and Dignity Commission established a record on Ben Ali–era abuses, including systematic corruption, and laid the groundwork for possible national criminal prosecutions (Toska 2017). These processes have arguably played a significant role in preventing the violent conflict that accompanied some other Arab Spring transitions. Some transitional justice processes were less effective in preventing violence overall but have provided a model for future mechanisms to alleviate social and political polarization. For example, exploration of historical injustice over more than 200 years, including state expropriation of land of the Bangsamoro community in Mindanao, the Philippines, was part of the comprehensive peace agreement in 2014.

Conclusion

Most violent conflicts today play out in four arenas of contestation where groups in society negotiate access to power, resources, services, and security. As the spaces where access to the means of livelihood and well-being are defined and defended, these arenas are critical sites of both risk and opportunity.

Governance of these arenas in large part shapes a society's pathway. As demonstrated in chapters 3 and 4, risk is heightened where shocks interact with underlying grievances. Chapter 5 has described how this interaction often plays out in the arenas of contestation. Because negotiations in the arenas reflect broader power dynamics in society, reform is often contested. Actors who are already at the table must agree to change the rules, institutions, or structural factors that define the power balance in the arenas, and they may see little benefit in challenging the status quo.

Preventing violent conflict requires targeted, flexible, and sustained attention to all of the arenas. When the risks of violent conflict build up across arenas of contestation, an effective state has a responsibility to ensure that conflicts and contestations remain nonviolent and that the outcome is conducive to the well-being of all citizens. Even if improving institutions can take decades, states can play an important role by signaling that they are focusing on equal access to political process, natural resources, services, security, and justice irrespective of sex, age, region of domicile, ethnicity, religion, or other group identity. National plans to implement the 2030 Agenda can be useful in that regard. This aspect of the role of the state is at the heart of the social contract that ties citizens to the state. Where the state does not play this role effectively, it will become a source of contestation in itself and can become the object of violent conflict between groups within society.

Conflict in the security and justice arena poses particular challenges for prevention. These challenges are discussed in greater detail in chapter 6, which reviews the experiences of countries that have managed conflict. They relate to actors' political and physical survival; as such, security and justice reforms have proven sensitive and politically charged. Domestic actors in countries that have successfully made changes have had to make risky trade-offs. Short-term capability has been sacrificed for the potential of longer-term effectiveness. Reforms focused on inclusivity, transparency, accountability, and management of security institutions have boosted the resilience and legitimacy of the state.

Reform of any institution is a long-term exercise. In the case of security and justice institutions, it usually takes roughly 5–10 years for significant and noticeable improvements in effectiveness and accountability to become evident (DCAF 2017). Reconciling the pressure from external supporters of SSR, who want to see change, with on-the-ground realities in specific contexts has been an ongoing challenge for many countries. In the Central African Republic, the uneven approach from both the government and donors contributed to an escalation of conflict (DCAF 2017). To navigate such competing demands, Sierra Leone signed a memorandum of understanding with the United Kingdom, which provided assurance of long-term commitment and space for incremental and flexible approaches (DCAF 2017) and helped to enable important incremental progress on accountable and effective institutions.

This chapter has given an overview of the particular risks that can accumulate in each of the arenas, some technical aspects of reform of the arenas, and potential trade-offs that are often present when addressing risks. The next chapter draws experiences from specific countries to illustrate how incentives for peace have been built and maintained by paying careful attention to the arenas of contestation as well as other measures.

Notes

1. These arenas were selected following consultations within the UN and the World Bank and are based on an analysis of all Uppsala Conflict Data Program (UCDP) identified violent conflicts since 2000. The choice also builds on literature that has examined these issues, including Aall and Crocker (2017); Marc, Verjee, and Mogaka (2015); Parks, Colletta, and Oppenheim (2013).

2. Power sharing is often associated with Lijphart's (1977) concept of "consociational" democracy, but is a broader concept encompassing other mechanisms of guaranteed access to state authority.

3. McEvoy and O'Leary (2013) define power sharing "broadly as any set of arrangements that prevents one political agency or collective from monopolizing power, whether temporarily or permanently."

4. Other key factors were the ongoing war and general scarcity of arable land for the population.

5. Many papers cite research supporting the assertion that the appropriation and mismanagement of high-value natural resources have been key factors in triggering, escalating, or prolonging conflicts, especially in Sub-Saharan Africa. See, for example, those referenced in Bannon and Collier (2003); Collier and Hoeffler (2000); Elbadawi and Sambanis (2002); Fearon (2004); Maconachie, Srinivasan, and Menzies (2015, 5); Ross (2003).

6. Vasquez (2016) defines "local content" as "the advantage given to local businesses and local employment in procurement processes for the oil or gas industries; the preference given to local hiring where possible; and the development of mechanisms for improving local skills as needed."

7. The EITI standard requires information along the extractive industry value chain. This includes how licenses and contracts are allocated and registered, who are the beneficial owners of those operations, what are the fiscal and legal arrangements, how much is produced, how much is paid, where are those revenues allocated, and what is the contribution to the economy, including employment. See http://www.eiti.org/about/who-we-are.

8. According to the terms of the KPCS, each participating government must issue a certificate to accompany all rough diamonds being exported from within its borders, to ensure that they are "conflict free." Each country must therefore be able to track the diamonds being exported to their place of origin or to the point of import, and it must meet a set of standards for these internal controls. All participating countries must also agree not to import any rough diamonds without an approved KPCS certificate (Maconachie 2008, 7). See www.kimberleyprocess.com/en/about for more information.

9. Service delivery is not the only influence on legitimacy: state or government can gain political legitimacy through several sources, including elections, charismatic leadership, good economic performance, improved security, and political inclusion, among others. See Baker (2017).

10. Chapter 3 discusses in greater detail the prevention issues arising in areas where the state does not fully govern and where nonstate actors actively create insecure areas.

11. No single model of a security sector exists, and it is the primary responsibility of the country concerned to determine the national approach to and priorities of the security sector. SSR should be a nationally owned process and could include defense, law enforcement, corrections, intelligence services, and institutions responsible for border management, customs, and civil emergencies. In some cases, elements of the judicial sector responsible for cases of alleged criminal conduct and misuse of force are included. See UN Security Council (2014).

12. A case in point is the Global Focal Point for Police, Justice, and Corrections Areas in the Rule of Law in Post-Conflict and other Crisis Situations, established in 2012, which is designed to do just that: marry the operational and developmental dimensions in joint programming and implementation in support of both security and development

(see Bryden and Olonisakin 2010; UNDP Geneva n.d.).

13. As Security Council Resolution 2151 notes, with the bulk of Security Council–mandated UN assistance in the area of security sector reform taking place in, and directed to, countries in Africa, some African countries are becoming important providers of such assistance (UN Security Council 2014).

14. Democratic control over security forces also presupposes that the government and parliament are legitimate and have the capacity and knowledge to make informed decisions on security matters. Where this is not the case, SSR needs to address legitimacy and capacity deficits, or it is likely to be only of marginal benefit. The mutual distrust between the government and the armed forces that hampered progress on military and intelligence reform in Guatemala in the late 1990s is a case in point (Nathan 2007).

15. Nathan (2007) argues that this was a deciding factor in the Intelligence White Paper's lack of impact.

16. SIPRI (2017) highlights the fact that regional and gender-related differences are also important factors in the way that many perceive their security.

17. While national dialogue processes depend on host government, external funding, and expertise on planning and implementation, dialogue processes have proven useful in several cases, including in Liberia and Sierra Leone (Permanent Secretariat and the Advisory Panel 2014).

18. More than 10 million people are stateless in dozens of low-, middle-, and high-income countries around the world, although the exact numbers are not known (UNHCR 2017).

19. For example, national postconflict, truth-seeking processes have identified the breakdown of the rule of law at local and national levels as the driver of conflicts.

20. The UN defines transitional justice as "the full range of processes and mechanisms associated with a society's attempt to come to terms with a legacy of large-scale past abuses, in order to ensure accountability, serve justice, and achieve reconciliation (UN 2010).

21. See, for example, the case of Sierra Leone (Ainley, Friedman, and Mahony 2015).

22. Examples are Argentina and Colombia, among others (De Greiff 2008).

23. The small number of international and foreign prosecutions could not render significant statistical results.

References

Aall, P., and C. A. Crocker, eds. 2017. *The Fabric of Peace in Africa: Looking Beyond the State*. Waterloo: Centre for International Governance Innovation.

Abrahamsen, R. 2005. "Blair's Africa: The Politics of Securitization and Fear." *Alternatives* 30 (1): 55–80.

Adepoju, A., A. Boulton, and M. Levin. 2007. *Promoting Integration through Mobility: Free Movement under ECOWAS*. Geneva: United Nations High Commissioner for Refugees.

Ainley, K., R. Friedman, and C. Mahony, eds. 2015. *Evaluating Transitional Justice: Accountability and Peacebuilding in Post-Conflict Sierra Leone*. London: Palgrave Macmillan.

Ali, D., K. Deininger, and M. Goldstein. 2014. "Environmental and Gender Impacts of Land Tenure Regularization in Africa: Pilot Evidence from Rwanda." *Journal of Development Economics* 110 (C): 262–75.

Arriola, L. R., and C. Johnson. 2012. "Electoral Violence in Democratizing States." Working Paper, University of California, Berkeley, CA.

Bagayoko, N., E. Hutchful, and R. Luckham. 2016. "Hybrid Security Governance in Africa: Rethinking the Foundations of Security, Justice, and Legitimate Public Authority." *Conflict, Security, and Development* 16 (1): 1–32.

Bahout, J. 2016. *The Unravelling of Lebanon's Taif Agreement: Limits of Sect-Based Power Sharing*. Washington, DC: Carnegie Endowment for International Peace.

Baker, P. 2017. *Reframing Fragility and Resilience: The Way Forward*. Washington, DC: Creative Associates.

Ballentine, K., and H. Nitzschke. 2004. "Business and Armed Conflict: An Assessment of Issues and Options." *Die Friedens-Ware* 79 (1-2): 35–56.

Bannon, I., and P. Collier. 2003. *Natural Resources and Violent Conflict: Options and Actions*. Washington, DC: World Bank.

Barnes, C., and H. Hassan. 2007. "The Rise and Fall of Mogadishu's Islamic Courts." *Journal of Eastern African Studies* 1 (2): 151–60.

Bates, R. 2008. *When Things Fell Apart: State Failure in Late-Century Africa*. New York: Cambridge University Press.

Bell, C. 2015. "Governance and Law: The Distinctive Context of Transition from Conflict and Its Consequences for Development Interventions." PSRP Briefing Paper 4, Global Justice Academy, Edinburg.

———. 2017. *Navigating Inclusion in Peace Settlements, Human Rights, and the Creation of the Common Good*. London: British Academy.

Bell, C., and J. Pospisil. 2017. "Negotiating Inclusion in Transitions from Conflict: The Formalised Political Unsettlement." Research Paper 2017/04, Edinburgh School of Law, Edinburgh.

Bell, C., and K. Zulueta-Fülscher. 2016. *Sequencing Peace Agreements and Constitutions in the Political Settlement Process*. Stockholm: International IDEA.

Bellina, S., D. Darbon, S. Sundstøl Eriksen, and O. J. Sending. 2009. *The Legitimacy of the State in Fragile Situations. Norad Report/Discussion Paper*. Oslo: Norwegian Agency for Development Cooperation.

Berry, M., Y. Bouka, and M. M. Kamuru. 2017. "Kenyan Women Just Fought One of the Most Violent Campaigns in History." *Foreign Policy*, August 7.

Besley, T., and T. Persson. 2011. "The Logic of Political Violence." *Quarterly Journal of Economics* 126 (3): 1411–45.

Binford, L. 1993. "The Continuing Conflict over Land in Postwar El Salvador." *Culture and Agriculture* 13 (47): 13–16.

Boege, V., A. Brown, K. Clements, and A. Nolan. 2008. *On Hybrid Political Orders and Emerging States: State Formation in the Context of Fragility*. Berlin: Berghof Research Centre for Constructive Conflict Management.

Brack, D., and G. Hayman. 2006. "Managing Trade in Conflict Resources." In *Trade, Aid, and Security*, edited by O. Brown, M. Halle, S. Pena-Moreno, and S. Winkler. London: Earthscan.

Brancati, D., and J. Snyder. 2012. "Time to Kill: The Impact of Election Timing on Postconflict Stability." *Journal of Conflict Resolution* 57 (5): 822–53.

Breitung, C., W.-C. Paes, and L. van de Vondervoort. 2016. "In Need of a Critical Re-Think: Security Sector Reform in South Sudan." Working Paper 6/2016, Bonn International Center for Conversion, Bonn.

Brinkerhoff, D., and Goldsmith, A. 2005. "Institutional Dualism and International Development: A Revisionist Interpretation of Good Governance." *Administration and Society* 37 (2): 199–224.

Brinkerhoff, D., A. Wetterberg, and S. Dunn. 2012. "Service Delivery and Legitimacy in Fragile and Conflict-Affected States." *Public Management Review* 14 (2): 273–93.

Brown, O., and M. Keating. 2015. "Addressing Natural Resource Conflicts: Working towards More Effective Resolution of National and Sub-National Resource Disputes." *Chatham House*, June 19.

Bruce, J. 2017. "Preventing Land-Related Conflict and Violence." Background paper for the United Nations–World Bank Flagship Study, *Pathways for Peace: Inclusive Approaches to Preventing Violent Conflict*, World Bank, Washington, DC.

Bryden, A., and F. Olonisakin, eds. 2010. Security Sector Transformation in Africa. Geneva: Geneva Center for the Democratic Control of Armed Forces.

Bryden, M. 1999. "New Hope for Somalia? The Building Block Approach." *Review of African Political Economy* 26 (79): 134–40.

Burger, J. 2009. "The Reasons behind Service Delivery Protests in South Africa." *ISS Today*, July 29.

Call, C. T. 2012. "UN Mediation and the Politics of Transition after Constitutional Crises." Policy Paper, International Peace Institute, New York.

Cambodian Center for Human Rights. 2013. *Cambodia: Land in Conflict: An Overview of the Land Situation*. Phnom Penh: CCHR.

Carter, D. 2011. "Sources of State Legitimacy in Contemporary South Africa: A Theory of Political Goods." Working Paper 134, Afrobarometer.

Chabal, P., and J.-P. Daloz. 1999. *Africa Works: Disorder as a Political Instrument*. Bloomington, IN: Indiana University Press.

Charney, J. G. 1975. "Dynamics of Deserts and Drought in the Sahel." *Quarterly Journal of the Royal Meteorological Society* 101 (428): 193–202.

Cilliers, J., O. Dube, and B. Siddiqi. 2016. "Reconciling after Civil Conflict Increases Social Capital but Decreases Individual Well-Being." *Science* 352 (6287): 787–94.

Cingranelli, D., M. Gibney, P. Haschke, R. Wood, D. Arnon, and B. Mark. 2017. "Human Rights Violations and Violent Conflict." Background paper for the United Nations–World Bank Flagship Study, *Pathways for Peace: Inclusive Approaches to Preventing Violent Conflict*, World Bank, Washington, DC.

Cleaver, F., and D. Elson. 1995. "Women and Water Resources: Continued Marginalization and New Policies." International Institute for Environment and Development, Edinburgh.

Coburn, N. 2011. *The Politics of Dispute Resolution and Continued Instability in Afghanistan*. Washington, DC: United States Institute of Peace.

Colletta, N., and B. Oppenheim. 2017. "Subnational Conflict: Dimensions, Trends, and Options for Prevention." Background paper for the United Nations–World Bank Flagship Study, *Pathways for Peace: Inclusive Approaches to Preventing Violent Conflict*, World Bank, Washington, DC.

Collier, P., and A. Hoeffler. 2000. "Greed and Grievance in Civil War." Policy Research Working Paper WPS 2355, World Bank, Washington, DC.

———. 2004. "Aid, Policy, and Growth in Post-Conflict Societies." *European Economic Review* 48 (5): 1125–45.

Collier, P., A. Hoeffler, and D. Rohner. 2009. "Beyond Greed and Grievance: Feasibility and Civil War." *Oxford Economic Papers* 61 (1): 1–27.

Cordella, T., and H. Onder. 2016. "Sharing Oil Rents and Political Violence." Policy Research Working Paper 7869, World Bank, Washington, DC.

Corruption Watch. 2014. "Corruption Fuels Poor Service Delivery." Corruption Watch, Johannesburg, February 3.

DCAF (Geneva Centre for the Democratic Control of Armed Forces). 2017. "The Contribution and Role of SSR in the Prevention of Violent Conflict." Background paper for the United Nations–World Bank Flagship Study, *Pathways for Peace: Inclusive Approaches to Preventing Violent Conflict*, World Bank, Washington, DC.

De Greiff, P. 2008. *The Handbook of Reparations*. Oxford: Oxford University Press.

DeYoung, K. 2017. "US Pledges $60 Million to Build New African Counterterrorism Force." *Washington Post*, October 30.

Deininger, K., and R. Castagnini. 2006. "Incidence and Impact of Land Conflict in Uganda."

Journal of Economic Behavior and Organization 60 (3): 321–45.

Development Committee. 2015. "From Billions to Trillions: Transforming Development Finance; Post-2015 Financing for Development." DC2915-0002, World Bank Group, Washington, DC.

Diamond, L. 2006. "Promoting Democracy in Post-Conflict and Failed States." *Taiwan Journal of Democracy* 2 (2): 93–116.

Dix, S., K. Hussmann, and G. Walton. 2012. "Risks of Corruption to State Legitimacy and Stability in Fragile Situations." U4 Anti-Corruption Resource Centre, Chr. Michelsen Institute, Bergen.

Donnelly, C. 1997. "Defence Transformation in the New Democracies: A Framework for Tackling the Problem." *NATO Review* 1 (January): 15–19.

Dorner, P., and W. Thiesenhusen. 2005. "Selected Land Reforms in East and Southeast Asia: Their Origins and Impacts." *Asian-Pacific Economic Literature* 4 (1): 65–95.

Drew, E. 2017. "Assessing the Links between Extractive Industries and the Prevention of Violent Conflict: A Literature Review." Background paper for the United Nations–World Bank Flagship Study, *Pathways for Peace: Inclusive Approaches to Preventing Violent Conflict*, World Bank, Washington, DC.

Edwards, S. 2008. "Social Breakdown in Darfur." *Forced Migration Review* 31 (October): 23–24.

Elbadawi, I., and N. Sambanis. 2002. "How Much War Will We See? Explaining the Prevalence of Civil War." *Journal of Conflict Resolution* 46 (3): 307–34.

Elgin-Cossart, M., B. Jones, and J. Esberg, eds. 2012. *Pathways to Change: Baseline Study to Identify Theories of Change on Political Settlements and Confidence Building*. New York: New York University, Center on International Cooperation.

Elkins, Z., T. Ginsburg, and J. Melton. 2014. "Characteristics of National Constitutions, Version 2.0." Comparative Constitutions Project.

EU (European Union). 2008. *Climate Change and International Security*. Brussels: European Commission.

Fearon, J. 2004. "Why Do Some Civil Wars Last So Much Longer Than Others?" *Journal of Peace Research* 41 (3): 275–301.

Felter, C., and D. Renwick. 2017. *Colombia's Civil Conflict*. New York: Council on Foreign Relations.

Fergusson, J. 2015. "The World Will Soon Be at War over Water." *Newsweek*, April 24.

Fiedler, C. 2017. "The Effects of Specific Elements of Democracy on Peace." German Development Institute/Deutsches Institut für Entwicklungspolitik (DIE). Background paper for the United Nations–World Bank Flagship Study, *Pathways for Peace: Inclusive Approaches to Preventing Violent Conflict*, World Bank, Washington, DC.

Field, E. 2007. "Entitled to Work: Urban Property Rights and Labor Supply in Peru." *Quarterly Journal of Economics* 122 (4): 1561–602.

Fisk, K., and A. Cherney. 2016. "Pathways to Institutional Legitimacy in Postconflict Societies: Perceptions of Process and Performance in Nepal." *Governance* 30 (2): 2663–81.

Fjelde, H., and K. Höglund. 2016. "Electoral Institutions and Electoral Violence in Sub-Saharan Africa." *British Journal of Political Science* 46 (2): 297–320.

Gagnon, V. P. 1994. "Ethnic Nationalism and International Conflict: The Case of Serbia." *International Security* 19 (3): 130–66.

Gates, S., B. A. T. Graham, Y. Lupu, H. Strand, and K. W. Strøm. 2016. "Powersharing, Protection, and Peace." *Journal of Politics* 78 (2): 512–26.

Giannini, A., M. Biasutti, and M. Verstraete. 2008. "A Climate Model-Based Review of Drought in the Sahel: Desertification, the Re-greening, and Climate Change." *Global and Planetary Change* 64 (—4): 119–28.

Gilley, B. 2009. *The Right to Rule: How States Win and Lose Legitimacy*. New York: Columbia University Press.

Gillingham, P., and F. Buckle. 2014. "Rwanda Land Tenure Regularisation Case Study." *Evidence on Demand, UK*, March.

Gleditsch, K. S., and A. Ruggeri. 2010. "Political Opportunity Structures, Democracy, and Civil War." *Journal of Peace Research* 47 (3): 299–310.

Gleick, P. 1993. "Water and Conflict: Freshwater Resources and International Security." *International Security* 18 (1): 79–112.

———. 2014. "Water, Drought, Climate Change, and Conflict in Syria." *Weather, Climate, and Society* 6 (3): 331–40.

Global Voices. 2015. "Violent Clashes in Ethiopia over 'Master Plan' to Expand Addis." *Guardian*, December 11.

Global Water Forum. 2012. *Water Outlook to 2050: The OECD Calls for Early and Strategic Action*.

Hameiri, S. 2007. "Failed State or a Failed Paradigm? State Capacity and the Limits of Institutionalism." *Journal of International Relations and Development* 10 (2): 122–49.

Harborne, B., W. Dorotinsky, and P. M. Bisca, eds. 2017. *Securing Development: Public Finance and the Security Sector*. Washington, DC: World Bank.

Hartzell, C. A., and M. Hoddie. 2006. "From Anarchy to Security: Comparing Theoretical Approaches to the Process of Disarmament following Civil War." *Contemporary Security Policy* 27 (1): 155–167.

———. 2007. *Crafting Peace: Power Sharing Institutions and the Negotiated Resolution of Civil Wars*. University Park, PA: Penn State University Press.

Ho, S. 2017. "Introduction to 'Transboundary River Cooperation: Actors, Strategies, and Impact.'" *Water International* 42 (2): 97–104.

Hoddie, M., and C. Hartzell. 2005. "Power Sharing and Peace Settlements: Initiating the Transition from Civil War." In *Sustainable Peace: Power and Democracy after Civil War*, edited by P. Roeder and D. Rothchild, 83–106. Ithaca, NY: Cornell University Press.

Homer-Dixon, T. 1999. *Environment, Scarcity, and Violence*. Princeton, NJ: Princeton University Press.

Human Rights Watch. 2017. *Discrimination in Arakan*. New York: Human Rights Watch.

Hussmann, K., M. Tisne, and H. Mathisen. 2009. *Integrity in Statebuilding: Anti-corruption with a Statebuilding Lens*. Report prepared for the DAC Network on Governance—Anti-Corruption Task Team, OECD, Paris, August.

Hyeran, J., and B. A. Simmons. 2014. "Can the International Criminal Court Deter Atrocity?" *International Organization* 70 (3): 443–75.

IASC (Inter-Agency Standing Committee). 2015. *Guidelines for Integrating Gender-Based Violence Interventions in Humanitarian Action: Reducing Risk, Promoting Resilience, and Aiding Recovery*. Geneva: IASC.

ICRC (International Committee of the Red Cross). 2016a. "Armed Violence and the New Urban Agenda: The ICRC's Recommendations for Habitat III." ICRC, Geneva.

———. 2016b. "Protracted Conflict and Humanitarian Action: Some Recent ICRC Experiences." Report, ICRC, Geneva.

IDS (Institute of Development Studies). 2017. "Using Digital and Social Media to Monitor and Reduce Violence in Kenya's Elections." Policy Briefing Issue 144, IDS, Brighton, U.K.

Isser, D. 2011. *Customary Justice and the Rule of Law in War-Torn Societies*. Washington, DC: United States Institute of Peace Press.

Jarstad, A. K., and D. Nilsson. 2008. "From Words to Deeds: The Implementation of Power-Sharing Pacts in Peace Accords." *Conflict Management and Peace Science* 25 (3): 206–23.

Keenan, J. 2008. "Demystifying Africa's Security." *Review of African Political Economy* 35 (118): 634–44.

Keister, J. 2014. "The Illusion of Chaos: Why Ungoverned Spaces Aren't Ungoverned, and Why That Matters." Policy Analysis 766, Cato Institute, Washington, DC.

Kelsall, T. 2005. "Truth, Lies, Ritual: Preliminary Reflections on the Truth and Reconciliation Commission in Sierra Leone." *Human Rights Quarterly* 27 (2): 361–91.

Kethineni, S., M. Srinivasan, and S. Kakar. 2016. "Combating Violence against Women in India: Nari Adalats and Gender-Based Justice." *Women and Criminal Justice* 26 (4): 281–300.

Lake, D. A., and D. Rothchild. 2005. "Territorial Decentralization and Civil War Settlements." In *Sustainable Peace: Power and Democracy after Civil Wars*, edited by P. G. Roeder and D. Rothchild, 109–32. Ithaca, NY: Cornell University Press.

Le Billon, P. 2014. *Wars of Plunder: Conflicts, Profits, and the Politics of Resources*. Oxford: Oxford University Press.

Lijphart, A. 1977. *Democracy in Plural Societies: A Comparative Exploration*. New Haven, CT: Yale University Press.

———. 2008. *Thinking about Democracy: Power Sharing and Majority Rule in Theory and Practice*. Abingdon, U.K.: Routledge.

Lindemann, S. 2008. "Do Inclusive Elite Bargains Matter? A Research Framework for Understanding the Causes of Civil War in Sub-Saharan Africa." Discussion Paper 15, Crisis States Research Centre, London School of Economics and Political Science.

Lindenmayer, E., and J. L. Kaye. 2009. *A Choice for Peace? The Story of Forty-One Days of Mediation in Kenya*. New York: International Peace Institute.

Linder, W., and A. Bächtiger. 2005. "What Drives Democratization in Asia and Africa?" *European Journal of Political Research* 44 (6): 861–80.

Logan, C. 2017. "Ambitious SDG Goals Confront Challenging Realities." Policy Paper 39, Afrobarometer.

Lujala, P. 2009. "Deadly Combat Over Natural Resources: Gems, Petroleum, Drugs, and the Severity of Armed Civil Conflict." *Journal of Conflict Resolution* 53 (1): 50–71.

———. 2010. "The Spoils of Nature: Armed Civil Conflict and Rebel Access to Natural Resources." *Journal of Peace Research* 47 (1): 15–28.

Maconachie, R. 2008. *Diamond Mining, Governance Initiatives, and Post-Conflict Development in Sierra Leone*. Manchester, U.K.: University of Manchester.

Maconachie, R. A., R. Srinivasan, and N. Menzies. 2015. *Responding to the Challenge of Fragility and Security in West Africa: Natural Resources, Extractive Industry Investment, and Social Conflict*. Washington, DC: World Bank Group.

MacPherson, E. 2008. "Invisible Agents: Women in Service Delivery Reforms." *IDS Bulletin* 38 (6): 38–46.

Magalhaes, F., ed. 2016. *Slum Upgrading and Housing in Latin America*. Washington, DC: Inter-American Development Bank.

Mahmoud, Y. 2017. "Peace Operations and Prevention for Sustaining Peace: The Restoration and Extension of State Authority." Issue Brief, International Peace Institute, New York.

Mahony, C. 2015a. "A Case Selection Independence Framework for Tracing Historical Interests' Manifestation in International Criminal Justice." In *Historical Origins of International Criminal Law*. Vol. 4, edited by M. Bergsmo, C. W. Ling, S. Tianying, and Y. Ping, 865–903. Brussels: Torkel Opsahl Academic EPublisher.

———. 2015b. "If You're Not at the Table, You're on the Menu: Complementarity and Self-Interest in Domestic Processes for Core International Crimes." In *Military Self-Interest in Accountability for Core International Crimes*, edited by M. Bergsmo and S. Tianying, 229–60. Brussels: Torkel Opsahl Academic EPublisher.

———. 2016. "International Criminal Justice Case Selection Independence: An ICJ Barometer."

FICHL Policy Brief Series 58 (2016), Torkel Opsahl Academic EPublisher, Brussels.

Mahony, C., and Y. Sooka. 2015. "The Truth about the Truth: Insider Reflections on the Sierra Leonean Truth and Reconciliation Commission." In *Evaluating Transitional Justice: Accountability and Peacebuilding in Post-Conflict Sierra Leone*, edited by K. Ainley, R. Friedman, and C. Mahony, 35–54. London: Palgrave Macmillan.

Malik, A. 2017. "Electoral Violence and the Prevention of Violent Conflict." Background paper for the United Nations–World Bank Flagship Study, *Pathways for Peace: Inclusive Approaches to Preventing Violent Conflict*, World Bank, Washington, DC.

Mallinder, L., and C. O'Rourke. 2016. "Databases of Transitional Justice Mechanisms and Contexts: Comparing Research Purposes and Design." *International Journal of Transitional Justice* 10 (3): 492–515.

Mamdani, M. 1996. *Citizen and Subject.* Princeton, NJ: Princeton University Press.

Marc, A., N. Verjee, and S. Mogaka. 2015. *The Challenge of Stability and Security in West Africa.* Africa Development Forum series. Washington, DC: World Bank; Paris: Agence Française de Développement.

Matthew, R. A., O. Brown, and D. Jensen. 2009. "From Conflict to Peacebuilding: The Role of Natural Resources and the Environment." Briefing Paper, UN Environment Programme, Nairobi.

Maze, K. 2014. "Land Conflict, Migration, and Citizenship in West Africa: Complex Diversity and Recurring Challenges: A Desk Study." Fragility, Conflict, and Violence Group, World Bank, Washington, DC.

Mazzuca, S., and J. Robinson. 2009. "Political Conflict and Power Sharing in the Origins of Modern Colombia." *Hispanic American Historical Review* 89 (2): 285–321.

McEvoy, J., and B. O'Leary. 2013. *Power Sharing in Deeply Divided Places.* Philadelphia, PA: University of Pennsylvania Press, Project MUSE.

McFate, S. 2010. *The Link between DDR and SSR in Conflict-Affected Countries.* Special Report. Washington, DC: United States Institute of Peace.

McGovern, M. 2011. *Making War in Côte d'Ivoire.* Chicago, IL: University of Chicago Press.

Mcloughlin, C. 2015a. "Researching State Legitimacy: A Political Approach to a Political Problem." Research Paper 36, Developmental Leadership Program, Birmingham, U.K.

———. 2015b. "When Does Service Delivery Improve the Legitimacy of a Fragile or Conflict-Affected State?" *Governance* 28 (3): 341–56.

Mendeloff, D. 2009. "Trauma and Vengeance: Assessing the Psychological and Emotional Effects of Post-Conflict Justice." *Human Rights Quarterly* 31 (3): 592–623.

Menkhaus, K. 2006. "Governance without Government in Somalia: Spoilers, State-Building, and the Politics of Coping." *International Security* 31 (3): 74–106.

Menzies, N., and G. Harley. 2012. "'We Want What the Ok Tedi Women Have!' Guidance from Papua New Guinea on Women's Engagement in Mining Deals." Justice for the Poor Briefing Note 7 (2), World Bank, Washington, DC.

Merry, S. E. 2012. "Legal Pluralism and Legal Culture: Mapping the Terrain." In *Legal Pluralism and Development: Scholars and Practitioners in Dialogue*, edited by B. Z. Tamanaha, C. Sage, and M. Woolcock, 66–82. Cambridge, U.K.: Cambridge University Press.

Milliken, J., and K. Krause. 2002. "State Failure, State Collapse, and State Reconstruction: Concepts, Lessons, and Strategies." *Development and Change* 33 (5): 753–74.

Mukherjee, B. 2006. "Does Third-Party Enforcement of Domestic Institutions Promote Enduring Peace after Civil Wars? Policy Lessons from an Empirical Test." *Foreign Policy Analysis* 2 (2006): 405–30.

Nathan, L. 2007. "South African Case Study: Inclusive SSR Design and the White Paper on Defence." London School of Economics, London.

Ndaruhutse, S., J. Dolan, N. Pearson, C. Talbot, M. Ali, R. Bohara, G. Kayijuka, S. Mtisi, S. Musoke, and R. Scott. 2012. *Synthesis Research Report: State-Building, Peacebuilding, and Service Delivery in Fragile and Conflict-Affected States.* Rugby, U.K.: Practical Action Consulting.

Neudorfer, N. S., U. G. Theuerkauf, and S. Wolff. 2016. "Territorial Self-Governance: An Effective Approach to Territory-Centred Conflict Management?" Paper prepared for the International Studies Association, 57th Annual Convention, Atlanta, March 16–19.

Nixon, H., R. Mallett, and A. McCullough. 2017. "Are Public Services the Building

Blocks of State Legitimacy? Input to the World Bank's 2017 World Development Report." Working Paper 55, World Bank, Washington, DC.

NRGI (Natural Resource Governance Institute). 2016. *Natural Resource Revenue Sharing.* New York: NRGI.

Null, S., and L. H. Risi. 2016. *Navigating Complexity: Climate, Migration, and Conflict in a Changing World.* Office of Conflict Management and Mitigation Discussion Paper. Washington, DC: U.S. Agency for International Development and Woodrow Wilson International Center for Scholars.

Nygård, H. M., K. Baghat, G. Barrett, K. Dupuy, S. Gates, S. Hillesund, S. A. Rustad, H. Strand, H. Urdal, and G. Ostby. 2017. "Inequality and Armed Conflict: Evidence and Data." Background paper for the United Nations–World Bank Flagship Study, *Pathways for Peace: Inclusive Approaches to Preventing Violent Conflict,* World Bank, Washington, DC.

OECD (Organisation for Economic Co-operation and Development). 2005. "Water and Violent Conflict." OECD Issues Brief, Office of Economic Co-operation and Development, Paris.

————. 2015. *Fragile States 2014: Domestic Resource Mobilisation in Fragile States.* Paris: OECD.

OHCHR (Office of the United Nations High Commissioner for Human Rights). 2010. *National Human Rights Institutions: History, Principles, Roles, and Responsibilities.* New York: OHCHR.

Omoeva, C., and E. Buckner. 2015. *Does Horizontal Education Inequality Lead to Violent Conflict?* New York: United Nations Children's Fund.

OSCE (Organization for Security and Co-operation in Europe). 2008. *Assessing the Impact: Kosovo's Community Safety Action Teams.* Kosovo: OSCE.

Parks, T., N. Colletta, and B. Oppenheim. 2013. *The Contested Corners of Asia: Subnational Conflict and International Development Assistance.* San Francisco, CA: Asia Foundation.

Payne, L., A. Reiter, C. Mahony, and L. Bernal-Bermudez. 2017. "Conflict Prevention and Guarantees of Non-Recurrence." Background paper for the United Nations–World Bank Flagship Study, *Pathways for Peace: Inclusive Approaches to Preventing Violent Conflict,* World Bank, Washington, DC.

Pedraza, L. E., and M. Heinrich. 2016. "Water Scarcity: Cooperation of Conflict in the Middle East and North Africa." *Foreign Policy Journal,* September 2.

Permanent Secretariat and the Advisory Panel. 2014. *The Burundi Defence Review: Lessons Identified.* London: Conflict, Security, and Development Research Group (CSDRG), Department of War Studies, King's College London and Institute of Economic Development in Burundi, June.

Postel, S., and A. Wolf. 2001. "Dehydrating Conflict." *Foreign Policy* (September/October): 60–67.

Putzel, J., and J. Di John. 2012. *Meeting the Challenges of Crisis States. Crisis States Research Centre Report.* London: London School of Economics and Political Science.

Reno, W. 2002. "The Politics of Insurgency in Collapsing States." *Development and Change* 33 (5): 837–58.

Rosiny, S. 2016. "A Quarter Century of 'Transitory Power-Sharing:' Lebanon's Unfulfilled Ta'if Agreement of 1989 Revisited." *Civil Wars* 17 (4): 485–502.

Ross, M. 2003. "The Natural Resource Curse: How Wealth Can Make You Poor." In *Natural Resources and Violent Conflict: Options and Actions,* edited by I. Bannon and P. Collier, 17–42. Washington, DC: World Bank.

————. 2006. "A Closer Look at Oil, Diamonds, and Civil War." *Annual Review of Political Science* 9 (1): 265–300.

————. 2012. *The Oil Curse: How Petroleum Wealth Shapes the Development of Nations.* Princeton, NJ: Princeton University Press.

————. 2015. "What Have We Learned about the Resource Curse?" *Annual Review of Political Science* 18 (May): 239–59.

Rotberg, R., ed. 2004. *When States Fail: Causes and Consequences.* Princeton, NJ: Princeton University Press.

Sacks, A., and M. Larizza. 2012. "Why Quality Matters: Rebuilding Trustworthy Local Government in Post-Conflict Sierra Leone." Policy Research Working Paper 6021, World Bank, Washington, DC.

Samuels, K. 2005. "Post-Conflict Peace-Building and Constitution-Making." *Chicago Journal of International Law* 6 (2): 663–82.

Sargsyan, I. L. 2017. "Corruption, Lack of the Rule of Law, and Conflict." Background paper for the United Nations–World Bank Flagship Study, *Pathways for Peace: Inclusive Approaches to Preventing Violent Conflict*, World Bank, Washington, DC.

Sekiguchi, M., and N. Hatsukano. 2013. "Land Conflicts and Land Registration in Cambodia." In *Land and Post-Conflict Peacebuilding*, edited by J. Unruh and R. C. Williams, 437–50. London: Earthscan.

Seligson, M. A. 1995. "Thirty Years of Transformation in the Agrarian Structure of El Salvador." *Latin American Research Review* 30 (3): 43–74.

Sikkink, K. 2011. *The Justice Cascade: How Human Rights Prosecutions Are Changing World Politics*. New York: Norton.

SIPRI (Stockholm International Peace Research Institute). 2017. "SIPRI and CONASCIPAL Launch Preliminary Results of Security Perception Survey at National Forum in Bamako." SIPRI, Stockholm, March 11.

Snyder, J. 2000. *From Voting to Violence: Democratization and Nationalist Conflict*. New York: Norton.

Snyder, J., and L. Vinjamuri. 2003. "Trials and Errors: Principle and Pragmatism in Strategies of International Justice." *International Security* 28 (3): 5–44.

Sorens, J. 2011. "Mineral Production, Territory, and Ethnic Rebellion: The Role of Rebel Constituencies." *Journal of Peace Research* 48 (5): 571–85.

Stearns, J. 2012. *Dancing in the Glory of Monsters: The Collapse of Congo and the Great War of Africa*. New York: PublicAffairs.

Stel, N., and F. M. Abate. 2014. "Between Control and Cooperation: Multi-Stakeholder Service Provision and the Legitimacy of State Institutions in Ethiopia's Amhara National Regional State." *European Journal of Development Research* 26 (5): 743–60.

Stel, N., and R. Ndayiragiie. 2014. "The Eye of the Beholder: Service Provision and State Legitimacy in Burundi." *Africa Spectrum* 49 (3): 3–28.

Strategic Foresight Group. 2013. *Water Cooperation for a Secure World: Focus on the Middle East*. Mumbai: Strategic Foresight Group.

Straus, S., and C. Taylor. 2012. "Democratization and Electoral Violence in Sub-Saharan Africa, 1990–2008." In *Voting in Fear: Electoral Violence in Sub-Saharan Africa*, edited by D. A. O. Bekoe, 15–38. Washington, DC: United States Institute of Peace.

Sturge, G., R. Mallett, J. Hagen-Zanker, and R. Slater. 2017. *Tracking Livelihoods, Services, and Governance: Panel Survey Findings from the Secure Livelihoods Research Consortium*. London: Secure Livelihoods Research Consortium.

Tabak, S. 2011. "False Dichotomies of Transitional Justice: Gender, Conflict, and Combatants in Colombia." *International Law and Politics* 44: 103–63.

Taydas, Z., D. Peksen, and P. James. 2010. "Why Do Civil Wars Occur? Understanding the Importance of Institutional Quality." *Civil Wars* 12 (3): 195–217.

Thiesenhusen, W. C. 1995. *Broken Promises: Agrarian Reform and the Latin American Campesino*. Boulder, CO: Westview.

Thoms, O. N. T., J. Ron, and R. Paris. 2010. "State-Level Effects of Transitional Justice: What Do We Know?" *International Journal of Transitional Justice* 4 (3): 329–54.

Toska, S. 2017. "Sustaining Peace: Making Development Work for the Prevention of Violent Conflicts Cases: Egypt, Tunisia, Morocco, and Jordan." Case study for the United Nations–World Bank Flagship Study, *Pathways for Peace: Inclusive Approaches to Preventing Violent Conflict*, World Bank, Washington, DC.

Tyler, T. 2006. "Psychological Perspectives on Legitimacy and Legitimation." *Annual Review of Psychology* 57: 375–400.

UN (United Nations). 2010. "United Nations Approach to Transitional Justice." Guidance note of the UN Secretary-General, New York.

———. 2017. "Informal Justice." *United Nations and the Rule of Law*.

UNDP (United Nations Development Programme). 2003. *Conflict-Related Development Analysis (CDA)*. New York: Bureau for Crisis Prevention and Recovery.

———. 2013. *Human Development Report 2013: The Rise of the South: Human Progress in a Diverse World*. New York: UNDP.

UNDP Geneva. n.d. *Inter-Agency Working Group on Disarmament, Demobilization and Reintegration (DDR)*. Geneva: UNDP Geneva.

UN General Assembly. 2015a. *Strengthening the Role of the United Nations in Enhancing the Effectiveness of the Principle of Periodic and Genuine Elections and the Promotion of Democratization*. Report A/70/306 of the UN Secretary-General.

———. 2015b. "Transforming Our World: The 2030 Agenda for Sustainable Development." Resolution A/RES/70/1, adopted September 25, New York.

UN Human Settlements Programme. 2016. "Scoping and Status Study on Land and Conflict: Towards a UN-Wide Engagement at Scale." Working Paper, United Nations Human Settlements Programme, Nairobi.

UNHCR (United Nations High Commissioner for Refugees). 2017. *Global Trends: Forced Displacement in 2016*. Geneva: UNHCR.

UN Security Council. 2014. "The Maintenance of International Peace and Security: Security Sector Reform: Challenges and Opportunities." Resolution S/RES/2014/2151, adopted April 28, New York.

———. 2016. "Post-Conflict Peacebuilding." Resolution S/RES/2282, adopted April 27, New York.

UN Water. 2006. "Gender, Water, and Sanitation." Policy Brief, Inter-Agency Task Force on Gender and Water, New York.

UN Women. 2015. "The Effect of Gender Equality Programming on Humanitarian Outcomes." Academic Paper, UN Women, New York.

USAID (United States Agency for International Development). 2009. *Democratic Decentralization Handbook*. Washington, DC: USAID.

Van de Walle, S., and Z. Scott. 2011. "The Political Role of Service Delivery in State-Building: Exploring the Relevance of European History for Developing Countries." *Development Policy Review* 29 (1): 5–21.

Vasquez, P. I. 2016. "Four Policy Actions to Improve Local Governance of the Oil and Gas Sector." *International Development Policy* 7 (1).

Vetschera, H., and M. Damian. 2006. "Security Sector Reform in Bosnia and Herzegovina: The Role of the International Community." *International Peacekeeping* 13 (1): 28–42.

Vinjamuri, L. 2010. "Deterrence, Democracy, and the Pursuit of International Justice." *Ethics and International Affairs* 24 (2): 191–211.

Vogt, M. 2012. "Escaping the Resource Curse: Ethnic Inclusion in Resource-Rich States in West Africa." Working Paper, Swisspeace, Bern.

Vreeland, J. 2008. "The Effect of Political Regime on Civil War: Unpacking Anocracy." *Journal of Conflict Resolution* 52 (3): 401–25.

Walter, B. F. 2003. "Explaining the Intractability of Territorial Conflict." *International Studies Review* 5 (4): 137–53.

Wee, A., J. Lendorfer, J. Bleck, and C. Yaiche. 2014. "State Legitimacy, Stability, and Social Cohesion in Low Population Density Areas: The Case of Northern Mali." Paper prepared for the "Annual Bank Conference on Africa," World Bank, Berkeley, CA, June 8–9.

Wilson, E., and J. Van Alstine. 2014. *Localising Transparency: Exploring EITI's Contribution to Sustainable Development*. London: International Institute for Environment and Development.

Wolf, A., A. Kramer, A. Carius, and G. Dabelko. 2006. "Water Can Be a Pathway to Peace, Not War." Navigating Peace Paper 4, Woodrow Wilson International Center for Scholars, Washington, DC.

Wolff, S., S. Ross, and A. Wee. 2017. "Subnational Governance and Conflict." Background paper for the United Nations–World Bank Flagship Study, *Pathways for Peace: Inclusive Approaches to Preventing Violent Conflict*, World Bank, Washington, DC.

World Bank. 2008. *Liberia: Insecurity of Land Tenure, Land Law, and Land Registration in Liberia*. Report 46134-LR. Washington, DC: World Bank.

———. 2010. *Violence in the City: Understanding and Supporting Community Responses to Urban Violence*, Washington, DC: World Bank.

———. 2011. *World Development Report 2011: Conflict, Security, and Development*. Washington, DC: World Bank.

———. 2013. *World Development Report 2013: Jobs*. Washington, DC: World Bank.

———. 2016. *High and Dry: Climate Change, Water, and the Economy*. Washington, DC: World Bank.

———. 2017a. *Social Service Delivery in Violent Context: Achieving Results against the Odds*. Washington, DC: World Bank.

———. 2017b. *Turbulent Waters: Pursuing Water Security in Fragile Contexts*. Washington, DC: World Bank.

———. 2017c. *World Development Report 2017: Governance and the Law*. Washington, DC: World Bank.

Zacchia, P., B. Harborne, and J. Sims. 2017. "Somalia—Security and Justice Sector Public Expenditure Review." World Bank, Washington, DC.

Additional Reading

Asunka, J., S. Brierley, M. Golden, E. Kramon, and G. Ofusu. 2017. "Electoral Fraud or Violence: The Effect of Observers on Party Manipulation Strategies." *British Journal of Political Science* (February): 1–23.

Beaulieu, E., and S. D. Hyde. 2009. "In the Shadow of Democracy Promotion: Strategic Manipulation, International Observers, and Election Boycotts." *Comparative Political Studies* 42 (3): 392–415.

Bøås, M., S. S. Eriksen, T. Gade, J. H. Sande Lie, and O. J. Sending. 2017. "Conflict Prevention and Ownership: Limits and Opportunities for External Actors." Background paper for the United Nations–World Bank Flagship Study, *Pathways for Peace: Inclusive Approaches to Preventing Violent Conflict*, World Bank, Washington, DC.

Cassese, A. 1998. "Reflections on International Criminal Justice." *Modern Law Review* 61 (1): 1–10.

Daxecker, U. E. 2012. "The Cost of Exposing Cheating: International Election Monitoring, Fraud, and Post-Election Violence in Africa." *Journal of Peace Research* 49 (4): 503–16.

Hartzell, C. A., and M. Hoddie. 2003. "Institutionalizing Peace: Power Sharing and Post-Civil War Conflict Management." *American Journal of Political Science* 47 (2): 318–32.

Hyde, S. D. 2007. "The Observer Effect in International Politics: Evidence from a Natural Experiment." *World Politics* 60 (1): 37–63.

International Security Sector Advisory Team. 2017. "Colombia SSR Background Note." Geneva Centre for the Democratic Control of Armed Forces.

Interpeace. 2017. *Constitution Making for Peace: Guiding Principles for the Process.* Geneva: Interpeace.

Jarstad, A., and T. Sisk. 2008. *From War to Democracy: Dilemmas of Peacebuilding.* Cambridge U.K.: Cambridge University Press.

Lake, D. A., and D. Rothchild. 1996. "Containing Fear: The Origins and Management of Ethnic Conflict." *International Security* 21 (2): 41–75.

———. 1998. "Spreading Fear: The Genesis of Transnational Ethnic Conflict." In *The International Spread of Ethnic Conflict: Fear, Diffusion, and Escalation*, edited by D. A. Lake and D. Rothchild, 3–32. Princeton, NJ: Princeton University Press.

Lohde, L. 2015. *The Art and Science of Benefit Sharing in the Natural Resource Sector.* Discussion Paper. Washington, DC: International Finance Corporation.

Lynch, M. 2016. *The New Arab Wars: Uprisings and Anarchy in the Middle East.* New York: PublicAffairs.

Mogaka, S. 2017. "Competition for Power in Africa: Inclusive Politics and Its Relation to Violent Conflict." Background paper for the United Nations–World Bank Flagship Study, *Pathways for Peace: Inclusive Approaches to Preventing Violent Conflict*, World Bank, Washington, DC.

Muggah, R. 2017. "Revisiting Community Violence Reduction." Background paper for the United Nations–World Bank Flagship Study, *Pathways for Peace: Inclusive Approaches to Preventing Violent Conflict*, World Bank, Washington, DC.

Norris, P. 2008. *Driving Democracy: Do Power-Sharing Institutions Work?* Cambridge, U.K.: Cambridge University Press.

North, D. C., J. J. Wallis, and B. R. Weingast. 2009. *Violence and Social Orders: A Conceptual Framework for Interpreting Recorded Human History.* New York: Cambridge University Press.

Paez, D., and J. H. Liu. 2011. "Collective Memory of Conflicts." In *Intergroup Conflicts and Their Resolution: A Social Psychological Perspective*, edited by D. Bar-Tal, 105–24. New York: Psychology Press.

Serrano, R., F. Carbonari, M. Cavalcanti, and A. Willman. 2012. *Bringing the State Back into the Favelas of Rio de Janeiro.* Washington, DC: World Bank.

Simpser, A., and D. Donno. 2012. "Can International Election Monitoring Harm Governance?" *Journal of Politics* 74 (2): 501–13.

Sriram, C. L., and S. Pillay, eds. 2009. *Peace versus Justice? The Dilemma of Transitional Justice in Africa.* Scottsville, South Africa: University of KwaZulu-Natal Press.

Thurston, A. 2011. "Can a Military Coup Restore Democracy?" *Christian Science Monitor*, July 1.

UN General Assembly. 2016. "Review of United Nations Peacebuilding Architecture." Resolution A/RES/70/262, adopted April 27, New York.

von Borzyskowski, I. 2013. "Sore Losers? International Condemnation and Domestic Incentives for Post-Election Violence." Working Paper, Florida State University, Tallahassee, FL.

World Bank. 2015a. "Colombia Protects Land and Patrimony of Internally Displaced Persons." World Bank, Washington, DC, August 13.

———. 2015b. *Forced Displacement and Mixed Migration in the Horn of Africa*. Washington, DC: World Bank.

———. 2016. "World Bank Supports Colombia's Land Organization and Regional Finance Efforts." Press release, World Bank, Washington, DC, December 9.

CHAPTER 6

Country Approaches to Preventing Violent Conflict

The pathway to peace or conflict for each society is unique. The previous chapters introduce a framework explaining how societies create and maintain pathways via the unique interplay of structural factors, institutions, and actors. This chapter reviews the experience of countries that have avoided violent conflict, prevented its escalation, or rebuilt peace afterward.

Drawing on the 19 country case studies prepared for this study, this chapter draws out several commonalities from the experiences of countries that have successfully prevented violence, interrupted its escalation, or avoided its recurrence.[1] This chapter draws on country examples in several ways, including through a fine slicing of the country cases to apply to a particular aspect of prevention and illustrate a specific point and through a more integrated examination of selected cases—presented in text boxes—that bring together the multiple factors that have coalesced in order to steer a country's pathways for peace.

The discussion is not comprehensive and is not intended as an exhaustive examination of all possible actions that were taken to prevent conflict. This chapter highlights the experiences of countries in addressing the risks of exclusion and mobilization of grievances, especially within the arenas of contestation, as discussed in chapters 4 and 5. While the discussion highlights policy choices or transition moments in country pathways, it is understood that these were all

part of longer trajectories. The chapter focuses on domestic actors, including the state, the private sector, and civil society, and it emphasizes the comparative advantages of these different actors. Chapter 7 focuses on the role and contribution of the international community.

As part of efforts to sustain peace, prevention requires three areas of action: (1) influencing actors' incentives in favor of prevention, (2) reforming institutions, and (3) investing to address structural challenges. These areas must be addressed simultaneously, rather than sequentially. In most cases, this has involved constantly monitoring and mitigating short-term risks in order to anticipate shocks and prevent them from triggering violence and taking advantage of transition moments while also addressing structural risks.

This chapter describes country experiences in building on transition moments and engaging across the three areas of action: influencing incentives, transforming institutions, and targeting structural factors. This does not imply that all actions fall neatly or exclusively into these categories. In reality, many actions have multiple effects. For example, efforts to promote inclusion in the security forces address both an institutional factor (reform of the security sector) as well as a structural one (historical exclusion that underlies disproportionate access to security), while also shifting incentives (creating stronger sanctions against violence). This study does not assume that all actions referred to were undertaken for the sole purpose of preventing violent conflict, as many were guided by other objectives. However, all have demonstrated transformational[2] potential to curve a society's pathway toward sustainable peace.

Navigating Transition Moments

Transition moments enable new efforts to prevent or recover from violence (World Bank 2011, xvii). They may occur at any point along a country's trajectory and provide a window of opportunity whereby actors can change the direction of a pathway. As discussed in chapter 3, a peaceful pathway often results from actions taken during multiple transition moments rather than a single event. These moments open or facilitate opportunities for actors to address underlying grievances through institutional reform or investments, develop a national implementation plan, rally support for the plan among all segments of the population, and signal the importance of equitable and inclusive development. By their very nature, transition moments are difficult to predict and anticipate and, indeed, may present themselves when actors least expect them and are often ill-prepared to act on them.

Transition moments come in many forms and can be triggered by a confluence of internal or external factors. In some cases, they occur suddenly: natural disasters or economic shocks, political changes such as elections or new constitutions, or actor-related changes such as the death of a leader can shift incentives quickly. Other transition moments emerge more gradually. While the Revolution of 2011 in Tunisia, for example, represented a turning point for the country, it resulted from a buildup of grievances related to unmet expectations. This transition moment led to civil protests, which paved the way for a transition from authoritarianism toward a more open and inclusive political system (Toska 2017). A second transition moment occurred with the shared realization that political

deadlock put economic stability and political progress at risk, and a power-sharing agreement then opened a path to further reform.

Managing Outbreaks of Violence

In many cases examined for this study, the way in which national actors managed outbreaks of violence became a transition moment. Violence can bring society to a crossroads, with a choice between continuing to escalate the violence or interrupting the violence to create an opening for a shift in direction. The introduction of a peacekeeping mission or a cease-fire, as happened in Liberia and Timor-Leste in 2006, can alter the incentives toward negotiations. Mediation and diplomacy can also reroute an incendiary situation. For example, in Kenya, in 2008, the intervention of a coalition led by Kofi Annan interrupted tit-for-tat violence that was escalating and gaining momentum. It opened a window of opportunity for resolution via dialogue (Lindenmayer and Kaye 2009).

The ability to recognize a transition moment and act in a swift, decisive manner is key. The 2012 oil shutdown in South Sudan and border war with Sudan demonstrated the rapidity with which the situation could deteriorate in the nascent country (Verjee 2017). It also presented an opportunity for the international community, led by the African Union and widely supported by key donors and allies, to seal the September 2012 Cooperation Agreement between Sudan and South Sudan. While this was a crucial step forward, the agreement itself did not account for structural weakness and ongoing violence within South Sudan, and few of the commitments to the agreement have since been met (Verjee 2017).

Maintaining Macroeconomic Stability

The lead-up to violent conflict often puts tremendous pressure on macroeconomic equilibrium, particularly with respect to inflation and state budgets (Carey and

Harake 2017). A fiscal shock in these environments—for example, linked to a terms of trade adjustment, a collapse in commodity prices, or a fall in tax revenues—can force the government to make unexpected fiscal adjustments, cut consumption subsidies, or reduce the civil service wage bill.

In many of the country cases examined for this study, maintaining macrofiscal stability has created a hard imperative for transition in critical areas, for example, reform of subsidies. Such reforms offer a distinct development opportunity in that they free up public resources and allow countries to reap sizable benefits in terms of overall social welfare, economic efficiency, and fiscal stability.[3] However, subsidy reform is complex in itself (Carey and Harake 2017; Vagliasindi 2012) and can act as a trigger of violence (Clements et al. 2013; OECD 2011, 2012).[4] Cases of reform reversal in Jordan (2011), Indonesia (2012), and Thailand (2013) all point to the political difficulties of staying the course. Moreover, they underscore the fiscal risks associated with reversals in the reform process (Inchauste and Victor 2017).[5] The timing of cuts also needs to be chosen carefully—for example, when prices are already low—and the country should receive adequate support from the international community and multilateral institutions to be able to make these adjustments with sufficient flexibility.

In socially and politically polarized contexts, taking advantage of macroeconomic transitions requires careful management to avoid the perception that some groups may benefit disproportionately or be harmed. Combining subsidy reform with robust safety nets helps to mitigate the risk of destabilization. An effective communications strategy can help to secure buy-in from a broad set of domestic and international stakeholders.[6] Yet, social safety nets and direct compensation programs are rarely effective in identifying and properly targeting those who lose out from subsidy cuts.[7] This ineffectiveness can fuel grievances and fray the social contract that helps to maintain a measure of stability in many low- and middle-income countries, on the assumption that the public tolerates

less-than-perfect governance because essential goods are subsidized. The mismatch can also cause a backlash against subsidy reform, which can undermine social cohesion and escalate conflict. For these reasons, leaders have a strong incentive and imperative to maintain macroeconomic stability as a part of prevention, especially in situations at risk of violent conflict.

Capitalizing on External Shocks

Exogenous shocks such as natural disasters or major shifts in the global economy can paradoxically reset dynamics for prevention by altering incentives and shaking up entrenched positions. The Boxing Day tsunami in 2004 is often noted as having helped to push through agreement in Aceh, Indonesia. The tsunami damaged many existing institutions, including much of the military's control infrastructure, and precipitated a humanitarian crisis that incentivized the rebels to come to the negotiating table. The influx of some US$7 billion in aid resources for rebuilding, combined with a collective focus on common goals of recovery and reconstruction, provided a platform from which the community could renegotiate norms and expectations. It compelled the government and rebels to demonstrate willingness to make progress toward peace, especially given the scrutiny and support of international actors (Renner and Chafe 2006).

The earthquake that hit Nepal in April 2015, killing more than 8,000 people and leaving much of the center of the country in ruins, is another example of how a natural disaster can open a window of opportunity for prevention (von Einsiedel and Salih 2017). The Constituent Assembly had spent several years debating a new constitution, unable to agree on the federalist restructuring of the state. The inadequate response to the earthquake and the ensuing humanitarian disaster contributed to a hasty deal on a new constitution, which was eventually adopted in September 2015 (von Einsiedel and Salih 2017). As in South Sudan, however, the acute need translated into limited consultation and insufficient consideration of structures and institutional realities and thus undermined the ability to target underlying risks (Verjee 2017; von Einsiedel and Salih 2017).

Global shocks, even when not proximate to violent conflict, can also create transition moments for action. Northern Ireland's peace process was advanced by the September 11, 2001, terrorist attacks on the United States, which delegitimized the use of terror tactics (Walsh 2017; box 6.1) and increased pressure on all sides to seek solutions through peace talks. With time, a full-scale return to violence became unthinkable, as the benefits of institutional change and increased participation became more visible (Walsh 2017). Similarly, in both Indonesia and the Kyrgyz Republic, economic crises helped to tighten purse strings, hasten the process of bringing warring parties in alignment on a peace deal (Timor-Leste in Indonesia), and resolve an ongoing standoff (the Kyrgyz Republic) (Jaffrey 2017; Logvinenko 2017).

Exploiting Hurting Stalemates

When parties recognize that they cannot be victorious over one another, either militarily (when the losses from fighting outweigh

---

BOX 6.1 Political Inclusion in Northern Ireland

Improving political inclusion. Northern Ireland's path away from decades of conflict and armed violence was made possible by gradual political inclusion. The Anglo-Irish Agreement was struck in 1985, giving Ireland input into the administration of Northern Ireland, pending the development of devolved institutions accepted by both communities. In the Good Friday Agreement of 1998, Ireland deleted its territorial claim to Northern Ireland from its constitution, and the British government acknowledged that it would "stay out of the way" if both parties were for Irish unity. An elected assembly was established in Northern Ireland with a power-sharing executive chosen based on the proportional allocation of seats. In addition, a north-south ministerial council was established to promote cross-border cooperation.

Incentives for more inclusive politics. Arriving at an eventual power-sharing arrangement was motivated largely by mutual experience of trying other avenues for influence and control, for example, using ongoing violent tactics and internationalizing the struggle. Over time, resources on both sides were drained, the military conflict had reached a deadlock, and the international community was not going to take sides to resolve it. Inclusion in realistic settlement talks was a powerful incentive to consider ceasing violence, since exclusion from power or self-determination was a cause of conflict. Once the need for alternative approaches was recognized at government and nongovernment levels, enough momentum for change was created to consider compromise.

Important opportunities for changing the dynamics were created when the United Kingdom and Ireland joined the European Economic Community in 1973. Membership gradually strengthened Ireland's own sense of legitimacy and sovereignty, through interaction with and recognition of an important international institution on its own terms. This critical third-party relationship opened opportunities for informal discussions on social and economic changes. It helped to strengthen avenues for influence other than violence and to change the perception of violence as a worthwhile option. The fruit of this relationship was the Anglo-Irish Agreement of 1985. This 20-year relationship laid the groundwork for the approval of substantial resources from the European Union (EU), which were essential to putting the peace process into action.

(Box continued next page)

BOX 6.1 Political Inclusion in Northern Ireland *(continued)*

At the community level, one critical example of important trust-building opportunities came through the newly formed police service of Northern Ireland. A policy of equal recruitment and a completely new identity, including name and uniforms, helped to balance power institutionally and symbolically and to open doors for overcoming divisions.

Means for prevention were strengthened substantially by international resources. The EU's commitment over recent decades of some 2 billion provided a common concern for both sides. Through the relationship came an investment of both money and time. The first EU program, PEACE I, was an investment over 5 years (1994–99). PEACE II was for 7 years (2000–07), and PEACE III was for 13 years (2007–20), reflecting the gradual strengthening over two and half decades—the minimum timeframe in which transition toward sustainable peace can be expected. At the same time, the United States worked to reduce the means for violence by advocating that Irish Americans support the deal rather than provide tacit or financial support for a cause using violent tactics.

Short-term change with long-term vision. Both the Anglo-Irish Agreement and the EU support combined near-term changes with a vision for longer-term change, leading from greater political and social inclusion toward devolving power and resources. Education and community development projects created visible, relevant, and tangible changes that strengthened incentives to support cease-fires. Interim bodies were established to manage certain governance functions and enable the transfer of responsibilities over time. Transitioning away from EU funding will still present challenges in the future. Dependency on aid funds instead of the government for certain areas of social spending is heavy. Deep divisions also remain, especially with regard to housing and education. The U.K. vote in June 2016 to leave the EU is a further test of the political and economic dynamics. On the one hand, the decision could support the unionist cause. Reestablishing a hard border between Ireland and Northern Ireland could undermine a key pillar of the Good Friday Agreement and bring into question the funding that Northern Ireland receives from the U.K. government.

Trade-offs. Improving political inclusion necessitated trade-offs for both sides. Once incentives were strong enough, a key compromise was the British agreeing, on principle, to include "terrorists" in negotiations. The Irish Republican Army (IRA) had to relinquish the use of violence and, therefore, their main source of power. Early demands for decommissioning weapons, however, proved a step too far, resulting in a brief resurgence of IRA violence. Progress became possible again once decommissioning was renegotiated as a gradual process, rather than as a prerequisite to talks. This agreement aligned better with the time necessary to build trust and establish alternative institutions for conflict resolution.

Global events were powerful in both propelling the conflict early on and helping to improve political inclusion to prevent further violence later. The original protests against unionist rule drew inspiration from the U.S. civil rights movement. Global events such as the political and social changes that followed the fall of the Berlin Wall in 1989 caused a rethinking of dogmatism. Peace negotiations in other major conflicts such as the Middle East and South Africa in the 1990s and the terrorist attacks in the United States in 2001 also delegitimized revolutionary violence. This, in turn, lent legitimacy to nationalists moving away from violence and toward peace talks, but retaining the support of their base for the cause and avoiding major splits in the movement. The Good Friday Agreement called on democracy to decide Irish unity, requiring only a vote by the majority to change the situation.

(Box continued next page)

the sense of gains or when combatants, seeing the mounting costs of war, lose the desire to fight) or politically (when the risks of further conflict outweigh the potential gains of a peaceful settlement), space is created for a transition from violence to peaceful resolution of conflict. Those attuned to this dynamic can recognize and capitalize on such moments.

Hurting stalemates—situations where neither side can win, but neither wants to retreat—can play a decisive role in the decision to lay down arms (Brahm 2003; Day and Pichler Fong 2017; Zartman 2001). This was seen in the decision by combatants in Sierra Leone to end the conflict and sue for peace. In Liberia, too, growing fatigue among combatants and the public at-large contributed to termination of the civil war (Marc, Verjee, and Mogaka 2015). It galvanized civil society and women's groups to lend their influence and weight to a peace agreement. In Nepal, after almost a decade of civil war, a mutually hurting stalemate brought about a realization by both sides that violence was no longer a tenable path to power (von Einsiedel and Salih 2017). The warring parties finally entered serious peace negotiations, which paved the way for restructuring the centralized, unitary state toward inclusive, progressive democracy and full political participation of the Maoists (von Einsiedel and Salih 2017). In Indonesia, too, a sense of fatigue contributed to the Malino II Accord that halted hostilities between Christian and Muslim militias in

Maluku and Sulawesi after the parties had mutually exhausted one another's organizational capacity for violence (Jaffrey 2017). In the Central African Republic, the widespread desire among much of the population to see the back of violence has been cited as one of the glimmers of possibility for resolution in the war-torn country; there is hope in the mere existence of a strong desire among Central Africans to find a way out of vicious cycles of conflict (Lombard 2017).

Changing Actors' Incentives

The incentives and interests of actors go to the heart of whether prevention efforts are successful. Particularly when the threat of violence is imminent, incentives are often stacked against prioritizing prevention. Actions in favor of crisis prevention or mitigation are often heavy with risk, not least physical, and may have uncertain outcomes for the actors who control the means of violence. Decisions in favor of violence, in contrast, often have specific and tangible results. As such, mobilizing actors' incentives in favor of peaceful action involves managing difficult choices and trade-offs.

Strengthening Leadership

From Burkina Faso and Tunisia to Indonesia and Niger, the leadership of key actors has played an outsize role in preventive action. Leadership is more than occupying a position of institutional power. It includes the ability to mobilize others and to guide a process of political and social change. Clear, decisive leadership exerts a powerful influence on the calculus of other actors. For example, Mahatma Gandhi in India and Nelson Mandela in South Africa built and guided broad coalitions with a vision for social and political change.

Leaders can promote institutional change and build or activate coalitions that rally support, spread risk, and create opportunities. Leaders are often in a unique position to identify and act on transition moments or opportunities for prevention; through the careful use of narrative, they can invoke or shape norms and values that can underwrite prevention—both in moments of crisis and over time.

In many of the case studies examined for this chapter, decisive leadership has provided the incentives for peaceful contestation of power. For example, in Burundi, President Pierre Buyoya demonstrated political willingness to build an inclusive government that helped to bring about the Arusha Accords in 2000 (Nygård et al. 2017). His efforts succeeded where previous attempts at power sharing had failed and ushered in a transitional government that handed power to a democratically elected government in 2005. It was backed by a framework that addressed fundamental ethnic inequalities in politics, brought warring parties to the table, and strengthened the representative nature and oversight capacities of Parliament (Nygård et al. 2017).

Strong and visionary leadership following the flush of a peace agreement and cessation of hostilities remains a critical element in sustaining a country along a peaceful pathway and in building on early gains. The role of leadership was central to ensuring the continuation of peace in Liberia and Sierra Leone following the end of the bloody conflicts in the Mano River basin. In the wake of peace agreements in Liberia and Sierra Leone and the resolution of postelection tensions in Côte d'Ivoire, each country's president was credited with steering a pathway toward improved relations with donors, improved economic governance, and a more open and inclusive democratic environment (Marc, Verjee, and Mogaka 2015).

Decisive leadership also involves gambles that can sometimes come at steep personal cost. In Indonesia, President Bacharuddin Jusuf Habibie's surprise decision to hold the 1999 referendum on Timor-Leste, which had been forcefully annexed in 1975 with the death of almost 19,000 people, offered a solution to the long-held resentment on the part of the Timorese people. The move found favor with various elements in government, including the military leadership. However, the eventual secession was unpopular among some Indonesians and may have cost President Habibie, who had previously indicated that he was not in favor of full secession, his position two months later (Jaffrey 2017).

Changes in leadership can pave the way to an alternate course of action and enable a deescalation of tensions. The departure of leaders who have contributed to the escalation of violence and conflict through intransigence and self-interested behavior has created opportunities for transition toward prevention and peace. In Malawi, the death of President Bingu wa Mutharika in 2012 opened the door for new leadership in the form of his Vice President Joyce Banda. Her appointment—and strong connection to civil society—helped to defuse tensions and move the country away from the confrontation and violence that had been stoked by a combination of a crackdown on civil liberties, economic mismanagement, and efforts to centralize executive power (Stackpool-Moore and Bacalja Perianes 2017).

Critical moments that helped to open a path for more peaceful resolution of conflicts in The Gambia also hinged on the eventual decision of the president of the country to step down from office. In The Gambia, popular opposition backed by efforts of regional leaders and the United Nations (UN) special representative for West Africa and the Sahel, coupled with the imminent threat of military intervention by the Economic Community of West African States (ECOWAS), was sufficient to persuade President Yahya Jammeh to negotiate his departure from office after losing the election (Steven and Sucuoglu 2017). His decision to stand down led to a peaceful transition of power to the legitimate president, Adama Barrow. Therefore, just as Jammeh's decision to dig in precipitated a crisis, his decision to leave office—accompanied by suitable inducements—enabled its deescalation (Steven and Sucuoglu 2017).

Diplomacy and mediation have at times succeeded in shifting the incentives of leaders, especially during a crisis and in concert with pressure exerted by local and national actors:

- The mediation that followed Kenya's 2007–08 election violence is one example of this (Lindenmayer and Kaye 2009). When talks stalled, the lead mediator, Kofi Annan, made a public statement, emphasizing the agency and responsibility held by President Mwai Kibaki and the leader of the opposition, Raila Odinga. By underscoring that "peace lay on the shoulders of the two more powerful leaders in the country," he placed the onus on them to act in the best interests of the country and its people in the medium term (Lindenmayer and Kaye 2009).
- In Burkina Faso, the international community, regional partners, and domestic actors all worked via diplomatic means to influence the calculus of President Blaise Compaore, who had escalated tensions by pursuing efforts for constitutional change. His sudden decision to resign took the country by surprise and left the military to fill the void. International partners and local actors then successfully prevailed on the military, including through the threat of sanctions, to permit a civilian-led transition (Pichler Fong 2017).
- In the Republic of Yemen, in 2011, President Ali Abdullah Saleh was encouraged to step down from his post by the Gulf Cooperation Council in return for immunity from prosecution after multiple previous efforts to broker a deal had failed (Kasinof 2012). He also requested safe passage out of the country. This engineered compromise helped to transfer power to President Abed Rabbo Mansour Hadi, temporarily averted a slide into civil war, and opened

the possibility—albeit short-lived—of resolution (Toska 2012).

Success in prevention efforts relies on the presence and participation of leaders across all levels and segments of society, not just within the military or government. Leaders are needed in the private sector and among civil society. As social tensions deepen, it becomes critical to identify and support leadership that can mobilize needed social change at different levels and across sectors in a nonviolent manner, particularly to counter extreme narratives and ideologies. It is often "middle-range leadership"—ethnic or religious leaders, mayors, academic or intellectual leaders, or heads of prominent nongovernmental organizations—who wield power as interlocutors with excluded groups and the higher ranks of national leadership (Lederach 1997, 45). Investing in and supporting middle-range leaders is an important component of prevention.

Faith-based leaders can be particularly well placed to challenge violent narratives and, in particular, to prevent violent extremism within a culturally appropriate framework, as seen in Indonesia (Mirahmadi, Farooq, and Ziad 2012; box 6.2). In recognition of the critical role that such leaders play, some domestic actors have shifted attention to empowering moderate voices. Such leaders are less visible and therefore often have more room for maneuver and influence than those at the top of the power structure. In some contexts, these burgeoning or middle-range leaders are sidelined or imprisoned, as they may be perceived as representing a future threat to the established order.

Building Coalitions

Peaceful pathways have always required coalitions. Just as violent conflict mobilizes civil, government, military, religious, business, and social concerns to sustain violence, so too does preventive action. The comparative advantages, perspectives, relationships, and resources of each, across society and externally, have been instrumental for many

BOX 6.2 Community-Based Approaches to Preventing Violent Extremism

National approaches to preventing violent extremism have enjoyed some success where they have been rooted in the community and capitalized on the persuasive power and legitimacy of middle-range leaders. Trusted and influential voices within communities—such as women, religious scholars, youth leaders, and traditional chiefs—can help to educate the population and develop community-specific strategies for preventing violent extremism at the local level. Familiarity with the prevailing context, as well as the authority of and trust in these local formal and informal actors, has aided their efforts to provide peer-to-peer support and mentorship and to act as positive role models. Indeed, a recent investigation into extremism in Africa finds that recruits largely hold community and religious leaders in relatively high regard, as the custodians of informal, community-level institutions, while 78 percent of those interviewed reported having poor or zero trust in the police, military, and political elites (UNDP 2017).

Recruitment strategies vary by context, and violent extremist groups often spread by tapping into identity-based conflicts, mobilizing group-based grievances, and exploiting preexisting fractures in society. Weak states with limited presence over their territory and in their border regions can be particularly vulnerable to violent extremism. Amid growing recognition and acceptance that a solely security-based approach is insufficient and, in fact, may worsen the problem, governments also understand that the broader community context is important. Communities can play a role as incubators for potential extremists and as a source of recruits, just as they can act as a source of resilience. In particular, community-based approaches that focus on youth can be an effective part of a broader development plan or embedded in a program on slum upgrading in addition to more specific projects on rural or livestock development.

The influence of faith-based leaders in challenging narratives that can fuel violent extremism has been seen in Indonesia, where the government worked with religious leaders and community organizations that had credibility with their constituents to counter efforts by extremist groups to spread violent messages. These social organizations were critical to coordinating activities on various levels. Based on the concept of *pancasila*, or culture, the strategy helped to establish a counternarrative to promote the separation of church and state and foster religious tolerance. One organization, LibForAll, enlisted celebrity singers to write songs to counter extremist narratives. The resulting album sold 7 million copies and reached the top of the music charts in Asia, giving the antiextremism messages weeks of high-level publicity (Ranstorp 2009).

The example of Morocco also highlights growing recognition of the power and sway of moderate voices in influencing incentives. The state has worked to prevent the spread of extremist ideologies and violence by bringing religious leaders closer to state institutions. The program has been credited with limiting the reach and damage of extremist narratives by providing strong incentives for local elites to join the state's project (Wainscott 2017). As a means of regulating religious narratives, the central government also took control of educational institutions that can confer the title of religious scholar (*alim*). The program included training women as "spiritual guides" (females cannot be *imams*) to lead prayers in community mosques and to combat extremist messages, placing special emphasis on the sacred role of women in families and communities (Bano and Kalmbach 2011).

Efforts to counter extremism in the Kyrgyz Republic have focused on the role of women in preventing violent extremism, with Women Leadership Schools in 16 target communities educating more than 80 women to act as religious leaders. The initiative, developed by the government in conjunction with

(Box continued next page)

reasons: for example, sustaining prolonged action, gaining access to warring parties, acting as a vehicle for legitimate negotiations, monitoring commitments, or providing a network to identify, share, or mitigate risk.

Coalitions—both formal and informal—can involve any number and combination of actors, including civil society, private sector, and international actors. They can be effective in the immediate and short term in shifting and aligning incentives, while fostering a sense of collective ownership among disparate actors. Coalitions provide forums for resolving differences and a vehicle for actors to pull in the same direction. They can demonstrate unity of purpose and ensure that peace talks and leaders stay the course.

Coalitions are strengthened by wide-ranging participation from all corners of society. The uprising and political transition in Burkina Faso in 2014, dubbed the Burkina Spring, owes its peaceful character to the "determination and conciliation" of the Burkinabe people and an active and invested civil society backed by the international community (Pichler Fong 2017). President Blaise Compaore's plans to change the constitution mobilized a vocal civil society opposition, and socially networked young people in the cities, religious groups, and even traditional chiefs who had historically been on the side of the ruling party came together. The combined weight of the the African Union, ECOWAS, and the United Nations in support of the domestic push helped to shift the calculus of the military in favor of a civilian-led political transition and opened space for inclusive Burkinabe-led negotiations on the transition roadmap (Pichler Fong 2017).

At times, coalitions have drawn on the experience of countries with geographic proximity or common historical, cultural, or other linkages to influence incentives for initiating or perpetuating conflict. In the Middle East, specifically Tunisia, the Islamist party Ennahda learned from the mistakes made by the Muslim Brotherhood in the Arab Republic of Egypt, and notwithstanding the fact that it was relatively weaker and more inclined to compromise than the Muslim Brotherhood, it adopted a more participatory and accommodating approach (Toska 2017). In Jordan and Morocco, King Abdullah II and King Mohamed VI both moved rapidly and astutely to head off the popular protests of the Arab Spring by promising far-reaching reforms and signaling their receptiveness to demands for change, while at the same time playing to the fear of instability among the population (Toska 2017). The experiences of neighboring countries also loomed over the peace talks in Kenya in 2008, with observers to the mediation noting that the descent into genocide in Rwanda and the specter of decades-long conflict in Somalia were factors in giving impetus to talks when they flagged (Lindenmayer and Kaye 2009).

International and Regional Support for Coalitions

The Gambia is a case study of how African national, regional, and continental leaders, with the support of the United Nations, worked in concert to mobilize domestic and regional pressure for a peaceful transfer of power (Steven and Sucuoglu 2017). Hailed as a success of the regional preventive architecture, the effort was facilitated by coordination between internal and regional actors, led by ECOWAS, which balanced internal negotiations with diplomatic pressure. This engagement, backed by credible threats of military action, delivered clear preventive benefits in the immediate term and enabled longer-lasting, structural change, a task that would fall largely to domestic actors (Steven and Sucuoglu 2017).

In South Sudan, the Intergovernmental Authority on Development sought to provide an umbrella intervention ensuring that regional rivalries did not sabotage peace efforts (Verjee 2017). Although criticized for lack of results, the coalition it built constrained the pursuit of individual national interests by Sudan and Uganda, eliminated forum shopping by the parties, and produced a rare demonstration (albeit short-lived) of unity between all the regional actors, the African Union, and other international partners that led to the signing of a peace agreement in August 2015 (Verjee 2017).

Civil Society Actors in Coalitions

Civil society plays a strong role in fostering social cohesion and collective action for peaceful pathways (Aslam 2017) by building relationships across groups in everyday interactions. For example, analysis of interethnic and intraethnic ties in India finds that interethnic organizations are more effective at preventing the escalation of communal violence than intraethnic organizations, because they strengthen social and civic ties (Varshney 2002).[8] This social trust forms the basis for collective action. Several large-sample studies have demonstrated that civil society mobilization tends to be overwhelmingly peaceful and oftentimes more successful than movements that employ violence:

- A cross-country study of the 25 largest social mobilization campaigns between 1900 and 2006 shows that nonviolent movements achieve their objectives at least half of the time compared with 26 percent of the time for movements that turn to violence (Stephan and Chenoweth 2011).
- The greater the support that nonviolent moments can muster, the higher the chances that governments will seek accommodation, as seen in Serbia[9] in 2000 (Sombatpoonsiri 2015) and Ukraine in 2004 (Binnendijk and Marovic 2006; Zunes, Hardy, and Stephan 2010), and that security actors will choose to side with the nonviolent campaign (Dahl, Gates, and Nygård 2017).
- A global study of transitions from authoritarianism between 1972 and 2005 finds that nonviolent civic resistance was a key factor driving 50 of 67 transitions; it finds that transitions driven by civic resistance led to more and greater increases in political rights and civil liberties than did transitions that were elite-driven or transitions in which the political opposition engaged in violence (Karatnycky and Ackerman 2005; Zunes, Hardy, and Stephan 2010).

Civil society groups often play important roles in peace processes by increasing accountability among conflicting parties and potentially endowing the process with greater public credibility (Chataway 1998; Lanz 2011; Wanis-St. John and Kew 2008). Given the role that perceptions of exclusion play in increasing the risk of violence, several studies have shown that bringing civil society groups into peace negotiations or decision making can increase the chances of addressing the underlying causes of the conflict rather than focusing solely on managing the risk of immediate violence or the postwar distribution of power (Barnes 2005; Nilsson 2012; Paffenholz et al. 2017; Saunders 1999). Analysis of the impact of including civil society in peace negotiations shows that such inclusion is associated with greater durability of peace agreements:

- In Liberia, civil society groups were involved from the early stages of the civil war in trying to end hostilities, with faith-based groups among the first to intervene (Marc, Verjee, and Mogaka 2015). Women's groups campaigned actively against wartime rape and advocated on behalf of women's issues, while local and international civil society groups worked to defuse tensions at various junctures. Civil society was initially confined to the sidelines of the Liberian peace process, which contributed, in part, to flawed agreements that only reflected the interests of combatants (Marc, Verjee, and Mogaka 2015). Their eventual inclusion in the Accra peace talks in 2003 was due to widespread recognition of their contribution in making peace deals stick and the desire to represent the interests of a wide range of groups in society. Civil society was also ultimately included in the power-sharing agreement that emerged from those talks (Marc, Verjee, and Mogaka 2015).
- In Sierra Leone, too, the Inter-Religious Council of Sierra Leone played an active role in building confidence and trust between the government and rebels, during and after the 1991–2002 civil war there, and is credited with preventing the emergence of religious schisms in such a fraught environment (Marc, Verjee, and Mogaka 2015).

Inclusive coalitions consisting of civil society actors can also incentivize peaceful dialogue that can foster trust, hold different actors to account, and mobilize collective action. Civil society can provide a vehicle to mobilize groups around common values, purposes, and interests and to foster convergence across social cleavages and religious boundaries:

- The Tunisian Nobel Peace Prize–winning Quartet coalition represented a wide range of sectors and values in Tunisian civil society: working life and welfare,

principles of the rule of law, and human rights (Toska 2017). It was formed in 2011 to advance peaceful democratic development, just as the democratization process risked collapse. The Quartet brokered a national dialogue between the governing administration and the opposition, which resulted in a roadmap to new elections. Tunisia's strong civil society tradition and this broad spectrum of interests gave the Quartet moral authority in exercising its mediation role (World Bank 2015b). The Quartet was awarded the Nobel Peace Prize in 2015 "for its decisive contribution to the building of a pluralistic democracy in Tunisia in the wake of the Jasmine Revolution of 2011" (Norwegian Nobel Committee 2015).

- Before the conflict degenerated, youth organizations in the Republic of Yemen—some financed by the private sector—connected young people to one another for social support and help in searching for jobs, dealing with financial problems, and organizing community activities. These practices can instill a sense of cooperation, solidarity, and public spirit among participants and can help individuals to develop organizing, mobilizing, and problem-solving skills (Marc et al. 2012, 106).

Private Sector Presence in Coalitions

Peacebuilding organizations have increasingly identified the potential of private sector actors to work for peace and are seeking innovative ways by which to mobilize them to this end as part of coalitions. International Alert, for instance, works with private sector companies with the aim of helping a country to "turn its back on conflict and move towards lasting peace" (Wennmann 2017, 8). It has also issued guidance to help extractive companies to understand and manage better the risks of working in contexts of conflict and violence (International Alert 2005).

Participation by the business community as peace mediators and in conflict prevention has reaped results in contexts including Nepal, the Philippines, Rwanda, South Caucasus, Sri Lanka, and Uganda

(Wennmann 2017). In South Africa, a movement led by business leaders facilitated the country's transition from the apartheid era to a multiracial state. The Consultative Business Movement was born in August 1988, forged from an understanding that the traditional methods of interaction adopted by the business community with mainly black unions and political leaders were "inadequate" (Ganson 2017, 5). During 1988 and 1989, the movement initiated broad-based bilateral consultations with political parties, civil society, the media, and private sector actors. Together with the South African Council of Churches, it convened a process that led to the 1991 National Peace Accord, which set the stage for constitutional negotiations and put into motion South Africa's transition to democracy (Ganson 2017). In this case, the private sector was able to act as a "stabilizing agent" in the transition because it occupied the space between the apartheid regime and the African National Congress and thus could credibly promote dialogue, trust building, and consensus building.

The private sector can exert its influence within society to sue for peace in various ways and help to influence actors' incentives toward a peaceful pathway. In Kenya, private sector actors skillfully deployed their leverage and influence during the 2007–08 postelection crisis for peaceful ends (Austin and Wennmann 2017). The long-standing patronage system that has fostered strong bonds between actors in the private and public sectors gave business leaders an edge lacking in other actors (Bigsten and Moene 1996; Hope 2014). On this basis, private sector actors such as the Kenya Private Sector Alliance intervened to help to end the crisis and have since continued to engage in peacebuilding activities by funding peace forums, preventing incitement, disseminating conciliatory narratives, negotiating privately with political leaders, organizing presidential debates, and maintaining neutrality (Goldstein and Rotich 2008; Materu 2015; Owuor and Wisor 2014; Wachira, Arendshorst, and Charles 2010). Similarly, in Northern Ireland, the Confederation of Business Industry and other business associations formed the Group of Seven, which used media and publicity campaigns to highlight the benefits of a peace dividend and pushed for a resolution to the conflict (Peschka 2011).

As private sector activity cuts across all socioeconomic strata, it can also help to foster inclusion and social cohesion and to address grievances related to socioeconomic exclusion:

- In Sri Lanka, a group of members from regional chambers of commerce across the country promoted joint initiatives between Muslim, Sinhalese, and Tamil businesses as well as policy advocacy (Peschka 2011).
- In the Philippines, La Frutera and Paglas Corporation set up a banana plantation in a marginalized area and employed Christian and Muslim workers, some of whom were former combatants, and thus helped to promote religious tolerance and reconciliation (International Alert 2006).
- In Colombia, the Footprints of Peace project, run by the Federación Nacional de Cafeteros coffee guild, worked to build local peace between 2011 and 2015 in some of the country's most violent areas (Miklian 2016). It succeeded in mitigating some risks of conflict through "community development, economic engagement, and reconciliation-based peacebuilding" (Miklian 2016, 3).

Transparency and accountability are critical to ensure responsible business conduct and conflict prevention. The absence of information on the origin of output from firms doing business in fragile countries or on the use of revenue from their sales generates scope for illicit activities that contribute to the continuation of conflicts. Larger local and multinational firms can be subjected to such screenings—because of their operations—outside of the fragile states themselves. Information and certification can eliminate revenue from firms that cut corners with regard to social standards or that channel resources toward illicit activities. The Kimberley Process is one of the first such certification schemes to develop greater transparency in financial flows, with mixed results so far. Regulatory provisions within the 1977 Foreign Corrupt Practices Act and the 2010 Dodd-Frank Act in the United States, the 2010 Bribery Act in the United Kingdom, or similar regulation adopted recently by the EU on "conflict minerals" require importers to carry out due diligence and monitor their supply chains to prevent the financing of armed groups and human rights abuses. Similar initiatives focusing on human trafficking and slavery have also been introduced recently in California and the United Kingdom, requiring firms to disclose their efforts to monitor and prevent these activities within their supply chains. At the level of governments, 52 countries have also implemented the Extractive Industries Transparency Initiative (EITI) standard requiring them to disclose annually information on how the revenue from natural resources makes its way through the government and how it contributes to social spending. Dependence on foreign demand where issues are sensitive can also be a powerful tool for responsible business conduct and conflict prevention, as long as there is a flow of information on firms operating in sensitive markets (box 6.3).

BOX 6.3 Private Sector Contributions to Peacebuilding

The private sector has contributed to peacebuilding in various ways. In addition to their role as mediators and promoters of economic stability, private sector actors often adopt conflict-sensitive business practices. These practices require firms to desist from contributing to conflict dynamics, human rights violations, corruption, or any type of criminal activity. Impetus to observe such practices comes from growing recognition that being perceived to fuel or contribute to conflict can have commercial, reputational, and financial repercussions. Private businesses can operate in a conflict-sensitive manner by adapting to the local context and incorporating an understanding of conflict risks and a philosophy of "do no harm" into their operations. The private sector contributes to prevention when it aligns its activities with the Sustainable Development Goals (SDGs), for example, by adhering to the UN Guiding Principles for Business and Human Rights or joining the UN Global Compact, which helps companies align their strategies and operations with universal principles of human rights, labor, the environment, and anticorruption.

Some multinational firms have responded to reputational risk from public relations scandals or environmental disasters by developing stringent rules, while others have responded to global pressure by adopting a more socially conscious outlook. Over the years, some leading firms have gradually shifted their strategies from running "safe operations" (protecting their own employees and assets) to building "safe communities" (taking action to address conflict risks in local communities). One example of such an approach is the Niger Delta Partnership Initiative, established in 2010, to which Chevron committed millions of dollars of investment and leveraged additional funds from donor agencies (Chevron Corporation 2014). An independent assessment after six years found that its programs had helped to achieve widespread change by bringing international attention and private investment to the Niger delta. This oil-rich region has suffered the effects of extensive environmental damage from extractive industries, which has affected the livelihoods of the local populations. The partnership's greatest impact has been in development and peacebuilding, creating a positive environment for economic growth and peace to take hold. While some companies have gone beyond the minimum standard, the incentives for this type of behavior do not always exist in companies that are operating in emerging economies or that are smaller in size and not at the mercy of the same sort of reputational risks as large multinational companies.

Sources: Chevron Corporation 2014; Ganson and Wennmann 2012; Gifford et al. 2016.

Influencing Narratives and Norms

Whether enshrined in law or followed as a social practice, norms are among the most powerful forces by which to influence incentives. Norms provide a shared framework through which actors and leaders can manage contestation in an equitable manner, including through the UN 2030 Agenda for Sustainable Development, and thus reduce the risk of conflict becoming violent. Norms are often undergirded by narratives that appeal to core values and notions related to constructs of identity, making them a potent force both for prevention and for mobilization toward violence.

Given the well-recognized power of narrative to amplify values and norms in support of either peace or violence, leaders and those lobbying them have often looked to craft or sway narrative as a way to shift incentives (Sargsyan 2017). Narratives can draw on values of identity, belonging, rights, territory, or culture. They can be called on to respond to signs of conflict or to carve out an alternative pathway (Zartman 2015).

Many state and civil society actors have used narratives to strengthen norms of social cohesion and tolerance. Some countries have made notable efforts and investments to counter the destructive effects of narratives that can act as an echo chamber and reinforce exclusionary and violent narratives:

- With international support, Ghana's National Commission on Civic Education has engaged political party representatives in all 275 constituencies on peace, civic, and voter responsibilities, aiming to change the image and dialogue regarding electoral violence (Hounkpe and Bucyana 2014). Following the troubled 2012 elections in Ghana, a bodybuilder group called Macho Men for Peace and Justice promoted a narrative to change the image of "macho men" from the stereotype of thugs for hire at the bidding of corrupt politicians to constructive protectors of peace and democracy (Bob-Milliar 2017).

- The Media Foundation for West Africa's monitoring of hate speech and indecent campaign language is testament to the negative power of narrative and the need to reinforce efforts to counter it (Tietaah 2014).
- An examination of the blogosphere in Pakistan finds that, while peacebuilding efforts on the Internet might not match the level of blogging activity seen by extremists, peaceful social coalitions of citizens can and do emerge in the Internet space (Naseem, Arshad-Ayaz, and Doyle 2017).

Narratives have significant power to work for negative ends, too, and can be manipulated to engineer a context that encourages violence. This was exemplified in the insidious effects of hate speech or "coded language" that was used to deadly effect in Kenya during the preelection violence of 2007–08 and in Rwanda during the genocide in 1994 to deepen fissures in society, delegitimize certain groups within society, and justify the use of violence against them (Somerville 2011). Often, this speech is perpetuated by leaders and influential actors and disseminated through social and broadcast media (Deb, Donohue, and Glaisyer 2017).

The Internet is playing an increasingly influential role in transmitting and spreading hate speech, and this has led to a much-debated push in some countries, including Kenya and South Africa, toward greater regulation (Nyathi and Rajuili 2017). The more recent phenomenon of "fake news" experienced in many countries, including Germany and the United States, is another example of how information can be manipulated or instrumentalized to reinforce a certain narrative and further an agenda or attain a specific objective (Gu, Kropotov, and Yarochkin 2017).

New norms and values have arisen during conflict and changed the pathway of a society:

- South Africa has worked hard to foster an inclusive historical narrative as a direct way of restoring and nurturing social cohesion (Sisk 2017). As one example of many steps taken as a result of national leadership that articulated agendas of reconciliation, equality, and justice, the country has celebrated December 16 as a Day of Reconciliation and a public holiday since 1995, instead of using the day to commemorate war and symbols of division (Sargsyan 2017).

- Niger, too, has reinforced a national narrative of social cohesion, peace, and tolerance by building on some of the unique characteristics of Nigerien society. In times of crisis, the country's leadership leverages this sense of solidarity as a way of managing and mitigating tensions between groups (Pérouse de Montclos 2017).

Narratives and norms can be institutionalized and have a more sustainable impact on pathways to peace by promoting civic values and a culture of peace through peace education,[10] civic education, public memorialization, and arts and culture (UNHRC 2016). Reflexively promoting civic values and strengthening a sense of citizenship can help to maintain and safeguard institutions. When citizens regard the state and social institutions as effective in protecting their rights and delivering services, they will see themselves as a part of public life and promote a sense of common well-being (Brennan 2017; UNDP 2016).

Domestic actors have strategically used global norms, particularly human rights norms, but the 2030 Agenda also provides entry points for rallying support behind a push for change or warding off pressure from contesting forces:

- For the Kyrgyz Republic, government's public declaration of its intention and efforts to strengthen human rights protections helped to reinforce domestic and international support in the face of regional political pressures (Logvinenko 2017).
- A desire to be seen as abiding by human rights norms also formed the basis for a robust mission of the Office of the United Nations High Commissioner for Human Rights to Nepal in 2005.

The government of Nepal signed an agreement with the high commissioner for human rights to establish an office with a far-reaching mandate on human rights. The mission aimed to reduce impunity on both sides of the conflict and to strengthen the national capacity to protect human rights. Its presence is credited with helping to lessen abuses, torture, and disappearances and with encouraging both sides to do more to limit civilian deaths. It also engaged with nonstate actors and opened opportunities to promote inclusion, equality, and dialogue among parties to the conflict (von Einsiedel and Salih 2017).

Gender norms can also be called on to mitigate tensions and promote peace. One of the best-known examples is that of Liberian women evoking norms of masculinity to pressure men to continue peace negotiations and empowering women in their traditional conflict resolution roles (Marc, Verjee, and Mogaka 2015). Women came together to institutionalize a more permanent way of mediating local disputes and preventing violence, while nurturing an ethic of peace and fostering social cohesion (Alaga 2010; box 6.4).

Development and peacebuilding institutions have, in recent decades, placed a greater priority on mobilizing women's efforts for peace, drawing on the roles they often play in society as connecters and trust builders. National action plans for the implementation of UN Security Council Resolution 1325, designed to increase women's participation in dialogue and peacebuilding, draw on this role, while efforts to prevent violent extremism often focus on women as critical actors for moderating extremist messages and preventing radicalization (Sisk 2017; UN Security Council 2000). As discussed in chapter 4, preexisting gender and power norms heavily influence the space and weight accorded to women's participation in peacemaking (Nygård et al. 2017), which makes consideration of such norms, particularly in a domestic context, critical to successful prevention.

BOX 6.4 Cost Savings of Investing in Women's Grassroots Prevention:
Female-Led Peace Huts in Liberia

Women peace activists in Liberia started peace huts shortly after the end of the civil war in 2003. An adaptation of the traditional *palava* hut, women in peace huts mediate local disputes, monitor the police and justice services, refer victims of violence to counseling and other services, and raise awareness within communities regarding peacebuilding priorities, such as elections, decentralization, and natural resource concessions. According to the local police, peace huts have been key to reducing and even preventing violence in the community because they defuse tensions and alert police to potential outbreaks of conflict. A study was commissioned to look at the effectiveness of peace huts and to compare the modest investment in establishing and maintaining them to the costs of addressing violence once it breaks out. The total financial cost of peace huts is small, amounting to an estimated US$1.5 million per year, or approximately US$62,000 per hut per year, including the expense of establishing the hut, building capacity, and conducting training and monitoring. In comparison to the US$10 billion cost of overall peacekeeping and foreign aid or the US$95 million in domestic financial resources incurred by the justice sector per year, peace huts constitute a minor investment with significant potential cost savings. This study found the following:

- Peace huts reduce the workload of the police and justice systems by handling disputes and interpersonal conflicts before they require intervention by the security sector.

- Peace huts link traditional redress mechanisms and the formal justice system by facilitating reporting of serious cases and improving access to justice when required.

- Women working with peace huts have established connections with political leaders and opened avenues for improving women's participation in decision making.

- Peace huts are more sustainable and resilient than similar initiatives, including throughout the Ebola crisis, due in part to their indigenous and grassroots nature.

- The proximity of peace huts to the community means that their efforts directly respond to pressing security issues at the local level.

Fall (2017) suggests that a low-cost, local, and women-led intervention fulfills important roles in the community, including conflict mediation, community policing, awareness raising, and sensitization. These roles fill a gap where communities lack immediate access to state justice mechanisms such as the police and judicial system.

Sources: Douglas 2014; Fall 2017.

Several countries have drawn on global norms regarding human rights, tolerance, and inclusion through sports programming to build trust and cohesion. Particularly in postconflict settings, sports are seen as both a *method* of programming for reconciliation and development work (such as youth livelihood development) and a *symbolic metaphor* for peaceful coexistence and indeed "normality" in social relations. Practically, sports are used to spread the values of human rights, dignity, inclusion, and participation of all and the peaceful resolution of disputes. Recent research from Northern Ireland shows that appropriately designed sports interventions can help to overcome problems of symbolic competition and territorial segregation with the representation of new, less distinct, and divided identities (Mitchell, Summerville, and Hargie 2016).

Addressing Institutional Weaknesses

Efforts to address institutions' shortcomings for peace constitute the second broad area for action on sustained prevention. As the "immune system" of a society (World Bank 2011, 72), effective institutions strengthen resilience to shocks and enhance the capacity for peaceful mitigation of conflict. Institutions provide the regulatory framework, both formal and informal, governing actors' behavior and limiting the harm individuals and groups can inflict. The quality and legitimacy of institutions reflect social relationships in broader society, and institutions evolve together with those relationships. In contexts with deep tensions across groups, institutions may be more exclusionary, more biased, and less trusted by underrepresented groups. Reform of institutions, therefore, presents an important opportunity for prevention.

Across the country cases prepared for this study, efforts to increase the representativeness and reach of institutions have tended to see a reduction in the risk of violent conflict. However, as the country cases show, reform efforts can run into obstacles and experience setbacks and reversals, as groups contest processes of change. This underscores the lesson that *how* institutions are reformed matters at least as much as *what* technical reforms are implemented.

Implementing Power-Sharing Arrangements and Temporary Mechanisms

Broadening and improving political inclusion[11] at the national level is a key plank in virtually every successful case of effective long-term prevention and also is reflected in the 2030 Agenda, including SDGs 10 and 16. As described in chapters 4 and 5, increasing access to the power and governance arena creates strong disincentives for violence, especially when power-sharing arrangements are enshrined in formal agreements, such as new constitutions. Over time, the benefits of political inclusion, such as increased influence, greater access

to information, and the means to pursue collective interests nonviolently, can have a powerful effect on actors' incentives for prevention:

- In Northern Ireland, the experience of gaining influence through participating in political discourse and seeing the utility of compromise strengthened Sinn Fein's motivation to invest in more peaceful conflict resolution processes (Walsh 2017).
- In Ghana, greater political inclusion and openness created an enabling environment not only for a robust political opposition to form and unrepresented groups to participate, but also for a vibrant civil society to emerge and security sector reform to take place (Bob-Milliar 2017; Steven and Sucuoglu 2017).
- Colombia's more local-level, informal bargaining process between nonstate actors helped to implement demobilization. Thus, nontraditional and informal mechanisms of inclusion and outsourcing can also help to maintain regime stability and create an alternative kind of order that enables the conditions for averting immediate threats of violence (Ahram 2011).

In all countries, however, taking the further step of institutionalizing changes through reform of state institutions is what laid the foundation for lasting peace. Negotiated roadmaps, peace agreements, and postconflict settlements have often provided platforms for a renegotiation of institutional arrangements and provided public signals of intentions for reform, creating space for longer-term change. Enshrining them in institutions helps to ensure that they last over time:

- Ghana's new constitution ensured the empowerment of minority and marginalized ethnic groups within substantive local decision-making structures (Steven and Sucuoglu 2017).
- Northern Ireland established an elected assembly, structured to ensure power sharing across divided groups (Walsh 2017).

- Meanwhile, in South Africa, gradual increases in political inclusion helped the country to navigate long-held structural and racial divides (Daly and Sarkin 2007).
- In Tunisia, the national dialogue forum that helped Islamists and the secular government to overcome an increasingly violent stalemate and agree on a roadmap going forward also served as a platform for compromise, including a new constitution guaranteeing fundamental rights for the entire population irrespective of gender, political conviction, or religious beliefs (Norwegian Nobel Committee 2015; Steven and Sucuoglu 2017). Islamist leaders reached out to the secular camp to strike compromises on difficult issues such as the role of Shari'ah in the constitution and gender equality.

Both Burkina Faso and Tunisia also demonstrated inclusion by explicitly including past politicians, even from rival groups, in politics rather than excluding or prosecuting them (Pichler Fong 2017; Toska 2017). For Tunisia, this broadened accountability for a peaceful political transition, while giving the transition team access to institutional memory and a wealth of prior experience (Toska 2017). In Burkina Faso, although not popular with civil society leaders, the move to include moderate elements of the former ruling party meant that the Charter of the Transition was more inclusive and that the reconciliation process had broader buy-in (Pichler Fong 2017).

One of the factors that has helped Niger to maintain relative stability in a region beset by security crises has been the move to institutionalize greater political inclusion at the national level. The transition from a military regime to an inclusive civilian-led regime in 2011 saw a change in Niger's fortunes and helped to maintain stability in the face of various internal and external threats (Pérouse de Montclos 2017). The new president, Mahamadou Issoufou, ushered in a parliamentary regime that extended political inclusion to a range of groups and parties, including naming various opposition leaders to government posts and appointing a Tuareg, Brigi Rafini, to the post of prime minister in 2011 (Pérouse de Montclos 2017). The inclusion offered by the new government helped it to maintain an elite pact and also helped Niger to address specific grievances among the population and to develop greater accountability (box 6.5).

To be meaningful, inclusion needs to go deeper than mere participation. It should lead to an increased focus on the core issues that are central to managing risks and that

BOX 6.5 Niger: An Example of Resilience in a Troubled Neighborhood

Niger faces the threat of extremist groups on its border with Mali, is exposed to the lawless Sahara interior through its border with Libya and northern Mali, and has seen repeated incursions by Boko Haram into its territory from Nigeria in the south. Internally too, it has experienced two military coups in recent years, tensions with its Toubou and Tuareg populations have exacerbated internal divides in the past, and its battle with Boko Haram in the southeast and with armed groups from Mali in the southwest have stoked intercommunal tensions and deepened tensions over access to resources. Despite these risks, Niger has managed to remain stable over the last decade. The following factors help to explain how the country has managed to avoid sliding into open, violent conflict.

Fostering a sense of national unity. Niger has a robust national narrative regarding social cohesion. A grassroots

(Box continued next page)

BOX 6.5 Niger: An Example of Resilience in a Troubled Neighborhood *(continued)*

rural development program fostered by President Mahamadou Issoufou has strengthened the state's relationship with communities and increased its legitimacy. The separation of the church and state during colonial times helped to give rise to a secular state and a context that has partially contained the emergence of radical Islamist ideology. The state supports secularism but also engages in an active dialogue with religious authorities, with Islam playing a central role in Niger. The religious community has supported conflict mitigation activities in the southwest since 2011; today, most religious actors in the southeast reject the Islamist narrative of Boko Haram. However, this rejection has not entirely mitigated the risk of radicalization toward violent extremism among the youth. Overall, the combination of historical, economic, and religious factors in Niger has helped to contain a further polarization of groups along the north-south divide and diluted the appeal of extremist ideologies. The leadership has used these factors to build a narrative of peace and tolerance. At the local level, the wide dispersal of Niger's Tuareg population across the country, living and intermarrying with different communities, has also contributed to cohesive social dynamics.

Forging a development, security, and diplomacy nexus. Niger has engaged in a major push to forge a strong nexus between development, security, and diplomacy. The army in Niger is well trained and, on the whole, has a positive relationship with the population. It has made efforts to work with civilian authorities, especially with structures such as the Haute Autorité à la Consolidation de la Paix (HACP). The comprehensive economic and social development plan includes components on security and conflict resolution. A US$2.5 billion strategy for the security and development of the Sahara-Sahel region proposes an integrated approach to security and development and includes issues like pastoralism development and management of local conflicts related

to transhumance activities. Finally, a recovery plan for the Diffa region, which has suffered the effects of Boko Haram attacks, is currently being drafted and contains elements related to security, humanitarian assistance, and longer-term development.

Boosting political inclusion. Measures to boost political inclusion include the absorption of Tuaregs into the public sector and into administrative positions. The appointment of Brigi Rafini, a Tuareg leader, as prime minister in Niamey and the placement of a Tuareg as head of the HACP have helped to foster a sense of inclusion that cuts across divides, as have the election and appointment of some Tuareg leaders to local governance positions. The inclusion of dominant local elites and minority representatives at all levels has helped to achieve stability. This stability is a product of both the elite pact that lasted between 2011 and 2015, which ensured a fair distribution of power and rents between elites, as well as a tradition of nationalist sentiment that has helped to keep elites integrated and united. At the national level, Niger introduced multiparty politics in 1991 and returned to a parliamentary system in 2011, following the end of a military hiatus that lasted from 2010 to 2011.

Promoting early warning and mediation. Niger has developed an original mechanism for early warning and mediation that it implements through the HACP, which was created in October 2011 and replaces a previous similar structure. The HACP reports directly to the presidency and administers a range of programs, including intercommunal dialogue, demobilization and reintegration of former combatants, and development projects aimed at promoting peace and cohesion. The early warning mechanism supports early mediation through a network of local and community actors— some of whom are hired by the HACP as chargés de mission—who report back to the president of the HACP when there are signs of heightened tension in a particular region or community. It is highly dynamic and coordinates activities

(Box continued next page)

build confidence for further progress. The pressure for a regime to survive or persist can incentivize temporary mechanisms for inclusion over institutional reform. Inclusion through the redistribution of favors, privileges, or some control of the use of force can reduce tensions and increase incentives to refrain from violence. However, this redistribution can come at the expense of a comprehensive reform of institutions or improved state capacity and, ultimately, lasting prevention:

- For example, the Republic of Yemen's 2013 National Dialogue Conference ultimately failed to bring about much-needed structural changes, despite being hailed as an inclusive and representative process that brought in the political elite, traditional leaders, the Houthis, the southern militant group Al Hirak, civil society, and women's and youth groups (Steven and Sucuoglu 2017). Although the process agreed on a draft document and wide-ranging recommendations, the decision by a small presidential panel to divide the Republic of Yemen into a federation of six geographic entities perceived to enjoy unequal access to resources ultimately contributed to an escalation of violence and a full-fledged military conflict (Steven and Sucuoglu 2017).

- In the Democratic Republic of Congo, successive political regimes since the 1970s have relied on alternative strategies for political survival, such as patronage, corruption, aid, and mineral extraction, among others (Bøås et al. 2017).

Ultimately, though, without corresponding improvements in state capability, efficiency, and accountability or efforts to lay the groundwork for a more durable settlement, prevention is unlikely to be sustained. Such arrangements have tended to work only so long as the pool of elites to co-opt is of a manageable size, incentives remain aligned, or the arrangements have the backing of a strong or canny leader. In Côte d'Ivoire, for example, the founding president, Felix Houphouet-Boigny, ran an inclusive government and promoted national cohesion for decades through patronage mechanisms and temporary elite pacts (Marc, Verjee, and Mogaka 2015). However, the stability conferred by this arrangement came to an end following his death, contributing to the country's eventual descent into civil war.

Gender inclusion has proven a powerful element in helping to ensure that processes move beyond dialogue to meaningful change. UN Security Council Resolution 1325 articulates this approach and has enabled global norms on gender equality to influence many peace negotiations as well as broader development plans in a manner that goes beyond the simple inclusion of women at the table (OSAGI 2000; UN Security Council 2000). It provides international backing for greater women's leadership in decision making at the national, regional, and international levels. This backing has contributed to the credibility and durability of many peace agreements (O'Reilly, Ó Súilleabháin, and Paffenholz 2015).

Attempting supportive institutional reforms to sustain prevention can also come up against serious challenges. In the case of many such states, efforts to reform institutions have disrupted the precarious balance of power established by the patrimonial state. Development partners and the international community face the conundrum of either supporting such states for the temporary stability they can provide or attempting to encourage reforms that may incur instability via the process of change. The lessons in many cases, however, highlight that whether reforms are managed or imposed, reform is a fundamental part of sustaining peace.

The monarchies in Jordan and Morocco withstood the revolutions that swept the Middle East through the Arab Spring in part due to the plausible promise of political and economic reforms and the prospect of those reforms translating into real inclusion (Toska 2017). Both countries also rely on access to rents in the form of foreign aid as one means of maintaining stability, and their kings are protected, in part, by the dual elected and royal structure of their states.

These structures allow concessions to greater political reform, without undermining or threatening elites, and promote stability, at least while the arrangements endure (Toska 2017).

Decentralizing Power, Services, and Resources

As discussed in chapter 5, the decentralization[12] of power and resources to local and federal levels has been a significant force for preventing and mitigating conflict (Nygård et al. 2017). It represents a practical demonstration of reforms that boost political and social inclusion. Decentralization usually requires fundamental and, often, extensive institutional changes that have the power to address underlying conflict risks, shift actors' incentives, and navigate structural constraints to peace. It is therefore not without risks. In Ghana and Kenya, decentralization transferred greater resources and control to historically marginalized regions (Bob-Milliar 2017; Mogaka 2017):

- In Ghana, a gradual increase in transfers of funds from the central to local government, in particular, to poorer districts in the northern region, took place over a decade (Bob-Milliar 2017). The process was set in motion by President Jerry Rawlings and ratified four years later in the 1992 constitution. The president retained some powers, but the Regional Coordinating Councils, district assemblies, and even subnational bodies all have meaningful powers of decision making and resource distribution.
- Kenya's extensive program of devolution, adopted under its 2010 constitution, was aimed, in part, at addressing concerns related to perceptions of fairness and political inclusion in the multiethnic state (Mogaka 2017). It established 47 county governments and redistributed resources across the country, in a move that gave the historically marginalized north and northeast of the country control over its political and economic destiny for the first time. In 2013, new county governors and assemblies were elected, creating a new tier of government. Spatial diffusion

of power and resources to the counties offers the country's marginalized regions the opportunity for rapid development directed by local priorities.

In both cases, the focus was on fostering a sense of political inclusion at local levels. In Kenya, the National Cohesion and Integration Commission was established to ease concerns that the tendency to centralize national structures would be mirrored at the county level; it also helped to facilitate discussions on political cohesion in local communities (Mogaka 2017). A sense of political inclusion was reinforced through the so-called "negotiated democracy" model, whereby some counties brokered deals to ensure adequate community representation in positions of leadership, enabling individuals to vote across ethnic lines with the expectation that their community would be adequately represented regardless (Mogaka 2017).

Where decentralization has worked well, control of power and resources has been traded, first, to manage frustrations stemming from horizontal inequalities and long-standing tensions relating to exclusion from political power (Nygård et al. 2017) and, second, to manage resources more efficiently. While decentralization has been instrumental in averting potential violence or diffusing ongoing violence, it has also created short-run risks for violent conflict. This is particularly the case where elite competition is transferred to the local level or local governments lack legitimacy (Nygård et al. 2017):

- An extensive decentralization program in Indonesia in 2001 led to major transfers of administrative, political, and financial authority to district and municipal levels (box 6.6). In the short term, the devolution of power and funds increased opportunities for contestation at the local level, as groups jockeyed to position themselves favorably during the process (Bertrand 2004). Once implemented, decentralization heightened the stakes for access to resources from the central government, and political elites exploited

ethnic identity as a way to mobilize their bases (Jaffrey 2017). After 2004, however, the country moved into a stabilization phase, which was attributed to public satisfaction with decentralization, greater space for the expression of local identities, greater levels of state penetration, effective design of local elections, and strong leadership and institutional frameworks at the local level (Steven and Sucuoglu 2017).

- In Kenya, too, devolution brought challenges (Mogaka 2017). The absence of existing "rules of the game," combined with the scale of resource flows, created and exacerbated local-level contestations. It heightened the stakes of political office at the local level and raised the specter of violence around elections at the county level. Balancing the way in which power in the counties is shared by elites from different communities remains a significant challenge (World Bank 2017a).

Where decentralization has failed to take effect, the failure is largely because it has been implemented incompletely or because political actors and leaders have had little or no incentive to see such wide-ranging changes take effect. Decentralization in Mali, although viewed as the main vehicle for conflict prevention, did not achieve its aims due to incomplete implementation amid "considerable resistance to change from officials at central and regional levels who stand to lose power when the capacity of local authorities is increased" (Bøås et al. 2017). The resulting unmet expectations and grievances undermined state legitimacy. The Central African Republic's small Bangui-based elite is an example of how entrenched interests can block attempts at reform: the lack of state presence outside the capital should be addressed ahead of any decentralization attempt (Lombard 2017). In Afghanistan, where competition for devolved resources or power is high, the perseverance of warlords and local strongmen, as well as weak or no state presence, increased local-level corruption, which fed into local grievances and reinforced conflict.[13]

BOX 6.6 Decentralization and Security Reform as Prevention in Practice: Indonesia

Indonesia has undergone cycles of violence and repression, with four secessionist conflicts waged between 1999 and 2004, as the country transitioned from decades of authoritarian rule toward democracy and economic and political stability. The conflicts were due to an array of long-standing historical issues. Each was intensified by Indonesia's deep economic crisis in the late 1990s and widespread political uncertainty following President Hajji Suharto's sudden resignation.

Among Indonesia's subnational conflicts, Timor-Leste's struggle for independence became known, in part, for the violent referendum of 1999, whereby a strong-arm military response left up to 1,000 people dead and a quarter of the population dispersed. A temporary UN administration took over, and recognition of the outcome of the referendum by the Indonesian Parliament led to eventual independence in 2002. The negotiated peace processes of the other three conflicts—Aceh, Central Sulawesi, and Maluku—are considered to have been relatively successful, although those, too, where not without violence. While Indonesia continues to struggle with episodes of subnational violence, including in Papua's "postconflict" areas, two effective prevention strategies have had well-demonstrated success: decentralizing power and resources and paying attention to the security forces.

Political and fiscal decentralization. Long-standing local intergroup tensions and horizontal inequalities that underscored the major conflicts were exacerbated by political marginalization by the state and a desire for greater self-determination. To address the grievances that were intensifying secessionist sentiment, the government recognized that ceding some central control of both power and resources was necessary to improve social stability and find resolution. Further motivation to decentralize came from the economic crisis the country faced in the 1990s. In return for taking the political and practical risks of decentralizing, the government also recognized the potential of more fiscally efficient approaches to governance and resource management across the country's highly complex social makeup and geographic territory. The potential means to manage such extensive decentralization existed in Indonesia, due to its relatively high, although very uneven, human and institutional capacity.

Central Sulawesi and Maluku were given recovery aid (an estimated US$300 million from the central government) that was placed outside the government's regular disbursement mechanism, allowing local-district heads to allocate resources at their discretion. Simultaneously, Aceh enacted political and fiscal autonomy provisions as part of the peace agreements, including laws for balanced formulas for previously marginalized areas, direct election of regional heads, and high degrees of local discretion in managing regional budgets. The decentralization measures were conducted in districts instead of in ethnically bounded provinces to mitigate the chance of separatist sentiment and ethnic politics. These changes were underpinned over the longer term by gradually improving political inclusion.

In the case of Timor-Leste, resolution eventually came in the form of full secession, despite intense political resistance from Indonesia and the Indonesian military's use of violence to dissuade citizens from voting for secession. While international pressure played a pivotal role in the government's eventual decision, the economic crisis also played a role. The government recognized that granting Timor-Leste its independence entailed lower fiscal and political costs than maintaining it as territory.

Reform of security forces. Indonesia's military had long played an active role in the country's politics. As such, security sector reform was particularly important in the move away from military dictatorship and toward democratization and durable peace—an important

(Box continued next page)

FIGURE B6.6.1 Foreign Direct Investment Net Flows as a Proportion of Gross Domestic Product in Indonesia, 1980–2015

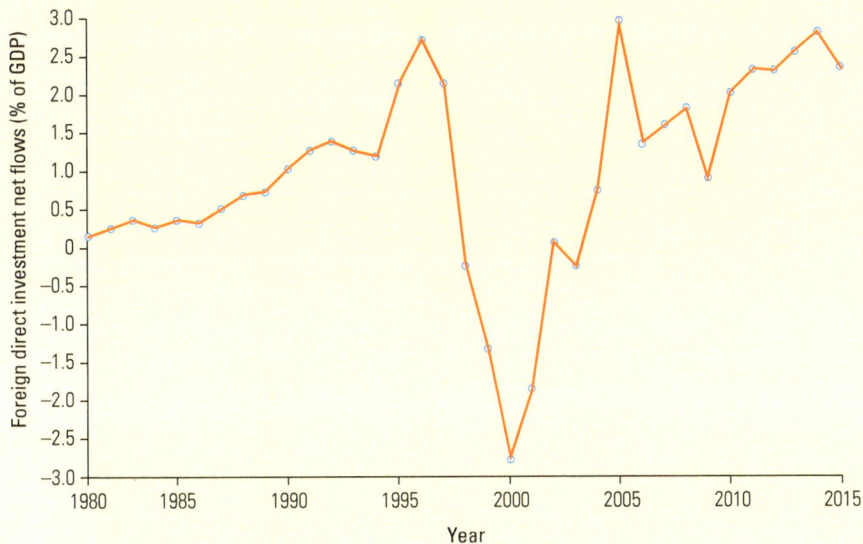

Note: GDP = gross domestic product.

political and practical complement to decentralization. Indonesia took the crucial step of ensuring political impartiality of its armed forces by separating the police and military and establishing parliamentary oversight. In exchange for conceding domestic security tasks to a newly formed police force, the military received significant budgetary concessions and was allowed to retain its territorial command structure.

Impact of peacebuilding on the economy. While at first, this substantial political and security risk was further destabilizing, follow-through on the changes paid off, with increasing inflows of foreign direct investment as a percentage of gross domestic

product (GDP) and balance of payments (figure B6.6.1). The eventual institutional clarity was critical to ensuring that the government had the means subsequently to form and enforce peace deals in other areas over the longer term. The resulting more even power balance between the military and the government further disincentivized the use of force as an option for resolving conflict. Decisive action by the Indonesian police in the early 2000s to improve surveillance and antiterror operations in response to terrorist attacks helped to improve citizen confidence in the security forces. Indonesia's relatively strong institutional capacity was critical to facilitating and following through on changes.

Sources: Jaffrey 2017; Nygård et al. 2017.

Like most approaches to prevention, the effectiveness of decentralization requires parallel attention to other social and economic factors (Nygård et al. 2017), as well as to the capacity, legitimacy, and interests of recipients to govern and manage resources. In many cases, this purpose has been served

by combining decentralization with community-driven development (CDD). If managed well, CDD can ensure that the benefits of decentralization, such as greater local decision making and direct control of resources, trickle down to the local level and potentially lead to more efficient delivery of services and, eventually, to measurable reductions in poverty. CDD projects can aim to reconfigure intergroup and state-community relations in order to influence local power relations and, as such, conflict dynamics. By addressing the risks of conflict related to an influx of resources, the goal is to make resources a force for progressive change. CDD in itself does not avoid violence; however, it can consolidate peace by promoting positive social change and influencing pathways through conflict (Barron, Diprose, and Woolcock 2006, 2007). It can also improve intergroup relations, help to share power at the village level, and even help to resolve disputes and conflicts.

Where CDD approaches have had limited success, this can be attributed largely to the low intensity of interventions, a mismatch in timeframes, or a lack of coherent and explicit theory of change (Bennett and D'Onofrio 2015; King and Samii 2014).

- In Afghanistan, the National Solidarity Program (NSP) created community councils and gave them small grants to start projects (Yemak, Gan, and Cheng 2013). The program—the largest development program in Afghanistan—has been credited with success for the fact that it is rooted in a local focus and scaled to existing capacity (Mashal 2015). It has brought CDD to all of Afghanistan's 34 provinces and, in doing so, has overcome security challenges, prevailing gender norms, and suspicion of the central government (Beath, Christia, and Enikolopov 2015). By dividing resources into small packages, the NSP has avoided pitfalls such as large-scale corruption, while ensuring local ownership over projects. Although NSP has had some beneficial effects, including increased acceptance of democratic processes and improved perceptions of economic well-being, the positive effects regarding attitudes toward central and subnational government fell off soon after the completion of NSP-funded projects (Beath, Christia, and Enikolopov 2015).
- Indonesia implemented a large CDD program that included conflict

resolution mechanisms. A two-province study in Aceh of the Kecamatan Development Project—a framework through which more than US$20 million in assistance was made available to more than 1,700 conflict-affected individual villages in block grants—finds that, while there is little evidence that the project itself has reduced levels of violent conflict, it has had "notable and positive" indirect impacts on the local institutional environment in the areas in which it operates (Barron, Diprose, and Woolcock 2006, 2007). CDD projects such as this can also complement local conflict mediation mechanisms, but they are unlikely to replace preexisting mechanisms. Where CDD projects complement ongoing governance reforms and local conflict mediation capacities, they can reinforce positive outcomes (Barron, Diprose, and Woolcock 2006, 2007).

Strengthening the Rule of Law

Security and justice issues have often been at the center of both challenges and solutions for violent conflict, as discussed in chapter 5. The country cases examined for this study underscore that there is no quick fix in addressing the risks of violent conflict that emerge from the security and justice arena or in realizing its full potential for prevention. Societies in high-risk or postconflict contexts must manage multiple, often competing, demands to address abuses of the past and demonstrate a clear departure from past practices, while simultaneously responding to the current security and justice needs of the population.

As discussed in chapter 3, violence is highly path-dependent; once it takes hold, incentives and systems begin to reorient themselves in ways that sustain violence. Violence often justifies beefing up military budgets and consolidating decision making within defense ministries. Altering the balance of power in favor of security forces has often worsened abuses during conflict and requires strong resistance to rebalancing power with other sectors once violence has ceased. To address this, many countries move to increase the accountability and transparency of the security forces to signal a change of direction.

In most cases, increasing accountability and transparency has involved paying closer attention to the separation between military and policing functions. Indonesia worked to increase citizen trust in security forces by dividing the police from the military and setting up an oversight body within Parliament (Jaffrey 2017; box 6.6). The reform of the security sector in Tunisia, where the abuses and impunity of the internal security institutions served as a catalyst for the protests that ended the rule of President Zine El Abidine Ben Ali, involved a move from "a police order to a police service" (Hanlon 2012, 8). The reform reorganized the security services into three bodies—the National Guard, the National Police, and Civil Protection (Hanlon 2012). Northern Ireland also underwent an extensive reform and transformation of police and policing mechanisms that involved creating an independent police ombudsman to encourage local accountability (Groenewald and von Tangen 2002).

Alongside such reforms, where ethnic or identity divides run deep, integrating marginalized ethnic or religious groups into the military has helped to defuse the salience of schisms (Brzoska 2006). Nepal's eventual integration of some 1,500 Maoist combatants into the army in 2012 was a major breakthrough in lowering the risk of return to fighting (von Einsiedel and Salih 2017).[14] The dissolution of the Maoist army was made significantly easier and less of a risk to the Maoists themselves by dint of the fact that it held political power at that stage (von Einsiedel and Salih 2017). In Burundi, a focus on maintaining parity in numbers between Hutus and Tutsis in military recruitment helped to promote inclusion and reconciliation (Samii 2013). In Kosovo, too, ethnic diversity in the police force was pursued as a deliberate policy by which to build community trust and create a less prejudiced institution (Heinemann-Grüder and Grebenschikov 2006; box 6.7).

Although the process of building trust takes time, decisive and clear measures to address failings can go a long way to restoring confidence and signaling intent.

BOX 6.7 Inclusion for Security Reform: Burundi, Kosovo, and Timor-Leste

Inclusion has proven indispensable to achieving lasting security sector reform, including with regard to establishing trust, as a critical ingredient for prevention. Inclusive approaches focus on transparency, view such reform as a public policy issue, and involve the full spectrum of social actors.

Burundi. Reforms began with the Arusha Peace and Reconciliation Agreement in 2000, which set the course for the country's emergence from 12 years of devastating civil war. After a long legacy of military domination of politics, the military itself was interested in professionalizing and rebuilding its reputation. Although still facing serious political and practical challenges, the relative success of the military reforms

is noteworthy for the level of broad acceptance they achieved. This appears due to the inclusive and integrated approach to reform. Burundian military reforms, with international support, set out to be inclusive in two main ways: first, in addition to operational capability, reforms explicitly considered governance across multiple areas of government, prioritized political dialogue, and gradually included civil society and the experiences of neighboring countries; second, the Arusha Agreement stipulated that no more than 50 percent of the armed forces could be drawn from any one ethnic group and that membership was open to all Burundian citizens, including rebel factions. Along with a gradual approach to building trust, educating

(Box continued next page)

citizens, and increasing local ownership of the process, the reforms have been a significant part of implementing the Arusha Agreement, which so far, has avoided a return to full-scale civil war.

Kosovo. The explicit efforts to ensure multiethnic representation in the newly formed Kosovo police service were critical factors of successful community-level policing in postconflict Kosovo. In order to gain the confidence and trust of all ethnic communities and prevent further conflict in a deeply divided society, the new police service was to have minimum quotas for Kosovo-Albanians and Kosovo-Serbs, as well as 20 percent female officers. Without this kind of inclusion, it would likely have been impossible to extend effective policing to all areas of the country. Through training, different ethnic groups were obliged to interact, motivated at least by the need to keep their new job. While achieving a relative ethnic balance was difficult and took time, by 2005 the share of women in the police force (16 percent) exceeded that of most European forces (around 10 percent). Over time, levels of comfort and even comradery grew in a way that outpaced those in the wider communities, despite ongoing political divisions. International support for development of the police service from the UN Interim Administration Mission in Kosovo and the Organization for Security and Cooperation in Europe, in particular, was crucial. It provided not only funding but also impartial expertise, which enabled depoliticization of the police service. By 2008, the police service was almost entirely locally led. Community confidence in the police grew significantly, especially for

Kosovo-Albanians who had not shown any confidence in police previously. Polls in 2009 and 2010 showed the police to be the most trusted institution, with low levels of corruption and good community relationships.

Timor-Leste. Greater local leadership and local inclusion were key to implementing security sector reforms in Timor-Leste. Over the first decade after independence, the technical and administrative capability of security forces improved with largely imported processes. The second-generation changes to security reforms put more emphasis on a holistic, locally led approach. Once the donors' footprint in the reform process had started to decline, many instrumental reforms were brought about, increasing public trust in the state security and justice institutions. National actors became more assertive in leading the reform process, leveraging civil society, and engaging both formal and informal security providers. These inclusive steps "fostered slower, but deeper, more multifaceted, and therefore more sustainable societal, political, and cultural transformations concerning the role of security sector institutions in Timorese society." Instituting community policing, devolving conflict resolution to communities where appropriate, and creating interlinkages between formal and informal institutions all sought to improve inclusion. Public confidence and trust in the security and justice institutions improved, along with the perception of legitimacy of security institutions, which was previously a key challenge and a key driver of conflict in Timor-Leste.

Sources: Ball 2014; DCAF 2017; Dewhurst and Greising 2017; Greene, Friedman, and Bennett 2012; Heinemann-Grüder and Grebenschikov 2006; Stodiek 2006.

Allegations of political partisanship and human rights violations, including rape and excessive use of force, following Kenya's postelection violence in 2007–08 provided the impetus for security sector reform as part of the 2010 constitution (Mogaka 2017). The reforms aimed to make the security institutions politically impartial and establish oversight over various security institutions, with the goal of restoring popular trust in these institutions. Increasing the visibility and transparency of the police through joint action and dialogue with communities can help to build trust and signal a change in direction while reforms are implemented, as in Jamaica by way of innovative community-policing approaches (DCAF 2017). The bottom-up approaches adopted in the Kyrgyz Republic, Timor-Leste, and Uganda are more likely to produce direct and visible results in regard to creating inclusiveness, legitimacy, and responsiveness in security and justice provision (DCAF 2017).

Gender inclusion—through increasing the number of women in the security forces—has boosted community trust and reduced both the misconduct of police and the use of excessive force to deal with emerging threats (DCAF 2017). Bougainville, Papua New Guinea, where women have traditionally played a core role in conflict resolution, has been especially effective in integrating women into its policing structure (DCAF 2017). Nicaragua, too, has used a multifaceted approach, including strong political commitment, revised recruitment procedures, training, and dedicated women's police stations, to attain a 26 percent female police staffing rate (DCAF 2017). This represents one of the highest proportions of female officers in the world and has contributed directly to Nicaragua having one of the lowest homicide rates in the region (DCAF 2017).

Establishing Forums for Peaceful Conflict Resolution

In the more successful cases, reforming institutions to foster incentives for peace has transcended a focus on national institutions and peace processes to focus on strengthening coordination across and building links between the myriad bodies that bear some responsibility for peacebuilding. A key lesson has been that, while national reforms play an important role, they are insufficient in themselves to support sustained peace. Local-level mechanisms offer a unique vantage point and cultural relevance for addressing conflict early on, while being contextually appropriate. However, they are limited in their reach if not embedded in a regional or national framework. Similarly, national policies and strategies that do not connect to local initiatives will struggle to gain traction on the ground (Giessmann, Galvanek, and Seifert 2017).

The process of establishing these interlinkages is often referred to as building "infrastructures for peace," defined as the organizational elements and linkages that form domestic "mechanisms of cooperation among all relevant stakeholders in peacebuilding by promoting cooperative problem solving to conflicts and institutionalizing the response mechanisms to conflicts in order to transform them" (van Tongeren 2001, 400; Giessmann 2016). Strengthening these infrastructures has meant aligning successful local initiatives with national strategies, ensuring that resources flow effectively, and enhancing coordination (box 6.8).

Ghana's comprehensive infrastructure for peace has succeeded in managing tensions and mitigating conflict risks, especially around elections, and has inspired neighboring countries to follow suit (Hopp-Nishanka 2012; box 6.9). The infrastructure includes a mediation, consensus-building, and advocacy role for the National Peace Council, with activities organized at national, regional, and district levels; a role for the judiciary; a role for the National Security Council; a traditional authority and alternative justice role for the National House of Chiefs; a watchdog and advocacy role for civil society; oversight by the legislature and independent national human rights body; and a role for the Electoral Commission. The national government also hosts a Peacebuilding Support Unit within the Ministry of the Interior to coordinate preventive efforts by all actors across the country. Electoral conflict and violence also provided Kenya with the impetus to transform its national conflict prevention and management architecture (Mogaka 2017). It has used district peace committees as the basis for a uniform national peace structure and has worked to build a multistakeholder approach (Mogaka 2017).

Niger provides another example of building effective infrastructures for peace

BOX 6.8 Infrastructures for Peace: Developing and Sustaining National Capacity

The concept of infrastructures for peace (I4P) encompasses the long-term, multilevel mechanisms and institutional structures for collaboration between stakeholders, including the state, civil society, and the private sector, to prevent and resolve violent conflict. There is no single ready-made model for I4P, and each country has to tailor it to its historical, institutional, and structural conditions. The concept was originally formulated in the 1980s by Lederach (1997), based on his experiences with local and national peace processes and the use of commissions in peace negotiations.

I4Ps can only be put in place through nationally owned and driven processes, but they are enhanced through global experience in building peace architectures to fit local needs. At different stages, they can also serve as an exit strategy for peacekeeping and political missions as well as development actors. They offer an assurance to national actors of the persistence of national institutions and constituencies that work for sustainable peace. National I4P can include various elements, including peace committees, peace secretariats, and national peacebuilding forums.

Peace committees bring together national and local institutions and focus on reducing violence, promoting dialogue, guiding problem-solving activities, encouraging community building, and working toward reconciliation. They typically capitalize on the skills of agents of change as mediators to bridge social, political, and economic divides. Peace committees are found at the national, regional, and local levels. They often include representatives of government, civil society, and political or traditional leaders and can be fully or partially integrated into the structures of the state.

Peace secretariats assist parties in negotiations by advancing and implementing the peace process. They fulfill their roles during peace negotiations by assisting in the creation of more permanent I4P entities. In particular, they coordinate with other institutions, create linkages between "tracks," and streamline peacebuilding approaches.

National peacebuilding forums are multistakeholder platforms for consultation and collaboration. They are based on inclusive and interactive relationships and networks that establish spaces for collective action and systemic engagement.

Sources: EU and UNDP 2014; Giessmann 2016; Lederach 1997.

BOX 6.9 Peace Committees and Early Warning Mechanisms: Kenya, Indonesia, and Ghana

Kenya has a history of bottom-up peacebuilding by local community structures. In the early 1990s the Women for Peace Committee was formed in response to an upsurge in communal conflict in what was then the Wajir District. Women worked across clans to mobilize youth and elders to work toward peace. Their efforts included establishing Al-Fatah leaders and creating the Al-Fatah Declaration, which became the basis for resolving future community conflicts. Local government recognized the value added by local actors and encouraged the formation of district peace committees, which integrated local peacebuilders into district development and security

(Box continued next page)

committees. This marked a milestone for introducing multistakeholder approaches to conflict prevention in Kenya. In the early 2000s, the government-established National Steering Committee on Peacebuilding and Conflict Management and a conflict early warning and response mechanism also became important platforms for conflict prevention. The latter, however, initially focused narrowly on cross-border conflict in the Karamoja and Somali clusters. This focus later expanded to national coverage of more than just cross-border pastoralist conflict. The National Council of Churches in Kenya has offered critical support to interethnic and interfaith dialogue at local and national levels, including mechanisms such as study tours to learn from the experience of ethnic violence in Rwanda. Civil society organizations and nongovernmental organizations played a prominent role prior to the 2013 election by promoting peace through various activities. Initiatives include their participation in the Uwiano platform—a multistakeholder platform that brought together government institutions, civil society, and development actors—ahead of the 2010 constitution to prevent political violence similar to what occurred during the 2005 referendum.

Indonesia also established programs to monitor, prepare for, and respond to violence that integrated civilian, state, and international mechanisms. The Aceh Monitoring Mission, composed of civilians, reported on violations of the memorandum of understanding between the Free Aceh Movement and the government. Aceh conflict monitoring updates, provided by the World Bank, tracked violent incidents across the province through local media reports. The National Violence Monitoring System, developed from the work of the World Bank and the National Planning Agency, collected data on postconflict violence in affected regions. These data were used to inform the future allocation of

resources, develop regional development plans, and enhance early mediation efforts in local conflict. Indonesia's police, concerned about increasing terrorist activity on Indonesian soil, worked to improve surveillance capacity (for example, in Central Sulawesi after the peace agreement, where several terror networks participated in anti-Christian violence).

Ghana's comprehensive institutional setup has been instrumental in preventing violence. The architecture combines regional-, national-, and local-level institutions with multiple dimensions of government, civil society, and dialogue mechanisms. The Northern Regional Peace Advisory Council was set up in 2004, followed by the National Peace Council, 10 regional peace councils, and district advisory councils. These mechanisms have featured prominently in preventing and addressing violence, including around the 2012 elections. Traditional and religious organizations play an important role as nonstate mechanisms in prevention of violent conflict. Chiefs or Queen mothers, the Earth priest, clan heads, family heads, and religious leaders are key stakeholders in the prevention process. Religious leaders are especially important in the northern savannah zone, where interethnic conflicts appear endemic. Early warning systems exist, with support from international actors. The National and Regional Peace Council set up the National and Regional Election Early Warning System in all regional capitals, along with response strategies to contain potential threats. The Media Foundation for West Africa also monitors campaign language on the radio during election time to keep track of hate speech and indecent campaign language. Military deployment appears to be used widely and effectively for conflict prevention. Security personnel have been sent to volatile areas to mitigate tensions, such as in the Yendi conflict.

Sources: Bob-Milliar 2017; Jaffrey 2017; Mogaka 2017.

(Pérouse de Montclos 2017). The Haute Autorité à La Consolidation de la Paix, led by a Tuareg since it was launched in 2011, has been successful in managing relations with the various communities in the north of the country (box 6.5). The HACP is one of the reasons the country has been more effective in managing conflicts with the Tuareg populations in the north than with Boko Haram in the south (Pérouse de Montclos 2017).

Civil society, religious bodies, and private sector actors can maximize their contributions by plugging into broader networks. The Christian Council of Lesotho has played the role of mediator and interlocutor between conflicting parties in the country for the last few decades (Giessmann, Galvanek, and Seifert 2017). Due to its success in mediating all election-related processes since the end of military rule in 1993, assisting with the nonviolent transition of power in 2012, and helping to build mediation and conflict resolution capacity across the country, the Christian Council of Lesotho was recognized as de facto mediator-in-chief by both Lesotho's state authorities and the Electoral Commission in 2009. Other influential actors have also recognized its role, including the Lesotho Council of Non-Governmental Organizations as well as international partners and regional organizations (Giessmann, Galvanek, and Seifert 2017).

The Peace Messengers program in the Kyrgyz Republic between 2010 and 2015 created teams of peace mediators drawn from local communities (Giessmann, Galvanek, and Seifert 2017). The teams were made up of local decision makers, community elders, religious leaders, informal neighborhood leaders, women's committees, head teachers, and others. Their prevention activities helped to keep local disputes from escalating and protected local mediation processes from external pressures. However, the program failed to create self-sustaining capacity for conflict prevention, in part because the external funding on which it was reliant dried up before it was firmly anchored into local structures (Giessmann, Galvanek, and Seifert 2017).

Comparative analysis suggests that local peace committees helped to lower the risk of violence overall and, in particular, to reduce the risk that localized insecurity could escalate.[15] Local-level structures often have the most immediate and pressing incentives to maintain peace and work toward prevention. Local peace committees can build on local incentives, capacity, and relationships. They provide "an alternative institutional framework for mediating local disputes, responding to crises, harnessing a range of local capacities through peacebuilding networks" (Sisk 2017), mapping resources and issues, and linking local and national contexts. For such committees, civil society and the private sector have proven indispensable as interlocuters and mediators, particularly in the presence of a high degree of political corruption, organized crime, and dysfunctional state institutions.

Challenges arise in several areas. Where peace committees are well resourced, they have become targets of capture by groups seeking rents or attempting to advance specific interests, which may not be in the interests of broader peace (Sisk 2017). In other cases, peace committees have suffered from weak capacity, unclear mandates, and politicization. Finally, peace committees can be seriously challenged if they result in a parallel structure to the formal conflict resolution mechanisms. For example, following the cessation of conflict in Nepal, the minister of peace and reconstruction—with support from the Nepal Peace Trust Fund—established local peace committees in almost all of the country's 75 districts to help to maintain peace at the local level. Although a few of these have had some success at inclusive peacebuilding, von Einsiedel and Salih (2017) argue that it would have been more effective to promote mediation activities within the established district- and local-level development committees rather than attempting to build a parallel structure.

Investing in Structural Factors

Tackling the structural challenges to achieving sustained peace is the final critical area for domestic action to be examined in this chapter. Structural factors comprise the foundational elements of society and shape the overall environment in which actors make decisions. These factors usually change slowly and require time, patience, and a long-term vision. However, it is possible to tackle these factors and to address the risks they present through targeted action. Economic reforms, redistributive policies, and infrastructure investments, for example, all can foster structural changes that reduce the risk of violence.

Chapters 3 and 4 discuss some of the structural factors that feature prominently in many conflicts, in particular, patterns of socioeconomic exclusion and inequality across groups, while chapter 5 examines the arenas of contestation in which these grievances accumulate. This section highlights the efforts of countries to manage structural factors by addressing social and economic grievances via reforms related to access to and redistribution of land, by increasing equity in the distribution of resource revenues, and by engaging in efforts to heal social divisions.

Addressing Economic and Social Grievances

Perceptions of exclusion present a major risk for violent conflict, as discussed in chapters 4 and 5. By focusing on the arenas of contestation—power and governance, access to land and natural resources, delivery of services, and justice and security—countries have taken various measures to address grievances by fostering greater access and redistributing benefits. In some cases, these measures have come about because of a peace agreement or a new constitution and have been incorporated into national development plans. The 2030 Agenda offers an important framework for addressing many grievances and building consensus around the ways to ameliorate them. In other cases, they have involved stand-alone, targeted efforts to address the source of a grievance.

Many countries have negotiated broad-based development plans that transcend peace agreements in a bid to address social and economic issues:

- Kenya recognized the destabilizing potential of regional imbalances and in Vision 2030, its national long-term development blueprint, committed to invest in marginalized areas to unlock their development potential, while contributing to spatial and national inclusion (Mogaka 2017). The 2010 constitution also made provisions for an equalization fund to improve the delivery of basic services to marginalized areas in a bid to bring service provision up to the levels experienced across the rest of the country.
- Indonesia's 2015–19 National Mid-Term Development Plan looks to address political, economic, security, and environmental dimensions through national, regional, and sectoral responses (Jaffrey 2017). Among other objectives, the plan aims to reduce inequality, develop peripheral areas, act against corruption, improve security, implement good governance, address law and justice, and advance social reform (Steven and Sucuoglu 2017).
- Niger's Renaissance project under President Issoufou attempts to reduce poverty across the nation as part of a strategy to address social and economic grievances that could translate into conflict risks (Pérouse de Montclos 2017).

Redistribution is always a contentious process because it necessarily creates winners and losers. In the country cases examined for this study, the process by which resources and access were redefined made a critical difference in determining the credibility, fairness, and sustainability of the reforms. These complex mechanisms pose major challenges for countries with limited fiscal space and limited capacities. They also require political will from the top level down to the local level. Some countries, such as Indonesia, found ways to mobilize political will while the reforms were implemented and eventually even garnered support for reforms from former opponents (Jaffrey 2017).

Specifically, three overarching lessons have emerged from successful cases: first, establishing a formula for redistribution that is viewed as fair by different groups; second, creating mechanisms to ensure that funds are distributed as the state claims they will be; and third, ensuring that the funds or services are delivered in an inclusive manner and viewed by the local population as appropriate. The 2030 Agenda offers entry points to apply all three lessons.

Leaders are often under intense pressure to deliver tangible results in the immediate term as they seek to influence incentives for peace.

- Following the conflict in Aceh, the Indonesian central government was aware of the importance of signaling its commitment to the peace process in Aceh (Jaffrey 2017). It prioritized highly visible projects that would serve the dual goal of neutralizing spoilers, while improving the image of the central government. It provided reintegration assistance to former combatants in an effort to stop them from sabotaging the agreement and assistance to civilians in order to boost popular support for the peace process. To avoid the impression that the Acehnese were being compensated for past abuses, much of the civilian aid was disbursed in the form of disaster recovery efforts (Jaffrey 2017). A particular challenge in this case was that postdisaster aid did not fully reflect the postconflict realities, as the funds provided were inadequate to address damage and losses caused by the conflict (MSR 2009).

- Similarly, Ghana focused funds for the north on the critical areas of improving services, health, education, and some economic infrastructure to create government visibility and legitimacy at the local level (Steven and Sucuoglu 2017). The comprehensive program of subnational investment, which helped the country to bridge a north-south divide and bolstered political inclusion at the local level, also saw the transfer of resources from the central to the local government between 1995 and

2014 (World Bank 2006). The program under the District Assembly Common Fund[16] weighs various factors, including "need," and accounts for differences in the quality of public services across districts. Between 2001 and 2007, more funds from the central government made their way to less prosperous districts than to those that were economically more robust. In all regions, an increase in external revenue from the government boosted the delivery of basic services.

In some countries, redistribution policies have taken the form of integrating neglected parts of urban centers into the broader city, as highlighted also in SDG target 11.1. In these cases, increasing the presence and responsiveness of the state via the rollout of basic services is critical. During the 1990s in Medellín, Colombia, a growing drug trade overtook many slum areas that were economically and socially disconnected from the rest of the city (Steven and Sucuoglu 2017). A decade later, "social urbanism" had transformed Medellín from one of the most violent cities in the world to one of the most progressive (Turok 2014). City institutions joined forces with other spheres of government to push a development approach based on a commitment to social inclusion and equity. The city government invested heavily in participatory processes to increase citizen voice in urban planning and in building infrastructure to connect slum areas with the broader city, including a cable car system, public parks, and libraries designed by world-renowned architects. Expansion of basic services, including a community policing initiative, and greater investment in schools and health services were credited with helping to bring down levels of violence and improving public perceptions of the state (Steven and Sucuoglu 2017). Economic development was also propelled by catalytic projects to rehabilitate former industrial sites and rundown buildings, generating jobs in the city (Turok 2014).

Broadening access and improving quality of education have been another important element addressing grievances around exclusion. The positive impacts seem to stem less from efforts to address a specific grievance (lack of education) than from indirect effects (the role of education in improving lives generally). Support for education signals government intent, providing conflict resolution tools, addressing the social acceptability of violence, and strengthening a sense of confidence in the future. The evidence is particularly strong for the link between government expenditure on education and availability of secondary education (particularly for young men) and peace (Nygård et al. 2017). Ghana and Northern Ireland both focused on education as a means of furthering social inclusion (Bob-Milliar 2017; Walsh 2017).

Resolving Land- and Resource-Related Grievances

Grievances relating to perceptions of unfairness and exclusion in access to and ownership of land can heighten the risks of violent conflict. Left unaddressed, they represent a major source of risk, particularly where grievances have deep historical antecedents, as seen in chapter 5. The centrality of addressing structural issues related to land distribution and sustained prevention is underscored in the example of Colombia, where the protection, formalization, and restitution of land to displaced people have been a core plank of Colombia's ongoing peace process (World Bank 2016d; box 6.10). Country efforts to address the sources of these grievances have focused

---

BOX 6.10 Land Protection for the Forcibly Displaced in Colombia

Colombia's long-running civil war between government forces, including paramilitary forces, and insurgent guerrilla groups caused large-scale displacement of the population. Land, territory, and the lack of institutional security for land tenure in rural areas were at the heart of the conflict. Disputes over land between tenants and large-scale farmers began as early as the 1920s and were core to the long-running civil war. Cycles of violence continued, fueled, in part, by unresolved land questions and calls for land reform, and were accompanied by massive land seizures and the forced displacement of roughly 2 million small-scale farmers from rural land to urban areas (World Bank 2016d). Tensions brought about by structural inequality, political exclusion, and forced dispossession of the land by large landowners erupted into war in the 1960s, spurred by the leftist ideology espoused by the Revolutionary Armed Forces of Colombia (FARC) and the National Liberation Army. The conflict escalated in the 1980s, as armed groups found new sources of financing in the illegal drug trade. The number of

displaced rural dwellers peaked in 2002 at 447,429. In all, the conflict displaced between 3 million and 5 million people.

In 1997, the government passed the first comprehensive law (Law 387) with measures to prevent forced displacement and to address challenges faced by its internally displaced citizens, including loss of productive assets. The Victims and Land Restitution Law of 2011 created the formal framework for the restitution of land to internally displaced persons. Between 2002 and 2014, donors supported and funded a three-part program to promote the protection, formalization, and restitution in order to support internally displaced persons and the peacebuilding process. Through systematic data collection and research to address specific land tenure issues, the project built the knowledge base and policy support for the Restitution Law. This law, and the land restitution process it promotes, despite having been associated with some violence against potential returnees, was a key plank of the 2016 peace deal between the government and FARC.

Source: Amnesty International 2014; Observatorio de Tierras 2017; World Bank 2015a, 2016d.

largely on land reform to promote redistribution of and expand access to land. For instance, in Uganda, the Commission for the Return of Properties to Departed Asians legally affirmed specific property rights, thus administering justice and serving the national interest of reestablishing international recognition and legitimacy of government (Colletta and Oppenheim 2017).

Some countries have had success in addressing the risks of violent conflict through schemes to redistribute underutilized land, as in Malawi, where the inheritance of colonial estates by a small number of large landowners created a situation of frequent land encroachments by a large number of land-poor citizens (Chinigò 2016; Machira 2009). In 2004, amid mounting social tensions, the government launched a community-based rural land development project, aimed to redistribute underutilized portions of large estates among the landless poor, around Blantyre, in southern Malawi. The project aimed to transfer land to about 15,000 poor, rural families through subsidized transactions, while also addressing titling and registration of the new holdings. In total, the government successfully reallocated 27,988 hectares to 12,656 families and helped to ease tensions among the landless poor in that region, despite coming up against some resistance from large landowners (Chinigò 2016; Machira 2009).

In Kenya, where contestations over land use and management have also formed the basis of much conflict, land is likened to the "fulcrum around which everything revolves" (Kanyinga 2005). To address this, the 2010 constitution provided for detailed policies and the creation of institutions designed to improve the management of land (Mogaka 2017). The National Land Commission was subsequently established to manage public land on behalf of the two levels of government, while the reforms also sought to address the grievances of communities and reduce the power of the executive over land management. Although the process has faced numerous challenges, and implementation remains incomplete, progress in land reforms has helped alleviate some of the risks related to land allocation that had been commonplace previously (Mogaka 2017).

Some countries have addressed the risk of extractives-related violent conflict by enhancing transparency in revenue sharing and dealing with perceptions of equity, as well as by devolving greater control of revenues to producing regions. Several SDGs offer entry points in this regard. Nigeria, for example, has instituted a formula for distributing the proceeds from extractives, in a bid to manage tensions related to perceptions of unfairness in the allocation of resource revenues. Although 95 percent of export earnings and 65 percent of government revenues in Nigeria came from the oil and gas sector in 2010, only 9 out of 36 states produced oil (Aguilar, Caspary, and Seiler 2011). The northern states have supported the principle of land mass and population as criteria for resource distribution, while the oil-producing states have argued in favor of a derivative principle by which they receive larger allocations. Since 1993, 13 percent of oil proceeds have been distributed among the 25 percent of states that produce oil (Eze 2013).

As discussed in more detail in chapter 5, the decentralization of natural resource revenues and decision making has been seen as a way to counter grievances related to resources at the local level. This approach has had mixed success, however, as in Ghana, where the Mineral Development Fund facilitated local-level revenue sharing but introduced new forms of inequality and reinforced elite capture (Standing and Hilson 2013).

Confronting the Past and Building Social Cohesion

Social relationships form the cornerstone of a society's ability to manage conflict constructively. Resilient relationships in which people and groups have an incentive to cooperate, or at least coexist, without violence, form the basis for effective institutions and pathways toward sustainable peace (Marc et al. 2012). Violent conflict deepens social divisions and erodes trust between social groups and the state. While physical infrastructure can be rebuilt over a period of months or years, repairing the damage to the social fabric can take generations. Rebuilding trust and cohesion is therefore a critical element in preventing further cycles of violence.

In the case studies prepared for this study, most countries have found it necessary to take some measures toward reckoning with the events of the past to build the trust to move forward. These efforts have taken a variety of forms. Formal truth commissions in Sierra Leone and Tunisia brought people together to help close and heal the divides between groups, lessening the threat of a relapse into violence (Ainley, Friedman, and Mahony 2016). In the Central African Republic, a hybrid national-international special criminal court is being set up to address grievances regarding impunity (Lombard 2017). However, it faces multiple challenges, not least being decisions regarding whom to prosecute, how to rebuild trust, and how to avoid the perception that its choices are politically motivated.

In some cases, addressing past abuse has been dealt with through less judicial processes, including official apologies and truth-telling processes, as in Sierra Leone (Ainley, Friedman, and Mahony 2016; ICTJ 2016) or recognition of suffering and material reparations for victims, as in Argentina (De Greiff 2008). Tunisia's Truth and Dignity Commission established a record on Ben Ali–era abuses, including on systematic corruption, with parallel intent for national criminal prosecutions (ICTJ 2016). These processes have helped to prevent violent outbreaks similar to other Arab Spring political changes. In the Philippines, the recognition of historical injustice over more than 200 years, including state expropriation of land of the Bangsamoro community in Mindanao, was part of the comprehensive peace agreement in 2014 and helped to alleviate social and political polarization (TJRC 2016). The work of the Truth, Justice, and Reconciliation Commission was carried out subsequent to signing of the peace agreement, in spite of the fact that implementation of the agreement had stalled.

As discussed in chapter 5, transitional justice mechanisms are often adopted in postconflict contexts in order to provide recourse for victims of crimes and promote reconciliation. While evidence on the value of transitional justice in preventing recurrence of violence is quite limited overall (Payne et al. 2017), the country experiences examined for this study suggest that such measures can help to increase confidence in a new government and rule-of-law institutions and to rebuild civic trust (World Bank 2011).

There are, however, cases where the *absence* of justice provisions for conflict-era crimes has helped to bring warring parties together in more informal forums. In Indonesia, the absence of justice provisions in peace agreements helped to bring combatants to the negotiating table in the short term (Jaffrey 2017). In the long term, however, the absence of acknowledgement and punishment for past abuses has remained an obstacle to the full reconciliation of religious communities in Maluku and Sulawesi. Lack of trust and the memory of ills done have led to a stratification of residential areas and hampered interaction of the two communities (Jaffrey 2017).

Conclusion

This chapter draws out some common elements of effective prevention based on an analysis of the country cases commissioned for this study. Drawing on the framework for the study, it describes the experience of national actors in three key areas: shaping the incentives of actors for peace, reforming institutions to foster inclusion, and addressing structural factors that feed into grievances. The chapter also highlights the possible role of the 2030 Agenda. From these experiences, common patterns emerge, even if specific prescriptions do not.

A central dilemma for all countries examined is that the incentives for violence are often certain and specific to an individual or group, while the incentives for peace are often uncertain and diffuse (World Bank 2017b). To shape incentives and reduce or share risk across a broader range of actors, the more successful cases mobilized a range of domestic actors, bringing in the comparative advantages of civil society, the faith community, and the private sector to manage tensions and influence incentives toward peace. Governments introduced both long-term reforms or investments targeting structural factors, at the same time implementing immediate initiatives that buttressed confidence in commitments to more inclusive processes.

Nevertheless, before or after violence, most of the countries examined that have found pathways to sustaining peace have eventually tackled the messy and contested process of institutional reform to address the risk of violence. Expanding access to the arenas of contestation has been a key part of this effort, in order to increase representation and alleviate grievances related to exclusion. Often, the transition moment that led to sustainable peace was based on a shift away from security-led responses and toward broader approaches that mobilized a range of sectors.

In many cases, governments planned socioeconomic development, undertook reforms, launched security operations, and managed political life, even while violence was ongoing. In these experiences, the greatest challenge lay not so much in accessing knowledge, but in the contentious process of identifying and prioritizing risks. Conflict did not bring a windfall of resources: a diversion of development investments into peaceful areas and a move to equip and support police, military, or security operations strained national budgets. Rather than creating the space for the more forward-looking decision making that is needed to establish the institutional or structural conditions for sustainable peace, violence narrowed the options. For this reason, preventive action was at times contrary to popular demands for visible and tangible security measures over longer-term, more complex responses that could address the causes of violence.

In these processes, formal political settlements—or at least durable settlements—were important, but also rare events on the pathway for peace. Approaches to preventing violence or resolving violent conflict, once started, often resulted from government policies of investment, security, and

diplomatic action put in place long before a political process was initiated or formalized. In some cases, political settlements were applied only to address specific aspects of conflict, while underlying causes were targeted more comprehensively through government action. In others, political settlements were not used as part of the prevention process at all.

In many cases, states sought international support in these endeavors. The next chapter turns to the role of international actors in supporting domestic processes.

Notes

1. These commonalities are derived from the country case studies and research commissioned for this study as well as broader relevant literature. The case studies cover Burkina Faso, Burundi, the Central African Republic, Côte d'Ivoire, the Arab Republic of Egypt, Ghana, Guatemala, Indonesia, Jordan, Kenya, the Kyrgyz Republic, Malawi, Morocco, Nepal, Niger, Northern Ireland, Sierra Leone, South Sudan, and Tunisia.

2. Here, "transformational" reflects the definition from World Bank (2016c), which defines transformational engagements as "interventions or series of interventions that support deep, systemic, and sustainable change with the potential for large-scale impact in an area of a major development challenge."

3. Since 2009 (Pittsburgh Communiqué), for instance, the G-20 has called on concerned countries to rationalize and phase out inefficient fossil-fuel subsidies, while compensating the poor and vulnerable and ensuring their access to energy. This commitment was reaffirmed in the 2010 summit in Busan, the 2012 meeting in Los Cabos, and the 2013 summit in Saint Petersburg.

4. According to OECD (2012), "An important condition for subsidy reform is the credibility of the government's commitment to compensate vulnerable groups … and to use the freed public funds in a beneficial way."

5. Once a social protection policy is introduced, it is hard to reverse, regardless of any changes in the underlying subsidy policy,

because such reversals entail political risks: the recipients now feel entitled to benefits.

6. Recent analysis reflecting best practices in subsidy reform calls for the use of social safety nets as a necessary element.

7. Clements et al. (2013) point to Indonesia as an example of successful and thoughtful planning of the use of social safety nets to overcome political economy and social concerns.

8. At the community level, civic organizations that cut across ethnic lines had a fundamental role in keeping a community stable and peaceful versus those communities that did not have such structures.

9. In 2000, Serbia was known as Serbia and Montenegro.

10. According to UNESCO (2008), "Education for non-violence and peace includes training, skills, and information directed towards cultivating a culture of peace based on human rights principles … The learning objectives of peace education may include an understanding of the manifestations of violence, the development of capacities to respond constructively to that violence, and specific knowledge of alternatives to violence. Two fundamental concepts of peace education are respect and skills. Respect refers to the development of respect for self and for others; skills refer to specific communication, cooperation, and behavioral skills used in conflict situations."

11. Political inclusion here is used broadly to describe meaningful inclusion of groups or individuals in politically salient dialogue or processes, whether part of formal governance institutions or informal processes (see Call 2012).

12. Here decentralization refers to territorially based autonomous political authority and decentralized political systems. Federalism or decentralization entails regional political autonomy from the capital; it is a combination of self-rule and shared rule that can preserve peace by "retain[ing] the territorial integrity of the state while providing some form of self-governance for disaffected groups" (Bakke and Wibbels 2006, 5).

13. See, for example, http://www.u4.no /publications/corruption-and-decentralisation -in-afghanistan/.

14. Serious challenges to the integration efforts remain, however, with continuing perceptions of unfairness spurring the formation of some splinter groups.

15. For a comparative analysis of peace committees, see Odendaal (2010, 2013); van Tongeren (2013).

16. External revenue comprises (1) the District Assembly Common Fund, (2) transfers from the central government to support the salaries of local government officials, (3) donor funds, (4) the Heavily Indebted Poor Countries fund, (5) school feeding, and (6) the District Development Facility. The District Assembly Common Fund is the main vehicle for intergovernmental transfers.

References

Aguilar, J., G. Caspary, and V. Seiler. 2011. "Implementing EITI at the Subnational Level." Extractive Industries for Development Series 23, World Bank, Washington, DC.

Ahram, A. I. 2011. "Learning to Live with Militias: Toward a Critical Policy on State Frailty." *Journal of Intervention and Statebuilding* 5 (2): 175–88.

Ainley, K., R. Friedman, and C. Mahony, eds. 2016. *Evaluating Transitional Justice: Accountability and Peacebuilding in Post-Conflict Sierra Leone.* Berlin: Springer.

Alaga, E. 2010. "Challenges for Women in Peacebuilding in West Africa." Policy Brief 18, Africa Institute of South Africa, Pretoria.

Amnesty International. 2014. "A Land Title Is Not Enough: Ensuring Sustainable Land Restitution in Colombia." Amnesty International, New York, November.

Antil, A., and M. Mokhefi. 2014. "Managing the Sahara Periphery." Sahara Knowledge Exchange Series, World Bank, Washington, DC.

Aslam, G. 2017. "Civic Associations and Conflict Prevention: Potential, Challenges and Opportunities—A Review of the Literature." Background paper for the United Nations–World Bank Flagship Study, *Pathways for Peace: Inclusive Approaches to Preventing Violent Conflict,* World Bank, Washington, DC.

Austin, J. L., and A. Wennmann. 2017. "Business and the Prevention of Violence in Kenya, 2007–2013." Background paper for the

United Nations–World Bank Flagship Study, *Pathways for Peace: Inclusive Approaches to Preventing Violent Conflict,* World Bank, Washington, DC.

Bakke, K., and E. Wibbels. 2006. "Diversity, Disparity, and Civil Conflict in Federal States." *World Politics* 59 (1): 1–50.

Ball, N. 2014. "Lessons from Burundi's Security Sector Reform Process." Africa Security Brief, Africa Center for Strategic Studies, Washington, DC.

Bano, M., and H. Kalmbach, eds. 2011. *Women, Leadership, and Mosques: Changes in Contemporary Islamic Society.* Leiden, the Netherlands: BRILL.

Barnes, C. 2005. "Weaving the Web: Civil-Society Roles in Working with Conflict and Building Peace." In *People Building Peace II: Successful Stories of Civil Society*, edited by P. van Tongeren, M. Brenk, M. Hellema, and J. Verhoeven, 7–24. Boulder, CO: Lynne Rienner.

Barron, P., R. Diprose, and M. Woolcock. 2006. "Local Conflict and Community Development in Indonesia: Assessing the Impact of the Kecamatan Development Project." Indonesian Social Development Paper 10, World Bank, Jakarta.

———. 2007. "Local Conflict and Development Project in Indonesia: A Part of the Problem or a Part of the Solution." Policy Research Working Paper 4212, World Bank, Washington, DC.

Beath A., F. Christia, and R. Enikolopov. 2015. "The National Solidarity Programme: Assessing the Effects of Community-Driven Development in Afghanistan." *International Peacekeeping* 22 (4): 302–20.

Bennett, S., and A. D'Onofrio. 2015. *Community-Driven? Concepts, Clarity, and Choices for CDD in Conflict-Affected Contexts.* International Rescue Committee Report. New York: International Rescue Committee.

Bertrand, J. 2004. *Nationalism and Ethnic Conflict in Indonesia.* Cambridge, U.K.: Cambridge University Press.

Bigsten, A., and K. O. Moene. 1996. "Growth and Rent Dissipation: The Case of Kenya." *Journal of African Economies* 5 (2): 177–19.

Binnendijk, A. L., and I. Marovic. 2006. "Power and Persuasion: Nonviolent Strategies to Influence State Security Forces in Serbia (2000) and Ukraine (2004)." *Communist and Post-Communist Studies* 39 (3): 411–29.

Bøås, M., S. S. Eriksen, T. Gade, J. H. S. Lie, and O. J. Sending. 2017. "Conflict Prevention and Ownership: Limits and Opportunities for External Actors." Background paper for the United Nations–World Bank Flagship Study, *Pathways for Peace: Inclusive Approaches to Preventing Violent Conflict,* World Bank, Washington, DC.

Bob-Milliar, G. 2017. "Sustaining Peace: Making Development Work for the Prevention of Violent Conflicts: Ghana and Côte d'Ivoire Compared." Case study for the United Nations–World Bank Flagship Study, *Pathways for Peace: Inclusive Approaches to Preventing Violent Conflict,* World Bank, Washington, DC.

Brahm, E. 2003. "Hurting Stalemate Stage." In *Beyond Intractability*, edited by G. Burgess and H. Burgess. Boulder, CO: Conflict Information Consortium, University of Colorado.

Brennan, J. 2017. "ESSA: Mapping Opportunities for Civic Education. Education Trends." Education Commission of the States, Denver, CO.

Brzoska, M. 2006. "Introduction: Criteria for Evaluating Post-Conflict Reconstruction and Security Sector Reform in Peace Support Operations." *International Peacekeeping* 13 (1): 1–13.

Call, C. 2012. *Why Peace Fails: The Causes and Prevention of Civil War Recurrence.* Washington, DC: Georgetown University Press.

Carey, K., and W. Harake. 2017. "Macroeconomic Environment and Policies." Background paper for the United Nations–World Bank Flagship Study, *Pathways for Peace: Inclusive Approaches to Preventing Violent Conflict,* World Bank, Washington, DC.

Chataway, C. 1998. "Track II Diplomacy: From a Track I Perspective." *Negotiation Journal* 14 (3): 269–87.

Chevron Corporation. 2014. "Chevron Increases Support for Niger Delta Partnership Initiative." Press Release, June.

Chinigò, D. 2016. "Rural Radicalism and the Historical Land Conflict in the Malawian Tea Economy." *Journal of Southern African Studies* 42 (2): 283–97.

Clements, B., D. Coady, S. Fabrizio, S. Gupta, T. Alleyne, and C. Sdralevich. 2013. *Energy Subsidy Reform: Lessons and Implications.*

Washington, DC: International Monetary Fund, September.

Colletta, N., and B. Oppenheim. 2017. "Subnational Conflict: Dimensions, Trends, and Options for Prevention." Background paper for the United Nations–World Bank Flagship Study, *Pathways for Peace: Inclusive Approaches to Preventing Violent Conflict,* World Bank, Washington, DC.

Dahl, M., S. Gates, and H. M. Nygård. 2017. "Securing the Peace." Background paper for the United Nations–World Bank Flagship Study, *Pathways for Peace: Inclusive Approaches to Preventing Violent Conflict,* World Bank, Washington, DC.

Daly, E., and J. Sarkin. 2007. *Reconciliation in Divided Societies: Finding Common Ground.* Philadelphia, PA: University of Pennsylvania Press.

Day, A., and A. Pichler Fong. 2017. "Diplomacy and Good Offices in the Prevention of Conflict." Background paper for the United Nations–World Bank Flagship Study, *Pathways for Peace: Inclusive Approaches to Preventing Violent Conflict,* World Bank, Washington, DC.

DCAF (Geneva Centre for the Democratic Control of Armed Forces). 2017. "The Contribution and Role of SSR in the Prevention of Violent Conflict." Background paper for the United Nations–World Bank Flagship Study, *Pathways for Peace: Inclusive Approaches to Preventing Violent Conflict,* World Bank, Washington, DC.

Deb, A., S. Donohue, and T. Glaisyer. 2017. "Is Social Media a Threat to Democracy?" Omidyar Group.

De Greiff, P., ed. 2008. *The Handbook of Reparations.* Oxford: Oxford University Press.

Dewhurst, S., and L. Greising. 2017. *The Gradual Emergence of Second Generation Security Sector Reform in Timor-Leste.* CSG Paper 16, Centre for Security Governance, Kitchener, Canada.

Douglas, S. 2014. "This Hut Is Working for Me: Liberian Women and Girls Make Peace in Their Communities." *International Feminist Journal of Politics* 16 (1): 148–55.

EU (European Union) and UNDP (United Nations Development Programme). 2014. "Supporting Insider Mediation: Strengthening Resilience to Conflict and Turbulence." UNDP, New York.

Eze, C. 2013. "Nigeria: New Revenue Formula—Niger Delta Demands 50 Percent Derivation." *Daily Trust*, October 11.

Fall, A. 2017. "Cost-Saving of Women-Led Conflict Prevention Mechanisms in Liberia." Background paper for the United Nations–World Bank Flagship Study, *Pathways for Peace: Inclusive Approaches to Preventing Violent Conflict,* World Bank, Washington, DC.

Ganson, B. 2017. "Business in the Transition to Democracy in South Africa: Historical and Contemporary Perspectives." Peace Research Institute Oslo, CDA Collaborative, and Africa Centre for Dispute Settlement.

Ganson, B., and A. Wennmann. 2012. "Confronting Risk, Mobilizing Action: A Framework for Conflict Prevention in the Context of Large-Scale Business Investments." Friedrich-Stiftung, Bonn.

Giessmann, H. J. 2016. *Embedded Peace. Infrastructures for Peace: Approaches and Lessons Learned.* New York: UNDP, SADC, and Berghof Foundation.

Giessmann, H.-J., J. Galvanek, and C. Seifert. 2017. "Curbing Violence. Development, Application, and the Sustaining National Capacities for Prevention." Background paper for the United Nations–World Bank Flagship Study, *Pathways for Peace: Inclusive Approaches to Preventing Violent Conflict,* World Bank, Washington, DC.

Gifford, A., A. DeVries, A. Knott, and H. Mant. 2016. *Pioneering New Operating Models and Measurement Techniques for Private Sector-Led Development: Assessing Impact in Nigeria's Niger Delta.* Washington, DC: Initiative for Global Development.

Goldstein, J., and J. Rotich. 2008. *Digitally Networked Technology in Kenya's 2007–2008 Post-Election Crisis.* Cambridge, MA: Berkman Klein Center for Internet and Society.

Greene, M., J. Friedman, and R. Bennett. 2012. "Rebuilding the Police in Kosovo: Case Studies." *Foreign Policy*, July 18.

Groenewald, H., and M. von Tangen. 2002. "Towards a Better Practice Framework in Security Sector Reform: Broadening the Debate." Occasional SSR Paper 1, Clingendael, International Alert, and Saferworld, The Hague.

Gu, L., V. Kropotov, and F. Yarochkin. 2017. "The Fake News Machine: How Propagandists Abuse the Internet and Manipulate the

Public." TrendLabs Research Paper, Trend Micro, Tokyo.

Guichaoua, Y., and M. Pellerin. 2017. "Faire la paix et construire l'etat: Les relations entre pouvoir central et périphéries sahéliennes au Niger et au Mali." Study 51, Institute de Recherche Stratégique de l'Ecole Militaire (IRSEM), Paris. http://www.defense.gouv.fr /content/download/509288/8603319/file /Etude_IRSEM_n51_2017.pdf.

Hanlon, Q. 2012. *Security Sector Reform in Tunisia.* Special Report. Washington, DC: United States Institute for Peace.

Heinemann-Grüder, A., and I. Grebenschikov. 2006. "Security Governance by Internationals: The Case of Kosovo." *International Peacekeeping* 13 (1): 43–59.

Hope, K. R. 2014. "Kenya's Corruption Problem: Causes and Consequences." *Commonwealth and Comparative Politics* 52 (4): 493–512.

Hopp-Nishanka, U. 2012. *Giving Peace an Address? Reflections on the Potential and Challenges of Creating Peace Infrastructures.* Berlin: Berghof Foundation.

Hounkpe, M., and O. Bucyana. 2014. "Electoral Management." Administration and Cost of Elections Project, IDEA, IFES, and UNDESA, New York.

ICG (International Crisis Group). 2013. "Niger: Another Weak Link in the Sahel?" Africa Report 208, ICG, Brussels.

———. 2017. "Niger and Boko Haram: Beyond Counter-Insurgency." Africa Report 245, ICG, Brussels, February 27.

ICTJ (International Center for Transitional Justice). 2016. "Revolutionary Truth: Tunisian Victims Make History on First Night of Public Hearings for TDC." ICTJ, New York.

Inchauste, G., and D. G. Victor. 2017. *The Political Economy of Energy Subsidy Reform.* Directions in Development— Public Sector Governance. Washington, DC: World Bank.

International Alert. 2005. *Conflict-Sensitive Business Practice: Guidance for Extractive Industries.* London: International Alert.

———. 2006. "Local Business, Local Peace: The Peacebuilding Potential of the Domestic Private Sector." International Alert, London.

Jaffrey, S. 2017. "Sustaining Peace: Making Development Work for the Prevention of Violent Conflicts. Case Study: Indonesia." Case study for the United Nations–World Bank Flagship Study, *Pathways for Peace: Inclusive Approaches to Preventing Violent Conflict,* World Bank, Washington, DC.

Kanyinga, K. 2005. "Speaking to the Past and the Present: The Land Question in the Draft Constitution of Kenya." In *The Anatomy of Bomas: Selected Analysis of the 2004 Draft Constitution of Kenya,* edited by K. Kindiki and O. Ambani. Nairobi: Claripress Ltd.

Karatnycky, A., and P. Ackerman. 2005. *How Freedom is Won: From Civic Resistance to Durable Democracy. A research study by Freedom House.*

Kasinof, L. 2012. "Yemen Legislators Approve Immunity for the President. Middle East." *New York Times,* January 22.

King, E., and C. Samii. 2014. "Fast Track Institution Building in Conflict Affected Countries? Insights from Recent Field Experiments." *World Development* 64 (December): 740–54.

Lanz, D. 2011. "Who Gets a Seat at the Table? A Framework for Understanding the Dynamics of Inclusion and Exclusion in Peace Negotiations." *International Negotiation* 16 (2): 275–95.

Lederach, J. P. 1997. *Building Peace.* Washington, DC: United States Institute for Peace Press.

Lindenmayer, E., and J. Kaye. 2009. *A Choice for Peace? The Story of Forty-One Days of Mediation in Kenya.* New York: International Peace Institute.

Logvinenko, I. 2017. "Conflict and Violence in Kyrgyzstan." Case study for the United Nations–World Bank Flagship Study, *Pathways for Peace: Inclusive Approaches to Preventing Violent Conflict,* World Bank, Washington, DC.

Lombard, L. 2017. "Case Study: The Central African Republic." Case study for the United Nations–World Bank Flagship Study, *Pathways for Peace: Inclusive Approaches to Preventing Violent Conflict,* World Bank, Washington, DC.

Machira, S. 2009. "Pilot Testing a Land Redistribution Program in Malawi." In *Agricultural Land Redistribution: Toward Greater Consensus,* edited by H. P. Binswanger-Mkhize, C. Bourguignon, and R. van den Brink, 367–95. Washington, DC: World Bank.

Marc, A., N. Verjee, and S. Mogaka. 2015. *The Challenge of Stability and Security in West Africa.* Africa Development Forum series. Washington, DC: World Bank; Paris: Agence Française de Développement.

Marc, A., A. Willman, G. Aslam, M. Rebosio, and K. Balasuriya. 2012. *Societal Dynamics and Fragility: Engaging Societies in Responding to Fragile Situations.* New Frontiers of Social Policy. Washington, DC: World Bank.

Mashal, N. 2015. "Afghan Jobs Program Aims to Stem Exodus of Young." *New York Times,* November 18.

Materu, S. F. 2015. *The Post-Election Violence in Kenya: Domestic and International Legal Responses.* London: Springer.

Miklian, J. 2016. "How Businesses Can Be Effective Local Peacebuilders: Evidence from Colombia." PRIO Policy Brief, Peace Research Institute Oslo.

Mirahmadi, H., M. Farooq, and W. Ziad. 2012. *Pakistan's Civil Society: Alternative Channels to Countering Violent Extremism.* WORDE Report. Washington, DC: World Organization for Resource Development and Education.

Mitchell, D., I. Summerville, and O. Hargie. 2016. "Sport for Peace in Northern Ireland? Civil Society, Change, and Constraint after the 1998 Good Friday Agreement." *British Journal of Politics and International Relations* 18 (4): 981–96.

Mogaka, S. 2017. "Kenya Case Study." Case study for the United Nations–World Bank Flagship Study, *Pathways for Peace: Inclusive Approaches to Preventing Violent Conflict,* World Bank, Washington, DC.

MSR (Multi-Stakeholder Review of Post-Conflict Programming in Aceh). 2009. *Identifying the Foundations for Sustainable Peace and Development in Aceh.* Washington, DC: World Bank, December.

Naseem, M. A., A. Arshad-Ayaz, and S. Doyle. 2017. "Social Media as Space for Peace Education: Conceptual Contours and Evidence from the Muslim World." *Research in Comparative and International Education* 12 (1): 95–109.

Nilsson, D. 2012. "Anchoring the Peace: Civil Society Actors in Peace Accords and Durable Peace." *International Interactions* 38 (2): 258.

Norwegiean Nobel Committee. 2015. "The Nobel Peace Prize for 2015." Press Release.

Nyathi, N., and K. Rajuili. 2017. "South Africa and Kenya's Legislative Measures to Prevent Hate Speech." Conflict Trends 2017/2, ACCORD, Mt. Edgecomb, South Africa, July 12.

Nygård, H. M., K. Baghat, G. Barrett, K. Dupuy, S. Gates, S. Hillesund, S. A. Rustad, H. Strand, H. K. Urdal, and G. Østby. 2017. "Inequality and Armed Conflict: Evidence and Data." Background paper for the United Nations–World Bank Flagship Study, *Pathways for Peace: Inclusive Approaches to Preventing Violent Conflict,* World Bank, Washington, DC.

Observatorio de Tierras. 2017. "Killings of Peasant Leaders Involved in Land Restitution Efforts." Observatorio de Tierras, June.

Odendaal, A. 2010. *An Architecture for Building Peace at the Local Level: A Comparative Study of the Use of Local Peace Forums.* New York: UNDP.

———. 2013. "The Political Legitimacy of National Peace Committees." *Journal of Peacebuilding and Development* 7 (3): 40–53.

OECD (Organisation for Economic Co-operation and Development). 2011. "Fossil-Fuel Support." OECD Secretariat background report for G-20 meeting of finance ministers, Paris.

———. 2012. "An OECD-Wide Inventory of Support to Fossil-Fuel Production or Use." OECD, Paris.

O'Reilly, M., A. Ó Súilleabháin, and T. Paffenholz. 2015. *Reimagining Peacemaking: Women's Roles in Peace Processes.* New York: International Peace Institute.

OSAGI (Office of the Special Adviser to the Secretary-General on Gender Issues and Advancement of Women). 2000. "Landmark Resolution on Women, Peace, and Security. Office of the Special Adviser on Gender Issues and Advancement of Women." OSAGI, UN, New York.

Owuor, V., and S. Wisor. 2014. *The Role of Kenya's Private Sector in Peacebuilding: The Case of the 2013 Election Cycle.* Broomfield, CO: One Earth Future Foundation.

Paffenholz, T., A. Hirblinger, D. Landau, F. Fritsch, and C. Dijkstra. 2017. "Preventing Violence through Inclusion: From Building Political Momentum to Sustaining Peace." Background paper for the United Nations–World Bank Flagship Study, *Pathways for Peace: Inclusive Approaches to Preventing Violent Conflict,* World Bank, Washington, DC.

Payne, L., A. Reiter, C. Mahony, and L. Bernal-Bermudez. 2017. "Conflict Prevention and Guarantees of Non-Recurrence." Background paper for the United Nations–World Bank Flagship Study, *Pathways for Peace: Inclusive Approaches to Preventing Violent Conflict,* World Bank, Washington, DC.

Pérouse de Montclos, M.-A. 2017. "The Republic of Niger: A Test-Case, with Reference to the Republic of Mali." Case study for the United Nations–World Bank Flagship Study, *Pathways for Peace: Inclusive Approaches to Preventing Violent Conflict,* World Bank, Washington, DC.

Peschka, M. 2011. "The Role of the Private Sector in Fragile and Conflict-Affected States." Background paper for *World Development Report 2011: Conflict, Security, and Development,* World Bank, Washington, DC.

Pichler Fong, A. 2017. "Burkina Faso: Popular Uprising and Political Transition (2014–2015)." Case study for the United Nations–World Bank Flagship Study, *Pathways for Peace: Inclusive Approaches to Preventing Violent Conflict,* World Bank, Washington, DC.

Ranstorp, M. 2009. "Preventing Violent Radicalization and Terrorism: The Case of Indonesia." Center for Asymmetric Risk Studies, Swedish National Defense College, Stockholm.

Renner, M., and Z. Chafe. 2006. "Turning Disasters into Peacemaking Opportunities." In *State of the World 2006,* edited by Worldwatch Institute. New York: W. W. Norton.

Samii, C. 2013. "Perils or Promise of Ethnic Integration? Evidence from a Hard Case in Burundi." *American Political Science Review* 107 (3): 558–73. doi: 10.1017/S0003055413000282.

Sargsyan, I. L. 2017. "Narrative, Perception and Emotion: A Review of Recent Political Science Studies." Background paper for the United Nations–World Bank Flagship Study, *Pathways for Peace: Inclusive Approaches to Preventing Violent Conflict,* World Bank, Washington, DC.

Saunders, H. H. 1999. *A Public Peace Process: Sustained Dialogue to Transform Racial and Ethnic Conflicts.* New York: St. Martin's Press.

Sisk, T. D. 2017. "Preventing Deadly Conflict in Ethnically Fractured Societies: An Overview and Analysis of International Development Assistance for 'Bridging' Social Cohesion." Background paper for the United Nations–World Bank Flagship Study, *Pathways for Peace: Inclusive Approaches to Preventing Violent Conflict,* World Bank, Washington, DC.

Sombatpoonsiri, J. 2015. *Humor and Nonviolent Struggle in Serbia.* Syracuse, NY: Syracuse University Press.

Somerville, K. 2011. "Violence, Hate Speech, and Inflammatory Broadcasting in Kenya: The Problems of Definition and Identification." *Ecquid Novi: African Journalism Studies* 32 (1): 82–101.

Stackpool-Moore, L., and M. Bacalja Perianes. 2017. "Malawi Case Study: Demonstrations July 2011." Case study for the United Nations–World Bank Flagship Study, *Pathways for Peace: Inclusive Approaches to Preventing Violent Conflict,* World Bank, Washington, DC.

Standing, A., and G. Hilson. 2013. *Distributing Mining Wealth to Communities in Ghana: Addressing Problems of Elite Capture and Political Corruption.* Bergen, Norway: Anti-Corruption Resource Centre.

Stephan, M., and E. Chenoweth. 2011. *Why Civil Resistance Works: The Strategic Logic of Nonviolent Conflict.* New York: Columbia University Press.

Steven, D., and G. Sucuoglu. 2017. "What Works in Conflict Prevention? Development-Security-Diplomacy Collaboration towards Better Results." Background paper for the United Nations–World Bank Flagship Study, *Pathways for Peace: Inclusive Approaches to Preventing Violent Conflict,* World Bank, Washington, DC.

Stodiek, T. 2006. "The OSCE and the Creation of Multi-Ethnic Police Forces in the Balkans." Core Working Paper 14, Centre for OSCE Research, Institute for Peace Research and Security Policy, University of Hamburg.

Tietaah, G. 2014. *Watching the Watchdog: Spotlighting Indecent Election Campaign Language on Radio.* Accra: Media Foundation for West Africa.

TJRC (Transitional Justice and Reconciliation Committee). 2016. *Report of the Transitional Justice and Reconciliation Committee.* Makati City, Kenya: TJRC.

Toska, S. 2012. "Building a Yemeni State While Losing a Nation: The Middle East Channel." *Foreign Policy,* October 29.

———. 2017. "Sustaining Peace: Making Development Work for the Prevention of Violent Conflicts Cases: Egypt, Tunisia, Morocco, and Jordan." Case study for the United Nations–World Bank Flagship Study, *Pathways for Peace: Inclusive Approaches to Preventing Violent Conflict,* World Bank, Washington, DC.

Turok, I. 2014. "Medellin's 'Social Urbanism' a Model for City Transformation." *Mail and Guardian,* May 16.

UNDP (United Nations Development Programme). 2016. *Citizen Engagement in Public Service Delivery: The Critical Role of Public Officials.* New York: UNDP.

———. 2017. *Journey to Extremism in Africa.* New York: UNDP.

UNESCO (United Nations Educational and Scientific Organization). 2008. "UNESCO's Work on Education for Peace and Non-Violence: Building Peace through Education." UNESCO, Paris.

UNHRC (United Nations Human Rights Council). 2016. "Report of the Special Rapporteur on the Promotion of Truth, Justice, Reparation, and Guarantees of Nonrecurrence, Pablo de Greiff." Report A/HRC/30/42, UNHRC, Geneva, September 7.

UN Security Council. 2000. "Women, Peace, and Security." Resolution S/RES/1325, adopted October 31, New York.

Vagliasindi, M. 2012. *Implementing Energy Subsidy Reform: Evidence from Developing Countries.* Directions in Development—Energy and Mining. Washington, DC: World Bank.

van Tongeren, P. 2001. "Infrastructures for Peace." In *Peacemaking: From Practice to Theory*, edited by S. A. Nan, Z. C. Mampilly and A. Bartoli. New York: Praeger.

———. 2013. "Potential Cornerstone of Infrastructures for Peace? How Local Peace Committees Can Make a Difference." *Journal of Peacebuilding* 1 (1): 39–60.

Varshney, A. 2002. *Ethnic Conflict and Civic Life: Hindus and Muslims in India.* New Haven, CT: Yale University Press.

Verjee, A. 2017. "Sustaining Peace: Making Development Work for the Prevention of Violent Conflicts South Sudan Case Study." Case study for the United Nations–World Bank Flagship Study, *Pathways for Peace: Inclusive Approaches to Preventing Violent Conflict,* World Bank, Washington, DC.

von Einsiedel, S., and C. Salih. 2017. "Conflict Prevention in Nepal." Case study for the United Nations–World Bank Flagship Study, *Pathways for Peace: Inclusive Approaches to Preventing Violent Conflict,* World Bank, Washington, DC.

Wachira, G., T. Arendshorst, and S. M. Charles. 2010. "Citizens in Action: Making Peace in the Post-Election Crisis in Kenya—2008." Nairobi Peace Group, Nairobi.

Wainscott, A. M. 2017. *Bureaucratizing Islam: Morocco and the War on Terror.* Cambridge, MA: Cambridge University Press.

Walsh, M. 2017. "Prevention of Conflict, Northern Ireland." Case study for the United Nations–World Bank Flagship Study, *Pathways for Peace: Inclusive Approaches to Preventing Violent Conflict,* World Bank, Washington, DC.

Wanis-St. John, A., and D. Kew. 2008. "Civil Society and Peace Negotiations: Confronting Exclusion." *International Negotiation* 13 (2008): 11–36.

Wennmann, A. 2017. "Assessing the Role of the Private Sector in Preventing Violent Conflict." Background paper for the United Nations–World Bank Flagship Study, *Pathways for Peace: Inclusive Approaches to Preventing Violent Conflict,* World Bank, Washington, DC.

World Bank. 2006. *World Development Report 2006: Equity and Development.* Washington, DC: World Bank.

———. 2011. *World Development Report 2011: Conflict, Security, and Development.* Washington, DC: World Bank.

———. 2015a. "Colombia Protects Land and Patrimony of Internally Displaced Persons." World Bank, Washington, DC, August 13.

———. 2015b. "Tunisia Risk and Resilience Assessment. Fragility, Conflict, and Violence Cross-Cutting Solutions Area." World Bank, Washington, DC.

———. 2016a. "An Integrated Framework for Jobs in Fragile and Conflict Situations." World Bank, Washington, DC.

———. 2016b. "Niger Risk and Resilience Assessment: Fragility, Conflict, and Violence Cross-Cutting Solutions Area." World Bank, Washington, DC.

———. 2016c. *Supporting Transformational Change for Poverty Reduction and Shared Prosperity Lessons from World Bank Group Experience.* Washington, DC: Independent Evaluation Group, World Bank.

———. 2016d. "World Bank Supports Colombia's Land Organisation and Regional Finance Efforts." World Bank, Washington, DC, December 12.

———. 2017a. *Mapping Conflict and Violence in Kenya.* Washington, DC: World Bank.

———. 2017b. *World Development Report 2017: Governance and the Law*. Washington, DC: World Bank.

Yemak, R., F. Gan, and D. Cheng. 2013. *Celebrating Ten Years of the National Solidarity Program (NSP): A Glimpse of the Rural Development Story in Afghanistan*. Washington, DC: World Bank.

Zartman, W. 2001. "The Timing of Peace Initiatives: Hurting Stalemates and Ripe Moments." *Global Review of Ethnopolitics* 1 (1): 8–18.

———. 2015. *Preventing Deadly Conflict Polity*. Hoboken, NJ. John Wiley and Sons.

Zunes, S., M. Hardy, and M. J. Stephan. 2010. "Nonviolent Struggle." In *International Studies Encyclopedia*, edited by R. A. Denmark. Oxford: Blackwell Publishing

Additional Reading

Anderlini, S. N. 2007. *Women Building Peace: What They Do; Why It Matters*. Boulder, CO: Lynne Rienner.

Baliqi, B. 2012. "Security Sector Reform in Kosovo: From Institutional Transitions to the Democratic Consolidation." *Iliria International Review* 2: 24–31.

Ballentine, K., and V. Haufler. 2009. *Enabling Economies of Peace*. New York: United Nations.

Banfield, J., A. Barbolet, R. Goldwyn, and N. Killick. 2005. "Conflict-Sensitive Business Practice: Guidance for Extractive Industries." International Alert, London.

Barnes, C. 2009. "Civil Society and Peacebuilding: Mapping Functions in Working for Peace." *International Spectator: Italian Journal of International Affairs* 44 (1): 131–47.

Batley, R., and C. McCoughlin. 2015. "The Politics of Public Services: A Service Characteristics Approach." *World Development* 74 (October): 275–85.

Binswanger-Mkhize, H. P., J. P. de Regt, and S. Spector. 2010. *Local and Community Driven Development: Moving to Scale in Theory and Practice*. New Frontiers of Social Policy. Washington, DC: World Bank.

Blattman, C., and L. Ralston. 2015. "Generating Employment in Poor and Fragile States: Evidence from Labor Market and Entrepreneurship Programs." World Bank, Washington, DC.

Boix, C., and D. Posner. 1996. "Making Social Capital Work: A Review of Robert Putnam's 'Making Democracy Work: Civic Traditions in Modern Italy.'" Harvard University, Cambridge, MA.

Collier, P., V. L. Elliott, H. Hegre, A. Hoeffler, M. Reynal-Querol, and N. Sambanis. 2003. *Breaking the Conflict Trap: Civil War and Development Policy*. Policy Research Report. Washington, DC: World Bank; Oxford: Oxford University Press.

Crespo-Sancho, C. 2017. "Conflict Prevention and Gender." Background paper for the United Nations–World Bank Flagship Study, *Pathways for Peace: Inclusive Approaches to Preventing Violent Conflict*, World Bank, Washington, DC.

Djordje, D. 2017. "Arendt on Prevention and Guarantees of Non-Recurrence." In *Philosophical Foundations of International Criminal Law*. Torkel Opsahl Academic EPublisher.

Dolan, C., and F. Cleaver. 2003. "Collapsing Masculinities and Weak States—A Case Study of Northern Uganda." In *Masculinities Matter! Men, Gender, and Development*, edited by F. Cleaver, 57–83. London: Zed Books.

Erk, J., and L. Anderson. 2009. "The Paradox of Federalism: Does Self-Rule Accommodate or Exacerbate Ethnic Divisions?" *Regional and Federal Studies* 19 (2): 191–202.

Fiedler, C. 2017. "The Effects of Specific Elements of Democracy on Peace." Background study, University of Essex and German Development Institute.

Fiedler, C., and K. Mross. 2017. "Post-Conflict Societies: Chances for Peace and Types of International Support." Briefing Paper 4/2017, German Development Institute/ Deutsches Institut für Entwicklungspolitik (DIE), Bonn.

Gettleman, J. 2008. "Death Toll in Kenya Exceeds 1,000, but Talks Reach Crucial Phase." *New York Times*, February 6.

Glover, T. D., K. J. Shinew, and D. C. Parry. 2005. "Association, Sociability, and Civic Culture: The Democratic Effect of Community Gardening." *Leisure Sciences* 27 (1): 75–92.

Hearn, S. 2017a. "CICIG in Guatemala." Case study for the the United Nations–World Bank Flagship Study, *Pathways for Peace: Inclusive Approaches to Preventing Violent Conflict*, World Bank, Washington, DC.

———. 2017b. "Inclusive Development for Conflict Prevention: The Case of Burundi." Case study for the United Nations–World Bank Flagship Study, *Pathways for Peace: Inclusive Approaches to Preventing Violent Conflict,* World Bank, Washington, DC.

———. 2017c. "Preventing the Recurrence of Conflict in Sierra Leone: How Did the UN Mission Succeed?" Case study for the United Nations–World Bank Flagship Study, *Pathways for Peace: Inclusive Approaches to Preventing Violent Conflict,* World Bank, Washington, DC.

Hegre, H., and H. M. Nygård. 2015. "Governance and Conflict Relapse." *Journal of Conflict Resolution* 59 (6): 984–1016.

ISDC (International Security and Development Committee). 2016. *Jobs Aid Peace.* Berlin: ISDC.

Kenya Red Cross Society. 2008. *Annual Report.* Nairobi: Kenya Red Cross Society.

Langer, A., A. R. Mustapha, and F. Stewart. 2007. "Horizontal Inequalities in Nigeria, Ghana and Côte d'Ivoire: Issues and Policies." CRISE Working Paper 45, Centre for Research on Inequality, Human Security and Ethnicity, Oxford University, Oxford.

Mcloughlin, C. 2015. "When Does Service Delivery Improve the Legitimacy of a Fragile or Conflict-Affected State?" *Governance: An International Journal of Policy, Administration, and Institutions* 28 (3): 341–56.

Paffenholz, T. 2014. "Civil Society and Peace Negotiations: Beyond the Inclusion–Exclusion Dichotomy." *Negotiation Journal* 30 (1): 69–91.

Parks, T., and W. Cole. 2010. *Political Settlements: Implications for International Development Policy and Practice.* Occasional Paper 2. San Francisco: Asia Foundation.

Parks, T., N. Colletta, and B. Oppenheim. 2013. *The Contested Corners of Asia: Subnational Conflict and International Development Assistance.* San Francisco: Asia Foundation.

Rakotomalala, O. 2017. "Local Level Mechanisms for Violent Conflict Prevention Literature Review." Background paper for the United Nations–World Bank Flagship Study, *Pathways for Peace: Inclusive Approaches to Preventing Violent Conflict,* World Bank, Washington, DC.

Sany, J. 2010. *Education and Conflict in Côte d'Ivoire.* Special Report 235. Washington, DC: United States Institute of Peace.

Stone, L. 2015. "Study of 156 Peace Agreements, Controlling for Other Variables, Quantitative Analysis of Women's Participation in Peace Processes." In *Reimagining Peacemaking: Women's Roles in Peace Processes,* by M. O'Reilly, A. Ó Súilleabháin, and T. Paffenholz, annex I. New York: International Peace Institute.

UNDP (United Nations Development Programme). 2015. *Joint UNDP-PDA Programme on Building National Capacities for Conflict Prevention.* New York: UNDP.

Wallensteen, P., and I. Svensson. 2014. "Talking Peace: International Mediation in Armed Conflicts." *Journal of Peace Research* 51 (2): 315–27.

Wilson, W. 1918. "President Wilson's Message to Congress, January 8, 1918." Records of the United States Senate, Record Group 46, National Archives, Washington, DC.

Yamagishi, T., and Yamagishi, M. 1994. "Trust and Commitment in the United States and Japan." *Motivation and Emotion* 18 (2): 129–66.

Zahra, S. A., E. Gedajlovic, D. O. Neubaum, and J. M. Shulman. "A Typology of Social Entrepreneurs: Motives, Search Processes, and Ethical Challenges." *Journal of Business Venturing* 24 (5): 519–32.

CHAPTER 7

The International Architecture for Prevention

Primary responsibility for mitigating shocks and reducing risks rests with states and national authorities. However, international and regional engagement has proven pivotal in supporting national pathways for peace. Most of this support has been bilateral, but where national interests align, the international community has come together around an international architecture to prevent violence and sustain peace.

Following World War II, the foundations for this architecture were put in place, rooted in the United Nations (UN) Charter and customary international law. The primary purpose of this architecture is to "maintain international peace and security, and to that end: to take effective collective measures for the prevention and removal of threats to the peace."[1] Over the last 70 years, this architecture has, arguably, succeeded at its primary aim by providing a framework for continuous consultation that has significantly reduced the risk of conflict between the great powers. This success has been achieved in large part by having provided a forum in which the major military powers of our era "debate international problems and seek constructive solutions" (von Einsiedel, Malone, and Ugarte 2015, 828).

Primarily focused on reducing the risks of interstate conflict, over the past 30 years, this system, with the support of member states, developed what scholars have recently identified as a "standard treatment" for intrastate conflict: the mediation of

political settlements, investment in peacekeeping operations to implement agreements reached, and a focus on prevention of abuses (Gowan and Stedman 2018). Despite criticism, this treatment has "achieved stability and security at relatively low cost" in many countries (Eikenberry and Krasner 2017, 9).

Today the international architecture deploys multilateral tools ranging from regional political offices to complex, multidimensional peace operations working across development, diplomatic, and security pillars. In an interconnected world, these efforts are increasingly based on cooperation between international and regional organizations and engage states in efforts to address international, regional, and subnational levels of conflict. However, despite these evolutions, changes in the nature of violent conflicts mentioned in chapter 1 and international affairs in chapter 2, this architecture is struggling to identify collective remedies to increasingly complex situations on the ground.

This chapter analyzes the international and regional architecture for prevention, as well as the tools developed to prevent violent conflict, in light of current challenges. In particular, with conflicts becoming increasingly protracted and transnational, as seen in chapters 1 and 2, and with strong correlations between intergroup grievances and violence, as seen in chapters 4 and 5, this chapter reexamines the relevance of the existing architecture and tools and provides examples of how they might further adapt to confront current challenges. In particular, the chapter highlights the potential benefits of engaging earlier, more comprehensively, and in a more sustained manner to address risks of violence.

As chapter 3 notes, the state is the central actor influencing a society's pathway and the point of reference for preventive action.[2] National governments have the authority and capacity to establish or reform institutions, allocate the resources necessary to tackle structural causes of violence, and address the processes by which the risks of violence manifest. Internationally, governments influence country pathways through direct bilateral relations and aid, including security assistance (box 7.1), and through international legal frameworks and multilateral institutions.

BOX 7.1 International Engagement through Military and Police Assistance

The most widespread form of international engagement in peace and security assistance across states occurs through the bilateral financing, equipping, and training of national military, police, and intelligence services by allies. The nature of such assistance can have a profound influence on the risks faced by a society and, more important, how national actors seek to manage such risks. Donor countries have used bilateral military cooperation to help institutionalize security systems that protect recipient countries, professionalize the security sector, and forge stronger alliances based on mutual military dependence (Anderson and McKnight 2014; Fisher and Anderson 2015; Poe 1991; Wendt and Barnett 1993).

The level of foreign military assistance is not included in the official development assistance (ODA) figures.[a] This division reflects a firewall between military and development resources and institutions, which contributes to the fact that these two streams often are not coordinated. Indeed, they often are at odds in the material effects and signals about international priorities that they send to the population and to the elites of recipient countries. Harmonizing decisions about military and development cooperation can make them more credible. Because of sensitivities regarding the core state function of security and circumscribed authority, external actors have only slowly become comfortable with expanding development assistance to the security sector. Development assistance is subject to greater scrutiny and different standards than military assistance.

While often essential for international security, military assistance has produced mixed results in addressing internal security challenges. As noted in chapter 5, a focus on creating accountable and professional security sector institutions with civilian oversight can facilitate effective conflict prevention. Most bilateral financing for military and police, however, has gone to enhancing operational capacities rather than to transformative reforms conducive to preventing conflict and building peace (Bryden and Olonisakin 2010, 9; Donnelly 1997). In addition, bilateral military and police assistance at the country level is not always effectively coordinated, resulting in conflicting or competing interests; a mismatch of standards and approaches with respect to training, equipment, and reform processes; and deficits in national ownership.

a. After 13 consecutive years of increases (from 1998 to 2011), world military spending has plateaued, at an estimated US$1,686 billion in 2016, equivalent to 2.2 percent of global gross domestic product or US$227 per person (Tian et al. 2017). No military equipment or services are reportable as ODA. Antiterrorism activities are also excluded. However, the cost of using the donors' armed forces to deliver humanitarian aid is included. Similarly, most peacekeeping expenditures are excluded in line with the exclusion of military costs. However, some closely defined developmentally relevant activities within peacekeeping operations are included (Development Assistance Committee 2017).

Systemic Prevention

Beyond the more visible deployments and actions by multilateral institutions, state engagement in preventive action has included a focus on systemic prevention, defined by United Nations Secretary-General Kofi Annan as "measures to address global risks of conflict that transcend particular states" (UN General Assembly 2006a, 1). Systemic prevention addresses transnational risks that can contribute to violent conflict and be dealt with effectively only by global partnerships. It includes, for example, measures to deal with illicit economies, including trafficking and the use and trade of arms, all of which are also addressed in the Sustainable Development Goals (SDGs), and weapons of mass destruction; address war crimes and crimes against humanity; respond to health epidemics such as human immunodeficiency virus/ acquired immunodeficiency syndrome (HIV/AIDS) and Ebola; and create broad coalitions to address climate change.

Understood this way, prevention lies at the heart of the rules-based international order. The international system, including the United Nations, the Bretton Woods institutions, regional security arrangements, and even development as a practice, was built, in part, around the notion that the world needed consensual norms and rules to minimize the risk that conflict could escalate into violence (Schlesinger 2004). The United Nations system—in particular, the UN Security Council—and specialized agencies like the International Atomic Energy Agency have played a significant role in facilitating intergovernmental treaties, enabling multilateral action, and fostering transnational advocacy networks. Together, this global infrastructure transmits and promotes norms against violence (Keck and Sikkink 1999; Risse, Ropp, and Sikkink 1999). This system, designed primarily to regulate interstate conflict (box 7.2), has evolved significantly to address broader risks associated with violent conflict (box 7.3).

BOX 7.2 Public International Law and Armed Conflict

International law establishes the obligations of signatory states and provides the most powerful framework for the conduct of states and organized armed groups in armed conflict.

Public international law. The following branches of public international law are directly relevant to situations of armed conflict.

International humanitarian law derives from customary international law, the four Geneva Conventions, three additional protocols, and other international treaties (ICRC n.d.). It regulates the conduct of states and organized nonstate armed groups that are party to an armed conflict. International humanitarian law applies during armed conflict to protect persons who are not or no longer participating in hostilities and restricts the means and methods of war between fighting parties.

International human rights law derives principally from the Universal Declaration of Human Rights (UN General Assembly 1948) and nine core UN human rights treaties as well as regional human rights instruments such as the African Charter on Human and Peoples' Rights. International human rights law recognizes fundamental rights for individuals and groups, which states must respect, protect, and fulfill. It applies during peacetime and during armed conflict.

International criminal law prohibits certain acts considered to be the most serious crimes (such as war crimes, crimes against humanity, the crime of aggression, and genocide) and regulates the investigation, prosecution, and punishment of individual perpetrators. The Rome Statute (UN Secretary-General 1998) establishes the jurisdiction of the International Criminal Court for the

(Box continued next page)

investigation and prosecution of crimes under international criminal law.

Rules on interstate use of force. The UN Charter prohibits the threat or use of force against another state. One exception to this rule is the right of a state to use force in self-defense in case of an armed attack (UN Charter, Art. 51). Short of this exception, only the UN Security Council is entitled to authorize the use of force against

another state to maintain or restore international peace and security (UN Charter, Ch. VII).

Peremptory norms. International law contains certain rules that are accepted and recognized by states as allowing for no derogation. The prohibitions of aggression, torture, slavery, racial discrimination, genocide, and crimes against humanity are examples of peremptory norms.

Source: McInerney-Lankford 2017.

As the primary multilateral body responsible for maintaining international peace and security and the sole international body, in principle, able to authorize the use of force

outside of self-defense, the UN Security Council possesses a range of tools for preventing, managing, and responding to violent conflict. Chapter VI of the UN Charter

Although the international system was, and remains, largely premised on the concept of state sovereignty, countries are increasingly interdependent, and risks are not confined to national borders. New and complex challenges have arisen since the end of the Cold War that range from terrorism and violent extremism to cybersecurity, from climate change to massive forced displacement, and from global illicit activities to outbreaks of disease.

These trends have motivated a new and explicit emphasis within the UN on addressing not only new forms of conflict, but also all phases of conflict. Secretary-General Boutros Boutros-Ghali highlighted this focus on conflict prevention in the 1992 Agenda for Peace, which identifies as guiding concepts preventive diplomacy,[a] peacemaking, peacekeeping, and postconflict peacebuilding (UN Secretary-General 2001). Secretary-General Kofi Annan's 2001 report on the prevention of armed conflict also emphasizes the mutually reinforcing nature of conflict prevention and sustainable and equitable development.

It states that the primary responsibility for prevention lies with national governments supported by civil society and distinguishes between *operational* prevention focused on an impending crisis and *structural* prevention focused on keeping crises from arising in the first place (UN Secretary-General 2001). The 2006 progress report on armed conflict prevention expands on these concepts, introducing *systemic* prevention or measures that address global risks of conflict that "transcend particular states" (UN General Assembly 2006a).

In 2014, the Security Council passed its first resolution explicitly on conflict prevention (S/RES/2150) (UN Security Council 2014). This recalled that the "prevention of conflict remains a primary responsibility of States" and further recalled their "primary responsibility to protect civilians and to respect and ensure the human rights of all individuals within their territory and subject to their jurisdiction." This resolution conceived of the UN's tools as including special political missions (such as regional offices), peacekeeping operations, and the Peacebuilding Commission,

(Box continued next page)

as well as regional and subregional organizations and arrangements and acknowledged that serious abuses and violations of international human rights or humanitarian law, including sexual and gender-based violence, can be an early indication of descent into conflict or escalation of conflict.

Despite these multiple commitments, three major strategic reviews of the UN's peace and security functions in 2015 found that prevention remains "the poor relative of better resourced peace operations deployed during and after armed conflict."[b] Building on these 2015 reports, the General Assembly and Security Council sustaining peace resolutions articulated a conceptual vision and operational guidance for member states and the United Nations

system. Advancing beyond linear understandings of conflict prevention, the resolutions concluded that *sustaining peace* should be "broadly understood as a goal and a process to build a common vision of a society, ensuring that the needs of all segments of the population are taken into account, which encompasses activities aimed at preventing the outbreak, escalation, continuation, and recurrence of conflict" (UN General Assembly 2016a; UN Security Council 2016). The sustaining peace resolutions underlined the importance of additional, urgent support in contexts where the risk of crisis is heightened, and the need for tools to address root causes, especially in societies having difficulties working toward the SDGs.

Source: Call 2017.

a. Defined as an "action to prevent disputes from arising between parties, to prevent existing dispute/s from escalating into conflicts, and to limit the spread of the latter when they occur."

b. The report of the High-Level Independent Panel on Peace Operations (HIPPO) underscored the importance of preventing conflict, concluding that the prevention of armed conflict was "the greatest responsibility of the international community" and yet remained underprioritized and underresourced (UN 2015). At the same time, an Advisory Group of Experts that conducted a review of peacebuilding architecture, under a mandate from the General Assembly and the Security Council, concluded, "A broader, comprehensive approach of sustaining peace is called for, all along the arc leading from conflict prevention ... through peacemaking and peacekeeping, and on to postconflict recovery and reconstruction" (UN General Assembly 2016a). The 2015 report of the Secretary-General regarding the global study on the implementation of Security Council Resolution 1325 underlined the importance of bringing women's participation and leadership to the core of peace and security efforts, including responses to new and emerging threats (UN Secretary-General 2015; UN Security Council 2000).

provides a framework for the Security Council's engagement in the peaceful settlement of disputes brought to its attention, including through investigative and fact-finding activities. Chapter VI also provides the framework for the Security Council's own direct engagements in recommending actions to the parties of a conflict or in support of the efforts of the secretary-general (see, for example, UN Department of Political Affairs 2015b). Chapter VII of the UN Charter provides the framework within which the Security Council may take enforcement action. It allows the Security Council to "determine the existence of any threat to the peace, breach of the peace, or act of aggression" and to make recommendations or to resort to nonmilitary and military action to

"maintain or restore international peace and security" (UN Department of Political Affairs 2015b).[3]

Through these frameworks, the Security Council can take decisions at all stages of the conflict cycle and within a wide array of responses, ranging from simply calling for parties to resolve a dispute peacefully, to directing the terms or principles by which a conflict will be resolved, to authorizing enforcement measures to ensure the implementation of its decisions (von Einsiedel, Malone, and Ugarte 2015). Ultimately the effectiveness of these tools, as with all other facets of the Security Council's work, depends on the collective willingness of states to respond to threats to international peace and security (Wood 2013).

In practice, absent a major crisis to mobilize collective action, the Security Council has tended to "stand back" (von Einsiedel, Malone, and Ugarte 2015). Actions have tended toward crisis management and response, and, as noted by the UN Security Council (2017, 2), "Despite strong rhetorical support for prevention, … concrete, meaningful preventive action is too often lacking." Tasked increasingly with dealing with conflicts within rather than between states, Security Council mechanisms can encounter resistance to actions that could challenge or weaken sovereign rights and responsibilities, both of council members and of states on the council agenda (von Einsiedel, Malone, and Ugarte 2015). At the same time, the number and complexity of ongoing conflicts in which the Security Council is engaged distracts from less immediate but potentially preventable conflicts (UN Security Council 2017).

Beyond crisis management, UN member states are also working through the Security Council to establish global norms related to conflict situations through thematic debates and resolutions. This work covers a range of topics, including protection of civilians; children and armed conflict; justice, rule of law, and impunity; women, peace, and security; and sexual violence in conflict (Keating 2015). Increasingly, the Security Council is addressing nontraditional security threats, such as piracy, illicit trafficking, and organized crime and climate change (von Einsiedel, Malone, and Ugarte 2015).[4]

Globally, the General Assembly has broad authority to consider conflict prevention within the framework of the UN Charter. It has held special or emergency sessions on a wide range of prevention-related thematic and geographic issues. It has adopted declarations on peace, the peaceful settlement of disputes, and international cooperation, notably the landmark resolution on sustaining peace in 2016 (UN General Assembly 2016a). As the leading intergovernmental body specialized in policy and coordination on economic, social, and environmental issues, the Economic and Social Council is the central UN platform for reflection, debate, and innovative thinking on sustainable development.

Beyond the traditional chambers of the United Nations system, the multilateral system has expanded and evolved within a broader trend of proliferation of actors on the global scene. This brings greater diversity of both instruments and forums engaging in systemic prevention, but also contributes to a fragmentation of global governance (Biermann et al. 2009; Koskenniemi and Leino 2002). There are four times as many state actors today as in 1945 and a growing number and diversity of nonstate actors (Thakur 2011). In 1951, there were only 123 intergovernmental organizations.[5] By 2013, there were 7,710 (ICM 2017). The emergence of bodies such as the G-20 speaks to a desire for wider global steering groups, while the growth of regional instruments—for example, the European Partnership process—has expanded the range of institutional frameworks engaged in promoting prevention.

The UN 2030 Agenda for Sustainable Development encapsulates the increased interlinkages between efforts at systemic prevention. The SDGs call for integrated solutions extending across development, peace, environment, and humanitarian realms and recognize the critical importance of sustainability to development progress as well as the importance of investing in global (and regional) public goods (Framtid 2015; Jenks and Kharas 2016). The SDGs also include specific targets on human trafficking, illicit financial and arms flows, and organized crime. The SDGs confirm that building resilience through investment in inclusive and sustainable development—including addressing inequalities, strengthening institutions, and ensuring that development strategies are risk-informed—is the best means of prevention.

Regional Action

Amid a changing global order and the mutation of conflict away from conventionally fought interstate wars, regional organizations have become increasingly important actors in preventive action. Conceived as a first resort for challenges to security that transcend national territories (Verjee 2017), regional capacities are also seen as critical to reducing the risks of regional contagion and instability caused by the rise of nonstate actors and intrastate conflict, with a focus on Africa. With the emergence of armed groups with transnational goals, the concentration of conflicts in regions where neighboring countries have endogenous risk factors, and the increase in international interference (Walter 2017), regional responses, whether positive or negative, are likely to remain important.

Long recognized as key partners of global institutions,[6] regional and subregional organizations have evolved considerably since the end of the Cold War. Differences in size, membership structure, and strategic objectives notwithstanding, many such organizations have experienced an expansion of their mandates, legal frameworks, and organizational capacities to address a broad range of regional political, security, and economic issues.

In particular, and with the support of the Security Council, some regional and subregional organizations have acquired considerable authority to engage in conflict management (Nathan 2010). These include the European Union (EU), which promotes peace through cooperation and integration in economic, political, and, increasingly, security matters; the African Union, which has developed specialized institutions and capacities to support political mediation, crisis management, postconflict reconstruction, and peacekeeping, the most notable example of which is the African Union Mission in Somalia (Anderson and McKnight 2014); and the Economic Community of West African States (ECOWAS), which is empowered to act in the case of threats to stability through political, economic, and military means (Fisher and Anderson 2015; box 7.4). The growing significance of regional and subregional organizations in conflict prevention is reflected in increasingly complex and multidimensional cooperation among them as well as with the United Nations.[7]

Other regional organizations serve more as forums for coordination between regional states, with their engagement and role in conflict management structured on an intergovernmental basis and with limited operational and institutional mandates or capacities for autonomous action. These include the League of Arab States and the Southern African Development Community, among others, which serve primarily as platforms for coordinated political, diplomatic, and sometimes military engagement in crises and conflicts.

While regional organizations vary in their normative frameworks and capacity, some have had success in forging a consensus on common priorities among states, sometimes serving as a pacesetter in transformative agendas. These include, for example, the African Union's legal provision of the right to intervene in grave human rights violations as contained in Article 4(h) of its Constitutive Act;[8] the development of an ambitious Agenda 2063 on regional integration (African Union Commission 2015); and the immediate priority of "Silencing the Guns by 2020."[9]

Regional and subregional economic communities, in particular, have gone beyond fostering economic cooperation and integration to providing important platforms for addressing regional threats to peace and security. Approximately 33 regional economic organizations have been founded since 1989, and 29 regionally based intergovernmental organizations have an established agenda related to peace and security. Part of the importance of regional economic communities has been their role in implementing regional integration agendas bridging peace, security, and economic cooperation. Based on this cooperation, regional economic communities are playing increasingly operational roles targeting subregional threats—for example, through regional coalitions such as the Multinational Joint Taskforce against Boko Haram, the G-5 Sahel, or the Regional Coalition Initiative against the Lord's Resistance Army.

The increasing role of regional organizations in addressing threats to stability and security in their regions is most evident in regional peacekeeping operations and regionally coordinated and negotiated security responses (box 7.3). The African Union and ECOWAS (box 7.4) peace operations have increased, especially in the initial stages of international deployments, and have at times proven quicker to deploy than other multilateral missions, as well as generally more willing to use military force, if necessary. However, these operations are at times poorly funded and equipped relative to the enormity of the task at hand, and a heavy strategic focus on military action has sometimes come at the expense of a holistic civilian-led approach (De Coning and Prakash 2016).

Salehyan and Gleditsch (2006), Salehyan (2009), and more recently Goldstone et al. (2010) have shown that one relatively good predictor of whether a country will experience a civil war is whether neighboring countries are experiencing civil war. Given their knowledge of the regional context and vested interest in preventing regional instability, regional and subregional organizations possess inherent attributes that often afford them greater efficacy and legitimacy to assume the role of mediators (Ibrahim 2016). Their proximity and access to regional and national stakeholders allow them to engage and intervene more quickly when crises occur. These advantages are reflected, for instance, in the success of the African Union in mediating an end to electoral violence in Kenya in

2008 (Lindenmayer and Kaye 2009) and the instrumental role of the Inter-Governmental Authority on Development (IGAD) in negotiations on ending the war in Sudan in 2005 (Healy 2009). However, when consensus among member states cannot be established, perceptions of partiality exist, or critical capacities are in short supply, regional and subregional organizations are faced with difficult challenges that may curtail their effectiveness in preventing and managing conflict.

International Tools for Prevention

Over the past decades, the international community has developed tools for preventing the outbreak, escalation, continuation, and relapse of conflict. While historically linked to international multilateral institutions, such tools are increasingly, if unevenly, shared with regional and subregional organizations.

These tools, ranging from remote monitoring of risks to deployments through in-country peace operations, have evolved considerably to deal with the growing complexity of conflicts.

Engagements are increasingly aimed at the entire cycle of conflict from outbreak to relapse, regional and subregional operations are more frequent, and multilateral deployments are increasingly recognizing the importance of multidimensional approaches integrating political, security, and development efforts.

Nevertheless, the current amount of attention to and spending on prevention amounts to a fraction of the quantity spent responding to crisis or on rebuilding afterward,[10] and the existing tools remain challenged by the changing nature of violent conflict. The following sections provide an overview of several operational instruments through which states provide support through multilateral frameworks for prevention, highlighting the evolution of policy, practice, and the extent and potential for greater convergence between international political, security, and development actors.

Early Warning Systems

Early warning systems (EWSs) play a significant role in the international field of conflict prevention. The Organisation for Economic Co-operation and Development defines early warning as "a process that (a) alerts decision makers to the potential outbreak, escalation, and resurgence of violent conflict and (b) promotes an understanding among decision makers of the nature and impacts of violent conflict" (OECD 2009, 22). EWSs are practical tools relying on qualitative or quantitative data on medium- and short-term risks, with the intention of directly informing or supporting preventive actions. EWSs help in formulating best- and worst-case scenarios and response options and then communicate the findings to decision makers (Mwaûra and Schmeidl 2002).

Initial models of early warning emerged in the 1970s. After the end of the Cold War, these systems developed rapidly, using both qualitative and quantitative data to improve the accuracy of predictions and extend their time horizons. Today diverse types of EWS exist: governmental, intergovernmental, and nongovernmental.[11]

- Government systems were designed, for example, in France (Système d'Alerte Précoce, located at the General Secretariat for National Defense) and Germany (BMZ Crisis Early Warning System).
- At the intergovernmental level, the African Union has developed a Continental Early Warning System to advise the Peace and Security Council on "potential conflict and threats to peace and security" and "recommend best courses of action." IGAD has designed the Conflict Early Warning and Response Mechanism (CEWARN) as an institutional foundation for addressing conflicts in the region. It is a collaborative effort of the member states of IGAD (Djibouti, Eritrea, Ethiopia, Kenya, Somalia, South Sudan, Sudan, and Uganda). ECOWAS has also developed ECOWARN to collect and analyze data and draft up-to-date reports on possible emerging crises, ongoing crises, and postcrisis transitions.
- Nongovernmental organizations have set up their own EWSs. The nonprofit organization International Crisis Group uses qualitative methods and field research to produce a monthly early warning bulletin, *Crisis Watch*, designed to provide global warnings of impending violence; the Forum on Early Warning and Early Response–Africa focuses on the Ituri region in the Democratic Republic of Congo; and the Early Warning and Early Response Project focuses on Timor-Leste (Defontaine 2017).[12]

Good practices of EWSs include (a) the use of field networks of monitors; (b) application of both qualitative and quantitative analytical methodologies; (c) use of technology; (d) regular monitoring and reporting, as conflict dynamics evolve rapidly; and (e) assurance of a strong interconnection between early warning and response, as emphasized in third-generation EWSs (Nyheim 2015).[13]

While converging qualitative and quantitative evidence suggests that EWSs can provide accurate information of impeding violent conflict in the short term (Chadefaux 2014; Ward et al. 2013), most models cannot make long-term projections (longer than two to three years) or predict the location, intensity, and trajectory of impending violence. At the same time, even when predictions are accurate, finding entry points for action, particularly in the context of current conflict dynamics, can be challenging. However, even the best EWS will have minimal effect if not used to inform preventive action. The short time horizons of warnings can limit the scope of relevant preventive action and make it difficult to sustain engagement beyond contingency planning. Likewise, EWSs rarely address how much uncertainty is associated with concrete predictions, with the result that action rarely immediately follows warning (box 7.5; Brandt, Freeman, and Schrodt 2011a, 2011b; King and Zeng 2001).

For this reason, some countries have developed dialogue processes among a variety of stakeholders to analyze data from different sources and channel this information into more coordinated action. In particular, violence observatories have become common tools to support the design and implementation of violence prevention actions, especially in urban areas. Observatories grew out of the experience of city governments in Latin America and have been central to government efforts to reduce gang and interpersonal violence in cities like Bogotá, Medellín, and Rio de Janeiro. Observatories usually involve regular meetings by stakeholders from different sectors—law enforcement, health, and urban development, for example—to analyze trends in violence and take coordinated actions to address it (Duque, Caicedo, and Sierra 2008; Sur 2014). They have been adapted to some situations of armed conflict, such as Indonesia (Barron and Sharpe 2005).

Protection of Civilians and Prevention of Mass Atrocities

Human rights violations, discrimination, and abuse are among the major warning signs of instability and conflict, and monitoring and reporting of such abuses provide the evidence base from which to devise actions. The UN Charter establishes a link between protection of human rights and maintenance of international peace and security,[14] and the Universal Periodic Review undertaken by the Human Rights Council is the main institutional review mechanism for all 193 UN member states.[15] The power of these systems lies not only in their triggering of action, but also their acceptance as a basis for standard setting across countries.[16] Recognizing that where preventive action fails, international action must protect the lives and dignity of civilians caught up in conflict, international action has advocated for enhanced respect for both international humanitarian law and international human rights law, prioritizing protection of civilians in UN peace operations and preventing forced displacement of refugees and internally displaced persons (UN Secretary-General 2017b).

More recently, systems have evolved to focus specifically on the prevention of large-scale and deliberate attacks on civilians. Even when conflict prevention has failed or no means of stopping armed conflict are available, prevention of mass atrocities remains a priority. In 2001, following the tragedies of the Balkans (A/54/549) and Rwanda (S/199/1257), the UN Security Council invited the secretary-general "to refer to the Council information and analyses within the United Nations system on cases of serious violations of international law" and on "potential conflict situations" arising from "ethnic, religious, and territorial disputes" and other related issues (UN General Assembly 1999a, 1999b; UN Security Council 2001). In 2004, following this instruction, the UN secretary-general appointed the first special adviser on the prevention of genocide, followed in 2008 by appointment of the first special adviser on the responsibility to protect. In 2014, the Office of Genocide Prevention and the Responsibility to Protect released the first United Nations Framework of Analysis for Atrocity Crimes (UN 2014).

This framework highlights that, like many other forms of violence, in most cases,

BOX 7.5 Challenges in Predicting Violent Conflict

Given the dynamics of violent conflict today, there has been a resurgence of interest in expanding beyond early warning systems to more accurate forecasting of medium- to long-term conflict risks.

Unlike early warning, forecasting relies on predictive capabilities of data monitoring tools and systems and is designed not to alert observers to impending violence, but to improve remote monitoring of underlying risks through data collection, multimethod and multidisciplinary research, adaption and revision of existing prediction models, and generation of policy-oriented analyses.

Prediction models vary, not only in their accuracy in predicting the onset of violent conflict, but also in their precision in determining location, intensity, and time. While conventional approaches rely on statistical analyses of a country's structural conditions, open-source information—that is, data from electronic news articles and web resources— is increasingly used for conflict risk assessment and near-time forecasting (Yi 2017c).

- The Political Instability Task Force, a macrostructural country-level forecasting model, has, for example, used a parsimonious selection of variables, focused on types of political regime and the existence of state-led exclusion to predict and explain large-scale violent conflict, destabilizing regime change, and genocide or politicide (Goldstone et al. 2010).

- Peace Research Institute Oslo has developed the Conflict Prediction Project to generate long-term simulation-based forecasts of armed conflict (Bosley 2016; Yi 2017c). Forecasting efforts have also been undertaken to identify risks of violence subnationally.

- In Liberia, for example, Blair, Blattman, and Hartman (2015) use 56 potential risk factors to predict locations of conflict, finding that ethnic diversity and polarization consistently predicted the location of violence over time. Another forecasting model using cross-sectional survey data in Liberia predicted up to 88 percent of actual local violence in 2012 and had an overall accuracy of 33–50 percent (Blair, Blattman, and Hartman 2011, 2015; Blattman 2012, 2014).[a]

The ability of qualitative sources to yield robust and policy-relevant predictions (Gibler 2016) is underscored in research that analyzed specialized newspaper content to predict political violence. News sources are not only available in real time, but also have strong country-specific elements. Therefore, by using topic models and focusing on within-country variation (or the timing of the occurrence of violence), researchers could predict accurately the onset of political violence one to two years before it occurred (Mueller and Rauh 2016).

Nevertheless, several different metrics[b] developed to evaluate predictive accuracy have shown that conflict forecasting still suffers from many limitations. Forecasting is most often based on complex models and is limited by technical and data issues—in particular, too many different variables are playing out in moving from risks to violence for simple modeling to provide a reliable basis for prediction.

a. Using cross-sectional surveys of respondents in 242 small rural towns and villages in Liberia in 2008, 2010, and 2012, researchers focused on communal, extrajudicial, and criminal violence. The team used the 2008 data to predict local violence in 2010 and then generated predictions for 2012, while collecting new data to compare the predictions with the reality.
b. Point forecast evaluations such as mean absolute error, root mean squared error, and receiver operator characteristic curves are among the most widely used metrics to assess the performance of forecasting models. These metrics are often complemented by interval and density forecast evaluations such as prediction interval, probability integral transform, and continuous ranked probability score (Yi 2017b).

atrocity crimes are not unforeseen and "tend to occur in similar settings and share several elements or features" (UN 2014, 6). The framework highlights eight common risk factors for atrocities, including previous serious violations of international human rights law, the capacity to commit atrocity crimes, and concrete preparatory action. In addition to these common factors, the framework identifies six risk factors relevant specifically to the international crimes of genocide, crimes against humanity, and war crimes. For example, crimes against humanity are often preceded by systematic attacks against specific civilian populations, and war crimes are often preceded by serious threats to humanitarian or peacekeeping operations. The framework also provides detailed indicators for assessing these risks.

Preventive Diplomacy and Mediation

Preventive diplomacy refers to early diplomatic action taken "to prevent disputes from arising between parties, to prevent existing disputes from escalating into conflicts, and to limit the spread of the latter when they occur" (UN Secretary-General 1992, 3). The UN secretary-general, for example, plays an essential and personal role in preventive diplomacy through the provision of "good offices" to all parties. Mediation is a process whereby a third party assists two or more parties, with their consent, to prevent, manage, or resolve a conflict by helping them to develop mutually acceptable agreements.

Using confidence building and leverage, preventive diplomacy and mediation can play a role in altering the incentives of actors that propel societies toward violence. Given that diplomatic action can be mobilized quickly, when consent is present, it is often a tool of first resort in response to high risks of conflict and sometimes the only approach, short of military intervention, that can be deployed to avert violence (Day and Pichler Fong 2017). Mediation has also been used increasingly frequently. Greig and Diehl (2012) conclude that there were more

mediation attempts during the 1990s (64 percent) than during the entire 1945–89 period, and this trend seems to have continued (Themmer and Wallensteen 2011).[17]

Within the United Nations, the establishment of regional political offices—the UN Office for West Africa and the Sahel (UNOWAS),[18] the UN Office for Central Africa (UNOCA), and the UN Regional Center for Preventive Diplomacy in Central Asia (UNRCCA)—has responded to the increasing regionalization of conflict. Given their standing presence, ability to deploy, and relationships with most key stakeholders across the region, these regional offices offer alternatives to peacekeeping operations. In the Kyrgyz Republic, the EU, the Organization for Security and Co-operation in Europe (OSCE), and UNRCCA responded to the 2010 crisis by focusing mainly on capacity building; tackling the rule of law; facilitating regional dialogues, especially around terrorism, water, and energy issues; and providing aid to displaced Uzbeks. This concerted effort enabled the government to end violence and commence a process of political reforms that led to parliamentary elections (Call 2012). Another example is the response of the UN Office for West Africa (UNOWA) to the crisis in Guinea in 2008 following the death of President Lansana Conté and the takeover of the country by a military junta. With the mediation of the head of UNOWA, Special Representative of the Secretary-General Saïd Djinnit, and ECOWAS, the situation was diffused. UNOWA subsequently provided expertise on conflict prevention, mediation, and security sector reform, which helped the country to hold successful national elections at the end of 2010.

Mediation is increasingly conducted by a range of organizations, including cadres of experienced envoys or mediators from the UN, regional and subregional organizations, individual states, and nongovernmental actors (box 7.6; Svensson and Lundgren 2015).[19] In a study undertaken using Uppsala Conflict Data Program (UCDP) data between 1989 and 2013, states were found to be the principal mediators in 59 percent of cases, while

Bilateral, subregional, and regional organizations and the United Nations often seek to work in tandem, rather than in parallel, to bring the legitimacy and weight of their respective bodies to bear in coordinated efforts. These efforts include other international and regional organizations as well as nongovernmental actors (in so-called track 2 approaches) and national actors (individual local mediators as well as civil society groups, for example, youth and women's groups). This collaboration has led to efforts to increase coordination at the international and national levels. At the country level, it has led to broader and more inclusive mediation approaches, including organization of national dialogue initiatives.

- In Kenya in 2008, Kofi Annan, former UN secretary-general, mediated the end of postelection ethnic violence on behalf of the Panel of Eminent African Personalities of the African Union, with technical support provided by experts from the United Nations and the nongovernmental Centre for Humanitarian Dialogue (Crocker and Aall 1999; Lanz and Gasser 2013; Lindenmayer and Kaye 2009).

- In the Kyrgyz Republic in 2010, after President Kurmanbek Bakiev's ouster, a triple mediation initiative of the EU, the OSCE, and the United Nations provided considerable leverage and legitimacy to the effort to ensure stability during the transition (Call 2012).

- In Guinea in 2009–10, the African Union, the International Contact Group, and the United Nations supported the ECOWAS-led mediation that persuaded a military junta to support a transition to civilian rule and constitutional order (Mancini 2011).

- In Colombia, the Cuban and Norwegian governments facilitated the peace agreement between the government of Colombia and the Revolutionary Armed Forces of Colombia (FARC) rebels, with technical assistance on thematic agreements and confidence building provided by various UN entities and other actors (Aguirre 2015).[a]

The broadening of the mediation environment (in terms of both mediators and parties) has improved the responsiveness and mobilization of international actors and facilitated broader ownership of peace processes. In The Gambia, for example, the national government, African Union, ECOWAS, the EU, Nigeria, and the United Nations played a decisive role in preventing violence and enabling a peaceful transition of power to the elected president, Adama Barrow. However, the growing number of stakeholders has also made the management of mediation more complex, increasing the need for coordination, leadership, and unified approaches to prevent confusion and efforts from working at cross-purposes to each other.

a. See also http://www.un.org/undpa/en/diplomacy-mediation.

intergovernmental organizations were principal mediators in 30 percent of cases. Private individuals and nongovernmental organizations such as the Geneva-based Centre for Humanitarian Dialogue, the Helsinki-based Crisis Management Initiative, or the Community of Sant'Egidio in Rome were the principal mediators in 11 percent of cases reported in the press (Svensson and Onken 2015).

In many processes, multiple mediators may be engaged, at times in a coordinated fashion in support of a lead mediator, at other times working at cross-purposes (Whitfield 2010).

The growing body of practice in preventive diplomacy has translated into stronger institutional frameworks supporting such actions. At the international level, groupings of member states and international organizations supporting the prevention or resolution of conflicts and leveraging financial and other resources, known variously as "groups of friends," "contact groups," and "core groups," grew from 4 to more than 30 between 1990 and 2009 (Whitfield 2010). At the same time, in some prominent cases—the Syrian Arab Republic most obviously, but also Libya and the Republic of Yemen—the breadth and complexity of the conflict and the multiplicity of actors involved have defied long-standing efforts to secure lasting political settlements.

Assessing the effectiveness of diplomacy and mediation faces inherent challenges, since it is hard to isolate the effects of such efforts from the conduct of the conflict, the parties, and other external actors. Data suggest that, while diplomatic engagement is the most common form of international recourse in violent conflict, evidence of its ability to halt the outbreak of conflict is mixed.[20] What is clearer is that mediation alone is insufficient to resolve underlying causes of violence. While mediators have the potential to help to generate settlement deals that can bring short-term stability, these deals are fragile and more likely to break down than military victories (Hoeffler 2014; Svensson and Lundgren 2015). Qualitative case studies show that diplomacy, which at its core relies on the "wisdom and appeal of its arguments" (Hinnebusch et al. 2016, 4), has helped to avert or end violence in specific cases, but that, even when successful, mediation and elite settlements often provide breathing space rather than long-term solutions (Day and Pichler Fong 2017).

These findings, however, require careful analysis of the definition of success.[21] A study using the International Crisis Behavior data set of interstate war finds that, in cases of conflict relapse after mediated settlement between 1945 and 2005, violence was often reduced in the first years after relapse.[22] Furthermore, when negotiated settlements are combined with third-party security guarantees, such settlements extended the duration of peace

(Hoeffler 2014; Walter 2017). In sum, diplomatic action can provide the framework for proposing measures that, if implemented, can consolidate peace.[23] When preventive diplomacy and mediation lead to settlements, they can provide much-needed space for other forms of action that address the underlying causes of violence. How diplomatic and other forms of engagements could work together is explored in more detail later in this chapter.

Despite these findings, preventive diplomacy and mediation face important challenges, including both the identification of entry points and the characteristics of the conflicts to be mediated. States can be sensitive to the engagement of outsiders in what are perceived as internal responsibilities. Preventive diplomacy also suffers from a bias toward the national level and underuse of dialogue processes at the subnational level that involve local actors, including trusted mediators (Harland 2016). In addition, international third-party contributions tend to come once a pathway to violence has been set and deviation from the path is more difficult.

Preventing Violent Extremism

There is a strong consensus on behalf of many national governments and multilateral organizations, including the UN General Assembly, the UN Security Council, and the World Bank, that violent extremism has reached a level of threat and sophistication that requires a comprehensive approach encompassing not only military or security measures, but also preventive measures that directly address development, good governance, human rights, and humanitarian concerns (Rosand 2016; UNDP 2017). Accordingly, the United Nations has developed an overarching Plan of Action to Prevent Violent Extremism (A/70/674), reinforcing the first pillar of the United Nations Global Counter-Terrorism Strategy (A/RES/60/288), which focuses on addressing the conditions conducive to the spread of terrorism (UN General Assembly 2006b; UN Secretary-General 2016a).

The Plan of Action recognizes that the risk of violent extremism often increases under the same conditions that lead to heightened risk of conflict and provides entry points for national and international actors to address key drivers of extremist violence. Where violent conflict exists, efforts must be redoubled to promote and sustain dialogue between warring parties, since persistent, unresolved conflict has proved to be a major driver of violent extremism (ICG 2016). Therefore, the first of the seven strategic priority areas consists of dialogue and conflict prevention.

The UN General Assembly, in Resolution 70/291 adopted on July 1, 2016, recommends that member states implement recommendations from the Plan of Action, as relevant to each national context (UN General Assembly 2016b; UN Secretary-General 2016a). It also invites member states, together with regional and subregional organizations, to develop national and regional plans of action to prevent violent extremism. As discussed in chapter 6, a growing number of member states and regional and subregional organizations are now developing national and regional plans to address the drivers of violent extremism, drawing on the UN Plan of Action to Prevent Violent Extremism, and are requesting UN support in their efforts. A High-Level Prevent Violent Extremism Action Group, chaired by the secretary-general and consisting of the heads of 21 UN agencies, funds, and programs, is taking the lead in implementing the Plan of Action in support of member states, at their request.

Peace Operations

Although not explicitly envisioned in the UN Charter, peace operations remain one of the most widely known international tools for prevention and have evolved significantly since 1990, from a narrow focus on monitoring cease-fires and peace agreements to complex multidimensional missions with mandates to consolidate peace, prevent relapse into conflict, and support the restoration of state authority.

While rarely deployed to avert the outbreak of violence, mandates today range from building institutions and facilitating peaceful dialogue to protecting civilians and upholding human rights (DPKO 2008).

Since 1945, most such deployments have been peacekeeping operations or special political missions led by the United Nations, although regional and subregional missions fielded by the African Union and ECOWAS and multinational forces with Security Council authorization have become increasingly common. Peacekeeping roles have ranged from the "classic" model of interpositioning forces and monitoring cease-fires all the way to conducting robust, peace enforcement operations with rules of engagement entailing the use of force. As of mid-2017, 16 peacekeeping operations are deployed (figure 7.1), comprising approximately 94,000 uniformed personnel and 15,000 civilian personnel and lasting on average three times longer than operations prior to 2000 (UN 2015, 4). The United Nation's special political missions, meanwhile—considered as "operations whose principal mandate is 'political'" (Johnstone 2010)—have steadily increased in the past two decades. While only 3 political missions were active in 1993, 21 were active in 2017, with more than 3,000 personnel.[24] Both peacekeeping and political missions have evolved considerably over time to support conflict prevention, mediation, and management across all phases of conflict (that is, from situations of active conflict to immediate postconflict and longer-term peacebuilding phases).

Most quantitative studies, drawing on different statistical models and definitions of peacekeeping, conclude that peace operations have a large and statistically significant impact on fostering the negotiated resolution of civil wars, preventing the escalation of violence against civilians, and preventing the recurrence of violence (Doyle and Sambanis 2000, 2006; Fortna 2004; Gilligan and Sergenti 2008; Hartzell, Hoddie, and Rothchild 2001; Walter 1997, 2017). Evidence also suggests that peace operations can prevent the spread of

FIGURE 7.1 **Overview of Deployment of UN Peacekeeping Forces, 1945–2015**

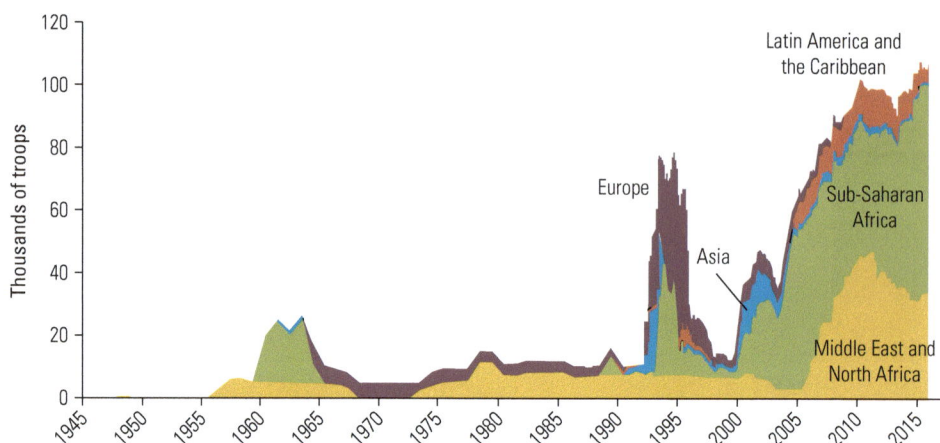

Sources: United Nations Department of Peacekeeping Operations; International Peace Institute; and Stimson Center.
Note: Data do not include civilian personnel or volunteers. The Middle East and North Africa region includes missions to Iraq, Israel, Lebanon, Sudan, Syria, and Western Sahara. All other missions are categorized according to UN regional divisions. Data for 1945–1990 show midyear values; data from 1991–2005 are monthly.

conflict within a country once violence has broken out.[25] These studies have been reinforced by analyzing different types of peace operations. For example, Collier and Rohner (2008), analyzing the correlation between peacekeeping expenditure and risks of recurrence of violent conflict, and Doyle and Sambanis (2000), considering different types of operations and the probability of peace breaking down within two years, have shown that robust mandates and larger missions in terms of budget and troop strength appear to perform better in preventing relapse into civil war (Beardsley 2011; Doyle and Sambanis 2000, 2006; Hultman, Kathman, and Shannon 2013). Qualitatively, the successes of peacekeeping are numerous, including Bosnia and Herzegovina, El Salvador, Kosovo,[26] Mozambique, Namibia, Nicaragua, and, more recently, Côte d'Ivoire, Liberia, Sierra Leone, and Timor-Leste.

The preventive value of these actions lies precisely in the creation of disincentives for the use of violence (box 7.7). As the complexity of conflicts has grown, however, multidimensional missions have increasingly been tasked with establishing institutional mechanisms for peacefully managing differences and disputes.[27] Both peacekeeping and political missions are, as a result, increasingly providing comprehensive support across areas as diverse as human rights, the rule of law, sexual violence in conflict, violent extremism, organized crime and drug trafficking, security sector reform, disarmament, demobilization and reintegration, and mine action.[28]

As highlighted in the 2015 report of the High-Level Independent Panel on United Nations Peace Operations, peace operations are increasingly deployed in protracted and complex conflicts, with peacekeepers and political officers operating in remote, unstable, and often dangerous environments (UN 2015). In these contexts, peace operations must actively engage in conflict prevention and management where there is no clear "peace to keep" or in unstable postconflict contexts characterized by fragile peace settlements, weak institutions, and high risk of future conflict. Peace operations in these environments play a role in (a) preventing the continuation of violence following a ceasefire or peace agreement and (b) preventing or managing new forms of conflicts and crises (outbreak, escalation, reoccurrence).

From the military side, this involvement has led to major changes in the rules of engagement and use of force, which have expanded to include the protection of civilians and the maintenance of access for providing humanitarian assistance, more robust engagement and use of force against armed actors, and capacity building of security forces.

These new circumstances have extended the duration of peacekeeping operations and increased the scale of operations required both to mitigate the impact of immediate violence and to reduce the risk of reoccurrence (box 7.8). While peace operations have prevented regional spillovers and supported postconflict transitions in many countries, they have been mandated to undertake tasks beyond their military and financial capabilities and often run the risk of overstretch. Some countries have experienced escalation of subnational conflict in spite of the deployment of large peacekeeping operations, such as the Central African Republic, the Democratic Republic of Congo, and South Sudan.

Taken together, the international system has developed tools designed to engage in preventive action across different phases of risk from outbreak to risk of continuation and relapse. Furthermore, the evidence shows that the various international tools and core functions have worked in specific circumstances. EWSs have provided short-term warning of impending violence, increased diplomatic efforts have secured settlements to conflict and reduced the risk of outbreaks, and peace operations have reduced spillover, escalation, and continuation of violence. Evidence also suggests that these tools have achieved greatest impact when deployed in a coordinated manner after the outbreak of violence (Hoeffler 2014), for example, when using mediation to encourage a cease-fire or technical support to reinforce policy reforms.

However, current trends are testing the limits of the existing tools, and the international system is struggling to adapt. For example, recent UN reviews highlighting the "primacy of politics" in guiding UN operations point to a more concerted need to address the underlying causes of conflict across multiple levels. Chapter 8 discusses recommendations for their adaptation and application in more detail.

International Development Assistance

International development assistance has long been a cornerstone of the international community's endeavors to create a peaceful and prosperous world. UN Secretary-General Kofi Annan's report on conflict prevention in 2001 highlighted that "one of the principal aims of preventive action should be to address the deep-rooted socioeconomic, cultural, environmental, institutional, and other structural causes that often underlie the immediate political symptoms of conflicts" (UN Secretary-General 2001, 2).

Development assistance has increased steadily over the past 60 years and is increasingly targeted at conflict-affected and fragile contexts. Where it is aligned with an understanding of conflict dynamics, aid is a very important mechanism to support national and local capacities to build pathways toward peace. This is especially the case when aid can be designed to address early risks of violent conflicts. Recent international commitments on aid, such as the Paris Declaration (2005), the Accra Action Agenda (2008), and the New Deal for Engagement in Fragile States (2011), have recognized the role of development aid in peacebuilding.

Over the past decade, the development focus among important bilateral and multilateral agencies has started to shift toward supporting national institutions and actors in conflict prevention. However, despite calls for greater investment in prevention (OECD 2015; World Bank 2011), most aid is still delivered after violence has occurred, and aid flows to fragile and postconflict settings tend to be unpredictable and inconsistent. Development aid is still not commonly viewed as a relevant tool for early prevention, and policies that stimulate growth and poverty reduction often are assumed to be sufficient in and of themselves to reduce the risk of violence.

In addition, international development actors and multilateral development banks, in particular, are still highly constrained from engaging on sensitive issues with governments by their mandates, institutional makeup, and internal culture. At early signs of risk and in precrisis contexts, these constraints often limit the scope for development programming to address causes of tension and sensitive areas such as security and justice. Aid for prevention also tends to be fragmented, short term, and seen as a complement to rather than an integral part of development efforts.

The Relationship between Aid and Conflict

The question of whether development assistance helps to prevent or fuel violent conflict has been a matter of debate for decades. Three main theories, discussed in chapter 3, have guided research in this area. Some (Calì and Mulabdic 2017; Dube and Vargas 2013) argue for a "rapacity effect," whereby aid essentially creates an incentive for violence because there are more resources to fight over. For example, Nunn and Qian (2014) find a positive effect of U.S. food aid on the incidence and duration of conflict.[29] Collier and Hoeffler (2004) and Dal Bo and Dal Bo (2011) counter that increasing the available resources (through aid or other measures) creates a disincentive for violence by raising the opportunity cost, especially if resources are allocated in a way that raises wages or redistributes them to would-be combatants.

A growing body of research suggests that the degree to which an increase in aid could fuel conflict depends on the extent to which the aid is fungible and the way the state uses it (Collier and Hoeffler 2006; Langlotz and Potrafke 2016). In particular, country-level aid, especially budget support, is sometimes seen as being much more political and therefore conflict-inducing than project-level aid, precisely because it allows a great deal of autonomy over use of the aid (Gehring, Kaplan, and Wong 2017). However, for governments that have a sound prevention strategy, budgetary support can be essential to providing the fiscal space and capability to implement their prevention strategy in a comprehensive way. A project-by-project approach can be unmanageable and lead to fragmentation.

The use of aid is critical, as is the relevance of the strategy that frames its delivery. If part of the budget support is channeled toward military spending, it could contribute to a decrease in violence if it effectively deters opposing groups from using violence. However, if the increased military funding is channeled toward more repressive measures seen as illegitimate by the population, it can have the opposite effect.

Aid at the project level is viewed as less political, although certainly not conflict-neutral. Aid projects that provide basic goods (food, water) or improve service delivery can have different effects depending on how the aid is used and what kind of aid it is. Aid that goes to individual projects can contribute to increased violence if rebel groups are able to appropriate and use it as an incentive for recruitment, or it can reduce violence if it helps to boost incomes and relieve economic stresses in conflict-affected regions (Anderson 1999; Fearon and Laitin 2003).

Because aid is part and parcel of the local context, differential benefits from aid can reinforce intergroup tensions and fuel divisive narratives of "us" versus "them" (Anderson 1999; Jenny 2017). Moreover, aid can reinforce grievances along identity lines when it lacks impartiality or when it is perceived as biased in favor of specific groups irrespective of their need for assistance (Carbonnier 2015). An OECD (2010) report on monitoring the principles for good international engagement in fragile states and situations highlights the uneven distribution of aid resources as problematic in five of the six countries reviewed (Afghanistan, the Central African Republic, the Democratic Republic of Congo, Haiti, and Timor-Leste). In Timor-Leste, for example, the "Dili-centric" development efforts were thought to worsen the urban-rural divide and contribute to pockets of exclusion (OECD 2010).

Aid can also create a substitution effect when an action takes over local capacity and reduces or replaces local efforts. This can have negative impacts by reducing the legitimacy of existing structures or authorities. For example, a dual or parallel public sector can detract from important state- and peacebuilding processes that are necessary for the country to earn legitimacy in the eyes of its constituents. Aid also can affect the local market, reinforce market distortions by feeding the war economy, and undermine peacetime production (Kang 2017).

Finally, aligning priorities for development aid can be difficult, depending on when crisis breaks out. For example, there could be political difficulties in realigning development aid in precrisis contexts or the often-dramatic reprioritization of aid that occurs when crisis breaks out (with emphasis placed on security or humanitarian expenditures). Even more worrisome are the disruptions of standard procedures in development coordination that occur when a crisis breaks.

Because of these potential negative impacts, linking the delivery of aid to do-no-harm measures is essential to help donors be sensitive to the specific contexts in which they operate. This process includes identifying issues, elements, or factors that divide societies as well as local capacity for peace that brings societies together. It also requires donors to consider what aid will do for whom, who are the responsible actors and stakeholders, and who has access to aid (Wallace 2015). A study conducted at the end of the five-year pilot phase of the New Deal took stock of how bilateral and multilateral donors have conceptualized and implemented their commitment to promote "inclusive and legitimate politics" (INCAF 2017). On the basis of empirical evidence acquired through case studies in four G-7+ pilot countries (Afghanistan, Somalia, South Sudan, and Timor-Leste), the study finds that, at best, donors work with an incomplete and inadequate understanding of the typically fragmented and contested politics of fragile societies beyond the formal representatives of their governments and administrations (INCAF 2017). The study also finds that, in response to perceived or real deficits in governance with regard to legitimacy or inclusivity, donors tend to offer standardized packages of political support that focus on the technical and procedural aspects of an idealized democracy (for example, pressuring national stakeholders to hold national elections as soon as possible after a political settlement) rather than on realities on the ground.

Overall, aid brings positive results when it is delivered with meaningful engagement with government and civil society. As described in chapter 6, civil society plays a critical role in conflict prevention. Donors have supported local peace committees and various conflict resolution platforms, including in postconflict situations. For such programs, civil society has proven to be an indispensable interlocutor, facilitator, and mediator, particularly in cases in which political corruption, organized crime, and dysfunctional state institutions are major issues. Donor-funded community-based conflict resolution has proved critical in various contexts. including Ghana, the Kyrgyz Republic, and Lesotho (Giessmann, Galvanek, and Seifert 2017). This involvement entails risks: when development aid is channeled primarily through nongovernmental organizations, it can undermine the state's capacity to play a central role in prevention.

A critical element of enhancing the impact of aid on peace is connecting aid from both development and security actors to national processes of prioritization. The New Deal for Engagement in Fragile States (box 7.9) provides a guiding framework for this connection. It emerged from the 2007 Principles for Good International Engagement in Fragile States and Situations, which sought to translate established principles of aid effectiveness—as per the Paris Declaration of 2005—to contexts of fragility and conflict. These initiatives and others are supported by bodies such as the International Network on Conflict and Fragility, established in 2009 by the Development Assistance Committee to enable its members to develop similar frameworks.

International actors are supporting national prioritization and planning processes in a growing number of countries. This can include support for national dialogues (box 7.10) as well as consultative processes to develop conflict and fragility assessments. Two relevant examples are the UN's conflict and development analysis and the World Bank's risk and resilience assessments, which inform programming.

Multistakeholder analytical and coordination platforms are increasingly being used to improve alignment of aid flows among multiple partners with identified conflict and peacebuilding priorities. Recovery and Peacebuilding Assessments (RPBAs), for instance, are assessments supported by the EU, the United Nations, and the World Bank to support countries in the development of holistic strategies for addressing the political, security, and development priorities related to stabilization and peacebuilding (box 7.11).

Supporting Peaceful Pathways with Development Assistance

As discussed in chapter 3, the path dependence of violence and of peace means that, as risks accumulate and intensify, the options for preventing violence become scarcer and more difficult to take. Because aid is channeled through national governments, international actors also experience this dynamic in supporting national processes; in higher-risk contexts, a smaller range of tools are applicable and feasible. To increase effectiveness, aid needs to be targeted sufficiently on supporting prevention policies and programs when early signs of risk appear and flexible enough to adapt as risks change. This targeting has proven difficult in the past, not least because it requires having a frank and engaged

---

BOX 7.9 The New Deal for Engagement in Fragile States

The New Deal for Engagement in Fragile States emerged from the recognition that ensuring effective development assistance requires a common international framework for all countries tackling the challenge of conflict and fragility. The New Deal is a global policy agreement formed with guidance from the International Dialogue on Peacebuilding and Statebuilding, which comprises conflict-affected and fragile countries, civil society, and international partners. It has been endorsed by more than 40 countries and organizations since 2011.

discussion with governments on issues of risk of violence that both sides too often perceive as being outside the realm of development efforts.[30]

A more formidable challenge arises when the state is the source of violence or a major obstacle to peace. In these situations, international actors are left with few options. They can halt aid entirely or confine it to priority regions or essential services, with the risk that doing so could reinforce divisions or give groups no alternative but to seek the support of the state. Conditioning aid on a change in course by the state is another option, but doing so can generate risks similar to the impacts of sanctions and has not proven effective in the recent past. Working through nonstate actors is another option, but this too risks ultimately undermining the state or increasing the vulnerability of those actors to state retaliation.

Finding ways to support national actors in changing course toward prevention, when incentives are strongly aligned against it, requires a level of coordination and sensitivity to local dynamics that is rarely seen. Calls for better coordination are consistently made, agreed on, and later ignored. In many cases, rather than enhancing coordination and efficiency, large-scale external aid has produced fragmentation, confronting government partners with thousands of projects, many of them short term, and parallel governance and fiduciary systems (Institute for State Effectiveness 2018). At the heart of this failure is a misalignment of incentives within both multilateral and national institutions.

The Central African Republic RPBA aimed to help the new government to promote peace and prevent a relapse of conflict following presidential elections in early 2016. The assessment was firmly grounded in a shared understanding of the conflict, building on a World Bank risk and resilience assessment, which informed the RPBA's conflict analysis and the UN's strategic assessment mission. It supported the planning for the United Nations Multidimensional Integrated Stabilization Mission in the Central African Republic (MINUSCA) operations. The joint EU, UN, World Bank scoping mission to Bangui in May 2016 met with the government, the international community, civil society, and the private sector. The findings of the conflict analysis were shared with the government and were used to define shared strategic objectives across development, peace, and security pillars.

The RPBA was innovative in its integration of the views of the population, gathered in a survey conducted in all 179 communes and through interviews with local authorities on local infrastructure and security and policy priorities.

The survey collected information on household socioeconomic well-being, perceptions of security and economic conditions, and opinions on policy priorities. The assessment reached more than 14,000 people across the country, resulting in a national plan that was adopted by the government and Parliament as basis for its recovery efforts.

The assessment recognized the limited outreach of government services and the significant role that the international community, including civil society organizations, played in security and service delivery. The RPBA established a basis for a renewed partnership between government and international partners, formalized in a framework for mutual accountability signed during a Brussels donor roundtable (November 17, 2016). This partnership focused on a limited number of critical priorities essential for the Central African Republic's transition toward peace, stability, and economic recovery. The financing and implementation arrangements recognized the country's need to transition away from international financing and to increase its revenue mobilization.

Source: "Central African Republic: National Recovery and Peacebuilding Plan 2017–21."

Allocation of Official Development Assistance

Official development assistance (ODA), as an external financial flow—along with foreign direct investment, remittances, and lending—is vital to countries with limited capacity to raise domestic resources, including countries affected by conflict.[31] In response to the increasingly complex challenges faced by many low- and middle-income countries, ODA—comprising concessional financing from donor governments to both governments and multilateral institutions—has been growing steadily, quadrupling since 1960 in real terms (OECD 2017).[32] Since 2000, the rate of increase has accelerated, with ODA measured in real terms (in constant 2015 prices and exchange rates) more than doubling between 2000 and 2016 from US$70.85 billion to US$143.3 billion, with a nearly 50 percent increase from 2007 to 2016 alone (OECD 2017).[33] The share of ODA going to multilateral institutions has increased, while bilateral aid has decreased slightly (falling by 5 percent from 2015).

As a result, multilateral aid is now roughly equal to bilateral aid (Development Assistance Committee 2017).

The rise in ODA has been boosted by an increase in humanitarian aid, particularly in response to the refugee crisis (box 7.12). Humanitarian aid increased by 8 percent between 2015 and 2016 in real terms, reaching US$14.4 billion. Still, humanitarian aid remains a small portion of overall ODA, only about 10 percent in 2016 (Development Assistance Committee 2017). In addition, ODA spent by donor countries to cover the costs of hosting refugees surged by 27.5 percent to US$15.4 billion between 2015 and 2016, representing roughly 10.8 percent of ODA (Development Assistance Committee 2017).[34]

The largest share of ODA is directed toward countries considered fragile or conflict-affected, where other sources of financing, especially foreign direct investment, tend to be more limited.[35] During 2011–14, 14 of the top 20 ODA recipients were considered fragile, according to the OECD framework (OECD 2016), and overall net ODA flows to fragile states increased by around 140 percent in real terms from 2000 to 2015 (Dugarova and Gulasan 2017).

Across fragile contexts, ODA tends to concentrate in a handful of countries. For instance, between 2003 and 2012, Afghanistan and Iraq received 22 percent of all ODA allocated to fragile contexts (OECD 2015). In per capita terms, 34 of 56 fragile

---

BOX 7.12 Humanitarian Assistance

The primary purpose of humanitarian assistance is to save lives, reduce suffering, and maintain human dignity. Since 2013, approximately 97 percent of humanitarian crises have been "complex emergencies," meaning that they are multifaceted humanitarian crises requiring multisectoral response (UNOCHA 2016). With humanitarian appeals lasting an average of seven years, humanitarian actors have been present in many crises for more than two decades, for example, in the Democratic Republic of Congo, Somalia, and Sudan (UNOCHA 2015).

As highlighted by the World Humanitarian Summit, this funding is unsustainable. Financing requirements for the UN-coordinated humanitarian appeals and refugee response plans increased significantly from US$5.2 billion in 2006 to US$22.1 billion in 2016 (UN 2017). Whereas humanitarian aid also increased from US$3.4 billion to US$12.6 billion during the same period, it increasingly falls short of needs, and only 56 percent of the UN appeals were met in 2016 (UN 2017).

Providing humanitarian aid and meeting international commitments to refugees are important responsibilities of countries, and in the absence of successful prevention of conflicts and disaster risk reduction, it is essential to mitigate the impact of conflict on the most vulnerable. Since the World Humanitarian Summit in 2016, important efforts have been under way to integrate the provision of humanitarian and development assistance more tightly, recognizing the need to respond simultaneously to life-saving needs, strengthen economic and social resilience, and, where possible, promote peacebuilding in conflict contexts. The World Humanitarian Summit resulted in important commitments in this regard, with member states and international organizations committing to improve joint planning and aid predictability and to ensure seamless transitions between humanitarian and development assistance. The summit secured, above everything else, key commitments to prevent and end conflicts and leave no one behind. Building on the summit, the World Bank and the United Nations have committed to "engaging earlier to prevent violent conflict and reduce humanitarian need" (World Bank 2017).

contexts attracted less than the average ODA per capita that the group as a whole received between 2011 and 2014—among them, 17 fragile contexts received less than half the average level (OECD 2016). The extent of aid dependency also varies significantly within the group. During the same period, the average aid dependency among fragile contexts was 10.5 percent of gross national income (GNI), compared with 2.5 percent of GNI for stable contexts; in Afghanistan, Liberia, and the Solomon Islands, it was around or above 30 percent (OECD 2016).

Despite strong arguments for increasing aid flows before violence takes hold (OECD 2015; World Bank 2011), most aid focuses on postcrisis situations. While humanitarian aid tends to spike during and immediately after conflict, development assistance, which represents the bulk of ODA, is most often disbursed only after violence has occurred and declines very rapidly (see, example, figure 7.2).

Aid volatility poses another set of challenges, especially for countries recovering from violent conflict. According to a report by the Brookings Institution, during the period 2007–14 aid volatility in fragile and conflict-affected settings was 7 percentage points higher and donors performed 10 percentage points fewer of their activities jointly with other donors than in other contexts (Chandy, Seidal, and Zhang 2016).

It has been argued that in high-risk contexts, volatile aid risks amplifying countries' internal instability (Chandy, Seidel, and Zhang 2016) and constrains the capacity for postconflict recovery. In many protracted conflicts, this volatility in the volume of aid can be exacerbated by sudden diversion of aid from developmental or institutional development to humanitarian service delivery, and back, as countries undergo repeated cycles of violence (Carver 2017). As the example of the Central African Republic (box 7.13) illustrates, unpredictable aid flows are creating major constraints on efforts to prevent the relapse of violent conflicts. Collier and Rohner (2008), noting the negative effects that violent conflict inflicts on a country's institutions and capacity, argue that aid flows would be much more productive if sustained over time, as countries rebuild institutions.

FIGURE 7.2 Aid Inflows (2002–15) and Conflict-Related Fatalities (2000–16) in the Democratic Republic of Congo

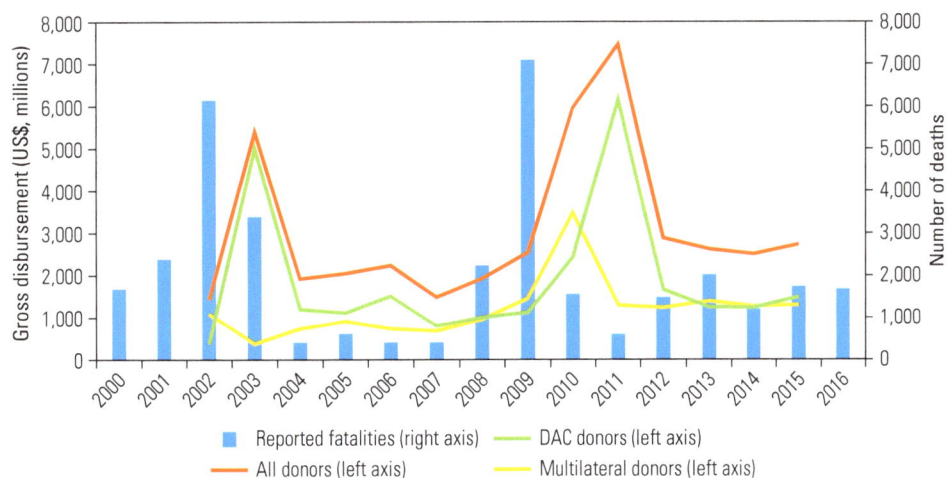

Sources: OECD Statistics; Armed Conflict Location and Event Data (ACLED) database; Yi 2017.
Note: DAC = OECD Development Assistance Committee.

The Central African Republic has been on the "fragile states" list of the OECD every year since the first year it was published in 2007. In 2013 the OECD identified the country as being potentially underaided—an "aid orphan"—according to two needs-based models using income per capita and population size as parameters.

In reality, however, the Central African Republic has been the recipient of often large, but extremely volatile, support. In 1998 a UN peacekeeping operation was deployed in the context of army mutinies and in the midst of controversial electoral preparations with a mission budget of approximately US$200 million in 2018 dollars. This mission was replaced on January 1, 2000, by a "peacebuilding office" with a budget 100 times smaller—approximately US$2 million.

At the same time, total flows of ODA to the country have been small. On average, the Central African Republic received US$286 million per year during the period 2002–14, amounting to US$65 per capita. The average, however, is biased upward by two large aid allocations: US$760 million in debt relief in 2009 and US$270 million in emergency relief in 2014.

Over the same period, ODA allocations to the first three Peacebuilding and State-building Goals of the New Deal on political, security, and justice institutions amounted to only US$3 per capita and an even more paltry US$1.4 per capita for 2002–05, immediately after withdrawal of the peacekeeping operation. Total ODA allocated to goals 1–3 amounted to only US$180 million over the 12-year period between 2002 and 2014.

Following the escalation of violence in 2013–14, a peacekeeping mission with more than 12,500 uniformed personnel and an annual operating budget of US$920 million was deployed, with US$2.2 billion of ODA pledged to support peacebuilding and recovery.

Sources: IMF 2009; OECD 2016.

Areas of Convergence between Diplomatic, Security, and Development Instruments

With violent conflict increasingly operating outside of state-based frameworks and the need for prevention to move beyond single actions and toward sustained engagement, no single policy realm is adequate to manage the risks of conflict (Griffin, forthcoming). Instead, successful conflict prevention strategies increasingly need to align security, development, and diplomatic action over the long term.

Recognizing the potential impact of more coordinated responses, diplomatic, security, and development actors increasingly seek to bridge divides and find areas of convergence between international tools in order to harness more coordinated action for prevention. This has been facilitated by the development of institutional platforms for interagency coordination and resource pooling. The UN Peacebuilding Commission and Peacebuilding Fund have played a strategic role in fostering greater coordination between peacekeeping and development actors and ensuring financial resources for integrated programs (box 7.14). This has been notably the case in Burundi, the Democratic Republic of Congo, and Sierra Leone, where support of the Peacebuilding Commission and Peacebuilding Fund has enabled peace consolidation and postconflict transition processes. Collaboration has also gone beyond UN development agencies to include partnerships with other multilateral development organizations, including the World Bank.

The evolution of both practice and policy points to some critical areas of convergence among security, development, and diplomatic action. This section

BOX 7.14 The Peacebuilding Commission

The Peacebuilding Commission was established on December 20, 2005, by Resolution 60/180 of the UN General Assembly (2005) and Resolution 1645 of the UN Security Council (2005), with the following mandate:

- Bring together all relevant actors to marshal resources and to advise on and propose integrated strategies for postconflict peacebuilding and recovery

- Focus attention on the reconstruction and institution-building efforts necessary for recovery from conflict and support the development of integrated strategies in order to lay the foundation for sustainable development

- Provide recommendations and information to improve the coordination of all relevant actors within and outside the United Nations, develop best practices, help to ensure predictable financing for early recovery activities, and extend the period of attention given by the international community to postconflict recovery.

Resolutions A/RES/70/262 (UN General Assembly 2016a) and S/RES/2282 (UN Security Council 2016) stress the importance of the Peacebuilding Commission to fulfill the following functions in this regard:

- Bring sustained international attention to sustaining peace and to providing political accompaniment and advocacy to countries affected by conflict, with their consent

- Promote an integrated, strategic, and coherent approach to peacebuilding, noting that security, development, and human rights are closely interlinked and mutually reinforcing

- Serve as a bridge between the principal organs and relevant entities of the United Nations by sharing advice on peacebuilding needs and priorities, in line with the respective competencies and responsibilities of these bodies

- Serve as a platform to convene all relevant actors within and outside the United Nations, including from member states; national authorities; UN missions and country teams; international, regional, and subregional organizations; international financial institutions; civil society; women's groups; youth organizations; and, where relevant, the private sector and national human rights institutions, in order to provide recommendations and information to improve their coordination, to develop and share good practices in peacebuilding, including on institution building, and to ensure predictable financing for peacebuilding.

Sources: UN General Assembly 2005, 2016a; UN Security Council 2005, 2016.

discusses how this convergence has contributed to the prevention of violent conflict over the long term.

Preconflict Mediation

Development actors have a standing presence in almost all countries at risk of conflict and maintain well-established relationships and contacts with a wide range of national actors. In some cases, development planning and assessments have been used to inform possible mediation planning, and development operations have directly undertaken or supported early mediation efforts. These efforts are particularly useful for addressing subnational disputes or latent tensions. A good example of this work is the Joint United Nations Development Programme (UNDP)–Department of Political Affairs Program on Building National Capacities for Conflict

Prevention (box 7.15), which has supported conflict analysis and early mediation efforts in countries including Chad and Kenya and has engaged national governments to build the capacity to address conflict risks (UNDP and Department of Political Affairs 2016).

Support for Postconflict Peacebuilding

Peace operations—particularly in contexts with tenuous or no peace agreements—increasingly have mandates to support the creation of a political, security, institutional, and economic environment conducive to peacemaking and longer-term peacebuilding.[36] In some countries, this has required technical advisory and development assistance across a range of thematic areas, including restoration of state authority, security and justice sector reform, disarmament, demobilization, and reintegration (DDR), and economic recovery, among others (box 7.16). Peace operations and development agencies have developed joint strategic frameworks to support multidimensional stabilization efforts, which have combined military, police, and civilian capacities and resources with development programming and financing to support improved security conditions and institutional capacities. Experience shows the importance of "bottom-up," community-driven conflict mitigation strategies with inclusive approaches to defining, reestablishing, and reforming institutions of governance and economic recovery strategies predicated on addressing inequality and exclusion.[37] This evolving approach to stabilization, which has been articulated operationally in the Central African Republic, the Democratic

---

BOX 7.15 **Strengthening National Capacities for Conflict Prevention**

Within the United Nations, the Program on Building National Capacities for Conflict Prevention is an example of conflict prevention programming that brings together political and developmental comparative advantage, capitalizing on the diversity within the United Nations system (UNDP and Department of Political Affairs 2016). Drawing on a cadre of peace and development advisers (PDAs), the joint program helps in-country UN personnel to strengthen national capacities and infrastructures for peace. Growing exponentially, 42 PDAs were deployed globally in 2016.

The role of PDAs is to adapt and respond to complex political situations and to develop and implement strategic prevention initiatives and programs. Broadly speaking, they engage in four core areas: (a) providing strategic advice and conflict analysis support to UN personnel in their relations with host government officials; (b) identifying areas of programmatic engagement with national stakeholders related to social cohesion, dialogue, conflict prevention, peacebuilding, or other relevant fields; (c) establishing strategic partnerships with key national stakeholders, regional and international actors, and development partners; and (d) strengthening the capacity of UNDP and the UN country team to undertake conflict analysis and mainstream conflict sensitivity in regular programming.

In 2016, for example, the joint program engagements ranged from strengthening dialogue, mediation, and national peace architectures in Kenya, Niger, the Philippines, and Ukraine to enabling strategic responses of the United Nations system through conflict analysis in Burundi and Tunisia and from conducting recovery and peacebuilding assessments with the World Bank and the EU in Cameroon and Nigeria to supporting the design of conflict prevention programs in Bangladesh, Sri Lanka, and Tajikistan.

Sources: Batmanglich 2017; UNDP and Department of Political Affairs 2016.

At the request of the Iraqi prime minister, UNDP established the Funding Facility for Stabilization (FFS) in June 2015 to help the government stabilize cities and districts liberated from the Islamic State in Iraq and the Levant (ISIL). The FFS is designed to help safeguard against the resurgence of violence and extremism, facilitate returns, and lay the groundwork for reconstruction and recovery.

FFS is an on-demand instrument overseen by a steering committee chaired by the secretary-general of the Iraqi Council of Ministers. Stabilization priorities are set by the Iraqi authorities who are directly responsible for stabilizing areas. As soon as a newly liberated area is declared safe and local authorities have identified priorities, UNDP uses fast-track procedures to bring local contractors on the ground, usually within weeks.

More than 95 percent of all stabilization projects are done through the local private sector employing local labor. This approach is highly effective, helping to inject liquidity into the local economy, generate local jobs, and reduce overall costs.

Nearly 1,550 projects are currently under way in 28 liberated towns in Anbar, Diyala, Nineveh, and Salah al Din governorates. More than half involve rehabilitation of electricity, water, and sewage grids. Rather than starting at the top of the grid and forcing families to wait for services, sometimes for years, households are being connected to the nearest functioning component of the grid.

Bridges, schools, health centers, pharmacies, hospitals, universities, and administrative buildings are being repaired, and thousands of people are employed on work crews, removing rubble and transporting debris. Destitute families, including women-headed households, are benefiting from cash grants, and thousands of houses are being rebuilt in destroyed neighborhoods.

The impact has been significant; half of the nearly 6 million Iraqis who were displaced during the fighting have returned to their homes and started to rebuild their lives.

Sources: Pillay and van der Hoeven 2017.

Republic of Congo, and Mali, attempts to provide a long-term commitment to reducing violence by identifying and managing the drivers of conflict alongside political negotiations.

Disarmament, Demobilization, and Reintegration and Community-Based Conflict Management

A core element of postconflict peacebuilding is the DDR of combatants. The United Nations, the World Bank, and other international organizations have been effective at monitoring and supporting demobilization and disarmament processes. When it comes to reintegration, however, their record is mixed (Berdal and Ucko 2009; Weinstein and Humphreys 2005). The current decade has seen heightened political and security challenges in settings where peace operations deploy (for example, no peace agreement or inclusive political process, transnational criminal networks, a rising number of armed nonstate actors, violent extremism, or regional armed group dynamics), making DDR more challenging to achieve (Colletta and Muggah 2009; Muggah 2010). Nonetheless, the Security Council continues to mandate DDR in situations of protracted conflicts, violent extremism, and generalized criminal violence.

One of the emerging challenges facing development, security, and diplomatic operations alike is the presence of organized armed groups and criminal gangs, often rooted in unsuccessfully reintegrated combatants. While these groups are usually small, they can create local conflicts that can rapidly escalate to the national level.

International partners, particularly peace operations, are increasingly working with national governments in formulating bottom-up, nonmilitary preventive "community engagement strategies." These initiatives may complement formal peace agreements and include approaches such as community violence reduction programs or community stabilization projects. These strategies are focused on "localizing" services in arenas of contestation, through protection of civilians, mitigation of intercommunal conflicts, and community violence reduction actions, while at the same time restoring state authority in sensitive areas. These initiatives have used field deployments of peace operations as platforms for engagement and have proven popular for their targeted and flexible nature. There is a clear point of convergence between these efforts and the actions of development partners focusing on local peacebuilding and reconciliation as well as broader community- or area-based economic recovery and social protection programming. However, questions remain as to their accountability and sustainability. Similar to other types of decentralized efforts to strengthen security at the local level, community violence reduction, in particular, has been criticized for inadvertently empowering gangs, stigmatizing certain communities, and lacking adequate oversight (Muggah 2017).

Security and Justice Reform

Another area of convergence between different operations has been in the area of security and justice reform as part of efforts to improve effectiveness, civilian oversight, and accountability of the state (UN Secretary-General 2013). While historically mandated in the context of peace operations, reform of security and justice institutions has increasingly been supported through development assistance. In policing, for instance, collaborative operations between peacekeeping and development actors have provided direct operational support to enhance national capacity to restore and maintain law and order, providing training and technical assistance for legal reform and institutional strengthening (UN Secretary-General 2016b). With respect to justice and corrections, technical advisory support from a wide range of sources has been deployed to support legal and institutional reforms and to boost professionalism and capacity through direct technical support and advice (DPKO 2016). This support changes significantly in contexts marked by the absence of a clear political settlement or peace agreement, as in Mali and South Sudan. In these cases, support for security and justice sector reform can be provided during peace negotiations or national dialogue processes through upstream provision of technical advice.

Building National Capacity for Mediation

The shift in mediation practice from a "state-centric" model toward inclusive processes involving governmental and nongovernmental actors has been complemented with stronger support for national and local mediation capacities. Provision of capacity development assistance—through training, development of guidance, and institutional strengthening—has been supported by civil society, development, and multilateral organizations alike, often forming part of governance or peacebuilding programming. Since 2012, for instance, the United Nations has partnered with the EU to support "national and local mediation" capacities in 14 countries with a focus on dialogue and negotiation. Together, the United Nations and the EU have supported national platforms for mediation and dialogue in Bolivia and Ghana; youth and women organizations in Chad, the Maldives, and Togo; and national dialogue processes in Guyana, Mauritania, Nepal, and the Republic of Yemen. Best-practice guidelines have been summarized in a joint publication by the United Nations and EU, joining similar guidelines for mediating conflicts over natural resources and guidance on gender and inclusive mediation strategies (UN Secretary-General 2012).

Development Support for Negotiations

Development assistance can be a useful resource for mediators seeking to facilitate comprehensive agreements on the social, economic, and governance provisions of a peace settlement or successor agreement. This support is particularly important, where multitier agreements are under negotiation (that is, where they focus not just on high-level political issues but also on broader social, economic, and institutional issues). Development institutions such as the World Bank have provided technical advice and guidance on the development of economic provisions of political settlements. In complex multilevel mediation efforts that span various stages of political negotiation toward a comprehensive settlement, development actors help to identify and frame technical issues, assess the developmental and fiscal impacts of negotiated settlements, and provide advisory assistance on options.

In the context of the 2011 Gulf Cooperation Council peace agreement in the Republic of Yemen, for instance, which included the organization of a national dialogue to achieve consensus on key national priorities, development partners actively supported the UN special envoy in identifying, framing, and organizing negotiations around key social and economic issues. Development assistance can also support the translation of political "blueprints" for governance arrangements into reality through investments in institutional development. Technical support and development of capacity of the parties in peace negotiations between the government of the Philippines and Mindanao Islamic Liberation Front was provided by the UN and the World Bank through the Facility for Advisory Support for Transition Capacities, or FASTRAC. In Burkina Faso, for example, the International Follow-up and Support Group for the Transition in Burkina Faso, established in December 2014, aimed to implement the transition roadmap and provided diplomatic, technical, and financial support to the transitional government in restoring peace and preparing for the 2015 presidential and legislative elections. This group was composed of the African Union, ECOWAS, and the United Nations, international and regional actors, and development partners, including the World Bank (Pichler Fong 2017).

Conclusion

Since the end of the Cold War, the multilateral architecture for conflict prevention and postconflict peacebuilding has struggled to adapt to a fast-changing situation in the field and globally. Despite many challenges, there have been some clear achievements. At a systemic level, comprehensive international normative and legal frameworks are in place to regulate the tools and conduct of war; protect human rights; address global threats including climate change, terrorism, and transnational criminal networks; and promote inclusive approaches to development (the SDGs). Several of these aspects are reflected in the 2030 Agenda.

Operationally, the United Nations and regional organizations such as the African Union and the EU have provided global and regional forums to coordinate international responses to threats to peace and stability. The results have been important tools stretching across the conflict cycle—including preventive diplomacy, protection of civilians, and peace operations—which have proven instrumental in preventing conflicts, mediating cease-fires and peace agreements, and supporting postconflict recovery and transition processes.

Growing collaboration between efforts to prevent violent conflict and development actors has been a key part of these developments. As conflicts have increasingly originated from and disrupted the core institutions of states, international and regional initiatives have accompanied these changes with greater coordination and resource pooling between development, diplomatic, and security efforts. In preventive diplomacy, this coordination has been demonstrated by the involvement of diverse stakeholders, the codification of mediation, and its broadening both thematically and in terms of its application at all levels and phases of conflict. Peacekeeping has evolved from a narrow focus on monitoring cease-fires and peace agreements to complex multidimensional missions with mandates to consolidate peace, stabilize the country, and support the restoration of state authority. Development assistance is shifting toward earlier engagement, more attention to socioeconomic and institutional drivers of fragility and conflict, and improved alignment with diplomatic, peace, and security efforts.

While this evolution is welcome, with conflicts becoming more fragmented, more complex, and more transnational, these tools are profoundly challenged—entry points for diplomatic engagement are harder to find (Gowan and Stedman 2018; Walter 2017), and peace operations are increasingly deployed to insecure environments. Meanwhile, multilateral engagement, per se, is tested by the emergence of nonstate actors uninterested in state-based power, ideologies at odds with international humanitarian law, and the increased sponsorship of proxy warfare by global and regional powers, as discussed in chapter 1. Each of these elements decreases the incentives of violent actors to accept mediation and increases the resistance of the international community to accept the terms of negotiated settlements.

These conclusions increase the need to focus on country pathways—the endogenous risk factors that engender violence and support for countries to address their own crises. Despite notable successes, current tools for international support are challenged with engaging effectively before the risks of violence become manifest. To some degree, this challenge reflects the difficulty of gaining accurate information, as even the most sophisticated EWSs offer only short time frames for averting crisis. However, in larger part, the lack of incentives of actors to identify and address broader risks presents the wider challenge.

At its core, preventive action now is instigated in large part by actions to mitigate violence and its impact on individual rights and by the international and regional system, rather than by countries' own development progress. When dealing with a new generation of conflicts, governance of

multilateral tools and the mandate to instruct engagements on developmental, peace, and security dimensions of conflict are often fragmented between institutions and actors.

Bringing the full power of international tools to bear on today's risks requires a much greater level of coordination and convergence than has been present historically. Achieving this demands a realignment of incentives to encourage greater collaboration among states and within the multilateral system. Chapter 8 turns to this challenge.

Notes

1. United Nations Charter, Art. 1.
2. See UN General Assembly (2016a) and Articles 2 and 3 of the UN Charter. The sustaining peace resolutions reaffirmed this principle, recognizing "the primary responsibility of national Governments and authorities in identifying, driving, and directing priorities, strategies, and activities for sustaining peace … emphasizing that sustaining peace is a shared task and responsibility that needs to be fulfilled by the Government and all other national stakeholders" (UN General Assembly 2016a; UN Security Council 2016).
3. Of the 63 resolutions adopted by the Security Council in 2014, 32 were adopted "acting under Chapter VII of the Charter" (approximately 51 percent), while in 2015, 35 of the 64 resolutions were adopted "acting under Chapter VII of the Charter" (approximately 55 percent). As in previous periods, most of those resolutions concerned the mandates of UN and regional peacekeeping missions or multinational forces and the imposition, extension, modification, or termination of sanctions measures (see, for example, UN Department of Political Affairs 2015b, 4).
4. The topics covered under these thematic debates are an arena of evolving multilateral agreement. During 2014 and 2015, for example, under the broad category of maintenance of international peace and security, the Security Council held 17 meetings, more than a fivefold increase with respect to the previous two years. Subagenda items

discussed in this period also multiplied and included the following: (a) war, its lessons, and the search for a permanent peace; (b) security sector reform; (c) conflict prevention; (d) inclusive development for the maintenance of international peace and security; (e) the role of youth in countering violent extremism; (f) peace and security challenges facing small islands developing states; (g) regional organizations and contemporary challenges of global security; and (h) trafficking of persons in situations of conflict (see, for example, UN Department of Political Affairs 2015b, 2).

5. According to the Union of International Associations, intergovernmental organizations are defined as bodies that are based on a formal instrument of agreement between national governments, include at least three nation states, and possess a permanent secretariat performing ongoing tasks. See http://www.uia.org/archive/types -organization/cc.

6. Chapter VIII of the UN Charter recognizes the importance of regional arrangements in support of the maintenance of international peace and security and stresses that "no enforcement action shall be taken under regional arrangements or by regional agencies without the authorization of the Security Council" (UN Charter, Ch. VIII, Art. 53).

7. In 2017, for instance, the African Union and the UN signed a framework agreement to strengthen their responses to emerging challenges in key areas such as peace and security, human rights, and development. See http://www.un.org/apps/news/story.asp? NewsID=56587#.WgsBnFtSzcs.

8. "The right of the Union to intervene in a Member State pursuant to a decision of the Assembly in respect of grave circumstances, namely: war crimes, genocide, and crimes against humanity" (African Union 2000).

9. "We pledge not to bequeath the burden of conflicts to the next generation of Africans and undertake to end all wars in Africa by 2020" (African Union 2013, art. E).

10. For example, official development assistance to countries with high risk of conflict averages US$250 million per year, only slightly higher than that to countries at peace, but increases to US$700 million during open conflict and US$400 million during recovery years. Similarly, peacekeeping support averages US$30 million a year for countries at high risk, compared with US$100 million for countries in open conflict and US$300 during recovery (Mueller 2017).

11. Many government-owned or government-sponsored conflict prediction systems are classified. Since the early 2000s, the United Nations has undertaken significant steps to anticipate and prevent violent conflict, and the World Bank is currently developing the Global Risk Scan, a tool designed to identify multifaceted fragility, conflict, and violence risks in countries across the globe.

12. Some governmental and intergovernmental early warning systems have civil society reporting components, for example, the African Union, CEWARN, and ECOWARN all have links to civil society networks, while early warning systems in the Southern African Development Community and the International Conference of the Great Lakes Region rely on state intelligence (ATF 2016).

13. Third-generation EWSs are located in conflict areas with strong local networks. The objective is to detect conflict and link EWS to response mechanisms, where monitors act as "first responders."

14. Article 55 of the UN Charter states that to support the "creation of conditions of stability and well-being which are necessary for peaceful and friendly relations among nations based on respect for the principle of equal rights and self-determination of peoples, the United Nations shall promote … universal respect for, and observance of, human rights and fundamental freedoms for all without distinction as to race, sex, language, or religion" (UN Charter, Preamble). See UN General Assembly (2003), also the "Vienna Declaration and Programme of Action" (World Conference on Human Rights 1993): "The efforts of the United Nations system towards the universal respect for, and observance of, human rights and fundamental freedoms for all, contribute to the stability and well-being necessary for peaceful and friendly relations among nations, and to improved conditions for peace and security as well as social and economic development,

in conformity with the Charter of the United Nations."

15. The potential of the Universal Periodic Review to contribute to conflict prevention and peacebuilding efforts was acknowledged in the sustaining peace resolutions (UN General Assembly 2016b, para. 11; UN Security Council 2016).

16. This has occurred gradually, with member states having ratified universal human rights instruments adopted under the aegis of the United Nations, and organizations like the African Union, the Council of Europe, and the Organization of American States having adopted regional instruments, the implementation of which is supported by civil society organizations and national human rights institutions.

17. Growing confidence in mediation has resulted in expanded capabilities to support such processes. Despite data gaps, there has been a significant increase in the number of deployed envoys, special advisers, and political missions over the past 10–15 years. These entities have taken up an increasingly broad range of functions, including early warning and analysis, coordination of regional mediation initiatives, and direct support for mediation before, during, and after crises and conflicts. Special political missions alone have increased in number by 70 percent, and spending has increased by a factor of 13, since 2000 (UN Secretary-General 2017a).

18. In 2016, the Security Council requested the United Nations Office for West Africa (UNOWA) and the Office of the Special Envoy for the Sahel to merge into a single entity, the United Nations Office for West Africa and the Sahel (UNOWAS).

19. Since 2008 the UN's Mediation Support Unit, with a standby team of senior mediation experts has provided tailored advice to national negotiators and international mediators (see www.peacemaker.un.org).

20. While qualitative cases indicate the potential importance of diplomatic engagement in both coordinating international and regional action and bridging conflict parties, few studies have assessed these cases against data. Regan (2010, 2012), building on Goldstone et al. (2010), assesses the success of interventions in countries and periods with a high risk of civil war. Regan (2012)

concludes that military interventions increase the likelihood of civil war, economic interventions have no effect on the likelihood of war, and diplomatic interventions decrease the likelihood of war (for example, Hoeffler 2013).

21. The meaning of success is much disputed among scholars of international mediation, and indicators vary substantially. Success rates of mediation have been measured on the basis of whether mediation has been accepted, whether violence has ended, whether conflicting parties have reached a formal agreement, and how long it holds. When measuring success against whether the parties reach any type of agreement (from cease-fire to comprehensive settlement), Wallensteen and Svensson (2014) conclude that 55 percent of mediated processes fail, in part, because they often do not result in such formalized outcomes. There are also signs that mediation successes are evolving. Building on the UCDP conflict termination data, Kreutz (2010) has calculated that, in the 1990s, 46.1 percent of conflicts that ended by negotiated settlement restarted, but the number of conflicts returning to violence decreased to 21.0 percent in the 2000s, suggesting that learning led to more lasting successes later.

22. Bercovitch and Wells (1993) find that in interstate conflicts, 29 percent of mediation attempts resulted in a cease-fire or more enduring peace. However, Svensson and Lundgren (2015) show that more than 60 percent of cases of mediation led to an abatement of crisis between 1945 and 2005. For other studies on the effectiveness of mediation, see, for example, Beardsley et al. 2006; Bercovitch and Wells 1993; Eisenkopf and Bachtiger 2013; Shrodt and Gerner 2004; Wilkenfeld et al. 2003.

23. Data confirm that multifaceted approaches used in tandem with other tools render mediation more effective. For instance, there is "strong empirical evidence" that mediation in combination with a peacekeeping operation highly correlates with nonrecurrence (DeRouen and Chowdhury 2016). Mediated agreements that encompass political, military, territorial, and justice provisions also decrease the risk of recurrence, although the likelihood of recurrence

rises over time in mediated cases (Beardsley 2011; DeRouen and Chowdhury 2016; Fortna 2003; Joshi and Quinn 2016a, 2016b).

24. See http://www.un.org/undpa/en/diplomacy-mediation.

25. Beardsley and Gleditsch (2015) explore whether the deployment of external peacekeepers can prevent violent conflict from spreading within a country once a civil war has broken out. Using geo-referenced conflict polygons between 1990 and 2010, the authors find that peacekeeping missions that are large, especially when there are many troops, have a strong containment effect.

26. All references to Kosovo should be understood in the context of UN Security Council Resolution 1244 (UN Security Council 1999).

27. The practice of peace operations in these areas has been codified in various policy and guidance documents, with support and resources provided through the Office of Rule of Law and Security Institutions at headquarters level (which also supports special political missions led by the Department of Political Affairs).

28. According to the *UN Peacekeeping Operations: Principles and Guidelines* (Capstone Doctrine; UN 2008), the role of multidimensional peacekeeping operations is to "create a secure and stable environment while strengthening the State's ability to provide security, with full respect for the rule of law and human rights; facilitate the political process by promoting dialogue and reconciliation and supporting the establishment of legitimate and effective institutions of governance; and provide a framework for ensuring that all United Nations and other international actors pursue their activities at the country-level in a coherent and coordinated manner" (POTI 2010).

29. More recent studies dispute this link, citing methodological questions (Christian and Barrett 2017) and arguing that the macro-level analysis hides important spatial distribution effects (Gehring, Kaplan, and Wong 2017).

30. In order to enable countries to access financing at early sign of risks of violent conflict, the World Bank has created a risk mitigation facility under IDA 18 to support countries in their prevention efforts. See http://ida .worldbank.org/financing/ida-special -allocation-index-isai-0.

31. ODA is composed of many elements including, for example, humanitarian aid, debt relief, and country programmable aid. When removing special-purpose flows such as humanitarian aid and debt relief, country programmable aid can provide a good estimate of funding used for development programming in recipient countries and thus is often used as a proxy for development aid at the country level.

32. While ODA flows fell in the mid-1990s because of fiscal consolidations in donor countries, overall flows rose again after 1998.

33. According to official data collected by the OECD Development Assistance Committee. Total ODA flows corresponded to 0.32 percent of GNI of member countries in 2016. Despite the sizable increases, this still falls short of the long-standing 0.7 percent of GNI commitment.

34. A 1988 rule allows donor countries to include the costs of hosting refugees in ODA for the first year after arrival. Development Assistance Committee (2017) notes that efforts are ongoing to revise ODA reporting rules to minimize the risk that spending on refugees diverts from spending on development.

35. The group of 56 fragile contexts defined by the OECD hosts approximately 22 percent of the world's population, but only attracts 5 percent of the global total of foreign direct investment (OECD 2016).

36. Relevant missions include MONUSCO in the Democratic Republic of Congo, MINUSMA in Mali, MINUSTAH in Haiti, UNMISS in South Sudan, and MINUSCA in the Central African Republic (Gorur 2016).

37. The shift to "bottom-up" approaches is a reaction to important failures of more state-centric approaches to stabilization that were tried in the Democratic Republic of Congo between 2008 and 2011, in which "top-down" approaches to state authority had the result of extending institutions that were perceived as illegitimate, reproduced certain "predatory" characteristics, and failed to provide frameworks for adequate governance of complex local conflict, social, and other dynamics (De Vries 2016).

References

Ackerman, A. 1999. *Making Peace Prevail: Preventing Violent Conflict in Macedonia.* Syracuse, NY: Syracuse University Press.

African Union. 2000. *Constitutive Act of the African Union.* Adopted in 2000 at the Lome Summit (Togo), entered into force in 2001. Addis Ababa: African Union.

———. 2013. "50th Anniversary Solemn Declaration." Assembly of the Heads of State and Government of the African Union, Addis Ababa.

African Union Commission. 2015. *Agenda 2063: The Africa We Want.* Addis Ababa: Africa Union Commission.

Aguirre, A. 2015. "Fiscal Policy and Civil Conflict in Africa." Paper prepared as part of the World Bank Regional Study, *Africa's Macroeconomic Vulnerabilities*, World Bank, Washington DC. http://alvaroaguirre.weebly.com/uploads/1/3/2/9/13298570/pf_conflict.pdf.

Anderson, D. M., and J. McKnight. 2014. "Kenya at War: Al-Shabaab and Its Enemies in Eastern Africa." *African Affairs* 114 (454): 1–27.

Anderson, M. B. 1999. *Do No Harm: How Aid Can Support Peace—or War?* Boulder, CO: Lynne Rienner.

ATF (African Task Force on the Prevention of Mass Atrocities). 2016. *African Regional Communities and the Prevention of Mass Atrocities.* Budapest: Budapest Centre for Mass Atrocities Prevention.

Babbitt, E. F. 2012. "Preventive Diplomacy by Intergovernmental Organizations: Learning from Practice" *International Negotiation* 17 (3): 349–88. doi: 10.1163/15718069-12341236.

Barron, P., and J. Sharpe. 2005. "Counting Conflicts—Using Newspaper Reports to Understand Violence in Indonesia." Social Development Paper, Conflict Prevention, and Reconstruction Series CPR 25, World Bank, Washington, DC.

Batmanglich, S. 2017. "Independent Review of Peace and Development Advisors and the Joint UNDP/DPA Programme on Building National Capacities for Conflict Prevention." U.K. Department for International Development, London.

Beardsley, K. 2011. "Peacekeeping and the Contagion of Armed Conflict." *Journal of Politics* 73 (4): 1051–64.

Beardsley, K., and K. S. Gleditsch. 2015. "Peacekeeping as Conflict Containment." *International Studies Review* 17 (1): 67–89.

Beardsley, K. C., D. M. Quinn, B. Biswas, and J. Wilkenfeld. 2006. "Mediation Style and Crisis Outcomes." *Journal of Conflict Resolution* 50 (1): 58–86.

Bercovitch, J., and R. Wells. 1993. "Evaluating Mediation Strategies." *Journal of Peace Research* 18 (1): 3–25.

Berdal, M., and D. Ucko. 2009. *Reintegrating Armed Groups after Conflict: Politics, Violence, and Transition.* New York: Routledge.

Biermann, F., P. Pattberg, H. van Asselt, and F. Zelli. 2009. "The Fragmentation of Global Governance Architectures: A Framework for Analysis." *Global Environmental Politics* 9 (4): 14–40.

Björkdahl, A. 2006. "Promoting Norms through Peacekeeping: UNPREDEP and Conflict Prevention." *International Peacekeeping* 13 (2): 214–28.

Blair, R. A., C. Blattman, and A. Hartman. 2011. *Patterns of Conflict and Cooperation in Liberia.* Part 2: *Prospects for Conflict Forecasting and Early Warning.* New Haven, CT: Innovations for Poverty Action.

———. 2015. "Predicting Local Violence." Brown University; University of Chicago; University College of London. https://papers.ssrn.com/sol3/papers.cfm?abstract_id=2497153.

Blattman, C. 2012. "Can We Predict Eruptions of Violence? Statistics and the Future of Conflict Early Warning." Harris School of Public Policy, University of Chicago. https://chrisblattman.com/2012/02/13/can-we-predict-local-conflict/.

———. 2014. "Can We Use Data and Machine Learning to Predict Local Violence in Fragile States? As It Turns Out, Yes." Harris School of Public Policy, University of Chicago. https://chrisblattman.com/2014/10/02/can-use-data-machine-learning-predict-local-violence-fragile-states-turns-yes/.

Bosley, C. C. 2016. "The 'New' Normal: Instability Risk Assessment in an Uncertainty-Based Strategic Environment." *International Studies Review* 19: viw038. 10.1093/isr/viw038.

Brandt, P. T., J. R. Freeman, and P. A. Schrodt. 2011a. "Racing Horses: Constructing and Evaluating Forecasts in Political Science." Paper presented at the 28th Summer Meeting of the Society for Political Methodology, Princeton University, Princeton, NJ, July. http://www.princeton.edu/politics/about/file-repository/public/RHMethods20110721.pdf.

———. 2011b. "Real Time, Time Series Forecasting of Inter- and Intra-State

Political Conflict." *Conflict Management and Peace Science* 28 (1): 41–64.

Bryden, A., and F. Olonisakin, eds. 2010. *Security Sector Transformation in Africa*. Geneva: DCAF.

Calì, M., and A. Mulabdic. 2017. "Trade and Civil Conflict: Revisiting the Cross-Country Evidence." Policy Research Working Paper 7125, World Bank, Washington, DC.

Call, C. T. 2012. "UN Mediation and the Politics of Transition after Constitutional Crises." Policy Paper, International Peace Institute, New York.

———. 2017. "The Evolution of Conflict Prevention in the United Nations." Background paper for the United Nations–World Bank Flagship Study, *Pathways for Peace: Inclusive Approaches to Preventing Violent Conflict*, World Bank, Washington, DC.

Carbonnier, G. 2015. *Humanitarian Economics: War, Disaster, and the Global Aid Market*. London: Hurst and Company.

Carver, F. 2017. "A 'Call to Peacebuilding': Rethinking Humanitarian and Development Activity in South Sudan." *Humanitarian Exchange* 68 (January): 7–10. https://odihpn.org/magazine/a-call-to-peacebuilding-rethinking-humanitarian-and-development/.

Chadefaux, T. 2014. "Early Warning Signals for War in the News." *Journal of Peace Research* 51 (1): 5–18.

Chandy, L., B. Seidel, and C. Zhang. 2016. "Aid Effectiveness in Fragile States, How Bad Is It and How Can It Improve?" Brooke Shearer Series, Brookings Institution, Washington, DC.

Christian, P., and C. B. Barrett. 2017. "Revisiting the Effect of Food Aid on Conflict: A Methodological Caution." Policy Research Working Paper 8171, World Bank, Washington, DC.

CIC (Center for International Cooperation). 2012. *Review of Political Missions 2012*. New York: Center for International Cooperation.

Colletta, N., and R. Muggah. 2009. "Context Matters: Interim Stabilisation and Second-Generation Approaches to Security Promotion." *Conflict, Security, and Development* 9 (4): 425–53.

Collier, P., and A. Hoeffler. 2004. "Greed and Grievance in Civil War." *Oxford Economic Papers* 56 (4): 563–95.

———. 2006. "Military Expenditure in Post-Conflict Societies." *Economics of Governance* 7 (1): 89–107.

Collier, P., and D. Rohner. 2008. "Democracy, Development, and Conflict." *Journal of the European Economic Association* 6 (2-3): 531–40.

Crocker, C., and P. Aall, eds. 1999. *Herding Cats*. Washington, DC: United States Institute of Peace Press.

Dal Bo, E., and P. Dal Bo. 2011. "Workers, Warriors, and Criminals: Social Conflict in General Equilibrium." *Journal of the European Economic Association* 9 (4): 646–77.

Day, A., and A. Pichler Fong. 2017. "Diplomacy and Good Offices in the Prevention of Conflict." Background paper for the United Nations–World Bank Flagship Study, *Pathways to Peace: Inclusive Approaches to Preventing Violent Conflict*, World Bank, Washington, DC.

De Coning, C., and C. Prakash. 2016. *Peace Capacities Network Synthesis Report*. Oslo: Norwegian Institute of International Affairs.

Defontaine, C. 2017. "Short Literature Review on Monitoring Risks of Violent Conflict." Background paper for the United Nations–World Bank Flagship Study, *Pathways for Peace: Inclusive Approaches to Preventing Violent Conflict*, World Bank, Washington, DC.

DeRouen, K., and I. Chowdhury. 2016. "Mediation, Peacekeeping, and Civil War Peace Agreements." *Defence and Peace Economics* (May 9): 1–17.

Development Assistance Committee. 2017. "Official Development Assistance: Definition and Coverage." OECD, Paris. http://www.oecd.org/dac/stats/officialdevelopmentassistancedefinitionandcoverage.htm#Coverage.

De Vries, H. 2016. *The Ebb and Flow of Stabilization in the Congo*. Nairobi: Rift Valley Institute.

Donnelly, C. 1997. "Defence Transformation in the New Democracies: A Framework for Tackling the Problem." *NATO Review* 1 (45): 15–19. http://www.nato.int/docu/review/1997/9701-4.htm.

Doyle, M. W., and N. Sambanis. 2000. "International Peacebuilding: A Theoretical and Quantitative Analysis." *American Political Science Review* 94 (4): 779–801.

———. 2006. *Making War and Building Peace: United Nations Peace Operations*. Princeton, NJ: Princeton University Press. http://www.jstor.org/stable/j.ctt7rtn4.

DPKO (Department of Peacekeeping Operations). 2008. *United Nations Peacekeeping Operations: Principles and Guidelines*. New York: UN DPKO.

———. 2016. "Support for Strengthening Justice and Corrections Systems." Non-Paper, UN DPKO, New York, January.

Dube, O., and J. F. Vargas. 2013. "Commodity Price Shocks and Civil Conflict: Evidence from Colombia." *Review of Economic Studies* 80 (4): 1384–421.

Dugarova, E., and N. Gulasan. 2017. *Global Trends: Challenges and Opportunities in the Implementation of the Sustainable Development Goals.* Geneva: United Nations Development Programme and United Nations Research Institute for Social Development.

Duque, L. F., B. Caicedo, and C. Sierra. 2008. "Sistema de vigilancia epidemiológica de la violencia para los municipios colombianos." *La Revista Facultad Nacional de Salud Pública* 26 (2): 196–208.

Eikenberry, K., and S. Krasner. 2017. "Civil Wars and Global Disorder: Threats and Opportunities." *Daedalus* 146 (4): 6–17.

Eisenkopf, G., and A. Bachtiger. 2013. "Mediation and Conflict Prevention." *Journal of Conflict Resolution* 57 (4): 570–97.

Eldridge, J. L. C. 2002. "Playing at Peace: Western Politics, Diplomacy, and the Stabilization of Macedonia." *European Security* 11 (3): 46–90. doi: 10.1080/09662830208407538.

Fearon, J., and D. Laitin. 2003. "Ethnicity, Insurgency, and Civil War." *American Political Science Review* 97 (1): 75–90.

Fisher, J., and D. M. Anderson. 2015. "Authoritarianism and the Securitization of Development in Africa." *International Affairs* 91 (1): 131–51.

Fortna, V. P. 2003. "Scraps of Paper? Agreements and the Durability of Peace." *International Organization* 57 (2): 337–72.

———. 2004. "Does Peacekeeping Keep Peace? International Intervention and the Duration of Peace after Civil War." *International Studies Quarterly* 48 (2004): 269–92.

Framtid, U. 2015. *From Billions to Trillions: MDB Contributions to Financing for Development.* Washington, DC: World Bank Group.

Gehring, K., L. Kaplan, and M. H. L. Wong. 2017. "Aid and Conflict at the Local Level—Mechanisms and Causality." Draft paper presented at Northeast Universities Development Consortium Conference, Harvard Kennedy School, Cambridge, MA. August 18. https://sites.tufts.edu/neudc2017/files/2017/10/paper_472.pdf.

Gibler, D. M. 2016. "Combining Behavioral and Structural Predictors of Violent Civil Conflict: Getting Scholars and Policymakers to Talk to Each Other." *International Studies Quarterly* 61 (1): 28–37.

Giessmann, H. J., J. B. Galvanek, and C. Seifert. 2017. "Curbing Violence: Development, Application, and the Sustaining of National Capacities for Conflict Prevention." Background paper for the United Nations–World Bank Flagship Study, *Pathways to Peace: Inclusive Approaches to Preventing Violent Conflict,* World Bank, Washington, DC.

Gilligan, M., and E. Sergenti. 2008. "Do UN Interventions Cause Peace? Using Matching to Improve Causal Inference." *Quarterly Journal of Political Science* 3 (2): 89–122.

Goldstone, J. A., R. H. Bates, D. L. Epstein, T. R. Gurr, M. B. Lustik, M. G. Marshall, J. Ulfelder, and M. Woodward. 2010. "A Global Model for Forecasting Political Instability." *American Journal of Political Science* 54 (1): 190–208.

Gorur, A. 2016. *Defining the Boundaries of UN Stabilization Missions.* Washington, DC: Stimson Center.

Gowan, R. 2011. "Multilateral Political Missions and Preventive Diplomacy." United States Institute of Peace, Washington, DC.

Gowan, R., and S. J. Stedman. 2018. "The International Regime for Treating Civil War, 1988–2017." *Daedalus* (Winter): 171–84.

Greig, J. M., and P. Diehl. 2012. *International Mediation.* Cambridge, MA: Polity.

Griffin, M. Forthcoming. "The UN's Role in a Changing Global Landscape." In *The Oxford Handbook on the United Nations,* 2d ed., edited by T. G. Weiss and S. Daws, ch. 45. Oxford: Oxford University Press.

Harland, D. 2016. "War Is Back: The International Response to Armed Conflict." *Horizons* 7 (Spring): 231.

Hartzell, C. A., M. Hoddie, and D. Rothchild. 2001. "Stabilizing the Peace after Civil War: An Investigation of Some Key Variables." *International Organizations* 55 (1): 183–208.

Healy, S. 2009. "Peacemaking in the Midst of War: An Assessment of IGAD's Contribution to Regional Security." Working Paper 59, Royal Institute of International Affairs, Chatham House, London, November.

Hinnebusch, R., and I. W. Zartman, with E. Parker-Magyar and O. Imady. 2016. "UN Mediation in the Syrian Crisis: From Kofi

Annan to Lakhdar Brahimi." International Peace Institute, New York, March.

Hoeffler, A. 2013. "Can International Interventions Secure the Peace?" ERSA Working Paper 31, Economic Research Southern Africa, Cape Town. http://citeseerx.ist.psu.edu/viewdoc/download?doi=10.1.1.357.3971&rep=rep1&type=pdf.

———. 2014. "Can International Interventions Secure the Peace?" *International Area Studies Review* 17 (1): 75–94.

Hultman, L., J. Kathman, and M. Shannon. 2013. "United Nations Peacekeeping and Civilian Protection in Civil War." *American Journal of Political Science* 57 (4): 875–91.

Ibrahim, R. 2016. *Regional Organizations and Internal Conflict: The Arab League and the Arab Spring*. Rio de Janeiro: BRICS Policy Center.

ICG (International Crisis Group). 2016. *Exploiting Disorder: Al-Qaeda and the Islamic State*. Geneva: ICG.

ICM (Independent Commission on Multilateralism). 2017. "The New Primacy of Partnerships: The UN, Regional Organizations, Civil Society, and the Private Sector." Policy Paper, International Peace Institute, New York.

ICRC (International Committee of the Red Cross). n.d. "The Geneva Conventions of 12 August 1949." ICRC, Geneva.

IMF (International Monetary Fund). 2009. "IMF and World Bank Support the Central African Republic's Completion Point under the Enhanced HIPC Initiative and Approve Debt Relief under the Multilateral Debt Relief Initiative." Press Release 09/245, IMF, Washington, DC, June 30.

INCAF (International Network on Conflict and Fragility). 2017. "Communiqué: INCAF Director-Level Meeting: 7 November 2017." OECD, Paris. http://www.oecd.org/dac/conflict-fragility-resilience/docs/INCAF_COMMUNIQUE.pdf.

Institute for State Effectiveness. 2018. "Sovereignty Strategies: Enhancing Core Government Functions as a Post-Conflict and Conflict Prevention Measure." ISE, Washington, DC.

Jenks, B., and H. Kharas. 2016. "Towards a New Multilateralism." Uppdrag Framtid background report, Brookings Institution, Washington, DC.

Jenny, J. 2017. "All Peacebuilding Is Local." *Global Peace Operations Review,* February 7. http://peaceoperationsreview.org/commentary/all-peacebuilding-is-local/.

Johnstone, I. 2010. "Emerging Doctrine for Political Missions." Thematic essay for Review of Political Missions 2010, a project of the Center on International Cooperation, New York.

Joshi, M., and M. Quinn. 2016a. "Is the Sum Greater than the Parts? The Terms of Civil War Peace Agreements and the Commitment Problem Revisited." *Negotiations Journal* 31 (1): 7–30.

———. 2016b. "Watch and Learn: Spillover Effects of Peace Accord Implementation on Non-signatory Armed Groups." *Research and Politics* 3 (January-March): 1–7. https://doi.org/10.1177/2053168016640558.

Kang, S. Y. 2017. "Aid Flow to Fragile and Conflict Affected Situations: How Does Aid Create Incentives or Disincentives for Conflict?" Background paper for the United Nations–World Bank Flagship Study, *Pathways for Peace: Inclusive Approaches to Preventing Violent Conflict,* World Bank, Washington, DC.

Keating, C. 2015. "Power Dynamics between Permanent and Elected Members." In *The UN Security Council in the 21st Century*, edited by S. von Einsiedel, D. M. Malone, and B. S. Ugarte. Boulder, CO: Lynne Rienner.

Keck, M. E., and K. Sikkink. 1999. "Transnational Advocacy Networks in International and Regional Politics." *International Social Science Journal* 51 (159): 89–101.

King, G., and L. Zeng. 2001. "Improving Forecasts of State Failure." *World Politics* 53 (4): 623–58.

Koskenniemi, M., and P. Leino. 2002. "Fragmentation of International Law? Postmodern Anxieties." *Leiden Journal of International Law* 15 (3): 553–79.

Kreutz, J. 2010. "How and When Armed Conflicts End: Introducing the UCDP Conflict Termination Dataset." *Journal of Peace Research* 47 (2): 243–50.

Langlotz, S., and N. Potrafke. 2016. "Does Development Aid Increase Military Expenditure?" CESifo Working Paper 6066, CESifo Group, Munich.

Lanz, D., and R. Gasser. 2013. "A Crowded Field: Competition and Coordination in International Peace Mediation." Centre for Mediation in Africa, University of Pretoria, Hatfield, South Africa.

Lindenmayer, E., and J. Kaye. 2009. *A Choice for Peace? The Story of Forty-One Days of Mediation in Kenya.* New York: International Peace Institute. https://peacemaker.un.org/sites/peacemaker.un.org/files/Kenya Mediation_IPI2009.pdf.

Lund, M. 2000. "Preventive Diplomacy for Macedonia, 1992–1999: From Containment to Nation Building." In *Opportunities Missed, Opportunities Seized: Preventive Diplomacy in the Post-Cold War World,* edited by B. Jentelson. New York: Rowman & Littlefield.

Mancini, F. 2011. "Managing Partnership (Partnerships – A New Horizon for Peacekeeping?) (Conclusion)." *International Peacekeeping* 18 (5): 627–33. https://ssrn.com/abstract=2902467.

Marc, A., N. Verjee, and S. Mogaka. 2015. *The Challenge of Stability and Security in West Africa.* Africa Development Forum series. Washington, DC: World Bank; Paris: Agence Française de Développement.

McInerney-Lankford, S. 2017. Background note for *Pathways to Peace: Inclusive Approaches to Preventing Violent Conflict,* World Bank, Washington, DC.

Mueller, H. 2017. "How Much Is Prevention Worth?" Background paper for the United Nations–World Bank Flagship Study, *Pathways for Peace: Inclusive Approaches to Preventing Violent Conflict,* World Bank, Washington, DC.

Mueller, H., and C. Rauh. 2016. "Reading between the Lines: Prediction of Political Violence Using Newspaper Text." INET Institute Paper, IAE (CSIC), Barcelona; University of Cambridge, Cambridge, MA.

Muggah, R. 2010. "Innovations in Disarmament, Demobilization, and Reintegration Policy and Research: Reflections on the Last Decade." Working Paper 774, Norwegian Institute of International Affairs, Oslo.

———. 2017. "Revisiting Community Violence Reduction." Background paper for the United Nations–World Bank Flagship Study, *Pathways for Peace: Inclusive Approaches to Preventing Violent Conflict,* World Bank, Washington, DC.

Mwaûra, C., and S. Schmeidl, eds. 2002. *Early Warning and Conflict Management in the Horn of Africa.* Trenton, NJ: Red Sea Press.

Nathan, L. 2010. "The Peacemaking Effectiveness of Regional Organizations." Working Paper 81, Crisis States Research Center, Development Studies Institute (DESTIN), London School of Economics.

Nunn, N., and N. Qian. 2014. "US Food Aid and Civil Conflict." *American Economics Review* 104 (6): 1630–66.

Nyheim, D. 2015. *Early Warning and Response to Violent Conflict. Time for a Rethink?* London: Saferworld.

OECD (Organisation for Economic Co-operation and Development). 2009. *Preventing Violence, War, and State Collapse. The Future of Conflict Early Warning and Response.* Paris: OECD.

———. 2010. *Monitoring the Principles for Good International Engagement in Fragile States and Situations, Fragile States Principles Monitoring Survey: Global Report.* Paris: OECD.

———. 2015. *States of Fragility 2015: Meeting Post-2015 Ambitions.* Paris: OECD.

———. 2016. *States of Fragility 2016.* Paris: OECD.

———. 2017. *Official Development Assistance, 2016.* Paris: OECD. http://www2.compareyourcountry.org/oda?cr=20001&cr1=oecd&lg=en&page=1.

Pichler Fong, A. 2017. "Burkina Faso: Popular Uprising and Political Transition (2014–2015)." Case study for the United Nations–World Bank Flagship Study, *Pathways to Peace: Inclusive Approaches to Preventing Violent Conflict,* World Bank, Washington, DC.

Pillay, R., and J.-J. van der Hoeven. 2017. *Stabilisation: An Independent Stocktaking and Possible Elements for a Corporate Approach for UNDP.* New York: UNDP.

Poe, SC. 1991. "Human Rights and the Allocation of U.S. Military Assistance." *Journal of Peace Research* 28 (2): 205–16.

POTI (Peace Operations Training Institute). 2010. *Principles and Guidelines for UN Peacekeeping Operations.* Williamsburg, VA: POTI. http://cdn.peaceopstraining.org/course_promos/principles_and_guidelines/principles_and_guidelines_english.pdf.

Regan, P. M. 2010. "Interventions into Civil Wars: A Retrospective Survey with Prospective Ideas." *Civil Wars* 12 (4): 456–76.

———. 2012. "Interventions before Civil Wars." Department of Political Science, University of Binghamton, Binghamton, U.K.

Risse, T., S. Ropp, and K. Sikkink. 1999. *The Power of Human Rights: International Norms* and *Domestic Change*. Cambridge, U.K.: Cambridge University Press.

Rosand, E. 2016. "Communities First: A Blueprint for Organizing and Sustaining a Global Movement against Violent Extremism." The Prevention Project, Washington, DC.

Salehyan, I. 2009. *Rebels without Borders*. Ithaca, NY: Cornell University Press.

Salehyan, I., and K. S. Gleditsch. 2006. "Refugees and the Spread of Civil War." *International Organisation* 60 (2): 335–66.

Schlesinger, S. 2004. *Act of Creation: The Founding of the United Nations*. New York: Basic Books.

Shrodt, P., and D. Gerner. 2004. "An Event Data Analysis of Third-Party Mediation in the Middle East and Balkans." *Journal of Conflict Resolution* 48 (3): 310–30.

Sokalski, H. J. 2003. *An Ounce of Prevention: Macedonia and the UN Experience in Preventive Diplomacy*, Washington, DC: United States Institute of Peace Press.

Stamnes, E. 2004. "Critical Security Studies and the United Nations Preventive Deployment in Macedonia." *International Peacekeeping* 11 (1): 161–81.

Sur, J., ed. 2014. "Que observan los que observan el delito." Banco Interamericano de Desarrollo IDB-DP-364, Inter-American Development Bank, Washington, DC. http://www.worldbank .org/en/news/video/2015/08/17/indonesias -national-violence-monitoring-system.

Svensson, S., and M. S. Lundgren. 2015. "Patterns of Peacemaking." Research report on Conflict Trends, Peace Research Institute of Oslo, Norway, April.

Svensson, I., and M. Onken. 2015. "Global Trends of Peace Negotiations and Conflict Mediation." In *Global Trends 2015. Prospects for World Society*, edited by M. Roth, C. Ulbert, and T. Debiel. Bonn: Development and Peace Foundation and Institute for Development and Peace; Duisburg: Centre for Global Cooperation Research. www.globale-trends.de/home.html.

Tardy, T. 2015. "United Nations Preventive Deployment Force (UNPREDEP-Macedonia)." In *The Oxford Handbook of United Nations Peacekeeping Operations*, edited by J. A. Koops, N. MacQueen, T. Tardy, and P. D. Williams. Oxford: Oxford University Press.

Thakur, R. 2011. "The United Nations in Global Governance: Rebalancing Organized Multilateralism for Current and Future Challenges." Paper prepared for "Thematic Debate on Global Governance," UN General Assembly, New York.

Themmer, L., and P. Wallensteen. 2011. "Armed Conflict, 1946–2010." *Journal of Peace Research* 48 (4): 525–36.

Tian, N., A. Fleurant, P. D. Wezeman, and S. T. Wezeman. 2017. "Trends in World Military Expenditure, 2016." SIPRI Factsheet, Stockholm International Peace Research Institute.

UN (United Nations). 2008. *United Nations Peacekeeping Operations: Principles and Guidelines*. New York: United Nations Secretariat.

———. 2014. *The UN Framework of Analysis for Atrocity Crimes: A Tool for Prevention*. New York: United Nations, October 30.

———. 2015. *Uniting Our Strengths for Peace—Politics, Partnership, and People*. Report of the High-Level Independent Panel on Peace Operations (HIPPO). New York: United Nations.

———. 2017. *Financing for Development: Progress and Prospects*. Report of the Inter-Agency Task Force on Financing for Development. New York: United Nations.

UN Department of Political Affairs. 2015a. *Annual Report—Multi-year Appeal 2015*. New York: UN DPA.

———. 2015b. "Repertoire of the Practice of the Security Council 19th Supplement 2014–2015." Security Council Affairs Division, Security Council Practices and Charter Research Branch, New York.

UNDP (United Nations Development Programme). 2017. *Journey to Extremism in Africa: Drivers, Incentives, and the Tipping Point for Recruitment*. New York: UNDP.

UNDP and Department of Political Affairs. 2016. *Joint UNDP-DPA Programme on Building National Capacities for Conflict Prevention: Annual Report*. New York: UNDP. http://www. undp.org/content/undp/en/home/librarypage/ democratic-governance/conflict-prevention/ joint-undp-dpa-programme-on-building-nati onal-capacities-for-con.html.

UN General Assembly. 1948. "Universal Declaration of Human Rights." Resolution RES 217, adopted December 10, Paris.

———. 1999a. "Report of the Independent Inquiry into the Actions of the United Nations during the 1994 Genocide in Rwanda." Report S/1999/1257, UN General Assembly, New York, December 15.

———. 1999b. "Report of the Secretary-General Pursuant to General Assembly Resolution 53/35: The Fall of Srebenica." Report A/54/549, UN General Assembly, New York, November 15.

———. 2003. "Prevention of Conflict." Resolution A/RES/57/337, adopted July 3, New York.

———. 2005. "Resolution on the Peace Commission." Resolution 60/180, adopted December 20, New York.

———. 2006a. "Progress Report on the Prevention of Armed Conflict: Report of the Secretary-General." Report A/60/891, UN General Assembly, New York, July 18.

———. 2006b. "The United Nations Global Counter-Terrorism Strategy." Resolution A/RES/60/288, adopted September 8, New York.

———. 2007. "Strengthening of the Economic and Social Council." Resolution A/RES/61/16, adopted January 9, New York.

———. 2016a. "Review of United Nations Peacebuilding Architecture." Resolution A/RES/70/262, adopted April 27, New York.

———. 2016b. "The United Nations Global Counter-Terrorism Strategy Review." Resolution A/RES/70/291, adopted July 1, New York.

UNIPSIL (UN Integrated Peacebuilding Office in Sierra Leone). 2017. "Background: The Conflict in Sierra Leone and the Engagement of the United Nations." UNIPSIL, New York. https://unipsil.unmissions.org/background.

UNOCHA (United Nations Office for the Coordination of Humanitarian Affairs). 2015. *World Humanitarian Data and Trends 2015.* New York: UNOCHA.

———. 2016. *World Humanitarian Data and Trends 2016.* New York: UNOCHA.

UN Secretary-General. 1992. "An Agenda for Peace: Preventive Diplomacy, Peacemaking, and Peacekeeping." Report A/47/277–S/24111 of Secretary-General Boutros Boutros-Ghali, United Nations, New York, June 17.

———. 1998. "The Rome Statute of the International Criminal Court." Adopted at a diplomatic conference, United Nations, Rome, July 17.

———. 2001. "Report on the Prevention of Armed Conflict." Report A/55/985-S/2001/574 of Secretary-General Kofi Annan, United Nations, New York.

———. 2012. "Report on Strengthening the Role of Mediation in the Peaceful Settlement of Disputes: Conflict Prevention and Resolution." Report of the Secretary-General A/66/811, United Nations, New York.

———. 2013. "Securing States and Societies: Strengthening the United Nations Comprehensive Support to Security Sector Reform." Report of the Secretary-General A/67/970, United Nations, New York, August 13. .

———. 2015. "Report on Women and Peace and Security." Report of the Secretary-General S/2015/716, United Nations, New York, September 16.

———. 2016a. "Plan of Action to Prevent Violent Extremism." Report of the Secretary-General A/70/674, United Nations, New York, January 15.

———. 2016b. "Report on United Nations Policing." Report of the Secretary-General S/2016/952, United Nations, New York, November 10.

———. 2017a. "Report on Arrangements for Funding and Backstopping of Special Political Missions." Report of the Secretary-General A/66/340, United Nations, New York.

———. 2017b. "Report on the Protection of Civilians in Armed Conflict." Report S/2017/414.2017, United Nations, New York.

UN Security Council. 1999. "Resolution on the Situation in Kosovo." Resolution S/RES/1244, adopted June 19, New York.

———. 2000. "Resolution on Women, Peace, and Security." S/RES/1325, adopted October 31, New York.

———. 2001. "The Role of the Security Council in the Prevention of Armed Conflicts." Resolution S/RES/1366, adopted August 30, New York.

———. 2005. "On Establishment of the Peacebuilding Commission." Resolution S/RES/1645, adopted December 20, New York.

———. 2014. "Threats to International Peace and Security." Resolution S/RES/2150, adopted April 16, New York.

———. 2016. "Post-Conflict Peacebuilding." Resolution S/RES/2282, adopted April 27, New York.

———. 2017. *Can the Security Council Prevent Conflict?* Research Report 1. New York: UN Security Council, February 9.

Verjee, N. 2017. "Regional Economic Communities in Conflict Prevention and

Management." Background paper for the United Nations–World Bank Flagship Study, *Pathways for Peace: Inclusive Approaches to Preventing Violent Conflict,* World Bank, Washington, DC.

von Einsiedel, S., D. M. Malone, and B. S. Ugarte. 2015. "Introduction." In *The UN Security Council in the 21st Century,* edited by S. Ensiedel, D. Malone, and B. S. Ugarte. Boulder, CO: Lynne Rienner.

Wallace, M. 2015. *From Principle to Practice, A User's Guide to Do No Harm.* Cambridge, MA: CDA Collaborative Learning Projects.

Wallensteen, P., and I. Svensson. 2014. "Talking Peace: International Mediation in Armed Conflicts." *Journal of Peace Research* 51 (2): 315–27.

Walter, B. 1997. "The Critical Barrier to Civil War Settlement." *International Organization* 53 (1): 335–64.

———. 2017. "The Role and Impact of Third Party Interventions in the Prevention of Violent Conflict." Background paper for the United Nations–World Bank Flagship Study, *Pathways for Peace: Inclusive Approaches to Preventing Violent Conflict,* World Bank, Washington, DC.

Ward, M. D. N. W. Metternich, C. L. Dorff, M. Gallop, F. M. Hollenbach, A. Schultz, and S. Weschle. 2013. "Learning from the Past and Stepping into the Future: Toward a New Generation of Conflict Prediction." *International Studies Review* 15 (4): 474–90.

Weinstein, J., and M. Humphreys. 2005. "Disentangling the Determinants of Successful Demobilization and Reintegration." Working Paper 69, Center for Global Development, Washington, DC.

Wendt, A., and M. Barnett. 1993. "Dependent State Formation and Third World Militarization." *Review of International Studies* 19 (4): 321–47.

Whitfield, T. 2010. *Working with Groups of Friends.* Washington, DC: United States Institute of Peace.

Wilkenfeld, J., K. Young, V. Asal, and D. Quinn. 2003. "Mediating International Crises: Cross-National and Experimental Perspectives." *Journal of Conflict Resolution* 47 (3): 279–301.

Wood, M. 2013. "International Law and the Use of Force: What Happens in Practice?" *Indian Journal of International Law* 53: 345–67.

World Bank. 2011. *World Development Report 2011: Conflict, Security, and Development.* Washington, DC: World Bank.

———. 2017. *World Development Report 2017: Governance and the Law.* Washington, DC: World Bank.

World Conference on Human Rights. 1993. "Vienna Declaration and Programme of Action," adopted June 25, Vienna.

Yi, J. 2017a. "Aid Flows to Conflict-Affected Situations: Exploring Cross-Country Empirical Studies and Updated Data." Background paper for the United Nations–World Bank Flagship Study, *Pathways for Peace: Inclusive Approaches to Preventing Violent Conflict,* World Bank, Washington, DC.

———. 2017b. "Evaluating Conflict Forecasts: Criteria, Approaches, and Tools." Background paper for the United Nations–World Bank Flagship Study, *Pathways for Peace: Inclusive Approaches to Preventing Violent Conflict,* World Bank, Washington, DC.

———. 2017c. "A Review of Conflict Forecasting Models." Background paper for the United Nations–World Bank Flagship Study, *Pathways for Peace: Inclusive Approaches to Preventing Violent Conflict,* World Bank, Washington, DC.

Additional Reading

Acholi Religious Leaders Peace Initiative. 2017. arlpi.org.

Biersteker, T., S. E. Eckert, and M. Tourinho. 2016. *Targeted Sanctions: The Impacts and Effectiveness of United Nations Action.* Cambridge, U.K.: Cambridge University Press.

Brandt, P. T., J. R. Freeman, and P. A. Schrodt. 2014. "Evaluating Forecasts of Political Conflict Dynamics." *International Journal of Forecasting* 30 (4): 944–62.

Brown, S., and J. Grävingholt, eds. 2016. *The Securitization of Foreign Aid.* New York: Palgrave Macmillan.

Brubaker, R., and T. Dorfler. 2017. "UN Sanctions and the Prevention of Conflict." Thematic paper for the United Nations–World Bank Study on Conflict Prevention, United Nations University, Tokyo.

Call, C. 2012. *Why Peace Fails: The Causes and Prevention of Civil War Recurrence.* Washington, DC: Georgetown University Press.

Cederman, L. E., and N. B. Weidmann. 2017. "Predicting Armed Conflict: Time to Adjust Our Expectations?" *Science* 355 (6324): 474–76.

Charron, A. Forthcoming. "The Evolution of Intrastate Conflict Sanctions Regimes: From Stopping Violence to Peacebuilding and

Beyond." In *The Sanctions Enterprise: Assessing a Quarter-Century of UN Action for Peace, Security, and Human Rights*, edited by S. Lopez and G. von Einsiedel. Tokyo: United Nations University.

Charron, A., and C. Portela. 2015. "The UN, Regional Sanctions and Africa." *International Affairs* 91 (6): 1369–85.

Comolli, V. 2017. "Transnational Organized Crime and Conflict." Background paper for the United Nations–World Bank Flagship Study, *Pathways for Peace: Inclusive Approaches to Preventing Violent Conflict*, World Bank, Washington, DC.

DPKO (Department of Peacekeeping Operations). 2017a. *DPKO Operations List and Deployment Statistics*. New York: United Nations. http://www.un.org/en/peacekeeping/documents/operationslist.pdf.

———. 2017b. "Overview of Peacekeeping Operations." UNDPKO, New York. https://www.unmissions.org/#block-views-missions-peacekeeping-missions.

Eriksson, M. 2016. "The Unintended Consequences of United Nations Targeted Sanctions." In *Targeted Sanctions: The Impacts and Effectiveness of United Nations Action*, edited by T. Biersteker, S. Eckert, and M. Tourinho, 190–219. Cambridge, U.K.: Cambridge University Press.

FEWER (Forum on Early Warning and Early Response). 1999. *FEWER Conflict and Peace Analysis and Response Manual*. London: FEWER.

Gartner, S. S., and M. M. Melin. 2009. "Assessing Outcomes: Conflict Management and the Durability of Peace." In *The Sage Handbook of Conflict Resolution*, edited by J. Bercovitch, V. Kremenyuk, and I. W. Zartman, 564–79. London: Sage.

Gleason-Roberts, M., R. Gowan, and A. Kugel. 2012. "Strategic Summary." In *Political Missions 2012*, edited by M. Gleason-Roberts, R. Gowan, and A. Kugel, 1–9. New York: Centre on International Cooperation.

Gordon, J. 2010. *Invisible War: The United States and Iraq Sanctions*. Cambridge, MA: Harvard University Press.

GPF (Global Policy Forum). 2017. "Peacekeeping Tables and Charts." GPF, New York. https://www.globalpolicy.org/security-council/peacekeeping/peacekeeping-data.html.

Hufbauer, C. G., J. J. Schott, K. S. Elliott, and B. Oegg. 2007. *Economic Sanctions Reconsidered*, 3d ed. Washington, DC: Peterson Institute for International Economics.

IISS (International Institute for Strategic Studies). 2016. *Armed Conflict Survey*. London: IISS.

Koskenniemi, M. 2006. "Fragmentation of International Law: Difficulties Arising from the Diversification and Expansion of International Law." Report of the Study Group of the International Law Commission, fifty-eighth session, International Law Commission, Geneva, May 1–June 9 and July 3–August 11.

Lombard, L. 2017. "Case Study: The Central African Republic." Case study for the United Nations–World Bank Flagship Study, *Pathways for Peace: Inclusive Approaches to Preventing Violent Conflict*, World Bank, Washington, DC.

Mueller, J., and K. Mueller. 1999. "Sanctions of Mass Destruction." *Foreign Affairs* 78 (3): 43–53.

Salehyan, I., and K. S. Gleditsch. 2014. "The Syrian Refugee Crisis and Conflict Spillover." *Political Violence at a Glance*, February 11. http://politicalviolenceataglance.org/2014/02/11/the-syrian-refugee-crisis-and-conflict-spillover/.

Sambanis, N. 2008. "Short- and Long-Term Effects of United Nations Peace Operations." *World Bank Economic Review* 1 (1): 9–32.

Shmueli, G. 2010. "To Explain or to Predict?" *Statistical Science* 25 (3): 289–310.

Sponeck, H.-C. 2000. "Ending the Iraq Impasse." *Global Dialogue* 2 (3): n.p.

Wallensteen, P., and C. Staibano. 2005. *International Sanctions: Between Wars and Words in the Global System*. New York: Routledge.

Zartman, I. W. 2000. "Ripeness: The Hurting Stalemate and Beyond." In *International Conflict Resolution after the Cold War*, edited by P. C. Stern and D. Druckman. Washington, DC: National Academies Press.

CHAPTER 8

Pursuing Pathways for Peace: Recommendations for Building Inclusive Approaches for Prevention

A surge in violent conflicts in recent years has left a trail of human suffering—displacing millions, fracturing societies, and suspending development progress in affected countries. The costs of destruction and lost economic growth are enormous. So, too, are the costs of response and recovery. Preventing these conflicts would have protected the lives and dignity of millions in addition to protecting substantial development gains that have, instead, been lost.

This study presents the evidence to support a renewed focus on prevention:

- Chapter 1 presents the evidence that violent conflict is increasing after decades of relative decline. Direct deaths in war, numbers of displaced populations, military spending, and terrorist incidents, among others, have all surged since the beginning of this century. Conflicts are more internationalized, are more protracted, cross borders more often, and are fought by more nonstate actors than in recent decades.
- Chapter 2 shows how this rise in violence is taking place in a rapidly evolving global context. Growing interdependence has created opportunities for development progress, but also amplified the impact of risks that transcend national borders,

such as climate change, population movements, and transnational organized crime.
- Chapter 3 presents the pathways framework, highlighting that conflict risks exist at various levels and that preventive action, as part of efforts to sustain development and peace, needs to identify solutions to imminent or ongoing violence and address underlying risks of conflict through incentives, institutional reforms, and investment in structural factors.
- Chapter 4 shows that grievances related to real and perceived exclusion and inequalities among groups are fueling many modern conflicts. Groups and elites are mobilizing around complex issues of identity and narrative to escalate and sustain conflict. The UN's 2030 Agenda for Sustainable Development is an important vehicle for addressing these risks.
- Chapter 5 shows that, to prevent cycles of violence, action must focus on the interaction among different dimensions of risk across arenas of power, opportunity, services, justice, and security. States hold the primary responsibility for resolving conflicts peacefully in these arenas, sometimes with the support of coalitions of actors.

- Chapter 6 provides evidence that preventive strategies are most effective and can only be sustained when they come from within societies. Many governments at differing levels of capacity are working in concert with national, and often international, partners to implement a variety of strategies that reduce the risks of violent conflict by addressing structural factors, institutions, and incentives of actors.

- Chapter 7 demonstrates that international efforts have helped countries to emerge from violence in many settings, but are challenged by the growing complexity of conflicts today. Effective preventive action must be grounded in national processes, be implemented when early risks are perceptible, and support initiatives, at various levels, to prevent the escalation of violence.

At the center of this study is the appreciation that, to be effective, prevention needs to be recognized as the collective responsibility of all actors of society and an integral part of our efforts to achieve the Sustainable Development Goals (SDGs). Prevention must be based on inclusive partnerships in all sectors and at all levels. States need to improve collaboration in the development of multilateral solutions when unilateral solutions will not suffice. Collaborating to revitalize systemic prevention—addressing those risks that no country can address alone and that are in nature international—as well as committing to cooperation and collaboration in the development of tools supporting preventive action in countries and regions at risk of violence are vital. This study posits that prevention enhances sovereignty by relying on national capacity and ensuring that international support is based on engagement with states and national actors.

The first section of this chapter sets out three principles for prevention. Above all, prevention must be *sustained* over the time needed to build more peaceful, just, and inclusive societies. Prevention must be *inclusive* and build broader partnerships across groups to identify and address the grievances that fuel violence. Prevention must actively and directly *target* patterns of

exclusion and institutional weaknesses that increase the risk of violent conflict.

The second section presents an agenda for action for national actors. Prevention strategies are successful when they increase capacity for constructive contestation, allow disputes to be managed peacefully, and protect people from the threat of violence. This section offers options available for supporting peaceful pathways by targeting the interaction between grievances and contestation across key arenas of power, opportunity, services, and security and justice.

The third section explores how international actors can effectively organize for prevention to overcome incentives that undermine their support for national partners. It includes a critical look at the organizational incentives that frustrate effective collective action and prevent engagement before a crisis reaches its acute phase.

Principles for Prevention

The evidence amassed by this study indicates, overwhelmingly, that, to address the complex and integrated nature of contemporary conflict-related risks, prevention must be sustained, inclusive, and targeted.

Prevention must be sustained. It is easy, but wrong, to see prevention as a trade-off between the short and long term. Preventive action must address immediate crises while investing to reinforce a society's pathway toward peace. Achieving prevention goals requires flexibility, and development investments should be integrated into overarching strategies, with politically viable short-term and medium-term actions. The need for sustainability requires balancing effort and resources so that action does not reward only crisis management. Those working on prevention face irrelevance if their time horizons stretch beyond political and investment cycles (table 8.1).

Prevention must be inclusive. Too often, preventive action is focused on elites. In complex, fragmented, and protracted conflicts, an inclusive approach to prevention puts an understanding of grievances and agency at the center of national and international engagement. It recognizes the

TABLE 8.1 A New Paradigm for Prevention

Today's challenges		A new paradigm
Short term Aspires to be long term, but the short term dominates	**Sustained**	**Short *and* long term** Shorter-term results increase the attractiveness of sustained and strategic approaches to prevention
Slow and inflexible Lacks flexibility and agility to act in or create windows of opportunity		**Adaptive** More agile approaches adapt in the face of changing risks and opportunities
Top down Risks identified by elites and direction set by a small group of specialists	**Inclusive**	**People-centered** Partnerships at all levels identify risks and develop solutions
Fragmented Highly technical, isolated in silos		**Integrated** Solutions increase resilience to multiple forms of risk, with effective prevention tools often in the hands of actors for whom conflict is not a primary focus
Delayed Dominated by crisis response, with prevention focused only on the most immediate risks	**Targeted**	**Proactive** Early and urgent action is taken to tackle and manage directly the full range of risks that could lead to violent conflict
Weakens leadership Prevention seen as undermining national sovereignty		**Strengthens leadership** Prevention enhances national sovereignty and expands the scope of action for governments

importance of understanding people and their communities: their trust in institutions, confidence in the future, perceptions of risk, and experience of exclusion and injustice. It uses this understanding to disaggregate risks and build inclusive responses to risk that enhance state legitimacy, reduce polarization, and avert violence.

Prevention must be targeted. Preventive action must actively and directly target grievances and exclusion across key arenas of contestation before, during, and after violence. Once group grievances become entrenched, it is harder for leaders and other national actors to find common ground and build consensus for actions that can reduce the risk of violence.

An Agenda for Action: Prevention in Practice

The principles—sustained, inclusive, and targeted—help to shift thinking about prevention; to effect real change, they must be put into practice. This section presents an agenda for action that can guide national actors as they partner for prevention.

Preventive action requires comprehensive approaches that respond simultaneously to the causes and impacts of violence, while mitigating the risks of future outbreak and escalation. Prevention of violent conflict should be a collective outcome, bringing together security, development, and political efforts around shared priorities, with development policy as a central instrument for addressing the risk of violent conflict.

The lessons of successful prevention that come across in the study show how national actors, to be effective, need to target several important policy and program areas:

1. Monitoring risks
2. Addressing multidimensional risks
3. Aligning peace, security, and development efforts
4. Implementing a people-centered approach to prevention
5. Sustaining prevention across levels of risks

Monitoring Risks of Violent Conflict

Engaging in preventive action early, before the outbreak of violence, requires a shift from early warning of violence to awareness of risk. Development planning should integrate the identification of risk and enable multisectoral responses. Risk management systems should not be limited to information sharing; instead, they should support decision making geared toward rapid response, policy change, and redirecting of investment.

Monitor exclusion. Preventive strategies need to be based on an understanding of the dynamics of exclusion and, more generally, the grievances of social groups. This understanding should be based on regular monitoring of horizontal inequalities among groups or geographic areas and other forms of exclusion, as well as assessment of societal cleavages such as gender inequality and youth exclusion. As much as possible, exclusion should be monitored around access to power, resources, services, and security. These efforts should be based on SDG indicators, targeting horizontal inequalities across economic, political, and social dimensions. Several SDGs, including most notably, but not exclusively, SDG 5, SDG 10, and SDG 16, address exclusion.[1] This monitoring requires assessing the intersection of exclusion with broader risks such as climate change.

Monitor perceptions and grievances of social groups. Perceptions matter, are not always related to objective data, and are often missed by traditional surveys and regular assessment tools. Innovative techniques, such as high-frequency surveys, polling, and focus groups can facilitate monitoring of public perceptions over time.[2] While monitoring perceptions has become a valuable tool of public policy formulation, assessments of individual or group perceptions need to be mainstreamed in preventive action. Perception monitoring needs to be undertaken with full awareness of the need for safeguards related to the security and privacy of individuals, so that the data cannot be used for repression or exclusion based on identity; it also needs to be undertaken with sensitivity to the context in which these surveys have been carried out (Sartorius and Carver 2008).

Strengthen early warning systems. Early warning systems (EWSs) are designed to initiate rapid actions to support prevention from the community level to the regional level. Noting that the risks of conflicts are

escalating rapidly and becoming protracted, particularly in border or remote areas, early warning systems that monitor short- and medium-term risks need to be reinforced and linked to appropriate action (Defontaine 2017).

Harness technology to improve monitoring. Considerable progress has been made in applying information and communication technologies to collect perception data; such technologlies can be particularly efficient in remote and conflict-affected areas, where exclusion can be felt acutely and where access is often most difficult. Real-time data collection methods such as crowdsourcing[3] and crowdseeding,[4] social media monitoring, geospatial technology, and mobile data collection tools provide opportunities—many of them low cost—to improve timeliness, detail, and nuance in monitoring.

Ensure that survey and data collection is sensitive to conflict and capacity.[5] The way data are accessed and shared requires strategies that balance risks and opportunity. The dissemination of data on group perceptions of security, services, resources, and power can, if not carefully used, reinforce polarization (Haider 2014; Putzel 2010). At the same time, limiting data to the use of a narrow group of technocrats can reduce the benefit of data collection, as the many actors that can play a key role in prevention would not benefit from this information. Finally, adding complex risk-monitoring systems where data collection capacity is already challenged can be counterproductive. Where possible, it is advisable to integrate risk monitoring into ongoing data collection efforts—for example, household surveys and price data collection—or to combine their setup with careful attention to long-term capacity building and financial sustainability.

Addressing the Multidimensionality of Risk

National actors are dealing with multiple risks simultaneously and are constrained by limited budgets, political capital, and time. Chapter 3 emphasizes that risks, whether exogenous to a country, such as climate change and cross-border movements, or endogenous, such as contested elections, can intersect and accumulate to increase vulnerability to violence.

Develop integrated peace and development plans. Responding to complex interrelated risks almost inevitably requires that institutions act in concert in support of common objectives using different instruments. This requires a level of integrated planning that is often challenging. Actors working on poverty reduction, disaster risk reduction, social service delivery, and environmental management need to come together, at different levels of government, to identify and prioritize conflict risks and responses under a single framework aligned with the SDGs. Such plans should identify collective outcomes across the humanitarian, development, and peace nexus, while respecting their mandates, bringing together mandates around shared objectives and, where possible, reinforcing and strengthening capacities at national and local levels. At the same time, addressing risks of conflict that evolve and change relatively rapidly requires adaptability and flexibility. The New Way of Working launched at the World Humanitarian Summit in 2016 provides a possible framework for such actions based on the Agenda for Humanity.[6] The New Way of Working advocates for pooled and combined data, analysis, and information; better coordination of planning and programming processes; effective leadership for collective outcomes; and financing modalities to support closer collaboration across humanitarian, development, and peacebuilding operations.

Target border and periphery areas. Border areas and zones of low population density tend to be particularly vulnerable to risks of violence, as state presence is often weak, delivering services is often expensive, and identifying economic investments with positive rates of return is also a challenge. However, the benefits of addressing perceptions of exclusion and grievances can be well worth the investment. Such efforts often require innovative ways of delivering services and strong

community involvement in development efforts. Border regions, specifically, can often benefit from improved regional connectivity, if investments are made alongside transport infrastructure so that growth is inclusive and benefits are widely shared. Given the positive influence that trade can have on mitigating conflict, measures should be taken to reduce trade barriers and facilitate logistics.

Mitigate the impact of shocks when tensions are high. Shocks, whether economic, political, or security related, can act as triggers for violence. One crucial factor in preventing a shock from triggering a violent response is the ability of governments to address the impact of shocks in a way that is timely and distributes impact fairly. People increasingly expect governments to play a significant role in mitigating the effects of shocks. For governments with limited fiscal space and capability to respond flexibly and quickly, the support of the international community is key. In all of these cases, it is important to ensure clear communication and outreach to the population to explain the nature of the shocks and the government response. How to do this will depend on the nature of the shock and the specific context. Price shocks are particularly sensitive, and macroeconomic management is an important tool for prevention. The ability of governments to introduce compensation rapidly to the groups most affected and to adjust the regulatory framework to address speculative behaviors can play a central role in preventing violence from starting or escalating.

Target action and resources to arenas of contestation: power, resources, security, and services. As the spaces where access to livelihoods and well-being are determined and where power imbalances manifest most clearly, these arenas present both risks and opportunities. These are areas of focus where governments can effectively use redistributive policies to address underlying risks of conflict. Resolving complex disputes in these arenas requires inclusive policy and institutional reforms as well as solid management of conflict. Table 8.2

lays out guidance on specific actions in each arena where governments can help to ensure that contestation is productive (nonviolent) instead of destructive (violent). These actions are far from exhaustive, but indicate some possible entry points.

Aligning Peace, Development, and Security

In addressing the risk of violent conflict, much stronger synergies need to be established between peacebuilding efforts, security provision, and economic and social

TABLE 8.2 Ensuring Productive Contestation in Key Arenas

Arena 1: Power and governance	Arena 2: Land and natural resources
• Placing a premium on responsible political leadership, encouraging the broad participation of all political actors, and mitigating "winner takes all" processes are key. • Inclusive, representative, and embedded power-sharing arrangements create greater chances for peaceful pathways. • Institutionalizing power-sharing arrangements via constitutions and other legal frameworks, rather than ad hoc arrangements, improves their sustainability. • Decentralizing, devolving, or allowing autonomy of subnational regions or groups can help to accommodate diversity and lower the risk of violence at the national level. • Space for civil society engagement, itself diverse and contested, has to be preserved (or opened up where lacking) as a vital link to local constituencies. • An independent and involved private sector can moderate the behavior of actors and facilitate connections where tensions manifest. • Credible and robust electoral authorities, preelection mediation, and protection of the right to vote, especially for women and marginalized groups, help to create incentives for peaceful elections. • Dialogue and consensus to agree on the "rules of the game" help to ensure nonviolent power sharing.	• Tensions around resources tend to be strongest at the local level. Community and local dispute resolution mechanisms can help to manage disputes in the short to medium term, while longer-term reforms are agreed upon, designed, and trialed. • Land and housing reforms and policies to improve access to water have different impacts on women and disadvantaged groups; these groups need to be integral to decision making. • Securing land rights can reduce tensions, recognizing that a continuum of a wide range of different types of land tenure rights exist and should be protected. • Robust mechanisms to ensure multiple uses of land and water can manage contestations between groups such as pastoralists and farmers. • Cooperation and negotiations between riparian countries and subregions on water sharing can provide the foundation for peaceful relations. • Climate change, population growth, urbanization, and the expansion of large-scale agriculture can exacerbate tensions around water access and use. • Equitable oversight mechanisms regarding the use and management of extractives, including with regions on the division of benefits, can offset tensions; involvement from the private sector is essential.
Arena 3: Service delivery	**Arena 4: Security and justice**
• Equitable service delivery can exert an indirect influence on reducing the risk of violence by reinforcing the legitimacy of the state. • How services are delivered and how fair they are perceived to be matter at least as much for state legitimacy as who delivers them or their quality. • Participatory processes and redress mechanisms can help to lessen grievances around service delivery. • Issues related to local corruption can often be reduced through community control mechanisms and empowerment of citizens. • The local community can play a role in the delivery of services, but the state must retain an overall presence to be seen as legitimate. • Concerted effort should be made to reach an increasing number of remote or underserved communities to ameliorate grievances and ensure human capacity. • Exclusion in education represents a particularly strong risk for fueling grievances and is central to preventing violent conflict. • Education for peace and citizenship can play a key role for prevention.	• Enhanced parliamentary, civilian, and internal oversight of security institutions can boost reform. • Broad-based consultations improve the sustainability and effectiveness of security reform. • Greater transparency in public expenditure of the security sector can support greater accountability of security forces and increase public confidence. • Antidiscrimination legislation, access to free legal aid, and inclusion in the judiciary of marginalized groups can help to manage risks around exclusionary justice systems. • In the context of heightened social tensions, addressing grievances related to systematic abuses in the past can help to alleviate the risks of renewed violence. • Bottom-up approaches to justice reform should be rooted in an understanding of the way people resolve conflicts in their everyday lives. • Greater diversity, consideration of gender, and community representativeness can strengthen the legitimacy and quality of security forces.

development. Local or national planning should be integrated within single guiding documents to ensure synergies among various actors and actions. Specific national-level coordination platforms should help to ensure complementarity between these different components of prevention in the field.

Ensure that security and development objectives are compatible. In high-risk contexts, development planners should recognize that groups with grievances might not be the poorest and might not be in areas of high potential for economic growth, yet failing to make investments that could channel their grievances into productive contestation can lead to violent conflict, which can wipe out larger development gains. Stability poles should become an important focus of development actions in areas where risks of violence are high and security is an issue. Security, implemented as a service to the local population, not only serves to identify and address security threats but also is key to protecting rights, property, and economic livelihoods. When security interventions are warranted, social services and economic support should be provided in tandem, so that armed forces are not the only interface between the state and the population. To avoid the perceptions that development actions are only done to facilitate the acceptance of a securitized approach, armed forces should not directly support or execute development programs that civilians could implement effectively.

Address the fiscal dimensions of prevention. In many countries dealing with high risk of violence or where violence is already high, domestic revenue is low or dependent on volatile commodity prices, and national finances are often in fiscally precarious situations. In order to implement preventive policies effectively, states need minimal fiscal space. Relying exclusively on donor financing for preventive programs and projects often results in a proliferation of programming that is outside state control and not sustainable. The state needs to have access to a certain level of

financing to be able to pay civil servants, especially those working in security and justice and other core services, to implement core state functions across the country, and to have the discretion necessary to disburse financing rapidly to geographic areas with higher risk. Budgetary support should be considered for well-designed policies for prevention, when they are sufficiently transparent and when they integrate accountability mechanisms.

Integrate security sector reform with other institutional reforms. While the status quo is that security sector reforms are often addressed separately from other institutional reforms, a shift toward preventive action will require that issues of accountability, procurement, payment, and others follow the same rules for security services as for the rest of the civil service. This is particularly important to ensure transparency and facilitate civilian oversight. In parallel, it is important that support to the security sector be conducted in line with principles of national ownership and in coordination with other sectors. In some cases, a recently concluded peace process can offer an opportunity to promote a culture of transparency and openness and to move toward a "people-centered" approach to security and justice sector reform. In such contexts, national actors can place priority on increasing the visibility and transparency of police services through community dialogue and joint action, integrating women and minorities into policing structures, and developing local security accountability forums. These measures can help to avoid the recurrence of violent conflict by increasing the accountability of the security sector.

Establish credible forums for dialogue and exchange. Prevention efforts should focus on strengthening the capacity of society for prevention—not just the state. Supporting local actors' efforts in prevention is a critical part of better understanding and addressing local grievances. Establishing forums at different levels of society for dialogue and exchange of ideas and building capacity through development assistance—training, development of guidance, and institutional strengthening—for national and local actors can build a society's capacity to mediate between social groups as well as between various elite interests. Many such efforts can be integrated into development programming (Rakotomalala 2017). Such capacity development assistance is already pursued in some instances by the United Nations and some development organizations and can help to build mediation capacity across lines of division or long-standing conflict. However, for this decentralized approach to mediation and peacebuilding to work, it is important to create synergies among various efforts at local, national, and regional levels and with diplomatic efforts.

Implementing a People-Centered Approach to Prevention

National actors should seek to reorient service delivery systems to make people partners in the design and delivery of public services. Emerging evidence appears to confirm the relative importance of *how* people are engaged as compared to *what* resources or services they receive, especially in areas of weak state presence or contested state legitimacy (Marshak et al. 2017; Mcloughlin 2015). National actors can contribute to addressing grievances through strengthening more inclusive and accountable approaches to development.

Mainstream people's engagement in community development programs and local conflict resolution. It is important to empower underrepresented voices such as women, youth, and marginalized groups and to increase the quality of people's engagement. An inclusive process for selecting representatives from diverse groups is critical for building trust and creating meaningful participation. Furthermore, service delivery should be reoriented to make people partners in the design and delivery of public services and to strengthen trust in local and central government. Making people partners is done most effectively through mainstreaming participatory and consultative elements for all planning and programming in areas at risk of violent conflict. Mainstreaming

these elements can help to ensure that all efforts are focused on locally defined problems and that proposed solutions are accepted as legitimate by all relevant stakeholders, thereby ensuring ownership and stronger trust in service providers, particularly central and local governments. Integrating local authorities—both informal and formal—in community development programs is important, so that the efforts improve the social contract at both local and national levels.

Link grievance-handling mechanisms to development actions. Programs need to allocate resources to ensure that grievances are mediated quickly and transparently. Development actors should integrate support for national and local mediation practices as part of existing governance and economic planning and programming. This effort should include addressing national issues—for example, establishing national development priorities targeting long-standing cleavages around resources, power, or equal access to services—as well as local grievances related to the functioning or distribution of services, land, and security. To this end, development and political actors should build on existing efforts with standing support for strengthening the mediation and negotiation capabilities of institutions as well as political leaders and supporting middle-range leadership with influence and authority—traditional or modern—to convene the relevant actors and build consensus around contested issues.

Engage nonstate actors in specific platforms for peacebuilding. In many countries, prevention requires new coalitions that more accurately reflect the importance of young people, women, and representatives from the private sector, civil society, and community-based organizations. The growing power and preponderance of nonstate actors mean that many actors in conflict today are not accessible by traditional diplomatic platforms or via state actors. Individuals and communities at the local level have the highest stakes in preventing violence, and effective, lasting solutions must begin with them. The inclusion of such partners is key to defusing tensions, restoring confidence, influencing a more peaceful narrative, providing access to local-level justice systems, and improving transparency and accountability through, among others, mechanisms such as participatory budgeting and third-party monitoring.

Sustaining Preventive Action across Levels of Risk

Different actions are needed in situations of emerging risk, high risk, and open violence and in postviolence contexts. As such, actors across development, security, political, and humanitarian sectors need to work more closely together across all levels of risk according to their comparative advantages. Figure 8.1 illustrates how this shift could look. In the current paradigm, development actors tend to decrease engagement, or halt altogether, when risks escalate, while political actors enter the scene only once violence is present. This study argues, instead, for a focus on early action by all actors, stronger partnerships, and shared financing platforms that spread prevention throughout policies and programs. This study posits that all actors have a role to play at all times, while acknowledging that different actors can be more or less prominent at different times.

This is not simply a call for better integration: exploiting comparative advantages across sectors has been acknowledged for decades and most recently, at the international level, in the 2015 review of United Nations peace operations (UN Security Council and UN General Assembly 2015). This requires differentiated approaches across levels of risks (described in table 8.3), where existing tools can converge to sustain prevention given the constraints and windows of opportunity that these categories of risk can create (figure 8.2).

Preventing Recurrence

The findings of the *World Development Report 2011* underscore the high risks of conflict recurrence in postconflict environments, particularly if underlying grievances are not addressed in the settlement that ended the conflict (World Bank 2011).

To break out of this cycle and prevent recurrence of violence, governments should focus on building more legitimate institutions and investing in people's security (World Bank 2011). Yet, building such institutions is a long-term process. Meanwhile, national reformers need to rebuild trust between the state and the population by focusing on confidence-building measures, support for livelihood activities, efforts to address the past, and development of sound security and justice institutions.

Civil society and informal institutions play a key role in reducing risks. International experience has shown that measures to strengthen inclusiveness of civil society institutions are effective in rapidly decreasing the risk of conflict recurrence (Paffenholz et al. 2017). For example, the inclusion of civil society in the negotiation, contents, and implementation of the agreement is a key factor for the success of peace agreements and can help induce governments to show commitment to addressing the grievances that have been at the origin of violent conflict (Lanz 2011; Wanis-St. John and Kew 2008). In many cases, informal institutions such as community leadership, religious institutions, and traditional governance systems can also play an important role in resolving conflicts and avoiding the breakout of violence.

Organizing for Prevention

The High-Level Independent Panel on United Nations Peace Operations calls for building a collective commitment to prevention (UN Security Council 2015; UN Security Council and UN General Assembly 2015). To do so, the international community should (1) align incentives; (2) share risks assessments openly and candidly; (3) build partnerships at local, national, regional, and international levels; and (4) provide financial and human resources support that is designed more appropriately for preventing crises than for responding to them.

Align Incentives

Development organizations should adjust incentives toward prevention. Chapter 7 shows

FIGURE 8.1 Siloed Approach to Prevention

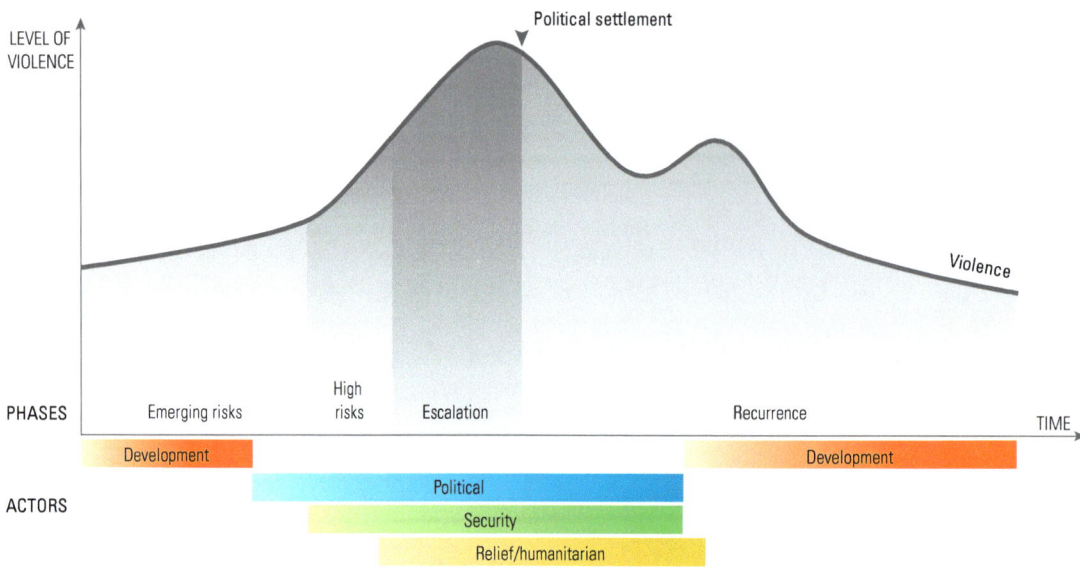

FIGURE 8.1 Siloed Approach to Prevention

that the current incentives of multilateral systems to engage in dialogue with national governments to facilitate a greater and earlier focus on risks remain weak, especially among development actors. Since the 1990s, the development focus among important bilateral and multilateral agencies started to shift toward supporting national institutions and actors in conflict prevention. However, international development actors and multilateral development banks are still constrained from engaging on sensitive issues with governments by their mandates, intergovernmental agreements, and institutional culture. In precrisis contexts, these constraints limit the scope for development programming and diplomatic efforts to address causes of tension, even when lessons from other countries are readily available. Pressure to disburse funds, resistance to addressing conflict risks that have not yet

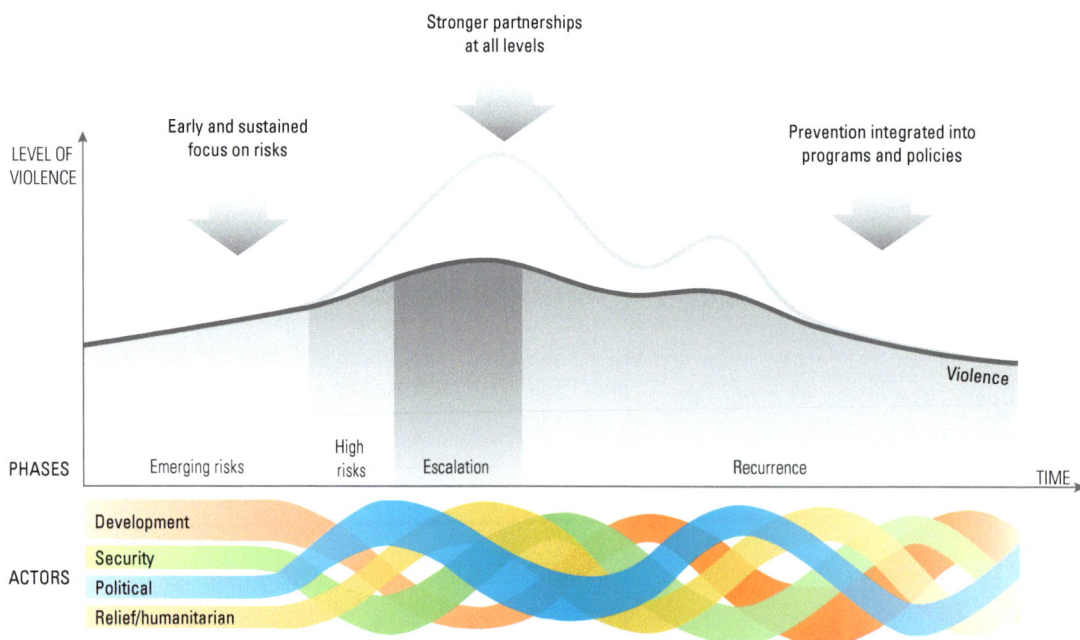

FIGURE 8.2 Sustained Approach to Prevention

TABLE 8.3 **Differentiated Approaches across Levels of Risk**

Area	Emerging risks	High risks	Escalation
Monitoring	Most violent conflicts today are rooted in grievances that stem from inequality among groups and political, economic, and social exclusion. Addressing risk early on means identifying and addressing inequality, exclusion, and feelings of injustice that arise when groups believe they are not getting their fair share.	Addressing actors' incentives for violence is key to averting outbreak, including perceptions of security. Scaling up mediation is central at various levels during this period. As tensions escalate, it is important to monitor and manage effectively potential conflict triggers, reinforce early warning systems, and ensure that they are connected to early action.	Addressing and reducing humanitarian needs are the priority during conflict. Where possible, development approaches should be undertaken simultaneously to reduce risks and vulnerabilities, build resilience, and maintain the capacities of institutions that are still able to function.
Shocks	As with a financial crisis, the reluctance to adjust in the face of external shocks may accelerate the onset of the fiscal and financial dimensions of the crisis. A preventive approach calls for the design of "slow and steady" policy adjustments to achieve sustainability, which get a head start on potential crises through earlier actions than is normally the case.	Prioritize macrofiscal stability, commodity price decline, and indicators of expectations such as capital flight, banking system stress, and exchange rate depreciation. Surveillance and enforcement to prevent financial flows linked to conflict financing are also important.	It is important to deescalate conflict; to avoid distributing resources that are likely to be perceived as exacerbating intergroup tensions; and to focus on fiscal, wage, and social protection programs that are aimed at reducing inequity among social groups within countries. Reductions in intergroup inequality are likely to protect against shocks.
Arenas	It is important to reform state institutions or legal structures and address narratives that could be contributing to violence mobilization at the central and local levels. Group-based exclusion from power and resources, land issues, abuses by security forces, limited or low quality of basic services, and lack of redress mechanisms often combine to increase the risks of violence.	Build confidence by signaling a change in direction and taking visible actions to show that grievances will be addressed. Hold transparent dialogue on areas of tension and demonstrate a commitment to peaceful change, inclusion, and collaboration, including holding actors, particularly security actors, accountable to the population.	Where possible, it is important to preserve the fiscal, physical, and political integrity of the state as a platform for political negotiation and service delivery. Establish parallel delivery mechanisms able to complement humanitarian assistance and reach insecure areas. This support may also consist of continuing to invest in development in areas not affected by conflict.
Partnerships	It is important to develop normative and legal mechanisms to respond to crisis and to bring various actors around common platforms to have a frank discussion on risks and how to address them.	Build coalitions with nonstate actors to reach areas and groups with limited state presence. Invest in innovative delivery mechanisms that can address grievances even in the midst of a conflict. Civil society and community networks can provide the basis for partnerships and help to bridge difficult divides.	It is important to engage international and regional partners.

resulted in violence, and the need to satisfy domestic constituencies in donor countries can undermine incentives to undertake preventive action. Assisting national governments in developing institutions that are just, inclusive, and capable of sustaining peace should be a mainstay of development to leave no one behind. The call for such a commitment should be made at the highest levels of management to signal a change in culture and approach.

Peace and security actors should work with development actors to incorporate longer-term perspectives. By nature of their mandates, international actors engaged in peacemaking and peace operations tend to have a stronger focus on immediate needs, whether that means finding entry points for political engagement or addressing security concerns.

While these efforts are critical to putting societies on pathways for peace, they should also assist the design of long-term development strategies to build capacity and create sustainable institutions and committed citizenship. For effective and sustained prevention, greater attention should be paid to increasing economic and social resilience. Collaboration between peace and security and development actors on long-term strategies for sustaining peace should respond to demands on the ground, supported by enhanced analysis and planning capacity.

Share Assessments of Risks

This study highlights the importance of monitoring risks of grievances and exclusion for preventing violent conflict by deploying more innovative approaches for data collection. Yet, if this information is to become the basis for more integrated action between different international actors and their national counterparts, the assessments of these risks must be shared and collectively agreed on.

International partners should commit to collective efforts to identify and understand risks at regional, country, and local levels. At present, action on prevention is defined by the absence of a common vision, objectives, systems, and capacities across development, crisis response, political, and peacekeeping work. The absence of collective efforts to assess and establish shared priorities translates into ad hoc and fragmented action. Nationally, these actions could include, for example, multistakeholder forums and processes bringing together governments; representatives from development, humanitarian, security, and diplomatic organizations; civil society; and private sector, academia, and regional organizations. In committing to joint risk assessments, it is important that international actors share key findings with the government and national actors. Engaging with the government and other stakeholders, including at the subnational level, through policy dialogue can help to generate a joint understanding of the challenges that need to be addressed.

Risk monitoring systems should be linked to resources and capacities to act. As described in chapter 7, EWSs have been set up in several regions at risk of violent conflict, often with the support of regional organizations. Such systems provide evidence for conflict prevention decision making, allowing stakeholders to anticipate trends and better understand the rapidly changing dynamics of situations. However, one of the main challenges of such systems is whether they can effectively influence response by actors at various levels. With the growing complexity of conflicts, the format of these systems needs to shift from information-sharing facilities toward effective monitoring of longer-term risks and vulnerabilities that is linked to decision making and cross-sectoral capacities to respond.

Joint risk assessments should articulate agreed priorities. Such assessments should be based on agreed indicators that allow trends to be monitored over time. The use of mutual accountability frameworks, or compacts, in countries such as Afghanistan and Somalia, have proven effective at galvanizing coordination and maintaining a sense of urgency of implementation once the media spotlight has moved on. The joint United Nations–European Union–World Bank Recovery and Peacebuilding Assessment (RPBA) offers such an approach. It provides an inclusive process to support dialogue and participation of a broad range of stakeholders in order to agree on the narrative related to the challenges and risks of conflict and uses this process to identify, prioritize, and sequence recovery and peacebuilding activities. The goal is not a technical output, but a joint narrative and shared prioritization framework between government and partners for how to mitigate and address conflict risks over time. Currently used mostly during and immediately following conflict, this approach could be used further upstream and developed into joint platforms for prioritizing risks. For example, in Cameroon, the RPBA methodology was used successfully to help the government to respond to subnational pressures and prevent an escalation and spillover of the security and displacement crisis created by Boko Haram.

Create Stronger Regional and Global Partnerships

Strengthen regional analyses and strategies for prevention. With an increasing number of conflicts taking on regional dimensions, approaches to prevention need to be coordinated across countries to develop regional strategies to address critical risks early on. To the extent possible, international development, security, and political actors should work together to share risk analyses at the regional level. Such analyses should lead to the provision of strategic, political, and operational guidance and to integrated operational support for prevention and sustainable development. This guidance and support requires commitment to improved regional analysis, strategies, and responses and enhanced cooperation with regional and subregional organizations.

Facilitate stronger cooperation with regional and subregional organizations. The United Nations should enable and facilitate others to play their role. UN facilitation should be achieved through deepened ties with regional and subregional organizations, including the African Union and subregional African organizations, as well as other partners such as the European Union, the Association of South East Asian Nations, the League of Arab States, the Organisation of Islamic Cooperation, the Organization of American States, and the Pacific Islands Forum. Enhanced cooperation should include encouraging the sharing of lessons, good practices, and methodologies as they relate to analyses and operations related to prevention.

Enhance diverse partnerships for prevention. International and regional action needs to leverage the comparative advantage of different groups and platforms, including civil society, the media, and the private sector, and to be more inclusive of groups that have not traditionally been part of development or diplomacy. Valuing women's leadership and including the contributions of youth are both essential to consolidating peace, as is mobilizing local mediation and conflict resolution forums.

Invest in anticipatory relationships with a range of stakeholders. In order to have access and influence when a crisis breaks out, international actors need to invest in relationships with a range of political and non-state groups as well as with regional stakeholders. While building these relationships takes time, such relationships can yield valuable information, strengthen sensitivity to context, and enhance the credibility of an envoy or mediator among the stakeholders whose buy-in is essential for conflict to be averted or assuaged. UN regional political offices are a good example of efforts to build such relationships.

Create stronger bridges between diplomatic and development actions. Peacemaking has advanced beyond "state-centric" models and increasingly is engaging through multi-track (or "horizontal") strategies. In some

circumstances, such strategies have created opportunities to align development planning with political processes. Linkages between mediation efforts and development assistance should be reinforced at national and subnational levels. For example, actors involved in mediation could complement their efforts by providing financing for development programming in priority areas to support confidence building and incentives for actors to engage in mediation. Enhanced attention to subnational grievances and conflicts, including through appropriate development or peacebuilding assistance, can forestall their escalation. Peace operations, through coherent approaches with development actors, can further the implementation of their political strategies and mandates and provide political leverage for shared prevention and sustaining of peace goals.

Improve Investment for Prevention

Financing for prevention remains risk-averse and focused on crises. Current models are too slow to seize windows of opportunity and too volatile to sustain prevention. Complex and multilevel prevention efforts are often constrained by the lack of readily available resources, resulting in ad hoc attempts to mobilize resources and too often in delayed and suboptimal responses.

Strengthen support for national financing capacity for prevention. Low-income countries face challenges related to limited fiscal space that also make investments in prevention difficult. As described in chapter 7, they are highly dependent on donor aid, which is unreliable and often comes in feast-or-famine cycles. Too frequently, budgetary support is provided quite narrowly for economic and institutional reforms without consideration of the efforts and reforms needed for prevention. International actors can offer support to national governments in retaining existing investments despite the risk for potential investors. Organizations like the Multilateral Investment Guarantee Agency can work with national governments and private investors to consider the type and reliability of insurance available for private investors in the country, what kind of arbitration system is available, and whether foreign investors can obtain insurance for political risk.

Combine different forms of financing. Financing for preventive action requires different forms of financing to work with each other to support short-term and long-term outcomes. Even when fiscal resources are available, national budgets are often slow to change and need to be supported by other resources. Another major challenge to the provision of the necessary resources for prevention relates to middle-income countries. As chapter 1 shows, conflicts are often seen in such settings, yet middle-income countries typically are not eligible for "softer" lending facilities, which can help to incentivize investments in conflict prevention—that is, concessional financing and grants—and are increasingly facing constrained access to financing. Appropriate forms of financing across different phases of risk are important to bridge the gap. For example, making concessional financing available to middle-income countries to prioritize action in key areas or risks is an innovative means to build national capacities.[7] This was done with the Concessional Financing Facility providing support for dealing with forced displacement in Jordan and Lebanon.

Support financing and help to foster an enabling environment for the private sector. The private sector, including small- and medium-size enterprises and international investors, can play an important role in preventing violent conflict. There is growing recognition that official development assistance (ODA) alone will not be sufficient to meet the SDGs and that much greater engagement from the private sector will be necessary to meet financing needs. It will be critical to prioritize private sector solutions where they can help to achieve development goals and to use scarce public finance where it is most needed. However, many countries that are most vulnerable to conflict face severe challenges in attracting private investment and financing. Sustainable and responsible private sector investments should help to grow more robust economies and build resilience in countries that are most vulnerable and least equipped to deal with the impacts of crises. Such innovative approaches will be needed to attract greater private investment and, when coupled with conflict-sensitive approaches, can maximize the private sector's contribution to peace. In addition to innovative financial solutions, the private sector also needs a strong enabling environment and complementary public investments to support the development of basic infrastructure and services.

Strengthen international financing mechanisms for prevention. Regardless of national financing strategies, dedicated funds for prevention and risk mitigation should be considered at the international level. Noting the lack of incentives for sustained and focused support for prevention, existing mechanisms like the International Development Association's IDA18 Risk Mitigation Regime and or the UN Peacebuilding Fund should be scaled up. These funds could provide a vehicle for incentivizing investments in prevention. Targeted financial support can strengthen government policies that recognize and address emerging risks more proactively as well as build institutional resilience to sustain prevention efforts over time.

Strengthen financing for regional prevention efforts. Financing strategies should be designed to account for the risk of cross-border spillovers posed by regional conflict. There may be opportunities to learn from recent innovations for providing insurance for regional pandemics, such as the World Bank's Pandemic Emergency Financing Facility, which funds coverage through financial markets and a complementary cash window. A financing facility that provides insurance coverage within a region destabilized by conflict could offer predictable, coordinated, and scaled-up disbursements of funds for countries with escalating risk in the key arenas described in this study, to be defined further for specific activation criteria. To receive the coverage, countries could be required to have a risk management plan in place that integrates development, diplomacy, and security sectors as well as a risk-monitoring platform with regional actors.

A Call for Action

This study shows that the 2030 Agenda for Sustainable Development is the paradigm shift on prevention. If the 1992 Agenda for Peace and the 2005 World Summit were the precursors, the time is ripe to deal collectively with the challenges and to capitalize on the opportunities of an increasingly interdependent world.[8]

This study highlights and elaborates how synergies between peace and development can be effectively pursued. Where the SDGs call for inclusivity and for the imperative of leaving no one behind, this study provides evidence that forms of exclusion create risks of violent conflict. As the SDGs underscore the importance of protecting our environment, renewing our infrastructure, and combating climate change, this study highlights how structural factors intersect with exclusion and can increase the risks of violence. Where the 2030 Agenda envisages broad-based partnerships as a prerequisite for its implementation, the study puts agency at the focus of attention and calls for a recognition and inclusion of the growing diversity of actors in building coalitions for action from the local to the global level.

While there is no single formula for effectively preventing violent conflict, based on expert analyses of country cases, the study demonstrates that prevention works, saves lives, and is cost-effective. It estimates that "savings" generated from prevention range from US$5 billion to US$69 billion a year. The study establishes that efforts must be *sustained, inclusive, and targeted*. Preventing violent conflict is a continuous process requiring long-term domestic efforts to promote inclusive societies and institutions. Targeted engagement, through different entry points, is critical.

Implementing these principles requires a shift in policies and practices on the part of national and international actors. The case for prevention has been made. National and international actors have before them an agenda for action to ensure that attention, efforts, and resources are focused on prevention. It is time to address distorted incentives and to do the utmost to prevent immense human suffering and avoid the exorbitant costs of conflict. The time to act is now.

Notes

1. A host of SDG targets and indicators could have relevance for assessing the risks of horizontal inequalities. Specifically, the following set of core targets for SDG 5, SDG 10, and SDG 16, respectively, are key: 5.1: end all forms of discrimination against all women and girls everywhere; 10.2: by 2030, empower and promote the social, economic, and political inclusion of all, irrespective of age, sex, disability, race, ethnicity, origin, religion, or economic or other status; 10.3: ensure equal opportunity and reduce inequalities of outcome, including by eliminating discriminatory laws, policies, and practices and promoting appropriate legislation, policies, and action in this regard; 16.3: promote the rule of law at the national and international levels and ensure equal access to justice for all; and 16.7: ensure responsive, inclusive, participatory, and representative decision making at all levels. In addition, many indicators collected through household surveys, including mortality rates, could be used to monitor horizontal inequalities, including among geographic areas.

2. Many governments use perception surveys, mini surveys, focus groups, key informant interviews, community maps, and other techniques in policy making and testing. These methodologies can also be helpful in assessing risks in challenging contexts (Van de Walle and Van Ryzin 2011).

3. The most well-known example is Ushahidi, an open-source software program to collect information and do interactive mapping. It was first used after the 2007 presidential election in Kenya.

4. This term was first used in the Voix des Kivus project in the Democratic Republic of Congo (2009–11). See http://cu-csds.org/projects/event-mapping-in-congo/.

5. Implementing monitoring of perceptions and issues such as horizontal inequality requires several important safeguards to be in place. Governments or other actors can use questions on perceptions, identity, and

aspirations to identify certain groups, target them for security purposes, deny people rights, or support implementation of exclusionary policies. It is essential that very strong attention be given to protecting the individual and collective rights of both the population interviewed and the people collecting the information. There are increasingly sophisticated methodologies to do this, such as asking the region of origin more than identity or asking difficult questions in a way that people can respond to directly or indirectly.

6. The Agenda for Humanity is a five-point plan that outlines the changes needed to alleviate suffering, reduce risk, and lessen vulnerability on a global scale. In the 2030 Agenda, humanity—people's safety, dignity, and right to thrive—is placed at the heart of global decision making around five core responsibilities, including the prevention and ending of conflicts.

7. The World Bank's Global Concessional Financing Facility (GCFF), launched in April 2016, provides concessional or "International Development Association–like" financing to help middle-income countries to address the influx of refugees, with Jordan and Lebanon being among the first to receive assistance to manage spillovers from the refugee crisis in the Syrian Arab Republic. Although concessional lending hinges primarily on income level, with the lowest rates reserved for the world's poorest nations, the GCFF alters this equation by offering concessional financing to countries like Jordan and Lebanon that promote a global public good by opening their borders to refugees. Facilities such as the GCFF will be important sources of funding going forward, especially for incentivizing investments in preventative measures. See http://globalcff.org/about-us/objectives-and-scope.

8. Since the mid-1990s, the UN "culture of peace" resolutions have recognized the fundamental link between peace, development, and human rights. In particular, the Programme of Action on a Culture of Peace, adopted in 1999, details how actions taken through education; economic and social development; human rights; gender equality; democratic participation; understanding and tolerance; the free flow of information; and international peace and security can serve to build a culture of peace. Only recently has a concerted effort been made to embed this mind-set and operational approach into the work of the United Nations.

References

Defontaine, C. 2017. "Short Literature Review on Monitoring Risks of Violent Conflict." Background paper for the United Nations–World Bank Flagship Study, *Pathways for Peace: Inclusive Approaches to Preventing Violent Conflict*, World Bank, Washington, DC.

Haider, H. 2014. *Conflict Sensitivity. Topic Guide.* Birmingham, U.K.: GSDRC, University of Birmingham.

Lanz, D. 2011. "Who Gets a Seat at the Table? A Framework for Understanding the Dynamics of Inclusion and Exclusion in Peace Negotiations." *International Negotiation* 16 (2): 275–95.

Marshak, A., D. Mazurana, J. H. Opio, R. Gordon, and T. Atim. 2017. "Tracking Change in Livelihoods, Service Delivery, and Governance: Evidence from a 2013–2015 Panel Survey in Uganda." Working Paper 59, Secure Livelihoods Research Consortium, London.

Mcloughlin, C. 2015. "Researching State Legitimacy: A Political Approach to a Political Problem." Research Paper 36, Developmental Leadership Program, University of Birmingham, U.K., November.

Paffenholz, T., A. Hirblinger, D. Landau, F. Fritsch, and C. Dijkstra. 2017. "Preventing Violence through Inclusion: From Building Political Momentum to Sustaining Peace." Background paper for the United Nations–World Bank Flagship Study, *Pathways for Peace: Inclusive Approaches to Preventing Violent Conflict*, World Bank, Washington, DC.

Putzel, J. 2010. *Conflict and Fragility. Do No Harm: International Support for Statebuilding.* Paris: OECD.

Rakotomalala, O. 2017. "Local Level Mechanisms for Violent Conflict Prevention." Background paper for the United Nations–World Bank Flagship Study, *Pathways for Peace: Inclusive Approaches to Preventing Violent Conflict*, World Bank, Washington, DC.

Sartorius, R., and C. Carver. 2008. *Monitoring, Evaluation, and Learning for Fragile and Peacebuilding Programs: Practical Tools for*

Improving Program Performance and Results. Arlington, VA: Social Impact Inc. http://pdf .usaid.gov/pdf_docs/pnady656.pdf.

UN (United Nations) Security Council. 2015. The *Future of United Nations Peace Operations: Implementation of the Recommendations of the High-Level Independent Panel on Peace Operations.* New York: United Nations.

UN Security Council and UN General Assembly. 2015. *Uniting Our Strengths for Peace: Politics, Partnership, and People; Report of the High-Level Independent Panel on Peace Operations.* New York: United Nations. http://www.un.org/en/ga /search/view_doc.asp?symbol=S/2015/446.

Van de Walle, S., and G. Van Ryzin. 2011. "The Order of Questions in a Survey on Citizen Satisfaction with Public Services: Lessons from a Split-Ballot Experiment." *Public Administration* 89 (4): 1436–50.

Wanis-St. John, A., and D. Kew. 2008. "Civil Society and Peace Negotiations: Confronting Exclusion." *International Negotiation* 13 (2008): 11–36. http://www.american.edu/sis/faculty/upload /Wanis-Kew-Civil-Society-and-Peace-Negotiat ions.pdf.

World Bank. 2011. *World Development Report 2011: Conflict, Security, and Development.* Washington, DC: World Bank.

Additional Reading

Babbitt, E. F., I. Johnstone, and D. Mazurana. 2016. "Building Legitimacy in Conflict Affected and Fragile States." Policy Brief 1, Institute for Human Security, Fletcher School of Law and Diplomacy, Tufts University, Medford, MA.

Blair, R. A., C. Blattman, and A. Hartman. 2011. *Patterns of Conflict and Cooperation in Liberia.* Part 2: *Prospects for Conflict Forecasting and Early Warning.* New Haven, CT: Innovations for Poverty Action.

———. 2015. "Predicting Local Violence." Brown University; University of Chicago; University College of London. https://papers.ssrn.com /sol3/papers.cfm?abstract_id=2497153.

Blattman, C. 2012. "Can We Predict Eruptions of Violence? Statistics and the Future of Conflict Early Warning." Harris School of Public Policy, University of Chicago. https:// chrisblattman.com/2012/02/13/can-we -predict-local-conflict/.

———. 2014. "Can We Use Data and Machine Learning to Predict Local Violence in Fragile States? As it Turns Out, Yes." Harris School of Public Policy, University of Chicago. https://chrisblattman.com/2014/10/02/can -use-data-machine-learning-predict-local -violence-fragile-states-turns-yes/.

Bush, K., and C. Duggan. 2013. "Evaluation in Conflict Zones: Methodological and Ethical Challenges." *Journal of Peacebuilding and Development* 8 (2): 5–25.

Calì, M., and A. Mulabdic. 2017. "Trade and Civil Conflict: Revisiting the Cross-Country Evidence." *Review of International Economics* 25 (1): 195–232.

DFID (Department for International Develop ment). 2010a. "Interim Guidance Note: Measuring and Managing for Results in Fragile and Conflict-Affected States and Situations." DFID, London.

———. 2010b. "Working Effectively in Conflict-Affected and Fragile Situations." Briefing Paper I: Monitoring and Evaluation, DFID, London. https://www.gov.uk/government /uploads/system/uploads/attachment_data /file/67695/building-peaceful-states-I.pdf.

FEWER (Forum on Early Warning and Early Response). 1999. *FEWER Conflict and Peace Analysis and Response Manual.* London: FEWER.

Goldwyn, R., and D. Chigas. 2013. *Monitoring and Evaluating Conflict Sensitivity: Methodological Challenges and Practical Solutions (CCVRI Practice Product).* Cambridge, MA: CDA.

Hagen-Zanker, J., R. Mallett, and R. Slater. 2015. "The First Round of the SLRC Panel Survey: The Process Paper." Secure Livelihoods Research Consortium, Overseas Development Institute, London. https://assets.publishing .service.gov.uk/media/57a0898f40f0b652dd0 002ae/SLRC-Panel-Survey-Process-Paper.pdf.

Herbert, S. 2013. *Perception Surveys in Fragile and Conflict-Affected States.* Birmingham, U.K.: GSDRC, University of Birmingham.

Institute for State Effectiveness. 2018. "Sovereignty Strategies: Enhancing Core Government Functions as a Post-Conflict and Conflict Prevention Measure." Institute for State Effectiveness, Washington, DC.

Kakachia, K., and L. O'Shea. 2012. "Why Does Police Reform Appear to Have Been More Successful in Georgia Than in Kyrgyzstan or Russia?" *Journal of Power Institutions in Post-Soviet Societies* 13: n.p.

Lainé, A. 2002. "Biological Identities, Social Identities, and Ethnic Conflicts in Sub-Saharan Africa." *Journal des Anthropologues* 1 (88-89): 29–39.

Lavoix, H. 2007. *Etude sur l'alerte précoce.* Paris: Ministère des Affaires Etrangères.

Letouzé, E. 2012a. "Can Big Data from Cellphones Help Prevent Conflict?" IPI Global Observatory, November 8. https://theglobalobservatory.org/2012/11/can-big-data-from-cellphones-help-prevent-conflict/.

———. 2012b. *Big Data for Development: Challenges and Opportunities.* New York: UN Global Pulse.

Letouzé, E., P. Meier, and P. Vinck. 2013. "Big Data for Conflict Prevention: New Oil and Old Fires." In *New Technology and the Prevention of Violene and Conflict,* edited by F. Mancini, 4–27. Washington, DC: United States International Peace Institute, United Nations Development Programme, and U.S. Agency for International Development

Meier, P. 2013. *Artificial Intelligence for Monitoring Elections (AIME).* https://irevolutions.org/2013/04/17/ai-for-election-monitoring/.

———. 2015. *Digital Humanitarians: How Big Data Is Changing the Face of Humanitarian Response.* London: Routledge.

Morel, A. 2016. *Violent Incidents Monitoring Systems: A Methods Toolkit.* San Francisco: Asian Foundation.

Moser, C., and C. Mcilwaine. 2006. "Latin American Urban Violence as a Development Concern: Towards a Framework for Violence Reduction." *World Development* 34 (1): 89–112.

Mwaûra, C., and S. Schmeidl, eds. 2002. *Early Warning and Conflict Management in the Horn of Africa.* Trenton, NJ: Red Sea Press.

Nyheim, D. 2015. *Early Warning and Response to Violent Conflict: Time for a Rethink?* London: Saferworld.

OECD (Organisation for Economic Co-operation and Development). 2008. *Guidance on Evaluating Conflict Prevention and Peace Building Activities: Working Draft for Application Period.* Paris: OECD, Development Assistance Committee.

———. 2009. *Preventing Violence, War, and State Collapse. The Future of Conflict Early Warning and Response.* Paris: OECD.

———. 2012a. "Checklist to Commission, Design, and Run a Perception Survey."

OECD, Paris. http://www.oecd.org/governance/regulatory-policy/49217483.pdf.

———. 2012b. *Evaluating Peacebuilding Activities in Settings of Conflict and Fragility: Improving Learning for Results.* Paris: OECD.

Parks, T., N. Colletta, and B. Oppenheim. 2011. *The Contested Corners of Asia: Subnational Conflict and International Development Assistance.* San Francisco: Asia Foundation.

Pattison, C., and N. W. Myint. Forthcoming. "Community-Driven Development in Situations Affected by Fragility, Conflict, and Violence: Magic or Mirage?" Social Development Working Paper, World Bank, Washington, DC.

Puig Larrauri, H. 2013. "New Technologies and Conflict Prevention in Sudan and South Sudan." In *New Technology and the Prevention of Violence and Conflict,* edited by F. Mancini, 71–86. Washington, DC: United States International Peace Institute, United Nations Development Programme, and U.S. Agency for International Development.

Richards, S., A. Morrice, and T. Carr. 2016. *Conflict Sensitivity Monitoring in Myanmar. Findings for OECD-DAC INCAF.* Prangins, Switzerland: PeaceNexus Foundation.

Scharbatke-Church, C., and A. Patel. 2016. "Technology for Evaluation in Fragile and Conflict Affected States: An Introduction for the Digital Immigrant Evaluator." Working Paper, Fletcher School of Law and Diplomacy, Tufts University, Medford, MA.

Schmeidl, S., and J. C. Jenkins. 1998. "The Early Warning of Humanitarian Disasters: Problems in Building an Early Warning System." *International Migration Review* 32 (2): 471–86.

Schmeidl, S., and E. Piza-Lopez. 2002. *Gender and Conflict Early Warning: A Framework for Action.* Kampala, Uganda: International Alert.

Smith, R. 2003. "The Impact of Hate Media in Rwanda." *BBC,* December 3. http://news.bbc.co.uk/2/hi/africa/3257748.stm.

U.K. Stabilisation Unit. 2016. *Conflict Sensitivity Tools and Guidance.* London: U.K. Stabilisation Unit.

UN (United Nations). 2013. *The Report of the High-Level Panel of Eminent Persons on the Post-2015 Development Agenda.* New York: United Nations. http://www.post2015hlp.org/wp-content/uploads/2013/05/UN-Report.pdf.

———. 2017. *Restructuring of the United Nations Peace and Security Pillar.* Report of the Secretary-General A/72/525. New York: United Nations.

United States Institute of Peace. 2015. *Lessons and Opportunities from the Tokyo Mutual Accountability Framework.* Washington, DC: United States Institute of Peace. https://www .usip.org/sites/default/files/SR378-Lessons-and -Opportunities-from-the-Tokyo-Mutual-Acco unztability-Framework.pdf.

Villanueva, S. D. 2009. *Managing Performance in Peacebuilding: Framework for Conflict Sensitive Monitoring and Evaluation.* GoP-UN ACT for Peace Programme.

Weber, M. 1919. "Politics as a Vocation." Duncker and Humblodt, Munich.

World Bank. 2001. *Low-Income Countries under Stress.* Washington, DC: World Bank.

———. 2010. *Crime and Violence in Central America.* Vol. II. Washington, DC: World Bank.

———. 2018. *Pilot Toolkit: Measuring and Monitoring in FCV Environments.* Washington, DC: World Bank. http://fcvindicators .worldbank.org/.

APPENDIX A

Thematic Papers and Case Studies

Thematic Papers

Aslam, G. 2017. "Civic Associations and Conflict Prevention: Potential Challenges and Opportunities: A Review of the Literature." Background paper for the United Nations–World Bank Flagship Study, *Pathways for Peace: Inclusive Approaches to Preventing Violent Conflict*, World Bank, Washington, DC.

Austin, J. L., and A. Wennmann. 2017. "Business and the Prevention of Violence in Kenya, 2007–2013." Background paper for the United Nations–World Bank Flagship Study, *Pathways for Peace: Inclusive Approaches to Preventing Violent Conflict*, World Bank, Washington, DC.

Banim, G., and I. Magnusson. 2017. "Low Road to Peace: The Potential of Peace Mediation in Revitalizing Prevention." European Institute of Peace. Background paper for the United Nations–World Bank Flagship Study, *Pathways for Peace: Inclusive Approaches to Preventing Violent Conflict*, World Bank, Washington, DC.

Betz, M. 2017. "Media Noise and the Complexity of Conflicts: Making Sense of Media in Conflict Prevention." Background paper for the United Nations–World Bank Flagship Study, *Pathways for Peace: Inclusive Approaches to Preventing Violent Conflict*, World Bank, Washington, DC.

Black, C., and K. Powell. 2017. "Macroeconomic Policies in Conflict-Affected Contexts: A Review of the Evidence." Deetken Group. Background paper for the United Nations–World Bank Flagship Study, *Pathways*

for Peace: Inclusive Approaches to Preventing Violent Conflict, World Bank, Washington, DC.

Bøås, M., S. S. Eriksen, T. Gade, J. H. S. Lie, and O. J. Sending. 2017. "Conflict Prevention and Ownership: Limits and Opportunities for External Actors." Norwegian Institute of International Affairs (NUPI). Background paper for the United Nations–World Bank Flagship Study, *Pathways for Peace: Inclusive Approaches to Preventing Violent Conflict*, World Bank, Washington, DC.

Boggero, M. 2017. "Technologies for Conflict Prevention." Background paper for the United Nations–World Bank Flagship Study, *Pathways for Peace: Inclusive Approaches to Preventing Violent Conflict*, World Bank, Washington, DC.

Brubaker, R., and T. Dorfler. 2017. "How and Why Have Sanctions Been Effective in Helping Prevent the Escalation, Continuation, and Recurrence of Conflict?" United Nations University (UNU). Background paper for the United Nations–World Bank Flagship Study, *Pathways for Peace: Inclusive Approaches to Preventing Violent Conflict*, World Bank, Washington, DC.

Bruce, J. 2017. "Preventing Land-Related Conflict and Violence." Background paper for the United Nations–World Bank Flagship Study, *Pathways for Peace: Inclusive Approaches to Preventing Violent Conflict*, World Bank, Washington, DC.

Call, C. 2017. "The Evolution of Conflict Prevention in the United Nations." Background paper for the United Nations–World Bank

Flagship Study, *Pathways for Peace: Inclusive Approaches to Preventing Violent Conflict*, World Bank, Washington, DC.

Carey, K., and W. Harake. 2017. "Macroeconomic Environment and Policies." Background paper for the United Nations–World Bank Flagship Study, *Pathways for Peace: Inclusive Approaches to Preventing Violent Conflict*, World Bank, Washington, DC.

Cingranelli, D., M. Gibney, P. Haschke, R. Wood, D. Arnon, and B. Mark. 2017. "Human Rights Violations and Violent Conflict." Background paper for the United Nations–World Bank Flagship Study, *Pathways for Peace: Inclusive Approaches to Preventing Violent Conflict*, World Bank, Washington, DC.

Cockayne, J., L. Bosetti, and N. Hussain. 2017. "Preventing Violent Urban Conflict." Background paper for the United Nations–World Bank Flagship Study, *Pathways for Peace: Inclusive Approaches to Preventing Violent Conflict*, World Bank, Washington, DC.

Colletta, N., and B. Oppenheim. 2017. "Subnational Conflict: Dimensions, Trends, and Options for Prevention." Background paper for the United Nations–World Bank Flagship Study, *Pathways for Peace: Inclusive Approaches to Preventing Violent Conflict*, World Bank, Washington, DC.

Comolli, V. 2017. "Transnational Organized Crime and Conflict." Background paper for the United Nations–World Bank Flagship Study, *Pathways for Peace: Inclusive Approaches to Preventing Violent Conflict*, World Bank, Washington, DC.

Crespo-Sancho, C. 2017. "Conflict Prevention and Gender." Background paper for the United Nations–World Bank Flagship Study, *Pathways for Peace: Inclusive Approaches to Preventing Violent Conflict*, World Bank, Washington, DC.

Dahl, M., S. Gates, and H. M. Nygård. 2017. "Securing the Peace." Peace Research Institute Oslo (PRIO). Background paper for the United Nations–World Bank Flagship Study, *Pathways for Peace: Inclusive Approaches to Preventing Violent Conflict*, World Bank, Washington, DC.

Day, A., and A. Pichler Fong. 2017. "Diplomacy and Good Offices in the Prevention of Conflict." Background paper for the United Nations–World Bank Flagship Study, *Pathways for Peace: Inclusive Approaches to*

Preventing Violent Conflict, World Bank, Washington, DC.

DCAF (Geneva Centre for the Democratic Control of Armed Forces). 2017. "The Contribution and Role of SSR in the Prevention of Violent Conflict." Background paper for the United Nations–World Bank Flagship Study, *Pathways for Peace: Inclusive Approaches to Preventing Violent Conflict*, World Bank, Washington, DC.

Defontaine, C. 2017. "Short Literature Review on Monitoring Risks of Violent Conflict." Background paper for the United Nations–World Bank Flagship Study, *Pathways for Peace: Inclusive Approaches to Preventing Violent Conflict*, World Bank, Washington, DC.

Demetriou, S. 2017. "Towards Convergence between Preventive Diplomacy, Peace Operations and Development in Conflict Prevention." Background paper for the United Nations–World Bank Flagship Study, *Pathways for Peace: Inclusive Approaches to Preventing Violent Conflict*, World Bank, Washington, DC.

Drew, E. 2017. "Assessing the Links between Extractive Industries and the Prevention of Violent Conflict: A Literature Review." Background paper for the United Nations–World Bank Flagship Study, *Pathways for Peace: Inclusive Approaches to Preventing Violent Conflict*, World Bank, Washington, DC.

Fall, A. 2017. "Cost-Saving of Women-Led Conflict Prevention Mechanisms in Liberia." Background paper for the United Nations–World Bank Flagship Study, *Pathways for Peace: Inclusive Approaches to Preventing Violent Conflict*, World Bank, Washington, DC.

Fatima, Q. 2017. "Conflict Prevention/Management Literature Review." Background paper for the United Nations–World Bank Flagship Study, *Pathways for Peace: Inclusive Approaches to Preventing Violent Conflict*, World Bank, Washington, DC.

Fiedler, C. 2017. "The Effects of Specific Elements of Democracy on Peace." German Development Institute/Deutsches Institut für Entwicklungspolitik (DIE). Background paper for the United Nations–World Bank Flagship Study, *Pathways for Peace: Inclusive Approaches to Preventing Violent Conflict*, World Bank, Washington, DC.

Fiedler, C., J. Gravingholt, and K. Mross. 2017. "Identifying Pathways to Peace: How Post-

Conflict Support Can Help Prevent Relapse of War." German Development Institute/ Deutsches Institut für Entwicklungspolitik (DIE). Background paper for the United Nations–World Bank Flagship Study, *Pathways for Peace: Inclusive Approaches to Preventing Violent Conflict*, World Bank, Washington, DC.

Giessmann, H.-J., J. Galvanek, and C. Seifert. 2017. "Curbing Violence: Development, Application, and Sustaining National Capacities for Prevention." Berghof Foundation. Background paper for the United Nations–World Bank Flagship Study, *Pathways for Peace: Inclusive Approaches to Preventing Violent Conflict*, World Bank, Washington, DC.

Hammond, D., and D. Hyslop. 2017. "Understanding Multi-Dimensional Risks and Violent Conflict Lessons for Prevention." Institute for Economics and Peace (IEP). Background paper for the United Nations–World Bank Flagship Study, *Pathways for Peace: Inclusive Approaches to Preventing Violent Conflict*, World Bank, Washington, DC.

Justino, P. 2017. "Linking Inequality and Political Conflict: The Role of Social Mobilization and Collective Action." Institute of Development Studies (IDS), University of Sussex. Background paper for the United Nations–World Bank Flagship Study, *Pathways for Peace: Inclusive Approaches to Preventing Violent Conflict*, World Bank, Washington, DC.

Kang, S. Y. 2017a. "Aid Flow to Fragile and Conflict Affected Situations: How Does Aid Create Incentives or Disincentives for Conflict?" Background paper for the United Nations–World Bank Flagship Study, *Pathways for Peace: Inclusive Approaches to Preventing Violent Conflict*, World Bank, Washington, DC.

———. 2017b. "Cultural and Religious Identity, and Its Implications for Understanding Conflicts Today." Background paper for the United Nations–World Bank Flagship Study, *Pathways for Peace: Inclusive Approaches to Preventing Violent Conflict*, World Bank, Washington, DC.

Kelly, J. 2017. "Intimate Partner Violence and Conflict: Understanding the Links between Political Violence and Personal Violence." Background paper for the United Nations–World Bank Flagship Study, *Pathways for Peace: Inclusive Approaches to Preventing Violent Conflict*, World Bank, Washington, DC.

Khosrokhavar, F. 2017. "Humiliation and Its Multiple Dimensions." Background paper for the United Nations–World Bank Flagship Study, *Pathways for Peace: Inclusive Approaches to Preventing Violent Conflict*, World Bank, Washington, DC.

Malik, A. 2017. "Electoral Violence and the Prevention of Violent Conflict." California State University San Marcos (CSUSM). Background paper for the United Nations–World Bank Flagship Study, *Pathways for Peace: Inclusive Approaches to Preventing Violent Conflict*, World Bank, Washington, DC.

Min, E., M. Singh, J. N. Shapiro, and B. Crisman. 2017. "Understanding Risk and Resilience to Violent Conflicts." Empirical Studies of Conflict Project (ESOC), Princeton University. Background paper for the United Nations–World Bank Flagship Study, *Pathways for Peace: Inclusive Approaches to Preventing Violent Conflict*, World Bank, Washington, DC.

Mogaka, S. 2017. "Competition for Power in Africa: Inclusive Politics and Its Relation to Violent Conflict." Background paper for the United Nations–World Bank Flagship Study, *Pathways for Peace: Inclusive Approaches to Preventing Violent Conflict*, World Bank, Washington, DC.

Mueller, H. 2017. "How Much Is Prevention Worth?" Barcelona Graduate School of Economics. Background paper for the United Nations–World Bank Flagship Study, *Pathways for Peace: Inclusive Approaches to Preventing Violent Conflict*, World Bank, Washington, DC.

Müller, L. 2017. "Conflict Prevention and the Legitimacy of Governance Actors." Freie Universitat Berlin. Background paper for the United Nations–World Bank Flagship Study, *Pathways for Peace: Inclusive Approaches to Preventing Violent Conflict*, World Bank, Washington, DC.

Muggah, R. 2017. "Revisiting Community Violence Reduction." Background paper for the United Nations–World Bank Flagship Study, *Pathways for Peace: Inclusive Approaches to Preventing Violent Conflict*, World Bank, Washington, DC.

Nezam, T. 2017. "Alternatively Governed Spaces." Background paper for the United Nations–

World Bank Flagship Study, *Pathways for Peace: Inclusive Approaches to Preventing Violent Conflict*, World Bank, Washington, DC.

Nygård, H. M., K. Baghat, G. Barrett, K. Dupuy, S. Gates, S. Hillesund, S. A. Rustad, H. Strand, H. Urdal, and G. Østby. 2017. "Inequality and Armed Conflict: Evidence and Data." Peace Research Institute Oslo (PRIO). Background paper for the United Nations–World Bank Flagship Study, *Pathways for Peace: Inclusive Approaches to Preventing Violent Conflict*, World Bank, Washington, DC.

Paffenholz, T., A. Hirblinger, D. Landau, F. Fritsch, and C. Dijkstra. 2017. "Preventing Violence through Inclusion: From Building Political Momentum to Sustaining Peace." Inclusive Peace & Transition Initiative (IPTI), Geneva Graduate Institute of International and Development Studies. Background paper for the United Nations–World Bank Flagship Study, *Pathways for Peace: Inclusive Approaches to Preventing Violent Conflict*, World Bank, Washington, DC.

Payne, L., A. Reiter, C. Mahony, and L. Bernal-Bermudez. 2017. "Conflict Prevention and Guarantees of Non-Recurrence." Background paper for the United Nations–World Bank Flagship Study, *Pathways for Peace: Inclusive Approaches to Preventing Violent Conflict*, World Bank, Washington, DC.

Rakotomalala, O. 2017. "Local-Level Mechanisms for Violent Conflict Prevention." Background paper for the United Nations–World Bank Flagship Study, *Pathways for Peace: Inclusive Approaches to Preventing Violent Conflict*, World Bank, Washington, DC.

Sargsyan, I. L. 2017a. "Corruption, Lack of the Rule of Law, and Conflict." Background paper for the United Nations–World Bank Flagship Study, *Pathways for Peace: Inclusive Approaches to Preventing Violent Conflict*, World Bank, Washington, DC.

———. 2017b. "Narrative, Perception, and Emotion: A Review of Recent Political Science Studies." Background paper for the United Nations–World Bank Flagship Study, *Pathways for Peace: Inclusive Approaches to Preventing Violent Conflict*, World Bank, Washington, DC.

Sisk, T. D. 2017. "Preventing Deadly Conflict in Ethnically Fractured Societies: An Overview and Analysis of International Development Assistance for 'Bridging' Social Cohesion." Background paper for the United Nations–

World Bank Flagship Study, *Pathways for Peace: Inclusive Approaches to Preventing Violent Conflict*, World Bank, Washington, DC.

Steven, D., and G. Sucuoglu. 2017. "What Works in Conflict Prevention? Development-Security-Diplomacy Collaboration towards Better Results." Center on International Cooperation (CIC), New York University. Background paper for the United Nations–World Bank Flagship Study, *Pathways for Peace: Inclusive Approaches to Preventing Violent Conflict*, World Bank, Washington, DC.

Verjee, N. 2017. "Regional Economic Communities in Conflict Prevention and Management." Background paper for the United Nations–World Bank Flagship Study, *Pathways for Peace: Inclusive Approaches to Preventing Violent Conflict*, World Bank, Washington, DC.

Walter, B. 2017. "The Role and Impact of Third-Party Interventions in the Prevention of Violent Conflict." Background paper for the United Nations–World Bank Flagship Study, *Pathways for Peace: Inclusive Approaches to Preventing Violent Conflict*, World Bank, Washington, DC.

Wennmann, A. 2017. "Assessing the Role of the Private Sector in Preventing Violent Conflict." Background paper for the United Nations–World Bank Flagship Study, *Pathways for Peace: Inclusive Approaches to Preventing Violent Conflict*, World Bank, Washington, DC.

Wolff, S., S. Ross, and A. Wee. 2017. "Subnational Governance and Conflict." Background paper for the United Nations–World Bank Flagship Study, *Pathways for Peace: Inclusive Approaches to Preventing Violent Conflict*, World Bank, Washington, DC.

Yi, J. 2017a. "Aid Flows to Conflict-Affected Situations: Exploring Cross-Country Empirical Studies and Updated Data." Empirical Studies of Conflict Project (ESOC), Princeton University. Background paper for the United Nations–World Bank Flagship Study, *Pathways for Peace: Inclusive Approaches to Preventing Violent Conflict*, World Bank, Washington, DC.

———. 2017b. "Evaluating Conflict Forecasts: Criteria, Approaches, and Tools." Empirical Studies of Conflict Project (ESOC), Princeton University. Background paper for the United Nations–World Bank Flagship Study, *Pathways for Peace: Inclusive Approaches to Preventing Violent Conflict*, World Bank, Washington, DC.

———. 2017c. "A Review of Conflict Forecasting Models." Empirical Studies of Conflict Project (ESOC), Princeton University. Background paper for the United Nations–World Bank Flagship Study, *Pathways for Peace: Inclusive Approaches to Preventing Violent Conflict*, World Bank, Washington, DC.

Country Case Studies

Bob-Milliar, G. 2017. "Sustaining Peace: Making Development Work for the Prevention of Violent Conflicts: Ghana and Côte d'Ivoire Compared." Case study for the United Nations–World Bank Flagship Study, *Pathways for Peace: Inclusive Approaches to Preventing Violent Conflict*, World Bank, Washington, DC.

Hearn, S. 2017a. "CICIG in Guatemala." Case study for the United Nations–World Bank Flagship Study, *Pathways for Peace: Inclusive Approaches to Preventing Violent Conflict*, World Bank, Washington, DC.

———. 2017b. "Inclusive Development for Conflict Prevention: The Case of Burundi." Case study for the United Nations–World Bank Flagship Study, *Pathways for Peace: Inclusive Approaches to Preventing Violent Conflict*, World Bank, Washington, DC.

———. 2017c. "Preventing the Recurrence of Conflict in Sierra Leone: How Did the UN Mission Succeed?" Case study for the United Nations–World Bank Flagship Study, *Pathways for Peace: Inclusive Approaches to Preventing Violent Conflict*, World Bank, Washington, DC.

Jaffrey, S. 2017. "Sustaining Peace: Making Development Work for the Prevention of Violent Conflicts. Case Study: Indonesia." Case study for the United Nations–World Bank Flagship Study, *Pathways for Peace: Inclusive Approaches to Preventing Violent Conflict*, World Bank, Washington, DC.

Logvinenko, I. 2017. "Conflict and Violence in Kyrgyzstan." Case study for the United Nations–World Bank Flagship Study, *Pathways for Peace: Inclusive Approaches to Preventing Violent Conflict*, World Bank, Washington, DC.

Lombard, L. 2017. "Case Study: The Central African Republic." Case study for the United Nations–World Bank Flagship Study, *Pathways for Peace: Inclusive Approaches to Preventing Violent Conflict*, World Bank, Washington, DC.

Mogaka, S. 2017. "Kenya Case Study." Case study for the United Nations–World Bank Flagship Study, *Pathways for Peace: Inclusive Approaches to Preventing Violent Conflict*, World Bank, Washington, DC.

Pérouse de Montclos, M.-A. 2017. "The Republic of Niger: A Test-Case, with Reference to the Republic of Mali." Case study for the United Nations–World Bank Flagship Study, *Pathways for Peace: Inclusive Approaches to Preventing Violent Conflict*, World Bank, Washington, DC.

Pichler Fong, A. 2017. "Burkina Faso: Popular Uprising and Political Transition (2014–2015)." Case study for the United Nations–World Bank Flagship Study, *Pathways for Peace: Inclusive Approaches to Preventing Violent Conflict*, World Bank, Washington, DC.

Stackpool-Moore, L., and M. Bacalja Perianes. 2017. Watipa Community Interest Company. "Malawi Case Study: Demonstrations July 2011." Case study for the United Nations–World Bank Flagship Study, *Pathways for Peace: Inclusive Approaches to Preventing Violent Conflict*, World Bank, Washington, DC.

Toska, S. 2017. "Sustaining Peace: Making Development Work for the Prevention of Violent Conflicts Cases: Egypt, Tunisia, Morocco, and Jordan." Case study for the United Nations–World Bank Flagship Study, *Pathways for Peace: Inclusive Approaches to Preventing Violent Conflict*, World Bank, Washington, DC.

Verjee, A. 2017. "Sustaining Peace: Making Development Work for the Prevention of Violent Conflicts; South Sudan Case Study." Case study for the United Nations–World Bank Flagship Study, *Pathways for Peace: Inclusive Approaches to Preventing Violent Conflict*, World Bank, Washington, DC.

von Einsiedel, S., and C. Salih. 2017. "Conflict Prevention in Nepal." United Nations University. Case study for the United Nations–World Bank Flagship Study, *Pathways for Peace: Inclusive Approaches to Preventing Violent Conflict*, World Bank, Washington, DC.

Walsh, M. 2017. "Prevention of Conflict, Northern Ireland." Case study for the United Nations–World Bank Flagship Study, *Pathways for Peace: Inclusive Approaches to Preventing Violent Conflict*, World Bank, Washington, DC.

www.ingramcontent.com/pod-product-compliance
Lightning Source LLC
Chambersburg PA
CBHW040841040426
42336CB00032B/15